SHAKESPEARE: THE CRITICAL HERITAGE
VOLUME 3 1733–1752

THE CRITICAL HERITAGE SERIES

GENERAL EDITOR: B. C. SOUTHAM, M.A., B.LITT. (OXON.)

Formerly Department of English, Westfield College, University of London

For a list of books in the series see the back end paper

SHAKESPEARE

THE CRITICAL HERITAGE

VOLUME 3 1733–1752

Edited by
BRIAN VICKERS
Professor of English, University of Zürich

ROUTLEDGE & KEGAN PAUL : LONDON AND BOSTON

First published in 1975
by Routledge & Kegan Paul Ltd
Broadway House, 68–74 Carter Lane,
London EC4V 5EL and
9 Park Street,
Boston, Mass. 02108, USA
© Brian Vickers 1975
No part of this book may be reproduced in
any form without permission from the
publisher, except for the quotation of brief
passages in criticism

ISBN 0 7100 7990 7

Set in Monotype Bembo 11/12 pt
and printed in Great Britain by
Richard Clay (The Chaucer Press) Ltd, Bungay, Suffolk

General Editor's Preface

The reception given to a writer by his contemporaries and near-contemporaries is evidence of considerable value to the student of literature. On one side we learn a great deal about the state of criticism at large and in particular about the development of critical attitudes towards a single writer; at the same time, through private comments in letters, journals or marginalia, we gain an insight upon the tastes and literary thought of individual readers of the period. Evidence of this kind helps us to understand the writer's historical situation, the nature of his immediate reading-public, and his response to these pressures.

The separate volumes in the *Critical Heritage Series* present a record of this early criticism. Clearly, for many of the highly productive and lengthily reviewed nineteenth- and twentieth-century writers, there exists an enormous body of material; and in these cases the volume editors have made a selection of the most important views, significant for their intrinsic critical worth or for their representative quality— perhaps even registering incomprehension!

For earlier writers, notably pre-eighteenth century, the materials are much scarcer and the historical period has been extended, sometimes far beyond the writer's lifetime, in order to show the inception and growth of critical views which were initially slow to appear.

Shakespeare is, in every sense, a special case, and Professor Vickers is presenting the course of his reception and reputation extensively, over a span of three centuries, in a sequence of six volumes, each of which will document a specific period.

In each volume the documents are headed by an Introduction, discussing the material assembled and relating the early stages of the author's reception to what we have come to identify as the critical tradition. The volumes will make available much material which would otherwise be difficult of access and it is hoped that the modern reader will be thereby helped towards an informed understanding of the ways in which literature has been read and judged.

B.C.S.

Contents

Preface

As with previous volumes in this series, the Shakespeare criticism of the period 1733 to 1752 has been collected under four categories: literary criticism of Shakespeare; adaptations of his plays; theatrical criticism (both of the original texts and of the adaptations); and textual criticism (the explanatory notes either appended to editions of his plays or issued separately). In the last of these this is an uneventful period, with the great edition of Theobald behind it (cf. Vol. 2) and that of Dr Johnson before it (cf. Vol. 5), for the editions of Hanmer and War-burton were throw-backs to the worst of Pope's practices as an editor. Theobald's influence, however, was widespread, and can be found here in the critics and commentators of the 1740s, such as Whalley, Upton, Holt and Seward. Other areas of new growth in criticism include George Stubbes's essay on *Hamlet* (No. 87), remarkably fresh and independent in many ways, and the first publications by two of the critics who will figure largely in subsequent volumes: Dr Johnson (Nos 105, 128) and Arthur Murphy (Nos 124, 133).

In the theatre the decline in the quantity and quality of new adaptations continues, Cibber's *King John* (No. 102) being the only substantial alteration in the period which I considered to be worth including. The single new force in this field is David Garrick, who began tentatively enough with what I have called 'presentations' rather than adaptations proper, small-scale alterations at major emotional climaxes in the tragedies (Nos 100, 101, 117). Garrick is one of the focal points, too, of the theatre criticism of the period, which reflects the general fascination with his interpretations of Shakespeare and also an increasing dissatisfaction with the adaptations, both reactions that will figure prominently in the next volume of the series. In almost every field the material presented in this volume represents a stage of transition: to await Vols 4 and 5 then, is to look forward to the flowering of several important strands in the eighteenth century's appreciation of Shake-speare. The exception to this general sense of transition is the actual performance of Shakespeare in the theatre, which reached a peak of frequency in this period that has never been equalled.

Once again I have to thank the founders, donors and staff of the major Shakespeare collections in England: the British Museum, the Bodleian, the Cambridge University Library and the Birmingham Shakespeare Library. For his help in checking references and quotations in English libraries I am grateful to Mr Ian Thomson, and for help with the proofs and index I thank Christian Casparis.

B.W.V.

Introduction

Comparing the Shakespeare criticism of this period with that covered in the previous volume, it is striking to see the emergence of much more liberal attitudes. This is not to say that neo-classicism is totally discredited but rather that the alternative judgments which I described in the last volume as 'escape-clauses' are invoked more frequently. The overall effect is much more liberated than in the previous twenty years.

True though this may be, we still find many of the neo-Aristotelian categories and the critical rejections which derive from them. Thus Aaron Hill confidently describes *Hamlet* as a most varied play which continues to please 'in spite of Errors and Absurdities, self-contradictory and indefensible' (No. 86: *Prompter*, 100). George Stubbes, in *Some Remarks on the Tragedy of 'Hamlet'*, in the following year, found many 'unnatural and absurd' elements in the play, such as the presence of armies on stage (No. 87). The anonymous author of an essay on *Edward the Black Prince* (1750) attacked the view that 'Rules are not at all necessary, since we are not offended at the Breach of them in Shakespeare. To which I answer, that every Man of true Judgment is offended at it, though we suffer or excuse his Faults, on account of his amazing Excellencies.' Had Shakespeare 'followed the Critical Rules' it would have given his work 'a great Addition both of Fame and Excellence' (No. 122). That devoted exponent of neo-classicism, William Mason, endorsed Voltaire's judgment that the English veneration for Shakespeare and his disregard for 'the necessary rules of the Drama' had led to a weakening of our literature (No. 131).

The Unities continued to be the easiest categories within which Shakespeare could be found lacking. For Mason 'good sense, as well as antiquity, prescribed an adherence to the three great Unities'. Conscious of the frequent criticism of Shakespeare for breaking the unity of time, John Upton excused Shakespeare by analogy with epic: in *Julius Caesar* the dramatist rightly continued beyond the death of Caesar, and as a result the plot of the play 'hangs together as in a heroic poem' (No. 114). Of course Upton is ignoring the specific neo-Aristotelian rules as to drama, but perhaps he intends that. (The orthodox would argue—as they still do over Sophocles' *Ajax*, say—that although a consideration of the consequences of a hero's death gives a play unity of theme, this is not the same as unity of action or time. The dramatist ought to choose a smaller span of history. . . .) Upton can cite *The Tempest* and *Measure for Measure* as examples of the unity of action, and John Holt (No. 118) agrees as to the former. Here are two critics otherwise liberal in their attitudes who still have sufficient respect for the rules to want to record Shakespeare's having occasionally observed them.

The mixture of comedy and tragedy in Shakespeare had aroused the wrath of many neo-classic critics, as the first two volumes in this series have shown. George Stubbes, in his full-length essay on *Hamlet* in 1736 (No. 87)—a piece which is in many ways free of the critical canons—is nevertheless upset by the presence of humour, as in the presentation of Polonius as a buffoon, in Hamlet's letter to Ophelia, his antic humour, his comments during the play-scene, his punning with Polonius and bawdy with Ophelia, his wit in the scene with Osric, and worst of all in the grave-diggers' scene. The writer of the less perceptive *Miscellaneous Observations on 'Hamlet'* in 1752 is equally offended by the unsuitable 'low comedy' of the grave-diggers (No. 134). Both writers deplore Shakespeare's weakness for puns, as does Mallet (No. 84), while Dr Johnson launches a most dignified exposure of 'low terms' in *Macbeth* (No. 129: *Rambler*, 168). The other vice of style distinguished by Dryden was bombast, but we hear less of that criticism in this period, with the exception of Upton's strictures on Shakespeare's 'faulty sublime', crowding 'metaphor upon metaphor' (No. 114), and of Pope's similar attack in his conversation with Spence (No. 88).

The traditional defence of Shakespeare under this head was still open: those were the faults of his age, a period of low taste and cultural barbarism. This explanation continues to satisfy William Popple in 1735 (No. 85), George Stubbes in 1736 (No. 87), William Guthrie in 1747 (No. 107), and Thomas Seward in 1750. Only Upton in 1748 has sufficient historical sense to see that this tradition makes a travesty of English humanism in the sixteenth century (No. 114).

That is, in brief, the sum of orthodox neo-classical attitudes in this period. Continuing my survey at this level will show how much more space and energy was spent opposing orthodoxy.

In 1751 John Brown turned upside down the tradition in neo-classicism which held that Shakespeare's irregularity made him a dangerous model:[1]

In England . . . our unrestrained Warmth of Imagination and habitual Reverence for the noble Irregularities of *Shakespeare*, concur to make us despise the rigid Laws of the Stage: On the contrary, in *France*, the Severities of the *Academy* have utterly quenched the high Tragic Spirit. . . .

In much the same vein Upton, Guthrie (No. 107) and Akenside (No. 119) attacked the whole French influence on English culture, although the latter example is perhaps not wholly free from the chauvinism which I remarked on in the previous volume. More significant are the attacks on the Unities. We might not agree with George Stubbes when he argues that *Hamlet* has unity of action in as much as every scene in it contributes to the main design, but we are happy to find him challenging the laws of place and time since these 'Arbitrary Rules' fail to perceive that 'no Dramatick Piece can affect us but by the Delusion of our Imagination'. Farquhar's argument of 1702 (No. 45 in Vol. 2) is thus taken up and re-applied. Samuel Foote attacked the Unities in 1747 (No. 110), arguing that Shakespeare had observed the only one that mattered, that of character. The following year Upton argued that 'dramatic poetry is the art of imposing', that the author practises an 'innocent deceit' and that as for the spectators 'he is the wisest man, who is easiest imposed on'. The author of the 1752 essay on *Hamlet* echoed this argument, that the unity of time is not necessary 'if we suffer ourselves to be deceived' (No. 134). In *Rambler*, 156 Dr Johnson attacked the arbitrary edicts of critics who would limit the action of a play to twenty-four hours, and he also defended the mingling of tragedy and comedy (No. 129). On this head he was in agreement with Upton, who again cited the example of epic to justify Shakespeare's practice.

Increasingly critics invoked the concepts of Shakespeare's genius, nature, imagination. (As in the four effusive examples which I have included of a genre which might be called 'The Shakespeare Poem', usually a 'survey' or 'progress' piece which sketches the history of drama in such a way as to place Shakespeare at the peak, or reviews his most famous characters or plays, or attacks contemporary taste: cf. Nos 94, 95, 97, 125.) The argument made by Sir William Temple, and applied to Shakespeare by Rowe and others,[2] that genius is positively aided by ignorance of learning (which might otherwise impede it) is made again by William Guthrie (No. 107) and more extensively by Richard Hurd: 'great reading prevents' the development of invention 'by demanding the perpetual exercise of the *memory*'. Only 'inferior wits' need training (No. 128):

The truly inspired . . . have need only of their *touch* from heaven. And does not the example of the first of *our* poets, and the most honoured for his invention, of *any*, give a countenance to this enthusiastic conclusion? It is possible, there are, who think *a want of reading*, as well as a vast superiority of genius, hath contributed to lift this astonishing man, to the glory of being esteemed the most original THINKER and SPEAKER, since the times of Homer.

Praise of Shakespeare's imagination is frequent, if seldom quite so ecstatic. William Smith celebrates Shakespeare's achievement 'by the natural strength of his own Genius . . . without any Imitation of these great Masters' (No. 91). For William Guthrie 'The field of imagination lyes higher than that of truth', and Shakespeare, 'like his own winged Mercury, vaults from the level soil into his seat' (No. 107). Shakespeare's unique ability to create fairies, witches, magic and the whole world of fantasy—a skill first singled out by Dryden in his prologue to *The Tempest* (No. 9 in Vol. 1)—is praised again by Smith (No. 91), by Holt (No. 118) and by Seward (No. 126), with the interesting primitivist argument that the deficiency of Beaumont and Fletcher in this mode derived from the 'accidental *Disadvantage of a liberal and learned Education*'—Shakespeare had only a 'low Education', lost in the primitive, archaic wilderness of Stratford-upon-Avon. Fallacious though that biographical inference may be, it typifies the general image of a dramatist who was able to strike direct at the audience's emotions, without any intermediate obstacle. In the words of James Thomson:[3]

> Thrice happy! could we catch great Shakespeare's art,
> To trace the deep recesses of the heart;
> His simple plain sublime, to which is given
> To strike the soul with darted flame from heaven.

The identity of Shakespeare with nature is even more often invoked, especially by the poets. Thus Thomson in *The Seasons* (1727) addressing Britannia, where reign 'the Queen of Arts' and 'Liberty':[4]

> For lofty sense,
> Creative fancy, and inspection keen
> Through the deep windings of the human heart,
> Is not wild Shakespeare thine and Nature's boast?

So, too, Dr Johnson, in his prologue for Garrick (1747):[5]

> When Learning's Triumph o'er her barb'rous Foes
> First rear'd the Stage, immortal SHAKESPEARE rose;
> Each Change of many-colour'd Life he drew,
> Exhausted Worlds, and then imagined new:

Existence saw him spurn her bounded Reign,
And panting Time toil'd after him in vain:
His pow'rful Strokes presiding Truth impress'd,
And unresisted Passion storm'd the Breast.

And a few years later Christopher Smart made his offering:[6]

Methinks I see with Fancy's magic eye,
The shade of Shakespeare, in yon azure sky.
On yon high cloud behold the bard advance,
Piercing all Nature with a single glance:
In various attitudes around him stand
The passions, waiting for his dread command.

Similar claims are made in the poems printed here (Nos 94, 95, 97).

An equal supremacy is awarded by the critics. So Pope's variation on the *topos* in his Preface ('he is not so much an Imitator, as an Instrument, of Nature', vol. 2, p. 404) becomes in turn a topic to be varied, expanded, as in William Guthrie's exercise in panegyric:

It is not Shakespeare who speaks the language of nature, but nature rather speaks the language of Shakespeare. He is not so much her imitator, as her master, her director, her moulder. Nature is a stranger to objects which Shakespeare has rendered natural.

—and so on (No. 107). Similar praise can be gleaned from Smith (No. 91), Whalley (No. 113) and the author of the 'Essay on Passions' in *The Museum* (No. 108). The corollary of this point is that Shakespeare excels in presenting 'the manners', that is, in vivid, realistic characterisation and behaviour. Many critics subscribe to this judgment: George Stubbes (No. 87), Aaron Hill (No. 86: *Prompter*, 100), Corbyn Morris in his extended examination of Falstaff as an illustration of humour (No. 98), Guthrie, with characteristic energy ('The genius forgetting that he is a poet wraps himself up in the person he designs; he becomes him; he says neither more nor less than such a person, if alive and in the same circumstances would say; he breathes his soul; he catches his fire; he flames with his resentments'); Whalley (No. 113), Holt (No. 118) and the 1752 critic of *Hamlet* (No. 134). A further point is that success here implies success in moral instruction through the characters, whether the just revenge of the ghost and the evil of Claudius (Nos 87, 134) or throughout the tragedies, in Shakespeare's moral presentation of the vices of his villains and the virtues of his heroes and heroines (No. 116).

These more liberal attitudes served to weaken the asperities of neo-classic criticism but can hardly be said to have created a detailed and viable alternative. But in one area they came near to doing this, an area in which such a demonstration was badly needed: Shakespeare's language. We find in this period, as a by-product of changing concepts of genius and inspiration, a more direct response to his poetry, and a new spirit of detailed, systematic analysis. The most important figure is John Upton, who in the middle of a rambling and fatally digressive book, his *Critical Observations on Shakespeare*, observed some of the disadvantages arising from England's lack of an adequate dictionary and grammar. 'No one can write without some kind of rules,' Upton argued, and although Shakespeare did not publish his *English Grammar*, as Ben Jonson did, his working rules can be deduced from his writings. Upton follows Theobald in seeing the value of such an enquiry as establishing a writer's norms, so that his usage can be tested against himself rather than against some arbiter's standard of correctness (No. 114):

when these [norms] are known, we shall be less liable to give a loose to fancy, in indulging the licentious spirit of criticism; nor shall we then so much presume to judge what Shakespeare *ought* to have written, as endeavour to discover and retrieve what he *did* write.

Upton lists fourteen 'rules', with some sub-divisions, and although they are not all equally valuable the exercise does alert us to characteristic Shakespearian linguistic formations and conventions, and it had some influence later in the century. Just as important in criticising that invocation of arbitrary, external criteria which neo-classicism was inherently prone to, is Upton's extensive citation of parallel grammatical liberties in the writing of the most admired ancient authors: Homer, Sophocles, Euripides, Virgil, Horace, Propertius, Terence, Plautus, Cicero, St Paul, Milton. The invocation of linguistic authority in order to put down the fallacy of Shakespeare's lawlessness could hardly continue to be made after such a demonstration. Credit must also be given to Upton for making the first examination of Shakespeare's metrical conventions, and if his enthusiasm in identifying what will appear to most modern readers abstruse classical metres seems excessive we should remember how little the study of this topic has advanced since his day.[7]

Upton's work on Shakespeare's language can be supplemented by other insights, whether general or particular. He had praised 'the masculine and nervous' style of Shakespeare, and those terms recur in the movement which opposes the traditional denigration of his puns or bombast. George Stubbes, in his 1736 essay on *Hamlet*, describes

Horatio's speech on omens at Rome as 'very nervous and Poetical', and uses the word 'nervous' as a term of praise twice elsewhere; he finds Ophelia's description of Hamlet's madness 'excellently good in the *Pictoresque* Part of Poetry'. James Holt described Shakespeare's language as 'copiously nervous' (No. 118). As examples of more detailed comment we could cite William Popple's note that punning is typical of Polonius, 'a Part of his natural Character' (No. 85; and Warburton's notes on Polonius, No. 111), or William Smith's perceptive analysis of the function of the rhetorical figure *hyperbaton* in Hamlet's first soliloquy, his defence of Shakespeare's use of 'low Terms', or his account of hyperbole (No. 91). William Dodd adds some further examples to Theobald's list of Shakespeare's use of the figure *aposiopesis* (No. 136), while Dr Johnson gives a remarkably acute explanation of the significance of the 'forced and unnatural Metaphors' given by Shakespeare to Macbeth after the murder of Duncan 'as a mark of Artifice and Dissimulation' (No. 105: Note XXIII).

Such a growth of interest and perception concerning Shakespeare's language is refreshing. While there is, perhaps, no criticism of the first rank in this volume, the over-all advance is considerable, and in the work of Upton we have an achievement which deserves more recognition than it has yet received.

II

On one point there is a strong link between literary criticism and discussions of the theatre in this period, the increasing dissatisfaction with the adaptations of Shakespeare. The author of theatrical criticism in *The Daily Journal* for 1736 and 1737 (who signed himself 'The Occasional Prompter': No. 89) has some very pointed criticism of the principles on which adaptations continued to be produced (versions of the comedies in these years are especially feeble). Of the literary critics Upton attacked those poets who, 'when their own little stock is spent . . . set themselves to work on new-modelling Shakespeare's plays, and adapting them to the tast of their audience', so producing 'a poet of shreds and patches'. Thomas Seward varied the metaphor: 'the very best Plays of *Shakespeare* were forced to be dressed *fashionably* by the *Poetic Taylors* of the late Ages . . .' (No. 126). The author of one of the many poems addressed to Garrick (No. 125) exhorted him, as from Shakespeare's ghost,

... to vindicate my injur'd song ...
To save me from a dire impending fate,
Nor yield me up to Cibber and to Tate:
Retrieve the scenes already snatched away,
Yet, take them back, nor let me fall their prey.

The 1752 essayist on *Hamlet* attacked Dryden and D'Avenant for their *Tempest*, Buckingham for his two-part *Julius Caesar*—'the most wretched Performances that were ever exhibited on the *English* Stage' (unfortunately for his rhetoric, Buckingham's versions were never acted), and savaged Tate (No. 134). In the same year William Dodd also attacked Buckingham's version (No. 136), while an anonymous journalist ironically praised Tate and others for attempting to 'reduce [Shakespeare] to common sense'.[8]

In 1750 Arthur Murphy produced the most intelligent criticisms of the adaptations yet made (No. 124), particularly concerning the distortions of Shakespeare's structure and meaning which they involved. He singled out Garrick's versions for special blame, and the role of this key theatrical figure in maintaining the adaptations was commented on increasingly. Richardson used the postscript to *Clarissa* to appeal to Garrick to have 'the courage to try the Public Taste' on this topic by banishing Tate's version (No. 115). Tate's 'vile Alterations' were attacked by the author of a pamphlet discussing the comedy success *The Suspicious Husband* (No. 112), who asks Garrick: 'How can you keep your Countenance when you come to the *Spheres stopping their Course, the Sun making halt, and the Winds bearing on their rosy Wings*, that Cordelia is a Queen?' He urged that Garrick could not plead that Tate seduced him: 'tho' you are not the Principal, you are accessary to the Murder, and will be brought in Guilty.'

These objections are the first widespread sign of dissatisfaction with the heavily transformed 'vehicles' which still held the stage. Yet they were to be made for many years in vain. Some writers, such as Elizah Haywood (No. 104), actually preferred the adaptations, and even Arthur Murphy confessed to liking Otway's ending to *Romeo and Juliet* better than Shakespeare's (No. 124). Certainly the theatre public made no concerted objection, and so the managers went on keeping them happy. Tate's *Lear*, the Dryden–D'Avenant *Tempest*, Otway's *Caius Marius*, Shadwell's *Timon*, all held the stage with frequent success in this period.[9]

Yet there was a lessening of impetus both in the number of new adaptations produced and in their extent. Compared to the 1680s or

1700s there are few large-scale adaptations, those total transformations of structure, values, character and language. For his *Macbeth* (No. 100) Garrick included a witch scene from D'Avenant's version, and followed him in omitting the Porter's wit, but otherwise he contented himself with shortening the scene in which Lady Macduff and her child are murdered[10] (this no longer takes place on stage) and adding a death-speech for the hero (which reads like an expansion of D'Avenant's added one-line curse on ambition).[11] For his *Othello* Garrick cut the 'antres vast and deserts idle' speech (which Rymer had objected to and which William Dodd in 1752 found unpleasing) and added a less 'marvellous' passage. He took greater liberties with *Romeo and Juliet* (No. 117),[12] and showed the influence of critical taste in rejecting the original's 'Jingle and Quibble', and that of theatrical taste in the added funeral processions and the retention of Otway's device of reviving Juliet before Romeo dies. (A device which Theophilus Cibber had used for his revival of the play in 1744, in a version which plagiarised from Otway, as his contemporaries soon pointed out.) We note the absence of any crusade to restore 'pure Shakespeare', but at least the situation is better than it was. Perhaps the best comment on the actors' divided position is given by Garrick in his Drury Lane prologue of 1750 (No. 121). On the one hand we have adulation for the bard—

> Sacred to SHAKESPEARE was this spot design'd,
> To pierce the heart, and humanize the mind

—and on the other the claim to be materially dependent on the audience's taste:

> If want comes on, importance must retreat;
> Our first great ruling passion is—to eat.

Exit Lear, enter Harlequin.

To come across Cibber's *King John* in the mid-40s, then, is to find a throw-back to a previous age. (Indeed there is evidence for productions of some version of this adaptation in 1703, and rehearsals of it in 1723 and 1736,[13] as mentioned in No. 89 below.) Cibber works with the free hands of the generation of Tate. The first act of Shakespeare's play is cut altogether, and with it the character of Queen Elinor; the Duke of Austria is also removed, which facilitates the cutting of the indecorous wit of Falconbridge; and Cibber adds much political bickering, partly designed to mirror England's relationship with France at that time. The element of the play which I have chosen to

9

represent is the heightened emotionalism, seen in the murder-plot between King John and Hubert, and in the recriminations and laments of
Constance. The style of this new material echoes the point which I
made in the last volume concerning adaptations by Theobald and Aaron
Hill in the 1720s, that when the playwrights attempted to intensify
Shakespeare's emotions there seemed to be only one style available, that
inaugurated by Tate.

In fact Cibber's adaptation was no more popular than others done in
this period (with the special exception of *Romeo and Juliet*, in which the
rival companies ran a night-by-night competition, Garrick finally
defeating Cibber). An able critique of Cibber's version was provided
by an anonymous writer (No. 103), who shows himself in tune with
the more liberal critics by affirming that, since the original play does
not keep to the Unities, the adapter will not find it easy to reduce it 'to
Rule'. (Yet, on the other side, he defends Tate's *Lear* and Hill's *Henry V*,
and advocates a policy of cutting offensive word-play.) The '*wild
Greatness*' of Shakespeare's characters is seen in Falconbridge and Constance, and has been trivialised by the adapter. Cibber, he argues, has
reduced the shock of the scene in which the King asks Hubert to murder
Arthur by giving a preliminary description of Hubert's evil, and has
distracted us still further by the melodramatic ploy of making the King
close the window before embarking on his plot. This sensitivity to the
way in which a dramatic effect can be achieved or ruined in the theatre
is shared by a number of critics in this period, in which theatrical
criticism first establishes itself as a genre. As already mentioned, Arthur
Murphy attacked absurdities of structure and motive produced in the
adaptations of *Romeo and Juliet*, and denounced the actors for their
crude exaggerations of character (No. 124). Bonnell Thornton amus-
ingly exposed the misunderstandings created by the appearance of the
Ghost (No. 135: *Drury Lane Journal*, 10), while everyone must remember Partridge's experience in *Tom Jones*.

The general value of the theatre reviewer to the historian of literature
is that he records styles of acting or producing and shows the nature of
contemporary taste. While the reviews can often be ephemeral, and
sometimes of little more use than to document actors or events of which
we would otherwise have no record, the special value of these mid-
eighteenth-century theatre critics is that they frequently evaluate actual
performances by reference to a critical concept of how a play or
character ought to be performed, according to their idea of what the
author intended. That is, they attempt to define the spectrum of viable

interpretations. Thus William Popple (No. 85) attacks the usual presentation of Polonius as a buffoon, complete with grimace and drawl,
and argues that Shakespeare shows him to be a man of understanding
and knowledge. Aaron Hill (No. 86: *Prompter*, 100) urges that the actor
of Hamlet has to reproduce both the serious and the gay aspects of his
personality. The major tragic roles drew the most comment. Garrick
attempted to parody in advance the commonplace criticisms of his
Macbeth (No. 99), but he certainly did not silence criticism of his Lear,
both sides of which will be represented in this and subsequent volumes.
One attack on his version (No. 109) argues that the cause of Lear's madness was his desire for royalty: he was answered by another anonymous
critic in that year who refuted him by pointing to the effects of ingratitude (No. 112). The earlier critic also defended Othello as being a
lover not a savage, and was supported by 'Sir' John Hill in 1750 (No.
123), who made a competent analysis of the process by which Shakespeare punctuates Othello's plans for revenge with self-reminders of his
love for Desdemona.

I have no wish to make any exaggerated claims for the theatrical
criticism. But, as it has been neglected by historians of formal criticism
for so long, I think that many readers will be surprised at its freshness
and cogency; and obviously enough, if we are to try to understand the
total presence of Shakespeare in any period, we cannot ignore the stage.

Contemporary criticism will help us to appreciate Shakespeare's
presence on the eighteenth-century stage, but to gauge its full extent
we have to turn from past opinion to modern scholarship, to that im-
pressively full documentation of the day-by-day performances in the
theatres compiled by a group of American scholars and presented in
The London Stage, 1600–1800. Here, and in particular in the work of
A. H. Scouten,[14] we can trace a remarkable rise in the performance of
Shakespeare. This boom used at one time to be ascribed to the influence of Garrick, but it evidently ante-dates his arrival and is the
product of a number of factors, literary, social and political. First among
these was the double success of *The Beggar's Opera* and *The Provoked
Husband* in the spring of 1728. These two plays may be said to have
created an expansion of the theatre, for the managers realised what a
potential audience they had, if only the crowds who flocked to them
could be induced to come regularly. In the following season the two
companies had been increased to four, and by 29 November 1729 five
companies were performing, a number which for the first time began
to approach the popularity of the theatre in Elizabethan and Jacobean

London. The number of actors increased accordingly: from 130 (in the two companies before 1728) to 250 in the 1729 season, and averaging 300 up to 1737.

Within this general boom in the theatre some special pressure was exerted on Shakespeare's behalf. A key figure here, who has never received due recognition, was Henry Giffard, an actor turned manager, who controlled the theatre at Goodman's Fields from 1731 to 1736 and from 1740 to 1742, and ran Lincoln's Inn Fields theatre from 1736 to 1737. In addition to offering much more contemporary drama than did either Rich at Covent Garden or the managers at Drury Lane, Giffard performed more Shakespeare than the large houses did, and revived the original plays rather than the adaptations. In the 1732–3 season, for instance, Drury Lane performed Shakespeare on 14 nights, Covent Garden on 23, but Goodman's Fields under Giffard on 40 nights out of the 171 on which the company performed (a proportion of 23 per cent). Another source of pressure for performing Shakespeare was the Shakespeare Ladies' Club, whose activities have been well researched by E. L. Avery.[15] Active from about 1736 to 1738, this group of women (evidently of some social status and education) wanted to have Shakespeare performed more often, and from authentic texts. In the season of 1737 they bespoke a performance at Drury Lane and actually raised money for a production at Covent Garden. They were praised by several distinguished contemporaries, including Fielding and James Ralph (see No. 89 below).

Before 1737, then, a clear increase in Shakespeare performances can be traced. In 1737 occurred an event which was disastrous for many causes in English theatre but which, paradoxically, increased the number of Shakespearian productions still further. Having long been taunted on stage by the opposition satirists (especially Fielding), Walpole succeeded in having the Theatrical Licensing Act passed on 21 June 1737, by which effectively only those theatres (Covent Garden and Drury Lane) already possessing patents were allowed to perform, and the Lord Chamberlain was given both the power to prohibit individual performances, and the duty of licensing all new plays and additions to old plays. While some brave and ingenious individuals such as Lacy, Giffard, Macklin, Theophilus Cibber and Samuel Foote managed to evade the Act, the deterrent effect of the legislation—which was enforced more in the censorship of new plays than in the punishment of unlicensed performances—led to a distinct reduction in the number and quality of new plays performed. Given an increasing interest in the theatre before this date, a group of able and energetic managers in addition to the patentees—such all-round men of the theatre as Giffard, Aaron Hill, Charles Macklin, Theophilus Cibber and William Hallam; given a new and talented generation of actors trained by these managers, who made their débuts in the 1730s and 40s; given all these factors, together with an existing interest in Shakespeare, it is no wonder that the restrictions on new drama imposed by the 1737 Act should have led to a great spurt in performances of Shakespeare. From this point onwards his plays become safe choices, low-risk theatre, vehicles in which each new performer can make (or lose) a reputation. The ten or twelve plays which were most often performed were so familiar to the audience in this period (see Hill's *Prompter*, 100: No. 86) that the spectators' attention was more at liberty to appreciate individual performances, nuances of voice and gesture. The theatre criticisms of the 1740s are not only more numerous than they were earlier, they are also far more detailed, as critics who knew their *Lear* or *Macbeth*, *Romeo and Juliet* or *Othello* intimately could concentrate almost exclusively on evaluating interpretation.

It is this combination of factors, briefly stated, which accounts for the rise in performances of Shakespeare. In the period from 1703 to 1710 Professor Scouten estimates that 11 per cent of all performances were Shakespearian; between 1710 and 1717 the figure would be 14 per cent, and from 1723 to 1734 it would be 12 per cent. At first sight the figure of 17 per cent for the period from 1717 to 1723 seems to point to a Shakespeare revival, but there is evidence from the box-office takings that these performances were under-attended. With an average, otherwise, of about 13 per cent over the previous thirty years, the figure of 14 per cent for the 1735–6 season is up to the norm. But then for 1736–7 it rises to 17 per cent, for 1737–8 to 22 per cent, and in 1740–1 it reaches 25 per cent of all performances, probably an all-time peak in the production of Shakespeare. The range of plays performed widens accordingly. Henry Giffard revived *The Winter's Tale* on 15 January 1741, 'not acted 100 Years', while on the same night Drury Lane (which had just had a great success in reviving *As You Like It* for the first time since the Restoration) revived *Twelfth Night*: both plays ran simultaneously for nine nights. Giffard revived *The Merchant of Venice* on 14 February 1741, in which Macklin had his great success as Shylock: it was acted over twenty times that season. In 1741 Giffard also revived *All's Well that Ends Well*, produced for the first time since the closing of the theatres in 1642. By the end of the 1741 season—in which the popular

13

favourites such as *Hamlet*, *1 Henry IV* and *The Merry Wives* were being performed *at all three theatres*—only six Shakespeare plays had not been revived (and two of these were put on by Theophilus Cibber in 1744). Drury Lane devoted 44 per cent of its performances in the 1740–1 season to Shakespeare. Surely at no other time in any country has Shakespeare been performed so frequently and with such success.

David Garrick made his début on the London stage (as Richard III) on 19 October 1741, under Giffard at the Goodman's Fields theatre. He was born into a Shakespeare boom, and of course he did a great deal to further it. But the uncritical adulation which Garrick has been a victim of, and which continues to be more damaging to a true evaluation of him than all the malicious criticism, has given credit to him as a pioneer which is, properly, due to Henry Giffard. But credit cannot be given only to individuals, and not even to groups such as the Shakespeare Ladies' club. In fact the 'Shakespeare boom of 1740–1' is a phenomenon for which 'credit' may be an inappropriate term. For even dedicated Shakespearians must regret that, owing to Walpole's 1737 Act, the gain in Shakespeare productions was bought at the price of a reduction in the creative life of English drama.

III

A fundamental element throughout the criticism and production of Shakespeare is often taken for granted, although it is no less prone to the taste of the age: that is the text, the very words which, after many years of editing and emending, we unthinkingly accept as being what Shakespeare wrote. The eighteenth century was a good deal more alert to the fact that 'Shakespeare's text' is a construct which is still alive, still being moulded by scholars, always liable to change. Although this period may seem like an interlude, with Theobald behind it and Dr Johnson before it, there are a number of pointers to a developing sensitivity in these matters.

The two main editions of the period were both disappointing. Sir Thomas Hanmer (No. 96) followed Pope in rejecting 'as spurious' those passages 'which were stigmatized as such' by Pope, and indeed added to them. Hanmer offered more of a glossary, but otherwise, apart from a few emendations, his edition was of no consequence. His entirely uncritical inclusion of textual cruces without either solving or commenting on them was exposed by Dr Johnson (No. 105), who also

disposed of his trivial tinkerings with the text with this memorable
sentence: 'Such harmless Industry may, surely, be forgiven, if it cannot
be praised: May he therefore never want a Monosyllable, who can use
it with such wonderful Dexterity.'

Hanmer, like Theobald, had the misfortune to accept suggestions
from Warburton, and became involved in a dispute over the use of
them which ended more to his discredit than to Warburton's.[16] As can
be seen from his contribution to Birch's biography of Shakespeare in
1739 (No. 90), Warburton had continued to accumulate emendations
since his correspondence with Theobald ten years earlier, and Birch
announced then that Warburton would soon give a 'much more
correct edition' which would include 'the rules, which he observed in
correcting his author, and a large glossary'. This 'excellent Critic'
offered an excerpt from his glossary, but when his edition finally appeared in 1747 he announced that he had decided not to offer either the
rules ('*a body of Canons*, for literal Criticism') or the glossary. What he
did offer was an edition which was immediately exposed to satire for
its arrogance, its pretentiousness and its wild misuse of the prerogative
of an editor.

In defence of Warburton it can be said that some of his emendations
are good ('the god kissing carrion' in *Hamlet*, say, or 'patens' in *The
Merchant of Venice*) and that some of his notes are to the point: the
attack on Dryden's *Tempest*, for instance, the note on duelling in *As
You Like It*, the defence of *The Winter's Tale* (rare in this period), the
partial apologia for Shakespeare's 'incorrect style', the notes on
Polonius, the defence of Hamlet's Pyrrhus speech, his refutation of
Rymer. He is not a complete dunce, whatever his contemporaries said.
Yet on the other side we have to set his Pope-like rejection of 'trash'
supposedly inserted by the players, his coarse and brutal treatment of
other editors and, above all, his perverse rejection of entirely acceptable
readings in favour of eccentric word-coinages of his own. Thus
'Stephano' becomes 'Staffilato', 'here' becomes 'heryed', 'increase' is
changed to 'inchase', 'damp' to 'trempe', 'plague' to 'plage', 'stage' to
'strage', 'mother' to 'meether', and so on. Even today the reader will be
puzzled to know what Warburton thought he was doing, and why.

His contemporaries lost no time in pointing out his errors. In the
selections included here he is attacked by Upton (No. 114), Holt (No.
118), Seward (No. 126) and Dodd (No. 136), several of whom declare
the superiority of Theobald. I have not included much of the great
quantity of abuse which was piled on him, since this seldom produced

insights either into the text or into the process of editing. But the points were taken. In the second edition of his *Critical Observations* (1748) John Upton devoted over fifty pages of his Preface to itemising errors 'such as even the most inveterate enemy would pity, did not an unusual insolence destroy every degree of it' (p. viii). He showed that Warburton cited examples of words in modern and classical texts which simply did not exist there; that his English etymology was equally inventive; and that his glosses were ridiculous (as when Warburton glosses 'snipe' as ' "a diminutive woodcock"—which is as if I should define a duck to be a diminutive goose': p. xxxi). Commenting on Warburton's condescending claim to have enlightened 'the unlearned reader', Upton affirmed that 'there is not one *learned reader or writer*, I dare say, in the whole republic of letters but looks on our editor as *wantonly trifling with an art he is stranger to*' (*ibid.*).

The unanimity of eighteenth-century critics and scholars on this point is impressive. The most brilliant of all the refutations was that first published anonymously in 1748 as *A Supplement to Mr. Warburton's Edition of Shakespeare* 'By a gentleman of Lincoln's Inn'. Abused by Warburton as being neither a lawyer nor a gentleman, the author, Thomas Edwards, disclosed his identity for the third edition of 1750 (which is the version selected here: No. 127, although later additions to it will be dealt with in the next volume). The first edition had totalled 62 pages; the third, 176 pages; the sixth (1758) and seventh (1765) amounted to over 300 pages. Some of this is padding, but Edwards found no difficulty in expanding the work with more examples of Warburton's absurdities. His work is divided into two parts, developing the chink which Warburton had left in his armour by not offering the promised *Canons of Criticism and Glossary* (which is how Edwards named his book from 1750 onwards). For the first, Edwards summed up satirically Warburton's actual working rules as an editor:

A Professed Critic . . . has a right to alter any passage, which He does not understand.

Where He does not like an expression, and yet cannot mend it, He may abuse his Author for it.

He may find out obsolete words, or coin new ones, and put them in the place of such, as He does not like, or does not understand.

All these 'Canons of Criticism' are illustrated with plentiful examples from Warburton's notes, and the satirical glossary exposes the wild errors even more acutely, as in the entries which I have included under 'carbonado'd', 'frown', 'groth' and 'oats'. The success of Edwards's volume was decisive: 'Even Warburton's friend Birch admitted to Lord Orrery that it was "one of the most ingenious pieces of Satire" he had ever read, and that it had "extremely humbled Mr. Warburton's pretensions to Criticism in the opinion of the public".'[17]

These attacks on Warburton were constructive in the sense that they rid the public of an edition which was seriously misleading on almost every head. But they also made contributions to textual criticism in their own right. Edwards shows the validity of Shakespeare's text often by giving an explanation where Warburton could find none, and offers some useful emendations (as, for instance, correcting Menenius' 'I have ever *verified* my friends' to 'I have ever *varnished* my friends', seeing the connection with the metaphor of 'size' in the following lines). Upton offers several intelligent suggestions, applying Theobald's method of illustrating Shakespeare from his own work to good effect in pointing for the first time to the 'clusters' of words associated with 'candied' (Whiter was to develop this). John Holt made several useful glosses and emendations in *The Tempest*, as the reader will discover, while even lesser critics like Seward and Dodd had something to contribute.

To sum up the movement in this period, we should note that the links between literary criticism and theatre criticism on the one side, and textual criticism on the other, were much closer than they are today, or have been since the growth of specialisation in the nineteenth century. Clearly it would not be easy to reverse that trend, and it becomes increasingly hard to master all three disciplines. But if you believe, as I do, that we ought all to be as complete critics as possible— since many of these areas have inter-relations which the narrow specialist is unable to perceive—then these Shakespeare critics of the mid-century form no mean model for our study and imitation.

NOTES

1 Brown, *Essays on the Characteristics of the Earl of Shaftesbury* (1751), p. 34.
2 See Vol. 1, p. 13 (Temple, John Dryden Jr); Vol. 2, pp. 9f. (Rowe, Addison, Felton, Welsted, Dennis).
3 Thomson, Prologue to *Tancred and Sigismunda* (1745), Sig. A₄; *cit.* C. E. Hughes, *The Praise of Shakespeare* (1904), p. 222.
4 Thomson, *Summer*, lines 1563ff.
5 Johnson, *Prologue spoken by Mr. Garrick at the Opening of the Theatre in Drury Lane 1747*.

6 Smart, 'Prologue to *Othello*, As it was acted in the Theatre-Royal in Drury Lane, on Thursday the 7th of March 1751, by Persons of Distinction for their Diversion', in *Poems on Several Occasions* (1752), p. 217.

7 See my review of D. L. Sipe, *Shakespeare's Metrics*, in *Yearbook of English Studies* I (1971), pp. 241–3.

8 *The Weekly Miscellany*, 1737; *cit*. G. W. Stone, Jr, 'Shakespeare in the Periodicals (2)', *Shakespeare Quarterly* III (1952), p. 325.

9 For details of performances see *The London Stage 1660–1800, Part 3, 1729–1747*, ed. A. H. Scouten (Carbondale, Ill., 1961) and *Part 4, 1747–1776* ed. G. W. Stone Jr (Carbondale, Ill., 1962). I shall be dealing with Garrick's relationship to Shakespeare more fully in the next volume.

10 Kalman Burnim has observed that, although Bell's acting edition of 1776 keeps the scene up to Angus's warning to Lady Macduff, a prompt-book from Garrick's theatre eliminates it altogether: *David Garrick, Director* (Pittsburgh, 1961), p. 123.

11 See G. W. Stone, Jr, 'Garrick's Handling of *Macbeth*', *Studies in Philology* XXXVIII (1941), pp. 609–28.

12 See G. W. Stone, Jr, '*Romeo and Juliet*: The Source of its Modern Stage Career', *Shakespeare Quarterly* XV (1964), pp. 191–206; and G. C. Branam, *Eighteenth-Century Adaptations of Shakespearean Tragedy* (Berkeley, 1956).

13 See J. J. McAleer, 'Colley Cibber—Shakespeare Adapter', *Shakespeare Newsletter* XI (1961), p. 42. Odell refers to Fielding's satire on the play in *The Historical Register for 1736: Shakespeare from Betterton to Irving*, I, 348. It was in rehearsal again in 1739, but news of an organised movement by the law-students (Templars) to disrupt its performances caused Cibber to withdraw it again. See *The London Stage, 1729–1747*, I, p. clxxv, and C. W. Nichols, 'Fielding and the Cibbers', *Philological Quarterly* I (1922), pp. 278–89, especially pp. 284–9.

14 See A. H. Scouten, 'Shakespeare's Plays in the Theatrical Repertory when Garrick came to London', *Studies in English* (Austin, Texas, 1945), pp. 257–68; 'The Increase in Popularity of Shakespeare's Plays in the Eighteenth Century: A Caveat', *Shakespeare Quarterly* VII (1956), pp. 189–202; and 'The Shakespearean Revival', in *The London Stage, 1729–1747*, I, pp. cxlix ff. and *passim*.

15 E. L. Avery, 'The Shakespeare Ladies' Club', *Shakespeare Quarterly* VII (1956), pp. 153–8.

16 See John Nichols, *Illustrations of the Literary History of the Eighteenth Century*, volume 2 (London, 1817), and A. W. Evans, *Warburton and the Warburtonians. A Study in some Eighteenth-century Controversies* (Oxford, 1932), pp. 151ff.

17 A. W. Evans, *op. cit.*, p. 162, quoting from *The Orrery Papers* II, p. 44.

Note on the Text

The texts in this collection are taken from the first printed edition, unless otherwise stated. The date under which a piece is filed is that of the first edition, with two exceptions; plays, for which the first performance is used (for such information I have relied on *The London Stage* for the period 1660 to 1800); and those works for which the author gives a date of composition substantially earlier than its first printing. The place of publication is London, unless otherwise indicated.

Spelling and punctuation are those of the original editions except where they seemed likely to create ambiguities for the modern reader. Spelling has, however, been standardised for writers' names (Jonson not Johnson, Rymer not Rhimer), for play titles, and for Shakespearian characters.

Small omissions in the text are indicated by three dots: [. . .]; larger ones by three asterisks.

Footnotes intended by the original authors are distinguished with an asterisk, dagger and so on; those added by the editor are numbered. Editorial notes within the text are placed within square brackets.

Act-, scene- and line-numbers have been supplied in all quotations from Shakespeare, in the form 2.1.85 (Act 2, scene 1, line 85). The text used for this purpose was the *Tudor Shakespeare* ed. P. Alexander (Collins, 1951).

Classical quotations have been identified, and translations added, usually those in the Loeb library.

84. David Mallet, textual criticism attacked

1733

From *Of Verbal Criticism. An Epistle to Mr. Pope. Occasioned by Theobald's Shakespeare, and Bentley's Milton* (1733), lines 35–58; this text from Mallet's *Works* 3 vols (1759).

David Mallet (1705?–65), a poet and dramatist who wrote a life of Bacon and edited the works of Bolingbroke, was a member of Pope's circle and expressed its leader's prejudice in this satire (a later passage of which descends to crude abuse of Theobald).

> . . . If SHAKESPEARE says, the noon-day sun is bright,
> His *Scholiast* will *remark*, it then was light;
> Turn CAXTON, WINKIN, each old *Goth* and *Hun*,
> To rectify the reading of a *pun.*
> Thus, nicely trifling, accurately dull,
> How one may toil, and toil—to be a fool!
>
> But is there then no honour due to age?
> No reverence to great SHAKESPEARE's noble page?
> And he, who half a life has read him o'er,
> His mangled points and commas to restore,
> Meets he such slight regard in nameless lays,
> Whom BUFO treats, and Lady WOU'D-BE pays?
>
> Pride of his own, and wonder of this age,
> Who first created, and yet rules, the stage,
> Bold to design, all-powerful to express,
> SHAKESPEARE each passion drew in every dress:
> Great above rule, and imitating none;
> Rich without borrowing, Nature was his own.
> Yet is his sense debas'd by gross allay:
> As Gold in mines lies mix'd with dirt and clay.

Now, eagle-wing'd, his heavenward flight he takes;
The big stage thunders, and the soul awakes:
Now, low on earth, a kindred reptile creeps;
Sad HAMLET[1] quibbles, and the hearer sleeps.

85. William Popple on Polonius

May 1735

From *The Prompter*, No. 57.

William Popple (1701-64) was a minor dramatist and poet who collaborated with Aaron Hill in publishing this periodical from 1734 to 1736.

No. 57 (27 May 1735)

In tracing the Corruption of the Stage up to its Source, it may not be improper to take in every Error that may have introduced itself, and furnished its Contingent to the general Body.

It will not therefore be foreign to my Purpose to consider some Characters in our Dramatick Pieces as they were originally DESIGN'D by the Poets who *drew* them, and as they APPEAR to an Audience from the manner in which the Actor *personates* them.

A *Character falsified*, like a Stream of poisoned Water, instead of nourishing *kills* and *destroys* every thing it runs thro'. Actors and Managers have not always Penetration enough to dive into the *Truth* of *Character* and are therefore content to receive it from Tradition and MISACT it, as *Arlequin Astrologue* composes Almanacks, *de père en fils.*

This Branch of Corruption, when it relates to old Plays, is not directly chargeable on the present Actors or Managers but is one of those general *Errors* which Time has given a *Sanction* to, and is for that

---

[1] The first edition reads 'Othello quibbles'.

Reason the more *considerable* as well as *dangerous*. But tho' the *Error* itself does not cover them with *deserved Shame* the reforming of it might crown them with *deserved Applause*, and make their Penetration, like the Sun *long* eclips'd, *break out* to the *Admiration* of the *present Age* and the *Comfort of Posterity*.

I shall inforce the Truth of my Observation by the Character of *Polonius* in *Hamlet*, which I shall consider in its *double Presentation*.

Polonius, according to *Shakespeare*, is a *Man of a most excellent Understanding and great Knowledge of the World*, whose Ridicule arises not from any *radical Folly* in the old Gentleman's Composition but a certain *Affectation of Formality and Method*, mix'd with a smattering of the Wit of that Age (which consisted in playing upon Words), which being grown up with him is *incorporated* (if I may venture the Expression) with all his *Words* and *Actions*.

That this is the true Character of *Polonius*, the doubtful Reader may be satisfied if he will give himself the Trouble to peruse the Scenes between *Polonius*, *Laertes*, and *Ophelia*, and the first Scene in the second Act, between *Polonius* and *Reynaldo*. To save him Part of the Trouble I shall make bold to borrow a Couple of Speeches for the immediate Confirmation of this Character given of *Polonius*, which will both establish his *good Sense and Knowledge of the World*, and his *Affectation of Formality and Method*.

The first is his Advice to his Son:

> Pol.   *Give thy Thoughts no Tongue;*
> *Nor any unproportion'd Thought his Act.*
> *Be thou* familiar, *but by no means* vulgar.
> *The Friends thou hast, and their Adoption try'd,*
> Grapple *them to thy Soul with* Hooks *of* Steel.
> *But do not dull thy Palm with Entertainment*
> *Of each* new-hatch'd unfledg'd *Com'rade.—Beware*
> *Of Entrance to a Quarrel; but, being in,*
> *Bear't, that th' Opposed may beware of thee.*
> GIVE *ev'ry Man thine* Ear; *but few thy* Voice.
> Take *each Man's Censure; but* reserve *thy* Judgment—
> Costly *thy* Habit, *as thy Purse can buy,*
> *But not* EXPREST *in* FANCY; *rich, not* gaudy:
> FOR THE APPAREL OFT PROCLAIMS THE MAN.
> —*Neither a* Borrower, *nor a* Lender *be;*
> *For* Loan *oft loses both itself and Friend,*

And borrowing dulls the Edge of Husbandry.
This, above all, TO THINE OWNE SELF BE TRUE—
And it must follow, as the Night the Day,
Thou can'st not then be false to any Man.
Farewel, &c. [1.3.59ff.]

No Man that was really a Fool could ever make such a Speech, which would become the Mouth of the wisest and most experienced.

The next is where *Polonius* acquaints the *King* and *Queen* that he has found out *the very Cause of* Hamlet's *Lunacy.*

> Pol.   *My Liege and Madam, To expostulate*
> *What Majesty should be, what Duty is,*
> *Why Day is Day, Night, Night, and Time is Time,*
> *Were nothing but to waste Night, Day, and Time—*
> *Therefore, since Brevity's the Soul of Wit,*
> *And Tediousness the outward Limbs and Flourishes,*
> *I will be brief: Your noble Son is mad;*
> *Mad call I it; for to define true Madness,*
> *What is't but to be nothing else but mad?*
> *But let that go* ——
> Qu.   *More Matter, with less Art.*
> Pol.   *Madam, I swear, I use no Art at all;*
> *That he is mad, 'tis true; 'tis true, 'tis pitty;*
> *And pitty 'tis, 'tis true; a foolish Figure,*
> *But farewel it; for I will use no Art.*
> *Mad let us grant him then; and now remains,*
> *That we find out the Cause of this Effect;*
> *For this* EFFECT DEFECTIVE *comes by Cause—*
> *Thus it remains, and the Remainder thus—Perpend—*
> *I have, &c.* [2.2.86ff.]

Here is a visible Affectation of *Formality* and *Method*, with that particular sort of Wit above mentioned, that makes the old Man appear ridiculous at the same time that what he says has all the Probability in the World of being the Truth. If we examine the Speeches of *Polonius* throughout the whole Play we shall find them reducible to this *determinate Character* and to no other *Species* of Folly.

How does *Polonius* appear to an Audience at present? He never *looks* or *speaks* but the Fool *stares* out of his *Eyes*, and is *marked* in the *Tone* of his *Voice*. Even Words that have the strongest *Sense* as well as *Beauty* of

Sentiment and *Expression* lose their original *Stamp* and *Dignity*, as the Character is now represented, and are converted into the *Seeming* of Folly.

A few Quotations, with the Reader's *Recollection* in what manner the Speeches are deliver'd by Mr. *Griffin* and Mr. *Hippisley* (who perform this Roll at the two Theatres Royal) will illustrate this Truth.

In the very first Speech which *Polonius* makes, where I defy the most penetrating to find either a *Character of Folly* or any *Stamp of particular Humour* or, in short, any thing but a Concern which the old Gentleman expresses with great Beauty of Language and *proper Seriousness* at his Son's going to travel and leaving him, our improving Actors present us with the Image of an *Old Buffoon*.

> Pol. *He has, my Lord, by* WEARISOME *Petition,*
> WRUNG *from me my* SLOW LEAVE; *and at the last,*
> *Upon his Will, I seal'd my* HARD *Consent.*
> *I do beseech you, give him Leave to go.*   [1.2.58ff.]

Here is the most *simple, plain, unstudy'd, unaffected* Reply that cou'd be given: yet how is this *spoke* and *acted*? The Eyes are turn'd *obliquely* and drest up in a foolish Leer at the King; the Words *intermittently drawl'd* out with a very strong Emphasis, not to express a Father's Concern—which would be right—but something ridiculous to excite Laughter, tho' neither the *Words* nor the *Sense* have any *Comick Vein* in them; the *Voice ton'd* like the *Squeak* of a *Bag-Pipe*, and the whole Attitude suited to this false Notion of his Character!

In the Scene between him and his Daughter, where he questions her about *Hamlet*'s Love, he fares no better.—You see the Figure and the Manner of an Idiot join'd to the Prudence of a Parent giving Advice to his Daughter how to receive the Addresses of a presumptive Heir of a Crown; a most unnatural *Connection*, which *Shakespeare* never thought of! The only Vein of Humour discoverable in the Scene is a little playing on the Word *Tenders*, a Part of his natural Character.

> Pol. *Marry I'll teach you; think yourself a Baby,*
> *That you have ta'en his* Tenders *for true Pay,*
> *Which are not* Sterling: Tender *yourself more dearly,*
> *Or (not to crack the Wind of the poor Phrase,*
> *Wringing it thus) you'll* tender *me a Fool.*   [1.3.105ff.]

Immediately after

> Pol. *Affection! Pugh! You speak like a green Girl*
> *Unsifted in such* perillous *Circumstance!*   [1.3.101f.]

Every Spectator of *Hamlet* will easily recollect what a Horse-laugh the manner of repeating these two Lines never fails to occasion. Examine the Sense and Language and you'll sooner find the Weight and Authority of a Father reproving an unexperienc'd Child who does not know in what Light she ought to consider both *Hamlet* and his Love, and acquainting her how she ought to behave for the future, than any *Drollery* or *Folly*. Again,

> Pol. *Ay, Springs to catch* Wood-cocks; *I do know*
> *When* the Blood boils, how prodigal the Soul
> Lends the Tongue Vows. [1.3.115ff.]

What can be more *beautiful* as well as *serious* than this Sentiment! What render'd so *light* and *ridiculous* by the manner of speaking it at present!

In the first Scene in the second Act, where *Ophelia* gives *Polonius* an Account of *Hamlet*'s Disorder, every Reflection the old Man makes is of the serious kind, and does not give the Actor the least Cue for *Mirth* or *Folly*. Yet in the Representation we see a strong Cast of both, without a Shadow of that Gravity his uncertain Conjectures and Reflections upon the Nature of the Passion he imagines the Prince possest with should naturally give him.

Those who have seen *Hamlet* will easily recollect the Figure *Polonius* makes in this Scene, and the Tone of Voice with which he utters:

> Pol. *Mad for thy Love* —— [2.1.85]
> Pol. *This is the very Ecstacy of Love.* [2.1.102]

And in the Scene where *Polonius* comes to *Hamlet* with a Message from the Queen, tho' 'tis evident *Polonius* only flatters *Hamlet*'s supposed Lunacy, and *Hamlet* himself tells us so:

> Ham. *They fool me to the Top of my Bent*— [3.2.374]

Yet from the manner this is acted the Audience is taught to believe that *Polonius*, in pure Simplicity of Sight, sees the Cloud in the three different Shapes *Hamlet* gives it.

It wou'd be endless to carry *Shakespeare*'s *Polonius* along with the *Modern one* throughout the whole Play in this manner. Enough has been quoted to shew the judicious Reader how much this Character is falsify'd, and what an Intrusion of Foreign *false* Humour it labours under!

If it be said, it is more entertaining now than it wou'd be were it represented in its true Humour, then the Consequence will be that Actors are better Judges of Characters than the Poets who drew them, and ev'ry Character will be in their Power to represent as they please; which wou'd pour a Torrent of Corruption on Dramatick Performances.

It will avail them very little as to the Force of Argument to say the modern *Polonius* never fails to excite Laughter, since neither the Poet nor the Actor shou'd strive to please the *Quantity* of what *Shakespeare* calls BARREN SPECTATORS, by making the JUDICIOUS GRIEVE, the Censure of WHICH ONE (as the Motto expresses it) *must out-weigh a whole Theatre of others.* [3.2.26ff.]

I have already said that this false Edition of *Polonius* is the Error of Time and no wise chargeable on the present Representers, Mr. *Griffin* and Mr. *Hippisley*, who, bating some few *Exuberances* which I shall in the Course of this Work *lop off*, are the very best Comick Performers that we have, and that have the truest Notions of the *Vis Comica*; which consists in bringing out the *express* Humour of a particular Character, the Idea of which lies *increate* in the Sense of the Words 'till, called forth by the penetrating Genius of the Actor, it receives Life and Motion to the Delight of the judicious Spectator, who is ever ravished with *true Imagery* and *faithful Portraiture.*

But to shew that it is impossible *Polonius* could ever have been designed by *Shakespeare* the Fool and Idiot he appears now, we find him not only intrusted by the King with an Affair of the last Consequence to him (which no wise Prince wou'd ever commit to the Care of a Fool), but that in his younger Days he had acquired the Reputation of being *cunning* and *politick*—

> Pol. *Or else this Brain of mine,*
> *Hunts not the Trail of Policy so sure*
> *As I have us'd to do.* [2.2.46ff.]

Again

> Pol. *Has there been such a Time, I'd fain know that,*
> *That I have positively said, 'Tis so,*
> *When it prov'd otherwise.*
> King. *Not that I know.* [2.2.152ff.]

'Tis true these are but the Braggings of an old Man, and he was out in his Judgment in this Case; but he is not the first Politician with a very good Head that has been mistaken. But without this additional Proof the Speeches quoted are sufficient to exclude Folly from his Composition.

One great Cause of the Corruption of this Character of *Polonius* I take to lie in the obsolete Language, which being very different from the Phraseology of our Days the injudicious Spectator takes the Expressions to be what the *French* call *Recherchées*, chosen on Purpose to create Laughter. As, for Example—

> *Affection! Pugh! You speak like a green Girl,*
> Unsifted *in such* perillous *Circumstance.*   [1.3.101f.]

The Sense of which being only 'You speak like a raw Girl unacquainted with such Matters' does not create any Laughter at all in this modern Garb, nor with the *Judicious* in its antique one. But by the Help of the Figure *Polonius* makes, and for want of considering the Idiom of those Times, it acquires in the Opinion of the *many* a Comick Turn in spite of the serious and moral Sense it contains. And so of the rest.

The Compass of a Half-sheet will not allow me to give any further Reasons for the Recovery of *Polonius*'s true Character. Those that come to Plays merely to laugh, tho' at the Expence of Reason, will relish *Polonius* as he is now. Those who reflect on Propriety of Character, Truth of Circumstances, and Probability of Fable cannot bear the inconsistent, ridiculous, and foolish Buffoon mix'd so preposterously with the Man of Sense.

As this is not the only Character that has suffer'd as extraordinary a Metamorphosis, and others still may, I leave it to every Reader's Reflection how radically this Corruption affects the Stage.

86. Aaron Hill on King Lear and Hamlet

October 1735

From *The Prompter*, Nos 95, 100.

No. 95 (7 October 1735) on King Lear

I should be sorry if the mistaken *Gravity* of any of my Readers of a more rigid Cast of Mind than the rest shou'd suppose me too frequent in my *Theatric* Animadversions. Persons of this gloomy Disposition have not allow'd themselves to reflect how diffusively powerful the Influence of the *Stage* has in all Ages been found, and of what universal Good Consequence it wou'd be cou'd [I] promise myself such *Improvement* as I *wish* from the Success of my disinterested Endeavours.

Trusting, however, to *Time* the *Event* of my Purpose, *The* PROMPTER will impartially and resolutely persist to make War on *Mismanagements*, to detect and expose *Incapacity* or *Conceitedness*, and to point out and do Justice to the Claims of *unheeded Excellence*. The Reformation He aims at may not be *Sudden*, but it will be *Certain*. The MASTERS of our Theatres will not always be *able* to *misguide* the Taste of the Publick. The *Players* Themselves will gradually become wise enough to *see* and *correct* the Errors which Custom and Imitation have made general among them. And the AUDIENCES at length will be reason'd into a *Sense* of their *Authority*, take Alarm at the Indignity with which they are treated by the *obstinate* or *lazy* Actor, and *use the Means they are Masters of* to enforce and maintain *Decorum*.

It being reasonable to suppose that the *Players*, in respect to One who was an HONOUR to their *Profession*, wou'd consider with *Partiality* the Opinions and Instructions of SHAKESPEARE, I took Pleasure in a late Paper to do him Right against some of their Notions, and produc'd from his Writings one of those beautiful *Pictures* they abound with, in Proof that he *must have been* a most accomplish'd and exquisite ACTOR. Here follows another, from the 3d Act of his *Henry the 5th.*

In PEACE, *there's nothing, so* becomes *a Man,*
As modest *Stillness—and* Humility:
—But, when the Blast of WAR *blows in our Ears,*
Then—*imitate the* Action *of the* Tyger.
STIFFEN *the* Sinews—*Summon up the* Blood;
Disguise fair Nature, with hard-favour'd RAGE:
Then lend the Eye, *a dreadful Look—and let*
The Brow O'ERHANG *it, like a* jutting Rock.
Now, Set the Teeth—*and* stretch *the* Nostril *wide:*
Hold hard *the* Breath—*and* bend up *every Spirit,*
To his *full* Height.   [3.1.3ff.]

Let us suppose these Outlines of ANGER, so strongly express'd in the
Picture, to have been *understood* and *consider'd* by that Player of the first
Rate who took upon him, some time since, to act the Character of
KING LEAR to a numerous and elegant Audience. What *Emotions* of the
Heart, what Varieties of conflicting Passions, what Successions of *Grief,*
Pity, Hatred, Fear, Anger, and *Indignation* wou'd not have arisen like
Whirlwinds to agitate, transport, and convey here and there at Pleasure
the *commanded Minds* of his Hearers, till the Poet's intended Impression
producing its natural *Effects* the Theatre had been *shook with Applause,*
and the Thunder and Lightning in the *Play* but a *faint* Emulation of the
Tempest which that Actor's fine Voice (*so exerted*) wou'd have rais'd in
the *Pit* and *Boxes*!

How happened, then, that All was *Calm* and *Indolent,* that an *In-*
difference to the Character left the House in but a *languid* Attention? The
Reason for This was too plain: when the Actor is *Cold* why shou'd the
Audience be *animated*? The Idea which seems to have been form'd of
the Character was *mistaken.* But since it is certainly in this Player's *Power*
to give us all that we miss'd in the Part, after He shall have *weigh'd* it by
the *Author's Intention,* I will lend him what Light I can furnish: not
without Hopes to be re-paid by the Pleasure of assisting in his *Praises,*
which *Nature* has qualified him to *merit,* the next Time he appears in
That Character.

King LEAR's most distinguishing *Mark* is the violent IMPATIENCE of his
Temper. He is *Obstinate, Rash,* and *Vindictive,* measuring the Merit of
all Things by their Conformity to *his Will.* He cannot bear Contra-
diction: catches Fire at first Impressions: and inflames himself into
Frenzy by the Rage of his Imagination. *Hence all his Misfortunes.* He has
Mercy, Liberality, Courage, Wisdom, and Humanity, but His Virtues

are eclips'd and made useless by the *Gusts* which break out in his Trans-ports. He doats on *Cordelia* yet *disinherits* and *leaves* her to *Misery*, in the Heat of an ill-grounded Resentment, for a Fault of no Purpose or Consequence; and to punish his *Rashness* by its Effects on *Himself* was the *Moral* and *Drift* of all those Wrongs which are done him.

It is plain, then, that an *Actor* who wou'd represent him as the Poet has drawn him shou'd preserve with the strictest Care that chief Point of *Likeness*, his IMPATIENCE. He shou'd be turbulent in his *Passions*, sharp and troubled in his *Voice*, torn and anguish'd in his *Looks*, majestically broken in his *Air*, and discompos'd, interrupted, and rest-less in his *Motions*.

Instead of all this the unquicken'd Serenity of this popular Player seem'd to paint him as an Object of Pity, not so much from the *In-gratitude* of his unnatural *Daughters* as from the *Calmness* and *Resignation* wherewith He *submitted to* his Sufferings. We *saw* in his Action, we *heard* in his Voice, the *Affliction* of the Father, without the *Indignation*; the *Serenity* of the Monarch, without the *Superiority*; and the *Wrongs* of the Angry Man, without their *Resentment*.

Let his *Provocations* be weigh'd, *they* will give us a *Measure* whereby to judge of his *Behaviour*. After having been insulted almost to Madness by his Daughter GONERIL, on whom He had newly bestow'd *Half his Kingdom*, He comes (labouring with a meditated Complaint) to REGAN, in Possession of the other Half: fully convinc'd SHE wou'd atone her Sister's Guilt by an Excess of Submission and Tenderness. *Here*, instead of the *Duty* he expected He finds his first Wrongs *made light of* and more than *doubled* by new Ones. His Messenger put in the *Stocks*; and his Daughter and her Husband *refusing him Admission* under Pretence of being *weary* by *travelling*.

Remember the *Qualities* of the King thus provok'd. Remember that *Impatience* and *Peevishness* are the Marks of his Character. Remember that you have seen him, but just before, casting out to Destruction his most favourite and vertuous *Cordelia* only for expressing her Appre-hension that Her Sisters had *flatter'd* him. What STORMS of *just Rage* are not NOW to be look'd for from this violent, this ungovernable Man, *so* beyond Human Patience insulted! *So* despis'd! *so* ill treated? *See* what *Shakespeare* makes him answer when *Gloster* but puts him in mind of the *Duke* of *Cornwall's* fiery Temper!

> *Vengeance! Plague! Death! Confusion!*
> FIERY! What *fiery Quality? Breath, and Blood!*

Fiery! the FIERY *Duke!*
Go—tell the Duke *and's* Wife—*I'd* speak *with 'em;*
Now—presently—*Bid 'em come* forth, *and* hear *me:*
Or, at their Chamber Door, I'll beat *the* Drum,
Till it cry, Sleep to DEATH.   [2.4.93f., 101f., 114ff.]

When we see such Starts of Impetuosity *hush'd unfeelingly over* and delivered without *Fire*, without *Energy*, with a Look of *Affliction* rather than *Astonishment*, and a Voice of *patient Restraint* instead of *overwhelming Indignation*, we may *know* by the Calmness which we feel in *our* Blood that the *Actor's* is not enough agitated.

In fine, where-ever *King Lear* call'd for the BASS of his Representor's Voice all possible Justice was done him. When He *mourn'd, pray'd, repented, complain'd*, or excited *Compassion*, there was nothing deficient. But upon Every Occasion that requir'd the *Sharp* and the *Elevated*, the *Stretch'd* Note and the *Exclamatory*, The King *mistook*, like a Dog in a Dream, that does *but* SIGH when He *thinks* He is BARKING.

I wish I could effectually recommend to so *Excellent* yet *unexerted* a VOICE a deliberate Examination into the MEANINGS of *Shakespeare* in his first Lines above quoted. The *Musick* and *Compass* of an *Organ* might be the *infallible Reward* of his Labour did he once but accustom his *Nerves* to That SENSATION which impresses (*mechanically*, and by inevitable *Necessity*) the whole FRAME, SPEECH, and SPIRIT with the Requisites of Every Character. But (I appeal to the Sincerity of *his own* private Reflexion) He neither, according to the mentioned Advice, *Stiffen'd the Sinews*, nor *Summon'd up the Blood*, nor *lent a terrible Look to the Eye*, nor SET *the Teeth*, nor *Stretch'd the Nostrils wide*, nor *held the Breath hard*—by which Last *Shakespeare* had in his View a certain out-of-Breath *Struggle* in the Delivery of the Words, when *angry*, which is *not only natural* but disorders and stimulates the *Body* with the most alarming Resemblance of *Reality*.

Another Thing which I must recommend to his Notice is That He loses an Advantage He might draw from these *Swellings* and *Hurricanes* of the *Voice*, in Places where proper, compar'd with such opposite Beauties as its *Fall*, its *articulate Softness*, its *clear Depth and Mellowness*; all which He is fam'd for already. These CONTRASTS are in *Acting*, as necessary as in *Painting*—ALL LIGHT, or ALL SHADE, never finish'd a Picture.

I am loth to speak of *Absurdities*, since I touch but upon *Errors* with a View to do Service. Yet in One Single Remark I will indulge myself for *That* Reason, it being an unavoidable Consequence, when Men *Resolve* before they have *Reflected*, that they must be sometimes RIDICULOUS as well as *Mistaken*.

The poor King, in the Distraction of his Spirits, amidst the Agonies of ungovern'd Sorrow, provok'd, inflam'd, asham'd, astonish'd, and vindictive, bursts out into a Succession of CURSES against the unnatural Object of his Fury, striving to *ease* an overburthen'd Heart in the following *Torrent* of rash Wishes.

> *All the* Stored Vengeances of Heaven *fall*
> *On her ungrateful Head*—Strike *her young Bones*,
> *Ye* taking *Airs, with* Lameness—
> *Ye nimble Lightnings*, dart *your blinding* Flames
> *Into her Scornful* Eyes! *&c.*   [2.4.160ff.]

An Actor who, in this Place, *misled* by his Love of *Weight* and *Composure*, instead of grinding out the Curses from between his Teeth amidst the Rage and Agitations of a Man who has been *wrong'd* into *Madness*, advances deliberately forward to the Lamps in Front of the Pit, KNEELS with elevated Eyes and Arms, and pronounces *with the Calmness and the Reverence of a* PRAYER such a meditated String of *Curses* in the *Face* of Heaven—that Actor must *destroy* the *Pity* which he labours so injudiciously to *attract*, since the Audience, instead of *partaking* his *Agonies* and imputing his Words to his *Wrongs*, which they would have done had They *Seen* him *in Torture* and transported out of his *Reason*, now *mispoint* their Concern; and, in Place of hating the Daughter for reducing to such Extremities a Father so indulgent and generous, condemn, and are scandaliz'd at, a Father who *with a Malice so* UNDISTURBED and SERENE can invent all those *Curses* for his Daughter.

Of such extensive Importance are the *Mistakes* of a *Player*, as even to *pervert* and *destroy* the Purpose for which the POET has written!

I cannot close this Paper without confessing my Pleasure from the Applause which That Actor receiv'd who appeared in the Character of EDGAR. Hence forward I shall conceive warm Hopes in his Favour. It was once my Opinion that this *Edgar*'s Voice had no BOTTOM, and that *King Lear*'s had no TOP. But *Edgar* has now convinc'd a pleas'd Audience by the well-judg'd RESTRAINT of his *Risings* (except in Places where beautiful and necessary) and by a right-plac'd Distinction in his *Falls, Breaks,* and *Tendernesses* that there is nothing we may not expect from him when he *examines into Nature* with a View to *act naturally*.

I remark'd with no less Delight an unexpected and surprizing Improvement in *Cordelia*, who to a FORM that is soft and engaging has of late added *Spirit*, *Propriety*, and *Attitude*, to a Degree that is strikingly *picturesque* and *delightful*. I found the Audience most *sensible* of it, and *whispering* their Approbation. They will THUNDER it in Favour of this Lady when she thinks fit to make her *Utterance* as Expressive as her *Gesture*. She need only give us her *Voice* as she receiv'd it from *Nature*, without THEATRIC Embellishment.—While she aims to make it *softer* she but *thins* and *refines* it 'till we lose its *Articulation*, and are left to *guess at* the *Sense* of her Speeches. Cou'd she prevail on her Modesty to speak like HERSELF she wou'd speak *in her Character*, but while she imitates (too humbly) some Examples which mislead her she *postpones* the Admiration I foresee *she will rise to.*

No. 100 (24 October 1735): on Hamlet
[Motto: 'Sufficient unto the Day is the Evil thereof.']

Though the Reverence I retain for the *Clergy* is as *fix'd* as the *Reason* upon which it is founded, yet cannot I be blind to the *Injustice* of some of their *Complaints*. If I blame them, in particular, for the Clamour they affect to raise against the INFIDELITY of the present Age it is because the Accusation seems a *manifest* Mistake. For even in the *Devil's own Domains* (so some of those *grave* Gentlemen have been pleas'd to *describe the King's* THEATRES) Men regulate their Conduct by *Advice of* HOLY WRIT, and (most literally) *follow the Maxim* to which I am oblig'd for my *Motto*.

It cannot, surely, have been owing to any *less powerful* Inducement that instead of a provident Meditation which might *form* SCHEMES *in Summer* for our Winter Entertainment, The *Managers* suffer the Seasons for Playing to come on and *provide for Themselves*. Yet They *do* it, to say Truth, with *Propriety*! The *same* Plays *return*, like the *same Blooms repeated*, with the Return of Each Season.

Hence, *for-ever without End*, have we the *Othellos*, *Oroonokos*, *Tamerlanes*, *Jaffeirs*, *Hamlets*, *Castalios*, *Torrismonds*, *Lears*, *Catos*, and all the *long-long Line* of their COMIC *Cotemporaries*! And the *Joke* of the CONSEQUENCE is that Every gay Frequenter of Plays, being compell'd to *have 'em by Heart*, grows as *tired* of 'em as He does of his *Wife*: and That, too for the very same Reason—*He can find Nothing* NEW *in their Company*.

The Repetition of this *Mill-horse* Management wou'd be less offen-

sive if *less general*. But the most ridiculous Part of the Absurdity is that
It extends itself to *Every Theatre in Town*. The same STOCK of Plays in
All confines us to the melancholy Necessity of turning (like a Man in a
Fever) but from One weary Side to the Other. 'The SAME TRAGEDIES
need not always be seen': 'No—You may see the SAME COMEDIES!' The
Expedient is comfortable, and puts me in Mind of a Reflexion which the
Devil makes in MILTON:

> In LIQUID *Burnings* —— or in DRY—*to dwell*,
> Is all the sad Variety of HELL!

If any Thing can possibly be *Sillier* than the *Practice itself* it is the
MOTIVE from which it arises. This MOTIVE is, That *personal Attachment*
wherewith Every ACTOR, falling in *Love* with *Himself*, is convinc'd that
his shortest Road to *Distinction* is to appear at *one* House in a Capital
Part, against the Actor most fam'd for it at the *Other, and shew us the*
DIFFERENCE. The MANAGER mean while, partaking the Triumphs of His
Actor's encourag'd *Cock-Matches*, makes just such a *political* Figure in
the Gladness of his Heart upon Occasions so little to his Honour as *Sir
Paul Pliant*, in Raptures at the *Eloquence* of his *Wife* while she is pressing
on the Design of His *Cuckoldom*.

The fairest *Satisfaction* the Players cou'd make to the Town in Reward of its *Patience* wou'd be to gather new *Judgment* from so often
representing a Character, and give it us still stronger and stronger, till
improv'd to the utmost Perfection. But they *imitate* too servilely the
prescriptive Mistakes of Each other to *improve* any better Way than
downward; as a CHAIN must be said to *improve* in its *Length* where one
Link suspending another in a regular Gradation of *Sinking* the Last must
of Course be the LOWEST.

HAMLET is the *Play*, of all their dramatic Circulation, which may
be oftenest seen without *Satiety*. Here are *Touches of Nature* so numerous, and *mark'd* with so expressive a *Force* that Every *Heart* confesses
their Energy: and in spite of Errors and Absurdities *Self-contradictory*
and *indefensible* This Play has always pleas'd, still pleases, and will for-
ever continue to please while *Apprehension* and *Humanity* have Power
in *English* Audiences.

To what *Excess* then wou'd it not *move* were *Hamlet's Character* as
strongly *represented* as *written*! The *Poet* has adorn'd him with a Succession of the most *opposite* Beauties, which are *varied*, like *Colours* on
the *Cameleon*, according to the *different Lights* in which we behold him.
But the PLAYER, unequal to his *Precedent*, is for-ever *His unvaried* SELF.

We *hear* him, indeed, *call'd* HAMLET, but we *see* him *Mr. Such a One*, the ACTOR. The Man who wou'd act *any* Stage Character to Perfection must borrow the *Serpent*'s Dexterity, to *slip out of his Skin* and leave his *old Form* behind him.

What *Cæsar* meant of *Terence* when He said, He was *Half a Menander*, suits exactly to the Truth that ought to be spoke of any the best *Player* who, within *my* Remembrance, has taken upon him the Representation of *this Character*. The utmost *Praise* He has been able to deserve was, to have been HALF *a Prince Hamlet. Mr.* WILKS, for Example, *was* his GAY *Half*, And *Mr.* BOOTH might have been his SOLEMN had he appear'd in the Part. But It was in the Power of *neither* to do Right to *That Half* which suited the *Manner* of the *Other*. They were, therefore, tho' very strong yet but *Half-finish'd* Actors, Men who had their *Graces* and *Capacities* SPECIFICK, and to whom *Nature* seems to have set *Limits*, as God did to the *Ocean*,—HITHERTO shalt thou go:—and NO FARTHER.

The characteristic Distinction that *marks* the Temper of *Hamlet* is a pensive, yet *genteel* HUMANITY.—He is by *Nature* of a *melancholy Cast*, but His polite Education has illuminated the *Sable*, and, like the Sun through a *wet* MAY *Morning*, mix'd a *Gleam* with his *Sadness*. When he *grieves*, he is never *Sullen*; When He *trifles*, he is never *light*. When *alone* He is *seriously solid*; When in Company, *designedly flexible*. He *assumes* what he pleases, but he *is* what He ought to be: the Lamenter of his murder'd *Father*, the Discerner of his *Mother*'s Levity, and the Suspecter of his *Uncle*'s Baseness.

How *weigh'd*, then, and *significant* should he be found in his *Looks* and his *Actions!* When He counterfeits Distraction with *Ophelia*, and perceives that she is *observing* him, All his Air is as light and as empty of Purpose as if *really* as *mad* as He designs She should *think* him. But no sooner has he declin'd himself from the Glances of HER Eye than His OWN gives us Marks of his *Pity* and his *Prudence*. The WILDNESS He but *affects* quits his Air in a Moment, and a touching Sensation of SORROW *paints* his *Soul* in his *Gesture*: which again the next Moment He transforms into *Wantonness*, in the very Instant of Time while He *returns* toward the Lady.

In *this*, then, the Double Capacity of *Mr.* WILKS, and *Mr.* BOOTH shou'd *unite* in ONE Actor. The First cou'd be *wanton*; but He was *wanton* without *Weight*. The Second cou'd be *Weighty*; but He was *Weighty* without *Easiness. Mr. Wilks* had a Spirit that ran away with his Body: *Mr. Booth* had a Body that dragg'd too heavy on his Spirit. When the One was *most* delightful, He seem'd animated without *Pur-*

pose. When the Other was most strong, He gave IMPRESSION without *Briskness.*

I will make still more evident the Justice of my Remark by producing *two* Instances, in One of which *Mr. Wilks* must be remember'd to have been unpardonably *Deficient*, and in the other whereof *Mr. Booth* will be suppos'd *incapable* to have *succeeded* by Any judicious Reflector who *considers* his Qualities.

While *Horatio* and *Marcellus*, in the solemn Stillness of *Midnight*, on the *Platform*, are discoursing with *Hamlet* concerning the *Carousals* at Court the *Ghost* of his *Father* appears: and upon *Horatio's* sudden crying out—'*Look, my Lord, where it* COMES!' The Prince is suppos'd to turn eagerly toward the Spirit, with an unbelieving *Curiosity* rather than a terrified *Apprehension*. But upon the discover'd *Reality* of the Form He *starts back* a Step or two, and expresses his Amazement as follows: in a low Pitch of Voice, still, FIXING his Eyes with a kind of riveted DOUBT in their *Steadiness.*

<blockquote>

Angels! *and Ministers of* Grace! *defend me!*   [1.4.39]

</blockquote>

Here, no doubt, He shou'd STOP: and after a significant PAUSE, under *silent* Agitations of *Horror*, strive for Strength of Resolution to *attempt* an APPROACH; which He accompanies with these broken Sentences and one—Short—Slow—Step—at Each of them—delivering the whole (till the Word QUESTIONABLE) with a Voice *faint* and *trembling*, as if it *struggled* and found a *Difficulty* in forcing its Way against the Oppression of his *Terror.*

<blockquote>

Be *thou—a Spirit of Light,—or Goblin damn'd!—*
Bring with *thee—Airs, from Heaven—or Blasts from* Hell!—
Be *thy* Intents—*wicked, or charitable!—*
Thou comest—*in such a* QUESTIONABLE Shape— [1.4.40ff.]

</blockquote>

Mark the *Burst* upon the Word *Questionable!* It explains the *Author's Design*, and supports and justifies the *Necessity* of such a *gradual* Advance as I have describ'd. It is as if *Hamlet*, after an Utterance breaking (faintly, and tremblingly *Low*) thro' the *fear-frozen* Organs of Speech, after *labouring* (in what he had been saying *before*) against the *Weight* of his *Blood* half *congeal'd* by his *Terror*, now drew Comfort and Encouragement from the Reflexion that this Form of his *Father* was a QUESTION-ABLE *Shape*: that is, a Shape, to which he might SPEAK, *boldly*. And accordingly, in the very next Line, He assumes a *stronger* and *positive*

EMPHASIS, and cries out, *kneeling* at the Word *Father*, for the more earnest Effect of his Application.

> *I* WILL—speak *to thee*—*I'll* CALL *thee*—Hamlet?—
> King?—FATHER?—ROYAL Dane?— [1.4.44f.]

Stopping, anxious and *expectant* (after creeping a little onward with his Knee) upon the two Last of these Appellations, Examining (with his own Eye still FIX'D upon That of the *Ghost*) the wish'd *Effect* of them separately. But when neither of 'em procures him an *Answer* He grows *desperate*; and forcing WARMTH from his *Impatience* Strains his Voice into EXCLAMATION:

> OH! —— ANSWER *me*.
> LET *me not* BURST—*in* Ignorance:—*but*—TELL *me*—
> WHY—&c. [1.4.45ff.]

And from This Place to the End of the Speech All his Action is *Earnest*, All his Looks are *distracted*, All his Body is *convuls'd*, and His whole *Soul* pour'd out in the *pathetic* Delivery of his *Accents*.

But whoever remembers *Mr.* WILKS in this Part of the Character need not be put in mind with what a *Lightness*, quite *improper* to the Occasion, He *anticipated* the *Place* in which it would have been the Duty of his Friends to *restrain* him; causing them (*immediately*, at his *first Sight* of the Apparition) to *struggle* against his unseasonable Endeavours to break away and *advance upon* the Ghost—forgetful how little Necessity a Man's *half curdled* Blood wou'd leave him under of being *held back from* such an Appearance—supposing it *real*.

With the same ill-judg'd *Vivacity* of Error He threw out from the Beginning all the *Sharps* of a *precipitate Clamour*, without Pause, without Terror, without *Rub*, *Rest*, or *Marking*, hurrying on the whole *Smartness* and *Alacrity* of his own natural Temper in such an *unnatural* Misapplication of its *Spirit* that I never saw him, in this Place, without thinking on *Oedipus* prescribing NOISE as a *Midwife* to the *Moon* in *Eclipse*.

> *Beat, beat, a* thousand Drums, *to ease her Labour*

Nay, to such Excess of ill-timed *Defiance* did he carry his *Rapidity* that when He came to this following Menace

> *By Heaven, I'll* MAKE *a* Ghost, *of* HIM, *that* HOLDS *me*:
> *I say,* AWAY.—Go *on*—*I'll* follow *thee*. [1.4.85f.]

Instead of directing the three first Words in the second Line against *Horatio* and *Marcellus* He address'd 'em, in high Rage and with a Flourish of his drawn Sword, *against* the *Ghost of his* FATHER: toward whom, on the contrary, after the highest Rage of an Elevated Voice against his *With-holders* he ought to have *inclined* his transported Breast with an Air of *Obedience*, and pronounced in the most *soft* and *gentle* Delivery, *this* Part of the Sense *only*:

Go on—I'll follow *thee.*

Dropping, at the same Time, his *Tone* and his SWORD (the *Drawing* whereof wou'd be *ridiculous*, upon any Supposition but to prevent a Renewal of his *Restraint*, after having forced himself away). For against *any Ghost at all* a SWORD is a silly Defence:—but quite *horrible* and the most shocking *Indecorum* against *the Ghost of his Father.*

In all this foregoing *Scene*, where *Mr. Wilks* was by *Nature* (not *Negligence*) deficient *Mr. Booth* wou'd by Nature (not *Care*) have been admirable. Each had his *Half*, and *no more*, of the *Form, Turn*, and *Spirit* that must, as I said, be JOIN'D to compleat this Character.

But wou'd we *see*, on the other Hand, *where* the *First* of these two celebrated Actors reach'd an *Easy* and a *Graceful* EXCELLENCE, which in the *Last* must have been *constrain'd* and *heavy* had he gone about to *imitate* it, we need but recollect the *Gayety*, the unforc'd, soft, becoming NEGLIGENCE, with which, reclining at the Feet of *Ophelia* and toying with her Fan as if *genteely Insignificant*, He kept a *Guard* upon his *Uncle's* EYE and *watch'd* (unnotic'd) the *Effect* of his *Play's Influence.*

In short, the Province of an ACTOR is too *copiously extensive* for the Limits of these narrow Papers. To comprehend it in one *general* Idea, His *skill* shou'd be like That of a PILOT, the Rudder may be suppos'd his *Judgment*, the Ship his *Voice* or *Person*, the Sea may be the *Character*, and the Winds which his Course is steer'd by shou'd be the *Passions*, in their Powers and Changes.

87. George Stubbes on *Hamlet*

1736

From *Some Remarks on the Tragedy of Hamlet* (1736).

The ascription of this essay to the Rev. George Stubbes (born *c.* 1683), a fellow of Exeter College, Oxford from 1701 to 1725, subsequently a country clergyman and domestic chaplain to the Duke of Ormond and Frederick, Prince of Wales, was made by the antiquary Richard Rawlinson. See Bodleian MS. Rawl. J 4° 3, fols 401r–402r; *Alumni Oxonienses* ed. Joseph Foster (Oxford, 1891), IV, p. 1439; and N. Joost, 'The Authorship of the *Free-Thinker*', in *Studies in the Early English Periodical* (Chapel Hill, N.C., 1957), p. 125. Stubbes also published a poem, *The Laurel and the Olive* (1710), a Sermon, *A Constant Search after Truth* (1721), two Platonic dialogues (on beauty, 1731; on the understanding, 1734) and *A New Adventure of Telemachy* (1731). Rawlinson also ascribes to him a translation of Mme de Sévigné's letters.

I am going to do what to some may appear extravagant, but by those of a true Taste in Works of Genius will be approv'd of. I intend to examine one of the Pieces of the greatest Tragick Writer that ever liv'd (except *Sophocles* and *Euripides*), according to the Rules of Reason and Nature, without having any regard to those Rules established by Arbitrary Dogmatising Criticks only as they can be brought to bear that Test.

Among the many Parts of this great Poet's Character so often given by some of our best Writers I shall particularly dwell upon those which they have the least insisted on, which will, however, put every Thing he has produc'd in its true and proper Light.

He had (beyond Dispute) a most unbounded Genius, very little regulated by Art.

His particular Excellency consists in the Variety and Singularity of his Characters, and in the constant Conformity of each Character to itself from its very first setting out in the Play quite to the End. And

still further, no Poet ever came up to him in the Nobleness and Sublimity of Thought so frequent in his Tragedies, and all express'd with
the most Energick Comprehensiveness of Diction.

And it must moreover be observed, as to his Characters, that although
there are some entirely of his own Invention and such as none but so
great a Genius could invent yet he is so remarkably happy in following of Nature that (if I may so express it) he does it even in Characters
which are not in Nature. To clear up this Paradox, my Meaning
is that if we can but once suppose such Characters to exist then we
must allow they must think and act exactly as he has described
them.

This is but a short Sketch of the main Part of *Shakespeare*'s particular
Excellencies; the others will be taken Notice of in the Progress of my
Remarks. And if I am so happy as to point out some Beauties not yet
discovered or at least not put in the Light they ought to be I hope I shall
deserve my Reader's Thanks, who will thereby, I imagine, receive that
Pleasure which I have always done upon any new Discovery of this
sort, whether made by my own Labour or by the Penetration of others.
And as to those Things which charm by a certain secret Force and
strike us we know not how, or why, I believe it will not be disagreeable
if I shew to every one the Reason why they are pleas'd, and by that
Consideration they will be capacitated to discover still more and more
Charms in the Works of this great Poet, and thereby increase their
Pleasure without End.

I do not pretend, in Publishing these Remarks of mine, to arrogate
any Superiority of Genius. But I think every one should contribute to
the Improvement of some Branch or other of Literature in this Country
of ours, and thus furnish out his Share towards the Bettering of the
Minds of his Countrymen, by affording some Honest Amusements
which can entertain a Man, and help to refine his Taste and improve his
Understanding, and no Ways at the Expence of his Honesty and Virtue.
In the Course of these Remarks, I shall make use of the Edition of this
Poet given us by Mr. *Theobald*, because he is generally thought to have
understood our Author best, and certainly deserves the Applause of all
his Countrymen for the great Pains he has been at to give us the best
Edition of this Poet which has yet appear'd. I would not have Mr. *Pope*
offended at what I say, for I look upon him as the greatest Genius in
Poetry that has ever appear'd in *England:* but the Province of an Editor
and a Commentator is quite foreign to that of a Poet. The former
endeavours to give us an Author as he is; the latter, by the Correctness

and Excellency of his own Genius, is often tempted to give us an Author as he thinks he ought to be.

Before I proceed to the particular Parts of this Tragedy I must premise that the great Admirers of our Poet cannot be offended if I point out some of his Imperfections, since they will find that they are very few in Proportion to his Beauties. Amongst the former we may reckon some *Anachronisms*, and also the inordinate Length of Time supposed to be employ'd in several of his Pieces; add to all this that the Plots of his Plays in general are charged with some little Absurdity or other. But then, how easily may we forgive this when we reflect upon his many Excellencies! The Tragedy that is now coming under our Examination is one of the best of his Pieces, and strikes us with a certain Awe and Seriousness of Mind far beyond those Plays whose Whole Plot turns upon vehement and uncontroulable Love, such as are most of our modern Tragedies. These certainly have not the great Effect that others have which turn either upon Ambition, the Love of one's Country, or Paternal or Filial Tenderness. Accordingly we find that few among the Ancients, and hardly any of our Author's Plays, are built upon the Passion of Love in a direct Manner; by which I mean that they have not the mutual Attachment of a Lover and his Mistress for their chief Basis. Love will always make a great Figure in Tragedy, if only its chief Branches be made use of; as for instance Jealousy (as in *Othello*) or the beautiful Distress of Man and Wife (as in *Romeo and Juliet*), but never when the whole Play is founded upon two Lovers desiring to possess each other. And one of the Reasons for this seems to be that this last Species of that Passion is more commonly met with than the former, and so consequently strikes us less. Add to this that there may a Suspicion arise that the Passion of Love in a direct Manner may be more sensual than in those Branches which I have mention'd; which Suspicion is sufficient to take from its Dignity, and lessen our Veneration for it. Of all *Shakespeare*'s Tragedies none can surpass this as to the noble Passions which it naturally raises in us. That the Reader may see what our Poet had to work upon, I shall insert the Plan of it as abridged from *Saxo-Grammaticus*'s *Danish History* by Mr. *Theobald*.

[Summarises source: cf. Vol. 2, p. 520]

I shall have Occasion to remark in the Sequel that in one Particular he has follow'd the Plan so closely as to produce an Absurdity in his Plot. And I must premise also this, that in my Examination of the whole Conduct of the Play the Reader must not be surprised if I censure any Part of it, although it be entirely in Conformity to the Plan the Author has chosen; because it is easy to conceive that a Poet's Judgment is particularly shewn in chusing the proper Circumstances, and rejecting the improper Ones of the Ground-work which he raises his Play upon. In general we are to take Notice that as History ran very low in his Days most of his Plays are founded upon some old wretched Chronicler, or some empty *Italian* Novelist; but the more base and mean were his Materials so much more ought we to admire His Skill, Who has been able to work up his Pieces to such Sublimity from such low Originals. Had he had the Advantages of many of his Successors ought not we to believe that he would have made the greatest Use of them? I shall not insist upon the Merit of those who first broke through the thick Mist of *Barbarism* in Poetry which was so strong about the Time our Poet writ, because this must be easily sensible to every Reader who has the least Tincture of Letters; but thus much we must observe, that before his Time there were very few (if any) Dramatick Performances of any Tragick Writer which deserve to be remembered, so much were all the noble Originals of Antiquity buried in Oblivion. One would think that the Works of *Sophocles, Euripides, &c.* were Discoveries of the last Age only, and not that they had existed for so many Centuries. There is something very astonishing in the general Ignorance and Dullness of Taste which for so long a Time over-spread the World, after it had been so gloriously enlighten'd by *Athens* and *Rome*; especially as so many of their excellent Master-pieces were still remaining, which one would have thought should have excited even the Brutes of those barbarous Ages to have examined them, and form'd themselves according to such Models.

> *Bernardo* and *Francisco*, two Centinels.
> *Bernardo. Who's there?* &c.   [I.I.I]

Nothing can be more conformable to Reason than that the Beginning of all Dramatick Performances (and indeed of every other kind of Poesie) should be with the greatest Simplicity, that so our Passions may be work'd upon by Degrees. This Rule is very happily observ'd in this Play, and it has this Advantage over many others that it has Majesty and Simplicity joined together. For this whole preparatory Discourse to the Ghost's coming in, at the same Time that it is necessary towards laying open the Scheme of the Play creates an Awe and Attention in the Spectators, such as very well fits them to receive the Appearance of a Messenger from the other World with all the Terror and Seriousness necessary on the Occasion. And surely the Poet has manag'd the Whole in such a Manner that it is all entirely Natural. And tho' most Men are well enough arm'd against all Belief of the Appearances of Ghosts yet they are forced during the Representation of this Piece entirely to suspend their most fixed Opinions, and believe that they do actually see a Phantom, and that the whole Plot of the Play is justly and naturally founded upon the Appearance of this Spectre.

> Marcell. HORATIO *says 'tis but our Phantasie,*
> *And will not let Belief take hold of Him,*
> *Touching this dreaded Sight twice seen of Us;*
> *Therefore I have intreated him along*
> *With us to watch the Minutes of this Night;*
> *That if again this Apparition come,*
> *He may approve our Eyes, and speak to it.*
> Horatio. *Tush, Tush, 'twill not appear!*

[1.1.23ff.]

These Speeches help greatly to deceive us, for they shew one of the principal Persons of the Drama to be as incredulous in Relation to the Appearance of Phantoms as we can be; but that he is at last convinc'd of his Error by the Help of his Eyes. For it is a Maxim entirely agreeable to Truth, if we consider human Nature, that whatever is supernatural or improbable is much more likely to gain Credit with us if it be introduced as such and talk'd of as such by the Persons of the Drama, but at last prov'd to be true—tho' an extraordinary Thing—than if it were brought in as a Thing highly probable and no one were made to boggle at the Belief of it. The Reason of this seems to be that we can for once, upon a very great Occasion, allow such an Incident as this to have happen'd if it be brought in as a Thing of great Rarity; but we can by no means so suspend our Judgment and Knowledge, or deceive our Understandings, as to grant That to be common and usual which we know to be entirely Supernatural and Improbable.

Enter the Ghost.

Here it is certain nothing could be better tim'd than the Entrance of this Spectre; for he comes in and convinces *Horatio*, to save *Marcellus* the Trouble of repeating the whole Story, which would have been tiresome to the Spectators, as these Gentlemen were obliged soon after to relate the Whole to Prince *Hamlet*.

Horatio's speeches to the Apparition are exceeding Natural, Aweful, and Great, and well suited to the Occasion and his own Character.

44

> *What art Thou, that usurpest this Time of Night,*
> *Together with that fair and warlike Form,*
> *In which the Majesty of buried Denmark*
> *Did some Time march? By Heaven, I charge thee speak.*
>
> [1.1.46ff.]

The other is:

> *Stay Illusion!*
> *If thou hast any Sound, or Use of Voice,*
> *Speak to me! ...*
> [1.1.127ff.]

His desiring *Marcellus* to stop it is also much in Nature, because it shews a Perturbation of Mind very much to be expected at such an Incident. For he must know, being a Scholar (as they term him) that Spirits could not be stopp'd as Corporeal Substances can.
But to return:

> Bernardo. *How now* Horatio! *you tremble and look pale,* &c.
>
> [1.1.53]

This is entirely in Nature, for it cannot be supposed that any Man, tho' never so much endu'd with Fortitude, could see so strange a Sight, so shocking to human Nature, without some Commotion of his Frame, although the Bravery of his Mind makes him get the better of it.

> Horatio. *Before my God, I might not this believe,*
> *Without the sensible and true Avouch*
> *Of mine own Eyes.* [1.1.56ff.]

This Speech still helps on our Deception, for the Reasons I have already given.

> Horatio. *Such was the very Armour he had on,* &c.
> [1.1.60ff.]

I have heard many Persons wonder why the Poet should bring in this Ghost in complete Armour. It does, I own, at first seem hard to be accounted for; but I think these Reasons may be given for it, *viz.* We are to consider that he could introduce him in these Dresses only: in his Regal Dress, in a Habit of Interment, in a common Habit, or in some Phantastick one of his own Invention. Now let us examine which was most likely to affect the Spectators with Passions proper to the Occasion, and which could most probably furnish out great Sentiments and fine Expressions.

45

The Regal Habit has nothing uncommon in it nor surprising, nor could it give rise to any fine Images. The Habit of Interment was something too horrible, for Terror, not Horror, is to be raised in the Spectators. The common Habit (or *Habit de Ville*, as the *French* call it) was by no Means proper for the Occasion.

It remains, then, that the Poet should chuse some Habit from his own Brain. But this certainly could not be proper, because Invention in such a Case would be so much in Danger of falling into the Grotesque that it was not to be hazarded.

Now as to the Armour, it was very suitable to a King who is described as a great Warrior, and is very particular, and consequently affects the Spectators without being phantastick. Besides, if there were no other Reason, the fine Image which arises from thence in these Lines is Reason enough.

> *Such was the very Armour he had on,*
> *When He th' ambitious* Norway *combated,*
> *So frown'd He once, when in angry Parle,*
> *He smote the sleaded* Polack *on the Ice.*
> *'Tis Strange!* [1.1.60ff.]

There is a Stroke of Nature in *Horatio's* breaking off from the Description of the King, and falling into the Exclamation *'Tis Strange!* which is inimitably Beautiful.

> Marcellus. *Good now sit down,* &c. [1.1.70]

The whole Discourse concerning the great Preparations making in *Denmark* is very Poetical, and necessary also towards the introducing of *Fortinbras* in this Play, whose Appearance gives Rise to one Scene which adds a Beauty to the Whole; I mean That wherein *Hamlet* makes those noble Reflections upon seeing That Prince's Army. Besides, this Discourse is necessary also to give the Ghost Time to appear again in order to affect the Spectators still more, and from this Conversation the Interlocutors draw one Reason why the Spirit appears in Arms which appears rational to the Audience. It gives also *Horatio* an Opportunity of addressing the Ghost in that beautiful Manner he does:

> *Stay Illusion!* &c.

The Description of the Presages which happen'd to *Rome*, and the drawing a like Inference from this supernatural Appearance, is very nervous and Poetical.

Bernardo. *It was about to speak when the Cock crew*, &c.

[1.1.147ff.]

The Speeches in consequence of this Observation are truly beautiful, and are properly Marks of a great Genius, as also these Lines which describe the Morning are in the true Spirit of Poetry:

> *But, look, the Morn, in Russet Mantle clad,*
> *Walks oe'r the Dew of yon high* Eastern *Hill.*

[1.1.166f.]

And as to *Shakespeare's* complying with the vulgar Notions of Spirits amongst the *English* at that Time, so far from being low it adds a Grace and a *Naïveté* to the whole Passage which one can much easier be sensible of than know how to make others so.

The Palace, And Sequel.

Enter the King, Queen, Hamlet, *&c.*   [1.2.1ff.]

It is very natural and apropos, that the King should bring some plausible Excuse for marrying his Brother's Wife so soon after the Decease of his Brother, which he does in his first Speech in this Scene. It would else have too soon revolted the Spectators against such an unusual Proceeding. All the Speeches of the King in this Scene, to his Ambassadors *Cornelius* and *Voltimand*, and to *Laertes* and to Prince *Hamlet*, are entirely Fawning and full of Dissimulation, and makes him well deserve the Character which the Prince afterwards gives him of *smiling, damn'd Villain, &c.* when he is informed of his Crime.

The King's and Queen's Questions to *Hamlet* are very proper, to give the Audience a true Idea of the Filial Piety of the young Prince and of his virtuous Character; for we are hereby informed of his fixed and strong Grief for the Loss of his Father. For it does not appear that the Usurpation of the Crown from him sits heavy on his Soul, at least it is not seen by any Part of his Behaviour.

How his Uncle came to be preferred to him we are left entirely in the dark, but may suppose it to have been done in the same Manner as several things of the like Nature have been effected, *viz.* by Corruption and Violence, and perhaps upon the Pretence of the Prince's being too young.

I can by no Means agree with Mr. *Theobald*, who thinks that it is necessary to suppose a considerable Number of Years spent in this Tragedy because Prince *Hamlet* is said to desire to return to *Wittenberg* again, and is supposed to be just come from it; and that afterwards the Grave-Digger lets us know that the Prince is Thirty Years old. My Reasons are that as *Wittenberg* was an University and *Hamlet* is represented as a Prince of great Accomplishments, it is no wonder that he should like to spend his Time there in going on in his Improvements, rather than to remain inactive at *Elsinore*, or be immers'd in Sottishness, with which he seems to tax his Countrymen (as will appear in the Sequel). Besides, he might well desire to return there when he found his Throne usurped and his Mother acting so abominable a Part. And as to the Term of going to School, &c., that does not at all imply literally a School for Boys, but is poetically used for Studying at any Age.

Another Reason may be given why there cannot be supposed to be a great Length of Time in this Play; which is this, That we see in the First Act Ambassadors dispatch'd to old *Norway* concerning his Nephew *Fortinbras*'s Army, which was then ready to march; and in the Fourth Act we see this Prince at the Head of that Army which immediately, upon the Embassy from the *Danish* King to his Uncle, we are naturally to suppose he leads to that other Enterprize which is mentioned in that Scene. Now it is no ways likely that between the Embassy and the marching of an Army already assembled before that Embassy there should be a Number of Years. These Reasons and the whole Conduct of the Piece convince me that this is one of *Shakespeare*'s Plays in which the least Time is employ'd; how much there is I cannot pretend to say.

As to the *Prolepsis*, or in other Words the mentioning the University of *Wittenberg* long before its Establishment, thus antedating its Time, I shall not justify *Shakespeare;* I think it is a fault in him but I cannot be o Opinion that it has any bad Effect in this Tragedy. *See Mr.* Theobald's *Note*.

As to *Hamlet*'s Soliloquy, I shall set down the whole Passage, and shall subjoin the Remarks of a very eminent Author which are in the Spirit of true Criticism. (8-18)

[Quotes the 'solid flesh' soliloquy, and Steele's comments on it in *Tatler*, 106: Vol 2, pp. 209f.]

Enter Horatio, Bernardo *and* Marcellus, *to* Hamlet.

The Greeting between *Hamlet*, *Horatio*, and *Marcellus* is very easy, and expresses the benign Disposition of the Prince, and first gives us an Intimation of his Friendship for *Horatio*.

We'll teach you to drink deep, ere you depart.

[1.2.175]

This seems designed to reflect upon the sottish Disposition then encouraged amongst the *Danes* by the Usurper, as will appear in the Sequel, and gives us one Reason why *Elsinore* was disagreeable to Prince *Hamlet*; and certainly much confirms what I before said as to his going back to *Wittenberg*.

The Prince's Reflections on his Mother's hasty Marriage are very natural, and shew That to be one of the principal Causes of the deep fix'd Concern so visible in his Behaviour; and then they serve to introduce the Relation of the Appearance of his Father's Ghost.

Hamlet receives the Account they give him with such a Surprize as is very natural, and particularly his breaking off from the Consequence of his Question, viz. *Hold you the Watch to Night?* and saying *arm'd?* that is, returning to the main Question, is exceedingly in Nature.

Their differing in the Account of the Time the Spectre said throws an Air of Probability on the Whole which is much easier felt than described.

The Prince's Resolution to speak to the Phantom, let what will be the Consequence, is entirely suitable to his Heroical Disposition, and his Reflection upon his Father's Spirit appearing in Arms is such as one would naturally expect from him; and the Moral Sentence he ends his short Speech with suits his virtuous Temper at the same Time that it has a good Effect upon the Audience, and answers the End of Tragedy.

[1.3] In *Polonius*'s House

Enter Laertes *and* Ophelia, *and afterwards* Polonius.

It is evident by the whole Tenour of *Polonius*'s Behaviour in this Play that he is intended to represent some Buffoonish Statesman, not too much fraught with Honesty. Whether any particular Person's Character was herein aim'd at I shall not determine, because it is not to the Purpose; for whoever reads our Author's Plays will find that in all of them (even the most serious ones) he has some regard for the meanest Part of his Audience and perhaps, too, for that Taste for low Jokes and Punns which prevailed in his Time among the better Sort. This, I think, was more pardonable in him when it was confined to Clowns and such like Persons in his Plays, but is by no Means excusable in a Man supposed to be in such a Station as *Polonius* is. Nay, granting that such

Ministers of State were common (which surely they are not) it would even then be a Fault in our Author to introduce them in such Pieces as this, for every Thing that is natural is not to be made use of improperly: but when it is out of Nature this certainly much aggravates the Poet's Mistake. And to speak Truth, all Comick Circumstances, all Things tending to raise a Laugh are highly offensive in Tragedies, to good Judges. The Reason in my Opinion is evident, *viz.* that such Things degrade the Majesty and Dignity of Tragedy and destroy the Effect of the Intention which the Spectators had in being present at such Representations; that is, to acquire that pleasing Melancholy of Mind which is caus'd by them, and that Satisfaction which arises from the Consciousness that we are mov'd as we ought to be, and that we consequently have Sentiments suitable to the Dignity of our Nature. For these and many other Reasons too long to mention here I must confess myself to be an Enemy also to all ludicrous Epilogues and Farcical Pieces at the End of Tragedies, and must think them full as ridiculous as if we were to dress a Monarch in all his Royal Robes and then put a Fool's Cap upon him.

But to come to the Scene now under Examination. It is certain, that except it be in playing upon the Word *Tender* (of which too he is sensible himself) our old Statesman behaves suitably to his Dignity, and acts fully up to his Paternal Character; so here we shall not tax him.

The Advice of *Laertes* to his Sister contains the soundest Reasoning express'd in the most nervous and poetical Manner, and is full of Beauties; particularly, I can never enough admire the Modesty inculcated in these Lines:

> *The chariest Maid is prodigal enough,*
> *If She unmask her Beauty to the Moon.*

[1.3.36f.]

Ophelia's modest Replies, the few Words she uses, and the virtuous Caution she gives her Brother after his Advice to her are inimitably charming. This I have observed in general in our Author's Plays, that almost all his young Women (who are designed as good Characters) are made to behave with a Modesty and Decency peculiar to those Times, and which are of such pleasing Simplicity as seem too ignorant and unmeaning in our well taught knowing Age; so much do we despise the virtuous Plainness of our Fore-fathers!

Polonius and *Laertes* Behaviour to each other is exceeding natural; and I agree with Mr. *Theobald's* Emendation as to that Circumstance of *Polonius* Blessing his Son; but I can by no Means be of his Sentiment that it was a Circumstance which, if well managed by a Comick Actor, would raise a Laugh, for I am perswaded that *Shakespeare* was too good a Judge of Nature to design any Thing Comick or Buffoonish upon so solemn an Occasion as that of a Son's taking leave of his Father in the most emphatical and serious Manner. And thereupon, whatever Actor proceeds upon this Supposition (as I have seen some do in parallel Cases) does only shew his Ignorance and Presumption. This Assertion of mine will appear indisputable if my Reader considers well the whole Tenour of this Scene, with the grave and excellent Instructions which it contains from *Polonius* to *Laertes* and from both to *Ophelia*. It is impossible that any Buffoonry could be here blended, to make void and insignificant so much good Sense expressed in the true Beauties of Poetry. As to Prince *Hamlet*'s Love for *Ophelia*, I shall speak to it in another Place.

Concerning the Design of this Scene, we shall find it is necessary towards the whole Plot of the Play and is by no Means an Episode.

[1.4] *The Platform before the Palace*

Enter Hamlet, Horatio *and* Marcellus.

The Beginning of this Scene is easy and natural. The King's taking his Rowse seems introduced to fill up a necessary Space of Time, and also perhaps to blacken still more the Character of the Usurper, who had revived a sottish Custom (as appears by the Prince's Remarks upon it) omitted by several of his Predecessors; for it would have been improper to have had the Ghost appear the Minute the Prince was come on to the Platform. Some Time was requisite to prepare the Minds of the Spectators, that they might collect all their Faculties to behold this important Scene, on which turns the whole Play, with due Attention and Seriousness. Although, indeed, I must think that the Prince's Speech would not be much worth preserving but for That Reason: for expressed and amended, according to the best that can be made of it (as **Mr.** *Theobald* has done it) it is but of very obscure Diction and is much too long [1.4.13–38]; for a very short Moral is to be drawn from it.

Enter the Ghost.

We now are come to the sublimest Scene in this whole Piece, a Scene worthy of the greatest Attention: an Heroical Youth addressing the Shade of his departed Father, whom he tenderly loved, and who, we are told, was a Monarch of the greatest Worth. Surely there cannot be imagin'd any Scene more capable of stirring up our noblest Passions. Let us but observe with how much Beauty and Art the Poet has managed it. This Spectre has been once spoken to by the Friend of our young Hero, and it must be confessed that *Horatio*'s Speech to it is truly great and beautiful. But as the like Incident was again to happen—that is, as the Ghost was again to be addressed and with this Addition, by the Hero of the Play and Son to the King whose Spirit appears—it was necessary, I say, upon these Accounts that this Incident should be treated in a sublimer Manner than the Former. Accordingly we may take Notice that *Hamlet*'s Speech to his Father's Shade is as much superior to that of *Horatio* upon the same Occasion as his is to any Thing of that kind that I have ever met with in any other Dramatick Poet.

Hamlet's Invocation of the heavenly Ministers is extremely fine, and the begging their Protection upon the Appearance of a Sight so shocking to human Nature is entirely conformable to the virtuous Character of this Prince, and gives an Air of Probability to the whole Scene. He accosts the Ghost with great Intrepidity, and his whole Speech is so full of the Marks of his Filial Piety that we may easily observe that his Tenderness for his Father gets the better of all Sentiments of Terror which we could suppose to arise, even in the Breast of the most un-daunted Person, upon the seeing and conversing with so strange an Apparition.

His breaking from his Friends with that Vehemency of Passion in an Eagerness of Desire to hear what his Father could say to him is another Proof of his Filial Tenderness.

The Reader of himself must easily see why the Spectre would not speak to the Prince but a-part from those who were with him: for it was not a Secret of a Nature fit to be divulg'd. Their earnest Intreaties, and almost Force which they use to keep him from going are much in Nature; the Reasons they give him, and the Reflections they make after he is gone, are poetically express'd, and very natural.

The Ghost's Account of the base Murther committed on him is express'd in the strongest and most nervous Diction that Poetry can make use of; and he speaks with such Gravity and Weight of Language as well suits his Condition. The Ideas he raises in the Audience by his short Hint concerning the Secrets of his Prison-House are such as must cause that Terror which is the natural Effect of such Appearances, and must occasion such Images as should always accompany such Incidents in Tragedy.

The Ghost's bringing out the Account of his Murder by Degrees, and the Prince's Exclamations as he becomes farther acquainted with the Affair, are great Beauties in this Scene because it is all entirely conformable to Nature; that is, to those Ideas by which we naturally conceive how a Thing of this sort would be managed and treated were it really to happen.

We are to observe further that the King spurs on his Son to revenge his foul and unnatural Murder from these two Considerations chiefly, that he was sent into the other World without having had Time to repent of his Sins, and having the necessary Sacraments (according to the Church of *Rome*, as Mr. *Theobald* has well explained it[1]), and that consequently his Soul was to suffer if not eternal Damnation at least a long Course of Penance in Purgatory; which aggravates the Circumstances of his Brother's Barbarity. And, Secondly, That *Denmark* might not be the Scene of Usurpation and Incest, and the Throne thus polluted and profaned. For these Reasons he prompts the young Prince to Revenge; else it would have been more becoming the Character of such a Prince as *Hamlet*'s Father is represented to have been, and more suitable to his present Condition, to have left his Brother to the Divine Punishment, and to a Possibility of Repentance for his base Crime which, by cutting him off, he must be deprived of.

His Caution to his Son concerning his Mother is very fine and shews great Delicacy in our Author, as has been observ'd by a great Writer[2] of our Nation. The Ghost's Interrupting himself (*but soft, methinks, I scent the Morning Air, &c.*) has much Beauty in it, particularly as it complys with the received Notions that Spirits shun the Light, and continues the Attention of the Audience by so particular a Circumstance.

The Sequel of this Scene by no Means answers the Dignity of what we have hitherto been treating of. *Hamlet*'s Soliloquy after the Ghost has disappeared is such as it should be. The Impatience of *Horatio*, &c. to know the Result of his Conference with the Phantom, and his putting them off from knowing it with his Caution concerning his future Conduct, and his intreating them to be silent in Relation to this whole Affair; all this, I say, is natural and right. But his light and even ludicrous Expressions to them, his making them swear by his Sword, and shift their Ground, with the Ghost's Crying under the Stage, and *Hamlet*'s Reflection thereupon, are all Circumstances certainly inferiour to the preceeding Part.

But as we should be very cautious in finding Fault with Men of such

[1] See Vol. 2, p. 521.   [2] Rowe: Vol. 2, p. 201.

an exalted Genius as our Author certainly was, lest we should blame them when in reality the Fault lies in our own slow Conception, we should well consider what could have been our Author's View in such a Conduct. I must confess, I have turn'd this Matter on every Side, and all that can be said for it (as far as I am able to penetrate) is that he makes the Prince put on this Levity of Behaviour that the Gentlemen who were with him might not imagine that the Ghost had reveal'd some Matter of great Consequence to him, and that he might not therefore be suspected of any deep Designs. This appears plausible enough; but let it be as it will the whole, I think, is too lightly managed, and such a Design as I have mention'd might, in my Opinion, have been answered by some other Method more correspondent to the Dignity and Majesty of the preceeding Part of the Scene. I must observe once more, that the Prince's Soliloquy is exquisitely beautiful.

I shall conclude what I have to say on this Scene with observing that I do not know any Tragedy, ancient or modern, in any Nation, where the Whole is made to turn so naturally and so justly upon such a supernatural Appearance as this is. Nor do I know of any Piece whatever where a Spectre is introduced with so much Majesty, such an Air of Probability, and where such an Apparition is manag'd with so much Dignity and Art; in short, which so little revolts the Judgment and Belief of the Spectators. Nor have I ever met in all my Reading with a Scene in any Tragedy which creates so much Awe and serious Attention as this does, and which raises such a Multiplicity of the most exalted Sentiments. It is certain our Author excell'd in this kind of Writing, as has been more than once observed by several Writers, and none ever before or since his Time could ever bring Inhabitants of another World upon the Stage without making them ridiculous or too horrible, and the Whole too improbable and too shocking to Men's Understandings.

Act 2, Scene 1. *Polonius* and *Reynaldo*, and afterwards *Ophelia*.

Polonius's Discourse to *Reynaldo* is of a good moral Tenour, and thus far it is useful to the Audience. His forgetting what he was saying, as is usual with old Men, is extremely natural and much in Character for him.

Ophelia's Description of *Hamlet*'s Madness does as much Honour to our Poet as any Passage in the whole Play [2.1.77ff.]. It is excellently good in the *Pictoresque* Part of Poetry, and renders the Thing almost present to us.

Now I am come to mention *Hamlet*'s Madness I must speak my Opinion of our Poet's Conduct in this Particular. To conform to the Ground-work of his Plot *Shakespeare* makes the young Prince feign himself mad. I cannot but think this to be injudicious; for so far from Securing himself from any Violence which he fear'd from the Usurper, which was his Design in so doing, it seems to have been the most likely Way of getting himself confin'd, and, consequently, debarr'd from an Opportunity of Revenging his Father's Death, which now seem'd to be his only Aim; and accordingly it was the Occasion of his being sent away to *England*. Which Design, had it taken effect upon his Life, he never could have revenged his Father's Murder. To speak Truth, our Poet, by keeping too close to the Ground-work of his Plot, has fallen into an Absurdity; for there appears no Reason at all in Nature why the young Prince did not put the Usurper to Death as soon as possible, especially as *Hamlet* is represented as a Youth so brave, and so careless of his own Life.

The Case indeed is this: Had *Hamlet* gone naturally to work, as we could suppose such a Prince to do in parallel Circumstances, there would have been an End of our Play. The Poet therefore was obliged to delay his Hero's Revenge; but then he should have contrived some good Reason for it.

His Beginning his Scenes of Madness by his Behaviour to *Ophelia* was judicious, because by this Means he might be thought to be mad for her, and not that his Brain was disturb'd about State Affairs, which would have been dangerous.

[2.2] *Enter King*, *Queen*, Rosencrantz, Guildenstern, *&c.*

The King in this Scene seems to be but half perswaded that *Hamlet* is really mad; had he thoroughly believed it, it was to no Purpose to endeavour to sound his Mind; and the shortest and best Way and what, methinks, the King ought most to have wished for, was to have had him confin'd; and this was an excellent Reason to give the People for so doing.

The Queen seems to have no Design or Artifice in relation to her Son but mere Affection; which, considering all Things, one would little expect from her.

The Account of the Embassy to *Norway* was necessary towards the Introduction of *Fortinbras* in the Sequel, whose coming in at the Close of the Play winds up all very naturally.

Polonius's Character is admirably well kept up in that Scene where he pretends to have discovered the Cause of the Prince's Madness, and would much deserve Applause were such a Character allowable in such a Piece as this.

Hamlet's Letter to *Ophelia*, which *Polonius* reads, is none of the best Parts of this Play, and is, I think, too Comick for this Piece. The whole Conduct of *Hamlet's* Madness is, in my Opinion, too ludicrous for his Character, and for the situation his Mind was then really in. I must confess, nothing is more difficult than to draw a real Madness well, much more a feign'd one; for here the Poet in *Hamlet's* Case was to paint such a Species of Madness as should not give cause of Suspicion of the real Grief which had taken Possession of the Prince's Mind. His Behaviour to those two Courtiers whom the Usurper had sent to dive into his Secret is very natural and just, because his chief Business was to baffle their Enquiries, as he does also in another Scene, where his falling into a sort of a Pun upon bringing in the Pipe is a great Fault, for it is too low and mean for Tragedy. But our Author in this (as in all his Pieces) is glad of any Opportunity of falling in with the prevailing Humour of the Times, which ran into false Wit and a constant endeavour to produce affected Moral Sentences.

He was very capable of drawing *Hamlet* in Madness with much more Dignity, and without any Thing of the Comick; although it is difficult, as I said, to describe a feign'd Madness in a Tragedy, which is not to touch on the real Cause of Grief.

The Scene of the Players [2.2.312ff.] is conducive to the whole Scheme of this Tragedy, and is managed with great Beauty. We are to observe that the Speeches spoken by the Prince and one of the Players are dismal Bombast, and intended, no doubt, to ridicule some Tragedy of those Days.

The Poet's stepping out of his Subject to lash the Custom of Plays being acted by the Children of the Chapel is not allowable in Tragedy, which is never to be a Satire upon any modern particular *Foible* or Vice that prevails, but is to be severe upon Crimes and Immoralities of all Ages and of all Countries.

Hamlet's Speech after his Conversation with the Players is good, and by it we see that the Poet himself seems sensible of the Fault in his Plot. But that avails not, unless he had found Means to help it, which certainly might have been.

The Prince's Design of confirming by the Play the Truth of what the Ghost told him is certainly well imagin'd, but as the coming of these

Players is supposed to be accidental it could not be a Reason for his Delay.

Act 3

How smart a Lash, that Speech doth give my Conscience, &c.

[3.1.49ff.]

The Poet here is greatly to be commended for his Conduct. As consummate a Villain as this King of *Denmark* is represented to be yet we find him stung with the deepest Remorse, upon the least Sentence that can any ways be supposed to relate to his Crime. How instructive this is to the Audience, how much it answers the End of all publick Representations by inculcating a good Moral, I leave to the Consideration of every Reader.

Hamlet's Conversation with *Ophelia*, we may observe, is in the Stile of Madness; and it was proper that the Prince should conceal his Design from every one, which had he conversed with his Mistress in his natural Stile could not have been.

I am perswaded that our Author was pleas'd to have an Opportunity of raising a Laugh now and then, which he does in several Passages of *Hamlet's* satirical Reflections on Women; but I have the same Objections to this Part of the Prince's Madness that I have before mentioned, *viz.* that it wants Dignity. *Ophelia's* melancholy Reflections upon *Hamlet's* having lost his Sovereignty of Reason, is natural and very beautiful. As to the King's sending him to *England* See Mr. *Theobald's* Note. I purposely omit taking Notice of the famous Speech, *To be, or not to be,* &c., every *English* Reader knows its Beauties.

The Prince's Directions to the Players are exceeding good, and are evidently brought in as Lessons for the Players who were *Shakespeare's* Companions, and he thought this a very proper Occasion to animadvert upon those Faults which were disagreeable to him. Whoever reads these Observations of his, if one may prove a Thing by a negative Argument, must believe *Shakespeare* to have been an excellent Actor himself; for we can hardly imagine him to have been guilty of the Mistakes he is pointing out to his Brethren.

Notwithstanding all this, and that the Opportunity seems natural enough to introduce these Remarks, yet I cannot think them agreeable in such a Piece as this; they are not suitable to the Dignity of the Whole, and would be better plac'd in a Comedy.

Hamlet's Expression of his Friendship for *Horatio* has great Beauties;

it is with Simplicity and Strength, and the Diction has all the Graces of Poetry. It was well imagin'd, that he should let his Friend know the Secret of his Father's Murder, because thus his Request to him to observe the King's Behaviour at the Play is very naturally introduc'd as a prudent Desire of the Prince's. The Friendship of *Aeneas* for *Achates* in the *Aeneid* is found Fault with much for the same Reasons that some Criticks might carp at this of *Hamlet*'s for *Horatio*, *viz.* that neither of them are found to perform any great Acts of Friendship to their respective Friends. But I think that the Friendship of *Hamlet* and *Horatio* is far superior to that of *Aeneas* and *Achates*, as appears in the last Scene, where *Horatio*'s Behaviour is exceeding Tender, and his Affection for the Prince likely to prove very useful to his Memory.

Hamlet's whole Conduct during the Play which is acted before the King has, in my Opinion, too much Levity in it. His Madness is of too light a Kind, although I know he says he must be idle; but among other Things, his Pun to *Polonius* is not tolerable. I might also justly find Fault with the want of Decency in his Discourses to *Ophelia*, without being thought too severe. The Scene represented by the Players is in wretched Verse. This we may, without incurring the Denomination of an ill-natur'd Critick, venture to pronounce, that in almost every Place where *Shakespeare* has attempted Rhime, either in the Body of his Plays or at the Ends of Acts or Scenes, he falls far short of the Beauty and Force of his Blank Verse: one would think they were written by two different Persons. I believe we may justly take Notice, that Rhime never arrived at its true Beauty, never came to its Perfection in *England* until long since *Shakespeare*'s Time.

The King's rising with such Precipitation and quitting the Play upon seeing the Resemblance of his own foul Crime, is very much in Nature, and confirms the Penetration of our Author's Hero.

Hamlet's Pleasantry upon his being certified that his Uncle is Guilty is not a-propos in my Opinion. We are to take Notice that the Poet has mix'd a Vein of Humour in the Prince's Character which is to be seen in many Places of this Play. What was his Reason for so doing I cannot say, unless it was to follow his Favourite *Foible*, *viz.* that of raising a Laugh.

The Prince's Resolution upon his going to his Mother is beautifully express'd, and suitable to his Character.

What *Rosencrantz* says of the Importance of the King's Life is express'd by a very just Image.

The King's seeming so very much touch'd with a Sense of his Crime is supposed to be owing to the Representation he had been present at; but I do not well see how *Hamlet* is introduced so as to find him at Prayers. It is not natural that a King's Privacy should be so intruded on, not even by any of his Family, especially that it should be done without his perceiving it.

Hamlet's Speech upon seeing the King at Prayers has always given me great Offence. There is something so very Bloody in it, so inhuman, so unworthy of a Hero that I wish our Poet had omitted it. To desire to destroy a Man's Soul, to make him eternally miserable by cutting him off from all hopes of Repentance; this surely, in a Christian Prince, is such a Piece of Revenge as no Tenderness for any Parent can justify. To put the Usurper to Death, to deprive him of the Fruits of his vile Crime, and to rescue the Throne of *Denmark* from Pollution, was highly requisite. But there our young Prince's Desires should have stop'd, nor should he have wished to pursue the Criminal in the other World, but rather have hoped for his Conversion before his putting him to Death; for even with his Repentance there was at least Purgatory for him to pass through, as we find even in a virtuous Prince, the Father of *Hamlet*.

Enter the Queen and Polonius, *and afterwards* Hamlet.   [3.4]

We are now come to a Scene which I have always much admired. I cannot think it possible that such an Incident could have been managed better, nor more conformably to Reason and Nature. The Prince, conscious of his own good Intentions and the Justness of the Cause he undertakes to plead, speaks with that Force and Assurance which Virtue always gives; and yet manages his Expressions so as not to treat his Mother in a disrespectful Manner. What can be expressed with more Beauty and more Dignity than the Difference between his Uncle and Father! The Contrast in the Description of them both is exquisitely fine; And his inforcing the Heinousness of his Mother's Crime with so much Vehemence, and her guilty half Confessions of her Wickedness, and at last her thorough Remorse, are all Strokes from the Hand of a great Master in the Imitation of Nature.

His being obliged to break off his Discourse by the coming in of his Father's Ghost, once more, adds a certain Weight and Gravity to this Scene which works up in the Minds of the Audience all the Passions which do the greatest Honour to human Nature. Add to this the august and solemn Manner with which the Prince addresses the Spectre after his Invocation of the Celestial Ministers.

The Ghost's not being seen by the Queen was very proper; for we could hardly suppose that a Woman, and a guilty one especially, could be able to bear so terrible a Sight without the Loss of her Reason. Besides that, I believe the Poet had also some Eye to a vulgar Notion that Spirits are only seen by those with whom their Business is, let there be never so many Persons in Company. This Compliance with these popular Fancies still gives an Air of Probability to the Whole. The Prince shews an extreme Tenderness for his Father in these Lines,

> *On Him! on Him! &c.*
> *His Form and Cause conjoin'd, &c.*   [3.4.125ff.]

and really performs all the strictest Rules of Filial Piety thro' out the whole Play, both to Father and Mother; and particularly to the Latter in this Scene, whilst he endeavours to bring her to Repentance. In a Word, We have in this important Scene our Indignation raised against a vile Murderer, our Compassion caus'd for the inhuman Death of a virtuous Prince, our Affection is heighten'd for the Hero of the Play, and, not to enter into more Particulars, we are moved in the strongest Manner by every Thing that can gain Access to our Hearts.

Hamlet's killing *Polonius* was in Conformity to the Plan *Shakespeare* built his Play upon; and the Prince behaves himself on that Occasion as one who seems to have his Thoughts bent on Things of more Importance. I wish the Poet had omitted *Hamlet's* last Reflection on the Occasion, *viz. This Counsellor, &c.* It has too much Levity in it; and his *tugging* him away into another Room is unbecoming the Gravity of the rest of the Scene and is a Circumstance too much calculated to raise a Laugh, which it always does. We must observe that *Polonius* is far from a good Character, and that his Death is absolutely necessary towards the *Denoüement* of the whole Piece. And our Hero had not put him to Death, had not he thought it to have been the Usurper hid behind the *Arras;* so that upon the Whole this is no Blemish to his Character.

Hamlet's Behaviour to the King, &c. (Act *fourth*) concerning *Polonius's* Body, is too jocose and trivial.

Enter Fortinbras *with an Army.*   [4.4]
This is a Conduct in most of our Author's Tragedies, and in many other of our Tragedy Writers, that is quite unnatural and absurd; I mean, introducing an Army on the Stage. Although our Imagination will bear a great Degree of Illusion yet we can never so far impose on our

Knowledge and our Senses as to imagine the Stage to contain an Army. Therefore in such a Case the Recital of it, or seeing the Commander and an Officer or Two of it, is the best Method of conducting such a Circumstance. *Fortinbras*'s Troops are here brought in, I believe, to give Occasion for his appearing in the last Scene, and also to give Rise to *Hamlet*'s Reflections thereon, which tend to give some Reasons for his deferring the Punishment of the Usurper.

Laertes's Character is a very odd one. It is not easy to say whether it is good or bad; but his consenting to the villainous Contrivance of the Usurper's to murder *Hamlet* makes him much more a bad Man than a good one. For surely Revenge for such an accidental Murder as was that of his Father's (which from the Queen, it is to be supposed, he was acquainted with all the Circumstances of) could never justify him in any treacherous Practices. It is a very nice Conduct in the Poet to make the Usurper build his Scheme upon the generous unsuspicious Temper of the Person he intends to murder, and thus to raise the Prince's Character by the Confession of his Enemy, to make the Villain ten Times more odious from his own Mouth. The Contrivance of the Foil unbated (*i.e.* without a Button) is methinks too gross a Deceit to go down even with a Man of the most unsuspicious Nature.

The Scenes of *Ophelia*'s Madness are to me very shocking, in so noble a Piece as this. I am not against her having been represented mad; but surely it might have been done with less Levity and more Decency. Mistakes are less tolerable from such a Genius as *Shakespeare*'s, and especially in the very Pieces which give us such strong Proofs of his exalted Capacity. Mr. *Warburton*'s Note (in Mr. *Theobald*'s edition) on *Laertes*' Rebellion,[1] is very judicious, (as indeed are all those of that Gentleman) only I cannot think *Laertes* (for the Reasons I have given) a good Character.

The Scene of the Grave-Diggers I know is much applauded, but in my humble Opinion is very unbecoming such a Piece as this and is only pardonable as it gives Rise to *Hamlet*'s fine moral Reflections upon the Infirmity of human Nature.

Hamlet's Return to *Denmark* is not ill contriv'd; but I cannot think that his Stratagem is natural or easy by which he brings that Destruction upon the Heads of his Enemies which was to have fallen upon himself. It was possible, but not very probable; because methinks their Commission was kept in a very negligent Manner to be thus got from them without their knowing it. Their Punishment was just, because they

[1] See Vol. 2, p. 538.

had devoted themselves to the Service of the Usurper in whatever he should command, as appears in several Passages.

It does not appear whether *Ophelia*'s Madness was chiefly for her Father's Death or for the Loss of *Hamlet*. It is not often that young Women run mad for the Loss of their Fathers. It is more natural to suppose that, like *Chimene* in the *Cid*, her great Sorrow proceeded from her Father's being kill'd by the Man she lov'd, and thereby making it indecent for her ever to marry him.

In *Hamlet*'s leaping into *Ophelia*'s Grave (which is express'd with great Energy and Force of Passion) we have the first real Proof of his Love for her, which during this whole Piece has been forced to submit to Passions of greater Weight and Force and here is suffered to break out chiefly, as it is necessary towards the Winding up of the Piece. It is but an Under-Passion in the Play, and seems to be introduced more to conform to the Plan our Poet built upon than for any Thing else; tho' as the whole Play is managed, it conduces towards the Conclusion, as well as it diversifies and adds Beauties to the whole Piece.

The Scene of the Fop *Osrick* is certainly intended as a Satire upon the young Courtiers of those Days and is humourously express'd, but is, I think, improper for Tragedy.

Hamlet's feeling, as it were, a Presage in his own Breast of the Misfortune impending from his accepting *Laertes*' Challenge is beautiful. And we are to note that our Author in several of his Plays has brought in the chief Personages as having a sort of prophetick Idea of their Death; as in *Romeo and Juliet*. It was (I doubt not) the Opinion of the Age he lived in.

Laertes' Death, and the Queen's, are truly poetical Justice, and very naturally brought about; although I do not conceive it to be so easy to change Rapiers in a Scuffle without knowing it at the Time.

The Death of the Queen is particularly according to the strictest Rules of Justice, for she loses her Life by the Villany of the very Person who had been the Cause of all her Crimes.

Since the Poet deferred so long the Usurper's Death, we must own that he has very naturally effected it, and still added fresh Crimes to those the Murderer had already committed.

Upon *Laertes*' Repentance for contriving the Death of *Hamlet* one cannot but feel some Sentiments of Pity for him; but who can see or read the Death of the young Prince without melting into Tears and Compassion? *Horatio*'s earnest Desire to die with the Prince, thus not to survive his Friend, gives a stronger Idea of his Friendship for *Hamlet* in the few Lines on that Occasion than many Actions or Expressions could possibly have done. And *Hamlet*'s begging him to *draw his Breath in this Harsh World* a little longer, to clear his Reputation and manifest his Innocence, is very suitable to his virtuous Character and the honest Regard that all Men should have not to be misrepresented to Posterity; that they may not set a bad Example when in reality they have set a good one; which is the only Motive that can, in Reason, recommend the Love of Fame and Glory. . . .

Horatio's Desire of having the Bodies carried to a Stage, &c. is very well imagined, and was the best way of satisfying the Request of his deceased Friend. And he acts in this and in all Points suitably to the manly, honest Character under which he is drawn throughout the whole Piece. Besides, it gives a sort of Content to the Audience that tho' their Favourite (which must be *Hamlet*) did not escape with Life, yet the greatest amends will be made him which can be in this World, *viz.* Justice done to his Memory.

Fortinbras comes in very naturally at the Close of this Play, and lays a very just Claim to the Throne of *Denmark* as he had the dying Voice of the Prince. He in few Words gives a noble Character of *Hamlet*, and serves to carry off the deceased Hero from the Stage with the Honours due to his Birth and Merit.

I shall close these Remarks with some general Observations and shall avoid (as I have hitherto done) repeating any Thing which has been said by others, at least as much as I possibly can. Nor do I think it necessary to make an ostentatious Shew of Learning, or to draw quaint Parallels between our Author and the great Tragick Writers of Antiquity. For in Truth, this is very little to the Purpose in reviewing *Shakespeare*'s Dramatic Works, since most Men are I believe convinced that he is very little indebted to any of them; and a remarkable Instance of this is to be observed in his Tragedy of *Troilus and Cressida*, wherein it appears (as Mr. *Theobald*[1] has evidently demonstrated it) that he has chosen an old *English* Romance concerning the *Trojan* War as a worthier Guide than even *Homer* himself. Nature was our great Poet's Mistress; her alone has he followed as his Conductress; and therefore it has been with regard to her only that I have considered this Tragedy. It is not to be denied but that *Shakespeare*'s Dramatick Works are in general very much mix'd; his Gold is strangely mingled with Dross in

[1] See Vol. 2, p. 519.

most of his Pieces. He fell too much into the low Taste of the Age he liv'd in, which delighted in miserable Punns, low Wit, and affected sententious Maxims; and what is most unpardonable in him, he has interspersed his noblest Productions with this Poorness of Thought. This I have shewn in my Remarks on this Play. Yet, notwithstanding the Defects I have pointed out, it is, I think, beyond Dispute that there is much less of this in *Hamlet* than in any of his Plays; and that the Language in the Whole is much more pure, and much more free from Obscurity or Bombast, than any of our Author's Tragedies; for sometimes *Shakespeare* may be justly tax'd with that Fault. And we may moreover take Notice that the Conduct of this Piece is far from being bad; it is superior in that respect (in my Opinion) to many of those Performances in which the Rules are said to be exactly kept to. The Subject, which is of the nicest Kind, is managed with great Delicacy, much beyond that Piece wherein *Agamemnon*'s Death is revenged by his Son *Orestes*, so much admired by all the Lovers of Antiquity; for the Punishment of the Murderer alone by the Son of the murdered Person, is sufficient; there is something too shocking in a Mother's being put to Death by her Son, although she be never so guilty. *Shakespeare*'s Management in this Particular has been much admired by one of our greatest Writers,[1] who takes Notice of the beautiful Caution given by the Ghost to *Hamlet*,

> *But howsoever thou pursuest this Act*, &c.   [1.5.84ff.]

The making the Whole to turn upon the Appearance of a Spectre, is a great Improvement of the Plan he work'd upon; especially as he has conducted it in so sublime a Manner, and accompanied it with all the Circumstances that could make it most perfect in its kind.

I have observed in my Remarks, that the Poet has with great Art brought about the Punishment of the guilty Queen by the very Person who caused her Guilt, and this without Staining her Son's Hands with her Blood.

There is less Time employ'd in this Tragedy, as I observed else where, than in most of our Author's Pieces, and the Unity of Place is not much disturbed. But here give me leave to say that the Critick's Rules, in respect to those two Things, if they prove any Thing, prove too much; for if our Imagination will not bear a strong Imposition, surely no Play ought to be supposed to take more Time than is really employ'd in the Acting; nor should there be any Change of Place in the least. This

---

[1] See Vol. 2, p. 201 (Rowe).

shews the Absurdity of such Arbitrary Rules. For how would such a Genius as *Shakespeare*'s have been cramped had he thus fettered himself! But there is (in Truth) no Necessity for it. No Rules are of any Service in Poetry of any kind unless they add Beauties, which consist (in Tragedy) in an exact Conformity to Nature in the Conduct of the Characters, and in a sublimity of Sentiments and nobleness of Diction. If these two Things be well observed, tho' often at the Expence of Unity of Time and Place, such Pieces will always please, and never suffer us to find out the little Defects in the Plot. Nay it generally happens (at least Experience has shewn it frequently) that those Pieces wherein the fantastick Rules of Criticks have been kept strictly to have been generally flat and low. We are to consider that no Dramatick Piece can affect us but by the Delusion of our Imagination; which, to taste true and real Pleasures at such Representations, must undergo very great Impositions, even such as in Speculation seem very gross, but which are nevertheless allowed of by the strictest Criticks. In the first Place, our Understandings are never shocked at hearing all Nations on our Stage speak *English*; an Absurdity one would think that should immediately revolt us; but which is, however, absolutely necessary in all Countries where Dramatick Performances are resorted to, unless the Characters be always supposed to be of each respective Nation—as for instance, in all *Shakespeare*'s Historical Plays. I say, this never shocks us, nor do we find any Difficulty in believing the Stage to be *Rome* (or *Denmark*, for instance, as in this Play) or *Wilks* to be *Hamlet*, or *Booth* to be a Ghost, &c. These Things, I repeat it, appear difficult in Speculation; but we find that in Reality they do go down, and must necessarily do so or else farewel all Dramatick Performances. For unless the Distress and Woes appear to be real (which they never can if we do not believe we actually see the Things that are represented) it is impossible our Passions should be moved. Let any one fairly judge if these do not seem as great Impositions on our Reason as the Change of Place, or the Length of Time, which are found fault with in our Poet. I confess there are Bounds set to this Delusion of our Imaginations (as there are to every Thing else in this World), for this Delusion is never perform'd in direct Defiance of our Reason; on the contrary, our Reason helps on the Deceit. But she will concur no farther in this Delusion than to a certain Point which she will never pass, and that is, the Essential Difference between Plays which deceive us by the Assistance of our Reason, and others which would impose upon our Imaginations in Despight of our Reason. It is evident by the Success our Author's Pieces have always met with for so long a Course of Time, it is, I say, certain by this general Approbation that his Pieces are of the former not of the latter Sort. But to go to the Bottom of this Matter would lead me beyond what I propose.

Since therefore it is certain that the strict Observance of the Critick's Rules might take away Beauties, but not always add any, why should our Poet be so much blamed for giving a Loose to his Fancy? The Sublimity of Sentiments in his Pieces, and that exalted Diction which is so peculiarly his own, and in fine, all the Charms of his Poetry far out-weigh any little Absurdity in his Plots, which no ways disturb us in the Pleasures we reap from the above-mention'd Excellencies. And the more I read him the more I am convinced that, as he knew his own particular Talent well, he study'd more to work up great and moving Circumstances to place his chief Characters in, so as to affect our Passions strongly; he apply'd himself more to This than he did to the Means or Methods whereby he brought his Characters into those Circumstances. How far a general Vogue is the Test of the Merit of a Tragedy has been often considered by eminent Writers, and is a Subject of too complicated a Nature to discuss in these few Sheets. But I shall just hint two or three of my own Thoughts on that Head. (21-55)

★   ★   ★

In short, not to pursue a Subject that would carry me great Lengths, I conclude from this that a Piece which has no Merit in it but Nature will please the Vulgar; whereas exalted Sentiments and Purity and Nobleness of Diction, as well as Nature, are absolutely requisite to please those of a true Taste. And it is very possible that a Play which turns upon some great Passion seldom felt by the Vulgar, and wherein that Passion is treated with the greatest Delicacy and Justness; I say, it is very possible that such a Piece may please the Few and displease the Many. And as a Proof of the bad Taste of the Multitude we find in this Nation of ours, that a vile *Pantomime* Piece full of Machinery, or a lewd blasphemous Comedy, or wretched Farce, or an empty obscure low Ballad Opera (in all which, to the scandal of our Nation and Age, we surpass all the World) shall draw together crowded Audiences, when there is full Elbow-Room at a noble Piece of *Shakespeare*'s or *Rowe*'s.

Before I conclude I must point out another Beauty in the Tragedy of *Hamlet*, besides those already mentioned, which does indeed arise from our Author's conforming to a Rule which he followed (probably without knowing it) only because it is agreeable to Nature; and this is, that there is not one Scene in this Play but what some way or other conduces towards the *Denoüement* of the Whole; and thus the Unity of Action is indisputably kept up by every Thing tending to what we may call the main Design, and it all hangs by Consequence so close together that no Scene can be omitted without Prejudice to the Whole. Even *Laertes* going to *France*, and *Ophelia*'s Madness, however trivial they may seem (and how much soever I dislike the Method of that last mentioned) are Incidents absolutely necessary towards the concluding of all, as will appear to any one upon due Consideration. This all holds good, notwithstanding, it is my Opinion, that several of the Scenes might have been altered by our Author for the better; but as they all stand it is, as I said, quite impossible to separate them without a visible Prejudice to the Whole. I must add that I am much in Doubt whether Scenes of Prose are allowable, according to Nature and Reason, in Tragedies which are composed chiefly of Blank Verse; the Objection to them seems to be this, that as all Verse is not really in Nature, but yet Blank Verse is necessary in Tragedies to ennoble the Diction, and by Custom is become natural to us, Prose mixed with it serves only, me-thinks, to discover the Effects of Art by the Contrast between Verse and Prose. Add to all this, That it is not suitable to the Dignity of such Performances.

In short, Vice is punished in this excellent Piece, and thereby the Moral Use of it is unquestionable. And if *Hamlet*'s Virtue is not rewarded as we could wish, Mr. *Addison*'s Maxim ought to satisfy us, which is this, 'That no Man is so thoroughly Virtuous as to claim a Reward in Tragedy, or to have Reason to repine at the Dispensations of Providence; and it is besides more Instructive to the Audience, because it abates the Insolence of Human Nature, and teaches us not to judge of Men's Merit by their Successes.' And he proceeds farther, and says, 'that though a virtuous Man may prove unfortunate, yet a vicious Man cannot be happy in a well wrought Tragedy.' This last Rule is well observed here.

Another Reason why we ought to bear with more Patience the Sufferings of a virtuous Character is the Reflection on the future Rewards prepared for such, which is more suitable to the Moral Maxims established in a Christian Country. Besides, had it pleased our Author to have spared *Hamlet*'s Life, we had been deprived of that pleasing Sensation which always (as I have elsewhere observed) accompanies a Consciousness that we are moved as we ought to be;

which we most assuredly are when we feel Compassion rise in us for the young Prince's Death in the last Scene. I shall just touch upon one Thing more and then I shall end these Reflections.

I am very sensible that our Nation has long been censur'd for delighting in bloody Scenes on the Stage, and our Poets have been found fault with for complying with this vicious Taste. I cannot but own that there is a great deal of Justice in these Complaints; and must needs be of Opinion that such Sights should never be exhibited but in order, visibly, to conduce to the Beauty of the Piece. This is sometimes so much the Case that Action is often absolutely necessary. And to come more particularly to the Subject now in hand I desire any un-prejudiced Man, of any Nation whatever (if such can be found) who understands our Language, to consider whether the Appearance of the Ghost and the Deaths of the several principal Personages (with whatever else may offend the Delicacy I mention) could possibly have that great, that noble Effect, by being told to the Audience, as they most undoubtedly have by being brought on the Stage. If this Matter be well examined with all possible Candour I am well perswaded that it would be found in the End that this Piece would, by the Method I speak of, lose half its Beauty.

The *French* (as has been often observ'd) by their Rules of Criticism have voluntarily imposed on themselves an unnecessary Slavery; and when little Genius's among them have written Tragedies with these Chains on they have made most miserable work of it, and given Plays entirely void of Spirit. Even the great Genius's in that Nation, such as *Corneille* and *Racine*, and Mr. *De Voltaire* (which last being capacitated, by having liv'd among us and by learning our Language, to judge of the Defects and Merits of both Nations, is highly sensible of the Truth of what I now say, as appears in his Preface to his *Brutus*) even they have been forced to damp their Fire, and keep their Spirit from soaring in almost all their Pieces; and all this is owing to the false Notions of Decency and a Refinement of Taste among our Neighbours, which is getting now to such a Height that so far from being able to bear the Representation of Tragical Actions they are hardly able to bear any Subjects which turn upon the weightier Passions; such as Ambition, Revenge, Jealousy, &c. The Form of their Government, indeed, is of such a Nature that many Subjects cannot be treated as they ought nor work'd up to that Height which they are here, and were formerly at *Athens*, &c.; and Love, for that Reason among others, is made to be the Basis of almost all their Tragedies. Nay, the Education of the People

under such a Government prevents their delighting in such Performances as pleased an *Athenian* or a *Roman*, and now delight us *Britons*.
Thus every Thing conduces to debase Tragedy among them, as every
Thing here contributes to form good Tragick Writers; yet how few
have we! And what is very remarkable, each Nation takes Delight in
that which in the Main they the least excel in, and are the least fit for.
The Audience in *England* is generally more crowded at a Comedy, and
in *France* at a Tragedy; yet I will venture to affirm (and I shall be ready
upon Occasion to support my Assertion by good Reasons) that no
Comick Writer has ever equal'd *Molière*, nor no Tragick Writer ever
came up to *Shakespeare*, *Rowe*, and Mr. *Addison*. Besides the many
Reasons I have already given in Relation to the *French*, I might add
that their Language is less fit for Tragedy, and the Servitude of their
Rhime enervates the Force of the Diction. And as for Our Comedies,
they are so full of Lewdness, Impiety and Immorality, and of such complicated perplexed Plots, so stuffed with Comparisons and Similies, so
replenished with Endeavours at Wit and Smartness, that I cannot forbear saying that whoever sees or reads them for Improvement (I make
some Exceptions in this Censure) will find a contrary Effect; and whatever Man of a True Taste expects to see Nature either in the Sentiments
or Characters will (in general) find himself very much mistaken. (58–
63)

88. Alexander Pope, conversations

1736

From Joseph Spence, *Anecdotes, Observations, and Characters, of Books and Men. Collected From The Conversation of Mr. Pope, And Other Eminent Persons Of His Time*, ed. S. W. Singer (1820).

[*Spence*:] Rymer a learned and strict critic? [*Pope*:] Ay, that's exactly his character. He is generally right, though rather too severe in his opinion of the particular plays he speaks of; and is, on the whole, one of the best critics we ever had. (172–3)

*   *   *

[*Pope*:] Shakespeare generally used to stiffen his style with high words and metaphors for the speeches of his kings and great men: he mistook it for a mark of greatness. This is strongest in his early plays; but in his very last, his *Othello*, what a forced language has he put into the mouth of the Duke of Venice! This was the way of Chapman, Massinger, and all the tragic writers of those days. It was mighty simple in Rowe, to write a play now, professedly in Shakespeare's style, that is, professedly in the style of a bad age. (173–4)

89. Unsigned essays, Shakespeare and the actors

December 1736–March 1737

From *The Daily Journal* Nos 5881 (29 December 1736), 5919 (11 February 1737) and 5938 (5 March 1737).

These theatrical criticisms were signed 'The Occasional Prompter'. The 'Shakespeare Club' referred to in the first piece existed between 1736 and 1738 in order to promote the appreciation of Shakespeare (see E. L. Avery, *Shakespeare Quarterly* VII (1956), pp. 153–8). The adaptation discussed in the third piece is *The Universal Passion*, by James Miller, performed at Drury Lane on 28 February 1737. It is a conflation of *Much Ado* with Molière's *La Princesse d'Elide*.

The Occasional Prompter.

NUMBER X.

The following Letter, which is a genuine one from one Friend to another, complains so very justly of the monstrous Waste of Time occasioned by the Length to which our publick Exhibitions are of late Years spun out, that I cannot defer the Publication of it one Moment, tho' I can't say I expect any great Amendment of this Grievance, were its Inconveniences set forth in a much stronger Manner, if possible, than this Gentleman has done. Entertainments, as he very rightly observes, are exclaimed against by every body; but, to their Shame, *frequented* by the Exclaimers themselves. And while this continues to be an universal Practice I much fear the Duration of this Theatrick Monster that has almost laid the Stage waste, and made an *ingenious Carpenter* a more IMPORTANT and NECESSARY Man for the Support of it than a QUIN or a MILWARD, a CLIVE or a HORTON. Why should *these* or any other *excellent* Actors endeavour to render themselves famous in their Profession, when a great fat Fellow, for shewing a most *indecent Sight* (no less than

71

his B—ch) to an Audience with an affected Aukwardness shall set the House in an Uproar, while a Scene touched with all the Beauty of Action and Propriety of Expression shall be received with a *frosty Coldness*, except by a very few who have still Understanding enough to taste *Truth* and *Nature* in their genuine Dignity? 'Tis not the *Manager*, but the *Town*, that is in Fault. If they would resolve to banish Entertainments the *Managers* would not dare to bring them on any more; and the whole Band of *Tumblers* and *Carpenters* (the Shame and Disgrace of the Stage) would soon be obliged to retire to their old Seats of *Sadler's Wells* and *Fairs*, where they may *please* (whom alone they should please) an *illiterate, coarse, uneducated*, Mob; and no longer make a Part of the Pleasures of the *Great* or *Polite*, the *Wise* or the *Chearful*.

A noble Attempt to revive the Stage, by a Club of Women of the First Quality and Fashion, is now going forward. Would the Men of Fashion form a Club to extirpate Entertainments the *Shakespeare Club* (for so the Ladies have dignified themselves) would find a noble Association there; and an Union of both in all Probability might restore the Stage, and make the Profession of an Actor as valuable in publick Opinion as it is really in itself.

A Letter to a Friend in the Temple.

Dear JACK,   *Golden Square, Christmas-day.*
I had met you and our good Friends t'other Night at Nine, as I intended, but found my self unfortunately engaged at a Dish of ——
Mac'rel and *incoherent Gooseberries*; or, to speak out of Allegory, I mean at *Macbeth* and *Harlequin Restored*, from which I did not break loose till half an Hour after Ten; and then left a thousand or two of my honest Countrymen all *agape* at the *aerial Flights* of that admirable Mimick *Philips*; who, I think, deserves better of the Stage than to be sent back to his old little Tricks of *Bartholomew Fair* and *Sadler's Wells*. I wonder in my Heart how the Managers of our Theatres can find their Account in producing our Diversions to such a Length as to make them lose that Name and become Punishments; and yet they certainly do, or they would hardly be such Idiots as to lay out fifteen hundred or two thousand Pounds upon a *Pantomime*. I never was in a Company where *Theatrical Entertainments* were the Subject of Discourse but this Complaint was unanimously made by the whole Company. It spoils all Meetings after the Play at Taverns, to talk over and digest the Diversion

of the Night; which used to be half the Pleasure of frequenting the Theatre, and which now is absolutely impossible, as it consists of so many *party-coloured* Patches of *Sense* and *Nonsense* as no *Reason* can connect. *It breaks into the Regularity of Families intolerably*; and many a poor kind Mother goes to Bed with an aching Heart, and her Daughters without their Supper, because the *Manager* is so lavish of his *Carpenters Wit* and his *mechanical Conundrums*. How many honest Apprentices have journeyed from the other End of the City for their eighteen Pennyworth of Diversion, and after paying two Shillings for it have found their Masters Doors locked against them, and taken up their Lodgings with the next hospitable Lady they met? Is not this the Case, *Jack*? I have heard your poor Brother *Bob*, that was with old *Worthy* the Linen-draper in *Cornhill*, often lament it, when he otherwise had no more Thought of a Wench than he had of his dying afterwards of her *kind* Usage.

The other Night we had *Macbeth* (I had like to have said *Shakespeare*'s *Macbeth* but I beg his Pardon, for he would scarce know it as it is now acted) incomparably performed by Mr. *Quin*, whose Justness in Speaking I know you admire. We had all Mr. *Purcell*'s excellent Musick (which would be an agreeable Entertainment anywhere, but ridiculously introduced in the midst of so fine a Play) with all Mr. *Dryden*'s rhyming Nonsense (which is called, adapting to the Stage). We had *a real Entertainment* between the Acts, by the *best Dancer* in *Europe* and the *best Romp* in the World. Now you or I, *Jack*, or any other reasonable Play-hunter should think this a pretty good Pennyworth for our Penny; but this same *Mr. Town* is such an unconscionable Gentleman that he is never to be satisfied with Diversions till he falls fast asleep in the midst of them. After this (which lasted till half an Hour after Nine) we had a *dumb Thing*, which the facetious Managers miscall *An Entertainment*; in which was introduced (because not tedious enough in itself) a long new Scene of many Words, which made a great Noise both upon the Stage and in the Galleries. They told me in the House that I was not a competent Judge of the Wit of this Scene, not having yet honoured *Lincoln's-inn-fields* Playhouse with my Company. So that I can form no other Judgment of it than that it was too long; not but I must say that a certain *hoarsen-throated* Gentleman of the other End of the Town was INIMITABLY *imitated* by a pretty young Stripling, a little too tall now to be called *Master Green*. This was followed by Rope-dancing and Tumbling, and tho' I went out before it was finished I was

73

not at home till after eleven; where I found *old Ned* fast asleep, drawing in the Fumes of his Candle that was sputtering in the Socket, and waked my Sisters and an old maiden Aunt out of their first Sleep; who scolded at me all Breakfast-time the next Morning: and now—*facit Indignatio*. If the aforesaid *Mr. Town* insists upon this kind of Entertainments and yet is so frequent in his Complaints of the Length and Folly of them, I should imagine it worth the Manager's while to set apart two or three Days in a Week for them, and only act Pieces of two or three Acts before them. And if they would make some such Rule in the Theatres no doubt their Poets would think it so much Labour saved to confine their Pieces to two or three Acts, and our Stage might soon be supplied with as many pretty Things of that Length as the *French*. But if they go on to force *Jonson* and *Shakespeare* into such scurvy Company, those poor modest Men of Merit may be discountenanced, and the Theatre in a little while deserted by the *Friends of Shakespeare*. I should be glad, dear *Jack*, to have an Hour or two's Discourse with you upon this Subject, which I know you have at Heart. I am

Yours, &c.

PHIL. DRAM.

The Occasional Prompter.

NUMBER XXI.

It has been contested by the *Literati*, and is still undetermined, Whether our great Countryman *Shakespeare* had Learning enough to trace the Rules laid down for *Dramatick* Compositions from the *Spring-head*, or whether he was ignorant both of them and the Reasons alledged to support their Practice. Without entering into this Debate, which is foreign to my Purpose, it is evident he has *not* observed the three grand Unities of *Time*, *Place*, and *Action*, so necessary to the Execution of the Drama, and has chosen Subjects which it was impossible to reconcile to them. All his historical Plays come directly under this *Predicament*; and those which we owe to his own inventive Genius or to some fabulous Story are so contrived by him as to be equally repugnant to these known Rules. It will then result from hence that whether he knew them or not he has conducted all his Dramas as if there were no Rules for such Compositions.

The Inference I would draw from this general *Postulatum* is That *Shakespeare*'s Plays being avowedly out of Rule, and the *Incidents* in them to which we owe some of his greatest Beauties and strongest

Touches, very often quite distinct from the main Action, to attempt to reform his Plays with respect to *Time*, or *Incident*, is the *greatest of Absurdities*; and if we go so far as to cut out any of the Beauties of this great Poet, in this *Reformation*, it becomes the *highest Injustice* that can be done to his *Manes*.

Wherein then will this inimitable Author admit of Alteration, which his best Friends must allow he stands in need of?

The Editor of *Shakespeare*, in the Character he gives of him as a Writer, says very justly: *The Genius that gives us the greatest Pleasure, sometimes stands in need of our Indulgence. Whenever this happens with regard to* Shakespeare, *I would willingly impute it to a Vice of his Times.* WE SEE COMPLAISANCE ENOUGH IN OUR OWN DAYS PAID TO A BAD TASTE. *His Clinches, false Wit, and descending beneath himself, seem to be a Deference paid to reigning Barbarism.*[1]

There is scarce a Play of this Great Man in which he does not descend beneath himself and pay this Deference to the reigning Barbarism of his Times. In his gravest Pieces, where he displays his most exalted Genius he as constantly throws a Vein of low Humour, in complaisance to the low Capacities of the *coarse Laughers* of his Days, whom perhaps it was as much his Interest to keep in Temper by suiting himself to their Taste as it is now of modern Poets who would succeed. But the Case is at present widely different with his Amenders; and he that would attempt to reform *Shakespeare* has not the *Tie* he had on him, and may act without *Complaisance*.

Instead therefore of torturing *Shakespeare* into *Rule* and *Dramatick Law*, let his *Clinches, false Wit*, &c. be the Object of their Amendment. Where a grave Scene is interrupted by a low Vein of Humour that, by inciting the *Vulgar to laugh* draws off the Attention of the *Polite*, let the *Shears* be applied without Fear; where likewise a Character has not been raised to the Height it might reach, from the Poet's applying himself to some more favourite Character in the Play, let the *Alterer* bend his Care, and the Success will be answerable if his Genius is equal to the Task. An Influence of Improvement of Character we have in *Edgar* (in *K.Lear*) as well as in *Cordelia*, between whom a Love Affair is very beautifully introduced without wronging *Shakespeare*. Another yet stronger, is in *Catherine* (in *Henry V*) whose Character in *Shakespeare* has too much of Burlesque in it. The Improvement of *her*'s has necessarily raised that of *Harry*.[2] Other Instances might be brought to shew

[1] Theobald: see Vol. 2, p. 477.
[2] In Aaron Hill's *Henry V*: see Vol. 2, No. 69.

where *Shakespeare* might admit with great *Beauty* and *Propriety* of strong Alterations.

To apply this Reasoning to the Tragedy of *King John*, and to consider *Philo-Shakespeare's* two Letters on this Subject, I shall first observe That *King John* of all his Works is that which has the least of *Clinches, false Wit*, and *descending beneath himself*, and requires very little Indulgence from us on those Heads; for the Character of the Bastard *Faulconbridge*, tho' a humourous one, is not of that Kind hinted at by the Editor above-mentioned, and would sit very ill on one that had not a certain Dignity in him; his Humour of Spirit becoming that *Greatness* of Mind he discovers in his graver Walk.

King John then being principally deficient in the three *grand Unities* which, it has been before observed, *Shakespeare did not regard*, to attempt to bring this Play into Rule must be absurd, since the Time (viz. 17 Years), the Place (viz. sometimes in *England*, sometimes in *France*), and the Action (which contains some chosen Events which happened to that Prince during a Course of 17 Years) can never be reconciled to Dramatick Laws without losing almost every Incident in the Play and the Beauties which arise from those Incidents, where our Poet is always *strongest*. It has been before observed That there is not one *low* or *burlesque* Character in the Play: so that a Reformation must be very little necessary to cure that Defect our Author falls into.

Not to speak against the Merit of Mr. *Cibber's* Alteration of *King John*, which not having seen I am not entitled to say any thing to, I shall only observe that according to my Notions of *Shakespeare* I think it cannot be *altered* properly, for the Reasons above-mentioned.

As to the Letters of *Philo-Shakespeare* the first hints at an Alteration made in the Character of *Constance* in favour of the Actress designed to play that Roll; and on that Supposition sketches out the Character of that Princess from the Poet's own Draught, with a View, I suppose, to help the Comparison that would be made between the *old* and *modern* CONSTANCE when it should be represented. On which I then observed (and it has been since confirmed to me) that the Play was altered nine or ten Years ago, which takes away the Right of supposing a Change in that Character in favour of the Actress hinted at before the Trial whether it be so or no. If then there should appear to be no Alteration in that Character (and my Correspondent does not positively say there is) and the Alterer has kept close to the Character as it is originally drawn, the View of the Letter-writer must have been to examine how far such a Character might become his Conceptions of the Actress's Powers.

As to this Point I shall only say That if a Character is ill cast it will soon be seen by the Town and the Blame will fall on the Manager, whose Business it is to suit Characters to Persons and Talents. If the Character is *well cast* I scarce think that *private Opinion* will bias the general Judgment of a Town, nor can I be brought to believe such a Letter deserves to be called *A palpable, invidious, Design to prejudice the Town against the Actress*: which I think too hard a Censure on one who critically examines a Character with an Eye to its being properly personated.

The second Letter comes to Particulars of the Alteration (of which I presume the Writer well informed) which, if true, certainly must greatly weaken the Play.

As to his Criticisms of Style and Language in the Laureat's Letter I have received a private Hint, in which (on a Supposition I only wrote to myself) I am very roughly handled for descending, as my Monitor calls it, into *Grub-street Criticisms of Letters and Commas,* and advises to keep to Criticisms of a higher Kind. I confess I was tempted, when I received the Letter, to cut out the three Paragraphs about the *Comma* and come to the Point; but I thought myself not sufficiently authorized to assume so great a Privilege, and printed it as it was sent.

It remains then a Question, Whether any Adventurer in Criticism has a *Right* to make this *previous publick* Examination of a Character? But this I shall reserve to treat of some other Opportunity, as it affects publick Writers, not having Room to consider it fully in this Paper.

PS. *I just now hear the Laureat has withdrawn his Tragedy; which I hope is not true, as it would look very much like not daring to stand to the Judgments he applied to.*

The Occasional Prompter.

NUMBER XXIV.

> *So have I seen a deep,* sagacious, *Hound*
> (*To whose* full VOICE *th'* awaken'd *Woods resound*)
> LEAD THE GAY FIELD, *while,* IMPOTENT, AND BASE,
> *In* YELPS *the* PARSON'S CUR, *and* FOILS THE CHASE.
> EPIG. Anonym.

Peace be with the Soul of *Shakespeare,* and may no *Consciousness* of what passes here disturb his Quiet! *Amen, Amen, Amen.*

The Incident, of which the Lines in my Motto give so natural a Description, conveys the most ludicrous Idea in the World to one who has even no Taste for that kind of Diversion; but to a Lover of Hunting is a Subject of most violent Anger. To have a *gay Field lead on*, as it is poetically express'd, with *Horses, Hounds,* and *Men,* all animated, their Voices ecchoing to each other, the Sounds *knowingly* taken up and carried on, at once interrupted by the *yelping Joy* of an *illiterate* Cur that breaks in upon the Chase and expresses in *rude* Sounds its mongrel Sensations, has every provoking Circumstance in it that can possibly be conceived! The poor *Cur,* all the while, is not to be blamed; its Ears take in general Notes of Joy; it expresses its Sense of that Joy, and does not know but that its *Voice* is as good as the best, and from that Notion elevates its Cry to the highest Pitch and endeavours to *outvoice* them all in Demonstration of its *Feelings,* ignorant that it disturbs and disconcerts their's.

Not to pursue this Allegory any further, in which I might shew the Difference between *Ignorance* and *Taste* in Matters of an *ingenuous* Nature, I shall, as more immediate to the Design of this Paper, give Place to a Correspondent who treats it with a particular Eye to an Operation very unskillfully made on the Parent of the *English* Drama.

To the OCCASIONAL PROMPTER.

SIR,

As you promised in a late Paper to examine the Right of speaking to *Plays* or *Characters* before their Exhibition, I have waited with Impatience for your Decision on that Point; but finding you have not judged proper to publish your Thoughts I concluded you were in your own Mind against such a *previous* Examen, and have therefore forbore *characterizing Much-ado-about-Nothing* in the manner I did *King John,* with an Eye to a Comparison when it should come to be acted. As it has now appeared, and the Publick is become its Judge, I shall take the common Right every Spectator has to speak his Mind of it without enquiring into the first Question, which I still please myself you will at your Leisure discuss.

I observe first, in the *Reverend Alterer,* a total Change of Names, tho' I am at a Loss to conceive any Necessity for it; *Claudio* being just as good as *Bellario,* and *Hero* as pretty as *Lucilia. Beatrice* and *Benedick* convey as much to the Understanding as Lord *Proteus* and *Delia*; and so of the rest.

The Affectation of altering Names in *Shakespeare* is something too ridiculous to be gravely *noticed*; for which Reason I shall pass on to a *new Character*, by Name *Joculo*, introduced for no Purpose in the World but to say a good deal of *Common-place* Satire even below *common Discourse*. But to shew what an *infinite Void* of Invention there is in our Bard, and how much he covets his Neighbour's Goods (contrary to one of ten Commandments he should particularly be observant of) he has robbed *Molière* of the Character of *Moron* (in a dramatick Entertainment called *Les Plaisirs de l'Isle Enchantée* or *La Princesse d'Elide*) quite *necessary* and *diverting* in the *French* Poet, to form a most *stupid Jester* who has nothing at all to do in the *English*. Nor does his *felonious* Disposition stop in stealing a Character only; he has stole the *hunting Match*, and the Incident of the Father's being saved, and has affected to make *Joculo* as useful in forwarding the Love Intrigue as *Moron*, tho' it is very evident none of them wanted a Cast of his Office.

The next Alteration is the blending two Characters in one and by that means wronging his Original, and making a *Sovereign* appear scarce equal to a *Subject*, in receiving an Injury of so near a Concern, and not resenting it as a *Sovereign* should. *Leonato* indeed might measure his Resentment in proportion to the Respect due to a *Prince*, but why a *Prince* himself should be so *tame*, and let *Bellario* go off without instant Revenge for an Aspersion so *triflingly* founded, is not reconcileable to *Propriety* of Character; and as it is productive of no Sentiment or Incident of *new Beauty* is an Alteration injurious to *Shakespeare*, and shews the Poverty of the *Alterer's* Understanding.

His Love of *altering* shews itself with the same Delicacy in shifting the Scene from *Messina* to *Genoa*; for I believe no one Person in the Audience could find any Reason for it. But this, it seems, is called *altering Shakespeare, changing the Names of the Drama and Scene of Action; leaving out one or two Characters necessary to the Fable and adding one that has nothing to do with it.*

His usage of *Benedick* is abominable; and of a gay young Lord that laughs at Love from a *Sprightliness* of Temper,

> (MESS. speaking of him—*Oh! he's return'd, and as* PLEASANT *as ever*.
> BEAT. *He set up his Bills here in Messina, and challenged Cupid at the Flight—*) [I.I.31ff.]

he has formed a Character that has more of *Severity* and *Flout* in it than *Mirth* or *Pleasantry*. He has made a *rough, gallant* Soldier of the fine Gentleman of those Days.

The *Under-plot* of making *Benedick* and *Beatrice* fall in love with each other, as well as the principal Part of the Fable that relates to *Claudio* and *Hero*, he has indeed condescended to preserve; and to these Scenes, mangled as they are, and the *excellent Performance of the Actors in general* must be attributed the Town's Indulgence in seeing *Shakespeare*, whom they would not suffer to be murdered in the Person of King *John*, most miserably *hacked* and *defaced* (notwithstanding the Act against Maiming, &c.) by more *cruel*, as well as *unskilful*, Hands.

I cannot conclude without expressing some Surprize at the Name under which it now appears. *Shakespeare*, in that which he gave to it, seemed to acknowledge (which indeed is true) that the Fable or Subject was making *Much Ado about Nothing*, and pretended to no more. But why this Comedy should be called *Love the Universal Passion*, any more than any other Piece that has *Love* in it, can only be accounted for by the present Rule for *altering Shakespeare* hinted at above. I am,

SIR, Your's,

Mar. 3, 1736.   Philo-Shakespeare.

I did promise in the Paper referred to by my Correspondent to examine the Right of speaking to a *Character* before the Exhibition of the Piece itself; but as I proposed at first setting out to appear only OCCASIONALLY, I reserved to myself a Liberty of chusing the OCCASIONS. As to the Question I shall, when it becomes necessary to discuss it, consider it at large. In the mean time I shall, in addition to what *Philo-Shakespeare* has wrote of the Play itself, say a Word or two to an Assertion of some Friends of the Author, viz. *That most of the Hisses were levelled at what was* Shakespeare's *and not his Alterer's.*

If this proves any thing (supposing it a Fact) it proves that the Play is injudiciously altered, and that he has retrenched in the wrong Place; *That he has done those things which he ought not to have done, and left undone those things which he ought to have done.* But it is very possible *Shakespeare* may have been *hissed* by the Fault of the *Alterer*: for what would be very proper in the Mouth of a Character *of his drawing* may, when this Character is *modernized*, be very *unsuiting* to it and *improper* to it.

90. Thomas Birch and William Warburton on Shakespeare's life and works

1739

From *A General Dictionary, Historical and Critical*, Vol. IX (1739).

This translation of the *Dictionnaire histoire et critique* of Pierre Bayle (1647–1706) included 'several thousand lives never before published', especially designed to fill the gaps in British biography. For his life of Shakespeare, Thomas Birch (1705–66) used the accounts of Rowe, Theobald and Pope; for critical and scholarly comments he was furnished with manuscript remarks by Warburton.

SHAKESPEARE (WILLIAM) was son of Mr. John Shakespeare, and was born at Stratford upon Avon in Warwickshire in April 1564. His family, as appears by the register and public writings relating to that town, were of good figure and fashion there, and are mentioned as Gentlemen. His father, who was a considerable dealer in wool, had so large a family, ten children in all, that though our author was his eldest son, he could give him no better education than his own employment. He had him bred indeed for some time at a free-school, where it is probable he acquired what Latin he was master of. But the narrowness of his circumstances, and the want of his assistance at home, forced his father to withdraw him from thence, and unhappily prevented his farther proficiency in that Language.[1] Upon his leaving school he seems to have given entirely into that way of living, which his father proposed to him; and in order to settle in the world after a family manner he thought fit to marry while he was yet very young, viz. by that time he was turned of seventeen years. His wife was the daughter of one Hathaway, a substantial Yeoman in the neighbourhood of Stratford. In this kind of settlement he continued for some time, till an extravagance, which he was guilty of, forced him both out of the country and that way of living which he had taken up; and though it

[1] So far the compiler takes everything *verbatim* from Rowe (Vol. 2, p. 190); he continues to draw on Rowe, with some omissions.

seemed at first to be a blemish upon his good manners, and a misfortune to him, yet it afterwards happily proved the occasion of exerting one of the greatest genius's, which ever was known in dramatic Poetry. He had fallen into ill company; and amongst them some, who made a frequent practice of Deer-stealing, engaged him with them more than once in robbing a park, which belonged to Sir Thomas Lucy of Cherlecot near Stratford. For this he was prosecuted by that Gentleman, as he thought, somewhat too severely; and in order to revenge that ill usage, he made a ballad upon him. And though this, probably the first essay of his Poetry, be lost, yet it is said to have been so very bitter, that it redoubled the prosecution against him to that degree, that he was obliged to leave his business and family in Warwickshire for some time, and shelter himself in London. It was at this time, and upon this accident, that he is said to have made his first acquaintance in the Play-House. He was received into the Company then in being, at first in a very mean rank; but his admirable wit, and the natural turn of it to the stage, soon distinguished him, if not as an extraordinary actor, yet as an excellent writer. His name is printed, as the custom was in those times, amongst those of the other Players before some old Plays, but without any particular account of what sort of parts he used to play; and Mr. Rowe tells us that he could never meet with any farther account of him this way than that the top of his performance was the Ghost in his own *Hamlet*. We have no certain authority which was his first Play. He was highly esteemed by Queen Elizabeth; and received many great and uncommon marks of favour and friendship from the Earl of Southampton, famous in the histories of that time for his friendship to the unfortunate Earl of Essex. It was to that noble Lord that he dedicated his Poem of *Venus and Adonis*. There is a very remarkable instance of the generosity of this Patron of Shakespeare, related by Mr. Rowe upon the authority of Sir William D'Avenant; which was, that the Earl of Southampton at one time gave him a thousand pounds to enable him to go through with a purchase which he had heard he had a mind to. His dramatic writings are very numerous. There is no certain account when he quitted the stage for a private life. Some have thought, that Spenser's *Thalia* in his *Tears of the Muses*, where she laments the loss of her *Willy* in the comic scene, relates to our author's abandoning the stage.[1] But it is well known that Spenser himself died in the year 1598; and five years after this we find Shakespeare's name among the

---

[1] This 'Willy' is probably Richard Wills or Willey, poet and critic: see Ethel Seaton's edition of Abraham Fraunce's *Arcadian Rhetoric* (Oxford, 1950).

actors in Ben Jonson's *Sejanus*, which first made its appearance in the year 1603. Nor surely could he then have any thoughts of retiring, since that very year a licence under the Privy Seal was granted by King James I to him and Fletcher, Burbage, Philipps, Heming, Condel, &c. authorizing them to exercise the art of playing Comedies, Tragedies, &c. as well at their usual house called the Globe on the other side the water as in any other parts of the Kingdom, during his Majesty's pleasure. Besides, it is certain that Shakespeare did not exhibit his *Macbeth* till after the Union was brought about, and till after King James I had begun to touch for the evil; for he has inserted compliments on both these accounts upon his Royal Master in that Tragedy. Nor indeed could the number of the dramatic pieces which he produced admit of his retiring near so early as that period. So that what Spenser there says, if it relates at all to Shakespeare, must hint at some occasional recess he made for a time upon a disgust taken; or the *Willy* there mentioned must relate to some other favourite Poet. Mr. Theobald is of opinion that he had not quitted the stage in the year 1610; for in his *Tempest* our author makes mention of the *Bermuda* Islands, which were unknown to the English till in 1609 Sir John Summers made a voyage to North America and discovered them, and afterwards invited some of his countrymen to settle a plantation there. The latter part of Shakespeare's life was spent in ease, retirement, and the conversation of his friends. He had the good fortune to gather an estate equal to his occasion, and in that to his wish; and is said to have spent some years before his death at his native Stratford. His pleasurable wit and good nature engaged him in the acquaintance and entitled him to the friendship of the Gentlemen of the neighbourhood. He died in 1616 in the fifty-third year of his age, and lyes interred on the north-side of the chancel in the great Church at Stratford, where a monument is erected to him and placed against the wall; but another more considerable one is intended to be raised to his memory in Westminster Abbey at the public expence [*Note I*]. He had three daughters, of which two lived to be married; Judith, the elder, to one Mr. Thomas Quiney, by whom she had three sons, who all died without children; and Susanna, who was his favourite, to Dr. John Hall, a Physician of good reputation in that country. She left one child only, a daughter, who was married first to Thomas Nash Esq, and afterwards to Sir John Bernard of Abbington, but died without issue. In 1614 the greatest part of the town of Stratford was consumed by fire; but our Shakespeare's house, among some others, escaped the flames. This house was first built by Sir Hugh

Clopton, a younger brother of an ancient family in that neighbourhood, who took their name from the manor of Clopton. Sir Hugh was Sheriff of London in the reign of Richard III, and Lord Mayor in the reign of Henry VII. The estate had now been sold out of the Clopton family for above a Century at the time when Shakespeare became the purchaser; who having repaired and modelled it to his own mind changed the name to *New-place*, which the mansionhouse since erected upon the same spot at this day retains. The house and land which attended it continued in Shakespeare's descendants to the time of the Restoration; when they were repurchased by the Clopton family, and the mansion now belonging to Sir Hugh Clopton Knt. When the civil war raged in England, and King Charles I's Queen was obliged by the necessity of affairs to make a recess in Warwickshire, she kept her Court for three weeks in New-place. We may reasonably suppose it then the best private house in the town; and her Majesty preferred it to the College which was in the possession of the Combe-family, who did not so strongly favour the King's party. How much our author employed himself in Poetry after his retirement from the stage does not so evidently appear. Very few posthumous sketches of his pen have been discovered to ascertain that point. We have been told indeed in print, but not till very lately,[1] that two large chests full of this great man's loose papers and manuscripts, in the hands of an ignorant Baker of Warwick who married one of the descendants from our Shakespeare, were carelessly scattered and thrown about as garret-lumber and litter, to the particular knowledge of the late Sir William Bishop, till they were all consumed in the general fire and destruction of that town. But Mr. Theobald distrusts the authority of this tradition, because as Shakespeare's wife survived him seven years, and as his favourite daughter Susanna survived her twenty-six years, it is very improbable, that they should suffer such a treasure to be removed and translated into a remoter branch of the family without a scrutiny first made into the value of it. His dramatic writings were first published together in fol. in 1623, and since republished by Mr. Rowe, Mr. Pope, and Mr. Lewis Theobald. But we may expect a much more correct edition of them from the reverend and learned Mr. William Warburton, author of the *Divine Legation of Moses demonstrated*, who in his edition, besides a general character of Shakespeare and his writings prefixed, will give the

---

[1] In *An Answer to Mr. Pope's Preface to Shakespeare* (1729): No. 77 in Vol. 2. This apocryphal story derives from Sir William Bishop (1626–1700), who lived in Stratford and passed on other such tales.

rules which he observed in correcting his author [*Note K*], and a large glossary [*Note L*]. We shall give the reader a specimen of this intended edition in several curious remarks which this excellent Critic has communicated to us, and which we shall introduce by way of illustration on Mr. Pope's admirable character of our Poet; who in the *Preface* to his edition observes that Shakespeare, notwithstanding his defects, is justly and universally elevated above all other dramatic writers. If ever any author deserved the name of an original, it was he. [Quotes from Pope's preface: Vol. 2, pp. 403ff., 407, and 413ff.]

Mr. Pope concludes by saying of Shakespeare, that with all his faults, and with all the irregularity of his drama, one may look upon his works, in comparison of those that are more finished and regular, as upon an antient majestic piece of Gothic Architecture, compared with a neat modern building. The latter is more elegant and glaring; but the former is more strong and more solemn. It must be allowed, that in one of these there are materials enough to make many of the other. It has much the greater variety, and much the nobler apartments; though we are often conducted to them by dark, odd, and uncouth passages. Nor does the whole fail to strike us with greater reverence, though many of the parts are childish, ill-placed, and unequal to its grandeur. Mr. Rowe tells us, that in a conversation between Sir John Suckling, Sir William D'Avenant, Endymion Porter, Mr. Hales of Eton, and Ben Jonson, Sir John Suckling, who was a professed admirer of Shakespeare, had undertaken his defence against Ben Jonson with some warmth. Mr. Hales, who had sat still for some time told them, 'that if Shakespeare had not read the antients, he had likewise not stoln any thing from them; and that if he would produce any one topic finely treated by any of them, he would undertake to shew something upon the same subject at least as well written by Shakespeare.' Mr. Warburton observes, that there is no vice of style or composition, but what our Poet has in one place or other of his writings ridiculed or censured [*Note Z*].

NOTES

I Another more considerable one is intended to be raised to his memory in Westminster Abbey at the public expence.] For this purpose our author's tragedy of *Julius Cæsar* was acted at the Theatre Royal in Drury-Lane April 28, 1738, and the profits arising from it deposited in the hands of the Earl of Burlington, Mr. Pope, Dr. Richard Mead, and Charles Fleetwood Esq; in order to be laid out upon the said monument. A

new prologue and epilogue were spoken upon that occasion; which
were as follow.

The Prologue, written by Benjamin Martyn Esq;

> Whilst in the venerable dome we view
> The Sculptor's art Britannia's bards renew;
> Behold their names on speaking marble live,
> Their forms in animated stone revive;
> Shakespeare obscurely lies; his lawrel'd bust
> Neglected moulders like his bones to dust.
> No single hand durst claim to rear his stone,
> And fix in Shakespeare's monument his own.
> To you 'twas left to dignify the bard,
> And grace your Shakespeare with this late reward.
> Shakespeare! the father of the British stage!
> Shakespeare! the wonder of each rising age!
> Whose glowing fancy and whose various art
> With ev'ry passion governs ev'ry heart:
> Whose genius opens nature to our view,
> Whose charms, tho' still repeated, still are new.
> Tho' Shakespeare wants no stone to speak his praise,
> Your gratitude's the monument you raise.
> Think, when you fix a basis for his name,
> You fix one likewise for your country's fame.
> Rome by her statues rouz'd the Roman blood,
> And form'd new heroes by the old she shew'd.
> Let then this chief of our Dramatic band,
> As first in rank, the first in honours stand.
> Let every breast, that feels his sacred fire,
> Glow with the virtues, which his lines inspire,
> While Brutus bleeds for liberty and Rome,
> Let Britons crowd to deck his Poet's tomb.
> To future times recorded let it stand,
> This head was lawrel'd by the publick hand.
> To future times with pride transmit it down,
> Such public merit should the public own.

The epilogue, written by the Honourable James Noel Esq;

> These smiles bestow'd, these gen'rous honours paid
> To a dead bard, to long lost Shakespeare's shade;

To public worth such public favours shewn,
Confirm his merit, and proclaim your own.
Ev'n here a noble monument you raise;
The tomb of glory is a people's praise.
Perhaps some will,—perhaps? no, none will say,
'No dance, no song to decorate the play!'
No, Shakespeare scorns such common arts to use;
Sense gave it birth,—let sense preserve the muse.
If comic scenes divert, or tragic move,
With both delighted you by both improve.
Fir'd by the muse you raise each passion higher,
And pant to reach the virtues you admire.
When Portia weeps, all gentle breasts must mourn,
When Brutus arms, all gen'rous bosoms burn.
When Rome's firm Patriots on the stage were shewn,
With pride we trace the Patriots of our own;
From bondage sav'd when that bold state we see,
We glow to think that Britain is as free;
We mount by bright example glory's throne,
And make the cause of virtue all our own.
Such was the bard first grac'd the British stage,
First charm'd, and still shall charm thro' ev'ry age:
Whose verse is music, not at wit's expence,
But joins the charms of harmony with sense.
He wakes the passions, governs, and inspires,
Charms while he teaches, while he pleases fires.
But here what humble thanks, what praise is due,
Ow'd to such gen'rous virtue, ow'd to you!
With grief you saw a bard neglected lie,
Whom towring genius living rais'd so high.
With grief you saw your Shakespeare's slighted state,
And call'd forth merit from the grave of fate.
Let others boast they smile on living worth;
You give a buried bard a brighter birth.

[K] *The rules, which he observed in correcting his author.*] [WARBURTON]:
One part of these rules are general, and relate to the art of criticism at
large; the other part refer to this particular author, to his genius, his
manner of composing, to the way in which his writings were collected,
transcribed, and published; a peculiarity in Shakespeare's fate which

has given birth to such monstrous corruptions as no Greek or Roman manuscript ever laboured under. By which the learned reader will understand the method which the editor has pursued and the caution he has observed in reforming the text; and the English reader be shewn that criticism is not a licentious habit of conjecturing at random, and correcting an author on fancy and caprice (as he has been taught to imagine), but an art founded, as all others are, on very constant and reasonable principles.

[L] *A large Glossary.*] [WARBURTON]: It will be a Glossary of the words in Shakespeare which require explanation; not of *terms of art* or *obsolete expressions*, for these every common Dictionary or Glossary will supply; but of such words as Shakespeare has affixed peculiar significations of his own to, unauthorized by use and unjustified by analogy; and these being chiefly mixed modes, as they are most susceptible of abuse, so they throw the most impenetrable obscurity over the discourse. The instances of this are innumerable. To mention a few. As *austerely* for *precisely*; to *afflict* for to *affect* simply; *convenience* for *assistance*; *constancy* for *reality*. . . .

In these instances, the author only deviates singly and imposes but one new signification on each word. But he sometimes gives several, which much increases the embarrass. As *absolute* for *resolved, determined*, for *perfect*; *ceremony* for the *regalia*, for a *love-token*, for *reverence*, for *the rites of atonement*, for *omens*; *Motive* for *instrument*, for *part moved*, for *assistant*; *sense* for *resentment*, for *appearances*, for *power, abilities*. Sometimes again he exchanges the signification of words, as *ostent*, which signifies *omen*, he uses for *outward behaviour*; and *ostentation*, which signifies *outward behaviour*, he uses for *omen*.

In this Glossary the editor not only gives the explanation of each word, but likewise in a comment on each shews what it was that led the author to use it thus perversely. As for example, *bated* for *allowed, no leisure bated*; because the deduction from a bill or account is called the *allowance* or *'batement* he therefore uses to *'bate* and to *allow* as synonymous terms; though here improperly enough, for the not bating was allowing. *Constitution* for *complexion* or *colour of the face*; *complexion* in our author's time signified equally colour of the face or temperament, for the temperament consisting of a combination of the sanguine, flegmatic, choleric, that which predominated was by the old Physicians called the *complexion*; and because by the colour of the face the *complexion* or temperament was known, that colour was called complexion, which at this time is the usual signification of the word. So one sense of complexion being temperament, and temperament signifying constitution, he uses constitution for the other sense of temperament. This figure is extremely common with him; as again, *garb* for *custom*, for one sense of *habit* being *garb* he uses *garb* to signify the other sense of it, *custom*. To *calculate* for *foretel*. The custom of foretelling fortunes by judicial Astrology being then much in vogue, and that being done by long laborious calculations, he uses to *calculate* for to *foretel* or *predict* simply. *Comparisons* for *ornaments*. The difficulty of apprehending the meaning of this word here has made the editors substitute *caparisons* in its stead; but the word *declined* in the next line shews *comparisons* to be right. It may be presumed that Shakespeare coined this word by analogy from the Italian phrase *vestito positivamente*, by which is meant one clothed simply and modestly by opposition of the positive to the comparative and superlative. *Frame* for *capacity*, *abilities*; because the outward work of some machines is called the *frame* and is the *capacity* of the machine, he therefore uses *frame* to signify *mental capacity*.

Shakespeare's critics not observing the nature and cause of this uncommon licence have run into two different mistakes. Some of them seeing an obscurity which this has created run through all his writings have censured him for the confusion of his ideas and the inaccuracy of his reasoning; whereas no writer's ideas were ever more clear, or his reasoning more close. But he sometimes being carried away by the full torrent of his matter gave small attention to the propriety of his terms, being very apt, as we see by the examples given, to regard words as synonymous that had in their composition any one idea in common. Mr. Rymer's ignorance of this matter made him in his *Short view of Tragedy* fall into the most brutal censure of our author; 'In the neighing of an horse, *says he*, or in the growling of a mastiff, there is a meaning, there is as lively expression, and (may I say) more humanity, than many times in the tragical flights of Shakespeare.' [Vol. 2, p. 30] Others again are apt to reckon those anomalies, as we may call them, amongst the corruptions of his text, and so perplex themselves with conjectures without and to the depravation, not reform, of the author. In a word, this Glossary will remove the greatest obscurities in his writings, and be a continued comment on his text.

[M] *The poetry of Shakespeare was inspiration indeed.*] And hath often, says Mr. Warburton,* in it the obscurity of an oracle; but so much

* In his manuscript *Remarks*, communicated to us.

beauty when unriddled that these are not the least amiable parts of his writings. As in *Midsummer night's-dream*, A. 2. the King of Fairies says to his attendant:

> thou remember'st,
> Since once I sat upon a promontory,
> And heard a mermaid on a dolphin's back
> Uttering such dulcet and harmonious breath,
> That the rude sea grew civil to her song,
> And certain stars shot madly from their spheres
> To hear the sea-maid's music. [2.1.148ff.]

The compliment made to Queen Elizabeth in the lines that immediately follow is so obvious as to be taken notice of by every body. But the character of Mary Queen of Scots in the lines above was too allegorically, it seems, delivered to be understood; and yet nothing is truer than that both a compliment and a satyr on that unfortunate Lady were here intended, either of which was a sufficient reason to disguise the matter by an allegory. First, the laying of the scene shews it to be near the British island, for the speaker is represented as hearing the *mermaid* at the very time he saw Cupid's attempt on the *Vestal*. The *mermaid on the dolphin's back* plainly designs Queen Mary's marriage with the *Dauphin of France*. The poet designs her under the image of a mermaid on two accounts, because she was Queen of one part of the isle, and because of her mischievous allurements. *Uttering such dulcet and harmonious breath:* this alludes to her great parts of genius and learning, which rendered her the most accomplished woman of her time. The French writers tell us that while she was in the Court of France, wife to the Dauphin, she pronounced a Latin oration in the great hall of the Louvre with so much grace and eloquence, that the whole assembly were in admiration. *That the rude sea grew civil to her song:* by this is meant Scotland, long in arms against her. There is the greater justness and beauty in it because the common opinion is, that the mermaid sings in storms.

> *And certain stars shot madly from their spheres*
> *To hear the sea-maid's music:* [2.1.153f.]

This alludes in general to the many matches proposed to her, but more particularly to the Duke of Norfolk's famous negotiation with her; which bringing such destruction on him and on the Earl of Northumberland and Westmorland and many other noble families, it was said with the utmost propriety, that *certain stars shot madly from their spheres.*

[O] *We find him knowing in the customs, rites, and manners of antiquity.*]
He always, says Mr. Warburton, makes an ancient speak the language
of antiquity. So *Julius Cæsar*, Act I. Scene III.

> Ye Gods, it doth amaze me,
> A man of such a feeble temper should
> So get the start of the majestic world,
> And bear the palm alone.   [1.2.128ff.]

This noble image is taken from the Olympic Games. The *majestic world*
is a fine periphrasis for the *Roman Empire*: *majestic*, because the noble
Romans ranked themselves on a footing with Kings; and a *world*, because they called their Empire *Orbis Romanus*. But the whole seems to
allude to the known story of Cæsar's great exemplar, Alexander, who
when he was asked whether he would run the course of the Olympic
Games, replied, *Yes, if the Racers were Kings.*

So again in *Antony and Cleopatra*, Act I. Scene I. *Antony* says with infinite sublimity

> Let Rome in Tyber melt, and *the wide arch*
> *Of the raised Empire fall.*   [1.1.33f.]

taken from the Roman custom of raising triumphal arches to per-
petuate their victories.

And again in Act III. Scene IV. *Octavia* says to *Antony* of the difference between him and her brother,

> Wars 'twixt you twain would be
> *As if the world should cleave, and that slain men*
> *Should solder up the rift.*   [3.4.30ff.]

This is wonderfully sublime: the thought is taken from the story of
Curtius's leaping into the Chasm in the Forum in order to close it; so
that as that was closed by one Roman, if the whole world were to
cleave Romans only could solder it up. The metaphor of *soldering* is
extremely exact; for as metal is soldered up by metal that is more
refined than that which it solders; so the earth was to be soldered by
men, who are only a more refined earth. So very proper, and at the
same time so full of sense is all that Shakespeare says . . . .

[P] *The manners of other nations in general, the Egyptians, Venetians,
French, &c. are drawn with equal propriety.*] [WARBURTON]: An instance or
two of this shall be produced with regard to the Venetians. In the
Merchant of Venice, Act IV. Scene I.

his losses,
That have of late so huddled on his back,
Enough to press a *Royal Merchant* down.   [4.1.27ff.]

We are not to imagine the word *Royal* to be a random sounding epithet. It is used with great propriety by the Poet, and designed to shew him well acquainted with the history of the people whom he here brings upon the stage. For when the French and Venetians in the beginning of the thirteenth century had won Constantinople, the French, under the Emperor Henry, endeavoured to extend their conquests into the provinces of the Grecian Empire on the *Terra Firma*, while the Venetians, being masters of the sea, gave liberty to any subject of the Republic who would fit out vessels, to make themselves masters of the Isles of the Archipelago and other maritime places, and to enjoy their conquests in sovereignty, only doing homage to the Republic for their several principalities. In pursuance of this licence the Sanudo's, the Justiniani, the Grimaldi, the Summaripa's, and others, all *Venetian Merchants*, erected principalities in several places of the Archipelago (which their descendants enjoyed for many generations), and thereby became truly and properly *Royal Merchants*.

So again in *Othello* Act. I. Scene VIII. Brabantio accusing Othello before the Senate for running away with his daughter, says,

She is abused, stolen from me, and corrupted
By spells and medicines bought of Mountebanks.   [1.3.60f.]

These lines Mr. Rymer has ridiculed as containing a weak and superstitious circumstance unbecoming both the gravity of the accuser and the dignity of the tribunal. But all that he shews in his criticism is his own ignorance. This circumstance was not only exactly in character, but urged with the utmost address, as the thing chiefly to be insisted upon. For by the Venetian Law, the giving love-potions was very criminal, as Shakespeare without question well knew. . . .

[Q] *His descriptions are still exact, and his metaphors appropriated.*] This, says Mr. Warburton (MS. *Remarks*), may be seen even through the deformity of the most corrupted passages. So in the *First Part of Henry IV.* Act I. Scene I. Henry speaking of the late commotion, says,

Those opposed EYES,
Which like the meteors of a troubled heaven,
All of one nature, of one substance bred,

Did lately meet in the intestine shock,
And furious close of civil butchery,
Shall now in mutual well-beseeming *ranks*
March all one way.   [1.1.9ff.]

This beautiful similitude has been strangely deformed by the insertion
of those monstrous *eyes* in the front. The stupid transcribers seeing
meteors in the second line, the sun (called the eye of heaven) came across
their heavy imaginations and so they substituted *eyes* instead of FILES,
the true reading. But what are *eyes meeting in intestine shocks and marching all one way*? That FILES is the true word, appears not only from the
integrity of the metaphor, *well beseeming ranks march all one way*; but
from the nature of those meteors to which they are compared; namely,
long streaks of red, which represent the *lines* of armies; the appearance
of which, and their likeness to those lines, gave occasion to all the
superstition of the common people concerning them. . . .

And again in *Antony and Cleopatra* Act IV. Scene II. upon one of
Antony's extravagances in his distress, an Attendant says

'Tis one of those old TRICKS, which sorrow shoots
Out of the mind.   [4.2.14f.]

The uniformity of the metaphor leads us to see, that Shakespeare wrote
TRAITS, arrows, shafts. A similar expression we have in *Cymbeline, 'Twas
but a bolt of nothing, shot at nothing, which the brain makes of fumes.*
                                                      [4.2.301f.]

[R] *No one is more a master of the poetical story, or has more frequent
allusions &c.*] Mr. Warburton observes that in the *First Part of Henry IV,*
Act III. Henry IV telling his son of the arts he used to gain the crown,
says:

And then *I stole all courtesy from heav'n,*
And drest myself in such humility,
That I did pluck allegiance from men's hearts.   [3.2.50ff.]

The *stealing courtesy from heaven* is an allusion to the story of Prome-
theus's theft, who stole fire from thence; and as with *this* he made a
man so with *that* Bolinbroke made a King. As the Gods were supposed
to be fond of appropriating *reason* to themselves, the getting fire from
thence, which caused it, was called a theft; and as *power* is their prerogative, the getting courtesy from thence, by which power is procured,
is called a theft. The thought is exquisitely noble.

93

Again, in *King Lear* Act II. Scene II. the old King exclaims thus
against his daughters:

> O heavens!
> If you do love *old men*; if your sweet sway
> Hallow obedience; *if your selves are old*,
> Make it your cause. [2.4.187ff.]

The exclamation, *O heavens, if your selves are old*, may appear to the unlearned reader low and ridiculous. But we are to consider this Pagan
King as here alluding to the antient Heathen Theology, which teaches
that *Cœlus* or *Ouranos* was deposed by his son Saturn, who rebelled and
rose up in arms against him. His case then being the same with *Lear*'s
makes this exclamation exceedingly pertinent and fine.

Again, Act III. Scene II, when the good Earl of Glocester is outraged
in his own house by his guests *Cornwall* and *Regan*, he says,

> By the *kind Gods.* 'tis most ignobly done
> To pluck me by the beard. [3.7.34f.]

We are not to understand by *kind Gods* here the Gods in general, who
are beneficent and kind to men, but that particular species of them
called by the antients *Dii hospitales, kind Gods*. So Plautus *in Pœnulo*.

> *Deum hospitalem* ac tesseram mecum fero.[1]

This was a beautiful exclamation; for those who insulted him were his
guests, whom he had hospitably received in his own house.

But Shakespeare appears to have been as well versed in the sculpture
of the antients as in their writings. So in the *Merchant of Venice* Act I.
Scene I, Solario says,

> Now by *two headed Janus*,
> Nature hath framed strange fellows in her time,
> Some that will evermore peep thro' their eyes
> And laugh
> And others of such vinegar aspect. [1.1.50ff.]

By *double-headed Janus* is meant the antique bifrontine statues, which
generally represent a young smiling face and an old wrinkled frowning
one, being sometimes of Pan and Bacchus, of Saturn and Apollo, &c.
These are commonly to be met with in collections of antiques and
books of antiquities, as Montfaucon, Spanheim, &c.

[1] 958. But modern editions read 'ad eum hospitalem'.

So again in *Timon of Athens* Act IV. Scene V. *Timon* says,

> Common mother, thou
> Whose womb unmeasurable and *infinite breast*
> *Teems and feeds all;*
> Ensear thy fertile and conceptious womb;
> Let it no more bring out ungrateful man,
> Go great with tygers, dragons, wolves and bears, &c.
> [4.3.176ff.]

This plainly alludes to the antient statues of *Diana Ephesia Multimammia* . . . But he has not only given the very picture of the statues in these lines, but has likewise explained their meaning in a very good comment on those extraordinary figures. See *Montfaucon's L'Antiquité expliquée* L. III. C. 15.

[Z] *There is no vice of style or composition, but what our Poet has in one place or other of his writings ridiculed and censured.*] Two places only shall be taken notice of where he has done it with infinite humour.

In *All's well that ends well*, Act V. Scene II. *Parolles* represents his misfortunes to the *Clown* in a very coarse ill-mannered metaphor; and on the *Clown's* stopping his nose *Parolles* says,

> Nay, you need not stop your nose, Sir; I speak by a metaphor:

The Clown replies:

> Indeed, Sir, if your metaphor stink—I will stop my nose against any
> man's metaphor. [5.2.9ff.]

Nothing could be conceived with greater humour or justness of satyr. The use of these *stinking metaphors* is an odious fault, which grave writers often commit. . . . Our author himself is extremely delicate in this respect; who throughout his large writings, if you except one passage in *Hamlet*, has scarce used a metaphor that can offend the most squeamish reader.

In *Timon*, Act V. Scene III. the *Poet* flattering *Timon* by inveighing against the ingratitude of his friends says in the highest bombast

> I am rapt, and cannot
> Cover the monstrous bulk of this ingratitude
> With any size of words.
> TIMON. Let it go naked: men may see't the better. [5.1.62ff.]

The humour of this reply is incomparable: it insinuates not only the highest contempt of the flatterer in particular, but this useful lesson in general, that the images of things are clearest seen through a simplicity of phrase. (IX, 186–99).

91. William Smith, Shakespeare and the Sublime

1739

From *Dionysius Longinus*, *'On the Sublime'*: *Translated from the Greek, with Notes and Observations* (1739); this text from 'The Second Edition, Corrected and Improved' (1743).

William Smith (1711–87), a distinguished classical scholar, also translated Thucydides and Xenophon.

The Pathetic, as well as the *Grand*, is expressed as strongly by Silence or a bare Word as in a Number of Periods. There is an admirable instance of it in *Shakespeare's Julius Caesar*, Act 4, scene 4. The preceding scene is wrought up in a masterly manner: we see there in the truest Light the noble and generous Resentment of *Brutus*, and the hasty Choler and as hasty Repentance of *Cassius*. After the Reconciliation, in the beginning of the next scene, *Brutus* addresses himself to *Cassius*.

> Bru. *O Cassius, I am sick of many Griefs.*
>   . . . *Portia's dead.*   [4.3.142ff.]

The Stroke is heavier, as it comes unexpected. The Grief is abrupt because it is inexpressible. The Heart is melted in an instant, and Tears will start at once in any Audience that has Generosity enough to be moved or is capable of Sorrow and Pity. (119–20)

✴   ✴   ✴

Shakespeare, without any Imitation of these great Masters, has by the natural Strength of his own Genius described the Extent of Slander in the greatest Pomp of Expression, Elevation of Thought, and Fertility of Invention:

> —*Slander,*
> *Whose Head is sharper than the Sword . . .*
> [*Cymbeline,* 3.4.31f.] (122)

*   *   *

Shakespeare has, with inimitable Art, made use of a Storm in his Tragedy of *King Lear,* and continued it through seven Scenes. In reading it one sees the piteous Condition of those who are expos'd to it in open Air; one almost hears the Wind and Thunder, and beholds the Flashes of Lightning. The Anger, Fury, and passionate Exclamations of *Lear* himself seem to rival the Storm, which is as outrageous in his Breast, inflamed and ulcerated by the Barbarities of his Daughters, as in the Elements themselves. We view him

> *Contending with the fretful Elements . . .*   [3.1.4]

We afterwards see the distressed old Man exposed to all the Inclemencies of the Weather; Nature itself in Hurry and Disorder, but he as violent and boisterous as the Storm.

> *Rumble thy belly-full, spit Fire, spout Rain;*
> *Nor Rain, Wind, Thunder, Fire are my Daughters;*
> *I tax not you, ye Elements.*   [3.2.14ff.]

And immediately after,

> —— *Let the great Gods,*
> *That keep this dreadful thund'ring o'er our Heads,*
> *Find out their Enemies now. Tremble, thou Wretch . . .*
>   [3.2.49ff.]

The Storm still continues, and the poor old Man is forced along the open Heath to take shelter in a wretched Hovel. There the Poet has laid new Incidents, to stamp fresh Terror on the Imagination, by lodging *Edgar* in it before them. The Passions of the old King are so turbulent that he will not be persuaded to take any Refuge. When honest *Kent* intreats him to go in he cries:

Prithee go in thyself, seek thy own Ease;
This Tempest will not give me leave to ponder
On Things would hurt me more—
Nay, get thee in; I'll pray, and then I'll sleep—
Poor naked Wretches, wheresoe'er you are ...   [3.4.23ff.]

The Miseries and Disorders of *Lear* and *Edgar* are then painted with
such judicious Horror that every Imagination must be strongly affected
by such Tempests in Reason and Nature. I have quoted those Passages
which have the moral Reflexions in them, since they add Solemnity to
the Terror and alarm at once a Variety of Passions. (138–40)

★   ★   ★

The Distraction of *Orestes*, after the murder of his Mother, is a fine
Representation in *Euripides*, because it is natural. . . . The Poet who
can touch such Incidents with happy Dexterity, and paint such Images
of Consternation, will infallibly work upon the Minds of others. This
is what *Longinus* commends in *Euripides*; and here it must be added that
no Poet in this Branch of Writing can enter into a Parallel with *Shakespeare.*

When *Macbeth* is preparing for the murder of *Duncan* his Imagination is big with the Attempt, and is quite upon the Rack. Within, his
Soul is dismayed with the Horror of so black an Enterprize, and every
thing without looks dismal and affrighting. His Eyes rebel against his
Reason, and make him start at Images that have no Reality.

Is this a Dagger which I see before me,
The handle tow'rd my hand? come let me clutch thee!
I have thee not—and yet I see thee still.   [2.1.33ff.]

He then endeavours to summon his Reason to his Aid and convince
himself that it is mere Chimera; but in vain, the Terror stamped on his
Imagination will not be shook off.

I see thee yet, in form as palpable,
As this which now I draw—   [2.1.40f.]

Here he makes a new Attempt to reason himself out of the Delusion,
but it is quite too strong.

I see thee still,
And on thy blade and dudgeon gouts of blood,
Which was not so before.—There's no such thing—

[2.1.45ff.]

The Delusion is described in so skilful a manner that the Audience cannot but share the Consternation, and start at the visionary Dagger.

The Genius of the Poet will appear more surprizing if we consider how the Horror is continually worked up by the Method in which the Perpetration of the Murder is represented. The Contrast between *Macbeth* and his Wife is justly characterized, by the hard-hearted Villany of the one and the Qualms of Remorse in the other. The least Noise, the very Sound of their own Voices is shocking and frightful to both:

> *Hark! peace!*
> *It was the Owl that shriek'd, the fatal bell-man,*
> *Which gives the stern'st good-night—he is about it—*
>
> [2.2.2ff.]

And again immediately after,

> *Alack! I am afraid they have awak'd,*
> *And 'tis not done: th'attempt, and not the deed,*
> *Confounds us—Hark!—I laid their daggers ready,*
> *He could not miss them—*   [2.2.9ff.]

The best way to commend it as it deserves would be to quote the whole Scene. The Fact is represented in the same affecting Horror as would rise in the Mind at sight of the actual Commission. Every single Image seems reality, and alarms the Soul. They seize the whole Attention, stiffen and benumb the Sense, the very Blood curdles and runs cold thro' the strongest abhorrence and detestation of the Crime. (146–8)

*   *   *

How vehemently does the Fury of *Northumberland* exert itself in *Shakespeare*, when he hears of the Death of his Son *Hotspur*! The Rage and Distraction of the surviving Father shews how important the Son was in his Opinion. Nothing must be, now he is not: Nature itself must fall with *Percy*. His Grief renders him frantic, his Anger desperate.

> *Let heav'n kiss earth! . . .*
> *And darkness be the burier of the dead.*
>   [2 *Henry IV*, 1.1.153ff.]
>   (150–1)

*   *   *

Ghosts are very frequent in *English* Tragedies; but Ghosts, as well as Fairies, seem to be the peculiar Province of *Shakespeare*. In such Circles none but he could move with Dignity. That in *Hamlet* is introduced with the utmost Solemnity, awful throughout and majestic. At the appearance of *Banquo* in *Macbeth* (Act 3 Sc. 5) the Images are set off in the strongest Expression, and strike the Imagination with high degrees of Horror, which is supported with surprising Art through the whole scene. (152)

⋆　　⋆　　⋆

[In ch. 22 Longinus describes the rhetorical figure *hyperbaton*, which is 'a transposing of Words or Thoughts out of their natural and grammatical Order'. This occurs in human speech when men are upset by some strong passion and their minds 'fluctuate here, and there, and every where', and 'by this Flux and Reflux of Passion they alter their Thoughts, their Language, and their manner of Expression a thousand times.'] This fine Remark may be illustrated by a celebrated Passage in *Shakespeare's Hamlet*, where the Poet's Art has hit off the strongest and most exact Resemblance of nature. The Behaviour of his Mother makes such Impression on the young Prince that his Mind is big with Abhorrence of it, but Expressions fail him. He begins abruptly, but as Reflexions croud thick upon his Mind he runs off into Commendations of his Father. Some Time after, his Thoughts turn again on that Action of his Mother which had raised his Resentments, but he only touches it and flies off again. In short he takes up eighteen Lines in telling us that his Mother married again in less than two Months after her Husband's Death.

> *But two months dead! nay, not so much, not two—*
> *So excellent a King, that was to this*
> Hyperion *to a* Satyr: *so loving to my mother,*
> *That he permitted not the winds of heav'n*
> *Visit her face too roughly. Heav'n and earth!*
> *Must I remember?—why, she would hang on him,*
> *As if increase of appetite had grown*
> *By what it fed on; yet within a month—*
> *Let me not think—Frailty, thy name is Woman!*
> *A little month!—or ere those shoes were old,*
> *With which she follow'd my poor father's body,*
> *Like* Niobe *all tears—why she, ev'n she—*

Oh heav'n! a beast that wants discourse of reason,
Would have mourn'd longer—married with mine uncle,
My father's brother, no more like my father,
Than I to Hercules. Within a month!
Ere yet the salt of most unrighteous tears
Had left the flushing of her galled eyes,
She married. Oh most wicked speed!   [1.2.138ff.]
                                                         (158–9)

           *   *   *

[In ch. 28 Longinus says that Circumlocution, or Periphrasis, 'is a cause
of Sublimity', exalting 'the Sentiment'.] *Shakespeare*, in *King Richard the
Second*, has made sick *John* of *Gaunt* pour out such a Multitude [of
periphrases] to express *England* as never was nor ever will be met with
again. Some of them indeed sound very finely, at least in the Ears of an
Englishman. For Instance,

> *This royal throne of kings, this seat of Mars,*
> *This other Eden, demy paradise,*
> *This fortress built by nature for herself*
> *Against infection and the hand of war;*
> *This happy breed of men, this little world,*
> *This precious stone set in the silver sea.*   [2.1.40ff.]
                                                         (168–9)

           *   *   *

[In ch. 31 Longinus says that 'Vulgar Terms are sometimes much more
significant than the most ornamental could possibly be. They are easily
understood because borrowed from common Life'.] Images drawn
from common Life or familiar Objects stand in need of a deal of Judgment to support and keep them from sinking, but have a much better
Effect and are far more expressive, when managed by a skilful Hand,
than those of a higher Nature. The Truth of this Remark is visible
from these Lines in *Shakespeare's Romeo and Juliet*:

> *I would have thee gone,*
> *And yet no further than a wanton's bird,*
> *That lets it hop a little from her hand,*
> *Like a poor Prisoner in his twisted gyves,*
> *And with a silk thread pulls it back again,*
> *So loving jealous of its liberty.*   [2.2.177ff.]

Mr. *Addison* has made use of an Image of a lower Nature in his *Cato*, where the Lover cannot part with his Mistress without the highest Regret, as the Lady could not with her Lover in the former Instance from *Shakespeare*. He has touch'd it with equal Delicacy and Grace:

> *Thus o'er the dying lamp th'unsteady flame*
> *Hangs quiv'ring to a point; leaps off by fits,*
> *And falls again, as loth to quit its hold.*

I have ventured to give these Instances of the Beauty and Strength of Images taken from low and common Objects because what the Critic says of Terms holds equally in regard to Images. An Expression is not the worse for being obvious and familiar, for a judicious application gives it new Dignity and strong Significance. All Images and Words are dangerous to such as want Genius and Spirit. By their Management grand Words and Images improperly thrown together sink into Burlesque and sounding Nonsense, and the easy and familiar are tortured into insipid Fustian. A true Genius will steer securely in either Course, and with such bold Rashness on particular Occasions that he will almost touch upon Rocks yet never receive any Damage. This Remark, in that part of it which regards the Terms, may be illustrated by the following Lines of *Shakespeare*, spoken by *Apemantus* to *Timon*, when he had abjured all human Society and vow'd to pass the remainder of his Days in a Desert:

> *What? think'st thou*
> *That the bleak air, thy boist'rous chamberlain,*
> *Will put thy shirt on warm? will these moist trees,*
> *That have out-liv'd the eagle, page thy heels,*
> *And skip when thou point'st out? will the cold brook,*
> *Candied with ice, cawdle thy morning taste*
> *To cure thy o'er-night's surfeit? Call the creatures,*
> *Whose naked natures live in all the spite*
> *Or wreakful heav'n, whose bare unhoused trunks,*
> *To the conflicting elements expos'd,*
> *Answer meer nature; bid them flatter thee;*
> *Oh! thou shalt find—* [4.3.220ff.]

The whole is carried on with so much Spirit and supported by such an air of Solemnity that it is noble and affecting. Yet the same Expressions and Allusions in inferior Hands might have retained their original Baseness, and been quite ridiculous. (169–71)

*   *   *

[On hyperbole] It is the importance of a Passion which qualifies the Hyperbole, and makes that commendable when uttered in warmth and vehemence which in coolness and sedateness would be insupportable. So *Cassius* speaking invidiously of *Caesar*, in order to raise the Indignation of *Brutus*:

> *Why, man, he doth bestride the narrow world*
> *Like a* Colossus, *and we petty men*
> *Walk under his huge legs, and peep about*
> *To find ourselves dishonourable graves.*   [1.2.135ff.]

So again, in return to the swelling Arrogance of a Bully;

> *To whom? to thee? what art thou? have not I*
> *An arm as big as thine? a heart as big?*
> *Thy words I grant are bigger: for I wear not*
> *My dagger in my mouth—*   [*Cym.*, 4.2.77ff.]

Hyperboles literally are Impossibilities, and therefore can only then be seasonable or productive of Sublimity when the Circumstances may be stretched beyond their proper size, that they may appear without fail important and great. (180–1)

* * *

[Subsequently Longinus discusses the inverted hyperbole or 'Diasyrm', which 'increases the Lowness of any Thing, or renders Trifles more trifling'.] Shakespeare has made Richard III speak a merry Diasyrm upon himself:

> *I, that am rudely stamp'd, and want love's majesty . . .*
> *That dogs bark at me, as I halt by them.*   [1.1.16ff.]
>   (181–2)

92. Colley Cibber, Shakespeare in the theatre

1740

From *An Apology for the Life of Mr. Colley Cibber, Comedian, and Late Patentee of the Theatre-Royal. With an Historical View of the Stage during his Own Time. Written By Himself* (1740).

See head-note to No. 38, Vol. 2.

[Chapter IV]

*   *   *

King *Charles* II. at his Restoration granted two Patents, one to Sir *William D'Avenant* and the other to *Henry Killigrew*, Esq. and their several Heirs and Assigns, for ever, for the forming of two distinct Companies of Comedians. The first were call'd the *King's Servants*, and acted at the Theatre-Royal in *Drury-Lane*; and the other the *Duke's Company*, who acted at the Duke's Theatre in *Dorset-Garden*. About ten of the King's Company were on the Royal Houshold-Establishment, having each ten Yards of Scarlet Cloth with a proper quantity of Lace allow'd them for Liveries; and in their Warrants from the Lord Chamberlain were stiled *Gentlemen of the Great Chamber*. Whether the like Appointments were extended to the Duke's Company I am not certain; but they were both in high Estimation with the Publick, and so much the Delight and Concern of the Court that they were not only supported by its being frequently present at their publick *Presentations* but by its taking cognizance even of their private Government; insomuch that their particular Differences, Pretentions, or Complaints were generally ended by the *King* or *Duke's* Personal Command or Decision. Besides their being thorough Masters of their Art these Actors set forwards with two critical Advantages which perhaps may never happen again in many Ages. The one was their immediate opening after the so long Interdiction of Plays during the Civil War and the Anarchy that followed it. What eager Appetites from so long a Fast must the

Guests of those Times have had to that high and fresh variety of Entertainments which *Shakespeare* had left prepared for them! Never was a Stage so provided! A hundred Years are wasted, and another silent Century well advanced, and yet what unborn Age shall say *Shakespeare* has his Equal? How many shining Actors have the warm Scenes of his Genius given to Posterity, without being himself, in his Action, equal to his Writing! A strong Proof that Actors, like Poets, must be born such. Eloquence and Elocution are quite different Talents. *Shakespeare* could write *Hamlet*; but Tradition tells us That the *Ghost*, in the same Play, was one of his best Performances as an Actor. Nor is it within the reach of Rule or Precept to complete either of them. Instruction, 'tis true, may guard them equally against Faults or Absurdities, but there it stops; Nature must do the rest. To excel in either Art is a self-born Happiness, which something more than good Sense must be the Mother of.

The other Advantage I was speaking of is that before the Restoration no Actresses had ever been seen upon the *English* Stage. The Characters of Women on former Theatres were perform'd by Boys, or young Men of the most effeminate Aspect. And what Grace or Master-strokes of Action can we conceive such ungain Hoydens to have been capable of? This Defect was so well considered by *Shakespeare* that in few of his Plays he has any greater Dependance upon the Ladies than in the Innocence and Simplicity of a *Desdemona*, an *Ophelia*, or in the short Specimen of a fond and virtuous *Portia*. The additional Objects then of real, beautiful Women could not but draw a Proportion of new Admirers to the Theatre. We may imagine too that these Actresses were not ill chosen, when it is well known that more than one of them had Charms sufficient at their leisure Hours to calm and mollify the Cares of Empire. Besides these peculiar Advantages, they had a private Rule or Agreement which both Houses were happily ty'd down to, which was that no Play acted at one House should ever be attempted at the other. All the capital Plays therefore of *Shakespeare*, *Fletcher*, and *Ben. Jonson* were divided between them, by the Approbation of the Court and their own alternate Choice: so that when *Hart* was famous for *Othello*, *Betterton* had no less a Reputation for *Hamlet*. By this Order the Stage was supply'd with a greater Variety of Plays than could possibly have been shewn had both Companies been employ'd at the same time, upon the same Play; which Liberty too must have occasion'd such frequent Repetitions of 'em, by their opposite Endeavours to forestall and anticipate one another, that the best Actors in the World must have grown tedious and tasteless to the Spectator: for what Pleasure is not languid to Satiety? (53–5).

*　　*　　*

These two excellent Companies were both prosperous for some few Years, 'till their Variety of Plays began to be exhausted. Then of course the better Actors (which the King's seem to have been allow'd) could not fail of drawing the greater Audiences. Sir *William D'Avenant*, therefore, Master of the Duke's Company, to make Head against their Success was forc'd to add Spectacle and Musick to Action and to introduce a new Species of Plays, since call'd Dramatick Opera's, of which kind were the *Tempest*, *Psyche*, *Circe*, and others, all set off with the most expensive Decorations of Scenes and Habits, with the best Voices and Dancers.

This sensual Supply of Sight and Sound, coming in to the Assistance of the weaker Party, it was no Wonder they should grow too hard for Sense and simple Nature, when it is consider'd how many more People there are that can see and hear than think and judge. So wanton a Change of the publick Taste, therefore, began to fall as heavy upon the King's Company as their greater Excellence in Action had, before, fallen upon their Competitors: of which Encroachment upon Wit several good Prologues in those Days frequently complain'd. (57–8)

*　　*　　*

Betterton was an Actor, as Shakespeare was an Author, both without Competitors! form'd for the mutual Assistance, and Illustration of each other's Genius! How *Shakespeare* wrote, all Men who have a Taste for Nature may read and know—but with what higher Rapture would he still be *read* could they conceive how *Betterton play'd* him! Then might they know, the one was born alone to speak what the other only knew to write! Pity it is that the momentary Beauties flowing from an harmonious Elocution cannot, like those of Poetry, be their own Record! That the animated Graces of the Player can live no longer than the instant Breath and Motion that presents them; or at best can but faintly glimmer through the Memory or imperfect Attestation of a few surviving Spectators. Could *how* Betterton spoke be as easily known as *what* he spoke then might you see the Muse of *Shakespeare* in her Triumph, with all her Beauties in their best Array, rising into real

Life and charming her Beholders. But alas! since all this is so far out of the reach of Description how shall I shew you *Betterton*? Should I therefore tell you that all the *Othellos, Hamlets, Hotspurs, Macbeths*, and *Brutus*'s whom you may have seen since his time have fallen far short of him? This still would give you no Idea of his particular Excellence. Let us see then what a particular Comparison may do, whether that may yet draw him nearer to you?

You have seen a *Hamlet*, perhaps, who on the first appearance of his Father's Spirit has thrown himself into all the straining Vociferation requisite to express Rage and Fury, and the House has thunder'd with Applause; tho' the mis-guided Actor was all the while (as *Shakespeare* terms it) tearing a Passion into Rags. I am the more bold to offer you this particular Instance because the late Mr. *Addison*, while I sate by him to see this Scene acted, made the same Observation, asking me with some Surprize if I thought *Hamlet* should be in so violent a Passion with the Ghost, which tho' it might have astonish'd, it had not provok'd him? For you may observe that in this beautiful Speech the Passion never rises beyond an almost breathless Astonishment or an Impatience, limited by filial Reverence, to enquire into the suspected Wrongs that may have rais'd him from his peaceful Tomb, and a Desire to know what a Spirit so seemingly distrest might wish or enjoin a sorrowful Son to execute towards his future Quiet in the Grave. This was the Light into which *Betterton* threw this Scene which he open'd with a Pause of mute Amazement! then rising slowly, to a solemn, trembling Voice, he made the Ghost equally terrible to the Spectator as to himself! and in the descriptive Part of the natural Emotions which the ghastly Vision gave him the boldness of his Expostulation was still govern'd by Decency, manly but not braving; his Voice never rising into that seeming Outrage or wild Defiance of what he naturally rever'd. . . . (59–61)

A farther Excellence in *Betterton* was that he could vary his Spirit to the different Characters he acted. Those wild impatient Starts, that fierce and flashing Fire which he threw into *Hotspur* never came from the unruffled Temper of his *Brutus* (for I have more than once seen a *Brutus* as warm as *Hotspur*). When the *Betterton Brutus* was provok'd, in his Dispute with *Cassius*, his Spirit flew only to his Eye, his steady Look alone supply'd that Terror which he disdain'd an Intemperance in his Voice should rise to. Thus, with a settled Dignity of Contempt, like an unheeding Rock, he repelled upon himself the Foam of *Cassius*. Perhaps the very Words of *Shakespeare* will better let you into my Meaning:

> *Must I give way, and room, to your rash Choler?*
> *Shall I be frighted when a Madman stares?* [4.3.39f.]

And a little after,

> *There is no Terror,* Cassius, *in your Looks! &c.* [4.3.66]

Not but in some part of this Scene, where he reproaches *Cassius,* his Temper is not under this Suppression but opens into that Warmth which becomes a Man of Virtue; yet this is that *Hasty Spark* of Anger which *Brutus* himself endeavours to excuse. (62–3)

* * *

[Chapter IX]

* * *

Lest, therefore, the frequent Digressions that have broke in upon it may have entangled [the reader's] Memory I must beg leave just to throw together the Heads of what I have already given him, that he may again recover the Clue of my Discourse.

Let him then remember, from the Year 1660 to 1684, the various Fortune of the (then) King's and Duke's two famous Companies; their being reduced to one united; the Distinct Characters I have given of thirteen Actors which in the Year 1690 were the most famous then remaining of them; the Cause of their being again divided in 1695, and the Consequences of that Division 'till 1697; from whence I shall lead them to our Second Union in—Hold! let me see—ay, it was in that memorable Year when the two Kingdoms of *England* and *Scotland* were made one. And I remember a Particular that confirms me I am right in my Chronology. For the Play of *Hamlet* being acted soon after, *Estcourt,* who then took upon him to say any thing, added a fourth Line to *Shakespeare's* Prologue to the Play in that Play, which originally consisted but of three; but *Estcourt* made it run thus:

> *For Us, and for our Tragedy,*
> *Thus stooping to your Clemency,*
> [This being a Year of Unity,]
> *We beg your Hearing patiently.* [3.2.144ff.]

This new Chronological Line coming unexpectedly upon the Audience was received with Applause, tho' several grave Faces look'd a little out of Humour at it. However, by this Fact, it is plain our Theatrical Union happen'd in 1707. (172–3)

93. Thomas Gray, Shakespeare's language

1742

From Gray's letters to West, *The Works of Thomas Gray*, ed. J. Mitford, 5 vols (1835–43).

Thomas Gray (1716–71) produced no formal Shakespeare criticism other than the letters which he wrote to his literary friends, especially Mason, Walpole and West. But his poetry contains many Shakespearian echoes, as Roger Lonsdale has recently shown in his edition of *The Poems of Thomas Gray, William Collins, Oliver Goldsmith* (1969).

[From a Letter to West, 4 April 1742]

★   ★   ★

[Racine's] language is the language of the times, and that of the purest sort; so that his French is reckoned a standard. I will not decide what style is fit for our English stage; but I should rather choose one that bordered upon *Cato*, than upon Shakespeare. One may imitate (if one can) Shakespeare's manner, his surprising strokes of true nature, his expressive force in painting characters, and all his other beauties; preserving at the same time our own language. Were Shakespeare alive now he would write a different style from what he did. These are my sentiments upon these matters. Perhaps I am wrong, for I am neither a Tarpa, nor am I quite an Aristarchus. You see I write freely both of you and Shakespeare; but it is as good as writing not freely, where you know it is acceptable. (II, 148–9)

★   ★   ★

[From a Letter to West, 8 April 1742]

★   ★   ★

As to matter of stile, I have this to say: the language of the age is never the language of poetry; except among the French, whose verse, where the thought or image does not support it, differs in nothing from prose. Our poetry, on the contrary, has a language peculiar to itself; to which almost every one that has written has added something by enriching it with foreign idioms and derivatives: nay sometimes words of their own composition or invention. Shakespeare and Milton have been great creators this way; and no one more licentious than Pope or Dryden, who perpetually borrow expressions from the former. Let me give you some instances from Dryden, whom every body reckons a great master of our poetical tongue.—Full of *museful mopeings*—unlike the *trim* of love—a pleasant *beverage*—a *roundelay* of love—stood silent in his *mood* —with knots and *knares* deformed—his *ireful mood*—in proud *array*— his *boon* was granted—and *disarray* and shameful rout—*wayward* but wise—*furbished* for the field—the *foiled dodderd* oaks—*disherited*— *smouldering* flames—*retchless* of laws—*crones* old and ugly—the *beldam* at his side—the *grandam-hag*—*villanize* his Father's fame. But they are infinite. And our language not being a settled thing (like the French) has an undoubted right to words of an hundred years old, provided antiquity have not rendered them unintelligible. In truth, Shakespeare's language is one of his principal beauties; and he has no less advantage over your Addisons and Rowes in this than in those other great excellences you mention. Every word in him is a picture. Pray put me the following lines into the tongue of our modern Dramatics:

> But I, that am not shaped for sportive tricks,
> Nor made to court an amorous looking-glass:
> I, that am rudely stampt, and want love's majesty
> To strut before a wanton ambling nymph:
> I, that am curtail'd of this fair proportion,
> Cheated of feature by dissembling nature,
> Deform'd, unfinish'd, sent before my time
> Into this breathing world, scarce half made up—
>
> [*Richard III*, 1.1.14ff.]

and what follows. To me they appear untranslatable; and if this be the case, our language is greatly degenerated. However, the affectation of imitating Shakespeare may doubtless be carried too far; and is no sort of excuse for sentiments ill-suited, or speeches ill-timed, which I believe is a little the case with me.[1] (II, 152–4)

---

[1] Gray refers to his tragedy *Agrippina*.

94. Thomas Cooke, a panegyric to Shakespeare

1743

'A Prologue on Shakespeare and his Writings, Spoke by Mr. Garrick, At the Theatre-Royal in Drury Lane', in *An Epistle to the Countess of Shaftesbury, with a Prologue and Epilogue on Shakespeare and his Writings* (1743).

Thomas Cooke (1703–56) was a prolific poet and dramatist (see head-note to No. 79 in Vol. 2). The epilogue is a feeble witticism concerning the evil women in Shakespeare's plays.

The Sun without a Rival guides the Day,
And thro the Zodiac bears imperial Sway;
The lesser Planets which are seen by Night
Shine, tho they blaze not with a Flood of Light;
Some Stars there are than these of lesser Fame;
And some there are which twinckling have a Name;
Some shed so faint a Ray they're scarcely seen,
And nameless are, as if they ne'er had been.
'Tis thus with *Shakespeare*, our dramatic Soul,
And other Bards who in their Orbits roll;
They who approach him nearest are as far
From him as from the Sun the next bright Star.
Of our dramatic Race some have the Lot
Awhile to be remember'd, some forgot.
   Like the great Eye of Day that gladdens all,
From those who till the Earth to those who rule the Ball,
Shakespeare alike delights the lowest Clown,
To him whose Brows are circled with a Crown.
   In his historic Scenes ye strongly see
What Princes ought, what they ought not, to be;
From your affected Hearts what Praise ye send,
When for his Country *Brutus* slays his Friend!

Then glows the gen'rous Breast with noble Pride,
And all the vicious, selfish Dregs subside.
The various Passions he describes so well
Your Bosoms with *Othello*'s Tortures swell,
And tho her Loves, prepost'rous Loves, surprise,
Poor *Desdemona*'s Suff'rings fill your Eyes;
And who (so harden'd) can refuse to weep
When *Duncan* falls, and *Glamis* murders Sleep?
Or when distracted *Lear*, by Grief subdued,
Groans under Age and foul Ingratitude,
While his poor Fool, who will not him forsake,
Keeps by satiric Saws his Woes awake!

How bless'd, our Poet shews, are Love and Truth,
When Virtue blossoms on the Rose of Youth.
Whatever Picture of Distress he draws
You all are influenc'd in the Suff'rer's Cause.

The Scenes are chang'd; and he commands your Smile,
And brings ye pleas'd to his inchanted Isle.
Who grieves to see the *Jew* depriv'd of Rest,
When Av'rice and Revenge dilate his Breast?
What is to *Shylock* woeful is the Birth,
To you, of lively laughter-loving Mirth.
Shallow, *Malvolio*, bring ye Joy in Tides;
But *Falstaff*, with a Torrent, shakes your Sides.

Such *Shakespeare* is; and, as the Springs return,
With Violets, with Roses, deck his Urn;
His Busto crown with Wreaths, and grateful say,
Sweet is his Memory as the Breath of *May*. (5-6)

95. William Collins, a panegyric to Shakespeare

1743

Verses Humbly Address'd to Sir Thomas Hanmer. On his Edition of Shakespeare's Works (1743).

William Collins (1721–59) seems to have written this piece in an attempt to ingratiate himself with Oxford University. He reissued it the following year with substantial alterations: see R. Lonsdale (ed.), *The Poems of Thomas Gray, William Collins, Oliver Goldsmith* (1969).

Sir,
While, own'd by You, with Smiles the Muse surveys
Th' expected Triumph of her sweetest Lays:
While, stretch'd at Ease, she boasts your Guardian Aid,
Secure and happy in her sylvan Shade:
Excuse her Fears who scarce a Verse bestows,
In just Remembrance of the Debt she owes;
With conscious Awe she hears the Critic's Fame,
And blushing hides her Wreath at *Shakespeare*'s Name.

Long slighted *Fancy*, with a Mother's Care,
Wept o'er his Works, and felt the last Despair.
Torn from her Head, she saw the Roses fall,
By all deserted, tho' admir'd by all.
'And oh! she cry'd, shall Science still resign
Whate'er is Nature's, and whate'er is mine?
Shall *Taste* and *Art*, but shew a cold Regard,
And scornful Pride reject th'unletter'd Bard?
Ye myrtled Nymphs who own my gentle Reign,
Tune the sweet Lyre, and grace my airy Train!
If, where ye rove, your searching Eyes have known
One perfect Mind which Judgment calls its own:

There ev'ry Breast its fondest Hopes must bend,
And ev'ry Muse with Tears await her Friend.'

  'Twas then fair *Isis* from her Stream arose,
In kind Compassion of her Sister's Woes.
'Twas then she promis'd to the mourning Maid
Th' immortal Honours which thy Hands have paid:
'My best lov'd Son (she said) shall yet restore
Thy ruin'd Sweets, and Fancy weep no more.'

  Each rising Art by slow Gradation moves,
Toil builds on Toil, and Age on Age improves.
The Muse alone unequal dealt her Rage,
And grac'd with noblest Pomp her earliest Stage.
Preserv'd thro' Time the speaking Scenes impart
Each changeful Wish of *Phaedra*'s tortur'd Heart:
Or paint the Curse that mark'd the★ *Theban*'s Reign,
A Bed incestuous, and a Father slain.
Line after Line our pitying Eyes o'erflow,
Trace the sad Tale, and own another's Woe.

  To *Rome* remov'd, with equal Pow'r to please,
The *Comic* Sisters kept their native Ease.
With jealous Fear declining *Greece* beheld
Her own *Menander*'s Art almost excell'd!
But ev'ry Muse essay'd to raise in vain
Some labour'd Rival of her *Tragic* Strain;
Ilissus' Laurels, tho' transferr'd with Toil,
Droop'd their fair Leaves nor knew th' unfriendly Soil.

  When *Rome* herself, her envy'd Glories dead,
No more Imperial, stoop'd her conquer'd Head:
Luxuriant *Florence* chose a softer Theme,
While all was Peace by *Arno*'s silver Stream.
With sweeter Notes th' *Etrurian* Vales complain'd,
And Arts reviving told—a *Cosmo* reign'd.
Their wanton Lyres the Bards of *Provence* strung,
Sweet flow'd the Lays, but Love was all they sung.
The gay Description could not fail to move,
For, led by Nature, all are Friends to Love.

★ The *Œdipus* of *Sophocles*.

But Heav'n, still rising in its Works, decreed
The perfect Boast of Time should last succeed.
The beauteous Union must appear at length,
Of *Tuscan* Fancy, and *Athenian* Strength:
One greater Muse *Eliza*'s Reign adorn,
And ev'n a *Shakespeare* to her Fame be born!

Yet ah! so bright her Morning's op'ning Ray,
In vain our *Britain* hop'd an equal Day!
No second Growth the Western Isle could bear,
At once exhausted with too rich a Year.
Too nicely *Jonson* knew the Critic's Part;
Nature in him was almost lost in Art.
Of softer Mold the gentle *Fletcher* came,
The next in Order, as the next in Name.
With pleas'd Attention 'midst his Scenes we find
Each glowing Thought, that warms the Female Mind;
Each melting Sigh, and ev'ry tender Tear,
The Lover's Wishes and the Virgin's Fear.
His★ ev'ry Strain the Loves and Graces own;
But stronger *Shakespeare* felt for Man alone:
Drawn by his Pen, our ruder Passions stand
Th' unrivall'd Picture of his early Hand.

With gradual Steps and slow, exacter *France*
Saw Art's fair Empire o'er her Shores advance:
By length of Toil a bright Perfection knew,
Correctly bold, and just in all she drew.
Till late *Corneille* from Epick *Lucan* brought
The full Expression and the *Roman* thought;
And classic Judgment gain'd to sweet *Racine*
The temp'rate Strength of *Maro*'s chaster Line.

But wilder far the *British* Laurel spread,
And Wreaths less artful crown our Poet's Head.
Yet He alone to ev'ry Scene could give
Th' Historian's Truth, and bid the Manners live.
Wak'd at his Call I view, with glad Surprize,
Majestic Forms of mighty Monarchs rise.
There *Henry*'s Trumpets spread their loud Alarms,
And laurel'd Conquest waits her Hero's Arms.

★ Their Characters are thus distinguish'd by Mr. *Dryden*.

Here gentler *Edward* claims a pitying Sigh,
Scarce born to Honours, and so soon to die!
Yet shall thy Throne, unhappy Infant, bring
No Beam of Comfort to the guilty King?
The Time shall come, when *Glo'ster*'s Heart shall bleed
In Life's last Hours, with Horror of the Deed:
When dreary Visions shall at last present
Thy vengeful Image, in the midnight Tent:
Thy Hand unseen the secret Death shall bear,
Blunt the weak Sword, and break th' oppressive Spear.

   Where'er we turn, by Fancy charm'd, we find
Some sweet Illusion of the cheated Mind.
Oft, wild of Wing, she calls the Soul to rove
With humbler Nature in the rural Grove;
Where Swains contented own the quiet Scene,
And twilight Fairies tread the circled Green:
Drest by her Hand the Woods and Vallies smile,
And Spring diffusive decks th' *enchanted Isle*.

   O blest in all that Genius gives to charm,
Whose Morals mend us and whose Passions warm!
Oft let my Youth attend thy various Page,
Where rich Invention rules th' unbounded Stage.
There ev'ry Scene the Poet's Warmth may raise
And melting Music find the softest Lays.
O might the Muse with equal Ease persuade,
Expressive Picture, to adopt thine Aid!
Some pow'rful *Raphael* shou'd again appear
And Arts consenting fix their Empire here.

   Methinks ev'n now I view some fair Design,
Where breathing Nature lives in ev'ry Line:
Chaste and subdu'd the modest Colours lie,
In fair Proportion to th' approving Eye—
And see, where* *Antony* lamenting stands
In fixt Distress, and spreads his pleading Hands!
O'er the pale Corse the Warrior seems to bend,
Deep sunk in Grief, and mourns his murther'd Friend!
Still as they press, he calls on all around,
Lifts the torn Robe, and points the bleeding Wound.

* See the tragedy of *Julius Caesar*.

But* who is he whose Brows exalted bear
A Rage impatient, and a fiercer Air?
Ev'n now his Thoughts with eager Vengeance doom
The last sad Ruin of ungrateful *Rome*.
Till, slow-advancing o'er the tented Plain,
In sable Weeds appear the Kindred-train:
The frantic Mother leads their wild Despair,
Beats her swoln Breast, and rends her silver Hair.
And see he yields! . . . the Tears unbidden start,
And conscious Nature claims th'unwilling Heart!
O'er all the Man conflicting Passions rise,
Rage grasps the Sword while *Pity* melts the Eyes.

Thus, gen'rous Critic, as thy Bard inspires,
The Sister Arts shall nurse their drooping Fires;
Each from his Scenes her Stores alternate bring,
Spread the fair Tints, or wake the vocal String:
Those *Sibyl*-Leaves, the Sport of ev'ry Wind,
(For Poets ever were a careless Kind)
By thee dispos'd, no farther Toil demand,
But, just to Nature, own thy forming Hand.

So spread o'er *Greece*, th' harmonious Whole unknown,
Ev'n *Homer*'s Numbers charm'd by Parts alone.
Their own *Ulysses* scarce had wander'd more,
By Winds and Waters cast on ev'ry Shore:
When, rais'd by Fate, some former *Hanmer* join'd
Each beauteous image of the tuneful mind:
And bad, like Thee, his *Athens* ever claim
A fond Alliance with the Poet's Name.

* *Coriolanus.*

96. Sir Thomas Hanmer, preface to Shakespeare

1744

From *The Works of Shakespeare in six vols, carefully revised and corrected by the former editions, and adorned with sculptures designed and executed by the best hands* (1743–4).

Sir Thomas Hanmer (1677–1746) was a member of parliament from 1701 to 1727, and was appointed speaker in 1714. His edition of Shakespeare was the fruit of his retirement to his estate in Mildenhall, Suffolk.

What the Publick is here to expect is a true and correct Edition of *Shakespeare*'s works cleared from the corruptions with which they have hitherto abounded. One of the great Admirers of this incomparable Author hath made it the amusement of his leisure hours for many years past to look over his writings with a careful eye, to note the obscurities and absurdities introduced into the text, and according to the best of his judgment to restore the genuine sense and purity of it. In this he proposed nothing to himself but his private satisfaction in making his own copy as perfect as he could: but as the emendations multiplied upon his hands other Gentlemen equally fond of the Author desired to see them, and some were so kind as to give their assistance by communicating their observations and conjectures upon difficult passages which had occurred to them. Thus by degrees the work growing more considerable than was at first expected, they who had the opportunity of looking into it, too partial perhaps in their judgment, thought it worth being made publick; and he who hath with difficulty yielded to their perswasions is far from desiring to reflect upon the late Editors for the omissions and defects which they left to be supplied by others who should follow them in the same province. On the contrary, he thinks the world much obliged to them for the progress they made in weeding out so great a number of blunders and mistakes as they have done, and probably he who hath carried on the work might never have thought of such an undertaking if he had not found a considerable part so done to his hands.

From what causes it proceeded that the works of this Author in the first publication of them were more injured and abused than perhaps any that ever pass'd the Press hath been sufficiently explained in the Preface to Mr. *Pope's* Edition which is here subjoined, and there needs no more to be said upon that subject. This only the Reader is desired to bear in mind, that as the corruptions are more numerous and of a grosser kind than can well be conceived but by those who have looked nearly into them, so in the correcting them this rule hath been most strictly observed, not to give a loose to fancy, or indulge a licentious spirit of criticism, as if it were fit for any one to presume to judge what *Shakespeare* ought to have written, instead of endeavouring to discover truly and retrieve what he did write: and so great caution hath been used in this respect, that no alterations have been made but what the sense necessarily required, what the measure of the verse often helped to point out, and what the similitude of words in the false reading and in the true, generally speaking, appeared very well to justify.

Most of those passages are here thrown to the bottom of the page and rejected as spurious, which were stigmatized as such in Mr. *Pope's* Edition; and it were to be wished that more had then undergone the same sentence. The promoter of the present Edition hath ventured to discard but few more upon his own judgment, the most considerable of which is that wretched piece of ribaldry in *King Henry V* [3, 4] put into the mouths of the *French* Princess and an old Gentlewoman, improper enough as it is all in *French* and not intelligible to an *English* audience, and yet that perhaps is the best thing that can be said of it. There can be no doubt but a great deal more of that low stuff which disgraces the works of this great Author, was foisted in by the Players after his death, to please the vulgar audiences by which they subsisted: and though some of the poor witticisms and conceits must be supposed to have fallen from his pen, yet as he hath put them generally into the mouths of low and ignorant people so it is to be remember'd that he wrote for the Stage, rude and unpolished as it then was; and the vicious taste of the age must stand condemned for them since he hath left upon record a signal proof how much he despised them. In his Play of *The Merchant of Venice* a Clown is introduced quibbling in a miserable manner, upon which one who bears the character of a man of sense makes the following reflection: *How every fool can play upon a word! I think the best grace of wit will shortly turn into silence, and discourse grow commendable in none but parrots.* [3.5.38ff.] He could hardly have found stronger words to express his indignation at those false pretences to wit then in vogue; and therefore though such trash is frequently interspersed in his writings it would be unjust to cast it as an imputation upon his taste and judgment and character as a Writer.

There being many words in *Shakespeare* which are grown out of use and obsolete, and many borrowed from other languages which are not enough naturalized or known among us, a Glossary is added at the end of the work for the explanation of all those terms which have hitherto been so many stumbling-blocks to the generality of Readers; and where there is any obscurity in the text not arising from the word but from a reference to some antiquated customs now forgotten, or other causes of that kind, a note is put at the bottom of the page to clear up the difficulty.

With these several helps if that rich vein of sense which runs through the works of this Author can be retrieved in every part and brought to appear in its true light, and if it may be hoped without presumption that this is here effected; they who love and admire him will receive a new pleasure, and all probably will be more ready to join in doing him justice, who does great honour to his country as a rare and perhaps a singular Genius: one who hath attained an high degree of perfection in those two great branches of Poetry, Tragedy and Comedy, different as they are in their natures from each other; and who may be said without partiality to have equalled, if not excelled, in both kinds, the best writers of any age or country who have thought it glory enough to distinguish themselves in either.

Since therefore other nations have taken care to dignify the works of their most celebrated Poets with the fairest impressions beautified with the ornaments of sculpture, well may our *Shakespeare* be thought to deserve no less consideration: and as a fresh acknowledgment hath lately been paid to his merit, and a high regard to his name and memory, by erecting his Statue at a publick expence; so it is desired that this new Edition of his works, which hath cost some attention and care, may be looked upon as another small monument designed and dedicated to his honour. (I, i–vi)

97. Joseph Warton, Shakespeare: Nature's child

1744

From *The Enthusiast: or the Lover of Nature* (1744), lines 168–79.

Joseph Warton (1722–1800), one of a distinguished literary family, was a critic and essayist, a member of Dr Johnson's circle. He translated Virgil and wrote an important study of Pope.

What are the Lays of artful *Addison*,
Coldly correct, to *Shakespeare*'s Warblings wild?
Whom on the winding *Avon*'s willow'd Banks
Fair Fancy found, and bore the smiling Babe
To a close Cavern. (Still the Shepherds shew
The sacred Place, whence with religious Awe
They hear, returning from the Field at Eve,
Strange Whisperings of sweet Music thro' the Air.)
Here, as with Honey gather'd from the Rock,
She fed the little Prattler, and with Songs
Oft sooth'd his wond'ring Ears, with deep Delight
On her soft Lap he sat, and caught the Sounds.

98. Corbyn Morris, Falstaff's humour

1744

From *An Essay Towards Fixing the True Standards of Wit, Humour, Raillery, Satire, and Ridicule. To which is Added, an Analysis Of the Characters of An Humorist, Sir John Falstaff, Sir Roger de Coverly, and Don Quixote* (1744).

Corbyn Morris (d. 1779), who became commissioner of customs in 1763, was the author of numerous works on economics and statistics.

[Introduction]

*   *   *

As to the Character of Sir *John Falstaff*, it is chiefly extracted from *Shakespeare*, in his *1st Part of King Henry the IVth*. But so far as *Sir John* in *Shakespeare's* Description sinks into a *Cheat* or a *Scoundrel* upon any Occasion, he is different from that *Falstaff* who is designed in the following *Essay*, and is entirely an amiable Character.

It is obvious that the Appearance which *Falstaff* makes in the unfinished Play of *The Merry Wives of Windsor* is in general greatly below his true Character. His Imprisonment and Death in the latter Part of *King Henry the IVth*, seem also to have been written by *Shakespeare* in Compliance with the *Austerity* of the Times, and in order to avoid the Imputation of encouraging *Idleness* and mirthful *Riot* by too amiable and happy an Example. (xxviii)

*   *   *

[An Essay . . .]

*   *   *

For HUMOUR, extensively and fully understood, is *any remarkable* Oddity *or* Foible *belonging to a* Person *in* real Life; *whether this* Foible *be constitutional, habitual,* or *only affected; whether partial in one or two Circumstances or tinging the whole Temper and Conduct of the* Person.

It has from hence been observ'd that there is more HUMOUR in the *English* Comedies than in others; as we have more various odd *Characters* in real Life than any other Nation, or perhaps than all other Nations together.

That HUMOUR gives more Delight and leaves a more pleasurable Impression behind it than WIT, is universally felt and established, though the Reasons for this have not yet been assign'd. I shall therefore beg Leave to submit the following.

1. HUMOUR is more *interesting* than WIT in general, as the *Oddities* and *Foibles of Persons* in *real Life* are more apt to affect our Passions than any Oppositions or Relations between *inanimate* Objects.

2. HUMOUR is *Nature*, or what really appears in the Subject, without any Embellishments; WIT only a Stroke of *Art* where the original Subject, being insufficient of itself, is garnished and deck'd with auxiliary Objects.

3. HUMOUR, or the Foible of a *Character* in real Life, is usually insisted upon for some Length of Time. From whence, and from the common Knowledge of the Character, it is universally felt and understood. Whereas the Strokes of WIT are like sudden *Flashes*, vanishing in an Instant, and usually flying too fast to be sufficiently marked and pursued by the Audience.

4. HUMOUR, if the Representation of it be just, is compleat and perfect in its Kind, and entirely fair and unstrain'd. Whereas in the Allusions of WIT the Affinity is generally imperfect and defective in one Part or other; and even in those Points where the Affinity may be allow'd to subsist some Nicety and Strain is usually requir'd to make it appear.

5. HUMOUR generally appears in such Foibles as each of the Company thinks himself superior to. Whereas WIT shews the Quickness and Abilities of the Person who discovers it, and places him superior to the rest of the Company.

6. HUMOUR, in the Representation of the *Foibles of Persons* in *real Life*, frequently exhibits very *generous benevolent* Sentiments of Heart, and these, tho' exerted in a particular odd Manner, justly command our Fondness and Love. Whereas in all Allusions of WIT, *Severity, Bitterness,* and *Satire* are frequently exhibited. And where these are avoided, not worthy amiable Sentiments of the *Heart* but quick unexpected Efforts of the *Fancy* are presented.

7. The odd Adventures and Embarrassments which *Persons* in *real Life* are drawn into by their *Foibles* are fit Subjects of *Mirth*. Whereas in pure WIT the Allusions are rather *surprizing* than *mirthful*; and the *Agreements* or *Contrasts* which are started between Objects without any relation to the *Foibles* of *Persons* in real Life, are more fit to be *admired* for their *Happiness* and *Propriety* than to excite our *Laughter*. Besides, WIT, in the frequent Repetition of it, tires the Imagination with its precipitate Sallies and Flights, and teizes the Judgment. Whereas HUMOUR, in the Representation of it, puts no Fatigue upon the *Imagination* and gives exquisite Pleasure to the *Judgment*.

These seem to me to be the different Powers and Effects of HUMOUR and WIT. However, the most agreeable Representations or Compositions of all others appear not where they *separately* exist but where they are *united* together in the same Fabric; where HUMOUR is the *Ground-work* and chief Substance and WIT, happily spread, *quickens* the whole with Embellishments.

This is the Excellency of the *Character* of Sir *John Falstaff*. The *Ground-work* is *Humour*, or the Representation and Detection of a bragging and vaunting *Coward* in *real Life*. However, this alone would only have expos'd the *Knight* as a meer *Noll Bluff*, to the Derision of the Company, and after they had once been gratify'd with his Chastisement he would have sunk into Infamy, and become quite odious and intolerable. But here the inimitable *Wit* of Sir *John* comes in to his Support, and gives a new *Rise* and *Lustre* to his Character: for the sake of his *Wit* you forgive his *Cowardice*; or rather, are fond of his *Cowardice* for the Occasions it gives to his *Wit*. In short, the *Humour* furnishes a Subject and Spur to the *Wit*, and the *Wit* again supports and embellishes the *Humour*.

At the *first* Entrance of the *Knight* your good Humour and Tendency to *Mirth* are irresistibly excited by his jolly Appearance and Corpulency; you feel and acknowledge him to be the fittest Subject imaginable for yielding *Diversion* and *Merriment*. But when you see him immediately set up for *Enterprize* and *Activity* with his evident *Weight* and *Unweildiness* your Attention is all call'd forth, and you are eager to watch him to the End of his Adventures, your Imagination pointing out with a full Scope his future Embarrassments. All the while, as you accompany him forwards, he *heightens* your Relish for his future Disasters by his happy Opinion of his own Sufficiency, and the gay Vaunts which he makes of his Talents and Accomplishments; so that at last when he falls into a Scrape your Expectation is exquisitely gratify'd, and you have the full Pleasure of seeing all his trumpeted Honour laid in the Dust. When, in the midst of his Misfortunes, instead of being utterly demolish'd and sunk he rises again by the superior Force of his *Wit*, and begins a *new* Course with fresh Spirit and Alacrity, this excites you the more to *renew* the Chace, in full View of his *second* Defeat; out of which he recovers again, and triumphs with new Pretensions and Boastings. After this he immediately starts upon a *third* Race, and so on, continually detected and caught, and yet constantly extricating himself by his inimitable *Wit* and *Invention*; thus yielding a perpetual *Round* of Sport and Diversion.

Again, the genteel *Quality* of Sir *John* is of great Use in supporting his Character: it prevents his *sinking* too low after several of his Misfortunes. Besides, you allow him, in consequence of his *Rank* and *Seniority*, the Privilege to dictate and take the Lead, and to rebuke others upon many Occasions; by this he is sav'd from appearing too *nauseous* and *impudent*. The good *Sense* which he possesses comes also to his Aid, and saves him from being *despicable* by forcing your Esteem for his real Abilities. Again, the *Privilege* you allow him of rebuking and checking others, when he assumes it with proper Firmness and Superiority, helps to *settle* anew, and *compose* his Character after an Embarrassment; and reduces in some measure the *Spirit* of the Company to a proper *Level* before he sets out again upon a fresh Adventure—without this, they would be kept continually *strain'd* and *wound up* to the highest Pitch without sufficient Relief and Diversity.

It may also deserve to be remark'd of *Falstaff* that the *Figure* of his *Person* is admirably suited to the *Turn* of his *Mind*; so that there arises before you a perpetual *Allusion* from one to the other, which forms an incessant Series of *Wit* whether they are in *Contrast* or *Agreement* together. When he pretends to *Activity* there is *Wit* in the *Contrast* between his *Mind* and his *Person*, and *Wit* in their *Agreement*, when he triumphs in *Jollity*.

To compleat the whole, you have in this Character of *Falstaff* not only a free Course of *Humour*, supported and embellish'd with admirable *Wit*, but this *Humour* is of a Species the most *jovial* and *gay* in all Nature. Sir *John Falstaff* possesses Generosity, Chearfulness, Alacrity, Invention, Frolic and Fancy superior to all other Men. The *Figure* of his *Person* is the Picture of Jollity, Mirth, and Good-nature, and banishes at once all other Ideas from your Breast; he is happy himself, and makes you happy. If you examine him further, he has no Fierceness, Reserve, Malice or Peevishness lurking in his Heart; his Intentions are all pointed at innocent Riot and Merriment; nor has the Knight any inveterate Design, except against *Sack*, and that too he *loves*. If, besides this, he desires to pass for a Man of *Activity* and *Valour* you can easily excuse so harmless a *Foible* which yields you the highest Pleasure in its constant *Detection*.

If you put all these together, it is impossible to *hate* honest *Jack Falstaff*. If you observe them again, it is impossible to avoid *loving* him. He is the gay, the witty, the frolicksome, happy, and fat *Jack Falstaff*, the most delightful *Swaggerer* in all Nature. You must *love* him for your *own* sake, at the same time you cannot but *love* him for *his own* Talents. And when you have *enjoy'd* them you cannot but *love* him in *Gratitude*; he has nothing to disgust you, and every thing to give you Joy. His *Sense* and his *Foibles* are equally directed to advance your Pleasure, and it is impossible to be tired or unhappy in his Company.

This *jovial* and *gay* Humour, without any thing *envious, malicious, mischievous,* or *despicable,* and continually *quicken'd* and adorn'd with *Wit,* yields that peculiar Delight, without any *Alloy,* which we all feel and acknowledge in *Falstaff*'s Company. *Ben Jonson* has *Humour* in his *Characters,* drawn with the most masterly Skill and Judgment. In Accuracy, Depth, Propriety, and Truth he has no *Superior* or *Equal* amongst *Ancients* or *Moderns.* But the *Characters* he exhibits are of a *satirical* and *deceitful,* or of a *peevish* or *despicable* Species: as *Volpone, Subtle, Morose,* and *Abel Drugger,* in all of which there is something very justly to be *hated* or *despised.* And you feel the same Sentiments of *Dislike* for every other *Character* of *Jonson*'s, so that after you have been *gratify'd* with their *Detection* and *Punishment* you are quite tired and disgusted with their Company. Whereas *Shakespeare,* besides the peculiar *Gaiety* in the *Humour* of *Falstaff,* has guarded him from disgusting you with his *forward Advances* by giving him *Rank* and *Quality;* from being *despicable,* by his real good *Sense* and excellent *Abilities;* from being *odious,* by his *harmless Plots* and *Designs;* and from being *tiresome,* by his inimitable *Wit* and his new and incessant *Sallies* of highest *Fancy* and *Frolick.*

This discovers the *Secret* of carrying COMEDY to the highest Pitch of Delight, which lies *in drawing the Persons exhibited with such chearful and amiable* Oddities *and* Foibles *as you would chuse in your own* Companions *in* real Life. Otherwise, tho' you may be diverted at first with the *Novelty* of a Character and with a proper *Detection* and *Ridicule* of it, yet its *Peevishness, Meanness,* or *Immorality* will begin to disgust you after a little Reflection, and become soon *tiresome* and *odious*—it being certain that *whoever cannot be endured as an* accidental *Companion in* real Life *will never become, for the very same Reasons,* a favorite comic Character *in the Theatre.*

This *Relish* for *generous* and *worthy* Characters alone, which we all feel upon the *Theatre,* where no Biass of Envy, Malice or personal Resentment draws us aside, seems to be some Evidence of our *natural* and *genuin* Disposition to *Probity* and *Virtue;* tho' the Minds of most Persons being early and deeply *tinged* with vicious Passions, it is no wonder that *Stains* have been generally mistaken for *original Colours.*

It may be added that *Humour* is the most exquisite and delightful when the *Oddities* and *Foibles* introduc'd are not *mischievous* or *sneaking* but *free, jocund,* and *liberal,* and such as result from a generous Flow of Spirits and a warm universal *Benevolence.* . . .

It may be proper to observe in this Place that the *Business* of COMEDY is to exhibit the whimsical *unmischievous Oddities, Frolics,* and *Foibles* of *Persons* in *real Life;* and also to *expose* and *ridicule* their *real Follies, Meanness,* and *Vices.* The *former,* it appears, is more pleasurable to the Audience, but the *latter* has the Merit of being more instructive.

The *Business* of TRAGEDY is to exhibit the *Instability* of *human* Grandeur, and the unexpected *Misfortunes* and *Distresses* incident to the *Innocent* and *Worthy* in all Stations. And also to shew the terrible Sallies and the miserable Issue and Punishment of ungovern'd Passions and Wickedness. The *former* softens the Heart and fills it with Compassion, Humility and Benevolence. Compositions of this Sort are the highest, most admirable, and useful in all Nature when they are finish'd with Propriety and Delicacy and justly wrought up with the Sublime and Simplicity. The *latter* Species of *Tragedy* terrifies and shocks us in exhibiting both the Crimes and the Punishments. It threatens us into Moderation and Justice by shewing the terrible Issue of their Contraries. Pieces of this Sort, conducted with Propriety and carrying Application to ourselves, can scarcely be desirable; but as they are generally conducted they amount only to giving us an absurd Representation of a Murther committed by some furious foaming *Basha* or *Sultan.*

To return. *Jonson* in his COMIC Scenes has expos'd and ridicul'd *Folly* and *Vice; Shakespeare* has usher'd in *Joy, Frolic* and *Happiness.* The *Alchemist, Volpone* and *Silent Woman* of *Jonson* are most exquisite *Satires.* The *comic* Entertainments of *Shakespeare* are the highest Compositions of *Raillery, Wit* and *Humour. Jonson* conveys some Lesson in every Character, *Shakespeare* some new Species of Foible and Oddity. The one pointed his Satire with masterly Skill; the other was inimitable in touching the Strings of Delight. With *Jonson* you are confin'd and instructed, with *Shakespeare* unbent and dissolv'd in Joy. *Jonson* excellently concerts his Plots, and all his Characters unite in the one Design. *Shakespeare* is superior to such Aid or Restraint, his Characters continually sallying from one independent Scene to another, and charming you in each with fresh Wit and Humour.

It may be further remark'd that *Jonson*, by pursuing the most useful Intention of *Comedy*, is in Justice oblig'd to *hunt down* and *demolish* his own Characters. Upon this Plan he must necessarily expose them to your *Hatred*, and of course can never bring out an amiable Person. His *Subtle* and *Face* are detected at last, and become mean and despicable. Sir *Epicure Mammon* is properly trick'd, and goes off ridiculous and detestable. The *Puritan Elders* suffer for their Lust of Money and are quite nauseous and abominable, and his *Morose* meets with a severe Punishment after having sufficiently tir'd you with his Peevishness. But *Shakespeare*, with happier Insight, always supports his Characters in your Favour. His Justice *Shallow* withdraws before he is tedious; the *French* Doctor and *Welch* Parson go off in full Vigour and Spirit. Ancient *Pistol*, indeed, is scurvily treated: however, he keeps up his Spirits, and continues to threaten so well that you are still desirous of his Company; and it is impossible to be tir'd or dull with the gay unfading Evergreen *Falstaff*.

But in remarking upon the Characters of *Jonson* it would be unjust to pass *Abel Drugger* without notice. This is a little, mean, sneaking, sordid Citizen, hearkening to a Couple of Sharpers who promise to make him rich. They can scarcely prevail upon him to resign the least Tittle he possesses, though he is assur'd it is in order to get more; and your Diversion arises from seeing him *wrung* between *Greediness* to *get* Money and *Reluctance* to *part* with any for that Purpose. His Covetousness continually prompts him to follow the Conjurer, and puts him at the same Time upon endeavouring to stop his Fees. All the while he is excellently managed and spirited on by *Face*. However, this Character upon the whole is *mean* and *despicable*, without any of that free spirituous jocund Humour abounding in *Shakespeare*. But having been strangely exhibited upon the Theatre a few Years ago, with odd Grimaces and extravagant Gestures, it has been raised into more Attention than it justly deserved. It is, however, to be acknowledg'd that *Abel* has no Hatred, Malice or Immorality, nor any assuming Arrogance, Pertness or Peevishness, and his eager Desire of getting and saving Money by Methods he thinks lawful are excusable in a Person of his Business. He is therefore not odious or detestable but harmless and inoffensive in private Life; and from thence, correspondent with the Rule already laid down, he is the most capable of any of *Jonson's* Characters of being a Favourite on the Theatre.

It appears that in Imagination, Invention, Jollity and gay Humour *Jonson* had little Power, but *Shakespeare* unlimited Dominion. The first was cautious and strict, not daring to sally beyond the Bounds of Regularity. The other bold and impetuous, rejoicing like a Giant to run his Course through all the Mountains and Wilds of Nature and Fancy.

It requires an almost painful Attention to mark the Propriety and Accuracy of *Jonson*, and your Satisfaction arises from Reflection and Comparison; but the Fire and Invention of *Shakespeare* in an Instant are shot into your Soul, and enlighten and chear the most indolent Mind with their own Spirit and Lustre. Upon the whole, *Jonson's* Compositions are like finished Cabinets, where every Part is wrought up with the most excellent Skill and Exactness; *Shakespeare's* like magnificent Castles, not perfectly finished or regular, but adorn'd with such bold and magnificent Designs as at once delight and astonish you with their Beauty and Grandeur. (23–37)

99. David Garrick, How not to act Macbeth

1744

From *An Essay on Acting: In which will be consider'd The Mimical Behaviour of a Certain fashionable faulty Actor, and the Laudableness of such unmannerly, as well as inhumane Proceedings. To which will be added, A Short Criticism On His acting Macbeth* (1744).

This curious pamphlet seems to have been issued by Garrick as an attempt to anticipate the obvious criticisms of his appearance as Macbeth. The title-page carries two mottoes which express the attitudes he expected to meet:

> —*So have I seen a Pygmie strut,*
> *Mouth and rant, in a Giant's Robe.*
> Tom Thumb

> —*Oh! Macbeth has murder'd G—K.*
> Shakespeare

By the banal nature of the advice given Garrick satirises the crudities both of contemporary acting and of unthinking panegyrics on Shakespeare.

So much for *Dress* and *Figure*. Now I shall proceed to the more difficult and physical Parts of the Character, and shall consider the *Action, Speaking* and *Conception* of our *modern Heroe*.

The first Words of the Part,—*So foul and fair a Day I have not seen*, in my Opinion are spoke wrong. *Macbeth* before his Entrance has been in a great Storm of Rain, Thunder, &c. Now as the Audience have been appriz'd of this by the three Witches he should very *emphatically* describe the quick Transition from being *wet to the Skin* to being almost instantaneously *dry'd again*. Tho' I can't convey in Writing the Manner how it *should* be spoke yet every Reader may comprehend how it *ought* to be spoke, and know that in the Manner it is *now* spoke the Sentiment is *languid, unintelligible,* and *undescriptive*. I shall now examine

130

the most remarkable Scene in the whole Play, which is that of the *Air-drawn Dagger*. This I shall make appear he has mistook from the Beginning to the End.

Macbeth, as a Preparation for this Vision, is so prepossess'd from his Humanity with the Horror of the Deed, which by his more prevailing Ambition he is incited to, and for the Perpetration of which he lies under a promissary Injunction to his Lady that, his Mind being torn by these different and confus'd Ideas, his Senses fail, and present that *fatal Agent* of his Cruelty, the *Dagger*, to him. Now in this visionary Horror he should not rivet his Eyes to an *imaginary* Object, as if it *really* was there, but should shew an *unsettled Motion* in his Eye, like one not quite awak'd from some disordering Dream. His *Hands* and *Fingers* should not be *immoveable* but *restless*, and endeavouring to disperse the Cloud that over shadows his optick Ray and bedims his Intellects. Here would be Confusion, Disorder, and Agony! *Come let me clutch thee!* is not to be done by *one* Motion only but by several *successive Catches* at it, first with one Hand and then with the other, preserving the same Motion at the same Time with his Feet like a Man who, out of his Depth and half drowned in his Struggles, *catches* at *Air* for *Substance*. This would make the Spectator's Blood run cold, and he would almost feel the Agonies of the Murder himself. I have spoke of the Scene following the Murder in my *Essay on Acting*, and shall only say that the *Daggers* are near an Inch and half too long, in Proportion to the Heighth of the Murderer. The Night-Gown he appears in after the Murder ought to be a *Red Damask*, and not the frippery-flower'd one of a *Foppington*; but when *Taste* is wanting in *Trifles* and *Judgment* in *Essentials* how can we hope to see the THEATRE flourish?

I must make a Remark upon him in the *Banquet Scene*, which is the most glaring Absurdity that ever was committed by an Actor. When *Banquo's* Ghost gets Possession of *Macbeth's* Chair, and the latter, frighted at his Appearance by Words and Actions, says *Which of you have done this?*—meaning the Murder of *Banquo*—here the Actor should address himself to the *Guests* and not keep a *fix'd Eye* upon the *Ghost*. He should turn his Head *from Banquo* and say to the Lords at Supper *Which of you have done this?* For to speak to the *plural* Number and look at the *singular* (*Banquo* only) is most absurd and ridiculous. Then at the *second* Appearance of the Ghost, at the Words *Dare me to the Desart with thy Sword*, *Macbeth* should draw his Sword and put himself in a Posture of Defence; and when he comes to *Hence horrid Shadow!* he should make a home Thrust at him, recover himself upon the *Ghost's* moving and keep passing at him till he has got him quite out of the Room. The Manner it has been done *heretofore*, which is keeping the Hand upon the Sword and following him out, is not so natural and affecting as the Way I propose; and if any Objection is made that *Macbeth* should know that *Ghosts* are not *vulnerable* I answer, *Macbeth*'s Horror confounds him, and his Actions must denote the *Non Compos*. Here I must take Notice of an Omission in the Part of *Banquo*. When he appears at the Banquet he ought to rise in a *Red Cloak*, as he was seen to cross the Stage in one immediately before his Murder. This would throw a great Solemnity upon the Figure of *Banquo*, and preserve the Decorum of the Stage.

I must likewise observe that in *Shakespeare*'s Time the Actors wore their own Hair, and now, from the present Fashion of wearing Wigs, some Speeches are become absurd. Such, for Instance, is this of *Macbeth*, *Never shake thy Goary Locks at me*; when at the same Time the Ghost is seen in a *Tye Wig*. If I might be allow'd to propose an Alteration (with all imaginable Deference to the immortal *Shakespeare*) in order to avoid this Blunder, I would have the Actor say *Never shake thy Goary* TYE *at me*; if the Word *Wig* is thought more Poetical it will be equally good, as they are both Monosyllables.

As I have not yet left the *Banquet Scene*, I must observe that the *Attitude G—k* stands in at the second Appearance of the Ghost, is absolutely wrong. *Macbeth* here should *sink* into *himself*, or rather, if I may be allow'd the Expression, *hide* himself behind *himself*. Or, to illustrate it more by Example (*Si parvis componere*,[1] &c.), he should imitate the contracting Power of a *Snail*, preserving at the *same Time* a *slow awful manly* folding up of his Faculties, and as his *Body* gathers up gradually at the Vision his *Mind* should keep the same Time, and denote its strong Workings and Convulsions at his *Eyes*. The Glass of Wine in his Hand should not be dash'd upon the Ground but it should fall *gently* from him, and he should not discover the least Consciousness of having such a Vehicle in his Hand, his Memory being quite lost in the present Guilt and Horror of his Imagination. (16–21)

*   *   *

I think I cannot better finish a Criticism on *Macbeth* than with a succinct Description of the Talents and Capacity of its Author. *Shakespeare* was a Writer not to be confin'd by *Rule*; he had a *despotick Power* over all Nature; *Laws* would be an *Infringement* of his *Prerogative*; his

---

[1] Virgil, *Eclogue* 1.23: 'to compare great things with small.'

scepter'd Pen wav'd Controul over every *Passion* and *Humour*; his *Royal Word* was not only *Absolute* but *Creative*; *Ideas*, *Language*, and *Sentiment* were his *Slaves*, they were *chain'd* to the *Triumphal Car* of his *Genius*; and when he made his *Entry* into the *Temple of Fame* all *Parnassus* rung with *Acclamations*; the *Muses* sung his *Conquests*, crown'd him with never-fading *Laurels*, and pronounc'd him *Immortal*. AMEN. (24)

100. David Garrick, from his presentation of *Macbeth*

1744

From Bell's edition of Shakespeare (ed. Francis Gentleman), 9 vols (1773), I, p. 69.

First performed on 7 January 1744, and advertised as Shakespeare's play, Garrick's few additions include a new death scene for the hero. However, Garrick follows D'Avenant in retaining the dancing witches and omitting the drunken porter. Garrick also curtails the scene in which Lady Macduff and her son are murdered: this takes place off-stage, as in D'Avenant. For details of his other cuts and re-arrangements see C. B. Hogan, *Shakespeare in the Theatre, 1701–1800*, Vol. 2 (Oxford, 1957), p. 362.

> *Macb.*   Lay on *Macduff*,
> And damn'd be he that first cries, hold, enough.
> *Macd.* This for my royal master *Duncan*.
> This for my bosom friend, my wife; and this for
> The pledges of her love and mine, my children.
>   [Macbeth *falls*]

Sure there are remains to conquer—I'll
As a trophy bear away his sword, to
Witness my revenge.   [*Exit* Macduff]

   Macb. 'Tis done! the scene of life will quickly close.
Ambition's vain, delusive dreams are fled,
And now I wake to darkness, guilt and horror;
I cannot bear it! let me shake it off—
'Tw'o not be; my soul is clogg'd with blood—
I cannot rise! I dare not ask for mercy—
It is too late, hell drags me down; I sink,
I sink—Oh!—my soul is lost for ever!
Oh!   [*Dies*]

101. David Garrick, from his presentation of *Othello*

1745

From Bell's edition of Shakespeare (ed. Francis Gentleman), 9 vols (1773), I, p. 165.

First performed 7 March 1745, this was a pure text, except for the following speech which Garrick added in place of Othello's description of 'antres vast and deserts idle . . .' [1.3.140ff.].

   Oth.   . . . of my redemption thence;
Of battles bravely, hardly fought: of victories,
For which the conqueror mourn'd, so many fell;
Sometimes I told the story of a siege,
Wherein I had to combat plagues and famine;
Soldiers unpaid; fearful to fight,
Yet bold in dangerous mutiny.
All these to hear
Would *Desdemona* seriously incline. . . .

102. Colley Cibber, adaptation of *King John*

1745

From *Papal Tyranny in the Reign of King John* (1745).

Cibber's adaptation was performed on 15 February 1745, although there is evidence that it was completed earlier (see Introduction above, p. 9 and note 13).

[Dedication to Philip, Earl of Chesterfield]

*   *   *

I shall not trouble your Lordship with a critical Examen or Comparison between this Play and the *King John* of *Shakespeare*, any farther than just to mention the principal Motive that first set me to work upon it.

In all the historical Plays of *Shakespeare* there is scarce any Fact that might better have employed his Genius than the flaming Contest between his insolent *Holiness* and *King John*. This is so remarkable a Passage in our Histories that it seems surprizing our *Shakespeare* should have taken no more Fire at it; especially when we find from how much less a Spark of Contention in his first Act of *Harry the fourth* he has thrown his *Hotspur* into a more naturally fomented Rage than ever ancient or modern Author has come up to, and has maintain'd that Character throughout the Play with the same inimitable Spirit. How then shall we account for his being so cold upon a so much higher Provocation? Shall we suppose that in those Days, almost in the Infancy of the Reformation, when *Shakespeare* wrote—when the Influence of the Papal Power had a stronger Party left than we have reason to believe is now subsisting among us; that this, I say, might make him cautious of offending? Or shall we go so far for an Excuse as to conclude that *Shakespeare* was himself a Catholick? This some Criticks have imagin'd to be true from the solemn Description of Purgatory given us by his Ghost in *Hamlet*; yet here, I doubt, the Conjecture is too strong; that Description being rather to be consider'd simply as a poetical Beauty and critically proper to a *Catholick* Character than offer'd as a real Point or Declaration of his own Faith. Had *Shakespeare* been a *Romanist* he would scarce have let his King *John* have taken the following Liberty with his Holiness, where he contemns the Credulity of *Philip* the *French* King that can submit to

> Purchase corrupted Pardon of a Man,
> Who, in that Sale, sells Pardon from himself. [3.1.166f.]

This is too sharp a Truth to be suppos'd could come from the Pen of a *Roman Catholick*. If then he was under no Restraint from his Religion it will require a nicer Criticism than I am master of to excuse his being so cold upon so warm an Occasion.

It was this Coldness then, my Lord, that first incited me to inspirit his King *John* with a Resentment that justly might become an *English* Monarch, and to paint the intoxicated Tyranny of *Rome* in its proper Colours. And so far, at least, my Labour has succeeded that the additional Sentiments which King *John* throws out upon so flagrant a Provocation were receiv'd with those honest cordial Applauses which *English* Auditors I foresaw would be naturally warm'd to. My Success in this Point, which I had chiefly at heart, makes me almost unconcern'd for what may be judged of the farther Mechanism of the Play. I have endeavour'd to make it more like a Play than what I found it in *Shakespeare*, and if your Lordship should find it so my Ambition has no farther Views. (Sig. A₃–A₄)

*   *   *

PROLOGUE.

Spoke by the AUTHOR.

The hardy Wretch, that gives the Stage a Play,
Sails, in a Cockboat, on a tumbling Sea!
Shakespeare, whose Works no Play-wright could excel,
Has launch'd us Fleets of Plays, and built them well:
Strength, Beauty, Greatness were his constant Care;
And all his Tragedies were Men of War!
Such tow'ring Barks the Rage of Seas defy'd,
The Storms of Criticks, adverse Winds, or Tide!
Yet Fame nor Favour ever deign'd to say,
King John was station'd as a first rate Play;

Though strong and sound the Hulk, yet ev'ry Part
Reach'd not the Merit of his usual Art!
To cure what seem'd amiss a Modern Muse,
Warm'd by the Subject, lets his Rashness loose;
Takes on himself the Errors of to Day,
And, thus refitted, trusts it to the Sea!
The Purpose of his Voyage this, to shew,
How *England* groan'd five hundred Years ago!
When, veil'd with Sanctity, the Papal Sway
To wolvish Pastors made our Folds a Prey!
When *Roman* Prelates here like Princes reign'd,
Yet scarce e'er visited the Land they drain'd!
And while the Bigots Neck this Yoke endures,
Our Souls were sav'd by foreign Sinecures!
Thus while each Pontiff, like the Sun, from hence
Exhal'd the Vapours of his *Peter-pence*;
Their lock'd-up Heav'n they promis'd (such the Grace is!)
That Popes, like Box-keepers, secur'd you Places:
But not as here, their Laws more firm were made,
None were admitted there before they paid.
As if the Right divine of *Roman* Pow'r
Were first to blind their Flocks, and then devour!
This carnal Discipline the fi'ry *John*,
Determin'd to suppress, asserts his Throne!
Defiance to the lordly Pontiff flings,
And spurns his Legates that would cope with Kings!
Hence! roar'd the holy Thunder through the Land!
Aghast! the People hear the dread Command!
Terror, Confusion, Rage and civil War,
At once the Bowels of the Nation tear;
'Till the lost Monarch vanquish'd and alone,
His Subjects to regain resigns his Throne;
With vassal Homage at her Feet lays down,
To hold from *Rome* his Tributary-Crown!
These dire Disasters, this religious Rage
That shames our Annals, may become the Stage:
Where the wild Passions which these Contests raise,
If well presented, may deserve your Praise;
At least this Pleasure from the View may flow,
That long! long distant were those Scenes of Woe!

And as such Chains no more these Realms annoy,
Applaud the Liberty you now enjoy.

*　　*　　*

[Act I, Scene ii. A Camp near Angiers]

Enter Constance, *from the Tent of* Philip.

Const. Now hangs the Crown of *England* on a Moment!
Decisive War anon demands it fix'd
Upon the Brow of Right, or Usurpation!
How desp'rate, how tremendous is the Stake,
Depending on this instant Cast of Battle!
The Victor, the Defeated—Slave or Monarch!
The regal Sceptre, and the purple Robe
Against the cockled Pilgrim's Rug and Staff!
A Prince in Glory, or a high-born Beggar!
O! miserable, wide Distinction, hark!

[*Alarms, at great Distance.*

The wafting Winds, in audible Perception,
Set all the Terrors of the Field before me!
This Jar of Drums! the lofty Trumpets' Ardour!
The vaunting Echoes of the neighing Steed!
This Clang of Armour! these sky-rending Shouts
Of charging Squadrons speak the Battle raging!
Yet from the wild Confusion no kind Sound
Distinguishes where Victory inclines;
These sharp Vicissitudes of Hopes and Fears
Tear me with Torture insupportable!
Conquest suspended is Captivity!
O dreadful, agonizing Interval!—
Hear, Heav'n, my Pray'r! If thy dread Will decrees
Our House must fall, let not my riper Sins
On hapless *Arthur*'s Head be visited!
O! spare, protect his youthful Innocence,
That Life prolong'd may propagate his Virtues!
This sudden Silence in the vacant Air
Seems as if breathless Conquest sought Repose:
Now is our Cause successful, or abandon'd!
Hark! a Retreat is sounded! O! for News

To quell this Conflict of Uncertainty!
But see! where One 'fore-spent with Toil and Haste,
This way conducts a Youth in Form, my *Arthur*!
My Pray'rs are heard! 'tis he himself preserv'd,
And living, from the Battle!—O my Life!

Enter Melun *with* Arthur.

O! welcome! to thy Mother's painful Longings!
To fold thee thus is more Content than Empire!
Crowns are not worth the anxious Coils they cost us!
O say, my Boy! how could thy tender Limbs
Support the Onsets of this dreadful Day?
   Arth. O 'twas a gallant Horse I rode, train'd up
To War! had I known Fear he would have tam'd me!
He curl'd his Crest, and proudly paw'd the Ground,
And from his vocal Nostrils neigh'd such Fire!
To mount him seem'd the Transport of a Throne!
   Const. My little Soldier! how thy Spirit charms me!

★   ★   ★

[Act III, Scene ii]

SCENE changes to a Chamber in the Castle of ROAN.

Enter King John *with* Hubert.

   K. John. This strict Observance of my Orders, *Hubert*,
Commends thee to a better Charge: Men of
Such Vigilance are scarce, and should be cherish'd.
   Hub. The Trouble you have taken to convince your Eyes,
Coming in Person to observe my Care,
As it has made me proud to have been prov'd
So shews it, Sir, how near this Boy concerns you!
And therefore shall it mend my Vigilance.
   K. John. Think not a Doubt of thee has brought me hither!
I came, my *Hubert*, to assist thy Care!
T'inform—instruct thee—to explain my Orders!
Nay to conceal them from the World beside;
For not within my Realms know I a Soul,
Whose friendly Bosom I would sooner make
The Casket of my secret Deeds than *Hubert*.

Hub. I hope, Sir, you have many more as faithful!
Yet this I know! had I a Secret here,
Unfit for other Knowledge than your own;
If Force or Torture would insist to know it, this
Within my Heart should hide it from the World.   [*Shews a Dagger.*

K. John. *Hubert*, thy Hand, thou art thy Master's Master!
There's scarce a Joy or Sorrow in my Soul
But longs to find its Fellowship in thee!
I had a Thing to say—I know thou'rt secret:
Yet 'tis of such a Nature—now I dare not!
The Sun is in the Heav'ns! and his gay Beams,
Exciting Mirth and Pleasure through the World,
Are all too wanton and too full of Gauds
To give me Audience. No, *Hubert*, the Time
For Speech like mine were when the midnight Bell,
With Sound of iron Tongue, proclaim'd the dead
And drousy Truce of worldly Cares and Labour!
The Place—some dark Church-yard or Charnel-house,
Where Tombs, or Bones, and Skulls, might only catch
My Words! There could I meet thee, swoll'n with Wrongs,
When that thy surly Spirit Melancholy
Had bak'd thy Blood, and made it heavy, stagnate!
Which else runs trickling up and down the Veins,
Making that Idiot Laughter fill Mens Eyes,
Straining their Cheeks to idle Merriment,
A Passion hateful to my Purposes.

Hub. Have you a Purpose, Sir, more fell than Death?
To give, or to receive it, frights not *Hubert*;
Why then this Pause, this Diffidence of Soul?

K. John. O! *Hubert*! could'st thou without Eyes behold me;
Hear without Ears, or make without a Tongue
Reply, using Conceit alone, to sound my Wishes;
Then, in the Face of this broad beaming Day,
Would I into thy Bosom pour my Thoughts,
With the same Confidence my Brain conceives them:
But to a Man like thee, whose Sense compleat
Might weigh against his Deeds their Consequence,
I dare not, *Hubert*, O, I dare not hint them.

Hub. Then, Sir, to ease your Heart, I will be plain;
I guess the Secret that distresses you.

Fear not to trust me, Sir, I'll do the Deed.

  K. John. Thou flatter'st me—

  Hub.   I'll serve you, Sir, but yet—

  K. John. What yet? hast thou a Doubt of me?

  Hub.   I've none.

Howe'er, because 'tis possible I may

Mistake your full Intentions, you too must

Be plain, and trust me with each Circumstance:

And, Sir, to shew you how secure you are,

There's my Dagger; if, when you name the Deed,

You find me change, or shew Confusion in

My Looks, or start in my Reply a Doubt

Or Scruple, to alarm your Jealousy,

Then, from my craven Heart, rip out your Trust!

When you have kill'd me, you resume the Secret.

  K. John. Do I not know thee faithful? Keep thy Dagger,

It may be useful.

  Hub.   Where?

  K. John.   Must I then speak it?

  Hub. Or how shall I be sure that I obey you?

  K. John. And yet, methinks, in Darkness I could better—

This Light offends—Shut forth the Sun and hear me!

                             [Hubert *darkens the Windows.*

  K. John. So,—so,—this Gloom befits our Purpose—

  Hub.   Now, Sir.

  K. John. O! *Hubert! Hubert! Arthur*—is alive!

  Hub. There lies your Grief, and you would have him—

  K. John.   Dead!

He is a very Serpent in my Way!

A Pain to see, and Danger to my Steps!

If thou'rt my Friend, remove him.

  Hub.   When?

  K. John. This Night.

  Hub.   By Death?

  K. John.   A Grave.

  Hub.   He shall not live.

  K. John. Enough, my Fears are hush'd! and now with Joy,

I can embrace thee. O, think! think, my Friend!

Howe'er I've worn my Crown Thy Hand alone

Can make it easy on my Brow. This Night

To *England* set we forward. When 'tis done,
Bring thou the News: There full Reward shall wait thee.　　[*Exit.*
　Hub. Now to my Office, let me think upon't.
As to the Time—the Place—the Means—why not
This very Hour? There, where he is—by this!　　[*Drawing his Dagger.*
Yet hold—to see the Dagger ere he feels
The Blow his Screams may give Alarm without.
That—that we must avoid—unseen prevents it.
Perhaps he sleeps—then, without Noise, we end him.
Steal on him softly, and observe—he prays!
The fitter for his Fate. A second Thought
Determines to my Wish: suppose, when dead,
Some Proof were left that he destroy'd himself;
The Means, kept secret, will be half the Merit:
That crowns the Work. By this his Beads are counted—
List—no—he's praying still—ha—what is't I hear?
Distraction to my Sense! he prays for me!
For *Hubert*! who has made his Chains sit easy,
And thanks high Heav'n he has so kind a Keeper.
What means this damp Reluctance on my Brow?
These trembling Nerves, this Ague in my Blood?
Is Death more cruel from a private Dagger,
Than, in the Field, from murd'ring Swords of thousands?
Or does the Number slain make Slaughter glorious?
Why then is Conscience more restrain'd in me,
Than in a crown'd Ambition? Conscience there can sleep
Secure by Custom and Impunity.
Shall Custom, then, excuse the Crimes of Pow'r,
And shall the Brave be baffled by a Shadow?
Let sickly Conscience shake the vulgar Soul
That Brute-like plods the beaten Paths of Life
Without Reflexion on its Slavery—no,
Be *Hubert*'s Actions, like his Thinking, free.

Enter Arthur.

He's here. Young Prince, I have to talk with thee.
　Arth. O! *Hubert*, I'm glad thou art return'd;
Thou told'st me thou would'st move my Uncle for
My Liberty, and hast thou seen him?—Ha!
What means that thoughtful Brow? those folded Arms?

And why this Noon-tide Gloom? this doleful Shade?
Art thou not well? I prithee tell me, *Hubert*;
Or has my Uncle's Answer made thee sad?
For me bad News is better than Suspense.
    Hub. Be satisfy'd—for thou must die a Prisoner.
    Arth. A Prisoner! Tedious Life! O, cruel Uncle!
Is there no Hope, dear *Hubert*? must I pine
Away my Days within these lonesome Walls?
For Life a Prisoner, said'st thou?
    Hub.   Only Death
Can end thy Miseries.
    Arth.   Then Death were welcome!
    Hub. I take thee at thy Word. This Dagger shall
Release thee.
    Arth.   Ha! Why dost thou fright me, *Hubert*?
    Hub. Thy Fate is in my Hand; raise not thy Voice
On Pain of lingring Wounds. Now, then, observe me:
Those golden Tablets I have seen thee use—
Without Delay produce them, quick.
    Arth.   Here! here!
O! *Hubert*, I have a Diamond on my Finger too,
Take that. Within I've other Gems of Value;
My little Pray'r-book is with precious Stones
Beset, and clasp'd with Gold; I'll yield thee all.
Nay, more, my wretched Mother (give me Time
To write) I know will starve her State to save me!
Let me but live, though here in Misery;
And, *Hubert*, I will find the Means to make
Thy Life one live-long Age of Happiness.
    Hub. Think'st thou I came to rob thee of thy Toys?
    Arth. It is not Robbery. Why so harsh a Name?
It is thy Right, good *Hubert*; am I not
Thy Captive, fairly taken in the Field?
Therefore whate'er was mine, by the known Laws
Of War, is duly thine by glorious Claim,
Thy Right and Purchase of superior Valour.
    Hub. I let him talk too much: I must be speedy—   [*Apart.*
Down foolish Qualm.—Here, write as I shall dictate.
    Arth. Most willingly. O! any Thing t'appease thee.
    Hub. For secret Reasons we must make thy Death

Seem to the World thy voluntary Choice.
Nay, no Reluctance, do it.
    Arth.   Cruel *Hubert!*
Must I do more than die? O! Mercy! Mercy!
    Hub. Suppress thy Voice, or thou art Days in dying.
    Arth. I will; O, spare me, *Hubert,* but a Moment,
But while I call once more on Heav'n! indeed,
I'll not be loud! Alas, I need not, there
The softest supplicating Sigh is heard to Heav'n.
    Hub. First, as I bid thee, write; then shalt thou pray.
    Arth. What would thy Rage enjoin me?
    Hub.   Write me thus:
'From an injurious World and doleful Prison,
By my own Hand this Dagger set me free.'
Write.
    Arth. O, *Hubert,* kill not my Soul, nor let
Me send, in Death, a Falshood up to Heav'n!
    Hub. Write, or thou dy'st before a Pray'r can 'scape thee.
    Arth. Should I write this, what Pray'r could wash away
The Sin? No, *Hubert,* no, if I must die,
I dare not taint my Innocence; and since
Thy Heart has none—may Heav'n have Mercy on me!
                                [Drops the Tablets.

    Hub. Wilt thou provoke my Rage?
    Arth.   How can I help it?
If I refuse to write I can at worst but die,
And should I write next Moment thou wilt kill me.
Was it for this I sent my Pray'rs for *Hubert?*
    Hub.   Ha!
    Arth. This very Hour I pray'd. O! if an Angel
Should have dropp'd from Heav'n t' have told me this,
So well I thought of *Hubert,* O! I could not,
Could not have believ'd him!—

    [Hubert, *after some Pause of Confusion, throws down the Dagger.*

    Hub. I cannot bear this Innocence!
    Arth.   O Heaven!
My Prayer is heard, *Hubert* is what he was.
In his relenting Eyes his Virtue lives,
And, like my Guardian Angel, wakes me from

This Dream of Death.

Hub.   Short-sighted Wretch,   [*To himself.*
To think such Cruelty was practicable!
O! raise thee from the Earth, poor injur'd Prince!
Thy Youth, thy Innocence, thy blooming Virtue,
Have conquer'd and redeem'd my Soul from Ruin!

Arth. Now thou hast taught my Eyes to weep for thee!
O *Hubert*! wilt thou spare me? shall I live?

Hub. Not all thy Uncle's Treasure, nor his Honours
Shall tempt me to thy Harm! O Sleep secure!
Hence to some Fort in *England* will I bear thee:
There shall a short Concealment be thy Guard,
Till Fate and kinder Seasons may relieve thee.

Arth. O might I once behold the Fields of *England*,
Tho' from a Prison-Tower, the Prospect would delight me.

Hub. This Night shall speed us in our Voyage—Ha!
What knocking!

Arth.   How I tremble!

Hub.   Be compos'd.
Some Officer with notice from the Guard,
How now! the News?

Enter an Officer.

Off.   The Lady *Constance*, Sir,
Is taken.

Arth.   Ha! My Mother!

Hub.   Where? from whence?

Off. Hearing her Son was Pris'ner in this Castle,
Her Griefs have ventur'd, with a small Retinue,
To risk the Mercy of an Enemy
In hope to have a Sight of him. She waits
Without, and begs in Tears to have an Audience.

Hub. Conduct her to the Council Room—we attend her.
                                        [*Exit* Officer.

Come, Prince; to dissipate thy Terrors past,
We'll venture to admit this Interview.
Short must it be.

Arth.   It shall, indeed, dear *Hubert*.
I'll not misuse thy Goodness.

Hub.   O my Shame!

How will thy Terrors ever be aton'd?

   Arth. Despair not, *Hubert*! let thy Comfort be,
Howe'er thy Soul has wander'd into Error,
No Virtue claims more Praise than Penitence;
Has not the holy Parable declar'd
That one poor Soul recover'd, from astray,
Does more triumphant Joy to Heav'n convey
Than flows from ninety-nine that never lost their Way?

★   ★   ★

[Act IV, Scene ii]

King John [*discovered*] *in his Tent alone.*

   K. John. It must be so—the Contest is in vain!
Why should I risk a Kingdom for a People
That are themselves unwilling to be free?
Whose Zeal, enslav'd, not only courts the Chains
Of *Rome*, but thinks in Conscience Kings should wear them.
The moody Barons too, that head those Bigots,
Take this Advantage of the holy Ferment
To lop the Branches of Prerogative.
Then the reproachful Death of *Arthur*! There's
My jealous Fears have plung'd my Arm too far!
A rash and fruitless Policy! In Death
He is become more terrible than living!
Thence have I rais'd in *France* a stronger Claim;
The Guilt of *Hubert*, too, now dreads t'approach me!
Or may, to save himself, make me most odious.
There Evils join'd must in their Ends be fatal!
Rome! Rome, then, that has ruin'd must redeem me!
The Terms 'tis true are harsh and terrible
To Honour, to the Vulgar meritorious!
They think the Bulls of *Rome* the Voice of Heav'n,
And tremble for their King that dares contest them!
The Pride of *Becket* too subdu'd my Father;
And yet his warlike Reign lives fam'd in Story!
Princes should think no Price too dear for Pow'r;
And what are Kings without a People.—*Hubert*?

Enter Hubert.

146

Hub. At length, my Liege, I come to bring you News—
K. John. For which thy trait'rous Soul shall howl in Horrors!
Slave, thou hast undone me! were not the Flames
That *Rome* had rais'd sufficient to consume,
But thou must add thy Brand of Provocation,
Thy damn'd officious Murder, to the Ruin,
To give its Cause Pretence and fortify Rebellion?
    Hub. Sir, you mistake the Service I have done you;
'Tis not the Claim of *Arthur* to your Crown
But his reported Death provokes your People!
    K. John. Villain! dar'st thou insult me on the Crime
Thy Longing to commit seduc'd me to endure?
    Hub. Whate'er my Inclination was, you know.
    K. John. O! 'tis the Curse of Princes to be serv'd
By Slaves that take their Wishes for a Warrant;
That, on the bare Inquietude of Looks,
Presume t'expound our Passions into Law,
And on the Sanction of a Frown commit
Such Deeds as damns the Conscience that conceives them.
    Hub. Yet, Sir, be patient when you hear my Story.
    K. John. Think not involving me t'excuse thyself!
I had some Cause to wish him dead but thou
Hadst none, saving what thy Nature prompted!
How oft have evil Deeds, for want of Means
To give them Practice, dy'd in the Conception?
But thou being present to the curst Occasion,
Ere scarce the Thought could ripen into Purpose
Thy stony Heart made offer of the Deed
And mock'd my Fears with impious Resolution!
    Hub. My gracious Liege! I beg you be compos'd!
    K. John. Hadst thou but shook thy Head, or made a Pause,
When I obscurely murmur'd my Disquiet;
Hadst thou but shewn one Sign of inward Grace,
With one reluctant Shrug declin'd the Motion,
Pale Conscience then, retreating from the Guilt,
Had smother'd in my Breast the dreadful Deed
Never to rise in my Reflexion more!
But thou, like the curst Fiend in Paradise,
Laidst lurking in my Paths of Rumination,
To watch the secret Wishes of my Soul,

And tempt its Frailty to eternal Ruin!

Hub. Now, Sir, yourself be judge! had I obey'd
Your dread Commands, how wretched had I made you?
For know, to give your Soul its former Peace,
Young *Arthur* lives! my coward Heart has sav'd him!
I am but half the Villain you have spoke me.

K. John. Prove me this true, and thy whole Soul is Angel!

Hub. O! when I came to practise on his Life
I found the Execution was as far
Remov'd from what my first Conceit had form'd
As Danger from Delight! as Hell from Heav'n!
His blooming Form, his Youth, his Piety,
His Resignation, Innocence, and Tears,
Rush'd as from Ambush on my lifted Arm
And seiz'd me Captive to his Sufferings!
With melting Eyes I dropt the Poniard down,
And, at the hazard of your Rage, preserv'd him!

K. John. O! *Hubert! Hubert!* thou hast sav'd thy **Master!**
Redeem'd him from the deepest, hideous Plunge
That ever stain'd the Glories of Ambition!
The Rage thou feard'st now blushes into Joy,
And crowns thy Disobedience with Applause!

* * *

[Act V, Scene i]

Enter Arthur, *on the Walls of a Castle.*

Arth. O *Hubert! Hubert!* are my Hopes at last
Confin'd within these lonely, ragged Walls?
Was it for this thy fruitless Mercy spar'd me?
Ah, what is Life depriv'd of Liberty?
It shall be so, these Walls no more shall hide me.
The Mote beneath I've fathom'd with a Line,
And find its Depth proportion'd to my Stature;
At worst, the Danger's less attempting to escape
Than pining here in hourly Fear of Death.
Take Courage Heart! whatever Chance befal thee
Cannot be sorer than my Suff'ring here.
Eternal Providence, to thee I bow,

Extend thy gracious Arm to save my Fall!
But if thy sacred Pleasure has decreed
Thy sinful Creature must untimely bleed,
For a repentant Soul, ye Saints, make room,
Who seeks his Happiness in Worlds to come.

> [*He leaps from the Walls, and is cover'd by a Parapet between his Body and the Audience.*

Enter Falconbridge, Hubert, Salisbury, Pembroke *and* Arundel.

Salis. Prove him but living, and the Terms are welcome:
Nor think our Bodies have been cas'd in Steel
To wrong the native Course of royal Pow'r,
But to assert our Liberties and Rights,
As in the Laws of *Edward* they are cited.
Which if the King by Charter shall confirm,
And give Enfranchisement to Royal *Arthur*,
Nor mew him up to choke his Days
With barb'rous Ignorance, or deny his Youth
The princely Helps of graceful Exercise,
Then shall appeas'd Resistance sheath her Sword,
Or henceforth turn it on the Foes of *England*!

Fal. Spoke with the Spirit of an *English* Noble!
Nought then remains but that your Eyes have Proof
Of *Arthur's* Health and princely Liberty.
Hubert, conduct us.

> [*As they are passing to the Castle,* Salisbury *sees the Body of* Arthur *in the Ditch.*

Salis.   Ha! what Body's this,
That in the Water, 'mid'st the Weeds and Rushes,
Mischance or Malice has depriv'd of Life?

> [*They bring the Body forward.*

Ha! 'tis he! 'tis *Arthur*! royal *Arthur* breathless!
Pale, cold, and lost beyond Recovery!

Hub. O fatal Chance!

Fal.   *Hubert!* if thou hast done
This Deed, or but in Thought consented to it,
Thou art more deeply damn'd than *Lucifer*!

Hub. By Heav'n! within this Hour I left him living!

*   *   *

149

[Act V, Scene iv]

Enter King John *from his Tent, supported by two Attendants.*

   K. John. O feeble Frame! is this a Time to fail me?
When my collected Spirits should inflame
The Eye to lead and animate the War?
Why has the Monarch so much Use for Life,
Yet in his Health is levell'd with the Peasant?
O painful Majesty! unequal State!
Not all the gorgeous Pomp, thy Flags of Pow'r,
Thy Dignities, Dominions, Ceremonies,
The Crown, the Sceptre, and the Royal Ball,
The purple Robe, nor Princely Crowds, whose Press
Of Duty intercepts the wholsom Air;
Not all these Glories for one precious Hour
Can buy the Beggar's Health or Appetite.

★   ★   ★

[Act V, Scene v]

The SCENE *opening discovers the funeral Ceremony of* Arthur *moving towards* Swinstead-Abbey, *to a Dead-March;* Lady Constance *with the Abbot and Mourners attending.*

   Const. Down, down, thou rolling Sun, to Darkness down,
Lose in eternal Shades thy hateful Beams,
Never to give these Eyes more painful Day!
See there an Object stains thy conscious Lustre!
Not all thy Promises of blooming Springs
Or Autumn Fruit can this dead Flow'r supply,
Thus mercilessly cropp'd by fell Ambition!
O since the Birth of *Cain,* the first Male-Child,
To him that did but yesterday suspire,
There was not such a gracious Creature born.
   Abbot. Repine not at the Will of Heav'n, and this
Thy Comfort be, that in the World to come
The dearest Friends shall meet and know each other.
   Const. O didst thou see his chang'd and ghastly Semblance
Thy frighted Sense would not remember him;

That Canker Death has so devour'd his Beauties,
So blanch'd the damask Bloom upon his Cheek;
All the soft Smiles that wanton'd in his Eye,
The sweet and graceful Spirit of his Features,
So sunk, so faded from their native Hue
That e'en in Heav'n my Soul must pause to know him.

   Abbot. O yet retire! part from this Feast of Death,
Where solemn Rites and Forms on Forms succeeding,
Feed but the fatal Appetite of Grief!
Hark, the last Bell now calls us to the Grave.   *[Bell tolls.*

   Const. O piercing Sound! O agonizing Knell!
Stay your officious Haste! one Moment's Pause!   *[To the Bearers.*
And the same Service shall be sung for both
Our parted Souls! Inexorable Death!
I ask thee not for Mercy! No, be cruel still!
Behold in me the Wretch that dares thy Rage!
A grieving Mother, whose Distress defies thee!
That thus arrests thy Triumph o'er her Child,
And will not let it pass. The Grave shall not devour him;
O! we must never part, one Earth shall hold us,
Now seize me, strike me, and compleat the Tyrant!

   Abbot. Be watchful o'er her Health, gently support her
Till Grief subsiding may admit Repose.

                   [To her Attendants, who lead her off.
But hark, the Terrors of the Field are ended!
The hostile Wounds of *France* and *England* now
Are by the Trumpet's loud Retreat proclaim'd.
Behold the harass'd Barons from the Toil retiring.

                      [Exit after Constance.

        ★   ★   ★

[As they go off, Constance *re-enters to the Funeral, with the Abbot, &c.*

   Const. Thy holy Counsels, Father, have reliev'd me;
Misfortunes now, familiar to my Sense,
Abate their Terror. Now my peaceful Heart,
With tearless Eyes, shall wait him to the Grave.

Enter Falconbridge.

   Fal. O Reverend Father, haste, the dying King

Implores thy holy Aid.

   Abbot. Said'st thou the King?

   Fal. Dying he seems, or cannot long survive:
Whether by Heat of Action in the Field
His latent Fever is inflam'd to Danger,
Or, as Suspicion strongly has avouch'd,
The gloomy Monk who serv'd him with the Cup
Might impiously infuse some Bane of Life,
We know not; but his Interval of Sense
In Grones calls earnest for his Confessor.

   Const. In his accounted Sins be this★ remember'd.

                [★ *Pointing to the Corpse of* Arthur.

   Fal. If Grief or Prejudice could bear to hear me,
I could a Truth unfold would calm thy Sorrows.

   Const. Lies not my Child there murder'd?

   Fal.   Hear my Story.   [*He seems to talk apart with* Constance.

Enter Salisbury *with* Arundel, *&c.*

   Salis. How fortunate the Hour that he had Sense
To ratify our Rights and seal the Charter!

   Abbot. What News, my Lords? How fares the King?

   Salis. I fear me, poison'd! his whole Mass of Blood
Is touch'd corruptibly, and his frail Brain,
Which some suppose the Mansion of the Soul,
By the disjointed Comments that it makes,
Foreshews its mortal Office is expiring.

   Fal. And *Hubert* dying disavow'd the Deed.   [*Apart to* Constance.

   Const. Admitting this, that meer Mischance destroy'd him,
What but his Wrongs expos'd him to Mischance?
Nor therefore are my Sorrows more reliev'd
But as Oppression may be less than Murder.

Enter Pembroke.

   Pemb. The King seems more at Ease, and holds Belief
That were he brought into the open Air
It might asswage the Ferment that consumes him.

   Salis. Behold the sad Remains of Royalty!

   Fal. Let those who lov'd him not endure the Sight.
When he is gone my Hopes in Life are friendless.   [*Exit.*

King John *is brought in.*

Abbot. How fares your Majesty?

K. John. The Air's too hot.

It steams, it scalds, I cannot bear this Furnace!
Stand off, and let the Northern Wind have Way!
Blow, blow, ye freezing Blasts from *Iceland* Skies!
O blissful Region, that I there were King!
To range and roll me in eternal Snow,
Where Crowns of Icicles might cool my Brain,
And comfort me with Cold.

Abbot. O gracious Heav'n!

Relieve his Senses from these mortal Pangs,
That his reflecting Soul may yet look back
On his Offences past with Penitence!

K. John. Why am I tortur'd thus? I kill'd him not;
Was it so criminal to wish him dead?
If Wishes were effectual, O, my Crown,
My Crown should from the Grave with Joy redeem him!

Abbot. If Penitence, not Frenzy, prompts thy Tongue,
Behold this Object of Calamity
Whom thy Severities have sunk with Sorrow.
O carry not, beyond the Grave, your Enmity.

K. John. Constance, the mournful Relict of my Brother,
How do thy Wrongs sit heavy on my Soul;
But who was ever just in his Ambition?
Thou seest me now an Object of thy Triumph,
The vital Cordage of my Heart burnt up,
All to a single Thread, on which it hangs,
Consumed. Now may the fearless Lamb approach,
Now close the Lion Eye of Enmity.
Hence but a Moment all this Royalty,
This Pride of Pow'r will crumble into Ashes.

Abbot. In his Extremities Heav'n help the King.

Const. And may his contrite Soul receive its Mercy.

K. John. The Lamp of Life is dry.—Thy Pray'rs, O Father!
At *Worcester* let these mortal Bones have Rest.
My Eyes refuse the Light—the Stroke is giv'n.
O, I am call'd—I wander—Mercy, Heav'n! [*Dies.*

Const. He's gone.
The turbulent Oppressor is no more.
The Hour of heav'nly Justice has at last

Demanded his Account of *England*'s Empire;
But since he seem'd to pass in Penitence
Let all his Crimes be bury'd in his Grave.
Thou Pow'r ador'd, what Thanks shall I repay thee,
That my Afflictions have subdu'd my Soul
T'extend its Charity ev'n to my Enemies?
Now, Life, I have no farther Use for thee.
Defer a while the Obsequies of *Arthur*,
Pass but some Hours and I shall soon o'ertake him,
Then lay us in one peaceful Grave together.   [*Exit, led off.*

*   *   *

Epilogue.

Of all the Helps for Wit so much in Vogue
This Play has scarce one Hint for Epilogue!
Now after Tragedy, you know, the Way
Is to come forward with an Air so gay,
Not to support,—no, no,—to *ridicule* the Play.
With flirting Fan and pointed Wit so jolly,
Crack Jokes on Virtue as an unbred Folly.
How often has the *Grecian* Dame, distress'd,
Been dismal Company till made a Jest?
And when her prudish Pride warm Love has slighted,
How lusciously her Epilogue delighted!
O! what Enjoyment to a modern Sinner,
To have it prov'd at last—she'd nothing in her!
Then is the Proof of Wit's commanding Pow'r,
When *double Entendres* make an Aud'ence roar!
When chuckling Rakes and Witlings void of Grace
Stare all the blushing Boxes in the Face!
And when the luscious Stroke has kept them under,
Crack! goes the joyous Laugh, in Claps of Thunder!
    Since Arts like these have charm'd a merry Nation,
Why could not *Colley* play the Wag in fashion?
Shall he pretend to give the Stage new Modes?
Would he have Plays as chaste as annual Odes?
Shall he suppose there can be any Sin in
Th'warmest Meaning—wrapp'd in decent Linen?

Something he ought to have for ev'ry Taste; ⎫
John Trott's an honest, though a vulgar Ghost: ⎬
His strong Digest'on thinks fat Food the best. ⎭
And when his full Meal's made, cries—'After all
That Epilogue was dev'lish comical!
Better, by half, than all their hum-drum Sorrow!
I'cod I'll come and hear't again to-morrow!'
What could in Nature our Fool's Reason be, ⎫
To strike away this Prop from Tragedy? ⎬
Odso! I've found it now: 'twas Modesty! ⎭
Yes! modest as the Jay, when he presumes,
To deck his dowdy Muse with Peacock Plumes!
Yet hold!—that Fleer too hard a Censure flings; ⎫
He's but the Wren that mounts on *Shakespeare*'s Wings; ⎬
Where, while the Eagle soars, he safely sings. ⎭
Let then the modern Scenes on *Shakespeare* live,
And what you cannot praise, like Friends forgive.

103. Unsigned essay against Cibber's *King John*

1745

From *A Letter to Colley Cibber, Esq; on his Transformation of 'King John'* (1745).

This piece seems to be by the author of 'The Occasional Prompter' series in *The Daily Journal*, 1736–7: see No. 89 above.

As to your Endeavour to make it *more a Play than what you found it in Shakespeare*, I heartily wish it may be thought you have done so by your noble Patron, whose Judgment, more *candid* than his *Taste*, I am persuaded will make the proper Distinction. But of all *Shakespeare*'s Plays this is that which sins most against the three Grand Unities of the

Stage, *Time*, *Place* and *Action*, and is on that Account the less reducible to *Rule*. And if, dear *Colley*, the Height of your Ambition is to have done this, or something like this, your Ambition rises no higher than your Judgment. Lord have Mercy upon both!

I come now to point out the Particulars of *your Transformation*, in which you have shewn the most surprising Genius at Alteration that any of that great Poet's Amenders ever yet produced.

The Editor of *Shakespeare*, in the *Character* he gives of him as a Writer, says very justly—'The Genius that gives us the highest Pleasure, sometimes stands in need of our Indulgence.—Whenever this happens with regard to *Shakespeare*, I would willingly impute it to a Vice of his Times; we see Complaisance enough in our own Days paid to a bad Taste. His Clinches, false Wit, and *descending beneath himself*, seem to be a Deference paid to reigning Barbarism.'

There is scarce a Play of this great Man in which he does not descend beneath himself and pay this Deference to the *reigning Barbarism* of his Times. In his gravest Pieces, where he displays his most exalted Genius he as constantly throws in a Vein of *low Humour*, in Complaisance to the low Capacities of the *Coarse Laughers* of his Days, whom perhaps it was as much his Interest to keep in Temper by *dividing* himself to all Tastes as it is now of modern Poets who would succeed. But the Case is widely different with his *Amenders*, and he that attempts to reform *Shakespeare* has not the same Tye on him, and may act without this Complaisance.

Instead therefore of *torturing Shakespeare* into *Rule* and Dramatick Law, or making *his Plays more of Plays than he made them*, let his *Clinches*, *False Wit*, &c. be the Objects of Amendment. Where a fine Scene of Nature is interrupted by a low *Vein of Humour*, which by inciting the *Vulgar* to laugh draws off the Attention of the *Sensible*, let the Shears be apply'd without Mercy. Where likewise a Character has not been rais'd to the Height it might reach, by the Poet's applying himself to some more favourite Character in the Play, let the Alterer bend his Care and the Success will be answerable—if his Genius be equal to the Task.

An Instance of improving or heightning a Character we have in *Edgar* (in *King Lear*) as well as in *Cordelia*, between whom a Love Episode is not ill woven. Another yet stronger is in *Catharine* (in *Henry the Fifth*) whose Character in *Shakespeare* is abominably low and obscene. The Improvement of her's has naturally rais'd that of *Harry*. Other Instances might be produced to shew where *Shakespeare* might admit, with great Beauty and Propriety, of strong Alterations, nay Amendments.

But, dear *Colley*, what have you done of all this? You have indeed purg'd *Shakespeare* of his *low Stuff*, but have you not fill'd the Place up with *Flat*? You have altered Characters, but have you amended one? That will presently be seen in the Examen of those of *Falconbridge*, *Constance*, *Arthur*, and King *John*!

There is a *wild Greatness* in some of *Shakespeare*'s Characters, above the Reach of common Readers, of which one can better form to one's self an Idea than convey Description to another. Of this Kind is the Character of *Falconbridge*. Never was Character (for what it is) better drawn or stronger kept up to the last. *Shakespeare* seems to have taken as much Pains in forming (as he calls him) this *Mis-begotten Devil* as he did his and ev'ry Body's Favourite *Falstaff*. His Character, tho' an humorous One, has a certain Dignity in it that well becomes the Greatness of Mind he discovers in his graver Walk. . . . (9–14)

*   *   *

. . . What in the Name of Wonder cou'd induce you to treat *Constance* with so much Barbarity?

There is, dear *Colley*, in that Princess a Stamp of *Heroism* mixt with an *inimitable Sensibility* of Grief that woud sit very ill in any *meer* Representer of Grief, however *Pathetick*. For Grief (which possibly you may not know) is but an *Accident* and not a *Constituent* of Character, and takes its *Colour* from the natural Frame of Mind of the Person; and, according as such Person is from *Temper*, either shews itself *outragious* and *violent* or *soft* and *pathetick*.

To prove that *Constance* is a Character design'd to be *outragious* and *violent* in *Grief*, when *Salisbury* brings her the News of the Peace concluded by the Means of Lady *Blanch* between the Kings of *England* and *France*, she says:

> *Const.* Oh if thou teach me to believe this sorrow,
> Teach thou this sorrow how to make me die;
> And let belief and life encounter so,
> As doth the fury of two desp'rate men,
> Which in the very meeting, fall and die.
> *Lewis* wed *Blanch*! O boy, then where art thou?
> *France* friend with *England*! what becomes of me?
> Fellow be gone, I cannot brook thy sight.   [3.1.29ff.]

The Idea convey'd to the Spectator by the most beautiful Comparison of the *Fury* of two *desperate Men, which in their very Meeting fall and die,* is a Frame of Mind in *Constance* that shou'd make her *burst* the Moment she believes the Truth, and not *pathetically* whine under it. . . . (18–19)

After her Son *Arthur* is taken Prisoner she grows quite frantick in her Grief, and utters such forcible Passion that nothing but *Shakespeare's* Genius cou'd express it, (or Mrs. *Cibber's* act it).

> *Const.* No, I defie all counsel, all redress,
> But that which ends all counsel, true redress,
> Death; death, oh amiable, lovely death!
> Arise forth from thy couch of lasting night,
> Thou hate and terror to prosperity,
> And I will kiss thy detestable bones;
> And put my eye-balls in thy vaulty brows,
> And ring these fingers with thy household worms,
> And stop this gap of breath with fulsom dust,
> And be a carrion monster like thy self;
> Come grin on me, and I will think thou smil'st,
> And kiss thee as thy wife: thou Love of Misery!
> O come to me. [3.4.23ff.]

When the Cardinal tells her she utters Madness and not Sorrow, with how much Energy does she convince every Body she is not mad, and make ev'ry Body wish for her own Sake she was! Hear her Words.

> *Const.* Thou art not holy to belie me so.
> I am not mad; this hair I tear is mine;
> My name is *Constance,* I was *Geffrey's* wife:
> Young *Arthur* is my son, and he is lost!
> I am not mad, I would to heaven I were. [3.4.44ff.]

Again, when he tells her *she holds too heinous a Respect of Grief* how beautiful is her Reply!

> *Const.* He talks to me, *that never had a son.* [3.4.91]

But what closes all, and rends the Heartstrings, is what follows.

> *Const.* Grief fills the room up of my absent child;
> Lies in his bed, walks up and down with me;
> Puts on his pretty looks, repeats his words,
> Remembers me of all his gracious parts;

Stuffs out his vacant garments with his form,
Then have I reason to be fond of grief.
Fare you well; had you such a loss as I,
I could give better comfort than you do.
I will not keep this form upon my head,

                [*Tearing off her Head-cloaths.*

When there is such disorder in my wit.
O lord! my boy, my *Arthur*, my fair son!
My life, my joy, my food, my all the world,
My widow comfort, and my sorrow's cure!   [3.4.93ff.]

It is plain then from these Quotations, that *Constance* is a Character of *Fire* throughout! *Great* and *Impetuous* in ev'ry Thing! and masterly drawn!

What Reason, dear *Colley*, to alter this Character? Was it *above Proof* that you was forc'd to lower it? Is it more palatable now you have? (23–5)

        ★   ★   ★

I should now, dear *Colley*, cast my Eye upon *King John*, and observe in the same candid manner I have all along proceeded *wherein* you have *inspirited* him; for as this was the first Motive that induced you to meddle at all with him so I don't question but this has been the *hic Labor*, the *hoc Opus*, with you. But I have looked into the Scenes between him and King *Philip*, and between him and *Pandulph*, where this *inspiriting* Quality ought to have been, according to your Declaration, infused with a lavish Hand, and can find nothing of it. I observe indeed, you have considerably *lengthned* the Scene; spun out the Dialogue; made *John declaim, argue, confute, puzzle* the Cardinal himself with Doctrine: but what of all that? where is the *Inspiriting*? You have (to use a Figure that may make me better understood) cut *many* different Channels for the Torrent of *John*'s Wrath to flow thro' but then unfortunately by this very Act, as it happens in Nature, you have *lost* the TORRENT; you have the same *Quantity* of Anger but the *Quality* is gone. Instead of collecting the Rays to a Point in order to *burn*, you spread them so, they become quite *Lambent*. You forget that by making your Bottom *too broad* you make it *flat*.—In short, dear *Colley* (for I know you love quaint Expressions) give me a *Dram* of *Shakespeare*'s Spirit by itself, and deal about as largely as you please of your own Mixture: People's Tastes will distinguish sufficiently between.

I shall therefore forbear hunting any longer to find out this *inspiriting* Force you kindly intended to give King *John*; and shew him, as you have painted him in a particular Scene or two; wherein you have vary'd wonderfully, for Reasons best known to yourself, from the Conduct of *Shakespeare*.

Shakespeare's blunt, downright Method of never formally preparing an Audience for his most *capital* Scenes is a kind of Insolence that ought to be resented. To come full upon one, in this manner, and not give one Time to resist him! To make one's Heart, Head, Eyes, tremble and shake with *Horror, Agony, Tenderness,* or whatever Passion it is he *pours* upon our Faculties, is like ordering one to immediate Execution without Notice! One *feels* before one knows one is to *feel*! The *Effect* almost *precedes* the *Act*, at least *keeps pace* with *it*.

Instances of this are frequent in this curst Play of his. *Constance* plagues us in this manner, at every Entrance. *John* does the same. He no sooner takes *Arthur* Prisoner, and sends his Cousin to *England* upon Business of Moment, but in the very Field of Battle, on the Spot, attacks *Hubert* at once, gives him no time to Pause, works him to his bloody Purpose and speeds for *England* for fresh Business.

This, dear *Colley*, you have *wholly reform'd*; you give us long Notice beforehand of *John's Purpose*, and *Hubert's Fitness* for it.

> *K. John.* If features err not, *Hubert* is the man:
> 'Tis true, he's slow, has not the courtier's quickness,
> Or half the hints we gave had fir'd his brain
> T'have done the deed we tremble but to name!
> Some fitter time shall mould him to our purpose:
> Now actions, open to the day, demand us.

And when you come to the Scene itself, you *craftily qualify* it in such a Manner that if it was not for a few Lines here and there of *Shakespeare* retained we shou'd see the whole Scene without any *great Pain* or *Terror*. Nay, we might be tempted to smile almost at *John's Delicacy* of not speaking by Day-light, and at *Hubert's Complaisance* in shutting the Windows. It might put one in mind of that unaccountable Modesty, so natural to a young bashful Wench, who would do any thing in the Dark but is afraid of the Daylight! Yet methinks *Hubert* speaks plain enough where he says

> *Hub.* Then, sir, to ease your heart, I will be plain;
> I guess the secret that distresses you;
> Fear not to trust me, sir, I'll do the deed.

Tho' he seems afterwards to be a little *arch*, and to have a Mind to make *John* speak the Thing plain:

> *John.* Must I then speak it?
> *Hub.* Or how shall I be *sure* that I *obey* you?

The shutting of the Windows is quite your own Invention, and wond'rous is the Effect thereof. You took the Hint, no doubt, from these Words:

> The sun is in heav'n, and the proud day,
> Attended with the pleasures of the world,
> Is all too wanton, and too full of gawds
> To give me audience.   [3.3.34ff.]

Improving by this surprising Act of shutting the Windows upon King *John*'s Horror and Gloom of Mind, so finely described by *Shakespeare*.

In the next Scene between *John* and *Hubert*, on the Barons falling off and the Distress brought on *John* by the supposed Death of *Arthur*, you have observed pretty near the same Method, and, softning all the Parts that were too *strong* in *Shakespeare*, and pouring in a good deal of cool *descriptive* Declamation have made the Scene *tolerable* which in *Shakespeare* had *too great* an Effect.

I must now take Leave of *John*, for I cannot bear to see him on his Death-bed, wishing

> To range and roll him in eternal snow,
> With crowns of *Icicles* to cool his brain.

However, I heartily thank you for making him penitential, and die with *Mercy* and *Heaven* in his Mouth. A Stave or two, or one of *Pandulph*'s *Requiems* sung in his *Pontificalibus*, and set to soft Musick had graced his Exit finely, and would have been new.

I see nothing in the Cardinal's Character to take up your Time with any longer; I can't help smiling though, to see how *Falconbridge* and his Eminence *smoke*[1] each other at first Sight, before they begin to treat.

> *Pandulph.* The humble bearing of this minister,
> At length I see, bespeak an humble master.
> *Fal.* This temper of his eminence, this form
> Of stately charity, foretells success.
> He read from my *humility*, my errand,
> And darted from his eyes a conscious triumph.

[1] To smoke: 'To get an inkling of, to smell or suspect (a plot, design, etc.)' (*OED*).

These are the Things, dear *Colley*, that *speak* the *Genius*! that *stamp* the *Poet*! This is the *indelible* Mark! By this you have acquired the Laurel that adorns your Brows. By this you continue to deserve it. This will make it flourish with everlasting Green! This will preserve your Memory, dear to all Lovers of our immortal *Shakespeare*! This will inspire future Amenders of that Poet, and be as a Land-Mark to them to escape the Perils that wait upon such hardy bold Attempts! (40-7)

104. Elizah Haywood on the adaptations of *Romeo and Juliet*

1745

From *The Female Spectator*, Book VIII (1745), ii, pp. 90-3.

The Female Spectator was edited between 1744 and 1746 by Elizah Haywood (1693?-1756), who wrote plays, poems and numerous romances.

If the Eye could be satisfied with seeing, or the Ear with hearing always the same Things over and over repeated, it must be own'd there are many old Plays which the best of our modern Poets would not perhaps be able to excel; but Nature delights in Variety, and tho' it would be unjust and ungrateful to strip the Laurels from the Brows of *Shakespeare, Jonson, Beaumont* and *Fletcher, Dryden, Otway, Lee, Congreve*, and several other deservedly admired Authors, to adorn those who shall succeed them, yet we love to see a Genius the Growth of our own Times and might find sufficient Trophies for the Merits of such without any Injury to their Predecessors.

Those most impatient for new Plays desire not, however, that those which for so many Years have continued to divert and please should now be sunk and buried in Oblivion. The Poets I have mention'd will always preserve the same Charms, and would do so yet more were they less frequently exhibited. Some of *Shakespeare's* Comedies and all his Tragedies have Beauties in them almost inimitable; but then it must be confessed that he sometimes gave a Loose to the Luxuriancy of his Fancy, so that his Plays may be compared to fine Gardens full of the most beautiful Flowers but choaked up with Weeds through the too great Richness of the Soil. Those, therefore, which have had those Weeds pluck'd up by the skilful Hands of his Successors are much the most elegant Entertainments.

For which Reason I was a little surprized when I heard that Mr. *Cibber* junior had reviv'd the Tragedy of *Romeo and Juliet* as it was first acted; *Caius Marius* being the same Play, only moderniz'd and clear'd of some Part of its Rubbish by *Otway*,[1] appearing to so much more Advantage that it is not to be doubted but that the admirable Author, had he lived to see the Alteration, would have been highly thankful and satisfied with it.

It were indeed to be wished that the same kind Corrector had been somewhat more severe, and lop'd off not only some superfluous Scenes but whole Characters which rather serve to diminish than add to the Piece, particularly those of the *Nurse* and *Sulpitius*, neither of them being in the least conducive to the Conduct of the Fable, and all they say favouring more of Comedy than Tragedy. It is, methinks, inconsistent with the Character of a *Roman* Senator and Patrician to suffer himself to be entertained for half an Hour together with such idle Chat as would scarcely pass among old Women in a Nursery. Nor does the wild Behaviour and loose Discourse of *Sulpitius* at all agree with the Austerity of the Times he is supposed to live in, or any way improve the Morals of an Audience. The Description also of the Apothecary (tho' truly poetical) and his meagre Appearance always occasion a loud Laugh, and but ill dispose us to taste the Solemnity of the ensuing Scene.

Mr. *Otway* was doubtless fearful of going too far, or he had removed every thing which prevents this Piece from being perfect. It must be own'd he has improved and heightened every Beauty that could receive Addition, and been extremely tender in preserving all those entire which are above the reach of Amendment. Nor is his Judgment in this particular less to be admired than his Candour. Some Poets, perhaps, to shew their own Abilities, would have put a long Soliloquy

---

[1] For Otway's *Caius Marius* see Vol. 1, pp. 295–320.

into the Mouth of young *Marius* when he finds *Lavinia* at her Window at a Time of Night when it was but just possible for him to distinguish it was she. Whereas this judicious Emendator leaves his Author here as he found him; and indeed what could so emphatically express the Feel of a Lover on such an Occasion as is couch'd in this short Acclamation:

> *Oh 'tis my Love!*
> *See how she hangs upon the Cheek of Night*
> *Like a rich Jewel in an* Ethiop's *Ear.* [1.5.43ff.]

Nor is the Tenderness and Innocence of *Lavinia* less conveyed to us when in the Fulness of her Heart, and unsuspecting she was overheard by any body, she cries out

> *Oh* Marius! Marius! *wherefore art thou* Marius?
> *Renounce thy Family, deny thy Name,*
> *And in Exchange take all* Lavinia.

> [cf. Otway, Vol. 1, p. 297]

I mention these two Places merely because they strike my own Fancy in a peculiar manner, for the whole Piece abounds with others equally strong, natural, and pathetic, and is, in my Opinion and that of many others, the very best and most agreeable of all the Tragedies of that excellent Author.

105. Samuel Johnson on *Macbeth*

1745

From *Miscellaneous Observations on the Tragedy of 'Macbeth': with Remarks on Sir T.H.'s Edition of Shakespeare* (1745).

This pamphlet reads like a preliminary essay towards an edition, with a painstaking attempt to establish the relevant historical background: indeed Johnson retained many of the notes for his edition of twenty years later (see Arthur Sherbo in *Review of English Studies*, n.s. ii, 1951). Warburton made an approving reference to it in his edition of 1747 (No. 111 below), for which Johnson was grateful.

NOTE I.

ACT I, SCENE I. *Enter three Witches.*

In order to make a true Estimate of the Abilities and Merit of a Writer it is always necessary to examine the Genius of his Age, and the Opinions of his Contemporaries. A Poet who should now make the whole Action of his Tragedy depend upon Enchantment, and produce the chief Events by the Assistance of supernatural Agents, would be censured as transgressing the Bounds of Probability. He would be banished from the Theatre to the Nursery, and condemned to write Fairy Tales instead of Tragedies. But a Survey of the Notions that prevailed at the Time when this Play was written will prove that *Shakespeare* was in no Danger of such Censures, since he only turned the System that was then universally admitted to his Advantage, and was far from overburthening the Credulity of his Audience.

The Reality of Witchcraft or Enchantment—which, though not strictly the same, are confounded in this Play—has in all Ages and Countries been credited by the common People, and in most by the Learned themselves. These Phantoms have indeed appeared more frequently, in proportion as the Darkness of Ignorance has been more

165

gross; but it cannot be shown that the brightest Gleams of Knowledge have at any Time been sufficient to drive them out of the World. The Time in which this Kind of Credulity was at its Height seems to have been that of the Holy War, in which the Christians imputed all their Defeats to Enchantments or diabolical Opposition, as they ascribed their Success to the Assistance of their military Saints; and the Learned Mr *W——* appears to believe (*Suppl. to the Introduction to Don* Quixote)[1] that the first Accounts of Enchantments were brought into this Part of the World by those *who* returned from their eastern Expeditions. But there is always some Distance between the Birth and Maturity of Folly as of Wickedness. This Opinion had long existed, though perhaps the Application of it had in no foregoing Age been so frequent, nor the Reception so general. . . . (1-2)

The Reformation did not immediately arrive at its Meridian, and tho' Day was gradually encreasing upon us the Goblins of Witchcraft still continued to hover in the Twilight. In the Time of Queen *Elizabeth* was the remarkable Trial of the Witches of *Warbois*, whose Conviction is still commemorated in an annual Sermon at *Huntingdon*. But in the Reign of King *James*, in which this Tragedy was written, many Circumstances concurred to propagate and confirm this Opinion. The King, who was much celebrated for his Knowledge, had, before his Arrival in *England*, not only examined in Person a Woman accused of Witchcraft but had given a very formal Account of the Practices and Illusions of evil Spirits, the Compacts of Witches, the Ceremonies used by them, the Manner of detecting them, and the Justice of punishing them, in his Dialogues of *Dæmonologie*, written in the *Scottish* Dialect and published at *Edinburgh*. This Book was, soon after his Accession, reprinted at *London*, and as the ready way to gain K. *James*'s Favour was to flatter his Speculations the System of *Dæmonologie* was immediately adopted by all who desired either to gain Preferment or not to lose it. Thus the Doctrine of Witchcraft was very powerfully inculcated, and as the greatest Part of Mankind have no other Reason for their Opinions than that they are in Fashion, it cannot be doubted but this Persuasion made a rapid Progress, since Vanity and Credulity co-operated in its favour and it had a Tendency to free Cowardice from Reproach. The Infection soon reached the Parliament, who, in the first Year of King *James*, made a Law by which it was enacted, *Ch.* XII: That 'if any Person shall use any Invocation or Conjuration of any evil or wicked Spirit; 2. Or shall consult, covenant with, entertain, employ, feed or

---

[1] William Warburton, in Charles Jarvis's translation of *Don Quixote* (1742).

reward any evil or cursed Spirit to or for any Intent or Purpose; 3. Or take up any dead Man, Woman or Child out of the Grave, or the Skin, Bone, or any Part of the dead Person, to be employed or used in any Manner of Witchcraft, Sorcery, Charm, or Enchantment; 4. Or shall use, practise or exercise any Sort of Witchcraft, Sorcery, Charm, or Enchantment; 5. Whereby any Person shall be destroyed, killed, wasted, consumed, pined, or lamed in any Part of the Body; 6. That every such Person being convicted shall suffer Death.'

Thus, in the Time of *Shakespeare*, was the Doctrine of Witchcraft at once established by Law and by the Fashion, and it became not only unpolite but criminal to doubt it; and as Prodigies are always seen in proportion as they are expected Witches were every Day discovered, and multiplied so fast in some Places that Bishop *Hall* mentions a Village in *Lancashire* where their Number was greater than that of the Houses. The Jesuites and Sectaries took Advantage of this universal Error, and endeavoured to promote the Interest of their Parties by pretended Cures of Persons afflicted by evil Spirits, but they were detected and exposed by the Clergy of the established Church.

Upon this general Infatuation *Shakespeare* might be easily allowed to found a Play, especially since he has followed with great Exactness such Histories as were then thought true; nor can it be doubted that the Scenes of Enchantment, however they may now be ridiculed, were both by himself and his Audience thought awful and affecting. (4–6)

NOTE II.

SCENE II.

The merciless *Macdonel*, from the Western Isles
Of *Kerns* and *Gallow-glasses* was supply'd,
And Fortune on his damned *Quarry* smiling;
Shew'd like a Rebel's Whore.   [1.2.9ff.]

Kerns are light-armed, and *Gallow-glasses* heavy-armed Soldiers. The word *Quarry* has no Sense that is properly applicable in this Place, and therefore it is necessary to read

And Fortune on his damned Quarrel *smiling*.

Quarrel was formerly used for *Cause*, or for *the Occasion of a Quarrel*, and is to be found in that Sense in *Hollingshead*'s Account of the Story of *Macbeth*, who, upon the Creation of the Prince of *Cumberland*, thought, says the Historian, that he had *a just Quarrel* to endeavour after the Crown. The Sense therefore is *Fortune smiling on his execrable Cause*, &c. (6–7)

NOTE III.

> If I say sooth, I must report they were
> As Cannons overcharged with double Cracks,
> So they redoubled Strokes upon the Foe: [1.2.36ff.]

Mr *Theobald* has endeavoured to improve the Sense of this Passage by altering the Punctuation thus:

> They were
> As Cannons overcharg'd, with double Cracks
> So they redoubled Strokes

He declares, with some Degree of Exultation, that he has no Idea of a *Cannon charged with double Cracks*; but surely the great Author will not gain much by an Alteration which makes him say of a Hero that he *redoubles Strokes with double Cracks*, an Expression not more loudly to be applauded or more easily pardon'd than that which is rejected in its Favour. That *a Cannon is charged with Thunder* or *with double Thunders* may be written not only without Nonsense but with Elegance, and nothing else is here meant by *Cracks*, which in the Time of this Writer was a word of such Emphasis and Dignity, that in this Play he terms the general Dissolution of Nature the *Crack of Doom*.

There are among Mr *Theobald*'s Alterations others which I do not approve, though I do not always censure them; for some of his Amendments are so excellent that even when he has failed he ought to be treated with Indulgence and Respect. (7–8)

*   *   *

NOTE VI.

SCENE V.

The Incongruity of all the Passages in which the *Thane* of *Cawdor* is mentioned is very remarkable. In the second Scene the *Thanes* of *Ross*

and *Angus* bring the King an Account of the Battle, and inform him
that *Norway*,

> Assisted by that most disloyal Traytor
> The Thane of *Cawdor*, 'gan a dismal Conflict.   [1.2.53f.]

It appears that *Cawdor* was taken Prisoner, for the King says in the
same Scene

> Go, pronounce his Death,
> And with his former Title greet *Macbeth*.   [1.2.66f.]

Yet though *Cawdor* was thus taken by *Macbeth* in Arms against his
King, when *Macbeth* is saluted in the fourth Scene *Thane of Cawdor* by
the Weird Sisters, he asks,

> How of *Cawdor*? the *Thane of Cawdor lives*,
> A prosp'rous Gentleman.   [1.3.72f.]

And in the next Line considers the Promises that he should be *Cawdor*
and *King* as equally unlikely to be accomplished. How can *Macbeth* be
ignorant of the State of the Thane of *Cawdor* whom he has just defeated and taken Prisoner, or call him a *prosperous Gentleman* who has
forfeited his Title and Life by open Rebellion? Or why should he
wonder that the Title of the Rebel whom he has overthrown should be
conferred upon him? He cannot be supposed to dissemble his Knowledge of the Condition of *Cawdor*, because he enquires with all the
Ardour of Curiosity and the Vehemence of sudden Astonishment, and
because Nobody is present but *Banquo*, who had an equal Part in the
Battle and was equally acquainted with *Cawdor*'s Treason. However, in
the next Scene his Ignorance still continues, and when *Ross* and *Angus*
present him from the King with his new Title he cries out

> The *Thane* of *Cawdor* lives.
> WHY do you dress me in his borrowed Robes?
>   [1.3.108f.]

Ross and *Angus*, who were the Messengers that in the second Scene informed the King of the Assistance given by *Cawdor* to the Invader,
having lost, as well as *Macbeth*, all Memory of what they had so lately
seen and related, make this Answer

> Whether he was
> Combin'd with *Norway*, or did line the Rebels

With hidden Help and Vantage, or with both
He labour'd in his Country's Wreck, I know not.
[1.3.111ff.]

Neither *Ross* knew what he had just reported, nor *Macbeth* what he had just done. This seems not to be one of the Faults that are to be imputed to the Transcribers since, though the Inconsistency of *Ross* and *Angus* might be removed by supposing that their Names are erroneously inserted and that only *Ross* brought the Account of the Battle and only *Angus* was sent to compliment *Macbeth*, yet the Forgetfullness of *Macbeth* cannot be palliated, since what he says could not have been spoken by any other. (12–14)

NOTE VII.

The Thought, whose Murder yet is but fantastical,
Shakes so my single State of Man, [1.3.139f.]

The *single State of Man* seems to be used by *Shakespeare* for an *Individual*, in Opposition to a *Commonwealth*, or *conjunct Body* of Men. (14)

NOTE VIII.

Macbeth. Come what come may,
Time and the Hour runs thro' the roughest Day.
[1.3.147f.]

I suppose every Reader is disgusted at the Tautology in this Passage, *Time and the Hour*, and will therefore willingly believe that *Shakespeare* wrote it thus:

Come what come may,
Time! on!—the Hour runs thro' the roughest Day.

Macbeth is deliberating upon the Events which are to befal him, but finding no Satisfaction from his own Thoughts he grows impatient of Reflection, and resolves to wait the Close without harrassing himself with Conjectures,

Come what come may.

But to shorten the Pain of Suspense he calls upon Time, in the usual
Stile of ardent Desire, to quicken his Motion,

Time! on!

He then comforts himself with the Reflection that all his Perplexity
must have an End,

The Hour runs thro' the roughest Day.

This Conjecture is supported by the Passage in the Letter to his Lady in
which he says, *They referr'd me to the* coming on of Time *with Hail King
that shall be* [1.5.8]. (14–15)

*   *   *

NOTE XIII.

> Hie thee hither,
> That I may pour my Spirits in thine Ear,
> And chastise with the Valour of my Tongue
> All that impedes thee from the golden Round,
> That Fate and metaphysical Aid do *seem*
> To have thee crown'd withal.   [1.5.22ff.]

FOR *seem* the Sense evidently directs us to read *seek*. The Crown to
which Fate destines thee, and which preternatural Agents *endeavour* to
bestow upon thee. The *Golden Round* is the *Diadem*. (19)

NOTE XIV.

> *Lady Macbeth.* Come all you Spirits
> That tend on *mortal Thoughts*, unsex me here. . . .   [1.5.37f.]

Mortal Thoughts: this Expression signifies not *the Thoughts of Mortals*
but *murtherous, deadly,* or *destructive Designs.* So in Act 5th.

Hold fast the *mortal* Sword,   [4.3.3]

And in another Place,

With twenty *mortal* Murthers.   [3.4.81]

Nor keep Peace between

Th' Effect and it.   [1.5.43f.]

The Intent of Lady *Macbeth* evidently is to wish that no womanish Tenderness or conscientious Remorse may hinder her Purpose from proceeding to Effect, but neither this nor indeed any other Sense is expressed by the present Reading, and therefore it cannot be doubted that *Shakespeare* wrote differently, perhaps thus:

> That no compunctious Visitings of Nature
> Shake my fell Purpose, nor *keep pace* between
> Th' Effect and it.

To *keep pace between* may signify *to pass between*, to *intervene*. *Pace* is on many Occasions a Favourite of *Shakespeare*. This Phrase is indeed not usual in this Sense, but was it not its Novelty that gave Occasion to the present Corruption? (19–20)

NOTE XV.

SCENE VIII.

> *King.* This Castle hath a pleasant *Seat*; the Air
> Nimbly and sweetly recommends itself
> Unto our gentle Senses. . . .   [1.6.1ff.]

In this short Scene I propose a slight Alteration to be made by substituting *Site* for *Seat*, as the antient Word for *Situation*; and *Sense* for *Senses* as more agreeable to the Measure; for which Reason likewise I have endeavoured to adjust this Passage,

> Heaven's Breath
> Smells wooingly here. No jutting Frieze,   [1.6.6f.]

by changing the Punctuation and adding a Syllable thus,

> Heaven's Breath
> Smells wooingly. Here is no jutting Frieze.

Those who have perused Books printed at the Time of the first Editions of *Shakespeare* know that greater Alterations than these are necessary almost in every Page, even where it is not to be doubted that the Copy was correct. (15–16)

NOTE XVI.

SCENE X.

The Arguments by which Lady *Macbeth* persuades her Husband to commit the Murder afford a Proof of *Shakespeare*'s Knowledge of

Human Nature. She urges the Excellence and Dignity of Courage, a glittering Idea which has dazzled Mankind from Age to Age, and animated sometimes the Housebreaker and sometimes the Conqueror; but this Sophism *Macbeth* has for ever destroyed by distinguishing true from false Fortitude in a Line and a half, of which it may almost be said that they ought to bestow Immortality on the Author though all his other Productions had been lost.

> I dare do all that may become a Man,
> Who dares do more is none. [1.7.45f.]

This Topic, which has been always employed with too much Success, is used in this Scene with peculiar Propriety, to a Soldier by a Woman. Courage is the distinguishing Virtue of a Soldier, and the Reproach of Cowardice cannot be borne by any Man from a Woman without great Impatience.

She then urges the Oaths by which he had bound himself to murder *Duncan*, another Art of Sophistry by which Men have sometimes deluded their Consciences and persuaded themselves that what would be criminal in others is virtuous in them; this Argument *Shakespeare*, whose Plan obliged him to make *Macbeth* yield, has not confuted, though he might easily have shown that a former Obligation could not be vacated by a latter. (22–3)

* * *

NOTE XX.

ACT II. SCENE II.

(1) . . . Now o'er one half the World
Nature seems dead. [2.1.49f.]

That is, *over our Hemisphere all Action and Motion seem to have ceased.* This Image, which is perhaps the most striking that Poetry can produce, has been adopted by *Dryden* in his *Conquest of Mexico*:

> All things are hush'd as Nature's self lay dead,
> The Mountains seem to nod their drowsy Head;
> The little Birds in Dreams their Songs repeat,
> And sleeping Flow'rs beneath the Night-dews sweat.
> Even Lust and Envy sleep!

173

These Lines, though so well known, I have transcrib'd that the Contrast between them and this Passage of *Shakespeare* may be more accurately observed.

Night is described by two great Poets, but one describes a Night of Quiet, the other of Perturbation. In the Night of *Dryden* all the Disturbers of the World are laid asleep; in that of *Shakespeare* nothing but Sorcery, Lust, and Murder is awake. He that reads *Dryden* finds himself lull'd with Serenity, and disposed to Solitude and Contemplation. He that peruses *Shakespeare* looks round alarmed, and starts to find himself alone. One is the Night of a Lover, the other that of a Murderer. (24-6)

(2) Wither'd Murder,

... Thus with his stealthy Pace,
With Tarquin's ravishing Sides tow'rd his Design,
Moves like a Ghost.   [2.1.52ff.]

This was the reading of this Passage in all the Editions before that of Mr *Pope*, who for *Sides* inserted in the Text *Strides*, which Mr *Theobald* has tacitely copied from him, tho' a more proper Alteration might perhaps have been made. A *ravishing Stride* is an Action of Violence, Impetuosity, and Tumult, like that of a Savage rushing on his Prey. Whereas the Poet is here attempting to exhibit an Image of Secrecy and Caution, of anxious Circumspection and guilty Timidity, the *stealthy Pace* of a *Ravisher* creeping into the Chamber of a Virgin, and of an Assassin approaching the Bed of him whom he proposes to murder without awaking him. These he describes as *moving like Ghosts*, whose Progression is so different from *Strides* that it has been in all Ages represented to be, as *Milton* expresses it,

Smooth sliding without Step.

This Hemistick will afford the true Reading of this Place, which is, I think, to be corrected thus:

And wither'd Murder;
... Thus with his stealthy Pace,
With <i>Tarquin</i> ravishing, slides tow'rd his Design,
Moves like a Ghost.

Tarquin is in this Place the general Name of a Ravisher, and the Sense is, 'Now is the Time in which every one is asleep but those who are employed in Wickedness, the Witch who is sacrificing to *Hecate*, and the Ravisher and the Murderer, who, like me, are stealing upon their Prey.'

When the Reading is thus adjusted, he wishes with great Propriety in the following Lines that the *Earth* may not *hear his Steps.* (26–7)

> (3) And take the present Horror from the Time
>   That now suits with it. [2.1.59f.]

I believe every one that has attentively read this dreadful Soliloquy is disappointed at the Conclusion, which if not wholly unintelligible is at least obscure, nor can be explained into any Sense worthy of the Author. I shall therefore propose a slight Alteration.

> Thou sound and firm set Earth,
> Hear not my Steps, which way they walk, for fear
> Thy very Stones prate of my Where-about,
> And *talk*—the present Horror of the Time!—
> *That* now suits with it. [2.1.56ff.]

Macbeth has, in the foregoing Lines, disturbed his Imagination by enumerating all the Terrors of the Night. At length he is wrought up to a Degree of Frenzy that makes him afraid of some supernatural Discovery of his Design, and calls out to the Stones not to betray him, not to declare where he walks, nor *to talk*. As he is going to say of what, he discovers the Absurdity of his Suspicion, and pauses, but is again o'erwhelmed by his Guilt, and concludes that such are the Horrors of the present Night that the Stones may be expected to cry out against him.

> *That* now suits with it.

He observes in a subsequent Passage, that on such Occasions *Stones have been known to move.* It is now a very just and strong Picture of a Man about to commit a deliberate Murder under the strongest Convictions of the Wickedness of his Design. (27–9)

NOTE XXI.

SCENE IV.

. . . A *Prophecy* of an *Event new hatch'd,* [2.3.55ff.] seems to be a *Prophecy* of an *Event past.* The Term *new-hatch'd* is properly applicable to a *Bird,* and that Birds of ill Omen should be *new-hatch'd to the woful*

Time is very consistent with the rest of the Prodigies here mentioned, and with the universal Disorder into which Nature is described as thrown by the Perpetration of this horrid Murder. (30)

*   *   *

NOTE XXIII.

> *Macbeth*. Here lay *Duncan*,
> His silver Skin laced with his golden Blood,
> And his gash'd Stabs look'd like a Breach in Nature,
> For Ruin's wasteful Entrance; there the Murtherers
> Steep'd in the Colours of their Trade, their Daggers
> *Unmannerly breech'd with Gore:*   [2.3.110ff.]

An *unmannerly Dagger* and a *Dagger breeched*, or as in some Editions *breach'd with Gore*, are Expressions not easily to be understood, nor can it be imagined that *Shakespeare* would reproach the Murderer of his King only with *Want of Manners*. There are undoubtedly two Faults in this Passage which I have endeavoured to take away by reading,

> *Daggers*
> *Unmanly drench'd with Gore.*

I saw drench'd *with the King's Blood the fatal Daggers, not only Instruments of Murder but Evidences of Cowardice.*

Each of these Words might easily be confounded with that which I have substituted for it by a Hand not exact, a casual Blot, or a negligent Inspection.

Mr *Pope* has endeavoured to improve one of these Lines by substituting *goary Blood* for *golden Blood*, but it may easily be admitted that he who could on such an Occasion talk of *lacing the silver Skin* would *lace it* with *golden Blood*. No Amendment can be made to this Line of which every Word is equally faulty but by a general Blot.

It is not improbable that *Shakespeare* put these forced and unnatural Metaphors into the Mouth of *Macbeth* as a Mark of Artifice and Dissimulation, to show the Difference between the studied Language of Hypocrisy and the natural Outcries of sudden Passion. This whole Speech considered in this Light is a remarkable Instance of Judgment, as it consists entirely of Antitheses and Metaphors. (31-2)

NOTE XXIV.
ACT III. SCENE II.

Macbeth. Our Fears in *Banquo*
Stick deep . . .
                And under him,
My Genius is rebuk'd; (1) *as it is said*
Antony's was by Cæsar.   [3.1.48ff.]

Though I would not often assume the Critic's Privilege of being confident where Certainty cannot be obtained, nor indulge myself too far in departing from the established Reading, yet I cannot but propose the Rejection of this Passage, which I believe was an Insertion of some Player that, having so much Learning as to discover to what *Shakespeare* alluded, was not willing that his Audience should be less knowing than himself, and has therefore weakened the Author's Sense by the Intrusion of a remote and useless Image into a Speech bursting from a Man wholly possess'd with his own present Condition, and therefore not at leisure to explain his own Allusions to himself. If these Words are taken away, by which not only the Thought but the Numbers are injured, the Lines of *Shakespeare* close together without any Traces of a Breach.

My Genius is rebuk'd. He chid the Sisters.

(2) . . . The common Enemy of Man.   [3.1.68]

It is always an Entertainment to an inquisitive Reader to trace a Sentiment to its original Source, and therefore though the Term *Enemy of Man* applied to the Devil is in itself natural and obvious, yet some may be pleased with being informed that *Shakespeare* probably borrowed it from the first Lines of the Destruction of *Troy*, a Book which he is known to have read.[1] (32–4)

*   *   *

NOTE XXXIII.

It will have Blood, they say Blood will have Blood,
Stones have been known to move, and Trees to speak,

[1] Johnson here sides with Theobald's scholarship, derided by Pope and his circle: see Vol. 2 p. 519 and No. 84 above.

> Augurs, that understood Relations, have
> By Magpies, and by Choughs, and Rooks brought forth
> The secret'st Man of Blood.   [3.4.122ff.]

IN this Passage the first Line loses much of its Force by the present Punctuation. *Macbeth*, having considered the Prodigy which has just appeared, infers justly from it that the Death of *Duncan* cannot pass unpunished,

> *It will have Blood,*

Then, after a short Pause, declares it as the general Observation of Mankind that Murderers cannot escape.

> *They say, Blood will have Blood.*

Murderers, when they have practised all human Means of Security, are detected by supernatural Directions.

> Augurs, that understand Relations, &c.

By the word *Relation* is understood the *Connection* of Effects with Causes; to *understand Relations* as *an Augur* is to know how those Things *relate to* each other which have no visible Combination or Dependence. (42-3)

NOTE XXXIV.

SCENE VII.

> *Enter* Lennox *and another Lord.*   [3.6]

As this Tragedy, like the rest of *Shakespeare*'s, is perhaps overstocked with Personages, it is not easy to assign a Reason why a nameless Character should be introduced here, since nothing is said that might not with equal Propriety have been put into the Mouth of any other disaffected Man. I believe therefore that in the original Copy it was written with a very common Form of Contraction *Lennox* and *An.* for which the Transcriber instead of *Lennox* and *Angus*, set down *Lennox* and *another Lord*. The Author had indeed been more indebted to the Transcriber's Fidelity and Diligence had he committed no Errors of greater Importance. (44)

NOTE XXXV.
ACT IV. SCENE I.

As this is the chief Scene of Inchantment in the Play, it is proper in this Place to observe with how much Judgement *Shakespeare* has selected all the Circumstances of his infernal Ceremonies, and how exactly he has conformed to common Opinions and Traditions.

> Thrice the brinded Cat hath mew'd, [4.1.1]

The usual Form in which familiar Spirits are reported to converse with Witches is that of a Cat. A Witch who was tried about half a Century before the Time of *Shakespeare* had a Cat named *Rutterkin*, as the Spirit of one of those Witches was *Grimalkin*; and when any Mischief was to be done she used to bid *Rutterkin go and fly*. But once, when she would have sent *Rutterkin* to torment a Daughter of the Countess of *Rutland*, instead of *going* or *flying* he only cried *Mew*, from which she discovered that the Lady was out of his Power—the Power of Witches being not universal but limited, as *Shakespeare* has taken care to inculcate.

> Though his Bark cannot be lost,
> Yet it shall be Tempest tost. [1.3.24f.]

The common Afflictions which the Malice of Witches produced was Melancholy, Fits, and Loss of Flesh, which are threatned by one of *Shakespeare*'s Witches.

> Weary Sev'nnights nine times nine
> Shall he dwindle, peak, and pine. [1.3.22f.]

It was likewise their Practice to destroy the Cattle of their Neighbours, and the Farmers have to this Day many Ceremonies to secure their Cows and other Cattle from Witchcraft; but they seem to have been most suspected of Malice against Swine. *Shakespeare* has accordingly made one of his Witches declare that she has been *killing Swine*, and Dr *Harsenet* observes that about that Time *a Sow could not be ill of the Measles, nor a Girl of the Sullens, but some old Woman was charged with Witchcraft*.

> Toad, that under the cold Stone
> Days and Nights has forty one
> Swelter'd Venom sleeping got,
> Boil thou first i'th' charmed Pot. [4.1.6ff.]

179

Toads have likewise long lain under the Reproach of being by some Means accessary to Witchcraft, for which Reason *Shakespeare* in the first Scene of this Play calls one of the Spirits *Padocke* or *Toad*, and now takes care to put a Toad first into the Pot. When *Vaninus* was seized at *Tholouse* there was found at his Lodgings *ingens Bufo Vitro inclusus, a great Toad shut in a Vial*, upon which those that prosecuted him *Veneficium exprobrabant, charged him*, I suppose, *with Witchcraft*.

> Fillet of a fenny Snake
> In the Cauldron boil and bake;
> Eye of Neut, and Toe of Frog; . . .
> For a Charm, &c. [4.1.12ff.]

The Propriety of these Ingredients may be known by consulting the Books *de Viribus Animalium* and *de Mirabilibus Mundi*, ascribed to *Albertus Magnus*, in which the Reader who has Time and Credulity may discover very wonderful Secrets.

> Finger of birth-strangled Babe,
> Ditch-deliver'd by a Drab; [4.1.30f.]

It has been already mentioned in the Law against Witches that they are supposed to take up dead Bodies to use in Enchantments, which was confessed by the Woman whom King *James* examined, and who had of a dead Body that was divided in one of their Assemblies two Fingers for her Share. It is observable that *Shakespeare*, on this great Occasion which involves the Fate of a King, multiplies all the Circumstances of Horror. The Babe whose Finger is used must be strangled in its Birth; the Grease must not only be human, but must have dropped from a Gibbet, the Gibbet of a Murderer; and even the Sow whose Blood is used must have offended Nature by devouring her own Farrow. These are Touches of Judgement and Genius.

> And now about the Cauldron sing . . .
> Blue Spirits and White,
> Black Spirits and Grey
> Mingle, mingle, mingle,
> You that mingle may.[1]

And in a former Part,

> Weird Sisters Hand in Hand . . .
> Thus do go about, about

[1] These lines are from the song 'Black Spirits' in Middleton's play *The Witch*, excerpts from which were interpolated in the Folio text of *Macbeth* at 4.1.39ff.

Thrice to mine, and thrice to thine
And thrice again to make up nine. [1.3.32ff.]

These two Passages I have brought together, because they both seem subject to the Objection of too much Levity for the Solemnity of Enchantment, and may both be shown, by one Quotation from *Camden's* Account of *Ireland*, to be founded upon a Practice really observed by the uncivilised Natives of that Country. 'When any one gets a Fall,' *says the Informer of* Camden, 'he starts up, and *turning three times to the Right* digs a Hole in the Earth; for they imagine that there is a Spirit in the Ground, and if he falls sick in two or three Days, they send one of their Women that is skilled in that way to the Place, where she says, I call thee from the East, West, North, and South, from the Groves, the Woods, the Rivers, and the Fens, from the *Fairies red, black, white.*' There was likewise a Book written before the Time of *Shakespeare* describing, amongst other Properties, the *Colours* of Spirits.

Many other Circumstances might be particularised in which *Shakespeare* has shown his Judgment and his Knowledge. (44–9)

* * *

NOTE XLII.

Macbeth. I have liv'd long enough: My *Way* of Life
Is fall'n into the Sear, the yellow Leaf: [5.3.22f.]

As there is no Relation between the *Way of Life* and *fallen into the Sear*, I am inclined to think that the *W* is only an *M* inverted, and that it was originally written: My *May* of Life.

I am now passed from the Spring to the Autumn of my Days, but I am without those Comforts, that should succeed the Sprightliness of Bloom, and support me in this melancholy Season. (56)

NOTE XLIII.

SCENE IV.

Malcolm. 'Tis his main Hope:
For where there is *Advantage to be given*,
Both more or less have given him the Revolt;
And none serve with him but constrained Things,
Whose Hearts are absent too. [5.4.11ff.]

The Impropriety of the Expression *Advantage to be given*, instead of *Advantage given*, and the disagreeable Repetition of the Word *given* in the next Line incline me to read:

> Where there is *a Vantage* to be *gone*
> Both more and less have given him the Revolt.

Advantage or *Vantage* in the Time of *Shakespeare* signified *Opportunity*. *More and less is* the same with *Greater and Less*. So in the interpolated *Mandeville*, a Book of that Age, there is a Chapter of *India the more and the Less*. (56-7)

NOTE XLIV.

SCENE V.

> She should have died hereafter,
> There would have been a Time for such a *Word*.   [5.5.17f.]

This Passage has very justly been suspected of being corrupt. It is not apparent for what *Word* there would have been a *Time*, and that there would or would not be a *Time* for any *Word* seems not a Consideration of Importance sufficient to transport *Macbeth* into the following Exclamation. I read, therefore,

> (1) She should have died hereafter.
> There would have been a Time for—such a *World*!
> To-morrow, *&c.*

It is a broken Speech in which only Part of the Thought is expressed and may be paraphrased thus: *The Queen is dead.* Macbeth. *Her Death should have been deferred to some more peaceful Hour; had she lived longer,* there would at length have been a Time for *the Honours due to her as a Queen, and that Respect which I owe her for her Fidelity and Love. Such is the* World—*such is the Condition of human Life, that we always think to-morrow will be happier than to-day, but to-morrow and to-morrow steals over us unenjoyed and unregarded, and we still linger in the same Expectation to the Moment appointed for our End. All these Days, which have thus passed away, have sent Multitudes of Fools to the Grave, who were engrossed by the same Dream of future Felicity, and, when Life was departing from them, were like me reckoning on to-morrow.*

(2) To the last Syllable of recorded Time, [5.5.21]

Recorded Time seems to signify the Time fixed in the Decrees of Heaven for the Period of Life. The *Record* of *Futurity* is indeed no accurate Expression, but as we only know Transactions past or present, the Language of Men affords no Term for the Volumes of Prescience in which future Events may be supposed to be written. (57–9)

NOTE XLV.

Macbeth. I pull in Resolution, and begin
To doubt th' Equivocation of the Fiend. . . . [5.5.42f.]

I *pull* in Resolution—

Though this is the Reading of all the Editions, yet as it is a Phrase without either Example, Elegance or Propriety, it is surely better to read

I *pall* in Resolution—

I languish in my Constancy, my Confidence begins to forsake me. It is scarcely necessary to observe how easily *pall* might be changed into *pull* by a negligent Writer, or mistaken for it by an unskilful Printer. (59–60)

NOTE XLVI.

SCENE VIII.

Seyward. Had I as many Sons as I have Hairs,
I would not wish them to a fairer Death:
And so his Knell is knoll'd. [5.8.48ff.]

This Incident is thus related from *Henry* of *Huntingdon* by *Camden* in his *Remains*, from which our Author probably copied it.

When *Seyward*, the martial Earl of *Northumberland*, understood that his Son, whom he had sent in Service against the *Scotchmen* was slain, he demanded whether his Wound were in the fore Part or hinder Part of his Body. When it was answered in the fore Part, he replied, 'I am right glad; neither wish I any other Death to me or mine.' (60–1)

After the foregoing Pages were printed, the late Edition of *Shakespeare*, ascribed to Sir T. H.[1] fell into my Hands, and it was therefore convenient for me to delay the Publication of my Remarks till I had examined whether they were not anticipated by similar Observations, or precluded by better. I therefore read over this Tragedy, but found that the Editor's Apprehension is of a Cast so different from mine that he appears to find no Difficulty in most of those Passages which I have represented as unintelligible, and has therefore past smoothly over them without any Attempt to alter or explain them.

Some of the Lines with which I had been perplexed have been indeed so fortunate as to attract his Regard, and it is not without all the Satisfaction which it is usual to express on such Occasions that I find an entire Agreement between us in substituting [*See* Note II.] *Quarrel* for *Quarry*, and in explaining the Adage of the *Cat* [Note XVII]. But this Pleasure is, like most others, known only to be regretted; for I have the Unhappiness to find no such Conformity with regard to any other Passage.

The Line which I have endeavoured to amend, Note XI., is likewise attempted by the new Editor, and is perhaps the only Passage in the Play in which he has not submissively admitted the Emendations of foregoing Critics. Instead of the common Reading,

> Doing every thing
> *Safe* towards your Love and Honour,   [1.4.26f.]

he has published,

> Doing every thing
> *Shap'd* towards your Love and Honour.

This Alteration—which, like all the rest attempted by him, the Reader is expected to admit without any Reason alleged in its Defence—is, in my Opinion, more plausible than that of Mr *Theobald*; whether it is right I am not to determine.

In the Passage which I have altered in Note XL. an Emendation is likewise attempted in the late Edition, where, for

> And the Chance *of* Goodness
> Be like our warranted Quarrel,   [4.3.136f.]

is substituted—And the Chance *in* Goodness—whether with more or

---

[1] Sir Thomas Hanmer: No. 96 above.

less Elegance, Dignity and Propriety than the Reading which I have offered I must again decline the Province of deciding.

Most of the other Emendations which he has endeavoured, whether with good or bad Fortune, are too trivial to deserve Mention. For surely the Weapons of Criticism ought not to be blunted against an Editor who can imagine that he is restoring Poetry while he is amusing himself with Alterations like these:

For
> *This is the Serjeant,*
> *Who like a good and hardy Soldier fought,*   [1.2.3f.]

> This is the Serjeant, who
> Like a *right* good and hardy Soldier fought;

For
> Dismay'd not this
> Our Captains *Macbeth* and *Banquo?*—Yes.   [1.2.33f.]

> Dismay'd not this
> Our Captains *brave Macbeth* and *Banquo?*—Yes.

Such harmless Industry may, surely, be forgiven, if it cannot be praised: may he therefore never want a Monosyllable, who can use it with such wonderful Dexterity.

Rumpatur quisquis rumpitur Invidia![1]

The rest of this Edition I have not read, but from the little that I have seen, think it not dangerous to declare that in my Opinion its Pomp recommends it more than its Accuracy. There is no Distinction made between the antient Reading and the Innovations of the Editor; there is no Reason given for any of the Alterations which are made; the Emendations of former Criticks are adopted without any Acknowledgment, and few of the Difficulties are removed which have hitherto embarrassed the Readers of *Shakespeare*.

I would not, however, be thought to insult the Editor, nor to censure him with too much Petulance for having failed in little Things, of whom I have been told that he excells in greater. But I may, without Indecency, observe that no Man should attempt to teach others what he has never learned himself; and that those who, like *Themistocles*, have studied the Arts of Policy and *can teach a small State how to grow great*, should, like him, disdain to labour in Trifles, and consider petty Accomplishments as below their Ambition. (61-4)

---

[1] Martial, 9.97.12: 'Let anyone, whoever he is, who is bursting with envy, burst!'

106. Mark Akenside, Shakespeare weighed and measured

1746

'The Balance of Poets' from *The Museum: or, the Literary and Historical Register* (1746).

Mark Akenside (1720–71) was a doctor and poet, best known for his poem *The Pleasures of Imagination* (1744); he edited Dodsley's magazine *The Museum* in 1746 and 1747. His model here is the influential art historian Roger de Piles (1635–1709), whose major work, *Cours de peinture par principes avec une balance des peintres* (1708) was translated into English 'by a Painter' in 1743, as *The Principles of Painting*. For a convenient reprint of 'The Balance of Painters' see Elizabeth G. Holt, ed., *A Documentary History of Art* (New York, 1958), II, pp. 183–7.

No. 19 (6 December 1746)

To the Keeper of the MUSEUM.

SIR,

M. *De Piles* is one of the most judicious Authors on the Art of Painting. He has added to his Treatise on that Subject a very curious Paper, which he calls *The Ballance of the Painters*. He divides the whole Art of Painting into four Heads: Composition, Design or Drawing, Colouring, and Expression; under each of which he assigns the Degree of Perfection which the several Masters have attained. To this End he first settles the Degree of sovereign Perfection, which has never been attain'd and which is beyond even the Taste or Knowledge of the best Criticks at present; this he rates as the twentieth Degree. The nineteenth Degree is the highest of which the human Mind has any Comprehension, but which has not yet been expressed or executed by the greatest Masters. The eighteenth is that to which the greatest Masters have actually attained; and so downwards according to their comparative Genius and Skill. *Monsieur de Piles* makes four Columns of his four chief Articles or Parts of Painting; and opposite to the Names of the great Masters writes their several Degrees of Perfection in each Article. The Thought is very ingenious, and had it been executed with Accuracy and a just Rigour of Taste, would have been of the greatest use to the Lovers of that noble Art. But we can hardly expect that any Man should be exactly right in his Judgment through such a Multiplicity of the most delicate Ideas.

I have often wished to see a Ballance of this Kind that might help to settle our comparative Esteem of the greater *Poets* in the several polite Languages. But as I have never seen nor heard of any such Design I have here attempted it myself, according to the best Information which my private Taste could afford me. I shall be extremely glad if any of your ingenious Correspondents will correct me where I am wrong; and in the mean Time shall explain the general Foundations of my Scheme, where it differs from that of the *French* Author. For he has not taken in a sufficient Number of Articles to form a compleat Judgment of the Art of Painting; and though he had, yet Poetry requires many more. I shall retain his Numbers, and suppose twenty to be the degree of absolute Perfection; and eighteen the highest that any Poet has attained.

His first Article is Composition, in which his Ballance is quite equivocal and uncertain. For there are, in Painting, two sorts of Composition, utterly different from each other. One relates only to the Eye, the other to the Passions. So that the former may be not improperly stiled *picturesque* Composition, and is concerned only with such a Disposition of the Figures as may render the whole Group of the Picture intire and well united; the latter is concerned with such Attitudes and Connections of the Figures as may effectually touch the Passions of the Spectator. There are, in Poetry, two analogous kinds of Composition or Ordonnance. One of which belongs to the general Plan or Structure of the Work, and is an Object of the cool Judgment of a Connoisseur; the other relates to the most striking Situations and the most moving Incidents. And tho' these are most strictly connected in Truth and in the Principles of Art yet in Fact we see them very frequently disjoined, and they depend indeed on different Powers of the Mind. *Sir Richard Blackmore*, a Name for Contempt or for Oblivion in the Commonwealth of Poetry, had more of the former than *Shakespeare*, who had more of the latter than any Man that ever lived. The former we shall call *Critical Ordonnance*, the latter *Pathetick*. And these make the two first Columns of our Ballance.

It may perhaps be necessary to observe here that though, literally speaking, these two Articles relate only to Epic and Dramatic Poetry yet we shall apply them to every other Species. For in Lyric Poetry, in Satire, in Comedy, in the Ethic Epistle, one Author may excell another in the general Plan and Disposition of his Work and yet fall short of him in the Arguments, Allusions, and other Circumstances which he employs to move his Reader and to obtain the End of his particular Composition.

Our next Article answers to that which *Monsieur de Piles* calls *Expression*; but this likewise, in Poetry, requires two Columns. Painting represents only a single Instant of Time; consequently it expresses only a present Passion without giving any Idea of the general Character or Turn of Mind. But Poetry expresses this part as well as the other; and the same Poet is not equally excellent in both. *Homer* far surpasses *Virgil* in the general Delineation of Characters and Manners; but there are, in *Virgil*, some Expressions of particular Passions greatly superior to any in *Homer*. I shall therefore divide this Head of *Expression*, and call the former Part *Dramatic Expression* and the latter *Incidental*.

Our next Article answers to what the Painters call *Design*, or the Purity, Beauty, and Grandeur of the Outline in Drawing; to which the Taste of Beauty in Description, and the Truth of Expression are analogous in Poetry. But as the Term *Design*, except among Painters, is generally supposed to mean the general Plan and Contrivance of a work I shall therefore omit it, to prevent Mistakes; and substitute instead of it *The Truth of Taste*, by which to distinguish the fifth Column. And indeed this Article would likewise admit of several Subdivisions; for some Poets are excellent for the Grandeur of their Taste, others for its Beauty, and others for a kind of Neatness. But they may all be rang'd under the same Head, as *Michael Angelo*, *Raphael*, and *Poussin* are all characteriz'd from their *Design*. The *Truth of Taste* will, *cæteris paribus*, belong to the first in the highest Degree; but we must always remember that there can be no Greatness without Justness and Decorum; which is the Reason that *Raphael* is counted higher in *Design* than *Michael Angelo*. For though this latter had a grander and more masculine Taste yet *Raphael*, with a truely grand one, was incomparably more correct and true.

It is not easy to assign that part of Poetry which answers to the Colouring of a Painter. A very good judge of Painting calls the *Colouring* the Procuress of her Sister, *Design*; who gains Admirers for her, that otherwise might not perhaps be captivated with her Charms. If we trace this Idea through Poetry we shall perhaps determine Poetical Colouring to be such a general Choice of Words, such an Order of Grammatical Construction, and such a Movement and Turn of the Verse, as are most favourable to the Poet's Intention, distinct from the Ideas which those Words convey. For whoever has reflected much on the Pleasure which Poetry communicates will recollect many Words which, taken singly, excite very similar Ideas, but which have very different Effects according to their Situation and Connection in a Period. It is impossible to read *Virgil*, but especially *Milton*, without making this Observation a thousand times. The sixth Column of the Ballance shall therefore be named from this *Poetical* Colouring.

As for Versification, its greatest Merit is already provided for by the last Article; but as it would seem strange to many should we intirely omit it the seventh Column shall therefore be allotted for it as far as it relates to the meer Harmony of Sound.

The Eighth Article belongs to the *Moral* of the several Poets, or to the Truth and Merit of the Sentiments which they express, or the Dispositions which they inculcate, with respect to Religion, Civil Society, or Private Life. The Reader must not be suprized if he find the Heathen Poets not so much degraded as he might expect in this Particular; for tho' their Representations of Divine Providence be so absurd and shocking yet this Article is intended to characterize the comparative Goodness of their moral Intention, and not the comparative Soundness of their speculative Opinions. *Where little is given, little is required.*

The Ninth and last Column contains an Estimate of their comparative Value and Eminence *upon the Whole*. This is greatly wanting in the *French* Author. The Degrees of Perfection which he assigns to *Rubens* make up a Sum, when the four Articles are added to each other, exactly equal to what he calculates for *Raphael*; so that one not greatly versed in the Study of Pictures, might imagine from thence that *Rubens* was as great a Painter as *Raphael*. This general Estimate is also more necessary in the present Scheme, as some of the Articles, particularly that of Ordonnance, are applied equally to every Species of Poetry; so that a Satirist will be rated as high in that Article as an Epic Poet, provided his Ordonnance be as perfect for Satire as that of the other is for Heroic Poetry. Upon this Account Justice to the Manes of the diviner Poets requires that we should acknowledge their Pre-eminence upon the Whole, after having thus set their Inferiors upon a Level with them in particular Parts.

You see this general Method is here applied to a few, the greater

Names of Poetry in most polite Languages. I have avoided to bring in any living Authors because I know the Vanity and Emulation of the Poetical Tribe; which I mention lest the Reader should find fault with me for omitting *Voltaire, Metastasio*, or any favourite Author of our own Nation. I am, Sir,

Your most humble Servant

MUSIPHRON.

The Ballance.	Critical Ordonnance.	Pathetic Ordonnance.	Dramatic Expression.	Incidental Expression.	Taste.	Colouring.	Versification.	Moral.	Final Estimate.
Ariosto	0	15	10	15	14	15	16	10	13
Boileau	18	16	12	14	17	14	13	16	12
Cervantes	17	17	15	17	12	16	—	16	14
Corneille	15	16	16	16	16	14	12	16	14
Dante	12	15	8	17	12	15	14	14	13
Euripides	15	16	14	17	13	14	—	15	12
Homer	18	17	18	15	16	16	18	17	18
Horace	12	12	10	16	17	17	16	14	13
Lucretius	14	5	—	17	17	14	16	0	10
Milton	17	15	15	17	18	18	17	18	17
Moliere	15	17	17	17	15	16	—	16	14
Pindar	10	10	—	17	17	16	—	17	13
Pope	16	17	12	17	16	15	15	17	13
Racine	17	16	15	15	17	13	12	15	13
Shakespeare	0	18	18	18	10	17	10	18	18
Sophocles	18	16	15	15	16	14	—	16	13
Spenser	8	15	10	16	17	17	17	17	14
Tasso	17	14	14	13	12	13	16	13	12
Terence	18	12	10	12	17	14	—	16	10
Virgil	17	16	10	17	18	17	17	17	16

107. William Guthrie on Shakespearian tragedy

1747

From *An Essay upon English Tragedy. With Remarks upon the Abbé le Blanc's Observations on the English Stage* [1747].

William Guthrie (1708–70) began his career by reporting parliamentary debates for *The Gentleman's Magazine*, his reports being revised by Dr Johnson; subsequently he translated Quintilian and Cicero, and published treatises in geography, history and grammar. His opponent, Jean-Bernard Le Blanc (1706–81) visited England in 1737–8 and published a collection of letters describing English life (translated in 1747 as *Letters on the English and French Nations*), in which Shakespeare's tragedies were heavily criticised for their 'unnatural extravagances'.

Long before the French had illuminated all Europe with the true rules of the drama our Jonson knew and practised them to a greater perfection than the most distinguishing academician ever wrote of them in speculation. Jonson, at a time when critical learning was as strange in France as in Barbary, did what no Frenchman ever was able to do. He produced regular plays of five acts, complete in the unities of place and characters, and so complete in the unity of time that they are acted upon the stage in the same time which the same story would have taken up in real life. Where then is the merit of the French critical discoveries when an Englishman has so much the start of their academy, and such advantages in the execution?

But Jonson had an understanding which raised him next to genius. He was in the drama what Poussin is in painting. He studied the works of the antients to so much perfection that his drawing, though dry, is always correct; and his attitudes, however uncouth, are always just. Hence, whatever he took from living manners (of which he was sparing) was complete in its kind; while his force of judgment and observation of proportion give a warmth, sometimes, to his colouring as pleasing as when it is the result of nature itself.

Pardon this digression in favour of a poet whom I admire rather than love, but who is so unequal to himself that when he rambles from that severity which is so peculiar to himself you cannot find in Jonson the smallest vestige of his merit; so entirely was he supported upon the stilts of close observation of nature, and strict application to study.

Even the bird of nature, Shakespeare, when he neither soars to elevation nor sinks to meanness, flies with balanced pinions; he skims the level of dramatic rules; and his *Merry Wives of Windsor* demonstrates how much he acted against his better judgment when he stretched his wings into the extravagance of popular prepossessions.

This last expression brings me to a decisive observation. Persius, applying to moral characters, says, 'Ne te quæsiveris extra:'[1] To the reproachful experience of our own country the reverse is proper, when applied to intellectual characters. It is FROM WITHOUT that we are to seek for the reason of an absurd conduct in many of our English authors, and Shakespeare in particular.

By the expression FROM WITHOUT I mean the taste of the courts, and the people to whom the poets wrote; and what it was with regard to the theatre a short review will exhibit.

We are to date the revival of classical taste in Italy, and of classical learning in England, from the reign of Henry VIII. That prince affected to be a scholar, and had one quality in common with other tyrants, that he was as severe upon the rivals of his learning as upon the enemies of his government. The only two men of wit about his court, the earl of Surrey and Sir Thomas More, lost their heads upon a scaffold, and had Erasmus been Henry's subject he probably would have shared in their fate, and in that of Fisher and Cromwell. But as to learning Henry was an ignorant pedant; it was confined to school divinity; nor do we know that he had the smallest relish for works of wit or genius. Yet during all his reign the people had their *panem et circenses*, 'their plays and pastimes.' They had their entertainments, not indeed exhibited upon the stage but in justs and tournaments, in pageants, in largesses, and in conduits running with wine and hyppocras. When the public is liberally entertained, as they were in Henry's time, with such exhibitions they soon forget the stage; nay, the feats of arms and the pomp of pageants dwell so strongly on their minds that when they are

[1] Persius, 1.7: 'look to no one outside yourself.'

brought to theatrical entertainments those are the first objects for which they send their eyes abroad.

Edward the sixth had but a narrow education; and, by what appears from his puling letters, yet extant, he had the same aversion or indifference as to works of wit as his father had. But the same public entertainments, though more rare, were in his reign kept up to the people.

During the six years gloomy reign of Queen Mary the passion of the people for pompous exhibitions was redoubled by the great influx of Spaniards, who formed the manners of the court and encouraged the passion of the public for diversions that were so dear to themselves.

Such was the taste of the nation at the accession of Queen Elizabeth, who was a woman of wit as well as sense. But her sex discouraged, and her inclinations disliked, the martial entertainments so lately in vogue. She countenanced the patrons of the drama, and its poets began, though languidly, to rear their heads. Theatrical entertainments, however, in the beginning of her reign were but few. But the queen and her maids of honour made a shift to please themselves with the few that were, and among the rest with the play of Palamon and Arcite, in which was introduced a special good imitation of a pack of hounds in full cry.

While the stage was thus over-run with ignorance, impertinence, and the lowest quibble, our immortal Shakespeare arose. But supposing him to have produced a commission from that heaven whence he derived his genius, for the reformation of the stage, what could he do in the circumstances he was under? He did all that man, and more than any man but himself could do. He was obliged, indeed, to strike in with the people's favourite passion for the clangor of arms and the MARVELLOUS of exhibition; but he improved, he embellished, he ennobled it. The audience no longer gaped after unmeaning shew. Pomp, when introduced, was attended by poetry, and courage exalted by sentiment. But are we to imagine that Shakespeare could reform the taste of the people into chastity? No; they had the full, the wanton enjoyment of his genius, when irregular, and they were both too uninformed and too incontinent to exchange LUXURY for ELEGANCE.

This would undoubtedly have been the case, even supposing Shakespeare to have attempted a reformation of the drama. But I believe he attempted none. His houses were crouded; his applause was full, and his profits were great. His patrons were pleased with the conduct of his plays. Why then should he attempt a reformation which with the public must have been impracticable, and to his own interest might have been detrimental?

But, not withstanding all this, where is the Briton so much of a Frenchman as to prefer the highest stretch of modern improvement to the meanest spark of Shakespeare's genius? Yet to our eternal amazement it is true, that for above half a century the poets and the patrons of poetry in England abandoned the sterling merit of Shakespeare for the tinsel ornaments of the French academy. Let us observe, however, to the honour of our country that neither the practice of her poets nor the example of their patrons could extinguish in the minds of the people their love for their darling writer. His scenes were still admired, his passions were ever felt; his powerful nature knocked at the breast; fashion could not stifle affection; the British spirit at length prevailed; wits with their patrons were forced to give way to genius; and the plays of Shakespeare are now as much crowded as, perhaps, they were in the days of their author.

Nothing has contributed more to the reproachful, the ignominious fashion of neglecting Shakespeare's manner than the not understanding aright the character of that pride of human genius. A young gentleman naturally of a fine turn for letters goes to the university, where the amusements of wit mingle with, nay often lead, his other studies, and one of the first things his tutor tells him is That all poetry is or ought to be an imitation of nature; and he confirms this doctrine by a number of passages from poets antient and modern. This agrees perfectly well with all the flimsy French dissertations, or English ones stolen from the French, which fall into his pupil's hands upon the subjects of delicacy, taste, correctness, AND ALL THAT. When his head is quite warm with their notions and when he imagines his taste, or something which he takes to be taste, is entirely formed he applies his rules to Shakespeare, and finds many of them not answer. He is soon after turned over to a Swiss or a Scotsman, who LEADS him to travel; and in France he has all his notions of delicacy confirmed and rivetted. He returns to England, where he hears the praises of Shakespeare with silent contempt; he tacitly pities every man who loves so unnatural an author, and bursts for an opportunity to discharge his spleen among his French and foreign acquaintances.

In reality the gentleman is not to be blamed. He proceeds upon a maxim which, however true when applied to most other writers, fails in Shakespeare.

Shall I attempt to give the reason of this? It is not Shakespeare who speaks the language of nature, but nature rather speaks the language of Shakespeare. He is not so much her imitator as her master, her director, her moulder. Nature is a stranger to objects which Shakespeare has rendered natural. Nature never created a Caliban till Shakespeare introduced the monster, and we now take him to be nature's composition. Nature never meant that the fairest, the gentlest, the most virtuous of her sex should fall in love with a rough, blustering, awkward Moor; she never meant that this Moor, in the course of a barbarous jealousy, and during the commission of a detestable murder, should be the chief object of compassion throughout the play. Yet Shakespeare has effected all this; and every sigh that rises, every tear that drops, is prompted by nature.

Nature never designed that a complication of the meanest, the most infamous, the most execrable qualities should form so agreeable a composition, that we think Henry the fifth makes a conquest of himself when he discards Jack Falstaff. Yet Shakespeare has struck out this moral contradiction, and reconciled it to nature. There is not a spectator who does not wish to drink a cup of sack with the merry mortal, and who does not in his humour forget, nay sometimes love his vices.

Give me leave farther to observe that beauties have, in Homer and other authors, been magnified into miracles which, without being noted, are more perfect, more frequent, and better marked in Shakespeare than in Homer himself.

To what extravagance has that father of antient poetry been justly raised for making so many of his heroes extremely brave, yet assigning to each a different character of courage! But to what perfection has our heaven-instructed Englishman brought this excellency which the French critics are so proud of having discovered in Homer? He has not confined it to courage but carried it through every quality. His fools are as different from one another as his heroes. But above all, how has he varied guilty ambition in a species so narrow of itself, that it seems impossible to diversify it! For we see Hamlet's father-in-law, Macbeth, King John, and King Richard, all rising to royalty by murdering their kindred kings. Yet what a character has Shakespeare affixed to every instance of the same species. Observe the remorse of the Dane, how varied it is from the distraction of the Scot: mark the confusion of John, how different from both; while the close, the vigilant, the jealous guilt of Richard is peculiar to himself.

I shall now proceed in the review I undertook that I may at last come to the main design of those pages, which was to prove the different conduct of a great genius and a fine poet, that character which has so long stifled dramatic excellency among us in tragedy.

James the first with much reading had but little knowledge, and with some wit no taste. His ministers, or rather his favourites, were dunces and rascals, and matters of wit were indifferent to them. They were, however, glad of every occasion to encourage every thing that could divert the public attention from affairs of state, and therefore they did not discourage the stage. They left that entirely to the patronage and management of the people. Hence it is that in all the reign of James the first we find the theatre upon an excellent footing and, so far as we can judge, furnished with the best set of actors that ever adorned any one nation at any one time. In short, as to the drama, the public rather acquired a better taste than it had under queen Elizabeth. The strength of Shakespeare, the regularity of Jonson, the genteel manner of Fletcher were all encouraged, and each had his just proportion of applause; nor am I sure whether this was not the period in which, take it all in all, England did not see her stage in its highest perfection. (6-13)

*   *   *

We shall now proceed to the period (a mighty blank it is) to the accession of George the second from that of King William, from whence we may date the decay of tragic genius in poetry. I am afraid neither Rowe nor Addison can wipe that reproach from this period. But what it then lost in one branch of the drama it gained in another. For England then saw her comic scene brought to perfection, to such perfection that nature in giving it seems to have exhausted her stock of dramatic talents. The same encouragement was then given to tragedy, but the public had not the same taste for the one species as for the other. The dispute between the antients and the moderns, which in itself was idle and immaterial, came over from France and infected our great men, who most of them either had wit, or were its profest patrons. The favourers of French poetry then crawled out, and in that summer of their days under the pretext of CORRECTNESS helped to extinguish SPIRIT. The cry against the popular taste of poetry during the late reigns became now more and more in fashion. Ministers took up the pen to ridicule Dryden, statesmen employed their talents to recommend the academy. England became a party in a French dispute. France by her arts avenged herself of our arms. Our men of wit admitted her to be an arbiter, without seeming once to reflect that England had produced a Shakespeare, a name which must have been decisive in the dispute, and which ought to strike dumb all advocates for any other superiority in the province of the drama.

Power is decisive in wit as in politics when, like the ministers of king William and queen Anne, it is munificent and affable, and encourages what it loves. Correctness was now all the mode. I shall confine myself to the influence which this had upon tragedy alone.

It is within the compass of almost every writer's abilities to be correct. He who has no other perfection may attain to that; and it must be owned in those days to have covered a multitude of faults. To exemplify this in our modern tragedies would be endless. Its effect was that correctness was first looked upon to supply the place of poetry, and then poetry that of genius. Correctness without spirit is a distinction understood by every body, but that of poetry without genius is what I am now bound to establish.

The first thing, then, a poet does after he gets the subject of a tragedy, is to form his characters and then his conduct. He next makes a kind of a prose anatomy of his play, and then he sits down to give it expression, the flesh and blood of his performance. But in what follows the genius and the poet differ, and here we shall take them both up.

The genius, forgetting that he is a poet, wraps himself up in the person he designs; he becomes him; he says neither more nor less than such a person, if alive and in the same circumstances, would say; he breathes his soul; he catches his fire; he flames with his resentments. The rapid whirl of imagination absorbs every sensation; it informs his looks; it directs his motions. Like Michael Angelo, who, when carving any great design, wrought with an enthusiasm, and made the fragments of the marble fly round him, he is no longer himself; he flies from representation to reality; with* Shakespeare, he treads the sacred ground; he surveys the awful dome; he does not describe, but converse, with the stalking ghost, and the lawrelled dead; the hallowed vaults re-echo his steps, and the solemn arches repeat his sounds.

The genius that is not so staunch as not to ramble after the most inviting pursuit, after the finest sentiment that springs in the field of fancy, sinks into poetry. A great genius never can be diverted from its immediate object. It does not perhaps keep up the same intenseness in all the under characters of the same play. But that is immaterial. It is sufficient if one or two characters at most, in a play, are thus worked up; nor is it one of the least faults of our modern drama that the

---

* Alluding to the known tradition that Shakespeare shut himself up all night in Westminster Abbey when he wrote the scene of the ghost in *Hamlet*.

manners of the under characters are marked too strongly. The practice of the antients and a greater authority than the antients, that of Shakespeare, was otherwise. Among the Greeks their Œdipus, their Iphigenia, their Philoctetes, in their several plays, fill up all the measure of distress and employ all the force of attention. Shakespeare has indeed in one play very strongly marked one under character, I mean that of Iago in *Othello*; but the high finishing of the principal one required it, and none but a genius like Shakespeare could have executed such a plan. In *Julius Caesar* the chief character, which I take to be that of Brutus, is drawn to his hand in history as is that of Cassius; and therefore he had less difficulty in executing them to such high perfections. But this conduct, easy as it was to Shakespeare, obliged him to throw the greatest character that ever nature formed into an under part. The figure which Cæsar makes in that play is that of formal, empty pomp; and we see the poet has rid his hands of him as soon as he could, that he might have the more leisure to attend his favourite Brutus.

This leads me to observe, though I have the prepossession of a whole age against me, that there is not the least necessity for the chief personage in a play to have either courage, wisdom, virtue, passion, or any other quality above what is to be found in his real history, or in common life. It is a sign of a poverty in genius when a poet invents a dress of good or bad qualities for a favourite character. The antients always brought the same men upon the stage which they saw in the world. But the French and the modern English in their tragedies have peopled the poetic world with a race of mortals unknown to life. This aiming at super-eminent qualities, were there no other, is a proof of the defect of genius; but the eternal practice of the French has, in modern times, given it a shameful sanction.

The field of imagination lyes higher than that of truth, and our modern poets generally take advantage of the ground to mount their Pegasus. But Shakespeare, like his own winged Mercury, vaults from the level soil into his seat.

He has supported the character of Hamlet entirely by the force of sentiment, without giving him any of those strong markings which commonly form the chief modern personage in a tragedy. He has not even made use of those advantages with which the great historian from whom he took his subject might have furnished him. He has omitted part of the marvellous to be met with in that writer, but has made excellent use of the following beautiful description of Hamlet's mad-. ness. . . . 'For Hamlet', says Saxo, 'abhoring the imputation of a lye, so

mingled cunning with truth that what he said was neither void of veracity, nor could the measure of his wit be betrayed by the discoveries of
his sincerity.' Where is the poet but Shakespeare who could have
worked so insipid a character into life by the justness of reflection and
the strength of nature, without applying those colours which an inferior
genius must have used to mark a principal figure*? All that we see in
Hamlet is a well-meaning, sensible young man, but full of doubts and
perplexities even after his resolution is fixed. In this character there is
nothing but what is common with the rest of mankind; he has no
marking, no colouring, but its beautiful drawing, perhaps, cost Shakespeare more than any one figure he ever attempted.

In like manner Macbeth is the same in Shakespeare as in Boethius
and Buchanan. The poet keeps to the historian's fable and characters.
... 'For Macbeth,' says the history,' of himself impatient, was spurred
on by the almost daily reproaches of his wife, his bosom counsellor in
all his designs.' How nobly has Shakespeare improved this hint! how
finished are his characters of this wicked pair! and how artfully has he
conducted and described the human heart through every stage of guilt,
rising and reluctant in the man, ready and remorseless in the woman.

In one of the two plays wrote by the other genius of England for
tragedy, I mean the *Orphan*,[1] the characters, like the fable, are not
raised above the level of common life. Distressed innocence is all that
marks Monimia. Her brother, though a favourite part in the play-
house, has nothing about him but what any other gentleman of the
army ought to possess. In Otway's other tragedy, *Venice Preserved*, the
parts of Pierre and Jaffier, and the distress of Belvidera are indeed
strongly marked, but the effects their characters produce are owing to
the poet's admirable application to the experience of mankind in
common life, beyond which the distress of his fable does not rise; and
in bringing the woes which the guilty suffered, home to the breast of
the innocent.

Having thus endeavoured to explain what I mean by a genius in
tragedy, I shall now proceed to the description of a poet; and, if you

---

* It may be some satisfaction to the reader to know that Shakespeare has taken from
the Danish history the whole of Hamlet's disguised madness; the friendship betwixt him
and Horatio who was his foster-brother; the scene with his mother; the death of Polonius;
his banishment into England; his return, and his killing the usurper. The story of the ghost
was either Shakespeare's invention, or, as I am inclined to believe, he had it from the
songs of Danish bards which was all the history that people had before Saxo and Snorro
wrote.

[1] By Thomas Otway.

will, a fine poet, and take him where I dropt him, when he begins to colour, and to draw his characters.

He does not so much consult what a character would say were he in the poet's place, as what he would say were he in the place of the character. He does not consider so much, how things may be properly as how they may be finely said. His heroes and his princesses all speak his language, that is, the language of poetry without passion. He never touches upon an effect without describing the cause; he never starts a sentiment but instead of considering how the character, were it real, would express it he consults how Virgil, Lucan, Seneca, or any great antient or modern author would turn it. He then launches out into their beauties, and gives it all their embellishments.

But above all things, he is excessively fond of definitions; no great quality comes athwart his dialogue that we have not anatomised, and its rise and progress accounted for. He is very much enamoured, when his characters are virtuous, with virtue in all her shapes; he takes occasion to recommend her from the mouth either of his hero or some of his friends. But the misfortune is, he is extremely apt to overdo. His characters of this kind are all so very virtuous, so very brave, so very loving, and so very constant that they exclude all failing and all propensity to guilt, which, I will venture to say, ought to attend the most complete dramatic character, and are the true springs which captivate, engage, move, and animate the passions.

Were a modern poet to express that simple yet fine sentiment of Otway,

'O I could love thee, ev'n in madness love thee!'

how would he disdain the baldness of the expression! how would he dissect and define, first, the lady's worthiness to the object of love, then love itself; and ten to one but he would even step into Bedlam, that he might entertain us with a more lively picture of madness and its symptoms! Were he to express the horrors of the Lady Macbeth how would he smile, supposing he had never read the play, if he were told it could be done beyond what ever poet executed or imagination conceived, only by rubbing the back of her hand and repeating a deal of wild stuff in her sleep! With him all must be great, all must be philosophy, all must be poetry.

I cannot prove the truth of this observation better than by the example of a great poet, to which character he joined as true a judgment and as much critical knowledge as any man ever possessed; I mean Mr

Addison. That author has, to the immortal credit of his name and nation, exhibited upon the stage a Cato; but we must take the liberty to observe that he is not the Cato whom Rome produced, or Shakespeare would have drawn: he is so firm in virtue, so fortified in philosophy that he is above the reach of fate, and consequently he can be no object of compassion, one great end of tragedy. The poet seems to be aware of this, and endeavours to raise compassion in circumstances wherein he ought of all things to have avoided such an attempt in drawing the character of a professed stoic. With such, the cause of virtue gave supreme happiness, whatever was its success. The friends of the family of Cato therefore could never in the eyes of a stoic be touched with misery while embarked in such a cause. These, I imagine, were the real sentiments of Cato, as his illustrious cotemporaries have drawn him; and if I mistake not, Shakespeare without any other regard, would have attached himself to that character only, and have made Cato from an enthusiasm of public spirit, like the first Brutus, do something extremely shocking to natural affection, and to those private passions which ever mingle with the human frame and oppose the force of nature to that of philosophy. This tremendous virtue formed the real character of Cato; and we find in fact the commands of the senate, in the business of Cyprus, engaged him to accept of a mean, mercenary, inhuman commission.

The under characters of that admirable play are all of them highly finished, and each is fit for the qualities it possesses to stand as the head character in any other tragedy. But they stand in this play as yews did in our old gardens, each regularly opposing the other; and this perhaps was one of the means which pleased the gentlemen of taste at the time it was wrote. The cool, the steady, the reserved virtue of Portius is opposed to the noble, the sincere, the open manner of Marcus. The generous, humane, disinterested principles of Juba constrast the dark, designing, treacherous qualities of Syphax. The softness and candour of Lucius are designed to raise our hatred for the impetuous dissimulation of Sempronius. All is indeed extremely well executed, and all bears the mark of a fine poet, but not of a great genius.

For a particular instance of the difference betwixt the poet and the genius, let us go to two speeches upon the very same subject by those two authors; I mean the two famous soliloquies of Cato and Hamlet. The speech of the first is that of a scholar, a philosopher, and a man of virtue: all the sentiments of such a speech are to be acquired by instruction, by reading, by conversation; Cato talks the language of the porch and academy. Hamlet, on the other hand, speaks that of the human heart, ready to enter upon a deep, a dreadful, a decisive act. His is the real language of mankind, of its highest to its lowest order; from the king to the cottager; from the philosopher to the peasant. It is a language which a man may speak without learning; yet no learning can improve, nor philosophy mend it. This cannot be said of Cato's speech. It is dictated from the head rather than the heart; by courage rather than nature. It is the speech of pre-determined resolution, and not of human infirmity; it is the language of uncertainty, not of perturbation; it is the language of doubting; but of such doubts as the speaker is prepared to cut asunder if he cannot resolve them. The words of Cato are not like those of Hamlet, the emanations of the soul; they are therefor improper for a soliloquy, where the discourse is supposed to be held with the heart, that fountain of truth. Cato seems instructed as to all he doubts: while irresolute, he appears determined; and bespeaks his quarters, while he questions whether there is lodging. How different from this is the conduct of Shakespeare on the same occasion! (17-26)

* * *

There are few of our late poets (for I speak not of the living) who have not attempted to shine in tragedy, but with how little success we have already examined. Were the principal speeches of their plays to be cut out, they might pass for excellent blank verse poems on such and such subjects. But with Shakespeare as with Homer, every speech is made for the character and not the character for the sake of the speech; nor can any sentiment be pronounced but by the character that speaks it: none of the least proofs of a great genius, and the strongest indication how intensely and how abstractedly he studied.

But after all I have said I am far from denying the great beauty of chastity in the drama. The unities are now, perhaps, inseparable to its merits, and they are so easily practised that we could not readily forgive even the greatest genius who should neglect them. But is this chastity to attone for coldness? Is good sense to take the place of great sentiment, or poetry to banish passion?

I cannot take my leave of this subject without remarking in general upon the observations which the French have made as to our stage, and as to Shakespeare particularly. An author whose letters are published under the name of M. Abbé le Blanc, and which have met with a favourable reception, leads me to detain you longer than I intended.

The abbot in his letters resembles our modern poets in their plays; he is a very good writer, but a very ignorant informer. He says to his correspondent, when speaking of Shakespeare, 'Some passages of this poet translated into our language, cannot but give the highest idea of his merit.' For my own part, I doubt extremely of this fact; or whether, when Shakespeare is translated into another language, our ideas of his merit can be raised much above those of the best French tragedies, so peculiarly immediate is the connection betwixt his language and his sentiments. But how does this ingenious Frenchman justify what he has asserted? He gives us a scene in two thirds of which all the sentiment, all the character, all the spirit of Shakespeare is crippled by miserable rhyme. Could the Frenchman pretend to be a critic of the English taste and yet be ignorant that there is not in all the works of Shakespeare, or any other English poet, one rhyming scene in tragedy which is read, far less admired, by even the most indifferent judges in England?

The abbot next, with an oblique reflection, gives us the scene of Beaufort upon his death-bed, which, he says, rises almost to horror by the truth it contains. But had the abbot been acquainted with the history of England he would have given Shakespeare the praise of thus en-nobling a single fact in history, and giving such strong dramatic charac-ters as are those of the king and the cardinal on this occasion without rising one tittle above the level of their true histories. This is what no genius but Shakespeare ever could do. Notwithstanding the high finishing of all his chief historical characters there is not a feature, there is not a colour, there is not a manner, nor a passion added which they had not in life. So well could Shakespeare improve without altering nature.

What I have said of his great characters are equally applicable to his mean ones, such as those introduced in the scene which the abbot next gives us of Cade and his rabble. Ignorant and barbarously whimsical as they seem in Shakespeare's scene, they are not more so than they are in the historian's page. Though Shakespeare has had the art to make all such characters superlatively detestable yet has he not added one cir-cumstance, or exaggerated it, beyond what he found in our annals. The abbot therefore is mistaken in giving us this scene as a specimen of Shakespeare's comic. It is, in effect, a specimen of the tragic as carried by the lowest, the most ignorant, the most infamous of mankind. Was Shakespeare to write now his conduct in introducing such personages would be inexcusable; but at the time he did write it was, perhaps, proper. He wrote to a people that even but a few years before had in fact given him the subject; nor was Shakespeare dead many years before they lived over all his scenes of civil rage, and acted in the world what he described in his theatre. His representing such a people in the strongest, the most ridiculous, the most odious colours could not therefore but have the best effects upon his audience, and upon the public.

The same abbot in his 73d letter, as another specimen of Shakespeare's genius, gives an extract from *Titus Andronicus*, a play falsely attributed to Shakespeare, or if his, so justly condemned by all men of taste in England that it can be no specimen of the English taste. But the abbot is representing the English nation as they are at present, and has been sufficiently informed he would not have given the defects of the dead Shakespeare as instances of taste in the living English. He would have mentioned that the English in general, who have eyes either to see or read a play, are as much shocked with and as much condemn the faults of Shakespeare; nay are as much quick-sighted to them as any Academician in France can be.

But after all, I am not quite sure whether the French or the Englishman would agree together on the passages to be condemned. What the Frenchman may call low stuff and buffoonery from his ignorance of past English manners perhaps the Englishman may, with much better reason, defend as fine wit and true humour. Nay, I will go farther by supposing, what I believe, that an Englishman under King George and one under Queen Elizabeth, could it be possible for them to hold conversation together, would have very opposite sentiments with regard to what is called Shakespeare's low wit.

In the performance which the abbot gives us, called the supplement of genius, and which is supposed to be writ by an English wit, the criticisms are all trite and obvious and deserve no consideration, because those which are just are universally known and approved of by the English nation. Therefore this performance, whether the work of an Englishman or a Frenchman, gives us as little idea of the present taste in the English as of real beauties in Shakespeare. But, perhaps, even in criticism as founded both on truth and the practice of the antients, we may in many things differ widely both from the abbot and his author. The practice of one stage, the French for instance, ought never to be the rule for that of another. To lash the vices or expose the follies of mankind, ought in truth to be the ends of the drama, and where the vices or follies of one nation differ from those of another the remedies must differ likewise. But a Frenchman can have no idea of the remedy because he is ignorant of the disease.

As to the practice of the antients one may venture to enter the lists with any academician, and be judged by any of his body who understands Greek, whether he does not in the best comedy of Aristophanes produce a greater number of more execrable puns, more indecent expressions, and lower trifling than there is in the worst play of Shakespeare.

The Abbé in his 39th letter has the following passage: 'Before the battle of Philippi,' says he, 'is fought, there is a parley betwixt Brutus and Cassius on one side, and Octavius and Antony on the other. By the grossness of the abusive language they give each other at this interview, one can't take them for Romans.' This observation is far from partaking of the abbé's usual candor. It is not the want of information that can bring him into so capital a blunder as to imagine that there is in all the system of modern ribaldry any sort of words or phrases too coarse for the politest of the Romans to use, not only in private altercations but in their most awful and decent debates. This is a character stamped upon that people by their own historians; and the thing is liberally practised by their orators. Sallust, the finest gentleman in Rome, abuses Cæsar in the most gross terms; and Cicero, the fountain of eloquence and address, has, in the open senate, at the bar, and from the rostrum discharged against the greatest men in Rome torrents of abuse which would pollute the stile even of our Billingsgate.

I cannot have a fairer opportunity than this presents for observing how strongly national prepossessions operate upon judgment. The abbé could have no notion that heroes could ever fall a-scolding. Had they run one another through, provided it had not been upon the stage, they had acted very decently. But the Romans, who were at least as brave and as sensible a people as the French are, thought otherwise. They employed their tongues upon one another, and their swords upon their enemies. Hence it is that in all the glorious period of their history, though we meet with many scolding bouts amongst their heroes, we don't meet with one duel. Shakespeare seems to have been perfectly sensible of this characteristic of that great people; and though in the fine scene betwixt Brutus and Cassius our players have ever made a feint towards a duel or rencounter yet nothing could be more opposite to the poet's meaning; it is not encouraged by one syllable of the discourse, and in effect it destroys the cool steady temper which our author, to the honour of his judgment, has made Brutus preserve. (28–33)

108. Unsigned essay on jealousy in *Othello*

August 1747

'An Enquiry into the Nature of the *Passions*, and the Manner in which they are represented by the Tragick Poets, particularly with respect to Jealousy; including some Observations on *Shakespeare's Othello*'; from *The Museum*, No. 38 (29 August 1747). Perhaps by Akenside.

It is a very common Objection, and one which we find frequently insisted upon by most of our *Criticks*, that POETS are apt to exaggerate all *Passions* when they come to represent them in *Tragedy*, and strain them to such a Degree that the Persons they draw, ceasing to be Men distemper'd in their Minds, act like Monsters that by a kind of Enchantment are become Furies. But when we come to consider Things more closely we shall find this a Charge not easily maintained; for when once any Passion gains the despotic Empire of the human Breast there follows such a Series of wild and irrational Actions as, singly taken, would argue the Man absolutely mad that committed them. But because numbers are actuated by their Passions as well as he, it is agreed that a Series of intemperate Actions shall not be esteemed a Proof of *Madness*, but serve only to shew that a Man has very *strong Passions*. This is absurd enough indeed, but so it is, as we see and know from daily Experience.

Amongst these I know of none that, when it has usurped the Throne of Reason, acts with such tyrannical Rage and Licence as *Jealousy*. It is for this Reason that whenever Poets attempt to paint a Man under its Influence they seldom regard his *Rank*, his *Character*, or his *Temper*; but, confounding all Rules of Decency and Decorum, show him—however great or elevated in his Station—as brutal as one of the lowest Mob, forgetting what is *due* to *himself* or to the Person who is the Object of his *Jealousy*, fixing his Thoughts wholly upon the real or the supposed Injury, and, in Consequence of his fixing them, blind to all Rules of Behaviour and lost to all Sense of Reasoning, all Capacity of reflecting, or comparing his Actions with his Duty. Neither are they restrained from this by any Consideration of the Manners they have given him before he is supposed to be infected with this Disease of the Mind. If he was mild and gentle they make no Scruple of changing him in an Instant into a Creature fierce and cruel; if remarkable for Calmness and Circumspection they show him harsh and violent in a Moment; if not only courteous but ceremonious in his Demeanour they make him appear not barely blunt but surly, from the Minute he is struck with Jealousy, and in short, opposite in all Respects to what he was.

The Question is, whether our Poets are justified in this; that is to say, whether they follow Nature or outrun her; whether in Cases of this kind they draw the true Picture of a jealous Man or a hideous *Caracatura* of *Jealousy*, and consequently, whether they deserve to be commended or condemned. I must for my own part confess that it seems to me they are much better acquainted with the human Mind than those who have taken upon them to censure them; and that it may be very justly affirmed that the boldest Poets have not ventured to feign Actions more out of the Road of Reason than are related as Matters of Fact upon the same Topick by the most authentick Historians. Now if this can be made out, that is to say, if it can be shown from the Records of History, which are no other than *written Experience*, that when Men are stung with Jealousy they really act as wildly, as absurdly, and as inconsistently as the Poets represent them acting, then all Ground and Foundation of Criticism in this Respect will be taken away, and the Poets must be allowed to be better acquainted with the true Force of the Passions than those who have taken upon them to find Fault with their Productions, and even to chastise the Publick for the Applause they have vouchsafed to those Productions as supposing them just Representations of Nature.

Of all the inimitable *Shakespeare*'s Performances there is not one more highly or more generally admired than his *Othello*, yet this Play has fallen under the Hands of a merciless Critick, I mean Mr. *Rymer*[1] of wrangling Memory, who has perswaded a Multitude of People to believe that they not only applaud but feel this Tragedy by Infatuation, catch accidentally those Impressions of the Passions which Tragedy ought to move, weep without Cause, and pay that Tribute to the Author which only the Players have deserved. According to him the whole of this Tragedy is not only irregular and ill-writ but improbable, monstrous, and absurd. A Blackamoor, and he too in Years,

[1] See Vol. 2, No. 29.

talks a young Lady of great Quality into Love with him, carries her off in a boisterous manner from her native Country, suffers himself to fall into Suspicion of her upon trivial as well as groundless Causes, hears her Honour basely attacked by one in his Service, and instead of chastising takes him for his Bosom Counsellor; then suspects him too; believes again; behaves like a Brute to his Wife, before Company; is convinced by the slight Circumstance of a Handkerchief; and then deliberately, and with a Show of Caution and Circumspection, commits with his own Hands a most shocking and detestable Murder, and all this in direct Contradiction to the Character before given of him by his own Officers, by *Desdemona*, the Senators, and the Duke of *Venice*. This I take it is the Sum of the *Indictment* brought by Mr *Rymer*, *Attorney-General* of the Criticks, against *Shakespeare* as a Poet. Now to pursue this Simile, I will bring the Matter to an *Issue* and put it upon this short Question, *Whether* SHAKESPEARE *has followed* Nature *or not*? And in order to decide it, I think the fairest Way is to have Recourse to Evidence, which I will next produce.

The Marquis *Ornano*, or, as he is often stiled, *Sampietro*, a Native of the Island of *Corsica*, distinguished himself in the civil Wars that happened in his Country by a noble Zeal for Liberty and by all the military Virtues that form a great Captain, and which afterwards raised him in *France* (a Country never famous for overvaluing the Merit of Strangers) to the highest Ranks in their Service. This Nobleman had married a young Lady of great Quality, *Vaninna Ornano*, of whom he was passionately fond; a Lady whose exquisite Beauty was the least of her Perfections; whose Manners were as amiable as her Person, and whose Virtues were as conspicuous and as heroic as any the antient Writers have recorded or the Authors of modern Romances have feigned. In all the Dangers and Distresses of her Husband, which were many and great, she bore a part; and when he was obliged to retire as an Exile into *France* she followed him thither with her infant Son, afterwards so well known to the World by the Title of Marshal *Ornano*. Upon the Death of *Henry* the Second her Husband, despairing of any farther Succours from *France*, and finding himself proscribed and a Price set upon his Head by the *Genoese*, determined to ask the Assistance of the *Turk*; and for that Purpose made a Voyage to *Constantinople*. In his Absence the *Genoese* contrived to tamper with his Lady. She was related, and that very nearly too, unto some of the best Families of the Republick; and some of these suggested to her that in case she would return and bring her Son with her she might very possibly be able to procure a Pardon for the Marquiss, notwithstanding all that he had done, and was still doing, to the Prejudice of the State.

It is no great wonder that the Marchioness *Ornano* listened to these Proposals; but her Husband having gained Intelligence of the whole Design, and either distrusting (as he might well do) the Sincerity of the *Genoese*, or being determined in his Aversion to that Republick so far as to despise a Reconciliation sent immediately into *France* his Secretary *Antonio St. Florentine*, with Instructions to persuade his Wife to lay aside all Thoughts of returning to *Genoa*. The Marchioness was no sooner acquainted with her Husband's settled Resolution than she shewed her accustomed Obedience, and, at the Request of *Antonio*, removed from *Marseilles* to *Aix* in *Provence*. When the *Genoese* found that this Scheme of theirs of getting the Wife and Son of their capital Enemy into their Possession was defeated, they had recourse to another Project and, corrupting one of the Marquiss's Domesticks, engaged him to throw out such Hints as might make his Master jealous of *Antonio*. And in this they were but too successful; for he no sooner conceived a Suspicion of his Wife's Conduct than, forgetting his Concern for the Liberty of his Country, the important Negotiation in which he was engaged, and even the Injuries he had received from and the implacable Hatred he bore the *Genoese*, he suddenly returned to *France*.

Upon his Arrival at *Marseilles*, finding his Lady gone from thence with *Antonio* to *Aix*, he required nothing farther to convince him; but immediately repairing thither, brought back his Lady and her Son to *Marseilles* that he might the more easily escape when he had perpetrated the barbarous Fact that he intended. When he had her there he told her in Terms very coarse, as well as cold, that she had offended him and must die; the Lady submitted, and only made this Request that, as no Man had ever touched her but himself, she might die by his Hand. To this he consented, and dropping one Knee upon the Ground, calling her his Mistress, and showing in the midst of the most savage Cruelty a Tenderness of Mind and Horror of the Fact, asked her Pardon, as Executioners are wont to do, and then strangled her with her Handkerchief.

This is a bare historical Narrative of the Fact, as set down by the Writer of *Sampietro*'s Life, and by many other impartial and authentick Historians; and, I presume, whoever considers it attentively will see that there are as many Circumstances of Levity, Distraction of Mind, and an absurd Mixture of passionate Love and barbarous Resentment as *Shakespeare* has expressed in his Tragedy of *Othello*; and that the *Genoese* was, to all Intents and Purposes, as great a Monster in Nature as *the Moor*. I conclude, therefore, that our Poet has preserved his Character, has painted the Passion of Jealousy as it ought to be painted in such a Man; has copied faithfully, without exceeding or exaggerating; and has frighted us (which, by the way, is the very Essence of Tragedy) not with an imaginary Scene but with a real Spectacle of a wise and worthy Man made mad by Jealousy, and becoming a wild, ungovernable, brutal and blood-thirsty Monster; and yet accompanied with Circumstances that deservedly excite Compassion. So that if what the Criticks define about Tragedy, that it is the Art of instructing by exciting Terror and Pity, he has accomplished it beyond any Writer in our Language, and may be therefore justly stiled inimitable.

I might indeed observe that the Story upon which this Tragedy is built was not absolutely a Fiction, or at least no Fiction of *Shakespeare*'s; for he had it very nearly as he has represented it from *Cynthio*'s Novels. I might also observe that as this very Fact happened before he wrote his Play, and as it made a very great Noise in the World, it might have reached his Knowledge; and from certain Circumstances in this Tragedy one might be really tempted to think he had it in View. I might remark, too, that the Charge against him of neglecting a Moral is very ill founded, and arises rather from the Petulancy of the Critick than from any Obscurity in the Performance. But I waive all these Considerations, and keep close to the Point which I laid down, that the Tragick Poets are very unjustly charged with exaggerating the Passions and making Men appear either wilder or worse than they are when under their Influence; and that the Instance of *Othello* in support of this Doctrine is unjust, and the Reflections made upon the Author for drawing him as he has done, improper and ill founded. But this is one Species of Jealousy only, though it is indeed the worst Species, *viz.* the Suspicious. I shall hereafter take Occasion to consider the Subject farther, and bestow a few Remarks upon a Play of *Fletcher*'s, and perhaps upon a Tragedy of Mr. *Rowe*'s, with the same View as in this Essay; that is, to vindicate the Conduct of those Poets, and to show that *Horace* was in the right when he asserted that there was more true Morality to be learned from their Works than those of the Philosophers.

109. Samuel Foote, Shakespeare and the actors

1747

From *A Treatise on the Passions, So far as they regard the Stage; With a critical Enquiry into the Theatrical Merit of Mr. Garrick, Mr. Quin, and Mr. Barry* (1747).

Samuel Foote (1720–77) was a successful comic actor and author of numerous comedies and farces.

Thus much for the corporal Defects or Advantages of Mr. *G.*; let us now take a View of him in Action, and consider whether he is artful in the concealing his natural Blemishes, and judicious in the Application of his Talents; and for this Purpose it will be most convenient both to the Reader and myself to regard him in a single Light; let it be *Lear*, and I the rather chuse this Character because Mr. *G.*, where he is right, is nowhere so masterly.

The Portrait that *Shakespeare* has given us of *Lear* is that of a good-hearted Man, easily provoked, impatient of Contradiction, and hasty in Resolution. The Poet himself, who seldom fails to direct the Actor, has thought an Apology necessary at the opening of the Play for what might appear immoral in the Conduct or Expressions of his Hero, by laying the Blame on a natural Habit, *'tis said that I am Choleric*[1]; and then, as a Testimony of the Humanity and innate Goodness of his Disposition, upon hearing the tragical End of his unnatural Daughters at the Close of the Play this tender, this affectionate Expression is put into his Mouth:

> *Ungrateful as they were,*
> *Tho' the Wrongs they have heaped on me are numberless;*
> *I feel a Pang of Nature for them yet.*

This I take to be a Sketch of *Lear*'s moral Character, a Circumstance that never ought to escape the View of the Actor.

[1] From Nahum Tate's version: see Vol. 1, pp. 349, 385.

And here sorry I am to set out with an Observation that Mr. G. seems quite regardless of both *Lear*'s Attributes, and that at a juncture too where the Poet's Excuse is but barely sufficient, and the Player's Assistance absolutely necessary. The Passage I mean is the Curse at the End of the first Act, which in my Judgment, and I am not singular, should be utter'd with a Rage almost equal to Phrenzy, quick and rapid as a Whirlwind, no Mark of Malice, no Premeditation, no Solemnity; the Provocation, the Persons against whom the Curse is denounced, *Lear*'s Character, all conspire to render such a Behaviour absurd. Nor can I easily pardon the Tears shed at the Conclusion. The whole Passage is a Climax of Rage, that strange Mixture of Anger and Grief is to me highly unnatural; and besides, this unmanly Sniveling lowers the Consequence of *Lear*. This Practice may with Propriety be introduced in the Imitation of a vex'd Girl, who cries because she can't (in the vulgar Tongue) gain her Ends. But, dear G., get your Friend *H—ym—n*[1] to draw an enraged Monarch, and see whether he will make any Use of the Handkerchief; nor can I admit the ill-judged Applause of the Multitude as a Plea for the Continuation of this Trick. The Transition from one Passion to another, by the Suddenness of the Contrast throws a stronger Light on the Execution of the Actor; and thus the Groundlings, who are caught more by the Harmony and Power of the Voice than Propriety are easily drawn in to applaud what must grieve the Judicious. I have been the longer on the last Particular because it is not in this Place alone that Mr. G. traps the Unwary by the same Bait; his unreal Mockery in *Macbeth*, and two memorable Speeches in the first Scene of *Chamont* are Instances which I hope he will hereafter never suffer to rise in Judgment against him. We all now know how the Shilling came under the Candlestick, the Trick is discover'd.

It will now (I presume) be expected that I should, agreeable to my Promise, oppose to this Error in Mr. G. one of his Excellencies; but, for the sake of Method, permit me first to discover the Passages wherein I think him mistaken, and then we will proceed to the Recital of his Perfections without Fear of Interruption.

The next Scene in which *Lear* is capitally concern'd, and where I think Mr. G. sometimes erroneous, is the Middle of the Second Act.

The poor old King is introduced in a Storm, exposed to the Fury of the warring Elements, and that no Circumstance of Horror might be omitted he is surrounded by Darkness and has no Companion in his

---

[1] Francis Hayman (1708-76), scene-painter and illustrator.

Misery but a Man in whom he could place no Confidence, as having but just entertain'd him; and here one would think it impossible to aggravate the Distress or increase our Pity, and yet the Poet has artfully contrived to heighten both by throwing *Lear* into Madness.

Let us now take a View of the Actor's Deportment in this Situation; but it may not be improper first to observe that as Madness is defin'd to be right Reasoning on wrong Principles there is always a Consistency in the Words and Actions of a Madman. Thus much may be gathered from a Scene naturally drawn, tho' by no means a Subject for Comedy, in the *Pilgrim* of *Fletcher's*: the sottish *Englishman* does not command the Winds and Seas, nor the Scholar call for Beer; you find the whole Group of Lunaticks employ'd on the Circumstances that first disturb'd their Imaginations—the Parson, whom possibly a long Law-Suit for Tithes had drove to Poverty and Despair, does not quit his Claim to a tenth Pig. But we need not have Recourse to foreign Assistance, the Subject before us will sufficiently demonstrate what we want; the Use I would make of the Observation is, that it be a Direction to the Actor to employ his first Enquiry into the Cause of the Madness he is to represent, that his Deportment may be conducted suitably therewith. For example, in *Lear* we find *Lear's* Mind at first entirely possess'd with the Thoughts of his Daughters Ingratitude, which was the immediate Cause of his Distress. To this he subjoins some Reflections on the State and Nature of his Afflictions, and thus far his Reason holds. But when his Mind makes a farther Progress and looks back to the remote Cause, which was a voluntary Resignation of the Regal Power, then the Idea of his former Grandeur rises to his View; which, when he compares with his present Misery and observes the Impossibility of remounting the Throne he had quitted, then his Brains turn and his Reason forsakes him.

The Desire of Royalty, then, is the Point that distracts *Lear's* Judgment; and the Belief that he possesses that Royalty, the State of his Madness; all his Expressions are full of the Royal Prerogative.

> *I pardon that Man's Life.*
> *You cannot kill me for Coining, I am*
> *The King himself.*
> *Ay, every Inch a King.*   [4. 6. 109, 83f., 107]

How, then, is this mad Monarch to be employed in picking Straws, and boyish Trifling, or in Actions more *à-propos*, more suitable to his imaginary Dignity, such as frequent Musings with the Finger on the

Brow—as if the Welfare of Kingdoms depended on his Care—issuing Orders to his Attendants, or in some Act that expresses Regal Power. I own I am weak enough, tho' in Contradiction to Mr. G., to think the last Method best; and if my Advice might be taken, every Motion, every Look should express an Extravagance of State and Majesty. And when mad *Tom* is consulted as a learned *Theban Lear* should not, if he would be directed by me, pull his Rags, play with his Straws, or betray the least Mark of his knowing the real Man. But with great Solemnity, a contracted Brow, one Hand on *Edgar*'s Shoulder, his Finger on his Breast, or some Action that should denote Superiority, seem to consult him on a knotty Point: but no Sign of Equality, no Familiarity, no sitting down Cheek by Jowl; this might be a proper Representation of a mad Taylor, but by no means corresponds with my Idea of King *Lear*.

Nor should he be less in earnest in all his Stratagems. His Project for shoeing a Troop of Horse with Felt should be delivered with Rapture, as if he had hit on a masterly Expedient. Nor would I have him express less Joy, but with a Tincture of Bitterness and Rancour at surveying the Execution of his Scheme, when he should have it in his Power to revenge his Wrongs,

> *Steal upon his Sons-in-law,*

and then,

> *Kill, kill, kill.*   [4.6.107f.]

How far this Passage has been mistaken by Mr. G. I submit to the Judicious; and here let me add that I will undertake to demonstrate that *Shakespeare* has not put one Expression into the Mouth of *Lear* throughout the whole Course of his Madness but what bears a visible Relation to the first Cause of it.

As these are the principal Mistakes we have to lay to Mr. G.'s Charge, the Gratification of his Enemies is at an end; his Friends may now uncloud their Brow, throw aside their Chagrin, and prepare for a Recital of his Perfections.

Mr. G.'s whole Behaviour during the first Act (except as before excepted) is natural and masterly, the choleric Man happily marked in the Scenes with *Cordelia, Kent,* and at the Discovery of his eldest Daughter's Ingratitude. (And indeed, wherever quick Rage is to be express'd no Actor does the Poet so much Justice.) Nor is he less successful in tincturing all the Passions with a certain Feebleness suitable to the Age of the King, the Design of the Author, and the raising in the

Minds of the Audience a stronger Feeling and Compassion for *Lear*'s
Sufferings. And tho', in the general Conduct of the mad Scenes Mr. G.
is in my Opinion faulty, yet in many particular Instances his Judgment
and Execution demands the highest Applause. There is a Mixture of
Distraction, with the Joy, that he expresses at

> *Was it not pleasant to see a Thousand, with red-hot Spits, come hissing in*
> *upon them.*   [3.6.15f.]

that I have seldom seen equall'd; nor can he be easily excell'd where the
Tortures of *Lear*'s Mind and the Fatigues of his Body throw him into a
Swoon. G.'s Preparation is fine, and the Execution of the Thing itself
inimitable—such a Death-like Paleness in his Countenance, such an
Inactivity in his Limbs, that only *Shakespeare*'s Words can do him
Justice,

> *He is indeed Death's Counterfeit.*   [*Macbeth*, 2.3.74]

Nor can I leave him without my particular Thanks for the Entertainment he has given me at his Recovery from Madness, and Recollection
of *Cordelia*. The Passions of Joy, Tenderness, Grief, and Shame are
blended together in so masterly a Manner that the Imitation would do
Honour to the Pencil of a *Rubens*, or an *Angelo*.

The last Circumstance that I shall trouble the Reader with is the
fatigue, weariness, and at the same time soldier-like and manly Pleasure
that G. expresses at having vanquished the Ministers of his inhuman
Daughter's last Commands. I could add one Observation to the foregoing, but as I differ from the Actor (tho' I must own some Arguments
may be brought in his Defence), and I have promised to mention no
more of his Faults I shall be silent, and am, for once, pleased with *Tate*'s
Alteration of *Shakespeare*, because it has prevented my commenting on
Mr. G.'s Manner of Dying, about which, I am afraid, we should have
some Disputes.

At last then the Task is finished, and happy shall I esteem myself if
these loose Hints can contribute to improve the general Taste of the
Publick or convey the least Instruction to a very great, I wish I could
add, perfect Actor.

Mr. Q. next claims our Attention; and as his Superiority in the
Character of *Othello* had been universally allow'd, 'till a Caveat was
entered by a young and new Actor from *Dublin*,[1] it may not be un-

---

[1] Spranger Barry, who made his London début in the part on 4 October 1746, with
such success that he displaced James Quin as the leading Othello of the period.

entertaining to oppose these great Men in this Part, and examine to which the Laurel is due.

As G.'s Person is so insignificant and trifling, Q.'s is too cumbersome and unwieldy; as the first is deficient in Characters that require Consequence and Dignity, so is the last in those that demand Ease and Bustle.

G. has Variety, but wants Power or Continuation of Voice; Q. a Monitone that seldom fatigues him, but is now and then a little tiresome to his Hearers. G.'s Action is various, but sometimes extravagant; Q.'s the same in all Circumstances and Passions.

B. has more Obligations to Nature than either of these; he is tall without Awkwardness (I mean whilst his Limbs are in a State of rest) and handsome without Effeminacy; his Voice is sweet and permanent, but the Tone too soft for the Expression of any but the tender Passions, such as Grief, Love, Pity, &c. I would here consider the Disposition of the Features in these Gentlemen, but as the black Covering in this Part before us hinders our discerning the Action of the Muscles, we cannot determine to which the Preference ought to be given, only from a general Observation. Q. would, were the Blacking removed, be most successful in the Scenes of Rage, B. in those of Tenderness.

Arm'd with these Weapons, the Heroes set forth in *Othello*; Q. from a Knowledge of the Stage, and the Happiness of a good level Voice, gets in the Opinion of the Many the first Advantage; my private Judgment, to deal freely, condemns them both. (16-25)

*   *   *

But we must now prepare our Attention for the third Act, the great Scene of Business; and here I could wish for a larger Compass than this Tract will afford me; I would then endeavour to pay my little Tribute to the Genius of the Author at the same time that I am attempting to do Justice to the Skill of the Actor; but circumscribed as I am, I can take no Notice of the former but as it assists my Observations on the latter.

The great Fault I have to charge the Actors with in this Scene is their betraying a Consciousness of what is to succeed; or, in other Words, being jealous before they have reason. *Iago*, in all the Speeches that work up *Othello* to the Height he desires, does not drop the least Hint of the Disloyalty of *Desdemona* but only gives his Friend to understand that he has a Secret, which he is unwilling to communicate, that nearly concerns him. *Othello* may have some Doubts of the Integrity of *Cassio* but does not harbour the least Suspicion of his Wife's Virtue; the Mistake commonly begins at *Ha!*, which Mr. Q. utters as a Mark of Reflection, *B.* of Rage. To be the better able to determine which of their Judgments is best take the whole Passage.

> Oth. *I'll know thy Thoughts.*
> Iag. *You cannot, if my Heart was in your Hand,*
>   *Nor shall not, &c.*
> Oth. *Ha!*   [3.3.166ff.]

The Increase of Rage at the Obstinacy of *Iago* is natural enough, but why should the Jealousy be received here more than at any other foregoing Passage of the Play? And besides, the Artifice of *Iago* is destroyed by this Means; who, seeing the Reason of *Othello* dispossessed by a Torrent of contending Passions, seizes on the Opportunity of pouring into his Mind a Suspicion which at another Time would have been denied Admittance, and so with no other Preparation than the raising a Storm which he knew how to divert he comes plump at once with,

> *O! my Lord, beware of Jealousy.*   [3.3.169]

This I take to be the most obvious Explanation of the Passage, and therefore decree in Favour of *B. Q.*, in the Words of Mr. *Cibber*, is more than excellent in his Endeavour to conceal from *Iago* the Grief and Anguish that the Doubts of his Wife gave him,

> *Not a Jot, not a Jot.*   [3.3.219]

But then he is far short of his Rival in

> *This Fellow's of exceeding Honesty.*   [3.3.262]

This Speech is a Mixture of deliberate Reasoning and wild Starts of Rage; *Q.* considers it in the first Light only, whilst *B.* gives fire to the one Part and Sedateness to the other. His Fury begins at

> *If I do prove her Haggard.*   [3.3.264]

and subsides at,

> *Happ'ly for I am black.*   [3.3.267]

Then a sudden Reflection destroys his Coolness, and the Thoughts of her being gone and that his only Relief was to loath her hurries him into a fresh Tempest of Impatience and Despair. Nor has the Poet less Obligations to *B.* at the Entrance of *Desdemona*; his immediate Drop from a Whirlwind to a Calm, and the Tenderness that accompanies the Declaration of a Belief that it was impossible so divine a Form could delight in Pollution; this, with his whole Behaviour to her at going off, is masterly and affecting. Q. claims the Preheminence at the Opening of the next Scene,

What Sense had I.   [3.3.342]

Tears have no Business here. And in this Place a Caution which I have to offer Mr. *B.* may be properly introduced.

You have, Sir, I doubt not, been often told that your Expressions of Grief and Tenderness are very becoming, and they told you Truth. But let not this Persuasion draw you into a Prostitution of the Excellence; for, not to mention that your Judgment will suffer in the Eyes of the Discerning, your hackneying the Passion and applying it indiscriminately will take from its Weight and lower its Force, even with the Injudicious. If you cry one Minute for Joy and another for Sorrow, as in Lord *Townly,* a Man would be puzzled to know whether you were angry or pleased; and in the present Case a Degree of Anger is rather the Passion than Sorrow.

The Close of the second Speech has, indeed, some Distress; *Othello's Occupation's gone*; and is finely calculated by the Author for the Advantage of the Actor. The Rage that ensues upon the Sight of *Iago*, who was the immediate Cause of *Othello*'s Affliction, is a fine Opposition to the resign'd, calm Despair that preceeds it. I can't boast much of the Execution of either Q. or B. in the climactick Speech of

Villain, be sure.   [3.3.363]

I call it one Speech, for those little Breaks of

My noble Lord, is't come to this?   [3.3.367]

are not design'd as Interruptions, but artfully thrown in as breathing Places for *Othello*. B.'s Action and Attitude, with the Totterings of *Iago*, convey to my Mind a pretty strong Idea of Wrestling, but do not disturb my Tranquillity with any Emotions of Terror; nor does Q.'s Method of Collaring and quitting and then collaring again, correspond with my Conception of the Passage. There is a Connection through the whole Speech; and to give the Mind an Opportunity of cooling by a Walk cross the Stage is an Error that I could not have thought Mr. Q.'s Experience would have committed. Nor do I much admire the Utterance of either Q. or B. in this Place; the Growl of the first is as far from right as the Vociferation of the last; the former wants

Fury, and the latter a forcible Energy, which Loudness can never convey. An Octavo would scarce have Room enough for a minute and critical Enquiry into the Defects and Perfections of both these Gentlemen in this Part.

I shall therefore trouble the Reader with but a few more Remarks by which, and the foregoing, he will be able to make a tolerable Judgment to which *Shakespeare* is most obliged.

The great Difficulty that attends the Actor in this Part is the raising in the Minds of the Audience a Compassion for himself superior, if possible, to that they entertain for his Wife; and, for this Purpose, the Strugglings and Convulsions that torture and distract his Mind upon his resolving to murder her cannot be too strongly painted, nor can the Act itself be accompanied with too much Grief and Tenderness. In short, let the killing of *Desdemona* appear as a Sacrifice to the Hero's injur'd Honour, and not the Gratification of a diabolic Passion.

> *For naught did I in hate, but*
> *All in Honour.*   [5.2.298f.]

are almost the last Words of *Othello*. Sure never has there been a Character more generally misunderstood both by Audience and Actor than this before us, to mistake the most tender-hearted, compassionate, humane Man for a cruel, bloody, and obdurate Savage. Is there an Expression of his, even when he has no Doubt remaining of the Incontinence of his Wife, but what is strongly tinctured with Love and Pity? With what Difficulty, with what Anguish of Mind does he resolve to poison her, and that not before he has recounted her most minute Excellence, even to her Skill with the Needle. Nor does the Command of

> *Get me some Poison, Iago.*   [4.1.200]

come from him till he had used every Argument in her Excuse, and searched, but in vain, for any other Expedient.

How gladly does he exchange the Manner of her Death for that which appears more suitable to Justice:

> *Strangle her in the Bed she hath contaminated.*
> Oth. *Good! the Justice of it pleases.*   [4.4.204f.]

And what Anxiety and Care does he testify for the immortal Part of her, even at the Instant before her Death; in how pathetick a Manner does he caution her against the Commission of a Sin which would effectually damn her:

> *Sweet Soul, take Heed of Perjury.* [5.2.54]

And what an Earnestness does he express for the Success of her short Prayer:

> *Amen, with all my Heart.* [5.2.36]

With this, take a View of his Behaviour after the Discovery of her Innocence, and then tell me whether the Tenderness, Love, Grief and Pity that *B.* blends with every Incident in the two last Acts, or the stern, brutal, unfeeling Behaviour of *Q.* be most consistent with the true Character of *Othello*.

I cannot but confess, notwithstanding all I have said of Mr. *B.* that frequent Trips are made by him in several Passages of the Play. But as he has the Pleas of Youth and Inexperience in his Favour I shall leave him to Time for Amendment and private Correction; but if through Vanity he continues obstinate he must expect a publick Admonition. With one Hint more I shall leave him, and that is with regard to his Deportment. In the Passion of Grief, by a villainous Habit, he throws his Body out of the Line, his Head is projected, and his Body drawn tottering after. But for a more picturesque Description of his Figure take this Line of *Pope*'s:

> *And, like a wounded Snake, draws his slow Length along.*

Not to mention the clasping of the Hands together, which is either an aukward Action or aukwardly executed; but were it ever so graceful it is too frequently repeated.

There is no Part that I can at present recollect which so absolutely depends on what the Laureat figuratively calls the Returning of the Ball, as the Character in question. I defy the greatest *Othello* that ever was born, unless he be well provided with an Antient, properly to express either the Hero or the jealous Lover. Nor, indeed, can the Skill and Address of *Iago* be placed in a conspicuous Light without the Assistance of a judicious *Othello*. Suppose, then, as these Characters are so closely connected, we bestow a few Periods on the most artful, insinuating, thorough-paced Villain that ever was indebted for Detection and Infamy to the Pen of a Poet.

And here, were I inclined to favour the Prejudices of the Public, I should intreat, not demand their Regard to an Actor, who, in the Part of *Iago*, is at least equal to any *Othello* this Age has produced. But as my present Purpose is the Discovery of Absurdity and Ignorance, however protected by partial Popularity, and the drawing from Obscurity real Merit, however depressed by Folly or Faction, take my sincere Sentiments of *Macklin* in the Character of *Iago* without Apology.

Be it our first Care then to consider in what Light (I mean as to Quality and Fortune) *Shakespeare* has presented *Iago* to us. I think we may venture to affirm that the Ensign was a Dependant on the General; nay, perhaps a Domestick, from the Imployment assign'd to *Emilia*:

> *I pray thee let thy Wife attend on her.* [1.3.296]

This may be safely concluded. Besides, we find *Othello* frequently imploying *Iago* in Offices that bear no relation to his Command,

> *Go to the Port and disembark my Coffers.*
> *Fetch Desdemona hither,* &c. &c. &c. [2.1.206; 1.3.120]

My Penetration can discover but one Place where *Iago* offers at disobeying the Injunctions of his Master:

> *I do not like the Office.* [3.3.414]

And here so many other Reasons may be assigned besides Equality of Condition, that no Conclusion can be fairly drawn opposite to what has been advanced. I have been the longer on this Point because on the Settling of it depends the Propriety of *Macklin*'s Deportment thro' the whole Play.

If then there be no Difference between these Characters but what is given by a superior Commission; that is, was the State of the *Venetian* Army the same as with us, *Macklin*'s Conduct is wrong. But if *Iago*'s Situation was what I have presum'd it, his distant obsequious Behaviour is critically right, and the Judgment both of his Competitors and Censurers erroneous and absurd. (28–38)

110. Samuel Foote on the Unities

1747

From *The Roman and English Comedy Consider'd and Compar'd* (1747).

As to the Unities of Time, Place, and Action, I cannot say that we have strictly attended to them, unless in some particular Instances, such as the *Alchymist*, and most of the Plays of *Jonson*, *Shakespeare*'s *Merry Wives of Windsor*; to which I might add some others. But in general these Bonds do not hit the Taste and Genius of the free-born luxuriant Inhabitants of this Isle: they will no more bear a Yoke in Poetry than Religion.

No political nor critical Monarch shall give Laws to them. They have indeed sometimes given Proofs that they do not despise these Mandates of *Aristotle* because it is not in their Capacity to comply with them, but because they will not be indebted to any other Country for what they can obtain without its Assistance.

I do not believe that it ever was in the Power of Man to furnish out a more elegant, pleasing, and interesting Entertainment than *Shakespeare* has in many Instances given us without observing any one Unity but that of Character. His adhering to that alone, with the Variety of his Incidents, the Propriety of his Sentiments, the Luxuriancy of his Fancy, and the Purity and Strength of his Dialogue, have produced in one Instance alone more Matter for Delight and Instruction than can be collected from all the starv'd, strait-lac'd Brats that every other Bard has produc'd. Can then our Contempt and Resentment be too strongly expressed against that insolent *French* Panegyrist, who first denies *Shakespeare* almost every Dramatic Excellence, and then in his next Play pilfers from him almost every capital Scene? Let those who want to be informed of this Man and this Truth read the *Mahomet* of *Voltaire* and compare it with the *Macbeth* of *Shakespeare*. . . . (20–1)

111. William Warburton, edition of Shakespeare

1747

From *The Works of Shakespeare In Eight Volumes. The Genuine Text (collated with all the former Editions, and then corrected and emended) is here settled: Being restored from the Blunders of the first Editors, and the Interpolations of the two Last: with A Comment and Notes, Critical and Explanatory* (1747).

See head-note to No. 83, Vol. 2, and No. 90 above.

[From the Preface]

I am now to give some Account of the present Undertaking. For as to all those Things, which have been published under the titles of *Essays, Remarks, Observations,* &c. on *Shakespeare* (if you except some critical Notes on *Macbeth,* given as a Specimen of a projected Edition and written, as appears, by a Man of Parts and Genius) the rest are absolutely below a serious Notice.

The whole a Critic can do for an Author who deserves his Service is to correct the faulty Text, to remark the Peculiarities of Language, to illustrate the obscure Allusions, and to explain the Beauties and Defects of Sentiment or Composition. And surely, if ever Author had a Claim to this Service, it was our *Shakespeare,* who, widely excelling in the Knowledge of Human Nature, hath given to his infinitely varied Pictures of it such Truth of Design, such Force of Drawing, such Beauty of Colouring as was hardly ever equalled by any Writer, whether his Aim was the Use or only the Entertainment of Mankind. The Notes in this Edition, therefore, take in the whole Compass of Criticism.

I. The first sort is employed in restoring the Poet's genuine Text, but in those Places only where it labours with inextricable Nonsense. In which, how much soever I may have given Scope to critical Conjecture, where the old Copies failed me I have indulged nothing to Fancy or Imagination but have religiously observed the severe Canons of literal Criticism; as may be seen from the Reasons accompanying every Alteration of the common Text. Nor would a different Conduct have become a Critic whose greatest Attention, in this part, was to vindicate the established Reading from Interpolations occasioned by the fanciful Extravagancies of others. I once intended to have given the Reader a *body of Canons* for literal Criticism, drawn out in form, as well such as concern the Art in general as those that arise from the Nature and Circumstances of our Author's Works in particular. And this for two Reasons. First, To give the *unlearned Reader* a just Idea and consequently a better Opinion of the Art of Criticism, now sunk very low in the popular Esteem by the Attempts of some who would needs exercise it without either natural or acquired Talents; and by the ill Success of others who seemed to have lost both when they came to try them upon English Authors. Secondly, To deter the *unlearned Writer* from wantonly trifling with an Art he is a Stranger to, at the Expence of his own Reputation and the Integrity of the Text of established Authors. But these Uses may be well supplied by what is occasionally said upon the Subject in the Course of the following Remarks.

II. The second sort of Notes consists in an Explanation of the Author's Meaning when, by one or more of these Causes, it becomes obscure: either from a *licentious Use of Terms*; or a *hard or ungrammatical Construction*; or lastly, from *far-fetch'd or quaint Allusions*.

1. This licentious Use of Words is almost peculiar to the Language of *Shakespeare*. To common Terms he hath affixed Meanings of his own, unauthorised by Use and not to be justified by Analogy. And this Liberty he hath taken with the noblest Parts of Speech, such as *Mixed-modes*; which, as they are most susceptible of Abuse so their Abuse most hurts the Clearness of the Discourse. The Critics (to whom *Shakespeare*'s Licence was still as much a Secret as his Meaning which that Licence had obscured) fell into two contrary Mistakes, but equally injurious to his Reputation and his Writings. For some of them, observing a Darkness that pervaded his whole Expression, have censured him for Confusion of Ideas and Inaccuracy of reasoning. *In the Neighing of a Horse* (says *Rymer*), *or in the Growling of a Mastiff there is a Meaning, there is a lively Expression, and, may I say, more Humanity than many times in the tragical Flights of* Shakespeare.[1] The Ignorance of which Censure is of a Piece with its Brutality. The Truth is, no one thought clearer or argued more closely than this immortal Bard. But his Superiority of Genius less needing the Intervention of Words in the

[1] See Vol. 2, p. 30.

Act of Thinking, when he came to draw out his Contemplations into Discourse he took up (as he was hurried on by the Torrent of his Matter) with the first Words that lay in his Way; and if amongst these there were two *Mixed-modes* that had but a principal Idea in common, it was enough for him; he regarded them as synonimous, and would use the one for the other without Fear or Scruple. Again, there have been others, such as the two last Editors, who have fallen into a contrary Extreme; and regarded *Shakespeare's* Anomalies (as we may call them) amongst the Corruptions of his Text, which, therefore, they have cashiered in great Numbers to make room for a Jargon of their own. This hath put me to additional Trouble, for I had not only their Interpolations to throw out again but the genuine Text to replace and establish in its stead; which in many Cases could not be done without shewing the peculiar Sense of the Terms, and explaining the Causes which led the Poet to so perverse a use of them. I had it once, indeed, in my Design to give a general alphabetic *Glossary* of these Terms; but as each of them is explained in its proper Place there seemed the less Occasion for such an Index.

2. The Poet's hard and unnatural Construction had a different Original. This was the Effect of mistaken Art and Design. The Public Taste was in its Infancy; and delighted (as it always does during that State) in the high and turgid; which leads the Writer to disguise a vulgar expression with hard and forced construction, whereby the Sentence frequently becomes cloudy and dark. Here his Critics shew their modesty and leave him to himself. For the arbitrary change of a Word doth little towards dispelling an obscurity that ariseth not from the licentious use of a single Term but from the unnatural arrangement of a whole Sentence. And they risqued nothing by their silence. For *Shakespeare* was too clear in Fame to be suspected of a want of Meaning, and too high in Fashion for any one to own he needed a Critic to find it out. Not but in his best works, we must allow, he is often so natural and flowing, so pure and correct that he is even a model for stile and language.

3. As to his far-fetched and quaint Allusions these are often a cover to common thoughts, just as his hard construction is to common expression. When they are not so the Explanation of them has this further advantage, that in clearing the Obscurity you frequently discover some latent conceit not unworthy of his Genius. (I, xiii–xvii)

★   ★   ★

It seemed not amiss to introduce the following Observations with one general Criticism on our Author's Dramatick Works, by dividing them into four Classes, and so giving an estimate of each Play reduced to its proper Class.

COMEDIES.

Class I.

Tempest; *Merry Wives of Windsor*; *Measure for Measure*; *Merchant of Venice*; *Twelfth Night*.

Class II.

Midsummer Night's Dream; *Much Ado about Nothing*; *As You Like It*; *All's Well That Ends Well*; *Winter's Tale*.

Class III.

Two Gentlemen of Verona; *Love's Labour's Lost*.

Class IV.

Taming of the Shrew; *Comedy of Errors*.

TRAGEDIES.

Class I.

Henry IV. Part 1; *Henry IV. Part 2*; *King Lear*; *Macbeth*; *Julius Cæsar*; *Hamlet*; *Othello*.

Class II.

King John; *Henry V*; *Richard III*; *Henry VIII*; *Timon of Athens*; *Antony and Cleopatra*; *Cymbeline*.

Class III.

Richard II; *Coriolanus*; *Troilus and Cressida*; *Romeo and Juliet*.

Class IV.

Henry VI. Part 1; *Henry VI. Part 2*; *Henry VI. Part 3. Titus Andronicus*.

The Comedies and Tragedies in the last Class are certainly not of *Shakespeare*. The most that can be said of them is that he has here and there corrected the dialogue, and now and then added a Scene. It may be just worth while to observe in this place that the whole first Act of *Fletcher's Two Noble Kinsmen* was wrote by *Shakespeare*, but in his worst manner.

*   *   *

[Headnote to *The Tempest*]

These two first Plays, *The Tempest* and the *Midsummer Night's Dream*, are the noblest Efforts of that sublime and amazing Imagination, peculiar to *Shakespeare*, which soars above the Bounds of Nature without forsaking Sense; or, more properly, carries Nature along with him beyond her established Limits. (I, 3)

*   *   *

[On *The Tempest*, 1.2.321ff.]

> *Cal. As* wicked *dew, as e'er my mother brush'd*
> *With raven's feather from unwholsom fen,*
> *Drop on you both.*

Shakespeare hath very artificially given the air of the antique to the language of *Caliban* in order to heighten the grotesque of his character. As here he uses *wicked* for *unwholsome.* So Sir *John Maundevil*, in his travels *p. 334, Edit. Lond. 1725. at alle tymes brennethe a Vesselle of Cristalle fulle of Bawme for to zeven gode smalle and odour to the Emperour, and to voyden awey alle* WYKKEDE *Eyres and Corrupciouns.* It was a tradition, it seems, that Lord *Falkland*, Lord *C. J. Vaughan*, and Mr. *Selden* concurred in observing that *Shakespeare* had not only found out a new character in his *Caliban* but had also devised and adapted a *new manner of language* for that character. What they meant by it, without doubt, was that *Shakespeare* gave his language a certain grotesque air of the Savage and Antique, which it certainly has. But Dr. *Bentley* took this *of a new language* literally; for speaking of a phrase in *Milton* which he supposed altogether absurd and unmeaning he says *Satan had not the privilege as* Caliban *in* Shakespeare *to use new phrase and diction unknown to all others*—and again—*to practice distances is still a* Caliban *stile.* Note on *Milton's paradise lost*, l. 4. v.945. But I know of no such *Caliban stile* in *Shakespeare* that hath new phrase and diction unknown to all others. (I, 19)

*   *   *

[On *The Tempest*, 1.2.408ff.]

The fringed curtains of thine eyes advance,
And say, what thou seest yond.

The Daughters of *Prospero*, as they are drawn by *Dryden*, seem rather to have had their Education in a Court or a Playhouse than under the severe precepts of a Philosopher in a Desert. But the *Miranda* of *Shakespeare* is truly what the Poet gives her out. And his art in preserving the unity of her character is wonderful. We must remember what was said in the foregoing note of *Prospero*'s intention to make his Daughter fall in love at sight. And notwithstanding what the *wits* may say or the *Pretty-fellows* think on this occasion, it was no such easy matter to bring this naturally about. Those who are the least acquainted with human nature know of what force institution and education are to curb and even deface the very strongest passions and affections. She had been brought up under the rough discipline of stoical Morality, and misfortunes generally harden the morality of virtuous men into Stoicism. Such a one was *Prospero*. And he tells us that his daughter fully answered the care he bestowed upon her. So that there would be some difficulty for nature to regain its influence so suddenly as the Plot required. The Poet, therefore, with infinite address causes her to be softened by the tender story her father told her of his misfortunes. For pity preceeds love, and facilitates its entrance into the mind. But this was evidently insufficient. Therefore, to make the way the easier, she is supposed to be under the influence of her Father's charm, which was to dissolve, as it were, the rigid chains of virtue and obedience. This is insinuated to the Audience when *Prospero*, before he begins his story, says to her,

> *Lend thy hand*
> *And pluck this magick garment from me.*   [1.2.23f.]

The touch communicated the charm, and its efficacy was to lay her to sleep. This is the reason that *Prospero* so often questions her, as he proceeds in his story, whether she was attentive: being apprehensive the charm might operate too quick, even before he had ended his relation. Without this interpretation his frequent repetition will appear extremely cold and absurd. For the same reason, likewise, he says, in conclusion,

> *Thou art inclin'd to sleep. 'Tis a good dulness,*
> *And give it way: I know thou can'st not chuse.*
> [1.2.185-6] (I, 24-5)

*   *   *

[On *The Tempest*, 4.1.68]

Thy POLE-CLIPT *vineyard*,
And thy sea-marge steril, and rocky-hard

Gildon, who has made what he calls a *Glossary* on *Shakespeare*, says—
Pole-clipt—clipt in the head. What he had in his head is not worth in-
quiring. *Clipt* here signifies *embraced*: but *pole-clipt* is a corrupt reading.
It sounded well, because vines are supported by Poles, to say *pole-clipt*
vineyard. And sound was what the Player-Editors only attended to. But
a little sense might have taught them that *vines* could not be called *pole-*
clipt, tho' *Poles* might be called *vine-clipt. Shakespeare* wrote

Thy PALE-CLIPT *Vineyard.*

i. e. the *vineyard* inclosed or fenced with *Pales*, in opposition to the wide
and open *sea-marge* or coast. *Rocky hard* should be read with an hyphen.
It is one of the epithets to *sea-marge: as hard as a rock.* (I, 63–4)

*   *   *

[On *The Tempest*, 5.1.286]

O, touch me not: I am not Stephano, *but a* cramp.

In reading this play I all along suspected that *Shakespeare* had taken it
from some *Italian* writer; the *Unities* being all so regularly observed,
which no dramatic writers but the *Italian* observed so early as our
Author's time, and which *Shakespeare* has observed no where but in
this Play. Besides, the Persons of the Drama are all *Italians.* I was much
confirmed in my Suspicion when I came to this place. It is plain a joke
was intended; but where it lies is hard to say. I suspect there was a
quibble in the Original that would not bear to be translated, which ran
thus, *I am not* Stephano *but* Staffilato. *Staffilato* signifying, in *Italian*, a
man well lashed or flayed, which was the real case of these varlets.

Tooth'd briars, sharp furzes, pricking goss and thorns
Which enter'd their frail Skins.   [4.1.180f.]

And the touching a raw part being very painful he might well cry out
Touch me not, &c. In *Riccoboni*'s Catalogue of *Italian* plays are these, *Il*
Negromante di L. Ariosto, prosa e verso, & Il Negromante Palliato di Gio-
Angelo Petrucci, prosa. But whether the *Tempest* be borrowed from
either of these, not having seen them, I cannot say. (I, 87)

*   *   *

[On *A Midsummer Night's Dream*, 1.1.6]

Long WITHERING OUT *a young Man's revenue*

Long withering out is, certainly, not good *English*. I rather think *Shakespeare* wrote, *Long* WINTERING ON *a young man's revenue*. (I, 93)

★   ★   ★

[On *A Midsummer Night's Dream*, 2.1.101]

The human mortals want their winter HERE.

But sure it was not one of the circumstances of misery, here recapitulated, that the Sufferers wanted their *Winter*. On the contrary, in the poetical descriptions of the golden Age it was always one circumstance of their happiness that they wanted Winter. This is an idle blunder of the Editor's. *Shakespeare* without question wrote,

The human mortals want their winter HERYED,

i. e. praised, celebrated. The word is obsolete, but used both by *Chaucer* and *Spenser* in this signification:

Tho' wouldest thou learne to CAROLL *of love,*
And HERY *with* HYMNES *thy Lasse's glove.*
Spens. Cal. Feb. [61f.]

The following line confirms the emendation,

No night is now with Hymn *or* Carol *blest*;

and the propriety of the sentiment is evident. For the winter is the season of rural rejoicing, as the gloominess of it and its vacancy from country labours give them the *inclination and opportunity* for mirth; and the fruits, now gathered in, the *means*. Well therefore might she say, when she had described the dearths of the seasons and fruitless toil of the husbandmen, that

The human mortals want their winter heryed.

But, principally, since the coming of Christianity this season in commemoration of the birth of Christ has been particularly devoted to festivity. And to this custom, notwithstanding the impropriety, *Hymn or Carol blest* certainly alludes. Mr. *Theobald* says, *he should undoubtedly have advanced this conjecture unto the text, but that* Shakespeare *seems rather fond of hallow'd. Rather* than what? *hallowed* is not synonymous to *heryed* but to *blest*. What was he thinking of? The ambiguity of the *English* word *blest* confounded him, which signifies either *prais'd* or *sanctified*. (I, 110–11)

*   *   *

[On *A Midsummer Night's Dream*, 2.1.111ff.]

> *The Spring, the Summer,*
> *The childing Autumn, angry winter change*
> *Their wonted* Liveries; *and th' amazed World*
> *By their* INCREASE *now knows not which is which.*

Whose increase? or what increase?—Let us attend to the Sentiment. Spring, Summer, Autumn and Winter change their *Liveries*, i.e., Spring and Summer are unseasonably cold and Autumn and Winter unnaturally warm. This temperature he calls the *Liveries* or the covering of the Seasons. Which, he says, confounds the amazed world, that now knows not which is which. This being owing then to the Seasons changing their garb the last line was doubtless wrote thus,

> *By their* INCHASE *now knows not which is which.*

i.e. by the temperature in which they are *set*. The metaphor before was taken from *Clothing*, here from *Jewels*. *Inchase* coming from the *French*, *Enchasseure*, a term in use amongst Goldsmiths for the setting a stone in Gold.

The CHIDING *Autumn.*

The Quarto of 1600 and the Folio of 1623 read CHILDING, and this is right. It is an old word which signified teeming, bearing fruit. So *Chaucer*, in his *Ballade of our Ladie*, says,

> *Chosin of* Joseph, *whom he toke to wive,*
> *Unknowyng hym,* CHILDING *by miracle*

This is the proper epithet of Autumn, and not *chiding*. (I, 111)

*   *   *

[On *The Two Gentlemen of Verona*, 3.2.78]

> *For* Orpheus' *lute was strung with* poet's *sinews.*

This shews *Shakespeare*'s knowledge of antiquity. He here assigns *Orpheus* his true character of legislator. For under that of a poet only, or lover, the quality given to his lute is unintelligible. But considered as a lawgiver the thought is noble, and the imag'ry exquisitely beautiful. For by his *lute* is to be understood his *system of laws*: and by the *poet's sinews* the power of numbers, which *Orpheus* actually employed in those laws to make them received by a fierce and barbarous people. (I, 223)

* * *

[On *The Merry Wives of Windsor*, 2.1.129]

I will not believe such a Cataian.

Mr. *Theobald* has here a pleasant note, as usual. *This is a piece of satire that did not want its force at the time of this play's appearing; tho' the history on which it is grounded is become obsolete.* And then tells a long story of *Martin Frobisher* attempting the north-west passage, and bringing home a black stone, as he thought, rich in gold-ore: that it proved not so, and that therefore *Cataians* and *Frobishers* became by-words for vain boasters. The whole is an idle dream. All the mystery of the term *Cataian*, for a liar, is only this. *China* was anciently called *Cataia* or *Cathay* by the first adventurers that travelled thither; such as *M. Paulo*, and our *Mandeville*, who told such incredible wonders of this new discovered empire (in which they have not been outdone even by the *Jesuits* themselves, who followed them) that a notorious liar was usually called a *Cataian*. (I, 276)

* * *

[On *The Merry Wives of Windsor*, 3.3.18]

How now, my Eyas-musket.

Eyas is a young unfledg'd hawk, I suppose from the Italian *Niaso*, which originally signified any young bird taken from the nest unfledg'd, afterwards, a young hawk. The *French* from hence took their *niais*, and used it in both those significations; to which they added a third, metaphorically *a silly fellow; un garçon fort niais, un niais. Musket* signifies a *sparrow hawk*, or the smallest species of hawks. This too is from the Italian *Muschetto*, a small hawk, as appears from the original signification of the word, namely, *a troublesome stinging fly.* So that the humour of calling the little page an *Eyas-musket* is very intelligible. (I, 302)

* * *

[On *Measure for Measure*, 3.1.95ff.]

The PRINCELY *Angelo?*—PRINCELY *guards.*

The stupid Editors mistaking *guards* for satellites (whereas it here signifies *lace*) altered PRIESTLY, in both places, to PRINCELY. Whereas
Shakespeare wrote it PRIESTLY, as appears from the words themselves,

> *'tis the cunning* livery *of hell.*
> *The damned'st body to invest and cover*
> *With* PRIESTLY *guards.*

In the first place we see that *guards* here signifies *lace*, as referring to
livery, and as having no sense in the signification of *satellites*. Now
priestly guards means *sanctity*, which is the sense required. But *princely
guards* means nothing but *rich lace*, which is a sense the passage will not
bear. *Angelo*, indeed, as *Deputy*, might be called the *princely Angelo*:
but not in this place, where the immediately preceding words of *This
outward sainted Deputy* demand the reading I have here restored.
(I, 402–3)

*   *   *

[On *Much Ado About Nothing*, 5.1.80]

Ant. He shall kill two of us, &c.

This *Brother Anthony* is the truest picture imaginable of human nature.
He had assumed the Character of a Sage to comfort his Brother,
o'erwhelm'd with grief for his only daughter's affront and dishonour;
and had severely reproved him for not commanding his passion better
on so trying an occasion. Yet, immediately after this, no sooner does
he begin to suspect that his *Age* and *Valour* are slighted but he falls into
the most intemperate fit of rage himself: and all his Brother can do or
say is not of power to pacify him. This is copying nature with a
penetration and exactness of Judgment peculiar to *Shakespeare*. As to
the expression, too, of his passion, nothing can be more highly painted.
(II, 76)

*   *   *

[On *The Merchant of Venice*, 5.1.59]

. . . *with* PATTERNS *of bright gold*

We should read PATENS: a round broad plate of gold born in heraldry;
the cover of the sacramental-cup. (II, 177)

*   *   *

[On *As You Like It*, 5.4.85ff.]

O Sir, we quarrel in print, by the book.

The Poet has, in this scene, rallied the mode of formal dueling then so prevalent with the highest humour and address; nor could he have treated it with a happier contempt than by making his *Clown* so knowing in the forms and preliminaries of it. The particular book here alluded to is a very ridiculous treatise of one *Vincentio Saviolo*, intitled *Of honour and honourable quarrels*, in Quarto printed by *Wolf*, 1594. The first part of this tract he intitles *A discourse most necessary for all gentlemen that have in regard their honors, touching the giving and receiving the lye, whereupon the* Duello *and the* Combat *in divers forms doth ensue; and many other inconveniences, for lack only of true knowledge of honor, and the* RIGHT UNDERSTANDING OF WORDS, *which here is set down.* The contents of the several chapters are as follows: I. *What the reason is that the party unto whom the lye is given ought to become challenger, and of the nature of lies.* II. *Of the manner and diversity of lies.* III. *Of the lye certain,* or direct. IV. *Of conditional lies,* or the lye circumstantial. V. *Of the lye in general.* VI. *Of the lye in particular.* VII. *Of foolish lies.* VIII. *A conclusion touching the wresting or returning back of the lye,* or the countercheck quarrelsome. In the chapter of *conditional lies* speaking of the particle IF, he says— *Conditional lies be such as are given conditionally thus*—IF *thou hast said so or so, then thou liest. Of these kind of lies, given in this manner, often arise much contention, whereof no sure conclusion can arise.* By which he means, they cannot proceed to cut one another's throats while there is an IF between. Which is the reason of *Shakespeare's* making the *Clown* say, *I knew when seven justices could not make up a quarrel: but when the parties were met themselves, one of them thought but of an* IF, *as if you said so, then I said so, and they shook hands, and swore brothers. Your* IF *is the only peacemaker; much virtue in* IF. *Caranza* was another of these authentick Authors upon the *Duello. Fletcher* in his last Act of *Love's Pilgrimage* ridicules him with much humour. (II, 381–2)

*   *   *

[On *All's Well That Ends Well*, 1.3.11f.]

you lack not folly to commit *them, and have ability enough to make such knaveries* YOURS.

Well, but if he had folly to *commit* them he neither wanted knavery nor any thing else, sure, to *make* them *his own.* This nonsense should be read, *To make such knaveries* YARE; nimble, dextrous, *i.e.*, tho' you be fool enough to commit knaveries yet you have quickness enough to commit them dextrously: for this observation was to let us into his character. But now, tho' this be set right, and, I dare say, in *Shakespeare*'s own words, yet the former part of the sentence will still be inaccurate—*you lack not folly to commit* THEM. Them, what? the sense requires *knaveries*, but the antecedent referr'd to is *complaints*. But this was certainly a negligence of *Shakespeare*'s, and therefore to be left as we find it. And the reader who cannot see that this is an inaccuracy which the Author might well commit, and the other what he never could, has either read *Shakespeare* very little, or greatly mispent his pains. The principal office of a critick is to distinguish between these two things. But 'tis that branch of criticism which no precepts can teach the writer to discharge, or the reader to judge of. (III, 16–17)

*   *   *

[On All's Well That Ends Well, 2.3.129ff.]

> *She is* YOUNG, *wise, fair;*
> *In these, to nature she's immediate heir;*
> *And these breed honour;*

The objection was, that *Helen* had neither riches nor title. To this the King replies, she's *the* immediate heir of nature, from whom she inherits youth, wisdom, and beauty. The thought is fine. For by the *immediate* heir to nature we must understand one who inherits wisdom and beauty in a supreme degree. From hence it appears that *young* is a faulty reading, for that does not, like wisdom and beauty, admit of different degrees of excellence; therefore she could not, with regard to *that*, be said to be the *immediate* heir of nature, for in *that* she was only joint-heir with all the rest of her species. Besides, tho' *wisdom* and *beauty* may *breed honour*, yet *youth* cannot be said to do so. On the contrary, it is *age* which has this advantage. It seems probable that some foolish player when he transcribed this part—not apprehending the thought, and wondring to find *youth* not reckoned amongst the good qualities of a woman when she was proposed to a lord, and not considering that it was comprised in the word *fair*—foisted in *young* to the exclusion of a word much more to the purpose. For I make no question but *Shakespeare* wrote,

She is GOOD, wise, fair.

235

For the greatest part of her encomium turned upon her virtue. To omit this therefore in the recapitulation of her qualities had been against all the rules of good speaking. Nor let it be objected that this is requiring an exactness in our author which we should not expect. For he who could reason with the force our author doth here (and we ought always to distinguish between *Shakespeare* on his guard and in his rambles) and illustrate that reasoning with such beauty of thought and propriety of expression, could never make use of a word which quite destroyed the exactness of his reasoning, the propriety of his thought, and the elegance of his expression. (III, 42–3)

*   *   *

[On *All's Well That Ends Well* 3.6.66]

I will presently pen down my Dilemmas,

By this word *Parolles* is made to insinuate that he had several ways, all equally certain, of recovering this Drum. For a *Dilemma* is an argument that concludes both ways. (III, 71)

*   *   *

[Headnote to *The Winter's Tale*]

This play throughout is written in the very spirit of its author. And in telling this homely and simple, tho' agreeable, country tale,

> *Our sweetest* Shakespeare, *fancy's child,*
> *Warbles his native wood notes wild.*   Milton.

This was necessary to observe in mere justice to the Play, as the meanness of the fable and the extravagant conduct of it had misled some of great name into a wrong judgment of its merit; which, as far as it regards sentiment and character, is scarce inferior to any in the whole collection. (III, 277)

*   *   *

[On *The Winter's Tale*, 1.2.202ff.]

'tis powerful: think it.

After this there are four lines of infamous, senseless ribaldry stuck in by some profligate player, which I have cashier'd; and hope no learned critick or fine lady will esteem this a castrated edition for our having now and then on the same necessity, and after having given fair notice, taken the same liberty. (III, 287)

* * *

[On *The Winter's Tale*, 5.2.79ff.]

which angled for mine eyes, [caught the water, tho' not the fish,] was, &c.

I dare pronounce what is here in hooks a most stupid interpolation of some player that angled for a witticism; and therefore have struck it out of the text. (III, 376)

* * *

[On *Henry IV, Part 1*, 1.1.6]

Shall damp her lips

This nonsense should be read, *Shall* TREMPE, *i.e.* moisten, and refers to thirsty in the preceding line. *Trempe*, from the *French*, *tremper*, properly signifies the moistness made by rain. (IV, 97)

* * *

[On *Henry IV, Part 1*, 1.3.201ff.]

By heav'n, methinks, &c.

Gildon, a critic of the size of *Dennis* &c., calls this speech, without any ceremony, *a ridiculous rant and absolute madness.* Mr. *Theobald* talks in the same strain. The *French* critics had taught these people just enough to understand where *Shakespeare* had transgressed the rules of the *Greek* tragic writers; and on those occasions they are full of the poor frigid cant of *fable, sentiment, diction, unities,* &c. But it is another thing to get to *Shakespeare's* sense: to do this required a little of their own. For want of which they could not see that the poet here uses an allegorical covering to express a noble and very natural thought.—*Hotspur*, all on fire, exclaims against *huckstering* and *bartering* for honour, and dividing it into shares. O! says he, could I be sure that when I had purchased honour I should wear her dignities without a Rival—what then? why then,

237

By heav'n methinks, it were an easie leap,
To pluck bright Honour from the pale-fac'd Moon:

i.e., tho' some great and shining character in the most elevated orb was already in possession of her yet it would, methinks, be easy by greater acts to eclipse his glory and pluck all his honours from him;

Or dive into the bottom of the deep,
And pluck up drowned honour by the locks:

i.e., or what is still more difficult, tho' there were in the world no great examples to incite and fire my emulation, but that honour was quite sunk and buried in oblivion, yet would I bring it back into vogue and render it more illustrious than ever. So that we see, tho' the expression be sublime and daring, yet the thought is the natural movement of an heroic mind. *Euripides* at least thought so, when he put the very same sentiment, in the same words, into the mouth of *Eteocles—I will not, madam, disguise my thoughts; I could scale heaven, I could descend to the very entrails of the earth, if so be that by that price I could obtain a kingdom.* (IV, 116)

*   *   *

[On *Henry IV, Part 2*, 4.5.129]

England *shall double gild his treble Guilt*;

Evidently the nonsense of some foolish Player, for we must make a difference between what *Shakespeare* might be suppos'd to have written off hand, and what he had corrected. These Scenes are of the latter kind; therefore such lines by no means to be esteemed his. But except Mr. *Pope* (who judiciously threw out this line) not one of *Shakespeare*'s Editors seem ever to have had so reasonable and necessary a rule in their heads when they set upon correcting this author. (IV, 291)

*   *   *

[On *Henry VI, Part 1*, 2.5.122]

Here DIES *the dusky torch—*

The image is of a torch just extinguished and yet smoking. But we should read LIES instead of DIES. For when a dead man is represented by an extinguished torch we must say the *torch lies*: when an extinguished torch is compared to a dead man we must say the *torch dies*. The reason is plain, because integrity of metaphor requires that the terms proper to the thing *illustrating*, not the thing *illustrated*, be employed. (IV, 472)

*   *   *

[On *King Lear*, 1.2.3]

Stand in the PLAGUE *of custom,*

To stand in the plague of custom, is an absurd expression. We should read,

Stand in the PLAGE *of custom,*

i.e. the place, the country, the boundary of custom. As much as to say, Why should I, when I profess to follow the freedom of *nature* in all things, be confined within the narrow limits of custom? *Plage* is a word in common use amongst the old *English* writers. So *Chaucer*,

The PLAGIS *of the North by land and sea.*
from *plaga*. (VI, 15)

*   *   *

[On *King Lear*, 2.4.255f.]

Those WICKED *creatures yet do look well-favour'd,*
When others are more WICKED.

As a little before in the text [*like flatterers*] the editors had made a similitude where the author intended none so here, where he did, they are not in the humour to give it us, because not introduced with the formulary word *like*. *Lear's* second daughter proving still more unkind than the first, he begins to entertain a better opinion of this, from the other's greater degree of inhumanity; and expresses it by a similitude taken from the deformities which old age brings on.

Those WRINKLED *creatures yet do look* well-favour'd,
When others are more WRINKLED:

For so, instead of *wicked*, it should be read in both places: which correction the word *well-favour'd* might have led to. *Lear* considers the unnatural behaviour of his daughters under this idea, both in and out of his senses. So again, speaking of them in his distraction, he says *And here's another whose* WARPT *looks proclaim what store her heart is made of.* *Shakespeare* has the character of a very incorrect writer, and so indeed he is. But this character being received, as well as given, in the lump has made him thought an unfit subject for critical conjecture: which perhaps may be true with regard to those who know no more of his genius than a general character of it conveys to them. But we should distinguish. Incorrectness of stile may be divided into two parts: an inconsistency of the terms employed with one another; and an incongruity in the construction of them. In the first case he is rarely faulty; in the second negligent enough. And this could hardly be otherwise. For his ideas being the clearest, and his penetration in discovering their agreement, disagreement, and relation to each other the deepest that ever was in any Poet, his terms of course must be well put together: nothing occasioning the jumbling of discordant terms, from broken metaphors, but the cloudiness of the understanding and the consequent obscurity of the ideas, terms being nothing but the painting of ideas, which he who sees clearly will never employ in a discordant colouring. On the contrary, a *congruity* in the construction of these terms (which answers to *drawing*, as the use of the terms does to *colouring*) is another thing. And *Shakespeare*, who owed all to nature, and was hurried on by a warm attention to his ideas, was much less exact in the construction and grammatical arrangement of his words. The conclusion is that where we find gross inaccuracies in the relation of terms to one another there we may be confident, the text has been corrupted by his editors: and, on the contrary, that the offences against syntax are generally his own. Had the *Oxford Editor* attended to this distinction he would not perhaps have made it the principal object in *his restored Shakespeare* to make his author always speak in strict grammar and measure. But it is much easier to reform such slips as never obscure the sense and are set right by a grammar-rule or a finger-end, than to reduce a depraved expression which makes nonsense of a whole sentence, and whose reformation requires you to enter into the author's way of thinking. (VI, 66-7)

*   *   *

[On *Macbeth*, 1.3.137f.]

present fears
Are less than horrible Imaginings.

Macbeth, while he is projecting the murder which he afterwards puts in execution, is thrown into the most agonizing affright at the prospect of it: which, soon recovering from, thus he reasons on the nature of his disorder. But *Imaginings* are so far from being more or less than *present*

Fears, that they are the same things under different words. *Shakespeare* certainly wrote

present FEATS

Are less than horrible imaginings.

i.e., when I come to execute this murder, I shall find it much less dreadful than my frighted imagination now presents it to me. A consideration drawn from the nature of the *imagination*.

Is smother'd in surmise;

Surmise, for contemplation.

and nothing is,

But what is not.

i.e. I can give no attention to any thing but to the future prospect of the crown.

Time and the hour

Time is painted with an hour-glass in his hand. This occasioned the expression. (VI, 343)

*   *   *

[On *Macbeth*, 2.2.38]

The DEATH *of each day's life, sore labour's bath,* &c.

In this encomium upon sleep, amongst the many appellations which are given it, significant of its benificence and friendliness to life, we find one which conveys a different idea and by no means agrees with the rest, which is:

The Death *of each day's life,*

I make no question but *Shakespeare* wrote,

The birth *of each day's life,*

the true characteristic of sleep, which repairs the decays of labour and assists that returning vigour which supplies the next day's activity. The Player-Editors seem to have corrupted it for the sake of a silly gingle between *life* and *death*. (VI, 361)

*   *   *

241

[On *Macbeth*, 2.3.86]

What, in our house?

This is very fine. Had she been innocent, nothing but the murder itself and not any of its aggravating circumstances would naturally have affected her. As it was, her business was to appear highly disorder'd at the news. Therefore, like one who has her thoughts about her, she seeks for an aggravating circumstance that might be supposed most to affect her personally; not considering that by placing it there she discovered rather a concern for herself than for the King. On the contrary her husband, who had repented the act and was now labouring under the horrors of a recent murder, in his exclamation gives all the marks of sorrow for the fact itself. (VI, 367)

*   *   *

[On *Macbeth*, 2.3.111]

His silver *skin* laced *with his* golden *blood,*

The allusion is so ridiculous on such an occasion that it discovers the declaimer not to be affected in the manner he would represent himself. The whole speech is an unnatural mixture of far-fetch'd and commonplace thoughts, that shews him to be acting a part. (VI, 368)

*   *   *

[On *Macbeth*, 2.4.6]

Threaten this bloody stage:

One might be tempted to think the poet wrote *strage*, slaughter. But I, who know him better, am persuaded he used *stage* for *act*. And because stage may be figuratively used for *act*, a dramatic representation, therefore he uses it for *act*, a deed done. Threatens a tragedy. (VI, 370)

*   *   *

[On *Macbeth*, 3.2.50]

LIGHT *thickens,*

Either the poet or his editors were out in their philosophy: for the more *light* thickens or condenses the brighter it is. I should think the poet wrote

NIGHT *thickens.*

Tho, by *thickens*, in his licentious *English*, he might mean grows muddy, and take his idea from a clear transparent liquor's turning thick by the infusion of an inky substance into it. (VI, 380–1)

*   *   *

[On *Macbeth*, 5.2.22f.]

> *my* way *of life*
> *Is fall'n into the Sear,*

An *Anonymus* would have it [p. 181 above],

> *my* May *of life:*

But he did not consider that *Macbeth* is not here speaking of his *rule* or government or of any sudden change, but of the gradual decline of life, as appears from this line,

> *And that, which should accompany* old age.

And *way*, is used for course, progress. (VI, 417)

*   *   *

[On *Coriolanus*, 2.1.166]

> *My gracious silence, hail!*

The epithet to *silence* shews it not to proceed from reserve or sullenness but to be the effect of a virtuous mind possessing itself in peace. The expression is extremely sublime; and the sense of it conveys the finest praise that can be given to a good woman. (VI, 468)

*   *   *

[On *Coriolanus*, 2.2.132f.]

> *It then remains,*
> *That you* do speak to th' People.

Coriolanus was banished U.C. 262. But till the time of *Manlius Torquatus* U.C. 393, the Senate chose *both* the Consuls; and then the people, assisted by the seditious temper of the Tribunes, got the choice of one. But if he makes *Rome* a Democracy, which at this time was a perfect Aristocracy, he sets the balance even in his *Timon*, and turns *Athens*, which was a perfect Democracy, into an Aristocracy. But it would be unjust to attribute this entirely to his ignorance; it sometimes proceded from the too powerful blaze of his imagination, which when once lighted up made all acquired knowledge fade and disappear before it. For sometimes again we find him, when occasion serves, not only writing up to the truth of history, but fitting his sentiments to the nicest manners of his peculiar subject as well to the *dignity* of his characters, or the *dictates* of nature in general. (VI, 477)

*　　*　　*

[On *Julius Caesar*, 3.2.13ff.]

Countrymen and Lovers! &c.

There is no where, in all *Shakespeare*'s works, a stronger proof of his not being what we call a scholar than this; or of his not knowing any thing of the genius of learned antiquity. This speech of *Brutus* is wrote in imitation of his famed laconic brevity, and is very fine in its kind, but no more like that brevity than his times were like *Brutus*'s. The ancient laconic brevity was simple, natural and easy; this is quaint, artificial, gingling, and abounding with forced antithesis's. In a word, a brevity that for its false eloquence would have suited any character, and for its good sense would have become the greatest of our author's time; but yet in a stile of declaiming that sits as ill upon *Brutus* as our author's trowsers or collar-band would have done. (VII, 55)

*　　*　　*

[On *Antony and Cleopatra*, 1.2.30]

Char. *Oh, excellent! I love long life better than figs.*

Here *Shakespeare* has copied ancient manners with as much beauty as propriety, this being one of those *ominous* speeches in which the ancients were so superstitious: for the aspicks, by which *Charmian* died, and after her mistress, were conveyed in a basket *of figs*. Omens (a superstition which *Pythagoras* first taught the Greeks) were the undesigned consequence of words casually spoken. The words were sometimes taken from the speaker, and applied by the hearers to the speaker's own affairs, as in the case of *Paulus Æmilius*, after his conquest of *Macedon*. Sometimes again the words of the speaker were transferred to the affairs of the hearer, as in the case of the same *Paulus* before his conquest of *Macedon. Itaque rebus divinis quæ publicè fierent, ut faverent linguis, imperabatur.* Cicero de Divin. l. 1.[1] (VII, 101)

★   ★   ★

[On *Antony and Cleopatra*, 1.2.106]

When our quick WINDS *lye still;*

We should read MINDS. The *m* was accidentally turn'd the wrong way at the press. The sense is this, *While the active principle within us lies immerged in sloth and luxury, we bring forth vices instead of virtues, weeds instead of flowers and fruits: But the laying before us our ill condition plainly and honestly is, as it were, the first culture of the mind, which gives hopes of a future harvest.* This he says to encourage the messenger to hide nothing from him. (VII, 104)

★   ★   ★

[On *Antony and Cleopatra*, 4.12.20f.]

The hearts
That PANNELL'D *me at heels, &c.*

Pannelling at heels must mean here, *following*: but where was the word ever found in such a sense? *Pannel* signifies but three things that I know in the *English* tongue, none of which will suit with the allusions here requisite; *viz.* That roll or schedule of parchment on which the names of a Jury are enter'd, which therefore is call'd *empannelling*; a pane or slip of wainscot; and a packsaddle for beasts of burden. The text is corrupt, and *Shakespeare* must certainly have wrote;

That PANTLER'D *me at heels;*

i.e. run after me like footmen, or *pantlers*; which word originally signified the servants who have the care of the bread, but is used by our poet for a menial servant in general, as well as in its native acceptation.

Thus in *Cymbeline*,

A hilding for a liv'ry, a Squire's cloth,
A PANTLER;   [2.3.123f.]

---

[1] 1.45.102: 'At public celebrations of religious rites they gave the command, "Guard your tongues." '

And *Timon* [4.3.223f.],

> *page thy heels,*
> *And skip when thou point'st out.*

(VII, 193-4)

★ ★ ★

[On *Cymbeline*, 3.4.48]

Whose MOTHER *was her painting*

This puzzles Mr. *Theobald* much: he thinks it may signify *whose mother was a bird of the same feather*; or that it should be read, *whose mother was her planting*. What all this means I know not. In Mr. *Rowe*'s edition the *M* in mother happening to be reversed at the press, it came out *Wother*. And what was very ridiculous, *Gildon* employed himself (properly enough indeed) in finding a meaning for it. In short, the true word is MEETHER, a north country word signifying *beauty*. So that the sense of *her meether was her painting* is that she had only an appearance of beauty, for which she was beholden to her paint. (VII, 290-1)

★ ★ ★

[On *Troilus and Cressida*, 5.2.142ff.]

> *where reason can revolt*
> *Without perdition, and loss assume all reason*
> *Without revolt.*

A miserable expression of a quaint thought, *That to be unreasonable in love is reasonable; and to be reasonable, unreasonable. Perdition* and *loss* are both used in the very same sense, and that an odd one, to signify *unreasonableness.* (VII, 473)

★ ★ ★

[On *Romeo and Juliet*, 3.2.76ff.]

Ravenous Dove, feather'd Raven, &c.

'The four following lines not in the first Edition, as well as some others which I have omitted.'   Mr. *Pope.*

He might as well have omitted these, they being evidently the

Players trash, and as such I have marked them with a note of reproba-
tion. (VII, 64)

★   ★   ★

[On *Hamlet*, 1.3.79]

And it must follow, as the NIGHT *the Day,*

The sense here requires that the similitude should give an image not of
two effects of different natures that follow one another alternately, but of
a *cause and effect*, where the effect follows the cause by a *physical necessity*.
For the assertion is, Be true to thyself and then thou must *necessarily* be
true to others. Truth to himself then was the *cause*, truth to others the
effect. To illustrate this necessity, the speaker employs a similitude: but
no similitude can illustrate it but what presents an image of a *cause* and
effect; and such a cause as that where the effect follows by a *physical*, not
a *moral* necessity: for if only by a *moral* necessity the thing *illustrating*
would not be more certain than the thing *illustrated*; which would be a
great absurdity. This being premised, let us see what the text says,

And it must follow as the night *the Day.*

In this we are so far from being presented with an *effect* following a
cause by a physical necessity that there is no cause at all, but only two
different effects, proceeding from two different causes and succeeding
one another alternately. *Shakespeare* therefore, without question wrote

And it must follow as the LIGHT *the Day.*

As much as to say, Truth to thy self, and truth to others, are inseparable,
the latter depending necessarily on the former, as *light depends upon the
day!* where it is to be observed that *day* is used figuratively for the *Sun*.
The ignorance of which, I suppose, contributed to mislead the editors.
(VIII, 137)

★   ★   ★

[On *Hamlet*, 2.2.86ff.]

My Liege, and Madam, to expostulate

The strokes of humour in this speech are admirable. *Polonius*'s character
is that of a weak, pedant, minister of state. His declamation is a fine
satire on the impertinent oratory then in vogue, which placed reason in

the formality of method, and wit in the gingle and play of words. With what art is he made to pride himself in his *wit*:

> That he is mad, 'tis true; 'tis true, 'tis pity;
> And pity 'tis, 'tis true; A foolish figure;
> But farewel it.

And how exquisitely does the poet ridicule the *reasoning in fashion* where he makes *Polonius* remark on *Hamlet's* madness;

> *Though this be* madness, *yet there's* method *in't:*

As if method, which the wits of that age thought the most essential quality of a good discourse, would make amends for the madness. It was *madness* indeed, yet *Polonius* could comfort himself with this reflexion, that at least it was *method*. It is certain *Shakespeare* excels in nothing more than in the preservation of his characters. *To this life and variety of character* (says our great poet in his admirable preface to *Shakespeare*) *we must add the wonderful preservation of it.*[1] We have said what is the character of *Polonius*; and it is allowed on all hands to be drawn with wonderful life and spirit. Yet the *unity* of it has been thought by some to be grosly violated in the excellent *Precepts* and *Instructions* which *Shakespeare* makes his statesman give to his son and servant in the middle of the *first*, and beginning of the *second act*. But I will venture to say, these criticks have not entered into the poet's art and address in this particular. He had a mind to ornament his scenes with those fine lessons of social life; but his *Polonius* was too weak to be the author of them, tho' he was pedant enough to have met with them in his reading, and fop enough to get them by heart and retail them for his own. And this the poet has finely shewn us was the case where, in the middle of *Polonius's* instructions to his servant, he makes him, tho' without having received any interruption, forget his lesson and say

> And then, Sir, does he this;
> He does—what was I about to say?
> I was about to say something—where did I leave?

The servant replies,

> *At*, closes in the consequence.

This sets *Polonius* right, and he goes on,

> *At*, closes in the consequence—*Ay marry*,
> He closes thus;—I know the gentleman, *&c.*

[1] Pope: see Vol. 2, p. 404.

which shews they were words got by heart which he was repeating. Otherwise *closes in the consequence*, which conveys no particular idea of the subject he was upon, could never have made him recollect where he broke off. This is an extraordinary instance of the poet's art, and attention to the preservation of Character. (VIII, 160–1)

*   *   *

[On *Hamlet*, 2.2.145ff.]

a short tale to make,
Fell to a sadness, then into a fast, &c.

The ridicule of this character is here admirably sustained. He would not only be thought to have discovered this intrigue by his own sagacity but to have remarked all the stages of *Hamlet's* disorder, from his sadness to his raving, as regularly as his physician could have done; when all the while the madness was only feigned. The humour of this is exquisite from a man who tells us, with a confidence peculiar to small politicians, that he could find

Where truth was hid, though it were hid indeed
Within the centre.   (VIII, 164)

*   *   *

[On *Hamlet*, 2.2.180ff.]

For if the Sun breed maggots in a dead dog,
Being a GOOD *kissing carrion—*
Have you a daughter?

The Editors, seeing *Hamlet* counterfeit madness, thought they might safely put any nonsense into his mouth. But this strange passage, when set right, will be seen to contain as great and sublime a reflexion as any the poet puts into his Hero's mouth throughout the whole play. We shall first give the true reading, which is this,

For if the Sun breed maggots in a dead dog
Being a God, *kissing carrion*

As to the sense we may observe that the illative particle, *for*, shews the speaker to be reasoning from something he had said before: what that was we learn in these words, *to be honest, as this world goes, is to be one picked out of ten thousand.* Having said this, the chain of ideas led him to reflect upon the argument which libertines bring against Providence from the circumstance of abounding *Evil*. In the next speech, therefore, he endeavours to answer that objection and vindicate Providence, even on a supposition of the fact that almost all men were wicked. His argument in the two lines in question is to this purpose, *But why need we wonder at this abounding of evil? for if the Sun breed maggots in a dead dog, which tho' a God, yet shedding its heat and influence upon carrion*—Here he stops short, lest talking too consequentially the hearer should suspect his madness to be feigned; and so turns him off from the subject by enquiring of his daughter. But the inference which he intended to make was a very noble one, and to this purpose: If this (says he) be the case, that the effect follows the thing operated upon (*carrion*) and not the thing operating (a *God*;) why need we wonder that the supreme cause of all things diffusing its blessings on mankind, who is, as it were, a dead carrion, dead in original sin, man, instead of a proper return of duty, should breed only corruption and vices? This is the argument at length, and is as noble a one in behalf of providence as could come from the schools of divinity. But this wonderful man had an art not only of acquainting the audience with what his actors *say* but with what they *think*. The sentiment too is altogether in character, for *Hamlet* is perpetually moralizing, and his circumstances make this reflexion very natural. The same *thought*, something diversified, as on a different occasion, he uses again in *Measure for Measure*, which will serve to confirm these observations:

> The tempter or the tempted, who sins most?
> Not she; nor doth she tempt; but it is I
> That lying by the violet in the sun
> Do as the carrion does, not as the flower,
> Corrupt by virtuous season.   [2.2.163ff.]

And the same kind of *expression* in *Cymbeline*,

> Common-kissing Titan.   [3.4.162] (VIII, 165–6)

*   *   *

[On *Hamlet*, 3.2.125]

nay, then let the Devil wear black, FOR *I'll have a suit of sables.*

The conceit of these words is not taken. They are an ironical apology for his mother's chearful looks: two months was long enough in conscience to make any dead husband forgotten. But the editors, in their nonsensical blunder, have made *Hamlet* say just the contrary, that the Devil and he would both go into mourning tho' his mother did not. The true reading is this, *Nay, then let the Devil wear black,* 'FORE *I'll have a suit of sable.* 'Fore i.e. before. As much as to say, Let the Devil wear black for me, I'll have none. The *Oxford Editor* despises an emendation so easy, and reads it thus, *Nay, then let the Devil wear black, for I'll have a suit of* ERMINE. And you could expect no less when such a critic had the dressing of him. But the blunder was a pleasant one. The senseless editors had wrote *sables,* the fur so called, for *sable,* black, And the critic only changed this fur for that; by a like figure, the common people say, *You rejoice the cockles of my heart,* for *the muscles of my heart;* an unlucky mistake of one shell-fish for another. (VIII, 191)

★   ★   ★

[On Hamlet, 5.1.10f.]

> *an act hath three branches; it is to act, to do, and to perform;*

Ridicule on scholastic divisions without distinction; and of distinctions without difference. (VIII, 241)

★   ★   ★

[On Hamlet, 5.2.41f.]

> *As peace should still her wheaten garland wear,*
> *And stand a* COMMA *'tween their amities;*

Peace is here properly and finely personalized as the Goddess of good league and friendship; and very classically dress'd out. . . . But the placing her as a *Comma,* or stop, between the *amities* of two Kingdoms makes her rather stand like a cypher. The poet without doubt wrote

And stand a COMMERE 'tween our amities.

The term is taken from a traficker in love who brings people together, a procuress. And this Idea is well appropriated to the satirical turn which the speaker gives to this wicked adjuration of the King, who would lay the foundation of the peace of the two kingdoms in the blood of the heir of one of them. *Periers* in his Novels uses the word *Commere* to signify a she-friend. *A tous ses gens, chacun une* Commere. And *Ben Jonson,* in his *Devil's an Ass,* englishes the word by a *middling Gossip.*

251

Or what do you say to a middling Gossip
To bring you together.   (VIII, 253)

*   *   *

[On *Hamlet*, 2.2.446ff.]

The rugged Pyrrhus, *he* &c.

The two greatest Poets of this and the last age, Mr. *Dryden*, in the preface to *Troilus and Cressida*,[1] and Mr. *Pope*, in his note on this place,
have concurred in thinking that *Shakespeare* produced this long passage
with design to ridicule and expose the bombast of the play from whence
it was taken; and that *Hamlet*'s commendation of it is purely ironical.
This is become the general opinion. I think just otherwise; and that it
was given with commendation to upbraid the false taste of the audience
of that time, which would not suffer them to do justice to the simplicity and sublime of this production. And I reason, first, from the
Character *Hamlet* gives of the Play, from whence the passage is taken;
secondly, from the passage itself; and thirdly, from the effect it had on
the audience.

Let us consider the character *Hamlet* gives of it. *The Play, I remember,
pleas'd not the million, 'twas Caviar to the general; but it was (as I received
it, and others, whose judgment in such matters cried in the top of mine) an
excellent Play well digested in the scenes, set down with as much modesty as
cunning. I remember, one said, there was no salt in the lines to make the matter
savoury; nor no matter in the phrase that might indite the author of affection;
but called it an honest method.* [2.2.429ff.] They who suppose the passage
given to be ridiculed must needs suppose this character to be purely
ironical. But if so it is the strangest irony that ever was written. *It
pleased not the multitude.* This we must conclude to be true, however
ironical the rest be. Now the reason given of the designed ridicule is the
supposed bombast. But those were the very plays, which at that time
we know took with the multitude. And *Fletcher* wrote a kind of *Rehearsal* purposely to expose them.[2] But say it is bombast, and that therefore it took not with the multitude. *Hamlet* presently tells us what it
was that displeased them. *There was no salt in the lines to make the matter
savoury; nor no matter in the phrase that might indite the author of affection;
but called it an honest method.* Now whether a person speaks ironically or

[1] See Vol. 1, pp. 263ff.
[2] *The Knight of the Burning Pestle.*

no when he quotes others, yet common sense requires he should quote what they say. Now it could not be, if this play displeased because of the bombast, that those whom it displeased should give this reason for their dislike. The same inconsistencies and absurdities abound in every other part of *Hamlet*'s speech supposing it to be ironical: but take him as speaking his sentiments the whole is of a piece, and to this purpose: The Play, I remember, pleased not the multitude, and the reason was its being wrote on the rules of the ancient Drama; to which they were entire strangers. But, in my opinion, and in the opinion of those for whose judgment I have the highest esteem, it was an excellent Play, *well digested in the scenes, i.e.* where the three unities were well preserved, *Set down with as much modesty as cunning,* i.e. where not only the art of composition but the simplicity of nature was carefully attended to. The characters were a faithful picture of life and manners, in which nothing was overcharged into Farce. But these qualities, which gained my esteem, lost the public's. For *I remember one said, There was no salt in the lines to make the matter savoury, i.e.* there was not, according to the mode of that time, a fool or clown to joke, quibble, and talk freely. *Nor no matter in the phrase that might indite the author of affection,* i.e. nor none of those passionate, pathetic love scenes so essential to modern Tragedy, *But he called it an honest method. i.e.* he owned, however *tastless* this method of writing on the ancient plan was to our times yet it was chaste and pure, the distinguishing character of the *Greek* Drama. I need only make one observation on all this; that, thus interpreted, it is the justest picture of a good tragedy wrote on the ancient rules. And that I have rightly interpreted it appears farther from what we find added in the old Quarto, *An honest method, as wholesome as sweet, and by very much more* HANDSOME *than* FINE, *i.e.* it had a natural beauty, but none of the fucus of false art.

2. A second proof that this speech was given to be admired is from the intrinsic merit of the speech itself: which contains the description of a circumstance very happily imagined, namely *Ilium* and *Priam*'s falling, together with the effect it had on the destroyer.

> The hellish Pyrrhus &c.
> To, *Repugnant to command.*
> Th' unnerved father falls &c.
> To, *So after* Pyrrhus' *pause.*

Now this circumstance, illustrated with the fine similitude of the storm, is so highly worked up as to have well deserved a place in

Virgil's second Book of the *Æneid*, even tho' the work had been carried on to that perfection which the *Roman* Poet had conceived.

3. The third proof is from the effects which followed on the recital. *Hamlet*, his best character, approves it; the Player is deeply affected in repeating it; and only the foolish *Polonius* tired with it. We have said enough before of *Hamlet*'s sentiments. As for the player, he changes colour, and the tears start from his eyes. But our author was too good a judge of nature to make bombast and unnatural sentiment produce such an effect. Nature and *Horace* both instructed him,

> *Si vis me flere, dolendum est*
> *Primum ipsi tibi, tunc tua me infortunia lædent,*
> *Telephe, vel Peleu.* MALE SI MANDATA LOQUERIS,
> *Aut dormitabo aut ridebo.*[1]

And it may be worth observing that *Horace* gives this precept particularly to shew that bombast and unnatural sentiments are incapable of moving the tender passions, which he is directing the poet how to raise. For in the lines just before he gives this rule,

> *Telephus & Peleus, cùm pauper & exul uterque,*
> *Projicit Ampullas, & sesquipedalia verba.*[2]

Not that I would deny that very bad lines in very bad tragedies have had this effect. But then it always proceeds from one or other of these causes.

1. Either when the subject is domestic, and the scene lies at home. The spectators in this case become interested in the fortunes of the distressed; and their thoughts are so much taken up with the subject that they are not at liberty to attend to the poet; who otherwise, by his faulty sentiments and diction, would have stifled the emotions springing up from a sense of the distress. But this is nothing to the case in hand. For, as *Hamlet* says,

> *What's* Hecuba *to him, or he to* Hecuba?

2. When bad lines raise this affection, they are bad in the other extreme; low, abject, and groveling instead of being highly figurative

---

[1] *A.P.*, 102ff.: 'If you would have me weep, you must first feel grief yourself: then, O Telephus or Peleus, will your misfortunes hurt me: if the words you utter are ill suited, I shall laugh or fall asleep.'

[2] *A.P.*, 96f.: 'in Tragedy Telephus and Peleus often grieve in the language of prose, when, in poverty and exile, either hero throws aside his bombast and foot-and-half-foot words.'

and swelling; yet when attended with a natural simplicity they have force enough to strike illiterate and simple minds. The Tragedies of *Banks* will justify both these observations.

But if any one will still say that *Shakespeare* intended to represent a player unnaturally and fantastically affected, we must appeal to *Hamlet*, that is, to *Shakespeare* himself in this matter; who on the reflection he makes upon the Player's emotion, in order to excite his own revenge, gives not the least hint that the player was unnaturally or injudiciously moved. On the contrary, his fine description of the Actor's emotion shews he thought just otherwise.

> *this Player here*
> *But in a fiction, in a dream of passion,*
> *Could force his soul so to his own conceit,*
> *That from her working all his visage wan'd:*
> *Tears in his eyes, distraction in his aspect,*
> *A broken voice &c.* [2.2.544ff.]

And indeed had *Hamlet* esteemed this emotion any thing unnatural it had been a very improper circumstance to spur him to his purpose.

As *Shakespeare* has here shewn the effects which a fine description of Nature, heightened with all the ornaments of art, had upon an intelligent Player, whose business habituates him to enter intimately and deeply into the characters of men and manners, and to give nature its free workings on all occasions, so he has artfully shewn what effects the very same scene would have upon a quite different man, *Polonius: by nature* very weak and very artificial (two qualities, though commonly enough joined in life, yet generally so much disguised as not to be seen by common eyes to be together; and which an ordinary Poet durst not have brought so near one another), *by discipline* practised in a species of wit and eloquence which was stiff, forced and pedantic, and *by trade* a Politician, and therefore of consequence without any of the affecting notices of humanity. Such is the man whom *Shakespeare* has judiciously chosen to represent the false taste of that audience which had condemned the play here reciting. When the actor comes to the finest and most pathetic part of the speech *Polonius* cries out *this is too long*; on which *Hamlet*, in contempt of his ill judgment, replies *It shall to the barber's with thy beard* (intimating that by this judgment it appeared that all his wisdom lay in his length of beard), *Pry'thee, say on. He's for a jig or a tale of bawdry* (the common entertainment of that time, as well as this, of the people), *or he sleeps, say on.* And yet this man of modern taste, who stood all this time perfectly unmoved with the forcible imagery of the relator, no sooner hears, amongst many good things, one quaint and fantastical word (put in, I suppose, purposely for this end) than he professes his approbation of the propriety and dignity of it. *That's good. Mobled Queen is good.* On the whole then, I think it plainly appears that the long quotation is not given to be ridiculed and laughed at but to be admired. The character given of the Play by *Hamlet* cannot be ironical. The passage itself is extremely beautiful. It has the effect that all pathetic relations, naturally written, should have; and it is condemned or regarded with indifference by one of a wrong, unnatural taste. From hence (to observe it by the way) the Actors in their representation of this play may learn how this speech ought to be spoken, and what appearance *Hamlet* ought to assume during the recital.

That which supports the common opinion concerning this passage is the turgid expression in some parts of it; which, they think, could never be given by the poet to be commended. We shall therefore in the next place examine the lines most obnoxious to censure, and see how much, allowing the charge, this will make for the induction of their conclusion.

> Pyrrhus *at* Priam *drives, in rage strikes wide,*
> *But with the whiff and wind of his fell sword*
> *Th'unnerved Father falls.* [2.2.466ff.]

And again,

> *Out, out, thou strumpet Fortune! All you Gods,*
> *In general Synod, take away her power:*
> *Break all the spokes and fellies from her wheel,*
> *And bowl the round nave, down the hill of Heaven,*
> *As low as to the Fiends.* [2.2.487ff.]

Now whether these be bombast or not is not the question, but whether *Shakespeare* esteemed them so. That he did not so esteem them appears from his having used the very same thoughts in the same expression in his best plays, and given them to his principal characters, where he aims at the sublime. As in the following passages.

Troilus, in *Troilus and Cressida,* far outstrains the execution of *Pyrrhus's* sword in the character he gives of *Hector's,*

> *When many times the* cative *Grecians* fall
> Ev'n in the fan and wind of your fair sword,
> *You bid them rise and live.* [5.3.39ff.]

Cleopatra, in *Antony and Cleopatra,* rails at Fortune in the same manner:

> *No, let me speak, and let me rail so high,*
> That the false huswife Fortune break her wheel,
> *Provok'd at my offence.* [4.15.43ff.]

But another use may be made of these quotations, a discovery of the
Author of this recited Play: which, letting us into a circumstance of our
Author's life (as a writer) hitherto unknown, was the reason I have been
so large upon this Question. I think then it appears from what has been
said that the Play in dispute was *Shakespeare's* own: and that this was
the occasion of writing it. He was desirous, as soon as he had found his
strength, of restoring the chastness and regularity of the ancient Stage;
and therefore composed this Tragedy on the model of the *Greek*
Drama, as may be seen by throwing so much *action* into *relation.* But
his attempt proved fruitless; and the raw, unnatural taste then prevalent
forced him back again into his old *Gothic* manner. For which he took
this revenge upon his Audience. (VIII, 267–72)

* * *

[On *Othello,* 1.2.33]

By Janus, *I think, no.*

There is great propriety in making the double *Iago* swear by *Janus,* who
has two faces. The address of it likewise is as remarkable, for as the
people coming up appeared at different distances to have different
shapes, he might swear by *Janus* without suspicion of any other em-
blematic meaning. (VIII, 284)

* * *

[On *Othello,* 1.3.140ff.]

Wherein of antres vast, &c.

Discourses of this nature made the subject of the politest conversations
when voyages into, and discoveries of the new world were all in vogue.
So when the *Bastard Faulconbridge,* in *King John,* describes the behaviour of upstart greatness, he makes one of the essential circumstances of it to be this kind of table-talk. The *fashion* then running
altogether in this way, it is no wonder a young lady of quality should
be struck with the history of an adventurer. So that *Rymer,* who pro-

fessedly ridicules this whole circumstance, and the noble author of the *Characteristics*, who more obliquely sneers it, only expose their own ignorance.[1] (VIII, 293-4)

★   ★   ★

[On *Othello*, 5.2.370f.]

> *To you, lord Governor,*
> *Remains the censure of this hellish villain:*

Rymer, who had neither vigour of imagination to make a poet, or strength of judgment to make a critic, as appears from his *Edgar* and his *Remarks* on Shakespeare, had yet just enough of both to play the buffoon and caviller. His criticisms on the *Poets of the last age*, with only a mixture of trite remarks transcribed from the *French* commentators on *Aristotle*, are one continued heap of ignorance and insolence. Almost the only remark on *Shakespeare* which, I think deserves an answer, is upon *Iago*'s character, which he thus censures: *To entertain the audience* (says he) *with something new and surprising, against common sense and nature, he would pass upon us a close, dissembling, false, ungrateful Rascal instead of an open-hearted, frank, plain-dealing soldier, a character constantly worn by them for some thousands of years in the world.* [Vol. 2, p. 30] This hath the appearance of sense, being founded on that rule of *Nature* and *Aristotle* that each character should have manners convenient to the age, sex, and condition

Ætatis cujusque notandi sunt tibi mores, &c.[2]

says *Horace*. But how has our critic applied it? According to this rule it is confessed that a soldier should be brave, generous, and a man of honour. This is to be his dramatic character. But either *one* or *more* of any order may be brought in. If only one, then the character of the order takes its denomination from the manners of that *one*. Had therefore the only soldier in this play been *Iago* the rule had been transgressed, and *Rymer*'s censure well founded. For then this *eternal villain* must have given the character of the soldiery, which had been unjust and unnatural. But if a *number* of the same order be represented, then the character of the order is taken from the manners of the majority; and this, according to nature and common sense. Now in this play there are many of the order of the soldiery, and all, excepting *Iago*,

---

[1] See Vol. 2, pp. 28 and 264f.
[2] *A.P.*, 156: 'You must note the manners of each age.'

represented as open, generous, and brave. From *these* the soldier's character is to be taken and not from *Iago*, who is brought as an exception to it—unless it be unnatural to suppose there could be an exception, or that a villain ever insinuated himself into that corps. And thus *Shakespeare* stands clear of this impertinent criticism. (VIII, 404–5)

112. Unsigned essay, Shakespeare the dramatist

1747

From *An Examen of the New Comedy, Call'd 'The Suspicious Husband'. With Some Observations Upon our Dramatick Poetry and Authors* . . . (1747).

The Suspicious Husband, by Benjamin Hoadly (1706–57) was performed on 12 February 1747 and was a success on stage and in print for many years. This piece is largely directed against Foote's account of Garrick's Lear, No. 109 above.

Notwithstanding the many various and opposite Opinions that Men have concerning Works of Genius in general, yet 'tis unanimously agreed among those of real Taste that SHAKESPEARE was the greatest Dramatick Poet that ever was in this or any other Nation. He is Excellent (I won't say equally) both in the *Sock* and the *Buskin*. His Comedy is at least equal, if not superior to any; but his Genius in Tragedy, compar'd with that of others, is a Giant among Pigmies. His Powers there are more than Human; and tho' we have many good Poets yet so great is the Distance that it is almost absurd to say who is the Second to him.

He is himself alone!

This amazing Superiority in *Shakespeare* evidently lies in his great Knowledge and Use of the *Passions*. While other mistaken Authors are hunting after *Similies, Descriptions,* and *poetical Images,* he is ever in pursuit of *Nature* only. *They* ransack their *Heads,* but *he* consults his *Heart,* and while *they* are tickling the Ears, *he* is *harrowing up the Soul!*

We have several good *Poets,* but very few *Playwrights* (this Distinction is obvious); and we have many Tragedies which are fine Poems yet very indifferent Plays. But to return to *Shakespeare.* Tho' no Poet has such exalted Sentiments, such animated Descriptions, such strong Images, nervous Language, or such dramatick Numbers yet those are (in my Mind) to be admir'd only as the *Ornaments* of his Genius. But when you see him conducting a *Macbeth* from Ambition through Guilt, Horror, Remorse, and Despair! When you behold the Rage, Anguish, Madness, and miserable Death of his *Lear!* When you see the artful Villany of *Iago* imposing upon the honest Credulity of his General, the gradual Approaches of Jealousy upon *Othello's* Mind, with its dreadful Effects! You are lost in Admiration, and are too sensible of the Author's Powers! Nor is it possible for the greatest *Misanthrope* to have a contemptible Opinion of human Nature when he considers these Plays as the Production of a Man! I think I don't carry my Idolatry, Enthusiasm, or what you please to call it, too far when I aver to you I had rather be Author of one of those three Tragedies than of all the rest (his own excepted) which I have ever seen or read, in this or any other Language. It has been often objected to this divine Author by the low tasteless Cavillers, that he wrote without the *Rules*; and I have been always surpris'd that the Admirers of him have given up this Point so easily, and by their Silence suffered so unjust and paltry a Criticism to prevail. If they mean by the *Rules* the mechanical Ones, of *Place, Time,* and *Action* (which are the chief Merit of some of our Tragedies) and which he likewise has preserv'd in some of his Plays; if I say, they mean *these,* I own to you he has leapt their Boundaries and boldly set his Imagination at Liberty! He has permitted her to soar not only beyond the Critick's Limits but ev'n those of Earth and Heav'n, and to take her Flights into new Worlds of his own Creation! How exactly has he painted himself in his *Midsummer Night's Dream!*

> *The Poet's Eye with a fine Frenzy rowling,*
> *Doth glance from Heav'n to Earth, from Earth to Heav'n!*
> *And as Imagination bodies forth*

The Form of Things unknown; the Poet's Pen
Turns 'em to Shape, and gives to Airy Nothing,
A local Habitation and a Name!

[5.1.12ff.]

The more essential and noble Rules of the Drama are always regarded
by *Shakespeare*, the Preservation and Consistency of Character, the
working up of the Passions, their Rise, Progress, and Effects! The Variety of interesting Circumstances, the unexpected Changes in the
Conduct of his Fable, the Blood-thrilling and Heart-breaking Strokes
of Nature throughout the Whole, the Sublimity of his Thoughts and
Vastness of his Invention, have never yet been equal'd, and can never be
surpass'd! Therefore, to every Dabler in Poetry, and Pidler in Criticism
who (like other Coxcombs) glory in their Ignorance and Infidelity,
and who, not being able to taste *Shakespeare*'s Beauties, are for ever
talking at Second-hand of his Errors and Inequalities, I shall address the
Words of the greatest and best Critick among the Ancients.

In the SUBLIME, *as in great Affluence of Fortune, some minuter Articles*
will unavoidably escape Observation; but it is almost impossible for a low and
groveling Genius to be guilty of Error, since he never endangers himself by
soaring on high, or aiming at Eminence, but still goes on in the same uniform
secure Track; whilst its very Height and Grandeur exposes the Sublime to
sudden Falls!

Smith's Translation of Longinus.
Sect. 33. pag. 79.

These, Sir, are my loose Thoughts upon this great Master of the
Drama. I have not endeavour'd at a methodical Dissertation, nor have I
given you a Third of what I had to say. The Theme is inexhaustible,
and I find myself still so full of him, that you must give me leave to
make a short epistolary Digression concerning him, to Mr G——k the
Player.

SIR,
As well as I like you, I have some Faults to find with you; I have once
or twice (tho' unknown) communicated my Thoughts to you before, I
won't say with what Success. I shall address you in a candid friendly
manner, so have no Apprehension of your being offended; if you are,
you have more Vanity than you ought to have, and less Sense than I
thought you had. If you take me for the Author of a late *Treatise upon*

261

the Passions,[1] in which you are criticiz'd in the Character of *Lear*, you do me wrong; and to convince you that I am not only impartial but a friendly Adviser, I will first clear you from his Misrepresentations before I take you in Hand myself. The Author of this Treatise declares himself a *young Writer*; and were we not more convinc'd of it from the Matter of his Performance than his Modesty in treating it, his Veracity might be call'd in Question. What may we not hope from so intrepid a Genius, who at first setting out takes upon himself the Censorship of the Stage, and becomes at once Preceptor-general to the Publick and the Actors! However, with all proper Deference to his Judgment and a due Contempt to his Displeasure, I shall venture to say he has grossly mistook the Character of *Lear*, and either has not given himself the trouble to read the Original or (what is more unpardonable) has only quoted a few inconsiderable Passages to serve his own Ends and mislead the Ignorant. He opens his Criticism of *Lear* with *a short Account of the Passions*, which indeed is unanswerable; and if he had pursu'd this manner of Writing through the whole he had been secure; but by unfortunately having some Meaning in other Parts he imprudently discovers his weak Side, and lies open to the Attacks of every thinking Man in the Kingdom. In order to give us a Sketch of *Lear*'s moral Character, *a Circumstance which* (he says) *never ought to escape the View of an Actor*, he quotes a Passage that is not in SHAKESPEARE.

> *Ungrateful as they were,*
> *Tho' the Wrongs they have heaped on me are numberless,*
> *I feel a Pang of Nature for 'em yet.*

[See Vol. I, p. 385]

Is it not surprizing that this great Critick and Man of Taste should propose Lines for your Consideration which are in the vile Alterations by *Tate?* and which only mark that Tenderness and Affection which in other Parts of his Pamphlet he condemns in you as no Ingeredients of the Character? When *Kent* in the *Original* addresses himself thus to *Lear*,

> *Your eldest Daughters have foredone themselves,*
> *And desperately are dead!*

[5.3.291ff.]

The poor old King, quite senseless, and near his Death, only answers

> *Ay, so I think.*

---

[1] See No. 109 above.

Thus the *Censor* has not only injur'd *Shakespeare* by taking this *Sketch* from the unhallow'd Pencil of *Tate* but he has even injur'd poor *Tate* himself, for his Lines are thus:

> *Ungrateful as they were, my Heart feels yet*
> *A Pang of Nature for their wretched Fall!*

Where are our Critick's Ears, that he could not find out that *his* second Line (for it belongs to No-body else) is three Syllables too long, and is neither Prose or Poetry? He condemns you greatly for your Manner of uttering the Curse against *Goneril*; but had he look'd into *Shakespeare* he would not have been so severe upon *your Tears shed at the Conclusion,* or have said that the *strange Mixture of Grief and Passion was highly unnatural*; for this Speech immediately following the Curse is your Direction and Authority.

> Lear. *I'll tell thee—Life and Death, I am asham'd*
> *That thou hast Pow'r to shake my Manhood thus!*
> *That these hot Tears which break from me perforce*
> *Should make thee worth them—Blasts and Fogs upon thee,*
> *Th' untented Woundings of a Father's Curse*
> *Pierce every Sense about thee! Old fond Eyes*
> *Beweep her once again, I'll pluck ye out*
> *And cast you with the Waters that you lose*
> *To temper Clay—*
>
> [1.4.296ff.]

Has not the Author here most strongly pointed out the Mixture of Grief and Passion? But supposing he had not, who can be so unfeeling or so little acquainted with human Nature not to know that these Transitions from Rage to Grief were necessary to support the Character? *Lear* is old and choleric, and, of Consequence, when his Rage is spent and his Powers fail him he must naturally (from his Circumstances) sink into Sorrow. In the Second Act his Grief almost overpowers him, and he expresses himself in these strong Terms:

> Lear. *Oh how this Mother swells up tow'rd my Heart!*
> Hysterica Passio, *down, thou climbing Sorrow:*
> *Thy Element's below.*
>
> [2.4.55ff.]

> *You see me here, you Gods, a poor old Man,*
> *As full of Griefs as Age, &c.*
>
> [2.4.271ff.]

> *Oh let not Womens Weapons, Water-drops,*
> *Stain my Man's Cheeks—No, you unnatural Hags!*
> *I will have such Revenges on you both, &c.*

[2.4.276ff.]

Here he finds his Tears making their Way; and when they burst out his Pride endeavours to conceal 'em by saying that he won't weep.

> *You think I'll weep, &c.*
> No, *I'll not weep.*   [2.4.281ff.]

What can be more natural or affecting? In these last Words there is no Transition from one Passion to the other, but they are absolutely blended together; and I must take Notice that in this very Place your Manner and Execution equals any Thing you do in the whole Character.

In Act the Third:

> Lear. *But I'll punish home;*
> *No, I will weep no more—*   [3.4.16f.]

In these mix'd Passions (*so highly unnatural to our young Writer and Instructor*) the superior Abilities of *Shakespeare* appear. No Poet has 'em in any degree of Competition with him, and therefore no Poet so excellent. In the Fourth Act of *Othello* there is a stronger Instance of a Mixture of the same Passions.

> Othello. *I would have him nine Years a killing! A fine Woman, a fair Woman, a sweet Woman!*
> Iago. *Nay, you must forget that.*
> Othello. *Ay, let her rot and perish, and be damn'd to Night; For she shall not live; no, my Heart is turn'd to Stone: I strike it and it hurts my Hand—Oh the World hath not a sweeter Creature; she might lie by an Emperor's Side and command him Tasks!*   [4.1.173ff.]

I would fain ask the Critick whether this *unmanly Sniveling* (as he delicately terms it), these sudden Transitions from Rage to Tenderness, *lowers the Consequence of* Othello? And if a robust Warriour *drops Tears as fast as the Arabian Trees their medicinal Gums*, can it be *highly unnatural* in *Lear*, who is *Fourscore and upwards*? I could produce many more Proofs of his weeping almost in every Scene he appears; but it is as ridiculous and impertinent to tire you with Quotations upon an undoubted Point as it is to produce none in Defence of a strange and uncommon Opinion.

The Critick says, (Mr *G-rr-ck*), you should have no Mark of *Malice*, *Premeditation*, or *Solemnity* in uttering the Curse. Here one of us is greatly mistaken, for I always thought a Desire of Revenge imply'd *Malice*, and that there could be no Address or Prayer to Heaven (whether for Blessings or Curses) without some Mark of *Solemnity!* However, not to dispute upon Words, I shall recollect your Manner of executing that Part of the Play, and then let the Judges pronounce their Sentence. You fall precipitately upon your knees, extend your Arms— clench your Hands—set your Teeth—and with a savage Distraction in your Look—trembling in all your Limbs—and your Eyes pointed to Heaven (the whole expressing a fulness of Rage and Revenge) you begin

Hear Nature, Dear Goddess! [1.4.275]

with a *broken, inward, eager* Utterance; from thence rising every Line in Loudness and Rapidity of Voice 'till you come to

and feel
How sharper than a Serpent's Tooth it is,
To have a thankless Child. [1.4.277ff.]

Then you are struck at once with your Daughter's Ingratitude; and bursting into Tears, with a most sorrowful Heartbreaking Tone of Voice, you say

go, go, my People. [1.4.272]

This in my Opinion is the strongest Climax of Rage; and the Break from it at the End of the Speech gives a natural, necessary Variety, and was visibly design'd so by the Author, as I have prov'd before. But now (as *Bayes* says) *for as far-fetch'd a Fancy as ever you heard*; the Critick undertakes to demonstrate *that the Desire of Royalty is the Point distracts* Lear's *Judgment; and that* Shakespeare *has not put one Expression into his Mouth throughout the Madness, but what bears a visible Relation to this first Cause!* Now it unfortunately happens that there is not a single Word mention'd (except once) in the first and second Scene of his Madness that has the least Relation to Royalty. It is evidently the Usage of his Daughters that continually rankles in his Mind, and in the second Scene he fancies himself in a Court of Justice, and arraigns 'em for their Ingratitude:

I will arraign 'em strait.

. . . Now ye She Foxes!

Arraign her first; 'tis Goneril!

And here's another whose warpt Looks proclaim

What Store her Heart is made of—Stop her there!

. . . Let 'em anatomize Regan—*see what breeds about her Heart. Is there*

any cause in Nature for these hard Hearts?   [3.6.20, 22, 46, 52ff.]

What can stronger mark the Cause of his Disorder! I cannot help taking Notice how exquisitely and figuratively he describes the State of his Wretchedness in the following Lines of the Fourth Act!

But I am bound

Upon a Wheel of Fire, which my own Tears

Do scald like molten Lead!   [4.7.46ff.]

What a Picture of Distraction and Sorrow!

Tho' the Ingratitude of *Regan* and *Goneril* and not the desire of Royalty is incontestably the Cause of *Lear's* Madness yet it does not follow that you or any Actor should drop the Majesty of the Character to *pick Straws, play with 'em, or use boyish Actions:* these are the Critick's Allegations. But as his Credit has appear'd hitherto a little exceptionable I will examine your Behaviour in that Scene, and then have done with him. In order to come at the Truth, let us know how you came by your Straw and your fantastick Garlands?

Cord. *Alack 'tis he—Why he was met ev'n now*

As mad as the vext Sea, singing aloud,

Crown'd with rank Fumitory and Furrow Weeds,

With Burdocks, Hemlock, Nettles, Cuckow Flowers,

Darnel, and all the idle Weeds that grow

In our sustaining Corn.   [4.4.1ff.]

I should be glad to know what Part of the *Royal Prerogative* is particularly shewn in *singing aloud,* or *dressing in Weeds and Flowers?* The Critick will reply, perhaps, that he takes the Weeds for his Regalia, and therefore makes a Crown with them. I agree with him, and therefore he may very naturally fancy a Handful of Straw his Scepter: and this is the Use you make of it. You enter with all the Dignity your *insignificant trifling Person* is capable of; you throw yourself into many various Attitudes of Command, and tho' you have Straw in your Hand, yet we very plainly see that you take it for a *Scepter, Bow, Gauntlet, &c.* as the different Ideas rise in your Imagination.

But 'tis in vain to argue with one who has so much misrepresented the *Actor*, and so little regarded his *Author*, His proposing *Tate*'s Lines (which he has misquoted) for the Foundation of the Character, and his asserting that the *Curse* is at the End of the First Act (which in *Shakespeare* is neither at the End of the Act or the Scene) plainly prove that he wholly relied upon his own Head, and had recourse neither to the *Original* or *Alteration*; so great is the Impartiality, Judgment, and Modesty of our *young Writer*. Thus, Mr *G—rr—ck*, I have endeavour'd to vindicate you where I thought you justifiable, and shall now as freely censure where I think you erroneous. In the first Place, why will you do so great an Injury to *Shakespeare* as to perform *Tate*'s execrable Alteration of him? Read and consider the two Plays seriously, and then make the Publick and the Memory of the Author some Amends by giving us *Lear* in the *Original*, *Fool* and all (*Macklin* or *Chapman* will play it well). And as some small Recompence for your Conversion to the Ways of Truth I will convince you of some Errors you are guilty of in that capital Character.

When you appear in the Fourth Act with the Physician, *Kent*, and *Cordelia*, you should change your Dress:

> Cord. *Is he array'd?*
> Phy. *Ay, Madam, in the Heaviness of Sleep*
> *We put fresh Garments on him.*   [4.7.20ff.]

But supposing you had not this Direction, how could you speak the following Lines without discovering the Absurdity?

> Lear. *I'm mainly ign'rant*
> *What Place this is, and all the Skill I have,*
> *Remembers not these Garments.*   [4.7.65ff.]

Here he has a short Interval from Madness; and the Loss of his Reason before is a very poor Excuse for his not knowing, now he's in his Senses, the Garments he has wore for almost Four Acts. But this and many other Mistakes are owing to your Acquaintance with that sorry Fellow *Tate*. If you had look'd into Sir *Thomas Hanmer*'s Edition of *Shakespeare* you never surely could speak the following Speech in the Manner you do.

> *Dear Daughter, I confess that I am old,*
> *Age is unnecessary: On my Knees I beg,*
> *That you'll vouchsafe to give me Raiment, Bed, and Food.*
>   [2.4.152ff.]

This you speak as really imploring *Regan* (which is very unnatural), whereas 'tis strong *Irony*, in answer to her when she advises him to *return to her Sister, and ask her Forgiveness. How* (says *Lear*), *ask her Forgiveness? Does this become Us?* Would you have me fall upon my Knees and say,

> *Dear Daughter, I confess that I am old, &c.*

In this Sense the Speech is strong in Nature; in your and Mr *Tate's* 'tis Spiritless and out of Character. I agree with the Author of the *Treatise upon the Passions* in one part of an Observation, tho' utterly against him in the other. When you burst into Tears at the End of the Curse you need not make use of your Handkerchief; your Change of Voice sufficiently marks your Distress, and your Application to your Handkerchief is, perhaps, too minute a Circumstance, and makes you more present to Things than you ought to be at that Time. I could wish you would curb your Spirit a little in a long Speech in the Second Act that begins,

> *Inform'd 'em! do'st thou understand me Man?*
> *The King would speak with* Cornwall, &c.
>
> [2.4.97ff.]

The Violence of his Temper breaks out several times, and it is my Opinion that your full Power of Voice should be reserv'd for

> *Bid 'em come forth and hear me,*
> *Or, at the Chamber Door, I'll beat the Drum,*
> *Till it cry, sleep to Death!*   [2.4.115ff.]

Sleep to Death! ought to be your most forcible and dreadful Point of Rage.

In your first Scene of the Fifth Act there is something done and said by you that always displeas'd me. When *Kent* discovers to you that he was *Caius* you say (in the Nonsense of the Alteration)

> *Caius! Wer't thou my trusty* Caius?
> *Enough—Enough.*[1]

and then you faint away, because *Cordelia* takes notice of the *Blood leaving your Cheeks*, and calls for help. This *Second* Fit has no Effect, and you might as well cut a Caper. You will say the alter'd Play has mark'd it so; to which I answer that it can be no Mitigation of your

---

[1] Tate's version: see Vol. 1, p. 377.

Fault to plead that Mr *Nahum Tate* has seduc'd you. Tho' you are not the Principal you are accessary to the Murder, and will be brought in Guilty. How can you keep your Countenance when you come to the *Spheres stopping their Course, the Sun making halt,* and *the Winds bearing on their rosy Wings* that Cordelia *is a Queen?*[1] Surely you are not acquainted with your own Powers, for let the Censor say what he will the last Scene of *Shakespeare's Lear* must shew you to advantage; and I hope it is rather your Idleness than Judgment that makes you persist in the other.—Here I shall leave you, not I assure you for want of Subject-Matter (for I have more Remarks in Store), but for want of Room and Time; and so

SIR,
Your humble Servant.

Now (*George*) I shall return to you, and the Dramatick Poets; I'll endeavour to be as concise as possible, and so without more Ceremony I shall proceed to *Ben Jonson.*

Ben was *Shakespeare's* Contemporary and Rival. He has succeeded in Comedy, but greatly fail'd in the Buskin. His Tragedies are nothing but Historical Facts digested in Five Acts, and fill'd up with long Speeches, translated almost literally from the ancient Historians and Poets, and put into Blank Verse.

Beaumont and *Fletcher,* who liv'd at the same Time, have certainly great Merit, and though they have not one finish'd Play in all their Number yet they are far Superior to *Ben* in their Tragedies, and those serious Scenes which are interwove in their Comedies. Their Fables are generally interesting for the first Three Acts, but afterwards they fall into such low Extravagancies and monstrous Improbabilities 'tis scarcely possible to read 'em through. They have endeavour'd to ridicule *Shakespeare* in many of their Plays, and yet are such servile Imitators of him that they have been *modest* enough not only to borrow Sentiments and Speeches from him but even Plots and Characters! (20–40)

*   *   *

Dryden, tho' a very great *Poet,* is (in my Opinion) a very faulty *Playwright.* There are most delightful fine Passages, and some good Scenes in all his Tragedies; but consider 'em as Plays and they sink greatly in their Value. *All for Love* is esteemed his Master-piece, and has

[1] See Vol. 1, p. 384.

been generally look'd upon as a perfect Performance; I have seen it more than once represented to the greatest Advantage by *Booth*, *Old-field*, *&c*. And tho' my Ears have been delighted with the Poetry, and my Mind charm'd with the Sentiments, yet my Eyes have been dry, and my Heart quiet. Read *Antony and Cleopatra*, from which the other is taken, tho' one of the most incorrect and careless of *Shakespeare*'s Plays, and you will soon *feel* the Difference. *Dryden*'s Play is most correctly poetical with the Unities; *Shakespeare*'s is most pathetically Natural without 'em. The first is the finish'd Performance of a great Poet, the last the hasty Production of a true Dramatick Genius. (41-2)

★ ★ ★

Otway is call'd *Shakespeare*'s eldest Son! And is certainly a Genius; and tho' any body might be proud of such an Heir yet, if my information is right, they are not so nearly related. He wants Variety, and can touch none of the Passions masterly but Love. There is exquisite Tenderness and fine Distress in his *Jaffier* and *Belvidera*, and in *Castalio* and *Monimia*; the Rage of *Chamont* is often unnatural, but his Affection for his Sister is finely touch'd throughout. There is great Gallantry, Spirit, and Nature, in *Polydore*, and a strong characteristick Boldness in *Pierre*; his Poetry, tho' often low and creeping, yet is frequently sweet and harmonious, and sometimes nervous and elevated. But with this confin'd Merit, what Claim can he lay to the unbounded Possessions of the Other? No, no; *Shakespeare* left no Inheritor behind him, the Publick are his only Heirs, who now enjoy, and will enrich themselves with his Treasures for ever.(43)

113. Peter Whalley on Shakespeare's learning

1748

From *An Enquiry into the Learning of Shakespeare, with Remarks on Several Passages of his Plays. In a Conversation between Eugenius and Neander* (1748).

Peter Whalley (1722–91) was a fellow of St John's College, Cambridge, for some years, and also published an edition of Ben Jonson in 1756.

[Preface]

★   ★   ★

The Learning of the Poet having been long made a Question, I recollected many parallel Places which I had taken notice of in the Study of the Classics. Upon bringing them together I perceived a very manifest Conformity between them, sufficient in some Measure to persuade one that *Shakespeare* was more indebted to the Ancients than is commonly imagined. Favourite Prepossessions usually operate very strongly on the Mind, and Parties of all kinds are seldom satisfied without pushing their Sentiments to indefensible Extremes. This probably may be the real Case with regard to the Dispute about our Poet. From being thought to have no Learning he may be represented to have read too much, or at least to have read more than what may be fairly collected from his Plays. Thus his Advocates, through Excess of Zeal, may destroy that Cause they are desirous to support. Nothing is advanced in the Quotations I have produced but what struck me immediately upon the first reading. It had been an easy Matter to have multiplied Citations and to have poured in a Profusion of Learning in Defence of the present Opinion. But I was intirely unwilling to overcharge, and chose rather to rely on a few Witnesses of Credit than to call in a Multitude of suspected Testimonies.

That *Shakespeare* was not altogether unacquainted with the dead

Languages is plain from the Confession of his Adversaries; and from the Authority of *Jonson*, who allows him a small Portion both of *Greek* and *Latin*. We may venture to go somewhat further and say that he not only understood those Languages but that he arrived to a Taste and Elegance of Judgment, particularly in the Latter. Of this the Tragedy of *Hamlet* is an irrefragable Instance.

Saxo, the *Danish* Historian from whom he took the Plot, is remarkable for a Purity of Style beyond any other Writer of the Times in which he lived. And the Critics are surprized to find an Author of such Politeness in so rude and ignorant an Age. *Shakespeare* must certainly have read him in the Original; for no Translation hath been ever yet made into any modern Language. His rejecting certain marvellous Occurrences which the Historian has inserted from the Traditions of his Countrymen, shews that he not only read him for Information but that he studied him as a Critic. Though he hath taken from him the Fact of *Hamlet*'s counterfeited Madness, and many other Circumstances of the Play, yet he has varied from the Narration in several Incidents. The Addition of the Ghost is probably from his own Imagination; and the Conclusion of the whole is different from the Relation of *Saxo*. If I may be permitted, with Submission, to declare my Sentiment, the *Catastrophe* is exceedingly ill managed and very unequal to the rest of the Play. It differs as much likewise from the Truth of History, which informs us that *Hamlet* survived the Usurper, and died a natural Death. But the Departure from an ancient Fact is easily pardoned when it occasions a fine Distress or any extraordinary Scene of Action. Yet neither of these, I apprehend, is accomplished by the Death of *Hamlet*.

Upon reviewing my Remarks, which were wrote at a time when the Amusements of Wit were suffered to mingle with other Studies, I found that most of them continued to be unobserved by the Editors of *Shakespeare*, or were not considered in the same Light in which I saw them. Hence I imagined they might probably contain something which the Admirers of this Author would not be displeased to meet with. I have purposely avoided to make any Alterations in the Text, one or two Instances excepted: for after all that has been offered on this Head I believe it not impossible to make still some additional Corrections. I would not be understood to include the last Edition, which I denied myself the Pleasure of perusing. If, therefore, I have any thing in common with that it arises from the same general Fund of Observation. (iv–vii)

*   *   *

[*Enquiry*]

[*Eugenius* reports that he is reading an author] we are neither of us unacquainted with, yet I seldom take him into my Hand but I always meet with something *new*. From the Character you give me, returned *Neander*, I should do an Injury to the supreme Genius if I did not immediately conclude it to be a Volume of *Shakespeare*. This Author was their common Favourite; of whom *Neander* frequently would say that he thought him not more the Boast of his Country in particular than the Glory of human Nature in general. *Eugenius* was going to make Answer, when the other interposed with observing that he imagined the Merit of *Shakespeare* to be now indisputably owned: and the Fondness of the Public for him he thought was pretty evident from the various Editions which have been lately published, and the frequent Representations of his Plays upon the Stage. Do you suppose then, said *Eugenius*, that the Nation was ever prejudiced against *Shakespeare*, or had not a proper Relish of his Merit? That is my Sentiment, replied *Neander*; for it seems, methinks, to have happened to some great Authors as to certain Notions and Opinions in Philosophy: they have been entertained at their first Appearance in the World with a candid and honourable Reception, but through the popular Caprice they would soon have fallen into Darkness and Oblivion if Men of Learning had not arose to recover their Character, and fixed them in universal Credit and Reputation. And this is easily accounted for by the Decline or Perversion of Sense and Taste in one Age, and its Revival, Perfection, and Improvement in another. Such, in my Apprehension, has been the Fate of *Shakespeare* with Regard to his several Contemporaries and his Rivals in Fame and Poetry. The Age wherein he lived hardly allowed him any Equal, never a Superior; but that which immediately succeeded began to prefer others to him in its Esteem, and set *Ben. Jonson* and *Beaumont* and *Fletcher* far above him; so that in Mr *Dryden*'s Time the Plays of these last became the most frequent Entertainments of the Stage, two of them being usually acted throughout the Year to one of *Shakespeare*'s or *Jonson*'s. The Reason of that Prepossession, returned *Eugenius*, is not difficult to find, for the Court, which in these Cases commonly gives the Law, was sunk in Indolence and Pleasure. The Morality of *Shakespeare* appeared with too severe a Countenance; the Form was too solemn and gloomy for the Gaiety of Men of Wit, and was a Kind of Reproof to the Irregularity of their own Conduct. The Conversation of Gentlemen, the Genteelness of their Behaviour and

Discourse, and the Extravagance of their Gallantries were much better painted by *Fletcher* than by any other Poet who wrote before him. The tender and more pleasing Passions were described in a natural and lively Manner, and a certain Easiness and Pleasantry reigning through the whole conspired to recommend him to the general Applause. However, as you intimated, the Judgment and Inclination of the present Age declare universally for *Shakespeare:* and this seems to proceed from the Labours of his several Editors, and from that inimitable Propriety with which his chief Characters are represented by an incomparable Actor, whose excellent Expression is an admirable Comment upon the Plays of our Author. (10–11)

★   ★   ★

Mr *Hales* asserted in his Favour, that there was no Subject which any antient Poet had ever treated, but he would engage to shew it as well wrote by *Shakespeare* [see Vol. 1, p. 138].

If you were at Leisure I could point out some parallel Passages tending to confirm this Assertion, and I would make a previous Enquiry into the several Sources from which the Poet drew Materials to adorn his Plays. But such a Disquisition, continued *Eugenius*, would, I fear, demand more time than you can probably allow me; for undoubtedly you have many Compliments and Services from the Country to deliver, which the Ceremony of the Town must be obliged with at your first Arrival. What little Matters of that Kind, replied *Neander*, I have to do are dispatching by a Servant; and I have *dealt* out my *Cards*, I hope, with so much Art as to secure me your Company, if disengaged for the rest of the Day. I have no particular Appointment, returned *Eugenius*, to call me out, and with your Leave we may employ the rest of the Morning in our present Conversation. *Neander* acknowledging his Inclination, *Eugenius* proceeded in the following Manner.

Shakespeare has been deservedly esteemed the *Homer*, the Father of our Dramatic Poetry, as being the most irresistible Master of the Passions, possessed of the same creative Power of Imagination, abounding with a vast Assemblage of Ideas and a rich Redundancy of Genius and Invention. And I think, added *Neander*, that he may be considered to deserve that Title in another Light, as having, like him, furnished many Poets and Tragedians of succeeding Times with the noblest Images and Thoughts. . . . However, with all these Superiorities, and with a Dignity equal to the divinest of the Ancients, he had the Fortune to resemble them in the least desirable Part of their Circumstances as he met with the Fatality, peculiar almost to distinguished Writers, of being transmitted to Posterity full of Errors and Corruptions. It would appear almost incredible that the Writings of an Author of so late a Date should be thus extremely faulty and incorrect, and that his Works, like the Province of *Africa* to the ancient *Romans*, should yield his Commentators such a continual Harvest of Victory and Triumphs. But it happens at the same time to prevent all Surprize, that we are not only assured of the Fact but in some measure likewise both of the Cause and Manner of it. This then being the Case, returned *Eugenius*, can it be any longer a Wonder why certain Adventurers in Criticism have so ardent an Esteem for *Shakespeare*, when he gives them the most delightful Opportunity of trying their Skill upon his Plays and of indulging a Disposition for Guesses and Conjecture, the darling Passion of our modern Critics? Besides the Correctness of the Text, which is equally necessary to the right understanding him in common with all other Authors, it may not be improper to consider a few Particulars which may possibly explain the Singularity of some Places, and give us a little Insight into the Learning of *Shakespeare*.

To begin with his Plots, the Ground-work and Basis of the whole. These are usually taken from some History or Novel; he follows the Thread of the Story as it lies before him, and seldom makes any Addition or Improvement to the Incidents arising from it. He copies the old Chronicles almost *verbatim*, and gives a faithful Relation of the several Characters they have left us of our Kings and Princes. It is needless to remark how erroneous this must render the Plan of his Drama, and what Violation it must necessarily offer to the Unities as prescribed by *Aristotle*. Yet it does not in the least abate my Veneration for our Poet that the *French Connoisseurs* have fixed on him the Imputation of Ignorance and Barbarism. It would agree, I believe, as little with their Tempers to be freed from a sovereign Authority in the Empire of Wit and Letters as in their civil Government. An absolute Monarch must preside over Affairs of Science as well as over those of the Cabinet; and it is pleasant enough to observe what Pain they are put to upon the least Appearance of offending against the Laws of the *Stagyrite*. But notwithstanding the Imperfection and even the Absurdity of the Plots of *Shakespeare* he continues unrivaled for his masterly Expression of the Characters and Manners; and the proper Execution of these is undoubtedly more useful, and perhaps more conducive to the Ends of Tragedy, than the Design and Conduct of the Plot. A great

Part of this unjustifiable Wildness of the Fable must be placed to the Taste and Humour of the Times. The People had been used to the Marvellous and Surprizing in all their Shews and Sports. They had seen different Kingdoms in different Quarters of the World engaged in the same Scene of Business, and could not be hastily confined from so unlimited a Latitude to a narrower Compass. I allow their Appetites to have been much depraved, yet probably some kind of *Regimen*, not very different from what they were before accustomed to, was the properest Method to bring them to a better. Nevertheless, were we to make a Dissection of his Plays we should discover more Art and Judgment than we are commonly aware of, both in the Contrast and Consistency of his principal Characters and in the different Under-parts, which are all made subservient towards carrying on the main Design; and we should observe that still there was a Simplicity of Manner, which Nature only can give, and as wonderful a Diversity. *Homer* is admired for that Perfection of Beauty which represents Men as they are affected in Life, and shews us in the Persons of others the Oppositions of Inclination, and the Struggles between the Passions of Self-love and those of Honour and Virtue, which we often feel in our own Breasts. This is that Excellence for which he is deservedly admired, as much as for the Variety of his Characters. May we not apply this Remark with an equal Propriety to *Shakespeare*, in whom we find as surprizing a Difference and as natural and distinct a Preservation of his Characters? And is not this agreeable Display of Genius, interposed *Neander*, infinitely preferable to that studied Regularity and lifeless Drawing practised by our latter Poets? in whom we meet with either a constant Resemblance or Antithesis both of Scenes and Persons, the natural Result of a confined and scanty Imagination! I am tempted to compare such Performances to that perpetual Sameness or Repetition which prevails in our modern Taste of Gardens, where

> *Grove nods at Grove, each Alley has a Brother,*
> *And half the Plat-form just reflects the other.*

Yet I believe, however earnestly we contend for Nature, that we are neither of us inclined to exclude the Direction of Art from interposing in the Drama: it gives a heightning and *Relief* to Nature, and at the same time curbs the extravagance of Fancy and circumscribes it within proper Bounds. All I would establish by this Remark is the Opinion of *Longinus,* preferring a Composition with some Faults of this kind which is wrote with Genius and Sublimity, to one of greater Regularity and Correctness that is not animated with equal Life and Spirit. The Business and Design of Art, returned *Eugenius*, is undoubtedly to polish and improve the Beauties of Nature; and in some Cases, perhaps, it may be a more illustrious Mark of Skill not to weaken and destroy a natural Grace than to introduce an artificial one. Rules may probably assist and set off a Genius, tho' they can never give Perfection where that is wanting. But we seem, *Neander*, to justify our Principles by our Practice. It is reasonable we should now return to our Subject, from which we have been long wandering, as I have something to observe which hath a natural Connection with the Point we are discussing.

You must have remarked, I think, that the Poet himself was sensible of the Imperfections of his Plots, and of the Folly of the Multitude which he was obliged to comply with against his Knowledge, for he attempts in many Places to apologize for his Weakness, and reflects severely upon the Judgment of his Audience (particularly in the Prologue, and Chorusses of *Henry the 5th.* and in the Prologue to *Henry the 8th*). Sir *Philip Sidney* sometime before him had condemned the Ignorance and Faults of many Poets, and their notorious Violations of the Unities in the Design and Management of their Fable. As I have the Book at hand you will permit me to read the Passage. 'You shall have *Asia*, says he, of the one Side, and *Afric* of the other; and so many other under–King-doms, that the Player, when he comes in, must ever begin with telling you where he is, or else the Tale will not be conceived. Now you shall have three Ladies walk to gather Flowers, and then we must believe the Stage to be a Garden. By-and-by we hear News of a Ship-wreck in the same Place, then we are to blame if we accept it not for a Rock. Now of Time they are much more liberal; for ordinary it is, that two young Princes fall in Love; after many Traverses she is got with Child, delivered of a fair Boy, he is lost, groweth a Man, falleth in Love, and is ready to get another Child; and all this in two Hours space, which how absurd it is in Sense, even Sense may imagine.' If I might suppose, added *Eugenius*, that Sir *Philip* in this Criticism alluded to any particu-lar Performance, it is probable that he hints at *Pericles, Prince of Tyre*, which abounds with many such palpable Absurdities, and is in the Number of those spurious Pieces which are attributed to *Shakespeare*. If this Conjecture be admitted it may be considered likewise as a Proof of that Play's being none of his; but as I lay no great Stress upon the Thought I shall not claim your Thanks for the Discovery.

The next Instance of the Poet's Understanding and Art is in forming the Characters and Manners. In this Field *Shakespeare* is confessedly invincible; for it is not easy to frame any Idea of a more comprehensive Mind or of an exacter Knowledge of the World than what he displays upon this Head. It is his singular Excellence to mark every Character in the strongest manner with Sentiments peculiarly correspondent, and to maintain the Propriety of each in every Circumstance of Action. Even those which appear to be the most uniform and of the same Complexion will be found, upon a nearer View, to be totally and formally different. The Diversity of these is as great as that of his Comparisons and Similies, for in short he has no two alike; they are as distinct from each other as one Man is from a second in real Life. The Diction also is proportionably varied, and adapted to the Rank and Circumstances of the Speaker. He everywhere discovers a perfect Intimacy with the antient poetic Story, which he always introduceth by the justest Application. Nor does he appear less knowing in Philosophy, History, Mechanics and many other Branches of abstruser Learning. He seems, indeed, interrupted *Neander* with a Smile, to be acquainted with the several Kinds of Science to so great a Degree that were all Arts to be lost they might be recovered with as little Difficulty from the Plays of *Shakespeare*, as from the *Iliad* of *Homer*, or the *Georgics* of *Virgil*.

Your mentioning these antient Authors, replied *Eugenius*, reminds me of the resemblance which there is between the Plays of *Shakespeare* and the Comedians and Satyrists of Antiquity, as I apprehend the Difficulty of understanding both commonly proceeds from the same Causes. An Allusion familiar enough to every Body at the time of writing may be irretrieveably lost, and what Perplexity this must necessarily occasion is extremely obvious. I am apt to imagine there is a great deal of concealed Satire in the Plays of our Author, and frequently in those Places where we least expect it. For it is evident, I think, that many Reflections of this kind on the marvellous Performances of the Writers of that Age, and on the Humours and Opinions of the Times are interspersed in Numbers of his Scenes. And as these have commonly little or no Connection with the Plot and Incidents they receive their chief Grace and Beauty from the Characters who speak, or the Application they are put to. Hence is it that we often find his Clowns or Fools repeating Passages from Plays well known to the Audience of that Age, with a View to ridicule and expose them. And thus, as it were by a kind of Transmutation, what was originally Folly and Stupidity becomes Wit and Humour by the Parody of *Shakespeare*.

This last Remark which you have made, returned *Neander*, confirms a Notion which I have long entertained of *Ben Jonson*, whom I con-

ceive to be far the most obscure of any of our Dramatic Poets; and I
dare say you will heartily join with me in a Wish I have frequently
made, that some Gentleman of Learning would oblige the Public with
a correct Edition of his Works, attended with explanatory Notes in
their proper Places. Abundance of Allusions occur in his Writings, both
to the Customs of his own Age and to those of Antiquity; which being
often very remote, darken the Sentiments to so great a degree that we
have as much Perplexity almost in reading him as we meet with in
Aristophanes or *Plautus*. *Terence* I am sure is infinitely easier, tho' a
Man would not expect to see greater Difficulties in an Author of his
own Country who died but a Century ago, than in another who wrote
in a foreign Language and hath been dead near twenty times as long.
These Difficulties, replied *Eugenius*, are owing in a great Measure to his
Learning: he formed himself upon the antient Models and hath copied
as well their Manner as Expression. We have not, I confess, in *Shakespeare* such direct and visible Traces of Antiquity; and for the same
Reason we are free from that Obscurity which this extravagant Affectation hath created in the other. (14–23)

*   *   *

As it is evident from what hath been said that *Shakespeare* framed
the Sentiments of his Plays in Conformity to the Notions then in
vogue, and made his Kings and Counsellors speak the Language of the
Court, so he drew Descriptions and Images from the Entertainments
most in use, and borrowed Metaphors from the Diversions practised
by Men of Birth and Quality. This lets us into the Reason why we have
such frequent mention of Hawking, Hunting, Archery, and the like.
Falconry in particular was a favourite Diversion of that Age; and the
Poet seems equally fond to illustrate his Thoughts by Allusions to that
before the rest. A Passage in *Othello* is composed of Metaphors which
are all entirely so many Terms in Hawking:

> *If I prove her Haggard,*
> *Tho' that her Jesses were my dear Heart-strings,*
> *I'd whistle her off, and let her down the Wind*
> *To prey at Fortune.*   [3.3.264ff.]

He discovers himself in these Lines a perfect Master of the Sport, as
indeed he always does of every thing which he occasionally introduces
in a Play. And every thing, added *Neander*, which he takes upon him

to describe appears to receive, in my Judgment, an uncommon Lustre and Polish and to be endued with more delicate and softer *Traits* of Beauty than I often find in the Things themselves. Every Description is a capital Piece of Painting, and sometimes even a single Line contains almost the Beauties of a whole Landscape. Thus you may observe, resumed *Eugenius*, that he is equally excellent in his Imagery of hunting, for which I might appeal to so inimitable a Description of a Pack of Hounds that there is scarce a Country 'Squire in the Nation who hath heard of the Name of *Shakespeare* but can repeat it entirely by Heart. The Place which I refer to, is to be found in the *Midsummer Night's Dream*, Act IV. Sc. 2 [111ff.], and we may add to it the following one from *Titus Andronicus*:

> Tamora. *The Birds chaunt Melody on every Bush,*
> *The Snake lies rolled in the chearful Sun,*
> *The green Leaves quiver with the cooling Wind,*
> *And make a chequer'd Shadow on the Ground:*
> *Under their sweet Shade, Aaron, let us sit,*
> *And whilst the babbling Echo mocks the Hounds,*
> *Replying shrilly to the well-tun'd Horns,*
> *As if a double Hunt were heard at once,*
> *Let us sit down, and mark their yelling Noise.* [2.3.12ff.]

The Lines which you have quoted, interposed *Neander*, are taken, I perceive, from a Performance very unequal in itself; it was despised by the Contemporaries of the Poet and is conceived upon the Whole not to have been wrote by him. The Absurdity and Confusion of the Plot, returned *Eugenius*, together with the Meanness of many Parts in this Play, and the Contempt which *Ben Jonson* openly expressed of it when *Shakespeare* was yet living are good Reasons to suppose that all of it did not come from him. Yet the above-mentioned Verses, which were wrote by the most lively Imagination, and others which might be easily produced, are, I think, a sufficient Evidence that they could possibly proceed from no other Hand than his. The Vices of the swelling or low Speeches are redeemed by the Virtues of those which are more natural and simple. It may probably be his first Performance in the dramatic Way, because we are certain it was in Being when the Poet was arrived but to the 25th Year of his Age. The distinguishing Parts of the Play are intirely descriptive . . . (25–7)

*   *   *

I observed in the Beginning of our Conversation, pursued *Eugenius*, that many Passages are discovered in the Poet to be designed with a double Intention. They are proper and consistent if considered as natural in the Character where they are used; and have likewise the Force of a strong and well wrote Satire upon particular Affairs or Persons remarkable at the time of their Appearance. Of this kind is the counterfeited Madness of *Edgar* in the Tragedy of *Lear*, whose wild, grotesque, and incoherent Sentiments are intirely such as we should conceive a Lunatic of that Turn would utter. And they are further designed to ridicule an Imposture discovered about that time, in which the several Fiends mentioned by the Poet were raised up to carry on the Cheat. And perhaps the Character of the Fool is not altogether free from particular Satire and Reflection as where he says, I will speak a *Prophecy* or two before I go.[1] He may hint at certain Forgeries of that kind which were newly coined by the *Papists*; for the Jesuits of that Age were able Conjurers and Seers, and had Oracles upon every Occasion ready cut and dry, tho' they met with the Fate of their Devils, and became the Sport of the Populace and Entertainment of the Stage. I have seen a Book relating to this Subject intitled *Admirable and notable Prophecies uttered by twenty-four Roman Catholics*, by one *James Maxwell*, printed in 1615, the Year before our Poet died. (36–7)

*　　*　　*

Shakespeare wrote with greater Exactness than the Generality of his Readers may imagine, who seldom consider how nice and accurate a Painter he was, as well as the universal Master of Nature, and that he did not render great Subjects more elevated and surprizing by the Magnificence and Sublimity of his Descriptions than he made common and little ones agreeable by his Likeness and Propriety.

If all the Instances, continued *Eugenius*, which I shall hereafter mention do not come fully up to the Point which we propose to settle yet they will convince us at least that *Shakespeare* could not think like the Ancients, and express himself with an equal Simplicity: for I do not pretend to determine that he had his Eye in every Particular upon some ancient Author. I have placed here the Volumes all before me, with some Strictures which I have made from Antiquity, and shall begin with pointing out a Passage in the *Tempest* where the Sentiment is full in the Spirit of *Homer*. It is *Prospero*'s Answer to his Daughter.

---

[1] *King Lear*, 3.2.80. On Shakespeare's use of Harsenet see Theobald in Vol. 2, pp. 458, 507f., 509.

> *Be collected:*
> *No more Amazement; tell your piteous Heart,*
> *There's no Harm done.* [1.2.13ff.]

Would not you think that the Poet was imitating those Places in the other, where his Heroes are rouzing up their Courage to take Heart of Grace, and begin with a

> Τετλαθι δε κραδιη[1]

We may observe also in the same Play a remarkable Example of his Knowledge in the Ancient Poetic Story, when *Ceres* in the Masque speaks thus to *Iris* upon the Approach of *Juno*:

> *High Queen of State,*
> *Great* Juno *comes; I know her by her Gait.* [4.1.101f.]

Here methinks now is no small Mark of the Judgment of our Author in selecting this peculiar Circumstance for the Discovery of *Juno*. And was *Virgil* himself to have described her Motion he would have done it in the same manner, for probably the *Divûm incedo Regina*[2] of that Author might furnish *Shakespeare* with the Hint; and his *Decorum* of the Character is prefectly consistent, and her Attendance upon the Wedding intirely agreeable to her Office.

Let us turn now to the next Play, where a Passage stops us at the very Beginning. *Theseus* complains thus of the Tardiness of Time;

> *Oh, methinks, how slow*
> *This old Moon wanes! she lingers my Desires*
> *Like to a Stepdame, or a Dowager*
> *Long withering out a young Man's Revenue.*
> [*A Midsummer Night's Dream* 1.1.3ff.]

Suppose we were to put this into a *Latin* Dress, could any Words express it more exactly than these of *Horace*:

> *Ut piger Annus*
> *Pupillis, quos dura premit custodia matrum,*
> *Sic mihi tarda fluunt, ingrataque tempora.*[3]
> L. I. Ep. I. v. 21, & seq.

---

[1] *Odyssey*, 20.18: 'Bear up, my heart.'

[2] *Aeneid*, 1.46: 'I, who move as queen of gods.'

[3] 'As the year lags forwards held in check by their mother's strict guardianship: so slow and thankless flow for me the hours which defer my hope . . .'

Pass we on from these to *Measure for Measure*, where in the second Scene of the third Act *Claudio* gives us such an image of the intermediate State after Death as bears a great Resemblance to the *Platonic* Purgations described by *Virgil*.

> *Ay, but to die, and go we know not where; . . .*
>   *. . . the delighted Spirit*
> *To bathe in fiery Floods, or to reside*
> *In thrilling Regions of thick-ribbed Ice,*
> *To be imprison'd in the viewless Winds,*
> *And blown with restless Violence round about*
> *The pendant World, &c.*   [3.1.119ff.]

> *Ergo exercentur pœnis, veterumque malorum*
> *Supplicia expendunt. Aliæ panduntur inanes*
> *Suspensae ad ventos: aliis sub gurgite vasto*
> *Infectum eluitur scelus, aut exuritur igni.*[1]
>   Æneid, L. VI. 739, & seq.

The next Instance which I have observed to demand our Notice occurs in *Much ado about Nothing*, where the Thought is very natural and obvious, founded on a Failing common to Human Nature.

> *What we have we prize not to its worth*
> *While we enjoy it; but being lack'd and lost,*
> *Why, then we rack the Value; then we find*
> *The Virtue that Possession would not shew us*
> *Whilst it was ours.*   [4.1.218ff.]

You may have seen, perhaps, the same Sentiment in many Classic Authors; but the most analogous, and which would almost tempt one to believe the Poet had it directly before him, is the following from *Plautus*:

> *Tum denique homines nostra intelligimus bona,*
> *Quom quæ in potestate habuimus, ea amisimus.*[2]
>   Captiv. Act I. Sc. II. v. 29.

Shakespeare's Translation of these Verses, if I may take the Liberty to call it so, tho' something diffused and paraphrastical exceeds, in my

---

[1] 'Therefore are they schooled with penalties, and for older sins pay punishment: some are hung stretched out to the empty winds; from some the stain of guilt is washed away under swirling floods or burned out in fire.'

[2] 142f.: 'Ah, we mortals realise the value of our blessings only when we have lost them.'

humble Opinion, the Original; for the Proposition being diversified so agreeably makes a deeper Impression on the Mind and Memory.

If we compare the Description of the wounded Stag in *As you like it* with *Virgil*'s Relation of the Death of the same Creature, we shall find that *Shakespeare*'s is as highly finished and as masterly as the other:

> *The wretched Animal heav'd forth such Groans,*
> *That their Discharge did stretch his Leathern Coat*
> *Almost to bursting; and the big round Tears*
> *Cours'd one another down his innocent Cheeks*
> *In piteous Chase.*   [2.1.36ff.]

What an exquisite Image this of dumb Distress, and of a wounded Animal languishing in the Agonies of Pain! I cannot help thinking that the Lines of *Virgil* do not reach it altogether so perfectly.

[Quotes *Æneid* 7.500ff.: 'But the wounded creature fled under the familiar roof, and moaning crept into his stall, where, bleeding and suppliant-like, he filled all the house with his plaints.']

I now turn to the Tragedy of *King Lear*, where his passionate Exclamations against his Daughters appear to have been copied from the *Thyestes* of *Seneca*.

> *I will have such Revenges on you both*
> *That all the World shall—I will do such things;*
> *What they are yet I know not; but they shall be*
> *The Terrors of the Earth.*   [2.4.278ff.]

> *Fac quod nulla posteritas probet,*
> *Sed nulla taceat: aliquod audendum est nefas*
> *Atrox, cruentum:*[1]   Act II. v. 192, & seq.

> *Haud, quid sit, scio.*
> *Sed grande quiddam est.*[2]   Ibid. 270.

And in the fourth Act we meet with a Passage which deserves our Attention upon a double Account. *Gloster* lamenting the Abuses which had been put both on himself and his Son *Edgar*, wishes that he might find him, and expresseth himself thus,

> *O dear Son*, Edgar,
> *The Food of thy abused Father's Wrath;*
> *Might I but live to see thee in my Touch*
> *I'd say, I had Eyes again.*   [4.1.22ff.]

[1] '. . . do what no coming age shall approve, but none forget. I must dare some crime atrocious, bloody . . .'

[2] 'I know not what it is, but 'tis some mighty thing.'

To say nothing of the *Oculatæ Manus* of the Comic Poet,[1] you may remark in these Lines a Contrariety of Metaphor equally bold and elegant, of which you may find many Examples in the ancient Tragedians and particularly in *Æschylus*, the *Athenian Shakespeare*. The whole of it has a remarkable Affinity to the Lamentation of *Œdipus* in his Blindness, desiring that his Daughters might be brought him:

> *Oh, might I once but have them in my Touch,*
> *Weep o'er their Sorrows, and lament our Fate.*
> *With either Hand to touch their tender Forms,*
> *Would make me think that I had Eyes again.*
> [Oedipus Tyrannus, 1466ff.]

There is another Passage in *King Lear* which, though not taken expresly from any particular Author, is directly the Language of the Ancients upon such Occasions. They were frequently induced by Misfortunes to deny the Justice and Equity of Heaven; and when they poured forth their Complaints, we heard of nothing but *Superûm Crimina, & Deorum Iniquitas. Claudian*, who was sceptically inclined, and questioned the Knowledge and Wisdom of Providence, at length acquitted the Gods and was convinced by the Punishment of *Rufinus*:

> *Abstulit hunc tandem Rufini pæna tumultum,*
> ABSOLVITQUE DEOS.
> Claudian in Rufin. L. I. sub init.[2]

The Close of the Period in *Shakespeare* is exactly of the same kind:

> *Take Physic*, Pomp,
> *Expose thy self to feel what Wretches feel,*
> *That thou mayest shake the Superflux to them,*
> *And shew the Heavens more just.* [3.4.33ff.]

The Thought in both Poets is evidently false, not being founded upon Truth and Reason, and is parallel to many of the stoical Extravagancies of *Lucan*.

By continuing our Progress, we come to the first Part of *Henry the IVth*, where we have an humorous Application of a *Greek* Proverb: 'How long is't ago, *Jack*, says *Hal* to *Falstaff*, since thou saw'st thy own Knee? *Fal*. My own Knee? When I was about thy Years, *Hal*, I could

---

[1] Plautus, *Asinaria* 202: 'Our hands have eyes always: seeing is believing with them.'
[2] 1.20f.: 'At last Rufinus's fate has dispelled this uncertainty and freed the gods from this imputation.'

have crept into any *Alderman's Thumb Ring.*' Creeping through a Ring was a Phrase usually applied to such as were extremely thin; for this Reason the old Woman in *Aristophanes* makes use of it in that Sense: 'You may draw me, says she, very easily through a Ring. Ay, replies *Chremylus*, if that Ring was about the Size of a Hoop.' (*Plutus*, 1067ff.)

From this we may proceed to the *Second Part of Henry the IVth*, where we meet with a political Observation of *Warwick's*, who accounts for the Disloyalty of *Northumberland* by observing that he had proved faithless to King *Richard*:

> There is a History in all Men's Lives,
> Figuring the Nature of the Times deceased:
> The which observ'd, a Man may prophecy
> With a near Aim of the Main Chance of things
> As yet not come to Life; which in their Seeds,
> And weak Beginnings lie intreasured,   [3.1.80ff.]

A Section of *Antoninus* will confirm and illustrate the Remark of *Shakespeare*: I will read it to you as I find it translated by Mr *Collier*. 'By looking back into History, and considering the Fate and Revolutions of Government, you will be able to form a Guess, and almost prophesy upon the future; for things past, present, and to come are strangely uniform and of a Colour, and are commonly cast in the same Mould. So that upon the Matter, forty Years of Human Life may serve for a Sample of ten thousand.' *Lib*. VII. *Sect*. 49. And such is the Character which *Pliny* gives of *Mauricus*: 'Vir erat gravis, prudens, multis experimentis eruditus, & qui futura possit ex præteritis prævidere.' *L*. I. *Epist*. 5.[1] (53-61)

*   *   *

We come next to that celebrated Soliloquy in the third Act, Sc. 2. [*Hamlet*] which seems so peculiarly the Production of *Shakespeare* that you would hardly imagine it can be parallelled in all Antiquity. Yet I will produce some Examples of the same kind; one of which at least will shew how nearly two great Tragedians could think upon the same Subject. A learned Gentleman* has taken Notice of the Conformity which there is between a Passage in *Plato's* Apology for *Socrates*, and the following Lines in this Speech. The Sentiment of *Plato* is to this

---

[1] Letters, 1.5.16: 'His opinions carry weight and his wisdom is gained from experience, so that he can judge the future by the past.'

* Translation of Tryphiodorus, p. 76 [Oxford, 1739; by W. Merrick].

Purpose; *If*, says he, *there be no Sensation after Death, but as when one sleeps, and sees no Dream, Death were then an inestimable Gain* [*Apology*, 40 d–e]. And the Verses of the Poet are these which follow.

> *To die! to sleep!*
> *No more—and by a Sleep to say we end*
> *The Heart-ach, &c.—*
> > *To die! to sleep!*
> *To sleep! perchance to dream! Ay, there's the Rub, &c.*
>
> [3.1.64ff.]

And the whole has a remarkable Similitude with these Verses in the *Hippolytus* of *Euripides*.

> *How full of Sorrow are the Days of Man,*
> *Of endless Labour and unceasing Woe!*
> *And what succeeds, our Hopes but ill presage,*
> *For Clouds conceal, and Darkness rests upon it.*
> *Yet still we suffer Light, averse to Life:*
> *Still bend reluctant to those Ills we have,*
> *Thro' Dread of others which we know not of,*
> *And fearful of that undiscovered Shore.*   [190ff.]

And in particular,

> *The undiscovered Country from whose Bourn*
> *No Traveller returns,*

may be very well translated by this of the *Latin* Poet.

> *Nunc it per Iter tenebricosum,*
> *Illuc, unde negant redire quinquam.*[1]
>
> Catull. III. v. 11

I apprehend it was from the Frequency of these moral Reflections, interposed *Neander*, many of which were probably put into his Mouth by *Socrates*, that *Euripides* had the Appellation given him of the Dramatic Philosopher. The same Title may be attributed to *Shakespeare*, if we are determined by the Suffrage of a noble Author [Shaftesbury]; whose Opinion will not be hastily disputed if we think with his Admirers that he has reduced Morality to a less ungainly Form than what she usually had. His Judgment on this Tragedy would confirm us, which he properly considers, as a continued Moral[2]; a Series of deep

---

[1] 'Now he goes along the dark road, thither whence they say no one returns.'
[2] See Vol. 2, p. 264.

Reflections proceeding from the Mouth of one Person on the most important Subject. Every Person, returned *Eugenius*, has those particular Sentiments which constitute the Character: for even *Polonius* appears furnished with such Observations which long Experience naturally produces. What he observes of the Partiality of Mothers to their Children in the Commission of any Crime [*Hamlet*, 3.3.31ff.] is agreeable to a Remark of *Terence*.

> *Matres omnes filiis*
> *In Peccato adjutrices, Auxilio in Paterna injuria*
> *Solent esse.*[1]   Heauton. Act V. Sc. 2. v. 38.

We are at length, *Neander*, drawing near to the Conclusion of our Enquiry, for I shall end with an Instance from *Othello*, which is visibly parallel to a Thought of the like Nature in *Terence*.

> *If I were now to die*
> *'Twere now to be most happy: For I fear*
> *My Soul hath her Content so absolute,*
> *That not another Comfort like to this*
> *Succeeds in unknown Fate.*   [2.1.187ff.]

And thus *Chærea*, in an Extasy of Joy, breaks out in a like Exclamation.

> *Proh* Jupiter!
> *Nunc Tempus profecto est, cum perpeti me possum interfici:*
> *Ne Vita aliquâ hoc Gaudium contaminet ægritudine.*[2]
>   Eunuch. Act III. Sc. 5. (68–71)

*   *   *

I believe, continued *Neander*, that not only the Riches of *Shakespeare*'s Genius prevented him from borrowing from the Ancients in many Instances, but that he was prevented as much from doing so by his Judgment likewise. For marking every Character with Sentiments which cannot possibly be applied to any other he was under the less Necessity of having recourse to any common-place Topics, and especially to that curious Mixture of the fierce and tender, of ranting against the Gods, idolizing a Mistress, or unnaturally braving ones own Mis-

---

[1] 991ff.: 'mothers usually help their sons in face of a peccadillo, back 'em up when their fathers maltreat them.'

[2] 550ff.: 'O heavens! this is a moment when I could bear dissolution for fear life pollute this exultation with some distress.'

fortunes, than all which nothing can be more dextrous, it being as easy as lying. Nor was he obliged to call out in the Style of Patriotism, on *Liberty* and *Virtue*, sentiments which have stood many modern Poets in great stead, being suitable to every great Man, and equally proper either in the Mouth of a *Scipio* or *Hannibal*.

It will be alledged, perhaps, that *Shakespeare* took his Hints from the Translations which were made in the Reigns of Queen *Elizabeth* and King *James*. *Ovid* appears to have been a favourite Author with the Poet, whose Cause he pleads in the following Lines:

> *Let's be no Stoics, nor no Stocks I pray,*
> *Or so devote to* Aristotle's *Checks,*
> *As* Ovid *be an out-cast quite abjured.*
>
> [*The Taming of the Shrew*, 1.1.31ff.]

As his own Translations from this Poet prove him to be a Master of his Works I think it may be concluded he was a competent Judge of other Authors who wrote in the same Language. These are much superior to a Translation of the *Metamorphoses* by *Arthur Golding*, a Person of some Eminence for Learning in those Days, who translated also *Caesar*'s Commentaries. My Edition is printed in 1603, on a black Letter, and in the same Metre with *Phaer's Virgil*. (78–9)

114. John Upton on Shakespeare

1748

From *Critical Observations on Shakespeare*, this text from 'The Second Edition, with Alterations and Additions' (1748).

John Upton (1707–60), Prebendary of Rochester, published his *Critical Observations* in 1746; he is best known for his edition of *The Faerie Queene* in 1758 and for other Spenser criticism.

[From Book 1]

SECTION II.

I have often wondered with what kind of reasoning any one could be so far imposed on as to imagine that Shakespeare had no learning when it must at the same time be acknowledged that without learning he cannot be read with any degree of understanding or taste. At this time of day he will hardly be allowed that inspiration which his brother bards formerly claim'd, and which claim, if the pretensions were any ways answerable, was generally granted them. However we are well assured from the histories of his times that he was early initiated into the sacred company of the Muses, and tho' he might have small avocations yet he soon returned again with greater eagerness to his beloved studies. Hence he was possessed of sufficient helps, either from abroad or at home, to midwife into the world his great and beautiful conceptions and to give them birth and being. That a contrary opinion has ever prevailed is owing partly to Ben Jonson's jealousy, and partly to the pride and pertness of dunces who, under such a name as Shakespeare's, would gladly shelter their own idleness and ignorance.

He was bred in a learned age, when even the court ladies learnt Greek, and the Queen of England among scholars had the reputation of being a scholar. Whether her successor had equal learning and sense is not material to be at present enquir'd into; but thus far is certain, that letters, even then, stood in some rank of praise. Happy for us that our poet and Jonson came into life so early; that they lived not in an age when not only their art but every thing else that had wit and elegance began to be despised, 'till the minds of the people came to be disposed for all that hypocrisy, nonsense, and superstitious fanaticism which soon after like a deluge overwhelmed this nation. 'Twere to be wished that with our restored king some of that taste of literature had been restored which we enjoyed in the days of Queen Elizabeth. But when we brought home our frenchified king we did then, and have even to this day continued to, bring from France our models not only of letters but (O shame to free born Englishmen!) of morals and manners. Hence every thing, unless of French extraction, appears aukward and antiquated. Our poets write to the humour of the age, and when their own little stock is spent they set themselves to work on new-modelling Shakespeare's plays, and adapting them to the tast of their audience by stripping off their antique and proper tragic dress, and by introducing in these mock-tragedies not only gallantry to women but an endeavour to raise a serious distress from the disappointment of lovers; not considering that the passion of love, which one would think they should understand something of, is a comic passion. In short they make up a poet of shreds and patches, so that the ancient robe of our tragedian, by this miserable darning and threadbare patch-work resembles the long motley coat of the Fool in our old plays, introduced to raise the laughter of the spectators. And I am afraid, if the matter was minutely examined into, we should find that many passages in some late editions of our poet have been altered or added or lopped off entirely thro' modern and French refinement.

SECTION III.

The misfortune seems to be that scarcely any one pays a regard to what Shakespeare *does* write, but they are always guessing at what he *should* write; nor in any other light is he look'd on than as a poor mechanic, a fellow, 'tis true, of genius, who says now and then very good things, but wild and uncultivated; and as one by no means proper company for lords and ladies, maids of honour and court-pages, 'till some poet or other who knows the world better takes him in hand, and introduces him in this modern dress to *good company*. (3–8)

★　　★　　★

SECTION IV.

It seems no wonder that the masculine and nervous Shakespeare and Milton should so little please our effeminate taste, and the more I consider our studies and amusements the greater is the wonder they should ever please at all. The childish fancy and love of false ornaments follow us thro' life, nothing being so displeasing to us as nature and simplicity. This admiration of false ornaments is visibly seen even in our relish of books. After such examples can we still admire that rattle of the Muses, a jingling sound of like endings tag'd to every line? Whilst we have still preserved some noble remains of antiquity, and are not entirely void of true genius's among our own nation, what taste must it shew to fly for amusements to the crude productions of an enslaved nation? Yet this is our reigning taste; from hence our lawgivers are taught to form their lives and conduct, with a thorough contempt of ancient learning, and all those whose inclinations lead them thro' such untrodden paths.

But this perhaps will not appear so surprising when 'tis considered that the more liberal sciences and humane letters are not the natural growth of these Gothic and northern regions. We are little better than sons and successors of the Goths, ever and anon in danger of relapsing into our original barbarity. And how far the corruption of even our public diversions may contribute to the corruption of our manners may be an inquiry not unworthy the civil magistrate: lawgivers of old did not deem it beneath their care and caution . . . (15–16)

★   ★   ★

SECTION V.

But perhaps our poet's art will appear to greater advantage if we enter into a detail and a minuter examination of his plays. There are many who, never having read one word of Aristotle, gravely cite his rules and talk of the unities of time and place at the very mentioning Shakespeare's name; they don't seem ever to have given themselves the trouble of considering whether or no his story does not hang together, and the incidents follow each other naturally and in order; in short whether or no he has not a beginning, middle and end. If you will not allow that he wrote strictly tragedies yet it may be granted that he wrote dramatic heroic poems; in which, is there not an imitation of one action, serious, entire, and of a just length, and which, without the help of narration, excites pity and terror in the beholder's breast and by the means of these refines suchlike passions? So that he fully answers 'that end, which both at the first and now, was and is, to hold as 'twere the mirrour up to nature; to shew virtue her own feature, scorn her own image, and the very age and body of the time his form and pressure.'*

Let us suppose Shakespeare has a mind to paint the fatal effects of ambition. For this purpose he makes choice of a hero well known from the British chronicles, and as the story had a particular relation to the king then reigning 'twas an interesting story; and though full of machinery yet probable, because the wonderful tales there related were not only mention'd in history but vulgarly believed. This hero had conduct and courage, and was universally courted and caress'd; but his master-passion was ambition. What pity that such a one should fall off from the ways of virtue! It happened that he and his friend (from whom descended the Stewart family) one day, travelling thro' a forest, met three witches who foretold his future royalty. This struck his ambitious fancy; crowns, sceptres and titles danced before his dazled eyes, and all his visionary dreams of happiness are to be compleated in the possession of a kindom. The prediction of the witches he makes known by letter to his wife who, ten times prouder than himself, knew there was one speedy and certain way to the crown, by treason and murder. This pitch of cruelty a human creature may be work'd up to, who is prompted by self-love (that narrow circle of love, beginning and ending in itself), and by ambitious views. Beside, cruelty is most notorious in weak and womanish natures. As 'twas customary for the king to visit his nobles he came one day to our hero's castle at Inverness; where time and place conspiring, he is murdered; and thus the so much desired crown is obtained.

Who does not see that had Shakespeare broken off the story here it would have been incomplete? For his design being to shew the effects of ambition, and having made choice of *one* passion, of *one* hero, he is to carry it throughout in all its consequences. I mentioned above that the story was interesting, as a British story; and 'tis equally so as Macbeth, the hero of the tragedy, is drawn a man not a monster; a man of virtue, 'till he hearkened to the lures of ambition: then how is his mind agitated and convulsed, now virtue, now vice prevailing; 'till reason,

---

* *Hamlet*, Act III [2.20]; he seems to have had in his mind what Donatus in his life of Terence cites from Cicero, *Comoedia est imitatio vitae, speculum consuetudinis, imago veritatis.* ['Comedy is the imitation of life, the glass of custom, and the image of truth.']

as is usual, gives way to inclination. And how beautifully, from such a wavering character, does the poet let you into the knowledge of the secret springs and motives of human actions! In the soliloquy before the murder all the aggravating circumstances attending such a horrid deed appear in their full view before him.

He's here in double trust: [1.7.12ff.] (26–31)

*   *   *

There is such a cast of antiquity, and something so horridly solemn in this infernal ceremony of the witches, that I never consider it without admiring our poet's improvement of every hint he receives from the ancients or moderns. Then again those apparitions being* symbolical representations of what shall happen to him, are introduced paltering with him in a double sense, and leading him on, according to the common notions of diabolical oracles, to his confusion. And when the kings appear we have a piece of machinery that neither the ancients or moderns can exceed. I know nothing any where can parallel it, but that most sublime passage in Virgil, where the great successors of Aeneas pass in review before the hero's eyes. Our poet's closing with a compliment to James the first upon the union, equals Virgil's compliment to Augustus. (36–9)

*   *   *

SECTION IX.

. . . Other plays of our poet are called *First and second parts*, as *The first and second parts of King Henry IV*. But these plays are independent each of the other. *The first part*, as 'tis named, ends with the settlement in the throne of King Henry IV when he had gained a compleat victory over his rebellious subjects. *The second part* contains King Henry's death; shewing his son, afterwards Henry V, in the various lights of a good-natured rake, 'till he comes to the crown; when 'twas necessary for him to assume a more manlike character and princely dignity. To call these two plays *first and second parts* is as injurious to the author-character of Shakespeare as it would be to Sophocles to call his two plays on Oedi-

---

* The armed head represents symbolically Macbeth's head cut off and brought to Malcolm by Macduff. The bloody child is Macduff untimely ripp'd from his mother's womb. The child with a crown on his head, and a bough in his hand, is the royal Malcolm, who ordered his soldiers to hew them down a bough and bear it before them to Dunsinane.

294

pus, *first and second parts of King Oedipus*. Whereas the one is *Oedipus King of Thebes*, the other, *Oedipus at Athens*.

Julius Caesar is as much a *whole* as the *Ajax* of Sophocles: which does not end at the death of Ajax but when the spectators are made acquainted with some consequences that might be expected after his death; as the reconciliation between Teucer and the Grecian chieftains, and the honourable interment of Ajax. Nor does our poet's play end at the death of Julius Caesar but when the audience are let into the knowledge of what befel the conspirators, being the consequences of the murder of the hero of the play. The story hangs together as in a heroic poem.

The fable is one in *The Tempest*, viz. the restoration of Prospero to the dukedom of Milan: and the poem hastens into the midst of things, presenting the usurping duke shipwrecked on the inchanted island, where Prospero had long resided.

The unity of action is very visible in *Measure for Measure*. That reflection of Horace,

> *Quid leges sine moribus*
> *Vanae proficiunt?*[1]

is the chief moral of the play. How knowing in the characters of men is our poet, to make the severe and inexorable Angelo incur the penalty of that sanguinary law, which he was so forward to revive!

The three plays containing several historical transactions in the reign of K. Henry VI (if entirely written by Shakespeare, which I somewhat suspect) are only rude and rough draughts; and tho' they have in them many fine passages yet I shall not undertake to justify them according to the strict rules of criticism.

SECTION IX.

From what has been already observed it becomes less difficult to see into the art and design of Shakespeare informing and planning his dramatic poems. The unity of action he seems to have thought himself obliged to regard; but not at all the unities of time and place, no more than if he were writing an epic poem. Aristotle (our chief authority, because he drew his observations from the most perfect models) tells us that the epic poem has no determined time, but the dramatic he fixes to a

---

[1] *Odes* 3.24.35f.: 'of what avail are empty laws, if we lack principle?'

single day: the former is to be *read*, the latter to be *seen*. Now a man cannot easily impose on himself that what he sees represented in a continued action, at a certain period of time, and in a certain place, should take up several years and be transacted in several places. But dramatic poetry is the art of imposing; and he is the best poet who can best impose on his audience; and he is the wisest man who is easiest imposed on. The story therefore (which is the principal part, and as it were the very soul of tragedy) being made a *whole*, with natural dependance and connexion, the spectator seldom considers the length of time necessary to produce all these incidents but passes all that over; as in *Julius Caesar*, *Macbeth*, *Hamlet*, and in other plays of our poet.

To impose on the audience, with respect to the unity of place, there is an artificial contrivance of scenes. For my own part, I see no great harm likely to accrue to the understanding in thus accompanying the poet in his magical operations and in helping on an innocent deceit; while he not only raises or soothes the passions but transports me from place to place just as it pleases him, and carries on the thread of his story. (58–62)

*　　*　　*

SECTION X.

As dramatic poetry is the imitation of an action, and as there can be no action but what proceeds from the manners and the sentiments, manners and sentiments are its essential parts; and the former come next to be considered, as the source and cause of action. 'Tis action that makes us happy or miserable; and 'tis manners whereby the characters, the various inclinations, and genius of the persons are marked and distinguished. There are four things to be observed in manners.

I. That they be *good*. Not only strongly marked and distinguished but *good* in a moral sense, as far forth as the character will allow. . . . (65)

Upon these principles I cannot defend such a character as Richard III as proper for the stage. But much more faulty is the Jew's character in *The Merchant of Venice*, who is cruel without necessity. These are not pictures of human creatures, and are beheld with horror and detestation. . . . (67)

II. The manners ought to be *suitable*. When the poet has formed his character, the person is to act up to it. And here the age, the sex, and condition are to be considered. . . .

Shakespeare seems to me not to have known such a character as a fine lady; nor does he ever recognize their dignity. What tramontanes in love are his Hamlets, the young Percy, and Henry the Fifth? Instead of the lady Bettys, and lady Fannys, who shine so much in modern comedies he brings you on the stage plain Mrs Ford and Mrs Page, two honest good-humoured wives of two plain country gentlemen. His tragic ladies are rather seen, than heard; such as Miranda, Desdemona, Ophelia, and Portia. . . . (69–71)

III. The poet should give his manners that resemblance which history or common report has published of them. . . . Shakespeare very strictly observes this rule, and if ever he varies from it 'tis with great art. (73)

★   ★   ★

IV. The manners ought to be uniform and consistent: and whenever a change of manners is made care should be taken that there appear proper motives for such a change, and the audience are to be prepared before hand. . . .

Who does not all along see that when prince Henry comes to be king he will assume a character suitable to his dignity? And this change the audience expect.

> P. Henry. *I know you all, and will a while uphold*
> *The unyok'd humour of your idleness:*
> [1 *Henry IV*, 1.2.188ff.]

The uxorious and jealous Othello is easily wrought to act deeds of violence and murder. You know the haughty Coriolanus will persevere in his obstinacy and proud contempt of the commons: as well as that the resentful Achilles [in *Iliad*, IX] will never be prevailed on by any offers from Agamemnon to return to the field. Angelo, so severe against the common frailty of human nature, never turns his eye on his own character. What morose bigot or demure hypocrite ever did? From Hamlet's filial affection you expect what his future behaviour will be when the ghost bids him *revenge* his murder. The philosophical character of Brutus bids you expect consistency and steadiness from his behaviour. He thought the killing of Antony, when Caesar's assassination was resolved on, would appear too bloody and unjust:

> *Let us be* SACRIFICERS! *but not butchers:*
> *Let's carve him as a dish* FIT FOR THE GODS.
> [*Julius Caesar*, 2.1.166f.]

The hero, therefore, full of this idea of sacrificing Caesar to his injured country, after stabbing him in the senate tells the Romans to stoop and besmear their hands and their swords in the blood of the sacrifice. This was agreeable to an ancient and religious custom. So in Aeschylus we read, that the seven captains who came against Thebes sacrificed a bull and dipped their hands in the gore, invoking at the same time the gods of war, and binding themselves with an oath to revenge the cause of Eteocles. And Xenophon tells us that when the barbarians ratified their treaty with the Greeks they made a sacrifice, and dipped their spears and swords in the blood of the victim. By this solemn action Brutus gives the assassination of Caesar a religious air and turn; and history too informs us that he marched out of the senate house with his bloody hands, proclaiming liberty.

As there is nothing pleases the human mind so much as order and consistency, so when the poet has art to paint this uniformity in manners he not only hinders confusion but brings the audience acquainted, as it were, with the person represented; you see into his character, know how he will behave, and what part he will take on any emergency. And Shakespeare's characters are all thus strongly marked and manner'd. (76-9)

$$\star \quad \star \quad \star$$

SECTION XIII.

If we will consider Shakespeare's tragedies as dramatic heroic poems, some ending with a happy others with an unhappy catastrophe, why then, if Homer introduces a buffoon character both among his gods and heroes in his *Iliad*, and a ridiculous monster Polypheme in his *Odyssey*, might not Shakespeare in his heroic drama exhibit a Falstaff, a Caliban, or clown? Here is no mixture of various fables: tho' the incidents are many the story is one. 'Tis true, there is a mixture of characters, not all proper to excite those tragic passions, pity and terror; the serious and comic being so blended as to form in some measure what Plautus calls tragicomedy, where not two different stories, the one tragic, the other comic, are preposterously jumbled together, as in *The Spanish Fryar* and *Oroonoko*, but the unity of the fable being preserved, several ludicrous characters are interspersed, as in a heroic poem. Nor does the mind from hence suffer any violence, being only accidentally called off from the serious story to which it soon returns again, and perhaps better prepared by this little refreshment. The tragic episode of Dido is followed by the sports in honour of old Anchises. Immediately after the quarrel among the heroes, and the wrathful debates arising in heaven, the deformed Vulcan assumes the office of cup-bearer, and raises a laugh among the heavenly synod. Milton has introduced a piece of mirth in his battle of the gods, where the evil spirits, elevated with a little success, *stand scoffing* and punning *in pleasant vein*. But these are masterly strokes, and touches of great artists, not to be imitated by poets who creep on the ground but by those only who soar with the eagle wings of Homer, Milton, or Shakespeare.

But so far at least must be acknowledged true of our dramatic poet, that he is always a strict observer of *decorum* and constantly a friend to the cause of virtue: hence he shews in it's proper light into what miseries mankind are led by indulging wrong opinions. No philosopher seems ever to have more minutely examined into the different manners, passions, and inclinations of mankind; nor is there known a character, perhaps that of Socrates only excepted, where refined ridicule, raillery, wit, and humour were so mixed and united with what is most grave and serious in morals and philosophy. This is the magic with which he works such wonders. . . .

It seems to me that this philosophical mixture of character is scarce at all attended to by the moderns. Our grave writers are dully grave; and our men of wit are lost to all sense of gravity. 'Tis all formality, or all buffoonry. However this mixture is visible in the writings of Shakespeare; he knew the pleasing force of humour, and the dignity of gravity. (94–8)

*   *   *

SECTION XV.

. . . One could wish that Shakespeare was as free from flattery as Sophocles and Euripides. But our liberty was then in its dawn, so that some pieces of flattery which we find in Shakespeare must be ascribed to the times. To omit some of his rants about kings, which border on blasphemy, how abruptly has he introduced, in his *Macbeth*, a physician giving Malcolm an account of Edward's touching for the king's evil? And this to pay a servile homage to king James, who highly valued himself for a miraculous power (as he and his credulous subjects really believed) of curing a kind of scrophulous humours, which frequently are known to go away of themselves in either sex when they arrive at a certain age. In his *K. Henry VIII* the story which should have ended at the marriage of Anna Bullen is lengthened out on purpose to make a christening of Elizabeth and to introduce by way of prophecy a complement to her royal person and dignity: and what is still worse, when the play was some time after acted before K. James, another prophetical patch of flattery was tacked to it. If a subject is taken from the Roman history he seems afraid to do justice to the citizens. The patricians were the few in conspiracy against the many, and the struggles of the people were an honest struggle for that share of power which was kept unjustly from them. No wonder the historians have represented the tribunes factious and the people rebellious, when most of that sort now remaining wrote after the subversion of their constitution, and under the fear or favour of the Caesars. One would think our poet had been bred in the court of Nero when we see in what colours he paints the tribunes or the people: he seems to have no other idea of them than as a mob of Wat Tylers and Jack Cades. Hence he has spoiled one of the finest subjects of tragedy from the Roman history, his *Coriolanus*. But if this be the fault of Shakespeare 'twas no less the fault of Virgil and Horace; he errs in good company. Yet this is a poor apology, for the poet ought never to submit his art to wrong opinions and prevailing fashion.

And now I am considering the faulty side of our poet I cannot pass over his ever and anon confounding the manners of the age which he is describing with those in which he lived: for if these are at all introduced it should be done with great art and delicacy, and with such an antique cast as Virgil has given to his Roman customs and manners. Much less can many of his anacronisms be defended. Other kind of errors (if they may be so called) are properly the errors of great genius's: such are inaccuracies of language and a faulty sublime, which is surely preferable to a faultless mediocrity. Shakespeare labouring with a multiplicity of sublime ideas often gives himself not time to be delivered of them by the rules of *slow-endeavouring art*: hence he crowds various figures together, and metaphor upon metaphor, and runs the hazard of far-fetched expressions; whilst, intent on nobler ideas, he condescends not to grammatical niceties. Here the audience are to accompany the poet in his conceptions and to supply what he has sketched out for them. I will mention an instance or two of this sort. Hamlet is speaking to his father's ghost,

> *Oh! answer me,*
> *Let me not burst in ignorance; but tell*
> *Why thy canoniz'd bones, hearsed in death,*
> *Have burst their cearments? &c.* [1.4.45ff.]

Again, Macbeth in a soliloquy before he murders Duncan,

> *Besides, this Duncan*
> *Hath born his faculties so meek, hath been*
> *So clear in his great office, that his virtues*
> *Will plead, like angels, trumpet-tongu'd against*
> *The deep damnation of his taking off:*
> *And Pity, like a naked new-born babe,*
> *Striding the blast, or heav'n's cherubim hors'd*
> *Upon the sightless couriers of the air*
> *Shall blow the horrid deed in every eye;*
> *That tears shall drown the wind.* [1.7.16ff.]

Many other passages of this kind might be mention'd, which pass off tolerably well in the mouth of the actor while the imagination of the spectator helps and supplies every seeming inaccuracy; but they will no more bear a close view than some designedly unfinished and rough sketches of a masterly hand. (125–9)

⋆　　⋆　　⋆

[Book II, Section VII: on textual variants
and editors' mistakes]

And to add one instance more. In *The Tempest*, Act II.

> Ten consciences, that stand 'twixt me and Milan
> *Candy'd* be they, and melt, e'er they molest! [2.1.269f.]

We must read,

> *Discandy'd be they, and melt e'er they molest!*

Discandy'd. i.e. dissolved. Discandy and melt are used as synonomous terms in *Antony and Cleopatra*, Act IV.

> The hearts
> That pannell'd me at heels, to whom I gave
> Their wishes, do *discandy, melt* their sweets
> On blossoming Caesar. [4.12.20ff.]

By the bye, what a strange phrase is this,* *The hearts that pannell'd me at heels.* And how justly has Mr Theobald flung it out of the context! But whether he has placed in it's room a Shakespearean expression, may admit of a doubt.

> The hearts
> That pantler'd me at heels.

Now 'tis contrary to all rules of criticism to coin a word for an author, which word, supposing it to have been the author's own, would appear far fetched and improper. In such a case, therefore, we should seek remedy from the author himself: and here opportunely a passage occurs in *Timon*, Act IV.

> *Apem.* Will these moist trees
> That have outliv'd the eagle, *page thy heels*
> And skip when thou point'st out?   [4.3.222ff.]

From hence I would in the above-mention'd verses correct,

> The hearts
> That *pag'd* me at the heels, to whom I gave
> Their wishes, &c

But to return to the place in *The Tempest*: The verse is to be slurr'd in scansion, thus:

> *Discandy'd be they' and melt | e'ĕr thēy | mŏlēst.*

The printers thought the verse too long, and gave it

> *Candy'd be they and melt.*

But *candy'd* is that which is grown into a consistency, as some sorts of confectionary ware: Fr. *candir*, Ital. *candire*, hence used for congeal'd, fixt as in a frost. So in *Timon*:

> *Will the cold brook,*
> CANDIED *with ice*, &c.   [4.3.224f.]

---

* In this second edition I thought once to strike out this criticism, because I am persuaded Shakespeare's words ought not to be changed. Who is so unacquainted with our author as to be ignorant of his vague and licentious use of metaphors; his sporting (as it were) with the meaning of words?—The allusion here, licentious as it is, is to the pannel of a wainscot. But hear the poet himself in *As You Like It*. Act III. 'Jaq. This fellow will but JOIN you together, as they JOIN WAINSCOT,' [AYLI, 3.3.75] So that by *the hearts that pannell'd me at heels*, he means *the hearts that* JOIN'D *me, united themselves to me*, &c., This might have been lengthened into a simile, but he chooses to express it more closely by a metaphor.

Discandy'd therefore seems our poet's own word. (199–202)

★　　★　　★

In *King Lear*, Act I.

> Ingratitude! thou marble-hearted fiend,
> More hideous when thou shew'st thee in a child,
> Than the sea-monster.　　　　　　　　　[1.4.259ff.]

Read, 'Than i'th' sea-monster.' Meaning the river-horse, Hippopotamus*; the hieroglyphical symbol of impiety and ingratitude. (203)

★　　★　　★

SECTION IX.

'Tis a common expression in the western counties to call an ill-natured, sour person, VINNID. For *vinewed, vinowed, vinny* or *vinew* (the word is variously written) signifies mouldy. In *Troilus and Cressida*, Act II, Ajax speaks to Thersites, *thou vinnidst leaven* [2.1.14] i.e. thou most mouldy sour dough. Let this phrase be transplanted from the west into Kent, and they will pronounce it *Whinidst leaven*. So that it seems to me 'twas some Kentish person who occasioned this mistake, either player or transcriber, who could not bring his mouth to pronounce the V consonant, as 'tis remarkable the Kentish men cannot at this day. And this accounts for many of the Latin words, which begin with V, being turned into w, as *Vidua, widua*, Widow; *Ventus, wentus*, Wind; *Vallum, Wallum*, Wall; *Via, Wia*, Way, &c. In the same play, Act V, Thersites is called by Achilles, *thou crusty batch of nature* [5.1.5] i.e. thou crusty batch of bread of nature's baking: the very same ludicrous image as when elsewhere he is nick-named from his deformity *Cobloaf*. The word *Leaven* above-mentioned is a scriptural expression. Leaven is sour and salted dough, prepared to ferment a whole mass and to give it a relish: and in this sense used in *Measure for Measure*, Act I.

> Duke. *Come no more evasion*:
> *We have with a* prepared and leavened *choice*
> *Proceded to you.*　　　　　　　　　[1.1.51ff.]

---

* 'The River-horse signified, Murder, impudence, violence and injustice; for they say that he killeth his sire, and ravisheth his own dam.' Sandys *Travels*, p. 105.

i.e. before hand prepared and rightly season'd, as they prepare leaven. But in Scripture 'tis figurately used for the pharisaical doctrines and manners, being like leaven, of a sour, corrupting and infectious nature: so the Apostle, *a little leaven leaveneth the lump*, 1 Cor. v. 6. This explains the passage above, and another in *Cymbeline*, Act III.

> So thou, Posthumus,
> Wilt lay the leaven to all proper men;
> Goodly and gallant shall be false and perjur'd
> From thy great fail. [3.4.59ff.]

i.e. will infect and corrupt their good names, like sour dough that leaveneth the whole mass, and will render them suspected. The last line I would read,

> From thy great *fall*.

Because this reading is more poetical and scriptural; and more agreeable to our author's manner. (213-15)

*   *   *

SECTION XII.

Authors are not careful enough of their copies when they give them into the printer's hand; which, often being blotted or ill written, must be help'd out by meer guesswork. Printers are not the best calculated for this critical work, I think, since the times of Aldus and the Stephens's. What wonder therefore if in such a case we meet, now and then, with strange and monstrous words or highly improper expressions, and often contradictory to the author's design and meaning? (242)

*   *   *

It seems that some puns, and quibbling wit, have been changed in our author, thro' some such causes as mention'd in the beginning of this section. For instance, in *As You Like It*, [the Clown] is full of this quibbling wit through the whole play. In Act III he says

> I am here with thee, and thy *goats*; as the most *capricious* honest Ovid was among the *Goths*.
> *Jaq.* O knowledge ill-inhabited, worse than Jove in a thatch'd house. [3.3.5ff.]

Capricious is not here humoursome, fantastical, &c. but lascivious: Hor. *Epod.* 10. *Libidinosus immolabitur caper.*[1] *The Goths* are the Getae: Ovid. *Trist.* V, 7. *The thatch'd house* is that of Baucis and Philemon, Ovid. *Met.* VIII, 630.

Stipulis et cannâ tecta palustri.[2]

But to explain puns is almost as unpardonable as to make them: however I will venture to correct one passage more: which is in *Julius Caesar*, Act III.

> *Ant.* Here is a mourning Rome, a dangerous Rome:
>> No *Rome* of safety for Octavius yet.   [3.1.289f.]

I make no question, but Shakespeare intended it,
>> No *room* of safety for Octavius yet.

So in Act I.

>> Now is it *Rome* indeed; and *room* enough
>> When there is in it but one only man.   [1.2.156f.]

To play with words which have an allusion to proper names, is common with Shakespeare and the * ancients. Ajax in Sophocles, applying his name to his misfortunes, says,

>> ΑΙ, ΑΙ· τίς ἄν ποθ' ᾤεθ' ὧ δ' ἐπώνυμου
>> Τοὐμὸν ξυνοίσειν ὄνομα τοῖς ἐμοῖς κακοῖς[3]

Philoctetes, speaking to Pyrrhus has this quibble not inferior to any in Shakespeare—for badness.

>> Ω Πῦρ σὺ, καὶ ὧν δεῖμα.[4]

(257–9)

*   *   *

* See Aristot, Rhet. L. 2. c. 25. . . . . Allusions of this sort are frequent in Shakespeare. In *The Tempest*. Act III. *Ferd.* Admired Miranda. In the *Winter's Tale*. Act IV. *Perdita.* Even here undone. In *K. John*. Act II. *Aust.* Together with that pale, that *white-fac'd* shore. viz. *Albion, ab albis ripibus.*

[1] 10.23: 'a sportive goat . . . shall be offered.'

[2] 'thatched with straw and reeds from the marsh'.

[3] *Aj.*, 430f.: 'Ay me! Whoe'er had thought how well my name/Would fit my misery? Ay me! Ay me.'

[4] *Phil.*, 927: 'Thou fire, thou utter monster,/Abhorred masterpiece of Knavery.' [In fact, Philoctetes is speaking to Neoptolemus.]

There is a kind of pun in repeating pretty near the same letters with the preceding word, to which the rhetoricians have given a particular name, and in making a sort of a jingling sound of words [*paronomasia*]. Of this the sophists of old were fond. . . .

[Instances cited from Homer, Virgil, Terence]

And Milton frequently, as:

> And unfrequented left
> His righteous altar, *bowing lowly down*
> To bestial Gods; for which their heads *as low*
> *Bow'd down* in battel.   (*Paradise Lost*, I, 433)

> Which *tempted* our *attempt*, and wrought our fall.
>   (I, 642)

> And to begird th' almighty throne
> *Beseeching* or *besieging*.   (VI, 868)

> Serpent! we might have spar'd our coming hither,
> *Fruitless* to me, though *fruit* be here t'excess.
>   (IX, 647)

Instances in Shakespeare are without number; however I will mention one or two.
Macbeth, Act. I.

> What thou wouldst *highly*,
> That thou wouldst *holily*.   [1.5.17f.]
> And catch
> With its *surcease, success*.   [1.7.3f.]

Hamlet, Act. I.

> A little more than * *kin*, and less than *kind*.
>   [1.2.65] (263–6)

> *   *   *

* He seems to have taken this from *Gorboduc*, Act 1.
    In *kinde* a father, but not in *kindelyness*.   [1.1.18]

SECTION XVI.

But there are greater alterations than any yet mention'd still to be made. For the whole play intitled *Titus Andronicus* should be flung out the list of Shakespeare's works. What tho' a purple patch might here and there appear, is that sufficient reason to make our poet's name father this or other anonymous productions of the stage? But Mr Theobald has put the matter out of all question; for he informs us 'that Ben Jonson in the induction to his *Bartlemew-Fair* (which made its first appearance in the year 1614) couples *Jeronimo* and *Andronicus* together in reputation, and speaks of them as plays then of 25 or 30 years standing.[1] Consequently *Andronicus* must have been on the stage, before Shakespeare left Warwickshire to come and reside in London.' So that we have all the evidence, both internal and external, to vindicate our poet from this bastard issue; nor should his editors have printed it among his genuine works. There are not such strong external reasons for rejecting two other plays, called *Love's Labour's Lost*, and *The Two Gentlemen of Verona*: but if any proof can be formed from manner and style then should these be sent packing, and seek for their parent elsewhere. How otherwise does the painter distinguish copies from originals? And have not authors their peculiar style and manner, from which a true critic can form as unerring a judgment as a painter? External proofs leave no room for doubt. I dare say there is not any one scholar that now believes Phalaris' epistles to be genuine. (284–5)

✶   ✶   ✶

BOOK III

When one considers the various tribes of rhetoricians, grammarians, etymologists, &c. of ancient Greece [and Rome, and sees the advantages derived for literature and philosophy] . . . and then turn our eyes homeward, and behold every thing the reverse; can we wonder that the ancients should have a polite language, and that we should hardly emerge out of our pristine and Gothic barbarity?

Amongst many other things we want a good grammar and dictionary: we must know what is proper before we can know what is elegant and polite. By the use of these the meaning of words might be prefixed, the Proteus-nature, if possible, of ever-shifting language might

[1] 'He that will swear, *Jeronimo* [i.e., *The Spanish Tragedy*] or *Andronicus* are the best plays yet, shall pass unexcepted at here as a man whose judgement shows it is constant, and hath stood still these five and twenty or thirty years.'

in some measure be ascertained, and vague phrases and ambiguous sentences brought under some rule and regulation. But a piece of idle wit shall laugh all such learning out of doors: and the notion of being thought a dull and pedantic fellow has made many a man continue a blockhead all his life. Neither words nor grammar are such arbitrary and whimsical things as some imagine. And for my own part, as I have been taught from other kind of philosophers so I believe that right and wrong, in the minutest subjects, have their standard in nature not in whim, caprice or arbitrary will: so that if our grammarian or lexicographer should by chance be a disciple of modern philosophy should he glean from France and the court his refinements of our tongue, he would render the whole affair, bad as it is, much worse by his ill management. No one can write without some kind of rules: and for want of rules of authority, many learned men have drawn them up for themselves. Ben Jonson printed his English Grammar. If Shakespeare and Milton never published their rules yet they are not difficult to be traced from a more accurate consideration of their writings. Milton's rules I shall omit at present; but some of Shakespeare's which savour of peculiarity I shall here mention: because when these are known we shall be less liable to give a loose to fancy in indulging the licentious spirit of criticism, nor shall we then so much presume to judge what Shakespeare *ought to* have written as endeavour to discover and retrieve what he *did* write.

RULE I.

Shakespeare alters proper names according to the English pronunciation. (294-6)

... *Amleth*, he writes *Hamlet*; and *Cunobeline* or *Kymbeline*, he calls *Cymbeline*. ... (300)

The late Lord Shaftesbury, in his *Advice to an Author*, fell into a mistake concerning the name of the unfortunate *Desdemona*: 'But why (says he) amongst his Greek names, he should have chosen one which denoted the Lady *superstitious*, I can't imagine: unless, &c.' [See vol. 2, p. 265]. Her name is not derived from Δεισιδαίμων, but Δυσδαίμων: i.e. THE UNFORTUNATE: and *Giraldi Cinthio, in his novels, making the

---

* Novella VII. Deca terza. *Avēne, che una virtuosa Dōna, di maravigliosa bellezza, Disdemona chiamata, &c.* He calls her afterwards, in allusion to her name, *la infelice Disdemona.* And I make no question but Othello in his rapturous admiration, with some allusion to her name, exclaims, in Act III.

> Excellent *wretch*! perdition catch my soul,
> But I do love thee—   [3.3.91f.]

word feminine, calls her *Disdemona*, from whom Shakespeare took the name and story.

Thus the reader may see with what elegance, as well as learning, Shakespeare familiarizes strange names to our tongue and pronunciation. (303)

★   ★   ★

RULE II.

He makes Latin words English, and uses them according to their original idiom and latitude. . . .

In *A Midsummer Night's Dream*, Act III. he uses not a word form'd from the Latin, but the Latin word itself. Lysander speaks to Hermia,

> Get you gone, you dwarf,
> You *Minimus*.   [3.2.329f.]

> [Quotes Theobald's note: above, Vol. 2, p. 492.]

Mr Theobald, who was no bad scholar, might have remembered that the masculine gender is often used where the person is considered more than the sex, as here 'tis by Shakespeare. Milton's expression seems to be from Prov. xxx. 24. according to the vulgate, *Quatuor ista sunt minima terræ*. (308–9)

★   ★   ★

In *King Lear*, Act II.

> I tax you not, you elements—
> You owe me no *subscription*.   [3.2.16ff.]

Subscriptio is a writing underneath, a registering our names so as to take part in any cause, suit or service. Hence it signifies allegiance, submission, &c. And the verb *subscribere* is not only to write under but to aid and help, to abet and approve, &c. (312)

★   ★   ★

RULE III.

He sometimes omits the primary and proper sense, and uses words in their secondary and improper signification. (328)

★   ★   ★

The ancient tragedians are full of these allusions; some instances I have mention'd above [p. 305]. This rapturous exclamation and allusion too has something ominous in it; and instances of these presaging and ominous expressions our poet is full of.

RULE IV.

He uses one part of speech for another.

For instance, **he makes verbs of adjectives** as, *to stale*, i.e., to make stale and familiar. *To safe*, to make safe and secure, &c. *Antony and Cleopatra*, Act I:

> *Ant.*   My more particular,
> And that which most with you *should safe* my going,
> Is Fulvia's death.   [1.3.54ff.]

should safe, i.e. should make safe and secure.

So again, **he uses verbs for substantives.** *Accuse*, for accusation: *Affect*, for affection: *Deem*, for a deeming, an opinion: *Dispose*, for disposition: *Prepare*, for preparation: *Vary*, for variation: &c. And, *adjectives* for *substantives*. As *Mean*, for mediocrity or mean estate. In *K. Lear*, Act IV:

> *Glo.* Full oft 'tis seen
> Our *mean* secure us.   [4.1.20f.]

So *Private*, for privacy, &c. Nothing is more frequent among the Latins than to use substantively, *ardua, invia, avia, supera, acuta*, &c. In imitation of whom our poet in *Coriolanus*, Act I.

> As if I lov'd *my little* should be dieted
> In praises sauc'd with lies.   [1.9.52f.]

Again, **he makes verbs of substantives.** As, *to bench, to voice, to paper, to progress, to stage, to estate, to helm*, &c. . . .

In *Cymbeline*, Act I.

> *Iach.*   He *furnaces*
> The thick sighs from him.   [1.6.65f.]

i.e. his sighs come from him as thick as fire and smoke from a furnace. . . .

In *King Lear*, Act IV.

> *Glo.* Let the superfluous and lust dieted man
> That *slaves* your ordinance, that will not see,
> Because he does not feel, feel your power quickly.
>   [4.1.68ff.]

i.e. That makes a slave of your ordinance; that makes it subservient to his superfluities and lust.

Again, **he uses substantives adjectively;** or, **by way of apposition.**
[Instances cited from Homer, Virgil, Horace, Propertius and St Paul] Shakespeare in *Julius Caesar*, Act I, *Tyber bank*. And Act V, *Philippi fields*. In *Coriolanus*, Act II, *Corioli gates*. In *Hamlet*, *music vows*, *neighbour room*, &c. Hence we may correct some trifling errors, (if any errors can be called so) still remaining in Shakespeare. In *A Midsummer Night's Dream*, Act III:

> *Hel.* Is all the counsel that we two have shar'd,
>   *The sisters vows*, the hours that we have spent, &c.
>
> [3.2.198f.]

Read, *The sister vows*.

Again in *Antony and Cleopatra*, Act I:

>   *His captains heart*
> Which in the scuffles of great fight hath burst
> The buckles on his breast, reneges all temper.　　[1.1.6ff.]

Read, *His Captain heart*, i.e. His warlike heart, such as becomes a captain. There are other places of like nature that want to be corrected, but at present they do not occur. And sometimes **the substantive is to be construed adjectively when put into the genitive case;** *or*, **when governing a genitive case.** (330–3)

＊　　＊　　＊

He sometimes expresses one thing by two substantives; which the rhetoricians call [Hendiadys]*

    As Virgil:

> Patera libamus et auro,[1]

---

* This rule too our late editor forgot to note. In *Hamlet*, Act I:
>   Who by seal'd compact,
>   Well ratified *by law and heraldry*
>   Did forfeit, with his life, all these his lands.　　[1.1.86ff.]
i.e. By the Herald Law: *jure fetiali*. Cicero de Off. I, 2. Mr W. 'By law of heraldry', which is the gloss, or prosaic interpretation.

[1] *Georgics* 2, 192: 'we offer from bowls of gold.'

i.e. *pateris aureis.* In *Antony and Cleopatra,* Act IV:

> I hope well of tomorrow, and will lead you
> Where rather I'll expect victorious life
> Than *death and honour*   [4.2.42ff.]

i.e. than honourable death.   (336)

   Again, **he uses adjectives adverbially.** [Parallel instances quoted from Virgil and Milton]

   In *Hamlet,* Act III.

> I am myself *indifferent* honest   [3.1.123]

In *Macbeth,* Act I.

> by doing everything
> *Safe* toward your love and honour.   [1.4.26f.]

Safe, i.e. with safety, security and suretiship.

RULE V.

He uses the active participle passively.

So Cicero [example quoted]. In *The Tempest,* Act I.

> Had I been any God of power, I would
> Have sunk the sea within the earth; or ere
> It should the good ship so have swallow'd,
>   and
> The *fraighting* souls within.   [1.2.10f.]

i.e. *fraighted;* or *fraighting* themselves.

In *King Lear*

> Who by the art of known, and *feeling* sorrows,
> Am pregnant to good pity.   [4.6.224f.]

feeling, i.e. *causing themselves to be felt.*

In *Antony and Cleopatra*, Act IV.

> *Cleop.*   Rather on Nilus' mud
> Lay me stark naked, and let the water-flies
> Blow me into *abhorring*.   [5.2.58ff.]

i.e. into being abhorred and loathed. (337–40)

★   ★   ★

And the adjective passive actively.

In the *Twelfth Night*, Act I.

> *Viol.* Hollow your name to the *reverberate* hills
> And make the babling gossip of the air
> Cry out, Olivia!   [1.5.256ff.]

reverberate, i.e. causing it to be stricken back again. In *Macbeth*, Act I.

> Or we have eaten of the *insane* root,
> That takes the reason prisoner?   [1.3.84f.]

Insane, i.e. causing madness *ab effectu*, as the grammarians say. In *Othello*, Act I.

> *Brab.*   Gone she is;
> And what's to come of my *despised* time,
> Is nought but bitterness.   [1.1.161ff.]

i.e. of the time which I shall despise and hate: or rather, which will cause me to be despised; my daughter having run away with a black-amoor. In *K. Richard II*, Act II.

> Why have they dar'd to march
> So many miles upon her peaceful bosom,
> Frighting her pale-fac'd villages with war,
> And ostentation of *despised* arms.   [2.3.92ff.]

i.e. of arms despising the places they march through; or the laws of England.

RULE VI.

In his use of verbs there is sometimes to be understood intention, willingness and desire.

313

The Greek language has many instances fully to our purpose. [Instances quoted from Euripides] (341-2)

*   *   *

RULE VII.

He often adds to adjectives in their comparative and superlative degrees, the signs marking the degrees.

In *King Lear*, Act II.

    Corn. These kind of knaves I know, which in this plainness
Harbour more craft and *more corrupter* ends
Than twenty silly, &c.   [2.2.96ff.]

In *Henry VIII*, Act I.

        There is no English soul
    More stronger to direct you than yourself.   [1.1.146f.]

Nor is this kind of pleonasm unusual among the Latins and Grecians. [Virgil and Euripides cited] (344).

*   *   *

RULE VIII.

He frequently omits the auxiliary verb, am, is, are, &c., **and likewise several particles, as** to, that, a, as, **&c.**

In *Macbeth*, Act I.

      King. Is execution done on Cawdor yet?
      Or not those in commission yet return'd?   [1.4.1f.]

i.e. Or are not, &c. In *Hamlet*, Act III.

      But 'tis not so above,
    There is no shuffling, there the action lies
    In his true nature; *and we ourselves compelled*
    Even to the teeth and forehead of our faults
    To give in evidence.   [3.3.60ff.]

[Instances given from Sophocles and Horace] (346-7)

314

RULE IX.

He uses But, for *otherwise than*; **Or,** for *before*; **Once,** *once for all, peremptorily*; **From,** *on account of*; **Not,** for *not only*; **nor do two negatives always make an affirmative, but deny more strongly, as is well known from the Greek, and modern French languages.** (347)

*   *   *

RULE X.

He uses the abstract for the concrete, viz. *companies*, for *companions; youth*, for *young persons; reports*, for *people who made the reports.* (353)

*   *   *

RULE XI.

To compleat the construction, there is, in the latter part of the sentence sometimes to be supplied some word, or phrase from the former part, either expressed or tacitly signified. (355)

In *The Tempest*, Act IV.

The strongest *suggestion*
Our worser genius *can,*   [4.1.26f.]

i.e. can suggest. In *Macbeth*, Act IV.

I dare not speak much further,
But cruel are the times, when we are traitors,
And do not know ourselves.   [4.2.17ff.]

viz. to be traitors.

RULE XII.

He uses the Nominative case absolute; or rather elliptical.

The grammarians term this [*anacoluthon*]. Instances from the ancients are numberless, but it may be necessary to mention one or two. [Quotations from Terence, Plautus and others]

315

In *Hamlet*, Act III.

Your majesty and we, that have free souls, it touches *us* not. [3.2.236f.]

He begins with a nominative case, as if he would say, *what care we, it touches us not*: but cutting short his speech makes a solecism. Many kinds of these embarrassed sentences there are in Shakespeare. And have not the best authors their ἀκυρολογίαι, as the grammarians call them, seeming inaccuracies and departure from the common and trite grammar?

RULE XIII.

He makes a sudden transition from the plural number to the singular.

And so likewise do the most approved writers of antiquity. (356–8) [Instances cited from Terence, Sophocles, Euripides, St Paul, Cicero, Milton]

Of this mixture of the singular and plural, because it seems strange in Shakespeare, I will add an instance or two more from the Roman authors. [Tibullus, Catullus]

'Tis somewhat extraordinary that when we meet these kind of solecisms in the ancient writers we then try to reduce them to rule and grammar, but when we find the same in Milton or Shakespeare we then think of nothing but correction and emendation.

RULE XIV.

He shortens words by striking off the first or last syllable: and sometimes lengthens them by adding a Latin termination.

'Tis very customary in our language to strike off the first syllable. Hence we say, **sample,** for *example*: **spittle,** for *hospital*, &c. In Shakespeare among many others, **mends,** for *amends*: **fend,** for *defend*: **force,** for *inforce, reinforce*: **point,** for *appointments*: **sconce,** for *ensconce*, &c. . . .

In *Timon of Athens*, Act IV:

> *Apem.*   What a coil's here,
> *Serving* of becks and jetting out of bums?   [1.2.234f.]

i.e. observing one another's nods and bows. So *servans* for *observans*, among the Latins.

Nor is it unusual with Shakespeare to strike off a syllable or more from the latter part of words. So he uses **ostent,** for *ostentation:* **reverbs,** for *reverberates:* **intrince,** for *intrinsicate,* or *intricate.* . . . (361–2)

On the other hand he lengthens words by giving them a Latin termination. In *Hamlet,*

> Oh, such a deed,
> As from the body of *contraction* plucks
> The very soul, and sweet religion makes
> A rhapsody of words.   [3.4.45ff.]

contraction, i.e. contract. (363–4)

★   ★   ★

To these rules many others may easily be added; but what has already been said may lead the way to a right reading of our author. Concerning the strict propriety of all these rules, as being exactly suitable to the genius of our language, I am not at all concerned: 'tis sufficient for my purpose if they are Shakespeare's rules. But one thing more still remains of no little consequence to our poet's honour, and that is the settling and adjusting his metre and rhythm. For the not duly attending to this has occasion'd strange alterations in his plays: now prose hobbles into verse, now again verse is degraded into prose; here verses are broken, where they should be continued; and there joined, where they should be broken. And the chief reason of these alterations of his verses seems to proceed from the same cause as the changing his words and expressions, that is, the little regard we pay to our poet's art.

*Dryden says that Milton acknowledged to him, that Spenser was his original: but his original in what, Mr Dryden does not tell us: certainly he was not his original in throwing aside that Gothic bondage of jingle at the end of every line; 'twas the example of our† BEST ENGLISH TRAGEDIES here he followed; ‡HIS HONOURED SHAKESPEARE. And from him, as well as from Homer and Virgil, he saw what beauty would result from variety.

Our smoothest verses run in the iambic foot: *pes citus,* as Horace

---

* Dryden's preface to his *Fables.*
† Milton's preface to his *Paradise lost.*
‡ Milton's poem on Shakespeare, ann. 1630.

terms it; because we hasten from the first to the second syllable, that chiefly striking the ear. And our epic verse consists of five feet or measures, according to common scansion.

ĭt fā|dĕd ōn|thĕ crōw|ĭng of |thĕ cōck [*Hamlet*, 1.1.157]
1 | 2 | 3 | 4 | 5

Verses all of this measure would soon tire the ear, for want of variety: he therefore mixes the trochaic foot.

Náture|sĕems déad|ănd wĭc|kĕd drēams|ăbūse [*Macbeth*, 2.1.50]
1 | 2 | 3 | 4 | 5

And how beautifully are trochees intermixed in the following, where Lady Macbeth speaks in a hurry and agitation of mind!

Whĭch gīves|thĕ stērnest|gŏod nīght——|Hē's a|bōut it [2.2.4]
1 | 2 | 3 | 4 | 5

The tribrac is likewise used by our poets, as equivalent in time and measure to the iambic.

So Milton I, 91.
Now misery hath join'd
ĭn ē|quăl rŭĭn|īnto|whăt pīt|thŏu seēst
1 | 2 | 3 | 4 | 5

And Shakespeare very poetically in *K. Lear*, Act IV.

Edg. Sŏ mā|nў fā|thŏm|dōwn|prĕcĭpĭ|tătĭng. [4.6.50]
(364-7)

* * *

Shakespeare has several hemistiques; a poetical licence that Virgil introduced into the Latin poetry: but there have not been wanting hands to fill these broken verses up for both the poets. (369)

* * *

It ought not to be forgotten that Shakespeare has many words, either of admiration or exclamation, &c. out of the verse. Nor is this without example in the Greek tragedies. (370)

[Instances cited from Euripides and Sophocles, from *Hamlet* and *Othello*]

And in many other places exactly after the cast of the ancient plays.

There are some poetic liberties that our author takes, such as *lengthening words in scansion, as *wĭtĕnēss, fĭdēlēr, āngĕrȳ, Hēnĕrȳ, sārjĕānt, cāptăĭn, stātŭē, dēsĭrē, vĭllăĭn, fĭrē, hŏūr, grăcē, grĕāt,* &c. (371–2)

★   ★   ★

The greatest beauty in diction is when it corresponds to the sense. This beauty our language, with all its disadvantages, can attain; as I could easily instance from Shakespeare and Milton. We have harsh, rough consonants as well as the soft and melting, and these should sound in the same musical key. This rule is most religiously observed by Virgil; as is likewise that of varying the pause and cesura, or as Milton expresses it, *the sense being variously drawn out from one verse into another*: For it is variety and uniformity that makes beauty; and for want of this our riming poets soon tire the ear: for rime necessarily hinders *the sense from being variously drawn out from one verse to another*. They who avoid this Gothic bondage are unpardonable if they don't study this variety, when Shakespeare and Milton have so finely led them the way.

But to treat this matter, concerning his metre, somewhat more exactly: 'tis observed that when the iambic verse has its just number of syllables, 'tis called *acatalectic*; when deficient in a syllable *catalectic*; when a foot is wanting to compleat the *dipod*, according to the Greek scansion, *brachycatalectic*; when exceeding in a syllable, *hypercatalectic*. (374–5)

[Upton then argues that Shakespeare used the norm and variant forms of the following classical metres: iambic monometer, dimeter, trimeter; trochaic dimeter, tetrameter; anapestic monometer (375–84). The iambic trimeter acatalectic is said to have been used to characterise Caliban (379 note), the trochaic tetrameter catalectic, with its 'dancing measure, is very proper to the character of Polonius, a droll humourous old courtier' (382).]

These measures are all so agreeable to the genius of our language that Shakespeare's fine ear and skill are seen in what he gives us, as well as in what he omits. Sir Philip Sidney, who was a scholar (as noblemen were in Queen Elizabeth's reign) but wanted Shakespeare's ear, has dragged into our language verses that are enough to set one's ear on edge: thus for instance the elegiac verses,

* Our editors not knowing this have turned some passages into prose: viz. *Midsummer Night's Dream*, Act IV.

> Queen. I have a venturous Fairy that shall seek
> The squirrels *hŏārd*, and fetch thee new nuts.   [4.1.32f.]

Fōrtūne|nātūre|lōve lōng|hāve cōn|tēndĕd ă|boūt mē
Whĭch shoūld|mōst mĭsĕ|rīes|cāst ŏn ă|wōrme thăt ĭ |ām.

Sir Philip Sidney thought, like Vossius, that such a number of syllables was the only thing wanting, and that we had no long or short words in our language; but he was much mistaken. His sapphics are worse, if possible, than his elegiacs:

īf mĭne eȳs cān spēak tŏ dŏ heārtȳ ērrănd.

So much mistaken oftentimes are learned men, when they don't sufficiently consider the peculiar genius and distinguishing features, as it were, of one language from another.

The reader has now a plan exhibited before him partly intended to fix, if possible, the volatil spirit of criticism; and partly to do justice to Shakespeare as an artist in dramatic poetry. How far I have succeeded in this attempt must be left to his judgment. But it is to be remember'd that things are not as we judge of them but as they exist in their own natures, independent of whim and caprice. So that I except against all such judges as talk only from common vogue and fashion; 'why, really 'tis just as people like—we have different tastes now, and things must be accommodated to them.' They who are advanced to this pitch of barbarism have much to unlearn, before they can have ears to hear. Again, I can hardly allow those for judges who ridicule all rules in poetry; for whatever is beautiful and proper is agreeable to rule: nor those who are for setting at variance art and nature. And here I have Shakespeare's authority, who in *The Winter's Tale* says very finely, *The art itself is nature*: for what is the office of art but to shew nature in its perfection? Those only therefore seem to me to be judges who, knowing what is truly fair and good in general, have science and art sufficient to apply this knowledge to particulars.

If the plan likewise here proposed were followed the world might expect a much better, at least a less altered edition from Shakespeare's own words, than has yet been published. In order for this, all the various readings of *authority* should faithfully and fairly be collated and exhibited before the reader's eyes; and with some little ingenuity the best of these should be chosen and placed in the text. As to conjectural emendations I have said enough of these already. Nor can I but think that a short interpretation would be not amiss when the construction is a little embarrassed, or where words are used not strictly according to the common acceptation, or fetched from other languages: and some remarks could not but appear requisite to explain the poet's allusions to the various customs and manners, either of our own or foreign countries; or to point out now and then a hidden beauty: but this should be done sparingly; for some compliment is to be paid to the reader's judgment: and surely, if any critics are contemptible, 'tis such as with a foolish admiration ever and anon are crying out 'How fine! what a beautiful sentiment! what ordonnance of figures, &c!' For to admire without a reason for admiration, tho' in a subject truly admirable, is a kind of madness; and not to admire at all downright stupidity. (384–7)

[From the Appendix]

[Note to Book I, Section I; the allusion to 'the old Vice' is to the traditional stage-character. Upton adds further glosses to those already given by commentators.]

Some places of Shakespeare will from hence appear more easy: as in *The Ist Part of Henry IV*, Act II. where Hal, humourously characterizing Falstaff, calls him, *That reverend* VICE, *that grey* INIQUITY, *that father* RUFFIAN, *that* VANITY *in years* [2.4.438f.], in allusion to this buffoon character. In *K. Richard III*, Act III:

> *Thus like the formal Vice*, Iniquity,
> *I moralize two meanings in one word.*
>
> [3.1.82f.]

INIQUITY is the formal Vice. Some correct the passage

> *Thus, like the formal wise Antiquity,*
> *I moralize two meanings in one word.*

Which correction is out of all rule of criticism. In *Hamlet*, Act I, there is an allusion, still more distant, to THE VICE; which will not be obvious at first, and therefore is to be introduced with a short explanation. This buffoon character was used to make fun with the Devil; and he had several trite expressions, as, *I'll be with you in a trice: Ah, ha, boy, are you there,* &c. And this was great entertainment to the audience, to see their old enemy so belabour'd in effigy. In *K. Henry V*, Act IV. a boy characterizing Pistol says *Bardolph and Nim had ten times more valour, than this roaring Devil i' th' old play; every one may pare his nails with a wooden dagger* [4.4.68ff.]. Now Hamlet, having been instructed by his father's ghost, is resolved to break the subject of the discourse to none but Horatio; and to all others his intention is to appear as a sort of madman: when therefore the oath of secresy is given to the centinels, and the Ghost unseen calls out *swear*, Hamlet speaks to it as THE VICE does to the Devil. *Ah, ha boy, sayst thou so? Art thou there, truepenny?* Hamlet had a mind that the centinels should imagine this was a shape that the Devil had put on; and in Act III he is somewhat of this opinion himself,

> The Spirit that I have seen
> May be the Devil. [2.2.594f.]

This manner of speech therefore to the Devil was what all the audience were well acquainted with; and it takes off in some measure from the horror of the scene. Perhaps too the poet was willing to inculcate that good humour is the best weapon to deal with the Devil. *True penny* is either by way of irony, or literally from the Greek τρύπανον, *veterator*. . . . (393-6)

★ ★ ★

[On Shakespeare's crowding metaphors together: in Book I, Section XV; above pp. 300f.]

The crouding and mixing together heterogeneous metaphors is doing a sort of violence to the mind; for each new metaphor calls it too soon off from the idea which the former has rais'd: 'tis a fault, doubtless, and not to be apologized for; and instances are very numerous in Shakespeare. The poet is to take his share of the faults, and the critic is to keep his hands from the context. Yet 'tis strange to see how many passages the editors have corrected, meerly for the case of consonance of metaphor: breaking thro' that golden rule of criticism, *mend only the faults of transcribers*. Bentley shew'd the way to critics, and gave a specimen, in his notes on Callimachus, of his emendations of Horace by correcting the following verse,

> *Et male* tornatos *incudi reddere versus.*
>
> Hor. art. poet. 441.[1]

where he reads *ter natos*, for consonance of metaphor. But pray take notice, *ter natos*, is a metaphorical expression: for *nascor, natus*, signifies to be born: and are things *born* brought to the anvil? Is not here dissonance of metaphor with a witness?

[1] 'And return the ill-shaped verses to the anvil.'

This verse of Horace has been variously criticized. So at present I say no more concerning it; but return to our poet, whose vague and licentious use of metaphors is so visible to almost every reader that I wonder any editor, of what degree soever, should in this respect think of altering his manner of expression. Some few alterations of this kind I here exhibit to the reader, and leave it to him to make his own reflections.

Shakespeare, *Measure for Measure*, Act II:
> Look, here comes one; a gentlewoman of mine,
> Who falling in the *flaws* of her own youth,
> Hath *blister'd* her report.   [2.3.10ff.]

'Who doth not see that the integrity of metaphor requires we should read FLAMES *of her own youth*.'   Mr W. (397-8)

. . . In *Antony and Cleopatra*, Act I.
> The triple pillar of the world transform'd
> Into a strumpet's *fool*.   [1.1.11f.]

'The metaphor is here miserably mangled; we should read *Into a strumpet's* STOOL' Mr W.

There is much more of this kind of uncritical stuff in the late edition; but I am already weary with transcribing. (400)

115. Samuel Richardson on poetic justice

1748

From the 'Postscript' to volume 7 of *Clarissa Harlowe*.

Richardson was associated with the Shakespeare criticism of his day in a number of ways. He printed Wharton's *The True Briton* in 1723, *The Daily Journal* (above, No. 89) in 1736–7, and his friends included Warburton, Garrick, Dr Johnson, Aaron Hill and Thomas Edwards (below, No. 126). See T. C. D. Eaves and B. Kimbel, *Samuel Richardson. A Biography* (Oxford, 1971).

POSTSCRIPT.

The Author of the foregoing Work has been favoured in the course of its Publication with many Anonymous Letters, in which the Writers have *differently* expressed their wishes as to what they apprehended of the Catastrophe.

Most of those directed to him by the gentler Sex turn in favour of what they call a *fortunate Ending*; and some of them enamoured, as they declare, with the principal Character are warmly solicitous to have her *happy*.

These Letters having been written on the perusal of the first Four Volumes only, before the complicated adjustment of the several parts to one another could be seen or fully known, it may be thought superfluous, now the whole Work is before the Public, to enter upon this argument, because it is presumed that the Catastrophe necessarily follows the natural progress of the Story. But as the Notion of *Poetical Justice* seems to have generally obtained among the Fair Sex, and must be confessed to have the appearance of Good Nature and Humanity, it may not be amiss to give it a brief consideration.

Nor can it be deemed impertinent to touch upon this subject at the Conclusion of a Work which is designed to inculcate upon the human mind, under the guise of an Amusement, the great Lessons of Christianity in an Age *like the present*; which seems to expect from the Poets and

Dramatic Writers (that is to say, from the Authors of Works of Invention) that they should make it one of their principal Rules to propagate another Sort of Dispensation, under the Name of *Poetical Justice*, than that with which God, by Revelation, teaches us he has thought fit to exercise Mankind; whom, placing here only in a State of *Probation*, he hath so intermingled Good and Evil as to necessitate them to look forward for a more equal Distribution of both.

The History, or rather, The Dramatic Narrative of CLARISSA, is formed on this Religious Plan; and is therefore well justified in deferring to extricate suffering Virtue till it meets with the Completion of its Reward.

But we have no need to shelter our Conduct under the Sanction of Religion (an Authority, perhaps, not of the greatest weight with modern Critics) since we are justified in it by the greatest Master of Reason and the best Judge of Composition that ever was. The learned Reader knows we must mean ARISTOTLE; whose Sentiments in this matter we shall beg leave to deliver in the words of a very amiable Writer of our own Country.

'The English Writers of Tragedy, *says Mr Addison*, are possessed with a Notion, that when they represent a virtuous or innocent person in distress they ought not to leave him till they have delivered him out of his troubles, or made him triumph over his enemies. This *Error* they have been led into by a *ridiculous* Doctrine in *Modern Criticism*, That they are obliged to an *equal distribution* of *Rewards* and *Punishments*, and an impartial Execution of *Poetical Justice*.

Who were the first that established this Rule, I know not; but I am sure it has no Foundation in NATURE, in REASON, or in the PRACTICE of THE ANTIENTS.

'We find, that [*in the dispensations of* PROVIDENCE] Good and Evil happen alike to ALL MEN on this side the grave: And as the principal design of Tragedy is to raise Commiseration and Terror in the minds of the Audience we shall defeat this great end if we always make Virtue and Innocence happy and successful.'

[Richardson quotes further from *Spectator* No. 40: cf. Vol. 2, pp. 272ff.]

*   *   *

'*King Lear* is an admirable Tragedy of the same kind, as Shakespeare wrote it: But as it is reformed according to the *chimerical notion* of Poetical ⟨*or, as we may say, Anti-Providential*⟩ Justice, in my humble opinion it has lost half its beauty.*

At the same time I must allow, that there are very noble Tragedies, which have been framed upon the other Plan, and have ended happily; as indeed most of the good Tragedies which have been written since the starting of the above-mentioned Criticism, have taken this turn: As *The Mourning Bride, Tamerlane, Ulysses, Phædra and Hippolytus*, with most of Mr Dryden's. I must also allow, that many of Shakespeare's, and several of the celebrated Tragedies of Antiquity, are cast in the same form. I do not therefore dispute against this way of writing Tragedies; but against the Criticism that would establish This as the *only* method; and by that means would very much cramp the English Tragedy, and perhaps give a wrong bent to the Genius of our Writers.'

Thus far Mr Addison.

Our fair Readers are also desired to attend to what a celebrated Critic† of a neighbouring nation says on the nature and design of Tragedy, from the Rules laid down by the same great Antient.

'Tragedy, says he, makes man *modest* by representing the great Masters of the Earth humbled; and it makes him *tender* and *merciful* by shewing him the *strange accidents of life*, and the *unforeseen disgraces* to which the most important persons are subject.

But because Man is naturally timorous and compassionate he may fall into other extremes. Too much fear may shake his Constancy of Mind, and too much Compassion may enfeeble his Equity. 'Tis the business of Tragedy to regulate these two weaknesses. It prepares and arms him against *Disgraces*, by shewing them so frequent in the most considerable persons; and he will cease to fear extraordinary accidents, when he sees them happen to the *highest*. ⟨And still more efficacious, we may add, the example will be, when he sees them happen to the *best*⟩ part of mankind.

But as the End of Tragedy is to teach men not to fear too weakly *common Misfortunes*, it proposes also to teach them to spare their Com-

---

* Yet so different seems to be the Modern Taste from that of the Antients, that the altered *King Lear* of Mr Tate is constantly acted on the English Stage, in preference to the Original, tho' written by Shakespeare himself!—Whether this *strange* preference be owing to the false Delicacy or affected Tenderness of the Players, or to that of the Audience, has not for many years been tried. And perhaps the former have not the courage to try the Public Taste upon it. And yet, if it were *ever* to be tried, *Now* seems to be the Time, when an *Actor* and *Manager* in the *same person*, is in being, who deservedly engages the public favour in all he undertakes, and who owes so much, and is gratefully sensible that he does, to that great Master of the human Passions.

† Rapin, on Aristotle's Poetics.

passion for Objects that *deserve it*. For there is an *Injustice* in being moved at the afflictions of those who *deserve to be miserable*. We may see, without pity, Clytemnestra slain by her son Orestes in *Æschylus*, because she had murdered Agamemnon her husband; and we cannot see Hippolytus die by the plot of his stepmother Phædra, in *Euripides*, without Compassion, because he died not but for being chaste and virtuous.'

These are the great Authorities so favourable to the Stories that end unhappily. Yet the Writer of the History of Clarissa is humbly of Opinion that he might have been excused referring to them for the vindication of *his* Catastrophe, even by those who are advocates for the contrary opinion; since the notion of *Poetical Justice*, founded on the *Modern Rules*, has hardly ever been more strictly observed in works of this nature than in the present performance, if any regard at all be to be paid to the *Christian System* on which it is formed.

For, Is not Mr *Lovelace*, who could persevere in his villainous views against the strongest and most frequent convictions and remorses that ever were sent to awaken and reclaim a wicked man—Is not this great, this wilful Transgressor, condignly *punished*; and his punishment brought on thro' the intelligence of the very Joseph Leman whom he had corrupted; and by means of the very women whom he had debauched? Is not Mr *Belton*, who has an uncle's *hastened* death to answer for? Are not the *whole Harlowe family*— Is not the vile *Tomlinson*—Are not the infamous *Sinclair*, and her *wretched Partners*—And even the wicked *Servants* who, with their eyes open, contributed their parts to the carrying on of the vile schemes of their respective principals—*Are they not All likewise exemplarily punished?*

On the other hand, is not Miss HOWE, for her noble Friendship to the exalted Lady in her calamities—Is not Mr HICKMAN, for his unexceptionable Morals, and Integrity of Life—Is not the repentant and not ungenerous BELFORD—Is not the worthy NORTON—*made signally happy?*

And who that are in earnest in their Profession of Christianity, but will rather envy than regret the triumphant death of CLARISSA, whose Piety, from her early Childhood; whose diffusive Charity; whose steady Virtue; whose Christian Humility; whose Forgiving Spirit; whose Meekness, whose Resignation, HEAVEN *only* could reward?*
(VII, 425–31).

---

* It may not be amiss to remind the Reader, that so early in the work as Vol. II. p. 235, 236, 237. the dispensations of Providence in her distresses are justified by herself. And thus she ends her Reflections . . . 'I shall not live always . . . May my Closing Scene be happy!'
She had her wish. It was happy.

116. Unsigned essay on Shakespeare's morality compared with Otway's

November, December 1748

From 'Remarks on the Tragedy of the *Orphan*,' by 'N.S.', in *The Gentleman's Magazine*, xviii, pp. 502–6 (November 1748) and pp. 551–3 (December 1748).

[The author summarises the plot of Otway's play]

If we proceed to examine the above *Fable* it will be very difficult to find any *moral precept* that it tends to recommend or illustrate; tho' the Poet seems to have been aware that somewhat of this kind was necessary, and accordingly has, in the close of the 5th Act, in the person of *Chamont*, made a reflexion which seems to be at once very immoral and no necessary consequence of his Fable. I say immoral because it charges Providence as being the author of a series of misfortunes, which are altogether owing to the vicious and imprudent conduct of the persons concerned. The speech is as follows:

> Take care of good *Acasto*, whilst I go
> To search the means by which the Fates have *plagu'd* us.
> 'Tis *thus* that heav'n its empire does maintain:
> It may afflict, but man must not complain.

How much more properly might he have said with *Edgar*, in *K. Lear*,

> The Gods are just, and of our pleasant vices
> Make instruments to scourge us.   [5.3.170f.]

Which is a pious sentiment, and worthy of the stage.

That a tendency to promote the cause of Virtue is essential to Epic and Dramatic poetry will hardly be contested; and accordingly we find the great poets not content with barely holding up *the mirror to Nature*, and exercising the virtuous affections of mankind (which yet, it must be confess'd, are valuable ends of these species of writing) but that they have constantly endeavoured to inculcate some *prudential*

328

maxim, or *moral precept*. In this particular, our admirable *Shakespeare* seems to stand without an equal; in him we find the most instructive lessons inforced with all the art imaginable, and that not by a tedious and intricate deduction of consequences but barely by the necessary result of a well-wrought Fable. For instance, in *King Lear*, who does not at once see the fatal consequences of filial ingratitude, and that great error of parents who resign their power and trust to their children, for a support in the decline of life, upon so slender a foundation as flattering promises, and extravagant professions of affection and duty?—In *Othello*, the calamitous effects of Jealousy are represented; in *Richard III*, and several others, those of Ambition; in *Richard II* we view the instability of human Greatness; *Measure for Measure* contains an argument for the exercise of compassion towards offenders, the most powerful that can be thought of, *The frailty of human nature*: and this argument is exemplified in the character of the merciless *Angelo* in such a manner that we are at once convinced of its force, and excited to a just abhorrence of that cruelly inflexible disposition in magistrates, which is often mistaken for justice: but, above all, *Macbeth* teaches us a lesson the most important, namely, the fascinating power, and insensible progress of Vice. In the person of *Macbeth* we behold a man possess'd of many noble qualities, actuated by a most violent ambition, which, after a severe conflict, gets the better of his virtues in spite of the suggestions of a conscience naturally sensible and tender, and urges him on to the murder of his sovereign and benefactor. From this beginning of a vicious conduct we find all the sentiments of gratitude, love, friendship, humanity, &c. by insensible degrees, give place to his violent lust of power and the instigations of a wicked woman; 'till from a generous, noble, and (bating his ambition) a good man we find him transformed to perhaps as great a monster of wickedness as human nature ever produced. A precept more interesting, or of greater importance in the conduct of human life than what this story furnishes, surely never was inculcated by any moral or dramatic writer! What man, already engaged in a virtuous course of action, of a tender conscience, that startles at the thought of evil, and who perhaps is possess'd of many of those amiable qualities that adorn his nature; I say, what good man that surveys the fate of the unhappy *Macbeth* but must shudder to think on what a precarious tenure he holds the most valuable of all his possessions, and exert his utmost force to resist an enemy so wary in his conduct as scarce to be perceived 'till he has gain'd a complete victory?

Whoever considers the performance now under examination must confess that the story is admirably well calculated to excite compassion; but if we view it in the light abovemention'd, as *exhibiting some useful instruction*, we shall find it very deficient. For, what can be collected from it more than that in the business of Love it may be attended with very fatal consequences to conceal any thing from one's friends?—a maxim, which, at best, is greatly beneath the dignity of the Tragic Muse to inculcate. . . . (503-4)

Nor has the Poet [Otway] shewn any high idea of female excellence in that niggardly portion of the more lovely endowments which he has bestowed on *Monimia*. She is represented beautiful, and in general terms virtuous, and an orphan: yet there seems to be a want of that delicacy and simplicity which we admire in the *Desdemona* of *Shakespeare*! But whether a sense of the worth and dignity of *Monimia*'s character was the motive that determined the affection of *Castalio* or not 'tis pretty clear it did not at all influence the more courtly *Polydore*; he left such considerations to those dull fellows who could think of no way of possessing a mistress but marrying her. He, for his part, had *all the arts of fine persuasion, inherited his father's virtues, and was by nature mild and full of sweetness*; and as a proof of these qualities he with great calmness lays a design to corrupt a virtuous, innocent, unfortunate young lady, who had taken shelter in his father's family; and whom, by all the obligations of humanity, honour, and charity he was bound to protect. I know it will be urged, in defence of this part of the Poet's conduct (and this argument will be consider'd more at large hereafter), that he lived in a licentious age, when criminal gratifications were not looked on as derogatory from the character of a gentleman. I admit it; but who does not know that, as virtue is uniform, and entirely independent of custom, wherever they interfere, if a man will give way to the prevalence of vicious examples he may become a very fashionable gentleman; but will the wise and good part of mankind esteem him on this account? Will they not rather detest and shun the man who, with such confidence and assurance, tramples on those laws and obligations upon which the peace, order and happiness of society do so manifestly depend? (504)

*　　*　　*

That this was the current strain of dramatic writing for many years after the Restauration cannot be denied; and that an almost total extinction of genius and taste for poetry of every kind was the unhappy consequence of that event is no less certain. Can any one then, who is sensible of the dignity of this divine art and the excellent purposes it is capable of serving, with patience think on such a nest of pestilent vermin as, warmed by the sun-shine of court favours, crawled forth at that time, and spread their poisonous influence around them? Who, I say, can, without indignation, behold such shameless profligates as *Carew*, *Killigrew*, *Howard*, *Sedley*, *Etherege*, *Sheffield*, *D' Urfey*, the hasty *Shadwell*, and even the slow *Wycherley*, corrupting the taste, and consequently the manners of an age, and arrogating to themselves THE SACRED AND VENERABLE CHARACTER OF POETS?

But to return from a digression which the importance of the subject had insensibly led me into. The foregoing objections to the immorality of this celebrated tragedy may be carried much further; and will, if I mistake not, go a great way towards proving what the admirers of its author will, I suppose, be very unwilling to allow, *viz.* that he was but *a novice in his art*, and that it was owing to nothing less than the *meanness of his abilities* that his characters are so greatly deficient in regard to moral excellence.

Otway undoubtedly knew, as appears from the great pains he has taken to prejudice us in favour of *Monimia*, of the father, and indeed of both the brothers, that in order to interest the audience in the distress of his play it was necessary to excite in them the idea of something great and lovely in the suffering characters, and so far he was certainly right; but his great misfortune was that he had no clear conception of what he was about to represent, and in this particular seems to resemble a *bungling painter* or *statuary*, who knows well enough that there is such a thing as beauty, and that in that and an exact imitation of nature consist the perfections of his art, but for want of a distinct image or archetype of these perfections is unable to delineate them. Had not this been the case with our author he would most certainly have endowed his principal characters with such moral qualities as would *of themselves* have spoke their worth and merit, and render'd the testimony of the servants *Ernesto* and *Paulino* unnecessary. All that we are given to understand of this kind is that *Acasto* entertains a great regard for *the person of* his Prince; that the brothers are friends, and are fond of manly exercises; and that *Monimia* has just virtue enough to withstand the sollicitations of a lover who had neither gallantry or breeding to engage her affection.

On the contrary *Shakespeare*, who was perfectly skilled in the *moral science* and, consequently, knew how to delineate so resplendent a form as virtue, has exhibited to our view characters that command reverence, love and admiration, and reflect a lustre on human nature. Let us take a

view of his conduct in this particular. *Hamlet* is a courtier and a philosopher; *Othello* an image of a great mind, and a proof that tenderness
and humanity are no way inconsistent with an heroic temper. What
a delightful picture of patience under afflictions, and readiness to pardon
injuries, has he given us in the character of the wise and benevolent
Prospero! Who can choose but admire the disinterested friendship of
those illustrious gentlemen *Bassanio* and *Antonio?* and how is the character of the unhappy *Macduff* ennobled by the manly affection he discovers for his wife and slaughter'd infants! It is impossible to reflect on
this latter character without observing the singular art and judgment
with which the author paints the *domestic* virtues, if I may so call them,
or those affections of the soul which regard the welfare and preservation of a wife and family; an evident sign of the goodness of his heart,
and that he sensibly felt the force of

> Relations dear, and all the charities
> Of father, son and brother.

His women too, *Desdemona, Ophelia, Miranda, Hero, Imogen, Celia,
Portia, Jessica,* have tenderness and simplicity in the most exquisite
degree; even the humble cheerful Mrs *Ford* and Mrs *Page* deserve our
notice, the latter of whom, as a proof of her conjugal fidelity, speaking
of her husband, says

> He is as far from jealousy, as I am from giving him cause; and
> that, I hope, is an unmeasurable distance.
>
> *Merry Wives of Windsor* [2.1.92ff.]

His women, I say, are tender, modest, and delicate, and are endow'd
with every amiable quality the fair sex has to boast of.

It will be needless to say what must have been the consequence had
Otway's abilities been equal to his work; since in that case its effect on
our minds must in many respects have been the reverse of what it now
is; this at least must be allowed, that we should have neither been
shocked with *impiety* nor disgusted with *obscenity*, and that room would
have been given for the exercise of a degree of compassion for the
distress of the suffering characters far greater than it is now possible to
feel on their account.

Upon the whole, the conduct of this author seems to afford a powerful argument in favour of an opinion that has been entertained by the
wisest and greatest men in all ages, namely that Virtue and Genius,
especially that of the Poet, are very nearly, if not inseparably allied. To
paint the calamities of human life; to interest the affections in behalf of

suffering virtue; to excite just ideas of the superintendance of providence, and a resignation to the divine will; to raise an abhorrence of
vice, and animate the soul in its progress towards perfection, are the
proper ends of tragical representations, and these require a heart soften'd
and humanized by a tender sense of all the social and benevolent affections, an accurate knowledge of the distinctions and boundaries of
characters, together with *a high relish of moral excellence*. Whoever
considers the frame and structure of the human mind and the nature
and end of dramatic poesy will be convinced of the truth of this proposition, which in short is that to constitute a great Poet the primary
and essential qualification is TO BE A GOOD MAN.

117. David Garrick, adaptation of *Romeo and Juliet*

1748

From *Romeo and Juliet By Shakespeare. With Alterations, and an
additional Scene* . . .; this text from the second edition (1750).

Garrick's adaptation, first performed on 29 November 1748,
makes a number of cuts (omitting Lady Montague, and Romeo's
immature love for Rosaline) and re-arrangements. The major
additions are an elaborate funeral dirge and the awakening of Juliet
before Romeo's death.

Advertisement.

The Alterations in the following Play are few, except in the last act;
the Design was to clear the Original as much as possible from the
Jingle and Quibble which were always thought a great Objection to
performing it.

When this Play was reviv'd two Winters ago, it was generally thought that the sudden Change of *Romeo*'s Love from *Rosaline* to *Juliet* was a Blemish in his Character, and therefore it is to be hop'd that an Alteration in that Particular will be excus'd; the only Merit that is claim'd from it is that it is done with as little Injury to the Original as possible.

*   *   *

[Act I, Scene iv]

A Wood near Verona.

Enter Benvolio *and* Mercutio.

> *Mer.* See where he steals—Told I you not, *Benvolio*,
> That we should find this melancholy *Cupid*
> Lock'd in some gloomy covert, under key
> Of cautionary silence; with his arms
> Threaded, like these cross boughs, in sorrow's knot?

Enter Romeo.

> *Ben.* Good morrow, Cousin.
> *Rom.* Is the day so young?
> *Ben.* But now struck nine.
> *Rom.* Ah me! sad hours seem long.
> *Mer.* Prithee: what sadness lengthens *Romeo*'s hours?
> *Rom.* Not having that, which having makes them short.
> *Ben.* In love, me seems!

Alas, that love so gentle to the view,
Should be so tyrannous and rough in proof!

> *Rom.* Where shall we dine?—O me—Cousin *Benvolio*,

What was the fray this morning with the *Capulets*?
Yet, tell me not, for I have heard it all.
Here's much to do with hate, but more with love:
Love, heavy lightness! serious vanity!
Mis-shapen chaos of well-seeming forms!
This love feel I; but such my froward fate,
That there I love where most I ought to hate.
Dost thou not laugh, my cousin? Oh *Juliet, Juliet!*

> *Ben.* No, coz, I rather weep.
> *Rom.* Good heart, at what?
> *Ben.* At thy good heart's oppression.
> *Mer.* Tell me in sadness, who she is you love?

334

Rom. In sadness then, I love a woman.

Mer. I aim'd so near, when I suppos'd you lov'd.

Rom. A right good marksman! and she's fair I love:
But knows not of my love, 'twas thro' my eyes
The shaft empierc'd my heart, chance gave the wound,
Which time can never heal: no star befriends me,
To each sad night succeeds a dismal morrow,
And still 'tis hopeless love, and endless sorrow.

Mer. Be rul'd by me, forget to think of her.

Rom. O teach me how I should forget to think.

Mer. By giving liberty unto thine eyes:
Take thou some new infection to thy heart,
And the rank poison of the old will die,
Examine other beauties.

Rom. He that is strucken blind cannot forget
The precious treasure of his eye-sight lost.
Shew me a mistress that is passing fair;
What doth her beauty serve but as a note,
Remembring me, who past that passing fair;
Farewel, thou canst not teach me to forget.

Mer. I warrant thee. If thou'lt but stay to hear,
To night there is an ancient splendid feast
Kept by old *Capulet*, our enemy,
Where all the beauties of *Verona* meet.

Rom. At *Capulet*'s!

Mer. At *Capulet*'s, my friend.
Go there, and with an unattainted eye,
Compare her face with some that I shall show,
And I will make thee think thy swan a raven.

Rom. When the devout religion of mine eye
Maintains such falshoods, then turn tears to fires;
And burn the hereticks. All-seeing Phœbus
Ne'er saw her match, since first his course began.

Ben. Tut, tut, you saw her fair, none else being by,
Herself pois'd with herself; but let be weigh'd
Your lady's love against some other fair,
And she will shew scant well.

Rom. I will along, *Mercutio.*

Mer. 'Tis well. Look to behold at this high feast,
Earth-treading stars, that make dim heaven's lights.

335

Hear all, all see, try all; and like her most,
That most shall merit thee.
  Rom. My mind is chang'd—
I will not go to night.
  Mer. Why, may one ask?
  Rom. I dream'd a dream last night.
  Mer. Ha! ha! a dream!
O then I see queen Mab hath been with you.
She is the fancy's mid-wife, and she comes
In shape no bigger than an agat-stone
On the fore-finger of an Alderman. . . .

★   ★   ★

[Act V, Scene i]

Enter the funeral procession of *Juliet*, in which the following Dirge is
sung.

CHORUS.

Rise, rise!
Heart breaking sighs
The woe-fraught bosom swell;
For sighs alone,
And dismal moan,
Should echo *Juliet*'s knell.

AIR.

She's gone—the sweetest flow'r of *May*
That blooming blest our sight;
Those eyes which shone like breaking day,
Are set in endless night!

CHORUS.

Rise, rise! &c.

AIR.

She's gone, she's gone, nor leaves behind
So fair a form, so pure a mind;

How could'st thou, Death, at once destroy,
The *Lover*'s hope, the *Parent*'s joy?

CHORUS.

Rise, Rise! &c.

AIR.

Thou spotless soul, look down below,
Our unfeign'd sorrow see;
Oh give us strength to bear our woe,
To bear the loss of Thee!

CHORUS.

Rise, Rise! &c.

★　　★　　★

[Act V, Scene v.]

★　　★　　★

Bal. I will be gone, Sir, and not trouble you.
Rom. So shalt thou win my favour. Take thou that,
Live and be prosp'rous, and farewel, good fellow.
Bal. For all this same, I'll hide me near this place;　　　　[*Aside.*
His looks I fear, and his intents I doubt.　　　　[*Exit.*

Rom. Thou detestable maw, thou womb of death,
Gorg'd with the dearest morsel of the earth;
Thus I enforce thy rotten jaws to open.
　　　　　　　　　　[*Breaking open the monument.*

And in despight I'll cram thee with more food.
Par. [*Shewing himself.*] Stop thy unhallow'd toil, vile *Montague*:
Can vengeance be pursu'd further than death?
Condemned villain, I do apprehend thee;
Obey, and go with me, for thou must die.
Rom. I must indeed, and therefore came I hither—
Good gentle youth, tempt not a desp'rate man,
Fly hence and leave me:
By heaven I love thee better than myself;
For I come hither arm'd against myself.

Par. I do defie thy pity and thy counsel,
And apprehend thee for a felon here.
    Rom. Wilt thou provoke me? then have at thee, boy.

                                                      [*They fight,* Paris *falls.*

    Page. Oh lord, they fight! I will go call the watch.
    Par. Oh I am slain; if thou be merciful,
Open the tomb, lay me with *Juliet.*   [*Dies.*

    Rom. In faith, I will: let me peruse this face—
Mercutio's kinsman! Noble County *Paris!*
Give me thy hand,
One writ with me in sour misfortune's book,
I'll bury thee in a triumphant grave,
For here lies *Juliet*—Oh my love, my wife,
Death that hath suckt the honey of thy breath,
Hath had no power yet upon thy beauty:
Thou art not conquer'd, beauty's ensign yet
Is crimson in thy lips, and in thy cheeks,
And death's pale flag is not advanced there.
Oh *Juliet*, why art thou yet so fair—here, here
Will I set up my everlasting rest;
And shake the yoke of inauspicious stars
From this world-weary flesh.
Come bitter conduct, come unsavoury guide,
Thou desp'rate pilot, now at once run on
The dashing rocks my sea-sick weary bark:
No more—here's to my love—eyes, look your last;
Arms, take your last embrace; and Lips, do you
The doors of breath seal with a righteous kiss.
Soft—soft—she breathes, and stirs!   [Juliet *wakes.*

    Jul. Where am I? defend me, powers!
    Rom. She speaks, she lives; and we shall still be bless'd!
My kind propitious stars o'erpay me now
For all my sorrows past—rise, rise my *Juliet*,
And from this cave of death, this house of horror,
Quick let me snatch thee to thy *Romeo's* arms,
There breathe a vital spirit in thy lips,
And call thee back to life and love!   [*Takes her hand.*
    Jul. Bless me! how cold it is! who's there?

Rom. Thy husband,
It is thy *Romeo*, love; rais'd from despair
To joys unutterable! quit, quit this place,
And let us fly together—   [*Brings her from the tomb.*
  Jul. Why do you force me so—I'll ne'er consent—
My strength may fail me, but my will's unmov'd,—
I'll not wed *Paris*,—*Romeo* is my husband—
  Rom. Her senses are unsettl'd—restore 'em, Heav'n!
Romeo is thy husband; I am that *Romeo*,
Nor all th' opposing pow'rs of earth or man,
Can break our bonds, or tear thee from my heart.
  Jul. I know that voice—Its magic sweetness wakes
My tranced soul—I now remember well
Each circumstance—Oh my lord, my *Romeo*!
Had'st thou not come, sure I had slept for ever;
But there's a sovereign charm in thy embraces
That can revive the dead—Oh honest *Friar*!
Dost thou avoid me, *Romeo*? let me touch
Thy hand, and taste the cordial of thy lips—
You fright me—speak—Oh let me hear some voice
Besides my own in this drear vault of death,
Or I shall faint—support me—
  Rom. Oh I cannot,
I have no strength, but want thy feeble aid,
Cruel poison!
  Jul. Poison! what means my lord? Thy trembling voice!
Pale lips! and swimming eyes! death's in thy face!
  Rom. It is indeed—I struggle with him now—
The transports that I felt, to hear thee speak,
And see thy op'ning eyes, stopt for a moment
His impetuous course, and all my mind
Was happiness and thee; but now the poison
Rushes thro' my veins—I've not time to tell—
Fate brought me to this place—to take a last,
Last farewel of my love and with thee die.
  Jul. Die! was the *Friar* false?
  Rom. I know not that—
I thought thee dead; distracted at the sight,
(Fatal speed) drank poison, kiss'd thy cold lips,
And found within thy arms a precious grave—

339

But in that moment—Oh—

   Jul. And did I wake for this!

   Rom. My powers are blasted,

'Twixt death and love I'm torn—I am distracted!

But death's strongest—and must I leave thee, *Juliet*?

Oh cruel cursed fate! in sight of heav'n—

   Jul. Thou rav'st—lean on my breast—

   Rom. Fathers have flinty hearts, no tears can melt 'em.

Nature pleads in vain—Children must be wretched—

   Jul. Oh my breaking heart—

   Rom. She is my wife—our hearts are twin'd together—

Capulet, forbear—*Paris*, loose your hold—

Pull not our heart-strings thus—they crack—they break—

Oh *Juliet! Juliet!*   [Dies.

   Jul. Stay, stay, for me, *Romeo*—

A moment stay; fate marries us in death,

And we are *one*—no pow'r shall part us.   [*Faints on* Romeo's *body.*

Enter Friar Lawrence, *with lanthorn, crow and spade.*

   Fri. St. *Francis* be my speed! how oft to-night,

Have my old feet stumbled at graves! Who's there?

Alack, alack! what blood is this which stains

The stony entrace of this sepulchre?

   Jul. Who's there?

   Fri. Ah, *Juliet* awake, and *Romeo* dead!

And *Paris* too—Oh what an unkind hour

Is guilty of this lamentable chance!

   Jul. Here he is still, and I will hold him fast,

They shall not tear him from me—

   Fri. Patience, Lady—

   Jul. Who is that? Oh thou cursed *Friar*! patience?

Talk'st thou of patience to a wretch like me?

   Fri. O fatal error! rise, thou fair distrest,

And fly this scene of death!

   Jul. Come thou not near me,

Or this dagger shall quit my *Romeo*'s death.   [*Draws a dagger.*

   Fri. I wonder not thy griefs have made thee desp'rate.

What noise without? Sweet *Juliet*, let us fly—
A greater pow'r than we can contradict,
Hath thwarted our intents—come, haste away.
I will dispose thee, most unhappy lady,
Amongst a sisterhood of holy nuns:
Stay not to question—for the watch is coming,
Come, go, good *Juliet*—I dare no longer stay.   [*Exit.*

   Jul. Go, get thee hence, I will not away—
What's here! a phial—*Romeo*'s timeless end.
O churl, drink all, and leave no friendly drop
To help me after?—I will kiss thy lips,
Haply some poison yet doth hang on them—   [*Kisses him.*
[Watch *and* Page *within.*]

   Watch. Lead, boy, which way—
   Jul. Noise again!
Then I'll be brief—Oh happy dagger!
This is thy sheath, there rest and let me die.   [*Kills herself.*
   Boy. This is the place—my liege.

Enter Prince, &c.

   Prin. What misadventure is so early up,
That calls our person from its morning's rest?

Enter Capulet.

   Cap. What should it be that they so shriek abroad!
The people in the street cry *Romeo*,
Some *Juliet* and some *Paris*; and all run
With open outcry tow'rd our monument.
   Prin. What fear is this which startles in your ears?
   Watch. Sov'reign, here lies the County *Paris* slain,
And *Romeo* dead—*Juliet* thought dead before
Is warm and newly kill'd—
   Cap. Oh me, this sight of death is as a bell,
That warns my old age to a sepulchre.

Enter Montague.

   Prin. Come *Montague*, for thou art early up,

To see thy son and heir now early fall'n—
  Mon. Alas, my liege, my wife is dead to night,
Grief of my son's exile hath stop'd her breath:
What farther woe conspires against my age!
  Prin. Look there—and see—
  Mon. Oh thou untaught, what manners is in this,
To press before thy father to a grave?
  Prin. Seal up the mouth of outrage for a while
Till we can clear these ambiguities,
And know their spring and head—mean time forbear
And let mischance be slave to patience. . . .

118. John Holt, *Remarks on 'The Tempest'*

1749

From *Remarks on the Tempest: Or an Attempt to Rescue Shakespeare from the Many Errors falsely charged on him, by his several Editors* (1749). I prefer the straightforward title given to the second edition (1750) over the mock-Elizabethan one given to the first.

Nothing seems to be known about Holt's life.

[Preface]

*   *   *

In pursuing this Attempt *Shakespeare* alone shall be considered; and where any Ambiguity arises it shall be explained by the Poet himself. Always laying this down for a Rule, that as he was inspired *by* Nature so he wrote *to* Nature, and prided himself in it; as appears in

> Thou *Nature* art my *Goddess*, to thy *Law*,
> *My Services are bound:*   [*King Lear*, 1.2.1f.]

And as his Imagination was universal so were his Sentiments and Expressions; this is the only Key to unlock his Meaning and the truest Light to view him in.

If he wanted a regular Education his natural Talents were less cramped or fettered; unlearned, uninformed, but from his own keen Observation he scorn'd to be shackled by Rules, or, as he beautifully expresses it to have his

> unhoused, free Condition,
> Put into circumscription and confine.
>
> [Othello, 1.2.26f.]

and as his Conceptions were general and extensive his Language was copiously nervous, and his Diction proper; and what he thought greatly he uttered nobly, and boldy.

If he was deprived of the Advantages of School Learning his Knowledge of Nature was vast and comprehensive; and by a close and strong Application he had made himself intimately acquainted with most of the *living* Tongues of his Time, in many of which there were some very good Translations from the *Antients*, which seem to be the Springs from whence he drew his *Classical Knowledge*. How happily he has used it appears evident from its being now a moot Point whether he understood the Originals or not. Which would perhaps never have been doubted had not his snarling Contemporary, *Ben. Jonson*, taken such Pains to insinuate the Contrary, in order to set his own *Scholarship* in Opposition to *Shakespeare's* Fertility of *Invention*; though (*Learning* out of the *Question*) *Ben* himself in his utmost Rancour could not help paying Acknowledgments to *Shakespeare's* happy Endowments. . . . (viii–ix)

*   *   *

Remarks on The Tempest

This Play is allowed by all Judges to be one of the strongest Testimonials of *Shakespeare's* Poetic Power and of the Force of his Imagination, which on the Doctrine of Enchantment (in his Time firmly believed) has raised so noble a Structure, and from such immoral Agents has produced such fine Lessons of Religion and Morality as this Play abounds with.

The Plot is single: the making bad Men penitent, and manifesting that Repentance by restoring a deposed Sovereign Duke to his Dominions, with the additional Lesson that Patience under Afflictions meets in the

End its Reward, that Duke's Daughter by Marriage being entitled to a Kingdom; the Fable being built on this simple Story. (13-14)

[The plot is summarised.]

[The] whole Time of Action . . . is supposed to be about six Hours, *Shakespeare* having observed the Unities more in this Play than in any other he ever wrote.

The Manners are mix'd, and consequently the Sentiments, and Diction; but all proper to the Persons represented, and chiefly Moral, teaching a Dependance upon Providence in the utmost Danger and Distress, and the Blessings of Deliverance and Reward attending that Dependance.

The Language easy in the Narrative, but where the Passions are concerned, according to this Writer's usual Method, sublimely bold and figurative, though now and then something harsh in the Construction, and by that Means obscure to a cursory Reader.

The Characters admirably suited to their Business on the Scene, particularly *Caliban*'s; which is work'd up to a Height answerable to the Greatness of the Imagination that form'd it, and will always secure *Shakespeare*'s Claim to Poetic Fame, as abounding in every Part with Imagery and Invention, which two are the Support and Soul of Poetry. His Language is finely adapted nay peculiarized to his Character, as his Character is to the Fable, his Sentiments to both, and his Manners to all; his Curiosity, Avidity, Brutality, Cowardice, Vindictiveness, and Cruelty exactly agreeing with his Ignorance and the Origin of his Person.

The Plan mostly tragical, the Faculties being operated on by Amazement, Fear, and Pity; but not regular, being mixed with comic Interludes, and the Catastrophe happy. The Discovery is simple, and, allowing for Enchantment, very easily and naturally brought about. . . . (16-17)

REMARK I. ACT I. SC. I.

Enter a Shipmaster *and a* Boatswain.

The whole Dialogue here consisting of *Sea-Terms* and *Phrases*, though not quite perfect, is by much the best of that Kind ever introduced on the Stage; for unless where *Gonzalo* mentions the Cable (which is of no Use but when the Ship is at Anchor, and here it is plain they are under Sail) there is not one improperly used. (18)

*   *   *

REMARK III.

Boats. Lay her ahold, ahold; *set her two Courses off to Sea again*, lay her off. [1.1.46f.]

Set her two Courses] This is wrong pointed. What all the Editors in general understood by *Courses* here is something difficult to conceive. The Ship's *Course* is the Rhomb Line she describes in her Passage, or the Point of the Compass she sails upon, and the Sea Phrase for that is *she lays up*, or *steers* such or such *a Point of the Compass*; but that could not be intended here, for she could not steer *two Courses* at once. The Courses meant in this Place are two of the three lowest and largest Sails of a Ship, which are so called because, as largest, they contribute most to give her Way through the Water, and consequently enable her to feel her Helm and steer her Course better than when they are not set spread to the Wind. And therefore this Speech should be pointed thus

Lay her ahold, ahold; set her two Courses, off to Sea again; *lay her off.*

It being a Command to set those two larger Sails in order to carry *her off to Sea again*, she being too near in Shore. *To lay her ahold* signifies to bring her to lie as near the Wind as she can, in order to get clear of any Point or Head of Land. (18–19)

*   *   *

REMARK VIII.

Ar. (e) And for the rest o'th' Fleet
(Which I dispers'd) they all have met again,
And are upon the *Mediterranean* (f) Flote,
Bound sadly home for *Naples*;
Supposing they saw the King's Ship wrack'd,
And his great Person perish: [1.2.232ff.]

(e) *and for the rest o'th' Fleet,*] One of the heavy Charges against *Shakespeare* is his not attending over exactly to minute Circumstances in his Plots, (though he strictly observed them in his Characters) and by that Means offending Probability. But here he has been careful, even to Nicety, to avoid that Imputation; for had he not thus accounted for the Dispersion of the Fleet, either *Alonzo* and his People must have had Help or more have been shipwreck'd with him; either of which would by crouding the Scene have spoiled the Plot, and are both thus happily and skilfully avoided.

(f) Mediterranean *Flote*] *Flote* a *Saxon* Word for a Stream, River, or Flood; and here used by the Poet for the Sea.

REMARK IX.

> Pros. *Ariel*, thy Charge
> Exactly is perform'd; but there's more Work:
> *What* (g) *is the Time o' th' Day?*
> Ar. *Past the Mid-season.*
> Pros. *At least two Glasses:* the Time 'twixt six and now,
> Must by us both be spent most preciously.   [1.2.258ff.]

(g) *What is the Time o' th' Day?*] It is a very easy Thing to say this or that is done *impertinently*; but Care should be taken that the Charge should not rebound to the Accuser: Mr *Warb*[*urton*] says 'both the Question and Answer are made *impertinently*' in this Passage, because *Prospero* who asks it in some Degree answers it himself; and therefore gives the whole Answer to *Ariel.* Which though it might cure the Impertinence of the Answer, if it really wanted it, is no Remedy for that of the Question, which this Gentleman leaves as he found it. But both Question and Answer may stand as in the Fol. Edit. made by *Prospero* himself; who in the Hurry of his Mind might have forgot the general and yet, as soon as that was recalled to his Memory, very naturally recollect the particular Time, even to Minuteness, nothing being more common. And *Shakespeare* always kept Nature in his View, and pursued her in her Irregularities as well as her Beauties. And if this Gentleman had remembered some of his own Notes he would not sure have charged *Shakespeare*, or the *Player Editors*, with Impertinence, for making any one ask Questions merely for the Sake of answering them himself. But perhaps he makes his Forgetfulness an Evidence of his Wit.

REMARK X. SCENE IV.

Enter Caliban.

Mr *Warb.* would have done well to explain what he meant by *Antique* with Respect to the Language of *Caliban*; and also to have assign'd a Reason why he calls his Character *Grotesque.* Because there is nothing obsolete in Phrase or Idiom in his Speech, though his Stile is peculiarly adapted to his Origin; nor is there any Thing absurd, capricious, or unnatural in his Character, taking the Doctrine of Witches and their

346

engendering with Dæmons (which was fully credited in *Shakespeare*'s Time) for granted. And the traditionary Sentiment of Lord *Faulkland*, Lord Chief Justice *Vaughan*, and Mr *Selden*, that *Shakespeare* had given a *new* Language to this new invented Character, will hold good, notwithstanding that Gentleman's long Note [p. 227, above]. Nor is the Assertion so extravagant or obscure as to need his Comment.

REMARK XI.

> *Pros.* . . . *when thou did'st not*, Savage,
> *Know thy own meaning.* [1.2.355f.]

Mr *Warb*. changes *did'st* into *coud'st*, and *know*, into *shew;* following, tis to be presumed '*the severe* CANONS *of* LITERAL CRITICISM;' and indeed his *Criticisms* are so *literal* that he has often disguised and more often perverted the Sense of his Author, and no where much more than in this Passage. *Shakespeare*, he says, makes *Prospero* upbraid *Caliban* with only having taught him to *speak*; but surely there is another and a nobler Benefit here mentioned, instructing him to *think*:

> *taught thee* each Hour
> One Thing or other; [1.2.354f.]

and if *Prospero* was so exact and learned a Speaker as Mr *Warb*. contends for he hardly substituted *Thing* for *Word*, which last should have been the Term used if Language only had been taught. But it is pretty plain *Prospero* here speaks of Instruction in general, which *Caliban* was totally destitute of when first found; without any Arrangement of Ideas, which the Poet calls *Purposes*, and ignorant of every Thing (but what the Calls of Nature suggested to him) even of what was healthful or hurtful for him, as well as of Language. Which, when learnt, enabled him to sort and separate his Ideas and know his own Purposes, or those Meanings he had received from *Prospero* (as well as to make them known to others), which before he did not. . . . (26–30)

*   *   *

REMARK XIII.
ARIEL'*s Song*.

> *Full Fathom five thy Father lies*. . . [1.2.396ff.]

Mr WARB. is even prolix in justifying *Shakespeare* in this Song from *Gildon*'s Charge of trifling; and so far he deserves the Thanks of the

Public, nothing being more Poetical than this Method of fixing strongly in *Ferdinand*'s Mind at this Juncture the Idea of his Father's Death, the Belief of which is now absolutely necessary towards carrying on the Plot, as Mr. *Warb.* very justly observes. But then he grossly affronts every one who can read *Shakespeare* by asserting that he believes the general Opinion joins with Mr *Gildon*, when *Ferdinand* immediately after the Song tells the Design of it. '*This Ditty does* remember my drown'd Father;' and then directly acknowledges the magical Influence, here so beautifully supposed by the Author, to begin its Operation on the two Lovers,

> *This is* no mortal Business; *nor no Sound,*
> *That the* Earth owns.—   [1.2.406f.]

REMARK XIV.

Ferd.   . . . *If you be* Mayd *or no?*   [1.2.427]

Great Critics are frequently apt to over-shoot the Mark, and spy *Beauties* and *Blemishes* where no other Eye can; but the *Mischief* on't is that common Understandings, not being able to see Things in the same Light, are apt to give them different Names and to call their *Flowers* Faults: as 'tis likely may be the Case in this Place

Mr *Warb.* (following Mr *Pope*'s Alteration, but sure no Amendment) just after having taken Pains to clear his Author from trifling, here strenuously endeavours to make him guilty of the worst Sort, *punning*, by changing the Substantive *Mayd* (for *Maid*) into the Participle *made*; and has subjoin'd a long Note to this merry Blunder to illustrate his Author's (as he calls it) pleasant Mistake, for no Reason that appears, unless it is because (as *Shakespeare* finely observes, on another Occasion)

> Conceit *in* weakest Minds *still* strongest works.
>   HAMLET. [3.4.114]

For can any one reasonably imagine *Shakespeare* in this Conjuncture, on which the good or ill Fortune of *Prospero*, the chief Character of the Play depended, cou'd so far forget himself as to let the whole Plot stand still for the Sake of so low a Pun? The Knowledge whether *Miranda* was mortal or not might be proper enough to satisfy *Ferdinand*'s Curiosity (and, if the latter, to obtain Protection for him), but conduces nothing to the Business in Hand, the Marriage of *Ferdinand* and *Miranda*, and by that Match the Restoration of *Prospero* to his Dominions. But sure, the Knowledge whether she was single, which the Poet beautifully and justly phrases 'Maid or no', was very material to that Purpose, and very natural, and extremely proper for *Ferdinand* to enquire into. He felt a growing Passion, and was willing to be satisfied as soon as possible whether he might indulge it or not, or whether that grand Obstacle of her being already engag'd, stood in his Way. This appears clearly to be the Poet's Design, who makes both the Question and Answer naturally proceed from the Subject, the growing Love of the two Persons, whose Affections are hurried on towards each other by the Impulse of preternatural Powers, and not from the idle Curiosity of the one or the ignorant Simplicity of the other.

Ferdinand sees her in Company with *Prospero*, whom he does not yet know to be her Father; and though these are all the Persons he has yet seen in the Island he can't tell how well it may be peopled, and is naturally apprehensive so great a Beauty must have produced the same Effect on others he feels it has done on him; and desires to be informed of the Consequences.

The Author confirms this Sense strongly four Speeches after, by making *Ferdinand* say to her,

> O if a Virgin
> And your Affections *not gone forth*,— [1.2.447f.]

which would have follow'd her Answer immediately if the natural Surprize he was under at hearing her speak his Language, and what follows from *Prospero*, had not prevented it—which it is much so sharp-sighted a Critic should overlook. However, the *moral* Turn of his Note is very commendable. (32–5)

*   *   *

REMARK XVI.

> *Mir.* O dear Father,
> Make not too rash a Tryal of him, for
> *He's gentle and not fearful.* [1.2.466ff.]

He's *gentle*, and not *fearful*.] Mr *Warb.* says, 'This seems to be an odd Way of expressing her Sense of her Lover's good Qualities.' *i.e.* Mr *Warb.* is in some doubt whether good Breeding and Valour are neces- sary Requisites in a Gentleman, and seems to think it odd she shou'd esteem them so, and adds, 'It is certain the Beauty of it is not seen at

first View.' But sure, 'tis extremely obvious that she plainly acknowledges in these Words she is forcibly struck with the Humility of his
Address to her, his filial Piety in lamenting the Loss of his Father, and
his general Civility in Conversation (till *Prospero* threatens to treat him
indignantly), and with his Courage in doing what she had never seen
before, making a Shew of Resistance against *Prospero*'s Power. And
from these Qualifications, superior to any she had known but in her
Father, she is fearful of a Struggle between them lest the former shou'd
be hurt in the Action on the one Hand, or her Lover be destroy'd by
Magick on the other. Thus the Poet has clearly express'd, in five words,
all the tender Fear that Duty and a growing Affection cou'd shew. *He's
gentle*, and therefore ought not to be ill treated; *and not fearful*, and
therefore it may be dangerous to attempt it. (36–7)

* * *

REMARK XX.

* * *

 . . . The Lowness of the Dialogue, so frequent in our Poet and in all
his Contemporaries (the learned *Ben* not excepted), and which has been
so often lamented and condemn'd in *Shakespeare*, does not in the least
contradict but that it might be design'd as a Satire by the one—as it is
allow'dly by the other—on the vicious Prevalence of that snip-snap
Wit then so much in Vogue: And intended purely to expose it, rather
than any Fondness *Shakespeare* had for it, or that tame Compliance with
the Mode it has generally been attributed to.

And if what he makes *Gonzalo* say in the Close of this Scene be duly
attended to it gives a strong Turn that Way.

Alon. Pry'thee no more, thou dost talk nothing to me.

*Gonz. I do well believe your Highness: And did it to minister Occasion to
these Gentlemen, who are* of such sensible, and nimble Lungs, that they
always use to laugh at NOTHING.

Ant. 'Twas you we laugh'd at.

Gonz. Who in this Kind of MERRY FOOLING am *Nothing* to you: *So
you may* continue, and laugh at NOTHING still.

Ant. What a Blow was there given!   [2.1.164ff.]

Who does not see this evidently satirizes that Fault for which the Poet
has been so often unjustly upbraided?

Remark XXI.

   Gonz. I'th' Commonwealth, I wou'd by Contraries
Execute all Things: For no Kind of Traffick
Wou'd I permit; no Name of Magistrate;
Letters shou'd not be known; Riches, Poverty,
And Use of Service, none; Contract, Succession,
Bourn, Bound of Land, Tilth, Vineyard, none;
No Use of Metal, Corn, or Wine, or Oil;
No Occupation, all Men idle, all,
And Women too; but innocent and pure:
No Sovereignty.
   Seb. Yet he wou'd be King on't.
   Ant. The *latter End* of his *Commonwealth* forgets *the Beginning*.
                           [2.1.140ff.]

   The latter End *of his* Commonwealth, *&c.*] Mr *Warb.* says, 'All this
Dialogue is a fine Satire on the *Utopian* Treatises of Government;' but
it may perhaps, with greater Justice to the Poet, be look'd upon as a
Compliment to Sir *Philip Sidney*'s *Arcadia*, and Lord *Bacon*'s *New
Atlantis*, the praises being put in the Mouth of *Gonzalo*, who is drawn
as a good and a wise Man, and the Sneers in those of *Sebastian* and *Antonio*, two no very favourable Characters. (39–41)

⋆   ⋆   ⋆

Remark XXV.

   Ant. Then tell me
Who's the next Heir of *Naples?*
   Seb. Claribel.
   Ant. She that is Queen of *Tunis*; she that dwells
Ten Leagues beyond Man's Life; she that from *Naples
Can have no Note*, unless the Sun were Post,
(The Man i'th' Moon's too slow) till new-born Chins
Be rough and razorable;   [2.1.235ff.]

   Can have no Note] We are told by Mr *Warb.* that Mr *Pope* says this
means 'no Advice by Letter'; and he not contradicting it, approves it.
Thus all the Commentators cramp the extensive Scope of the Poet's
Expression to the narrow Limits of their own confin'd Ideas.
   Shakespeare here takes in the whole View of their then respective

Situations: *Ferdinand* drown'd (as is imagined); *Claribel* married in *Tunis*, out of the Reach of Information unless sent expressly (there being great Improbability, not to say Impossibility, she should hear by Report her Father and Brother were dead); *Alonzo* going to be destroy'd in an uninhabited Island; and *Sebastian* getting from that Island (if ever he gets off) King of *Naples*, and both till and after his Arrival there preventing by his Authority any Embassy (which, 'tis submitted, is rather a properer Way of notifying the Accession to a Throne than a Letter by the Post) from being sent to *Tunis*, and consequently *Claribel* from knowing her Right till *Sebastian* had securely fix'd his Power (unless she should learn it by Rumour, which the Poet supposes she could not do Time enough to be of any Use). And this is his Meaning of *no Note*; for *Shakespeare* was enough acquainted with *Geography* to know that a Courier might go from the remotest Part of *Italy* to the utmost known Extent of *Barbary* long before

> new-born Chins
> Grew rough and razorable,

if the *Distance* was the only Impediment.

And here the Poet has shewn his great Skill in Human Nature. *Antonio*, whose Tendency to Evil is described by himself in this Scene, forgets, in his strong Propensity to Power and Mischief, all the Circumstances that make against him: the being in a desart Place; nothing for his Monarch (when he has made him) to rule over, or to be enrich'd by; nor any reasonable Prospect of ever getting out of that Situation. And, beyond even this, he forgets that the rest of *Alonzo*'s Fleet (which he may believe have escaped the Storm, as he sees none of them wreck'd) are on their Passage homeward, with the melancholy Tidings of the Loss of their King and Prince; the Consequence of which must naturally be, the Vacancy in the State would be filled up, and all settled before *Sebastian*, in all human Probability, could put in his Claim. (44–6)

*   *   *

Remark XXXV.

Trin. . . . this is a very shallow Monster; *I afraid of him?* [2.2.134f.]

I afraid of Him?] Messrs. *Theob.* and *Warb.* say this is a Brag of *Trinculo*'s, which it is very far from; it being a direct Acknowledgment that he had been so, and now is angry with himself for it, being conscious it had been discovered by *Caliban*; and hence arises the Contempt

Caliban ever after has for *Trinculo*, and the Regard for *Stephano*'s Courage, which is often in his Mouth, and which without this Preparation would have been quite unnatural.

REMARK XXXVI.

Young Scamels [2.2.162]: Mr *Theob*. alters this to *young Shamois*, and assigns several Reasons for his Alteration; and Mr *Warb*. confirms the Change, *ex Cathedra*, with a magisterial Authority; 'We should read *Shamois*, i.e. young Kids.' But notwithstanding the Sentiments of the one, and the peremptory Decree of the other of these Gentlemen, it may be asked why we should read so? *Caliban* is no where in the Play fam'd for Swiftness, but frequently accused of Sloth, and here pretends to nothing but what may be done at great Leisure:

> . . . *bring thee where Crabs grow;*
>   . . . *dig thee Pig-nuts;*
> *Shew thee a Jay's Nest; and instruct thee how*
> *To snare the nimble Marmazet; I'll bring thee*
> *To clust'ring Filberts, and sometimes I'll get thee*
> *Young Scamels from the Rocks.*
>
>   [2.2.157ff.]

therefore *Shamois* cannot be right, their Celerity being remarkable, even to a standard for Swiftness. But then either something must be found that the Name *Scamels*, and the particular Situation here pointed out will suit, or else we must read with Mr *Theob. Seamel*, for *Sea-gull*, a Bird that builds amongst Rocks, from whence the young ones might be taken; and suppose that in transcribing or at the Press the [E] was chang'd into a [C]. But the Shell-Fish called the Limpet, (whose Shell is generally known by the Name of the nipple Shell) are called in some Countries SCAMS; they are found on the Rocks, and are by many reckoned delicious Food; and from these *Shakespeare* might take the Liberty to form a Diminutive, and make his Word SCAMELS. (55–7)

★ ★ ★

REMARK XXXIX.

I'll go no further off [3.2.69]: *Caliban* is proposing the Plot to murder *Prospero* to *Stephano* and *Trinculo*, who are both drunk. *Ariel*, supposed invisible, interrupts him, which Interruption he imputes to *Trinculo*; whereupon *Stephano* quarrels with *Trinculo*, and threatens to beat him, on which *Trinculo* insists he has done nothing and refuses to go farther from them. But Mr *Theob*. and Mr *Warb*. (probably following Mr *Pope*) have expung'd the Negative, and thereby defaced the strong Features of Nature here mark'd by the Poet, who all through the Character draws *Trinculo* a conscious Coward, and continually endeavouring to hide his Fear by Pretences to Bravery, though in vain; for even *Caliban* has found him out, and in this Scene tells him so more than once:

> *I'll not serve him, he is not* valiant.　　　　　　[3.2.23]

> *I wou'd my* valiant *Master wou'd destroy thee.*　　[3.2.42]

> *If thy Greatness will*
> Revenge *it on him, for I know* thou dar'st,
> *But* this Thing *dares not—*　　　　　　　　　　[3.2.50ff.]

> Beat him *enough, after a little Time*,
> I'll beat him too.　　　　　　　　　　　　　　[3.2.81f.]

The Humour of the Scene is greatly heightened by *Ariel*'s being supposed inaudible as well as invisible to *Trinculo*, whose Curiosity to hear *Caliban*'s Plot occasions the Refusal to go any farther from him and *Stephano*, till the latter by an actual Beating obliges him to shift his Ground. And there is little Room to doubt but this Speech was originally spoke as above pointed, or else *Stephano* to his first Threats added some Sign or Motion for *Trinculo* to remove to some farther Distance, to either of which his affected Resolution not to stir was a proper and pertinent Answer. Whoever has read this Poet attentively will find many Examples of this abrupt Manner of Address, as to *Ferdinand* and *Miranda* afterwards in this Play.

> *Fer., Mir.* We wish you Peace.
> *Pros.* Come with a Thought; *I thank you: Ariel*, come.
> 　　　　　　　　　　　　　　　　　　　[4.1.163f.]

Where he calls first on *Ariel*, and then abruptly breaks that Call to thank them for their kind Wishes, and then again calls his Spirit. (59–61)

*　　*　　*

REMARK XLI.

*   *   *

> Ariel. *You are three Men of Sin, whom Destiny,*
> *That hath to Instrument, this lower World*
> *And what is in't, the never-surfeited Sea*
> *Hath caus'd to belch up:*   [3.3.53ff.]

This whole Speech of *Ariel's* is beautifully imagined, to set the Sense of their Guilt in such a glaring Light as to awaken their Remorse (which all their Sufferings had not been able to do) and to point out the only Means of Relief,

>   *. . . Hearts Sorrow,*
> *And a clear Life ensuing.*   [3.3.81f.]

These moral Strokes which abound in *Shakespeare* prove him a good Man, as well as a great Poet.

REMARK XLII.

> *Gon.* All three of them are desperate; their great Guilt,
> Like Poison, given to work *a long Time after,*
> Now gin's to bite the Spirits.   [3.3.104ff.]

Like Poison, given to work a long Time after] This beautiful and apt Simile contains in it a Piece of Marine Tradition; the Seamen being strongly persuaded that the *Africans*, especially on the *Guiney Coast*, can temper Poison so as to operate at any precise Time and in any limited Degree, and that during the Interval between taking and operating, the Patient shall feel no Manner of Effect from the Dose.

REMARK XLIII.

> Pros. *Have given you here* a Third *of my own Life.*   [4.1.3]

Mr *Theob.* changes this to a *Thread*; and Mr *Warb.* adopts, and *n. a.* acknowledges whence he had it (a Condescension not common with this Gentleman). But the old Reading may be left in Repose, *A Third* being some certain proportional Part of what was dear and valuable to him, and which he could share with another. But query, if *Prospero* parted with the *Thread*, i.e. the *Whole* of his Life, Life itself, whether he could with any Propriety be said still to live, as in the next Line he is made to do? And the Instances produced by Mr *Theob.*

And let not Bardolfe's vital Thread *be cut.*   [*Henry V*, 3.6.46]

His Thread of Life *had not so soon decay'd.*   [*1 Henry VI*, 1.1.34]

Argo *their* Thread of Life *is spun.*   [*2 Henry VI*, 4.2.28]

. . . *shore his old* Thread *in Twain.*   [*Othello*, 5.2.209]

instead of supporting his Alteration of this Passage prove that *Shake-speare* constantly used *Thread of Life* in the strict poetick Sense, for Life, not for any Part or Portion of it: for that *by* and not that *for* which (as it is here expressed) any one liv'd. And though he found that *Prospero* had no Wife living, nor any other Child but *Miranda*, and that *Dimidium Animæ meæ*[1] cannot be construed into three Halves, yet if he had recollected *the Occasion* of this Speech and *to whom* the Speech was spoken (and *how many* interested in the Speech were present at the speaking), he might have thought perhaps the introducing such a Son-in-Law into *Prospero's* Family, who settled a Remainder Expectant of a Crown upon his Daughter and, delivering him from Wretchedness and Banishment, restored him to Power and princely Grandeur, might tempt the Old Gentlemen to imagine his Satisfaction was increased one full Third. And in the Height of that Imagination he might be induc'd, by a poetic Licence, to express himself so as to be clearly understood by an ordinary Reader to have such an Esteem for the Person to whom he was then giving an only Daughter he doated on as to reckon him absolutely as one of his own Family, and an essential *third* Part of his future Happiness, though such an Expression transgressed against the *severe Canons of literal Criticism.* And it is something strange Mr *Warb.* should so hastily adopt this Alteration, as he has prov'd in his Dedication to his Edition he has no private Reasons of his own why a Son-in-Law should not be so regarded. (64-6)

*   *   *

Remark XLIX.

Pros. *And like the baseless Fabrick of their Vision,*
The cloud-capt Towers, the gorgeous Palaces,
The solemn Temples, the great Globe itself,
Yea all which it inherit, shall dissolve;
And like this insubstantial Pageant faded,
Leave not a Rack behind.   [4.1.151ff.]

Mr *Warb.* has much to say about this Passage, condemning *Shakespeare*

---

[1] Horace, *Odes* 1.3.8: 'The half of my own soul'.

unless his Alteration shall pass for *Shakespeare's* Words) for '*wretched Tautology*, and *aukward Expression*;' and all to make Way for his imaginary pompous Reading,

> *And like the baseless Fabric of* TH' AIR VISIONS.

But does this mend the Matter, admitting it to want Amendment? Will the 'Vestige of an embodied Cloud, broken, and dissipated by the Wind,' prove any solider Basis, than the thin Air of which Spirits are said to be framed? Or can *a Vision* be said to be any other than Airy? The Term being strictly confined to that which has no Solidity, no Substance, but merely a Creature of the Brain and the Effect of super-natural Power.

The 'aukward Expression' (as this Gentleman is pleased to call it) *their Vision*, is surely used here with great Propriety; the Spirits who per-formed and contrived it (for any Thing that appears to the contrary) having the best Title to have it call'd theirs. The Tautology, also (mentioned with such Indignation), will melt into Air, into thin Air, if the Speech is divided into its proper Parts,

> *the* baseless Fabric *of their Vision*

referring to Air, which the Poet had just before said they were com-posed of, and returned to; and

> *this* insubstantial Pageant *faded*,

to the Scene they had just represented, which was now totally vanished. Both finely inculcating that all the Power, Wealth, Strength, and Beauty we know, morally considered, is but a Dream, a Vision, and like one shall dissolve and melt away; leaving not so much as a RACK, or smallest Part, behind to testify their having ever existed. As the PSALMIST, with equal Beauty and greater Strength expresses it:

Thou hast destroy'd Cities, *their* Memorial *is* perish'd *with them.* Ps.ix.v.6.

His Place *cou'd* no where *be found.* Ps. xxxvii. v. 37.

For the Wind passeth over it, and it is gone, *and the* Place *thereof shall* know it no more. Ps. ciii. v. 16.

And that the true Meaning of a *Rack* in this Place is a Fragment, a broken Remnant, the learned Gentleman himself admits by calling it, '*the* Vestige of an EMBODIED CLOUD, broken, *and* dissipated *by the Wind.*' Though what he means by an '*embody'd Cloud*,' or how the

'*Vestige*' (Footstep, or Trace) of '*Dissipation*' is to be discern'd, is left to himself to explain, when he thinks proper.

REMARK L.

> *Pros.* The Trumpery in my House, go bring it hither,
> For Stale to catch these Thieves. [4.1.186f.]

Mr *Warb.* says, 'If it should be asked what Necessity for this Apparatus? I answer, that it was the superstitious Fancy of the People, in our Author's Time, that Witches, Conjurers, &c. had no Power over those against whom they would employ their Charms, till they had got them at this Advantage, committing some Sin or other, as here of Theft.' Herein, forgetting on one Hand, all his own excellent Reasoning on the Sin of Ingratitude, and on the other that long before, in, and after *Shakespeare*'s Time the Power of Witchcraft was said to be frequently, nay, most commonly exercised on *Babes* and *Brutes*, neither of which were extremely liable to be had at this Advantage of '*committing some Sin or other*,' as being for the most Part incapable of doing any Act *Animo Peccandi*. But above all forgetting that without some '*Apparatus*' there would have been no manifest Reason why the Assassins should not immediately on their Appearance enter the Cave and perpetrate their Villany; which, if they had, the Stage must have stood still during that Time, and which this *Trumpery* alone totally prevents, as it diverts them from their main Design, and yet keeps the Scene busy, and shews *Shakespeare* perfectly understood the *Jeu du Théâtre*. (76–8)

★   ★   ★

REMARK LII.

SCENE II.

> *Pros.* Ye Elves of Hills, Brooks, standing Lakes, and Groves; [5.1.33ff.]

Shakespeare, in this beautiful Incantation, has shewn beyond Contradiction he was perfectly acquainted with the Sentiments of the Ancients on the Subject of Enchantments. *Ovid*'s Metamorphoses, *Book* vii. from *v.* 197 to *v.* 206 were his Foundation; but he has varied the Plan with a masterly Judgment, having omitted Circumstances which, though then supposed to be practised and therefore ornamental to the *Roman Poet*, would have made no Figure (being disused) in the *British Bard*; and by the happy Fire of his own Imagination, greatly improv'd those he thought fit to take Notice of . . . (80–1)

119. Mark Akenside, Shakespeare attacks Francophilia

1749

Ode: The Remonstrance of Shakespeare (1749) from *The Poems of Mark Akenside, M.D.* (1772), pp. 307–11.

See head-note to No. 106.

THE REMONSTRANCE OF SHAKESPEARE:

Supposed to have been spoken at the Theatre Royal, while the French Comedians were acting by Subscription.

MDCCXLIX.

If, yet regardful of your native land,
Old Shakespeare's tongue you deign to understand,
Lo, from the blissful bowers where heaven rewards
Instructive sages and unblemish'd bards,
I come, the ancient founder of the stage,
Intent to learn, in this discerning age,
What form of wit your fancies have imbrac'd,
And whither tends your elegance of taste,
That thus at length our homely toils you spurn,
That thus to foreign scenes you proudly turn,
That from my brow the laurel wreath you claim
To crown the rivals of your country's fame.
    What though the footsteps of my devious Muse
The measur'd walks of Grecian art refuse?
Or though the frankness of my hardy style
Mock the nice touches of the critic's file?
Yet, what my age and climate held to view,
Impartial I survey'd and fearless drew.

359

And say, ye skillful in the human heart,
Who know to prize a poet's noblest part,
What age, what clime, could e'er an ampler field
For lofty thought, for daring fancy, yield?
I saw this England break the shameful bands
Forg'd for the souls of men by sacred hands:
I saw each groaning realm her aid implore;
Her sons the heroes of each warlike shore:
Her naval standard (the dire Spaniard's bane)
Obey'd through all the circuit of the main.
Then too great commerce, for a late-found world,
Around your coast her eager sails unfurl'd:
New hopes, new passions, thence the bosom fir'd;
New plans, new arts, the genius thence inspir'd;
Thence every scene, which private fortune knows,
In stronger life, with bolder spirit, rose.

Disgrac'd I this full prospect which I drew?
My colours languid, or my strokes untrue?
Have not your sages, warriors, swains, and kings,
Confess'd the living draught of men and things?
What other bard in any clime appears
Alike the master of your smiles and tears?
Yet have I deign'd your audience to intice
With wretched bribes to luxury and vice?
Or have my various scenes a purpose known
Which freedom, virtue, glory, might not own?

Such from the first was my dramatic plan;
It should be your's to crown what I began.
And now that England spurns her Gothic chain,
And equal laws and social science reign,
I thought, Now surely shall my zealous eyes
View nobler bards and juster critics rise,
Intent with learned labour to refine
The copious ore of Albion's native mine,
Our stately Muse more graceful airs to teach,
And form her tongue to more attractive speech,
Till rival nations listen at her feet,
And own her polish'd as they own'd her great.

But do you thus my favorite hopes fullfil?
Is France at last the standard of your skill?

Alas for you! that so betray a mind
Of art unconscious and to beauty blind.
Say: does her language your ambition raise,
Her barren, trivial, unharmonious phrase,
Which fetters eloquence to scantiest bounds,
And maims the cadence of poetic sounds?
Say: does your humble admiration chuse
The gentle prattle of her Comic Muse,
While wits, plain-dealers, fops, and fools appear,
Charg'd to say nought but what the king may hear?
Or rather melt your sympathizing hearts
Won by her tragic scene's romantic arts,
Where old and young declaim on soft desire,
And heroes never, but for love, expire?
   No. Though the charms of novelty awhile
Perhaps too fondly win your thoughtless smile,
Yet not for you design'd indulgent fate
The modes or manners of the Bourbon state.
And ill your minds my partial judgment reads,
And many an augury my hope misleads,
If the fair maids of yonder blooming train
To their light courtship would an audience deign,
Or those chaste matrons a Parisian wife
Chuse for the model of domestic life;
Or if one youth of all that generous band,
The strength and splendor of their native land,
Would yield his portion of his country's fame,
And quit old freedom's patrimonial claim,
With lying smiles oppression's pomp to see,
And judge of glory by a king's decree.
   O blest at home with justly-envied laws,
O long the chiefs of Europe's general cause,
Whom heaven hath chosen at each dangerous hour
To check the inroads of barbaric power,
The rights of trampled nations to reclaim,
And guard the social world from bonds and shame;
Oh let not luxury's fantastic charms
Thus give the lye to your heroic arms:
Nor for the ornaments of life imbrace
Dishonest lessons from that vaunting race,

361

Whom fate's dread laws (for in eternal fate
Despotic rule was heir to freedom's hate)
Whom in each warlike, each commercial part,
In civil counsel, and in pleasing art,
The judge of earth predestin'd for your foes,
And made it fame and virtue to oppose.

120. Richard Hurd on Shakespeare and ordinary life

1749

From 'Notes on the Art of Poetry', in Q. *Horatii Flacci Ars Poetica. Epistola ad Pisones. With an English Commentary and Notes* (1749).

Richard Hurd (1720–1808) attracted the attention of William Warburton by this edition of the *Ars Poetica*, and was appointed Whitehall preacher on Warburton's recommendation. Subsequently Hurd became bishop of Lichfield and Coventry (1775) and Worcester (1781); in 1783 he was offered the primacy, which he refused. His literary works include the commentaries on Horace, several times enlarged, four 'Critical Dissertations', *Moral and Political Dialogues* (1759), *Letters on Chivalry and Romance* (1762), and editions of Warburton, Cowley and Addison. He was a friend of William Mason and Gray.

[On the dangers of not following nature]

For, in attempting to outdo originals, founded on the plan of simple nature, a writer is in the utmost danger of running into affectation and bombast. And indeed, without this temptation, our writers have generally found means to incur these excesses; most of them (except Shakespeare and Otway) filling their plots with unnatural incidents, and heightening their characters into caracatures. Though it may be doubted, whether this hath been owing so much to their own ill taste as to a vicious compliance with that of the public. . . . (68)

★   ★   ★

[On *domestica facta*, ordinary life as the subject-matter for drama]

This judgment of the poet, recommending domestic subjects, as fittest for the stage [*A.P.*, 286] may be inforced from many obvious reasons. As I. That it renders the drama infinitely more *affecting*: and this on many accounts. (1.) As a subject, taken from our own annals, must of course carry with it an air of greater probability, at least to the generality of the people, than one borrowed from those of any other nation. (2.) As we all find a personal interest in the subject. (3.) As it of course affords the best and easiest opportunities of catching our minds, by frequent and unavoidable references to our manners, prejudices and customs. And of how great importance this is, may be learned from hence, that, even in the exhibition of foreign characters, dramatic writers have found themselves obliged to sacrifice truth and probability to the humour of the people, and to dress up their personages, contrary to their own better judgment, in some degree according to the mode and manners of their respective countries. . . . And (4.) as the writer himself, from an intimate acquaintance with the character and genius of his own nation, will be more likely to draw the manners with life and spirit.

II. Next, which should ever be one great point in view, it renders the drama more generally useful in its moral destination. For, it being conversant about domestic acts, the great instruction of the fable more sensibly affects us; and the characters exhibited, from the part we take in their good or ill qualities, will more probably influence our conduct.

III. Lastly, this judgment will deserve the greater regard, as the conduct recommended was, in fact, the practice of our great models, the Greek writers; in whose plays, it is observable, there is scarcely a single scene, which lies out of the confines of Greece.

But, notwithstanding these reasons, the practice hath, in all times, been but little followed. The Romans, after some few attempts in this way (from whence the poet took the occasion of delivering it as a dramatic precept), soon relapsed into their old use; as appears from Seneca's, and the titles of other plays, written in, or after the Augustan age. Succeeding times continued the same attachment to Grecian, with the addition of an equal fondness for Roman, subjects. The reason in both instances hath been ever the same: that strong and early prejudice, approaching somewhat to adoration, in favour of the illustrious names of those two great states. The account of this matter is very easy; for their writings, as they furnish the business of our younger, and the amusement of our riper, years, and more especially make the study of all those, who devote themselves to poetry and the stage, insensibly infix in us an excessive veneration for all affairs, in which they were concerned; insomuch that no other subjects or events seem considerable enough, or rise, in any proportion, to our ideas of the dignity of the tragic scene, but such as time and long admiration have consecrated in the annals of their story. Our Shakespeare was, I think, the first that broke through this bondage of classical superstition. And he owed this felicity, as he did some others, to his want of what is called the advantage of a learned education. Thus, uninfluenced by the weight of early pre-possession, he struck at once into the road of nature and common sense: and without designing, without knowing it, hath left us in his historical plays, with all their anomalies, an exacter resemblance of the Athenian stage, than is anywhere to be found in its most professed admirers and copyists.

I will only add, that, for the more successful execution of this rule of celebrating domestic acts, much will depend on the æra, from whence the subject is taken. Times too remote have almost the same inconveniences, and none of the advantages, which attend the ages of Greece and Rome. And, for those of later date, they are too much familiarized to us, and have not as yet acquired that venerable cast and air, which tragedy demands, and age only can give. There is no fixing this point with precision. In the general, that æra is the fittest for the poet's purpose, which, though fresh enough in our minds to warm and interest us in the event of the action, is yet at so great a distance from the present times, as to have lost all those mean and disparaging circumstances, which unavoidably adhere to recent deeds, and, in some measure, sink the noblest modern transactions to the level of ordinary life. (125–8)

*   *   *

There was a time, when the art of JONSON was set above the divinest raptures of SHAKESPEARE. The present age is well convinced of the mistake. And now the genius of SHAKESPEARE is idolized in its turn. Happily for the public taste, it can scarcely be too much so. (145)

121. David Garrick on Shakespeare's temple

September 1750

'Occasional Prologue, Spoken by Mr *Garrick* at the Opening of
Drury-Lane Theatre, 8 Sept. 1750', from *The Poetical Works of
David Garrick* (1785), I, pp. 102–3.

As Heroes, States, and Kingdoms rise and fall,
So (with the mighty to compare the small)
Thro' int'rest, whim, or if you please thro' fate,
We feel commotions in our mimic state:
The sock and buskin fly from stage to stage;
A year's alliance is with us—an age!
And where's the wonder? All surprize must cease
When we reflect how int'rest or caprice
Makes real Kings break articles of peace.
    Strengthen'd by new allies, our foes prepare;
Cry havock! and let slip the dogs of war.
To shake our souls, the papers of the day
Drew forth the adverse pow'r in dread array;
A pow'r might strike the boldest with dismay.
Yet fearless still we take the field with spirit,
Arm'd *cap-a-pé* in self-sufficient merit.
Our ladies too, with souls and tongues untam'd,
Fire up like Britons when the battle's nam'd:
Each female heart pants for the glorious strife,
From Hamlet's* mother, to the Cobler's wife.†
Some few there are, whom paltry passions guide,
Desert each day, and fly from side to side:
Others, like Swiss, love fighting as their trade,
For beat or beating—they must all be paid.
    Sacred to SHAKESPEARE was this spot design'd,
To pierce the heart, and humanize the mind.

* Mrs Pritchard.
† Mrs Clive.

But if an empty House, the Actor's curse,
Shews us our Lears and Hamlets lose their force;
Unwilling we must change the nobler scene,
And in our turn present you Harlequin;
Quit Poets, and set Carpenters to work,
Shew gaudy scenes, or mount the vaulting Turk:
For tho' we Actors, one and all, agree
Boldly to struggle for our—vanity,
If want comes on, importance must retreat;
Our first great ruling passion is—to eat.
To keep the field, all methods we'll pursue;
The conflict glorious! for we fight for you:
And should we fail to gain the wish'd applause,
At least we're vanquish'd in a noble cause.

122. Unsigned essay, Shakespeare and the Rules

1750

From *An Examen of the Historical Play of Edward the Black Prince* ...
(1750).

I think it is necessary for this Purpose (as far as Rules can teach) if you
would melt your Audience in Tears, to draw the Character you would
make miserable, *faultless, amiable, tender, compassionate,* and unequal to
Misfortune, yet meeting those Miseries which it is least able to bear;
and such a Character is *Desdemona* in *Othello.* But if you would terrify
as well as melt the Soul, let the Character be stain'd with a Crime it
both abhors and is punish'd for: such a Character is *George Barnwell,*
and if his Crimes take away Part of our Pity it is certainly well supply'd
by the Terrour his Guilt occasions, and so happily are the Passions mixed

in that Play that I never knew it fail of drawing Tears from a whole Audience. Such is the Noble *Othello*, whose great Heart indeed disdains our Pity, yet how severe the Pleasure one feels from Admiration, Compassion, and Terrour! But would you give Terrour and Fear unmixed with other Passions, draw Guilt, enormous Guilt, and the Mind raging yet groaning under the Oppression of Conscience, and Furies, and Air-drawn Daggers presenting themselves to the tortured Imagination: in short study and copy *Macbeth.*—I shall make but one Observation more, and proceed to my Design.

It is very certain that *Shakespeare* never observed any Rule but that essential one of *Character*, and it is as certain perhaps that *Shakespeare* was the best Dramatick Writer the World ever produced; from hence it has been urged that Rules are not at all necessary, since we are not offended at the Breach of them in *Shakespeare*. To which I answer that every Man of true Judgment is offended at it, though we suffer or excuse his Faults on account of his amazing Excellencies. And it is absurd to suppose that if he had followed the Critical Rules (which are only Observations on Nature) and wrote with the same Spirit, that it would not have given to his Works a great Addition both of Fame and Excellence.

If it should be urged that no Man who wrote by Rules equall'd *Shakespeare*, who disdained all Curbs, and that therefore Rules are nothing but a Clog upon the Genius; the plain Answer, is, the Difference was in the *Men* and not in their *Methods*. But if after all it should be proved (which I believe it cannot) that Rules are really an undue Check to the free Mind, that they restrain instead of direct the Genius, I contend not for them, and wish they may be sent back to the Schools from whence they came with Ignominy and Disgrace, as I prefer the End to the Means, and had rather be hurried from *Venice* to *Cyprus* than lose one Start of Nature or exalted Sentiment. (6–7)

123. 'Sir' John Hill, Shakespeare and the actors

1750

From *The Actor: A Treatise on the Art of Playing* (1750).

John Hill, M.D. (1716?–75), who called himself 'Sir John', edited *The British Magazine* from 1746 to 1750 and contributed a daily letter called 'The Inspector' to *The London Advertiser and Literary Gazette* from 1751 to 1753. He quarrelled with Fielding, Garrick and Christopher Smart, but was, notwithstanding, a shrewd observer of the theatre.

If we would recollect, by way of contrast to the labour'd violence, the artificial heat with which these passages are deliver'd by this actor, the true spirit, the native fire with which a provok'd old man ought to deliver himself, let us look to the player we have just mention'd, Mr *Garrick*, in *King Lear*, at the conclusion of the second act, where, urg'd by the ingratitude and baseness of those whom he had rais'd to power, he cries out

> Heavens, drop your patience down!
> Ye see me here, ye gods, a poor old man,
> As full of grief as age: wretched in both—[1]

Perhaps nobody but *Shakespeare* could have well drawn a character in so strong a scene of rage and vehemence: certainly no man except the gentleman we have just mentioned in the character ever did, or ever could do him justice in the expressing it. The whole compass of the stage will not afford us so high a contrast of the true and the false fire, the native and the artificial violence we have been speaking of, as we see in these; therefore more specimens of this defect are needless. (30–1)

*   *   *

We are very willing that the heroes in tragedy should be culpable, but

---

[1] Tate's version, 2.2.320ff.; *King Lear*, 2.4.270ff.

we would always have them be criminal with great excuses, and as it were in spite of themselves: we expect that even in the very act of delivering themselves up to the ill they should preserve a kind of love and reverence for the good; and that they be led on artfully to the precipice, not that they plunge themselves voluntarily headlong into it.

The murder of *Desdemona* by *Othello* is one of the most brutal things done by the hero of a play that we have an instance of; but with what a judicious care does the author excuse it in this unhappy man by the thousand circumstances that he contrives to lead to it, and how nicely has he distinguished between the savage fury of a bravo, and the just resentment of an unoffending, injur'd husband, by making him in love with her even at the moment that he is about to destroy her. Whoever will *look into* the following passages with this view will find great reason to be satisfy'd with the conduct of this scene of revenge, savage and brutish as it is in the period. I say, whoever will *look into them in his closet* will find this, for the judgment of the people who prepare and cut plays for the actors is not quite enough to lead them to comprehend the necessity of some of those things which assist in the palliating the circumstances in this manner, so that we do not hear them on the stage.

When *Iago* has by his cunning rais'd the jealousy of the heroe to that pitch that he seems certain of his wife's crime, his resentment bursts out out not against her but the suppos'd villain who had wrong'd him with her:

> I would have him nine years a killing,   [4.1.174]

We expect some horrible threat next against the lady, but he melts into tenderness, and only says

> A fine woman! a fair woman! a sweet woman!   [4.1.175]

and 'tis with difficulty that *Iago*, who answers *Nay, you must forget that*, is able to conjure up any other thoughts in him. This is one of those soothing passages which shew how much against the nature of the heroe is the crime he is afterwards to commit; and it is one of the many of the same kind struck out by the *prompters* from his part.

Immediately after this, when he exclaims in the violence of his rage,

> Aye, let them rot and perish. Let her be damn'd to night;
> She shall not live; my heart is turn'd to stone.   [4.1.177ff.]

he immediately melts again, and adds,

Oh! the world has not a sweeter creature;
She might lie by an emperor's side, and command him tasks:
Oh! she will sing the savageness out of a bear,—
And then of so gentle a condition. The pity of it, *Iago*,
O! the pity of it!   [4.1.179ff.]

The poet gloriously contrives to make even the natural temper of his heroe assist in the taking off from the brutality of the action he is to be guilty of.

What can we expect of a worthy man, convinc'd of his belov'd wife's pretended adultery, but death as the punishment? When we hear the impetuosity of rage burst forth against the supposed adulterer,

O that the slave had forty thousand lives;
One is too poor, too weak for my revenge.   [3.3.446f.]

what are we to expect but the vows of vengeance against the other criminal, as we find them follow:

Now do I see it's true; look here, *Iago*,
All my fond love thus do I blow to heaven.
Arise, black vengeance, from the hollow hell!
Yield up, oh love, thy crown, and hearted throne
To tyrannous hate! swell, bosom, with the fraught,
For 'tis of aspicks' tongues.—O! blood, blood, blood!
                                               [3.3.448ff.]

When the subtle accuser of the lady works the deluded man up to a resolution of never stopping till he has done the suppos'd justice he intends by hinting to him that *his mind may change*, how nobly is the character kept up by the answer:

Never, *Iago*. Like to the *Pontick* sea,
Whose icy current and compulsive force,
Ne'er feels retiring ebb, but keeps due on,
To the *Propontick* and the *Hellespont*:
Even so my bloody thoughts with violent pace
Shall ne'er look back, ne'er ebb to humble love,
'Till that a capable and wide revenge
Swallow them up.   [3.3.457ff.]

How natural, nay how excusable does all this fury appear, under the circumstances in which the author has represented it; and how artful

is his conduct in binding him immediately after by a solemn vow to do
what must be done, tho' it was so very improper for the character of a
hero to perform it. We see *Shakespeare* in this noble instance throwing
the cruelty of the action that was to be committed upon the provok'd
and artfully-rais'd vengeance of the husband, and this so judiciously
that we could scarce have accused him of sinking into brutality had
Desdemona fallen by his hand at that instant. But this was not enough
for *Shakespeare*, how gloriously has he reconciled us to the heroe's
acting it by making him even tender and affectionate in the instant he
is about to do it, representing it to himself as an act of justice, not a
brutal revenge.

> She must die, else she'll betray more men.
> Put out the light, and then—
> Put out *the* light! if I quench thee, thou flaming minister,
> I can again thy former light restore,
> Should I repent me: but once put out *thy* light,
> Thou cunning'st pattern of excelling nature,
> I know not where is that *Promethean* heat
> That can thy light relumine.
> When I have pluck'd the rose
> I cannot give it vital growth again,
> It needs must wither: I'll smell it on the tree;
> O balmy breath, that dost almost persuade
> Justice to break her sword.
> Be thus when thou art dead, and I will kill thee
> And love thee after.
> I must weep, but they are cruel tears;
> This sorrow's heavenly, it strikes where it does love.
>
> [5.2.6ff.]

Whatever horror and brutality there may be in the act itself of killing
an innocent wife, the author has here perfectly reconciled it to the
character of a hero by his conduct of the circumstances that occasion it,
and that lead to it. It is evidently against the inclination of his heart that
Othello does it; and even while we see him about it we do not know
whether he or *Desdemona* be most to be pitied. (142–6)

*   *   *

There is the same defect in his playing *Lear*, and that from the same

371

cause. It is not that Mr *Garrick* is not equal to the task of keeping up the dignity of a king or a heroe—we find by the instances first cited that he is—but he gives way to thoughts of another kind in so great a degree that he frequently loses this part of his character. It is the same natural turn to be severe that robs us of the king in *Lear*, which before sunk the heroe in *Pierre*, as this gentleman plays it. *Shakespeare* has put some of the keenest things he ever wrote into the mouth of this enrag'd monarch, and this player gives them a peculiar strength and sharpness in the expression; but then the king is not found in the satyrist, they are rather sharp things deliver'd as any other character of the play might have said them.

Even in the mad scenes we know from another player's manner of conducting them that the majesty of the monarch may be kept up amidst the wildest sallies of the frantic lunatic; but surely the best friends of Mr *Garrick* will not dispute with us that in this whole part of the play he looks as like a mad any thing else, as a mad king. *Shakespeare* has every where kept up *Lear*'s remembrance of his regal state, even in his utmost ravings; he introduces him with the ornaments of royalty about him, tho' made of weeds and straw, and makes him remember that he is *every inch a king*. But 'tis *Shakespeare* only, not the actor in this case that does it: even when this player says,

> When I do stare, see how the subject quakes. . . . [4.6.108]

The judicious observer, tho' pleased with the just emphasis laid on the words, tho' charm'd with the spirit with which they are spoken, yet cannot but observe that they are not deliver'd with a kingly majesty. They seem rather the flights of a man whose madness made him fancy himself a monarch, than of one who ever really was so. (170–1)

*　　*　　*

[On the over-emphatic speaking of rhymed verse]

A more modern instance, and one which we wish to see mended, as it is of the number of the few things that displease us in a very pleasing play, is that of the *Friar* in *Romeo and Juliet*, who enters, at his morning employ of gathering medicinal herbs for the use of the poor, with these lines:

> The grey-ey'd morn smiles on the frowning night,
> Cheq'ring the eastern clouds with streaks of light; . . .
>
> > [2.3.1ff.]

The poet, according to the fashion of the times, has thrown this into rhyme; but we do not want the player to put us in continual mind of that blemish, or to preserve what we wish had not been exhibited. We dare pronounce it, that if the actor we have mentioned before had these lines to speak their sense would affect the audience as much more than it at present does as the rhyme would be less distinguish'd. (192)

*   *   *

The playhouses swarm with these mighty aristarchs, who, incapable of preserving their attention thro' a whole scene or of interesting themselves in the business of a play, are easily taken by accidental strokes, and turn'd out of their way by things of ever so little importance. *Shakespeare* himself does not escape these criticks, who in the course of a scene as full of true majesty and as interesting to the soul of every man who is capable of being mov'd as the world ever produc'd, will lose sight of all the beauties it abounds with in order to fix their attention upon some trifling imperfection; which, tho' they have not penetration enough to see it, is only such because the times and customs have chang'd since the author wrote it. . . .

If our players had courage enough to make the necessary alterations in their several parts that the changes of the customs of an age or two require, how many excellent plays might we see reviv'd that now lie dormant; while we in vain complain of wanting variety in our theatres, or what is worse, supply that want with new things too contemptible for censure.

What shou'd prevent a man of Mr *Garrick*'s judgment both as a player and a manager from reviving some play in which he finds much merit, tho' many imperfections, with all that merit preserv'd and all those blemishes struck out; instead of forcing upon us pieces which he knows he must despise us for being satisfy'd with. If a line is bad in an old play let it be struck out; if a dozen lines are bad in the midst of a good speech let them all be struck out, and let the good part of it be preserv'd. If there are scenes which his discernment knows wou'd please but which are made languid and tiresome by some long and lifeless speeches, let these be retrench'd or their whole necessary import be thrown into a few words, and the rest of the scene preserv'd. (252–3)

124. Arthur Murphy on *Romeo and Juliet*

October 1750

'Free Remarks on the Tragedy of *Romeo and Juliet*', from *The Student*, ii (1750). This essay (dated here 20 October) appeared in other journals at this time, e.g. *The Ladies Magazine*, ii (Nov./Dec. 1750), and *The Universal Museum*, i (October 1762).

Arthur Murphy (1727–1805), actor, essayist and prolific dramatist, who wrote *The Gray's Inn Journal* from 1752 to 1754, also edited the works of Fielding (1762), wrote a study of Dr Johnson (1792) and a biography of Garrick (1801). For the ascription of this essay to Murphy see A. Sherbo (ed.), *New Essays by Arthur Murphy* (Michigan, 1963), p. 190.

My design being chiefly to consider whether SHAKESPEARE has been improved by the alterations lately made in this play, I shall waive the dispute about the excellencies of this or that actor, *the little or the tall.* In my opinion neither of them are fitted for the characters as drawn by the poet, but particularly the hero and heroine of *Covent-Garden.*[1] They all seem to want what no actor can truly feign, no spectator can thoroughly be deceived in; I mean that degree of puberty, which is but just to be distinguished from childhood. That JULIET is no older than fourteen we are told by her nurse in the first act: '*Of all the days in the year, come Lammas-eve at night shall she be fourteen.*' [1.3.17f.] The age of ROMEO, tho' not expressly marked by our poet, we may suppose to be the same as represented in the original novel of BANDELLO on which this tragedy is founded, and which, as I remember, is eighteen. Indeed allowances should be made by considering that the scene is laid in *Italy*, a warm country, where the people arrive at maturity much sooner than in a colder northern climate: and let me add that in SHAKE-

---

[1] For twelve nights in 1750 the two companies performed rival productions of the play. At Drury Lane Garrick played Romeo to Mrs Bellamy's Juliet, with Woodward (a famous Harlequin) as Mercutio; at Covent Garden Spranger Barry was the Romeo, Mrs Susanna Arne Cibber the Juliet and Charles Macklin Mercutio.

SPEARE's time luxury, debauchery and effeminacy had not yet stinted the growth and retarded the maturity of our robust ENGLISH ancestors. However, such artless simplicity and innocence are so strongly characterized in our two lovers as plainly determine their age to be about the time beforemention'd. Who therefore can help laughing to see a mother of children endeavouring to impose herself upon us for a raw girl just in her teens, and to hear her whining in this strain:

> *Give me my* ROMEO, *night, and when he dies,*
> *Take him and cut him into little stars,* &c.   [3.2.21f.]

or a great huge tall creature about six foot high, and big in proportion, wishing

> *O that I were a glove upon that hand,*
> *That I might touch that cheek.*   [2.2.24f.]

with a thousand other instances of a like nature. But in this I may perhaps seem hyper-critical.

And here I could shew the impropriety of the actors in some other characters of this play. Particularly the gentleman, the wit,

> *That gallant spirit, brave* MERCUTIO,   [3.1.113f.]

in one house is an arch buffoon, and in the other a noisy impudent coxcomb. Thus many of SHAKESPEARE's characters have suffer'd from the ignorance of the players. BENEDICK is a mere woman-hater, HARRY *the eighth* a bluff bully; OTHELLO too was an unfeeling brute till lately, and POLONIUS is still a silly doating old idiot. Indeed it is a shame to common sense to suffer that sensible, tho' officious, old courtier to be so miserably burlesqued: sensible I call him on account of the whole tenour of his speeches, but particularly that in which he advises his son on his setting out to travel, and which is judiciously omitted in the acting (for such elegant sentiments would sound very aukwardly from the mouth of a MACKLIN or a TASWELL).

SHAKESPEARE has always suffered from unskilful alterations, as is plainly prov'd from many vain attempts which are buried in oblivion. But our theatre still furnishes us every season with a sad instance of this truth in *King Lear*. And I question whether *Romeo* and *Juliet* has gain'd much by the late amendments. 'Tis true, some superfluous sapless branches have been lopt off; but then the trunk itself has been wounded, and the root almost destroy'd.

The first and most palpable alteration [by Garrick] (*as it was repre-sented*) is of the very foundation of the plot. As the play is now acted ROMEO, as soon as he appears, lets us know that he is deeply smitten with the love of JULIET; but *when, where, or how* he came to be so we are left to guess as we can. This is striking at the very essence of the story. SHAKESPEARE had represented his young hero entirely devoted to ROSALINE, who returned not his passion; but after having seen JULIET at a feast of her father's he became as deeply enamour'd of her, and

> *She, whom now he loves,*
> *Doth give him grace for grace, and love for love,*
> *The other did not so.* [2.3.85ff.]

From this change of his affection arises the distress which continues to the catastrophe.

'*Many people* (says the editor in his preface to the last edition of this play)[1] *have imagined that the sudden change of* ROMEO'*s love from* ROSALINE *to* JULIET *was a blemish in his character: but* SHAKESPEARE *has dwelt particu-larly on it, and so great a judge of human nature knew that to be young and inconstant was extremely natural.*' But how ever the *judgment* of SHAKE-SPEARE may be impeached by small criticks his *invention* stands acquitted: for if this change be a fault he was led into it by BANDELLO, from whom he borrowed his story and who dwells much more on it than our author. But '*so great a judge of human nature*' knew that this was not only a *natural* but a *necessary* incident. He knew, indeed, '*to be young and in-constant was extremely natural;*' but he knew, too, that the fire of love must be extinguished except it be fed with fresh fuel, and that the cruelty of one mistress is a foil to the fondness of another. Nor in reality is there any *inconstancy* in forsaking one who slights your passion, and fixing it on another who returns it; for constancy must of necessity be mutual. With respect to the *suddenness* of the change, if any change is wrought it must, at the moment it is wrought, be instantaneous; for in so violent a passion as ROMEO's love for JULIET, and where their souls so entirely sympathized, there was no room for cool deliberation and doubtful demur.

And that this is a *necessary* incident appears from the absurdity which arises from the alteration in question. ROMEO, we find as soon as he enters, is in love with JULIET. But how came he to be so? He had *seen* her perhaps; but that he had never *talked* to her till the feast of the

---

[1] Theophilus Cibber: his adaptation was performed in 1744 and printed in 1748. For the position which Murphy is attacking, see Garrick above, pp. 333f.

CAPULETS at the end of the first act appears from what she says in the garden-scene afterwards:

> My ears have not yet drunk an hundred words
> Of that tongue's uttering, yet I know the sound.   [2.2.58f.]

And yet have the players represented him in the very first act so deeply smitten as to *steal into the covert of a wood, shut up his windows, lock fair day light out, &c.*

Again, by representing ROMEO so much enamour'd of JULIET before they actually meet on the stage half the *pathos* is lost, and we are but half prepared for the consequent distress. We are easy on ROMEO's account, we know he is already wounded, *captus est, habet*, and we only feel for JULIET: whereas according to SHAKESPEARE's original we are in pain for both the young lovers, watch every motion of their souls, and partake in every turn of their passions. By being the confidants of their love from the very beginning we are interested in the unhappy issue of it; and as we knew how much he had suffer'd before from ROSALINE's disdain we are now transported with his passion for JULIET, rejoice with him in a return of her affection, and lament with him in being separated from her.

I shall now proceed to point out a few mistakes (as they appear to me) in the other alterations, as well as in the performance of this play, without entering into a particular examen of the whole.

The next material objection I have to offer is with regard to the conduct of the actors in that scene wherein ROMEO takes his leave of JULIET They are brought in *tête à tête* on the platform of the stage; whereas in SHAKESPEARE they are supposed to converse together from a window. I cannot conceive but that this is as convenient a situation for both of them *now* as it was for JULIET in the *garden-scene* where they first met. In SHAKESPEARE's original ROMEO descends from his mistress's window by a ladder of ropes: but by the present management, as he is made to walk off the stage coolly a circumstance is destroyed which (in our author) is noble, sublime, truly tragical, and [in] the spirit of the ancients; a circumstance which must have had the finest effect imaginable on the audience, and have prepared them for the catastrophe. It is as follows: while ROMEO is descending JULIET cries,

> O heav'n! I have an ill-divining soul;
> Methinks I see thee, now thou'rt parting from me,
> AS ONE DEAD IN THE BOTTOM OF A TOMB.   [3.5.54ff.]

I now come to the grand raree-show at the end of the fourth act. But before I take notice of that ridiculous piece of pageantry, let me observe that the players have omitted one of the grandest thoughts, perhaps, which an inspired genius could conceive. This, forsooth, is removed for a common-place sentiment and hackney'd exclamation. Old CAPULET finding his daughter dead (as he believ'd), addresses himself to Count PARIS, who was that very morning to have married her, in this speech, as it stands alter'd from the original:

> O son, the night before thy wedding-day,
> Death has embrac'd thy wife: she, there she lies,
> Flower as she was, nipp'd in the bud by him!
> O JULIET, oh my child, my child!

Now the misfortune is that the old father had used almost the same expression not three lines before:

> Death lies on her, like an untimely frost
> Upon the sweetest flower of the field.   [4.5.28f.]

But in SHAKESPEARE the lines stand thus:

> O son, the night before thy wedding-day
> Has death lain with thy wife: see, there she lies
> (Flower as she was) deflower'd now by him!
> DEATH IS MY SON-IN-LAW.   [4.5.36ff.]

Can any thing be grander than this last hemistich? . . . Our poet is particularly fond of these figurative expressions. In this play we may find several images similar to that of *death is my son-in-law*. As for instance,

> Affliction is enamour'd of thy parts,
> And thou art wedded to calamity.   [3.3.2.f.]

> Happiness courts thee in her best array.   [3.3.142]

so when ROMEO sees JULIET lying (as he thought dead) in the tomb, he expresses his surprize at seeing her so beautiful in the following bold but just speech, which is omitted at our playhouses:

> Why art thou yet so fair?—shall I believe
> That unsubstantial death is amorous,
> And that the lean abhorred monster keeps
> Thee here in dark, to be his paramour?   [5.3.101ff.]

I now proceed to consider the grand funeral dirge, which is introduced in both houses with a rival magnificence and ostentation, of which I don't doubt but the managers took the hint from the concluding lines of the fourth act. Accordingly a long procession of monks, friers, &c. &c. &c., accompanied with musick, is made to pass over the stage. But what end is all this farce and shew to answer? If it be calculated to please the eye and ear only, and not designed to have a proper tragical effect on the mind of the audience, nor contributes to the carrying on or denouement of the plot, it is absurd and ridiculous. This is really the case: for instead of being affected with that seriousness which a *real* funeral might produce, we must rather laugh at so much pomp and expence bestowed on JULIET, whom *we* know is not dead, the frier and the audience being the only persons in the secret. In short, if there is any distress stirring, the candle-snuffers and scene-shifters who assisted as chief mourners have it all to themselves.

Before I conclude these remarks I must confess that the additional scene in the last act between the two lovers at the tomb is very happily imagined, and excites both pity and terrour, the two principal objects of tragedy. But the merit of it is chiefly due to OTWAY, who in his *Caius Marius* (founded on this drama) first gave the hint of it, and from whom the most striking passages are directly borrowed.[1] This the *Editor* might have had the honesty to own: for tho' he is pleased to say '*the favourable reception it had met with from the publick induced the* writer *to print it,*' any one who consults the abovementioned tragedy will see he is little more than a bare transcriber.

London, Oct. 20. 1750.   THEATRICUS.

[1] See Vol. 1, pp. 295–320. Murphy is quite correct about Theophilus Cibber's large-scale borrowing from Otway. But Garrick also borrowed: compare his final scene (above, pp. 338–9) with Otway's (Vol. 1, pp. 316–17).

125. Unsigned poem, 'Shakespeare's Ghost'

June 1750

From *The London Magazine* xix, pp. 278–9 (June 1750).

SHAKESPEARE's GHOST.

From fields of bliss, and that Elysian grove,
Where bards' and heroes' souls, departed, rove,
Fam'd Shakespeare seeks his native isle once more,
And views with filial eyes the parent shore:
"Hail happy land! thro' all the world renown'd,
The first in arms, the first in learning found;
Hail happy land! where ev'ry art maintains
Its sacred rule, where ev'ry science reigns;
Where first, in humble state my lyre I strung;
Where first the tragick muse unloos'd my tongue;
By her inspir'd, I charm'd a former age,
With Juliet's sorrows, and Othello's rage:
A monarch's toils my Falstaff's jests reliev'd,
With him she laugh'd, with pious Henry griev'd.
Nor was the pow'r to draw a nation's tears
Fixt to one circle of revolving years:
Nor cou'd so short a space my fame confine,
The present hours, nay, those to come, are mine.
Still shall my scenes show nature void of art,
Still warm to virtue ev'ry feeling heart.
    But whilst my lays instruct you on the stage,
Guard me, ye Britons, from the pedant's page;
Let not the critick charm your tastes away
To waste, on trifling words, the studious day:
No, to the idly busy bookworm leave
Himself with length of thinking to deceive;

Let him the dross and not the metal chuse,
And my true genius in his language lose:
Do you the unimportant toil neglect,
Pay to your poet's shade the due respect;
Go, to the lofty theatre repair,
My words are best explain'd and told you there;
By action rais'd, my scenes again shall live,
And a new transport to your bosoms give;
When all the critick race forgotten lie
The actors skill shall lift my fame on high.
    Come, let my triumph now in pomp begin:
Let the true Falstaff give you mirth in Quin;
Let Barry in *Othello* pity move,
Or melt in *Romeo* every breast to love;
Let Constance, mad with grief, your tears command,
When Cibber's looks those pitying drops demand:
Nor blush, when Juliet bleeds, her fate to weep,
And o'er her tomb attentive silence keep.
Nor less let Pritchard's silver voice invite
When Beatrice affords a chaste delight;
When Hamlet's mother shows her sex how frail!
When Edward's widow how her fears prevail;
Or the proud wife of Scotland's lawless king,
The dreadful ills which from ambition spring;
But let the modern Roscius stand the chief,
Who wins the soul alike to joy or grief.
    Garrick, whose voice inforces every thought,
By whom my sentiments are noblest taught,
Thou mighty master of dramatick art,
Help me to touch the passions of each heart;
Show conscious murd'rers, Richard struck with fear;
Show froward age, the fatal fault of Lear;
Let in Macbeth and English John be shown
The tyrant trembling on his ill-got throne;
In Hotspur, virtue by rebellion stain'd;
In Hamlet, duty by a son maintain'd;
The lurking traitor in Iago's fate,
What disappointments on the villain wait;
While sprightly minds attend a liv'lier lay
And Benedick diverts the young and gay.

O favour'd of Melpomene, pursue
The happy art reserv'd till now for you:
O only worthy me! my scenes rehearse,
And give new spirit to each tuneful verse.
The muse of fire which Henry's conquests sung
Receiv'd new force when summon'd by thy tongue:
Go on, and give a people more delight,
Produce each day fresh beauties to their sight.
Let Antony a thousand passions raise,
Urging the croud with bleeding Caesar's praise;
Let Imogen's unhappy, jealous lord
Too soon affiance to false signs accord,
Let guilty Beaufort die with conscious dread,
And toss distracted on th' unquiet bed.
Or freed from mirth, set savage rage to view,
In the fell vengeance of the bloody Jew.

 To thee, my great restorer, must belong
The task to vindicate my injur'd song,
To place each character in proper light,
To speak my words and do my meaning right,
To save me from a dire impending fate,
Nor yield me up to Cibber and to Tate:
Retrieve the scenes already snatched away,
Yet, take them back, nor let me fall their prey:
My genuine thoughts when by thy voice exprest,
Shall still be deemed the greatest and the best;
So by each other's aid we both shall live,
I fame to thee, thou life to me shalt give."

126. Thomas Seward on Shakespeare

1750

From the Preface to *The Works of Mr Francis Beaumont, and Mr John Fletcher*, 10 vols (1750).

Thomas Seward (1708–90), canon of Lichfield and Salisbury, completed this edition of Beaumont and Fletcher, which had been started by Theobald, and wrote the preface.

These *Authors* are in a direct *Mean* between *Shakespeare* and *Jonson*: they do not reach the *amazing Rapidity* and *immortal Flights* of the former, but they soar with *more Ease* and to *nobler Heights* than the latter. They have less of the *Os magna sonans*,[1] the *Vivida Vis Animi*,[2] the *noble Enthusiasm*, the *Muse of Fire*, the *terrible Graces* of *Shakespeare*, but they have much more of all these than *Jonson*. On the other hand, in *Literature* they much excel the former, and are excell'd by the latter; and therefore they are more *regular* in their *Plots* and more *correct* in their *Sentiments* and *Diction* than *Shakespeare*, but less so than *Jonson*. Thus far *Beaumont* and *Fletcher* are *One*, but as hinted above in this they differ. *Beaumont* studied and follow'd *Jonson*'s Manner, *personiz'd* the *Passions* and drew *Nature* in her *Extremes*; *Fletcher* follow'd *Shakespeare* and *Nature* in her *usual Dress* (this *Distinction* only holds with regard to their *Comic Works*, for in Tragedies they all chiefly paint from *real Life*). Which of these *Manners* is most excellent may be difficult to say. The former seems most *striking*, the latter more *pleasing*; the *former* shews *Vice* and *Folly* in the most ridiculous Lights, the *latter* more fully shews each Man himself, and unlocks the inmost Recesses of the Heart. (x-xi)

*　　*　　*

Many People read Plays chiefly for the sake of the *Plot*, hurrying

---

[1] Horace, *Satires* 1.4.43f., *os magna sonaturum*: 'tongue of noble utterance'.
[2] Lucretius, *de Rerum Natura*, 1.72: 'the lively force of his mind'.

still on for that Discovery. The happy Contrivance of surprising but natural Incidents is certainly a very great Beauty in the *Drama*, and little Writers have often made their Advantages of it. They could contrive *Incidents* to embarrass and perplex the *Plot*, and by that alone have succeeded and pleased, without perhaps a single Line of *nervous Poetry*, a single *Sentiment* worthy of Memory, without a *Passion* worked up with natural Vigour, or a Character of any distinguished Marks. The best *Poets* have rarely made this *Dramatic Mechanism* their Point. Neither *Sophocles, Euripides, Terence, Shakespeare, Beaumont, Fletcher* or *Jonson* are at all remarkable for forming a *Labyrinth* of *Incidents* and entangling their Readers in a *pleasing Perplexity*. Our late Dramatic Poets learnt this from the *French*, and they from *Romance Writers* and *Novelists*. We could almost wish the Readers of *Beaumont* and *Fletcher* to drop the Expectation of the Event of each Story, to attend with more Care to the Beauty and Energy of the *Sentiments, Diction, Passions* and *Characters*. Every good Author pleases more, the more he is examined (hence perhaps that *Partiality* of *Editors* to their *own Authors*: by a more intimate Acquaintance they discover more of their Beauties than they do of others); especially when the *Stile* and *Manner* are quite *old-fashioned* and the Beauties hid under the Uncouthness of the Dress. The *Taste* and *Fashion* of Poetry varies in every Age, and tho' our old Dramatic Writers are as preferable to the Modern as *Vandike* and *Rubens* to our Modern Painters, yet most Eyes must be accustomed to their *Manner* before they can discern their *Excellencies*. Thus the very best Plays of *Shakespeare* were forced to be dressed *fashionably* by the *Poetic Taylors* of the late Ages before they could be admitted upon the Stage, and a very few Years since his *Comedies* in general were under the highest Contempt. Few, very few, durst speak of them with any sort of Regard; till the many excellent *Criticisms* upon that Author made People study him, and some excellent *Actors* revived these Comedies, which compleatly open'd Mens Eyes, and it is now become as *fashionable* to admire as it had been to decry them.

Shakespeare therefore, even in his *second-best Manner* being now generally admired, we shall endeavour to prove that his *second-rate* and our Authors' *first-rate Beauties* are so near upon a Par that they are scarce distinguishable. A Preface allows not Room for sufficient Proofs of this, but we will produce at least some Parallels of Poetic *Diction* and *Sentiments*, and refer to some of the *Characters* and *Passions*.

The Instances shall be divided into three Classes: The first of Passages where our Authors fall short in comparison of *Shakespeare*; the second of such as are not easily discerned from him; the third of those where *Beaumont* and *Fletcher* have the Advantage. (xiv–xvi)

✳   ✳   ✳

[Quotes a passage from *The Maid's Tragedy*]

A Youth gazing on every Limb of the victorious Chief, then begging his Sword, feeling its Edge, and poising it in his Arm, are Attitudes nobly expressive of the inward Ardor and Ecstacy of Soul. But what is most observable is

> And in his Hand
> Weigh it——He oft, &c.

By this beautiful Pause or Break the *Action* and *Picture* continue in View, and the Poet, like *Homer*, is *eloquent in Silence*. It is a Species of Beauty that shews an Intimacy with that *Father of Poetry*, in whom it occurs extremely often. *Milton* has an exceeding fine one in the Description of his *Lazar-House*.

> Despair
> '*Tended the Sick, busiest from Couch to Couch,*
> *And over them triumphant Death his Dart*
> *Shook—but delay'd to strike, &c.*
>
> *Paradise lost*, Book II. lin. 492.

As *Shakespeare* did not study *Versification* so much as those Poets who were conversant in *Homer* and *Virgil*, I don't remember in him any striking Instance of this Species of Beauty. But he even wanted it not, his *Sentiments* are so amazingly striking that they pierce the Heart at once; and *Diction* and *Numbers*, which are the *Beauty* and *Nerves* adorning and invigorating the *Thoughts* of other Poets, to him are but like the *Bodies of Angels*, *azure Vehicles*, thro' which the whole *Soul* shines transparent. . . . (xvii–xviii)

✳   ✳   ✳

At the latter-end of *King John* the *King* has receiv'd a *burning Poison*; and being asked,

> How fares your Majesty?

> K. John. *Poison'd, ill Fare! dead, forsook, cast off;*
> *And none of you will bid the Winter come,*

385

To thrust his icy Fingers in my Maw;
Nor let my Kingdoms Rivers take their Course
Thro' my burnt Bosom; nor intreat the North
To make his bleak Winds kiss my parched Lips,
And comfort me with Cold—I ask not much,
I beg cold Comfort. [5.7.35ff.]

The first and last Lines are to be rang'd among the *Faults* that so much disgrace *Shakespeare*, which he committed to please the corrupt Taste of the Age he liv'd in, but to which *Beaumont* and *Fletcher's* Learning and Fortune made them superior. The intermediate Lines are extremely beautiful, and mark'd as such by the late great Editor, but yet are much improv'd in two Plays of our Authors, the first in *Valentinian*, where the *Emperor* poison'd in the same Manner, dies with more *Violence*, *Fury* and *Horror*, than King *John*. . . (xxxi–xxxii)

*   *   *

[Beaumont and Fletcher, in their '*Magic and Machinery* . . . fall shorter of *Shakespeare* than in any other of their Attempts to imitate him'.] What is the Reason of this? Is it that their *Genius*, improv'd by Literature and polite Conversation, could well describe *Men* and *Manners* but had not that *poetic*, that *creative Power* to form new Beings and new Worlds,

and give to airy Nothings
    A local Habitation and a Name.
[*A Midsummer Night's Dream*, 5.1.17f.]

as *Shakespeare* excellently describes his own Genius? I believe not. The *Enthusiasm of Passions* which *Beaumont* and *Fletcher* are so frequently rapt into, and the vast Variety of distinguish'd Characters which they have so admirably drawn, shew as strong Powers of Invention as the Creation of *Witches* and *raising* of Ghosts. Their Deficiency therefore in *Magic* is accountable from a Cause far different from a *Poverty of Imagination*: it was the accidental *Disadvantage of a liberal and learned Education*. Sorcery, *Witchcraft*, *Astrology*, *Ghosts*, and *Apparitions* were then the universal Belief of both the *great Vulgar and the small*, nay they were even the *Parliamentary*, the *National Creed*; only some *early-enlightened Minds* saw and contemn'd the whole superstitious Trumpery. Among these our *Authors* were probably initiated from their School-days into a deep-grounded Contempt of it, which breaks out in many parts of their Works and particularly in *The Bloody Brother* and *The Fair Maid of the Inn*, where they began that admirable Banter which the excellent *Butler* carry'd on exactly in the same Strain, and which, with such a *Second*, has at last drove the *Bugbears* from the Minds of almost all Men of common Understanding. But here was our Authors Disadvantage. The Taste of their Age call'd aloud for the Assistance of *Ghosts* and *Sorcery* to heighten the Horror of *Tragedy*; this Horror they had never felt, never heard of but with Contempt, and consequently they had no *Arche-types* in their own Breasts of what they were call'd on to describe. Whereas *Shakespeare* from his low Education had believ'd and felt all the Horrors he painted; for tho' the Universities and Inns of Court were in some degree freed from these Dreams of Superstition, the Banks of the *Avon* were then *haunted* on every Side.

> *There tript with printless Foot the Elves of Hills,*
> *Brooks, Lakes, and Groves; there Sorcery bedimn'd*
> *The Noon-tide Sun, call'd forth the mutinous Winds,*
> *And 'twixt the green Sea and the azur'd Vault*
> *Set roaring War, &c.* [*Tempest* 5.1.33ff.: adapted]

So that *Shakespeare* can scarcely be said to create a new World in his *Magic*; he went but back to his native Country, and only dress'd their *Goblins* in poetic Weeds. Hence ev'n *Theseus* is not attended by his own Deities, *Minerva*, *Venus*, the *Fauns*, *Satyrs*, &c. but by *Oberon* and his *Fairies*. Whereas our *Authors*, however aukwardly they treat of *Ghosts* and *Sorcerers*, yet when they get back to *Greece* (which was as it were their *native Soil*) they introduce the *Classic Deities* with Ease and Dignity. . . . (lii-liii)

*   *   *

But before I finish my Account of them, it is necessary to apologise for a Fault which must shock every modest Reader: it is their frequent use of *gross* and *indecent* Expressions. They have this Fault in common with *Shakespeare*, who is sometimes more gross than they ever are; but I think Grossness does not occur quite so often in him. (liii)

*   *   *

[On the development of textual criticism in the Eighteenth Century]
No sooner therefore were *Criticisms* wrote on our *English* Poets but each deep-read Scholar whose severer Studies had made him frown with contempt on Poems and Plays was taken in to read, to study, to

be enamour'd. He rejoic'd to try his Strength with the Editor, and to become a *Critic* himself. Nay, even Dr *Bentley*'s strange Absurdities in his Notes on *Milton* had this good Effect, that they engag'd a *Pierce* to answer, and perhaps were the first Motives to induce the greatest *Poet*, the most universal *Genius*, One of the greatest *Orators*, and One of the most *industrious Scholars* in the Kingdom each to become Editors of *Shakespeare*. A *Pope*, a *Warburton*, and a *Hanmer* did Honour to the *Science* by engaging in Criticism; but the Worth of that *Science* is most apparent from the Distinction Mr *Theobald* gain'd in the learned World, who had no other Claim to Honour but as a *Critic* on *Shakespeare*. In this Light his Fame remains fresh and unblasted, tho' the *Lightning* of Mr *Pope* and the *Thunder* of Mr *Warburton* have been both launch'd at his Head. Mr *Pope*, being far too great an *Original* himself to submit his own Taste to that of *Shakespeare*'s, was fairly driven out of the Field of Criticism by the plain force of Reason and Argument; but he soon retir'd to his *poetic Citadel*, and from thence play'd such a *Volley* of *Wit* and *Humour* on his *Antagonist* as gave him a very grotesque *Profile* on his Left; but he never drove him from his *Hold* on *Shakespeare*, and his Countenance on that Side is still clear and unspotted. Mr *Warburton*'s Attack was more dangerous, but tho' he was angry from the apprehension of personal injuries, yet his Justice has still left Mr *Theobald* in possession of great Numbers of excellent Emendations, which will always render his Name respectable. (lviii-lix)

* * *

[On the text of *Antony & Cleopatra*]

* * *

I have before observ'd that the Asiatic Stile and Sentiments are from the Scriptures adopted by the *English*, and particularly by *Shakespeare*; but he has given both *Antony* and *Cleopatra* a Rapidity and Boldness of Metaphors that approaches even to Phrensy, which was peculiarly proper to their Characters.

* * *

Alexas.   *So he nodded,*
And soberly did mount an Arm-gaunt *Steed . . .*

[1.5.47f.]

. . . Sir *Thomas* [Hanmer] makes another Change in these Lines, for *arm-gaunt* he reads *arm-girt*: I suppose he meant *with Arms or Shoulders bound round with Trappings*. The Expression is very stiff in this Sense, and justly rejected by Mr *Warburton*, who restores *arm-gaunt*, and explains it of a War-Horse grown gaunt or lean by long Marches and frequent Fights. But why must *Antony*, after a profound Peace and a long Revel in the Arms of *Cleopatra*, upon his Return to *Rome* have nothing to ride but an old batter'd lean War-Horse? Beside, lean Horses are seldom remarkable like this for neighing loud and vigorously. By *Arm* we all understand the *Shoulder*, in *Latin*, *Armus; gaunt* is *lean* or *thin*. It is common for Poets to mention the most distinguish'd Beauty of any thing, to express Beauty in general: by *Synecdoche* a Part is put for the whole. *Arm-gaunt* therefore signifies *thin-shoulder'd*, which we know to be one of the principal Beauties of a Horse, and the Epithet has, from the uncommon use of either part of the compound Word in this Sense, an *antique Dignity* and Grandeur in Sound that Poets much delight in. (lxvi-lxviii, notes)

*   *   *

[On the text of *Measure for Measure*]
Ay, but to die, and go we know not where;
To lie in cold Obstruction, and to rot:
This sensible warm Motion to become
A kneaded Clod, and the delighted *Spirit*
To bathe in fiery Floods, or to reside
In thrilling Regions of thick-ribbed Ice.   [3.1.119ff.]

The Epithet *delighted* in the fourth Line is extremely beautiful, as it carries on the fine Antithesis between the Joys of Life and the Horrors of Death. *This sensible warm Motion must become a kneaded Clod, and this Spirit, delighted* as it has hitherto been with the soothing Delicacies of Sense and the pleasing Ecstasies of youthful Fancy, *must bathe in fiery Floods*. This is peculiarly proper from a Youth just snatch'd from Revelry and Wantonness, to suffer the anguish and Horror of a shameful Death. But this beautiful Sense not being seen, Mr *Upton* makes the first Editor surprisingly blind indeed, for he says that he did not see the Absurdity of a Spirit's being *delighted to bathe in fiery Floods*. Upon supposition therefore of this Absurdity being chargeable on the old Text, he alters *delighted Spirit* to *delinquent Spirit*: a Change which totally loses the whole Spirit of the Poet's original Sentiment. (lxviii-lxix)

*   *   *

[On the future conduct of textual criticism]

Shakespeare alone is a vast Garden of Criticism, where tho' the Editors pull'd up great Numbers of Weeds and the View is much improv'd, yet many are still left, and each of the Editors have mistakingly pull'd up some Flowers which want to be replac'd. And this will be the Fate of every Critic who knows not every single *Word*, *History*, *Custom*, *Trade*, &c. that Shakespeare himself knew, which at this distance of Time is next to an Impossibility. What room therefore for Quarrels and Insults upon each other! (lxxii–lxxiii)

127. Thomas Edwards, Warburton exposed

1750

From *The Canons of Criticism, and Glossary, being a Supplement to Mr Warburton's Edition of Shakespeare. Collected from The Notes in that celebrated Work, And proper to be bound up with it* (1750).

Thomas Edwards (1699–1757) a barrister, published his exposure of Warburton's pretensions as a Shakespeare editor in 1748. An immediate success, a second edition was called for that year, and continually enlarged editions were put out in 1750 (two), 1753, 1758 and 1765. In the preface to the 1750 edition used here Edwards explains why he has been forced to abandon his anonymity.

CANONS OF CRITICISM.

I.

A Professed Critic has a right to declare that his Author *wrote* whatever He thinks he *ought* to have written, with as much positiveness as if He had been at his Elbow.

II.

He has a right to alter any passage which He does not understand.

III.

These alterations He may make in spite of the exactness of measure.

IV.

Where He does not like an expression, and yet cannot mend it, He may abuse his Author for it.

V.

Or He may condemn it as a foolish interpolation.

VI.

As every Author is to be corrected into all possible perfection, and of that Perfection the Professed Critic is the sole judge; he may alter any word or phrase which does not want amendment or which *will do*, provided He can think of any thing which he imagines *will do better.*

VII.

He may find out obsolete words, or coin new ones, and put them in the place of such as He does not like or does not understand.

VIII.

He may prove a reading or support an explanation by any sort of reasons, no matter whether good or bad.

IX.

He may interpret his Author so as to make him mean directly contrary to what He says.

X.

He should not allow any poetical licences which He does not understand.

XI.

He may make foolish amendments or explanations, and refute them, only to enhance the value of his critical skill.

XII.

He may find out a bawdy or immoral meaning in his Author where there does not appear to be any hint that way.

XIII.

He need not attend to the low accuracy of orthography or pointing; but may ridicule such trivial criticisms in others.

XIV.

Yet when He pleases to condescend to such work He may value himself upon it; and not only restore lost puns but point out such quaintnesses where, perhaps, the Author never thought of them.

XV.

He may explane a difficult passage by words absolutely unintelligible.

XVI.

He may contradict himself for the sake of shewing his critical skill on both sides of the question.

XVII.

It will be necessary for the professed Critic to have by him a good number of pedantic and abusive expressions to throw about upon proper occasions.

XVIII.

He may explane his Author or any former Editor of him by supplying such words or pieces of words or marks as He thinks fit for that purpose.

XIX.

He may use the very same reasons for confirming his own observations which He has disallowed in his adversary.

XX.

As the design of writing notes is not so much to explane the Author's meaning as to display the Critic's knowledge, it may be proper to shew his universal learning, that He minutely point out from whence every metaphor and allusion is taken.

XXI.

It will be proper, in order to shew his wit, especially if the Critic be a married Man, to take every opportunity of sneering at the Fair Sex.

XXII.

He may misquote himself, or any body else, in order to make an occasion of writing notes when He cannot otherwise find one.

XXIII.

The Professed Critic, in order to furnish his Quota to the Bookseller, may write Notes of Nothing; that is to say, Notes which either explane things which do not want explanation, or such as do not explane matters at all but merely fill-up so much paper.

XXIV.

He may dispense with truth in order to give the world a higher idea of his parts, or the value of his work.

PREFACE.

[To the Second Edition]

I now appear in public, not a little against my inclination; for I thought I had been quit of the task of reading the last edition of Shakepeare any more, at least till those who disapprove of what I have published concerning it should be as well acquainted with it as I am; and that perhaps might have been a reprieve for life. But Mr. Warburton has dragged me from my obscurity, and by insinuating that I have written a libel against him (by which he must mean the CANONS OF CRITICISM, because it is the only book I have written) I say, by this unfair insinuation he has obliged me to set my name to a pamphlet, which if I did not in this manner own before it was, I must confess, owing to that fault Mr. Warburton accuses me of; a fault which He, who like Cato can have no remorse for weaknesses in others which his upright soul was never guilty of, thinks utterly unpardonable; and that is *Modesty*. Not that I was either ashamed of the pamphlet, or afraid of my adversary; for I knew that my cause was just, and that truth would support me even against a more tremendous antagonist, if such there be; but I thought it a work which though not unbecoming a man who has more serious studies yet was not of that consequence as to found any great matter of reputation upon.

Since then I am thus obliged to appear in public I the more readily submit, that I may have an opportunity of answering not what Mr Warburton has written against me, for that is unanswerable, but some objections which I hear have been made against the *Canons* by some of his friends.

It is my misfortune in this controversy to be engaged with a person who is better known by his name than his works; or, to speak more properly, whose works are more known than read; which will oblige me to use several explanations and references, unnecessary indeed to those who are well read in him, but of consequence towards clearing myself from the imputation of dealing hardly by him, and saving my readers a task which I confess I did not find a very pleasing one.

Mr Warburton had promised the world a most complete edition of Shakespeare, and long before it came out raised our expectations of it by a pompous account of what he would do in the *General Dictionary*;[1] he was very handsomely paid for what he promised. The expected edition at length comes out, with a title-page importing that the Genuine Text *collated* with all the former editions, and then *corrected* and *emended* is there settled. His preface is taken up with describing the great difficulties of his work, and the great qualifications requisite to a due performance of it. Yet at the same time he very cavalierly tells us that these notes were among the amusements of his younger years: and as for the Canons of Criticism and the Glossary which he promised, he absolves himself, and leaves his readers to collect them out of his notes.

I desire to know by what name such a behaviour in any other commerce or intercourse of life would be called? and whether a man is not dealt gently with who is only laughed at for it? I thought then I had a right to laugh; and when I found so many hasty, crude, and to say no worse, unedifying notes supported by such magisterial pride, I took the liberty he gave me, and extracted some Canons and an essay towards a glossary from his work. If he had done it, he had saved me the labor. It is possible indeed that he might not have pitched upon all the same passages as I did to collect them from, as perhaps no two people who did not consult together would; but I defie him to say that these are not fairly collected, or that he is unfairly quoted for the examples. If Mr Warburton would have been more grave upon the occasion, yet I did not laugh so much as I might have done; and I used him with better

---

[1] See No. 90 above.

manners than ever he did any person whom he had a controversy with, except one gentleman[1] whom he is afraid of, if I may except even him. (3–5)

* * *

After being degraded from my gentility, I am accused of dulness, of being engaged against Shakespeare, and of personal abuse. For the first, *if*, as Audrey says, *the Gods have not made me poetical*, I cannot help it; every body has not the wit of the ingenious Mr Warburton, and I confess myself not to be his match in that species of wit which he deals out so lavishly in his notes upon all occasions. As to the charge of being engaged against Shakespeare, if he does not by the most scandalous equivocation mean HIS edition of Shakespeare, it is maliciously false; for I defy him to prove that I ever either wrote or spoke concerning Shakespeare, but with that esteem which is due to the greatest of our English Poets. And as to the imputation of personal abuse, I deny it, and call upon him to produce any instance of it. I know nothing of the man but from his works, and from what he has shewn of his temper in them I do not desire to know more of him. Nor am I conscious of having made one remark which did not naturally arise from the subject before me, or of having been in any instance severe but on occasions where every gentleman must be moved; I mean where his notes seemed to me of an immoral tendency, or full of those illiberal, common-place reflections on the fair sex, which are unworthy of a gentleman or a man, much less do they become a divine and a married man. And if this is called personal abuse, I will repeat it till he is ashamed of such language as none but libertines and the lowest of the vulgar can think to be wit; and this too flowing from the fulness of his heart, where honest Shakespeare gave not the least occasion for such reflections.

If any applications are made which I did not design, I ought not to be answerable for them; if this is done by Mr Warburton's friends they pay him an ill compliment; if by himself, he must have reason from some unlucky co-incidences which should have made him more cautious of touching some points; and he ought to have remembered, that a man whose house is made of glass should never begin throwing stones. (7–9)

* * *

[1] In the British Museum Malone copy this person is identified (in what is said to be Edwards's own hand) as 'Dr Middleton' (i.e. Conyers Middleton).

I thought it proper to hasten this new edition, which Mr Warburton's ungentleman-like attack made necessary for my defense, as much as possible; and am proud to acknowledge that I have received considerable assistance in it from a gentleman who in a very friendly manner resented the ill usage I have met with as much as if it had been done to himself. I have added a few new Canons, and given a great many more examples to the others: though because I would neither tire my reader or myself, nor too much incroach upon Mr Tonson's property, I have left abundant gleanings for any body who will give himself the trouble of gathering them. This I hope will answer one objection I have heard, that I had selected the only exceptionable passages, a few faults out of great numbers of beauties of which the eight volumes are full. This will never be said by any person who has read the eight volumes; and they who do not care to give themselves that trouble ought not to pass too hasty a judgment: whether it be true or no will appear to those who shall peruse these sheets. That there are good notes in his edition of Shakespeare I never did deny; but as he has had the plundering of two dead men,[1] it will be difficult to know which are his own; some of them, I suppose may be; and hard indeed would be his luck if among so many bold throws he should have never a winning cast. But I do insist that there are great numbers of such shameful blunders as disparage the rest, if they do not discredit his title to them, and make them look rather like lucky hits than the result of judgment.

Thus I have, for the sake of the public, at my own very great hasard, though not of life and limb yet of reputation, ventured to attack this giant critic; who seemed to me like his brother *Orgoglio*, of whom Spenser says,

> *The greatest Earth his uncouth Mother was,*
> *And blust'ring Æolus his boasted Sire;*

Book I. Canto 7. St. 9.

And she, after a hard labour,

> *Brought forth this monstrous Masse of earthly Slime,*
> *Puff'd up with empty wind, and fill'd with sinful Crime.*

I have endeavoured, like *Prince Arthur*, to squeeze him, and the public must judge whether the event has been like what happened to his brother on the same experiment.

[1] Theobald and Hanmer. The helper referred to may have been R. Roderick: see Vol. 4, No. 169.

But soon as breath out of his breast did passe,
The huge great body which the Giant bore
Was vanish'd quite; and of that monstrous Masse
Was nothing left, but like an empty bladder was.

Canto 8. St. 24.

The world will not be long imposed on by ungrounded pretenses to learning or any other qualification; nor does the knowledge of words alone, if it be really attained, make a man learned. Every true judge will subscribe to Scaliger's opinion: 'if,' says he, 'a person's learning is to be judged of by his reading, no-body can deny Eusebius the character of a learned man; but if he is to be esteemed learned who has shewn judgment together with his reading, Eusebius is not such.'

I shall conclude, in the words of a celebrated author on a like occasion;* 'It was not the purpose of these remarks to cast a blemish on his envied fame, but to do a piece of justice to the real merit both of the *work* and its *author*, by that best and gentlest method of correction which nature has ordained in such a case, of laughing him down to his proper rank and character.' (11–13)

SONNET.

Tongue-doughty Pedant; whose ambitious mind
   Prompts thee beyond thy native pitch to soar,
   And, imp'd with borrow'd plumes of Index-lore,
Range through the Vast of Science unconfin'd!

Not for thy wing was such a flight design'd:
   Know thy own strength, and wise, attempt no more;
   But lowly skim round Error's winding shore,
In quest of Paradox from Sense refin'd.

Much hast thou written—more than will be read;
   Then cease from *Shakespeare* thy unhallowed rage;
Nor, by a fond o'erweening pride mis-led,
Hope fame by injuring the sacred Dead:
   Know, who would comment well his godlike page,
Critic, must have a Heart as well as Head. (14)

* Remarks on the *Jesuit* Cabal, p. 57, 58.

INTRODUCTION

To the First Edition.

Shakespeare, an author of the greatest genius that our, or perhaps any other, country ever afforded, has had the misfortune to suffer more from the carelessness or ignorance of his editors than any author ever did. (15)

*   *   *

[Of Rowe's edition] it has been said that he rather yielded to the hasty publication of some notes which he had made *obiter* in reading of Shakespeare than performed the real work of an editor. If this be not so, what a prodigious genius must Mr Warburton be, who can supply what Mr Pope, 'by the force of an uncommon genius' and in his maturest age could not perform; merely by giving us observations and notes which, though they 'take in the whole compass of criticism,' yet (to use his own words) 'such as they are, were among his younger amusements, when many years ago he used to turn over these sort of writers to unbend himself from more serious applications.' And here I must do Mr Warburton the justice to say that however he may be slandered by the ignorant or malicious Tartufes it is very apparent that he has not interrupted his more serious studies by giving much of his time and attention to a playbook.

Mr Pope's however, I suppose, was as good an edition as a mere poet could produce; and nothing, as Mr Warburton justly observes, 'will give the common reader a better idea of the value of Mr Pope's edition, than the two attempts which have been since made by Mr Theobald, and Sir Thomas Hanmer, in opposition to it; who—left their author in ten times a worse condition than they found him.' And this will plainly appear to any one, who compares Mr Pope's first edition with Mr Theobald's, before the booksellers had an opportunity of transplanting the 'blunders' of the latter into the text of the former; as indeed no small number of readings from both those condemned editions have unluckily crept into Mr Warburton's also.

Mr Pope ambitiously wished that his edition should be *melted down* into Mr Warburton's, as it would afford him a fit opportunity of *confessing* his mistakes; but this Mr Warburton with prudence refused. It was not fit that the poet's and the critic's performances should be confounded; and though they are, as we may say, rivetted together, particular care is taken that they should never run the one into the other: they are kept entirely distinct, and poor Mr Pope is left

> disappointed, unanneal'd,
> With all his imperfections on his head. [*Hamlet*, 1.5.77ff.]

To conclude. Nothing seems wanting to this most perfect edition of Shakespeare but the CANONS or RULES *for Criticism*, and the GLOSSARY, which Mr Warburton left to be collected out of his Notes; both which I have endeavoured in some measure to supply, and have given examples to confirm and illustrate each Rule. And I hope when Mr Warburton's edition is thus completed by the addition of what his want of leisure only hindered him from giving the public it will fully answer the ends he proposed in it; which are, '*First, to give the *unlearned reader* a just idea, and consequently a better opinion, of the art of criticism, now sunk very low in the popular esteem by the attempts of some who would needs exercise it without either natural or acquired talents, and by the ill success of others who seem to have lost both when they come to try them upon English authors. And secondly, to deter the† *unlearned writer* from wantonly trifling with an art he is a stranger to, at the expence of his own reputation and the integrity of the text of established authors;' which, if this example will not do, I know not what will. (21–3)

✳   ✳   ✳

[On *Romeo and Juliet*, 4.2.31f.]

> 'Now afore God, this rev'rend holy friar
> All our whole city is much bound *to him*.

'*to him*.] For the sake of the grammar I would suspect Shakespeare wrote

> much bound to *hymn*.

i.e. praise, celebrate.' WARB. [VIII, 88]

And I, for the sake of Mr Warburton, would suspect that he was not thoroughly awake when he made this Amendment. It is a place that

---

* Mr W.'s *Pref.* [above p. 224].

† *N. B.* A writer may properly be called *unlearned*; who, notwithstanding all his other knowledge, does not understand the subject which he writes upon.

wants no tinkering; Shakespeare uses the nominative case absolute, or rather elliptical, as he does in *Hamlet*:

> Your Majesty and we that have free souls,
> It touches us not. [3.2.236f.]

> But yesternight, my Lord, she and that Friar
> I saw them at the prison. [*Measure for Measure*, 5.1.134f.]

> The trumpery in my house, go bring it hither.
> [*Tempest*, 4.1.186]

And this is a frequent way of speaking, even in prose. (6)

★   ★   ★

[On Hamlet, 5.2.352]

'And flights of angels *sing* thee to thy rest.
What language is this, of *flights singing*? We should certainly read,
And flights of angels *wing* thee to thy rest.
i.e. carry thee to heaven.' WARB. [VIII, 265]

What language is this? why English certainly, if he understood it. A *flight* is a flock, and is a very common expression, as a *flight* of woodcocks, &c. If it had not been beneath a profess'd critic to consult a Dictionary he might have found it rendered *Grex avium*, in Littleton; *Une volée*, in Boyer; and why a *flight* of angels may not *sing*, as well as a *flight* of larks, rests upon Mr Warburton to shew. (9)

★   ★   ★

[On A Midsummer Night's Dream, 1.2.23f.]

—'my chief humour is for a tyrant: I could play Ercles rarely, or a part to tear a *cat* in.'

We should read, A part to tear a *cap* in; for as a ranting whore was called a *tear-sheet*, (*2d part of Hen. IV*.) so a ranting bully was called a *tear-cap*.' WARB. [I, 104]

Nick Bottom's being called *Bully* Bottom seems to have given rise to this judicious conjecture; but it is much more likely that Shakespeare wrote, as all the editions give it, 'a part to *tear a cat in*' which is a burlesque upon Hercules's killing a lion. (12)

★   ★   ★

[On *Measure for Measure*, 3.2.46]

'*Is't* not *drown'd* in the last *rain?*] This strange nonsense should be thus corrected, *It's not down* i'th' last *reign*, i.e. *these* are severities unknown to the old Duke's time. *And this is to the purpose.*' WARB. [I, 411]

To what *purpose* it is, I cannot tell, except it be to make a passage absolute nonsense, which at least was sense before he meddled with it. Though it may be difficult to explane all that Lucio says in this scene Mr Warburton has had the luck to make matters harder than he found them.

Lucio says, 'How now, noble Pompey? What, at the wheels of Cæsar? &c.–What reply? ha? What sayst thou to this tune, matter, and method? [i.e. *what answer have you to make me?*] 'Is IT [*his reply or answer*] not drown'd in the last rain?' A proverbial phrase, to express a thing which is lost.

This explication seems easier than that *it* should signify *these severities,* and *down in the last reign,* unknown to the old Duke's time, as much as Mr Warburton assures us that it *is to the purpose.*

In his very next note he has, by arbitrarily altering the pointing, obscured a passage which was clear before, lost the real jest in hunting for humor where none was designed, and attributed a sentiment to one of the speakers which there is not the least foundation for, while he supports this only by a *This is in character.* (22)

*　　　*　　　*

[On *Richard II*, 1.1.154]

'This we prescribe, though no Physician, &c.

"I must make one remark in general on the rhymes throughout this whole play; they are so much inferior to the rest of the writing that they appear to me of a different hand. What confirms this is that the context does *every where exactly* (and frequently much better) connect without the inserted rhymes, except in a very few places; and just there too, the rhyming verses are of a much better taste than all the others, which rather strengthens my conjecture." Mr POPE.' [See Vol. 2, p. 416]

The professed critic might have seen, that this observation of Mr Pope's happens to be very unluckily placed here, because the context, without the inserted rhymes, will not connect at all. For example, let us read the passage as it would stand corrected by this rule.

K. Richard. Wrath-kindled Gentlemen, be rul'd by me,
Let's purge this choler without letting blood.

....

We were not born to sue, but to command,
Which since we cannot do to make you friends
Be ready, as your lives shall answer it,
At Coventry, upon St. Lambert's day;
There shall your swords and lances arbitrate, &c.   [1.1.152f., 196ff.]

Here we see that when the rhyming part of this dialogue is left out
King Richard begins with dissuading them from the duel, and in the
very next sentence absurdly enough appoints the time and place of
their combat. Nor are these rhyming verses in so despicable a taste as
they are represented; on the contrary, what both of the persons say
about the value of their good name and honour contains sentiments by
no means unworthy of their birth and nobility.

But Mr Warburton seizes on this licence of his friend to nibble at the
rhyming part of the play, and makes a needless alteration in defiance
of the rhyme, and, as it seems, merely in defiance.

As gentle and as jocund as to *jest*,
Go I to fight: Truth hath a quiet breast.   [1.3.95f.]

'Not so neither: we should read, to *just*, i.e. to tilt or tourny, which
was a kind of sport too.' WARB.

By the pertness of his '*Not so neither*' one would imagine he had some
smart reason to give against that expression to *jest*, yet his remark
'*which was a kind of sport too*' brings it as near as possible to the idea of
jesting and seems to have been suggested to him by his evil Genius,
merely to weaken the force of his own emendation. (26–8)

*   *   *

[On *Henry VIII*, 1.2.1]

'My life itself, and the *best heart* of it.'
'*and the best heart of it*] The expression is monstrous. The heart is
supposed the seat of life: But as if he had many lives, and to each of
them a heart, he says his *best heart*. A way of speaking, that would have
become a cat rather than a king.' WARB. [V, 353]
Poor Shakespeare! Your anomalies will do you no service when once

you go beyond Mr Warburton's apprehension; and you will find a profess'd critic is a terrible adversary when he is thoroughly provoked. You must then speak by the card, or equivocation will undo you. How happy is it that Mr Warburton was either not so attentive or not so angry when he read those lines in *Hamlet*,

> Give me that man,
> That is not passion's slave, and I will wear him
> In my heart's core; aye, in my heart of heart   [3.2.69ff.]

We should then perhaps have heard that this was a way of speaking that would have rather become a pippin than a prince. (30)

*   *   *

[On *King Lear*, 3.2.4ff.]

'You sulphurous and thought-executing fires,
Vaunt-couriers of oak-cleaving thunderbolts,
Singe my white head—

The second of these lines must needs be the players' spurious issue. The reason is *demonstrative*. Shakespeare tells us in the first and third lines, truely, that the flash does the execution; but in the second he talks of an imaginary thunderbolt, (distinct from the flash or fire, which fire he calls only the *vaunt-couriers* or fore-runners of *it*) which he falsely says does it. This is so glaring a contradiction as makes it impossible to be all of one hand.' WARB. [VI, 72]

The latter part of this note I subscribe to. It appears to be so in fact, for the contradiction is of Mr Warburton's hand, and if there be any spurious issue it must call him Father; Shakespeare's sense is as plain as words can make it.

O light'ning, thou fore-runner of thunder, singe me, &c.

What is there here that can possibly mislead Mr Warburton to think of thunder sing'ing him? The lightning and the thunder have two distinct offices allotted them by the speaker. He calls on the former to *singe his white head*, and on the latter to *strike flat the thick rotundity of the world*. And thus the sentiment rises properly throughout the speech, and the line in question is a very fine part of it; for however absurd thunderbolts may be in true philosophy their poetical existence is unquestionable, and their actual existence is still universally believed by the common people in the country, who every day gather up flints of a particular form which they call by that name. But Mr Warburton will make his *writing and reading* appear *when*, as honest *Dogberry* says, *there is no need of such vanity*. He had better have given a truce to his philosophy, and minded his Grammar a little better, and then he would not have set the numbers a tilting at each other in the manner he has done above.

—*Fire* (singular) is the *vaunt-couriers* (plural) but the low care of Grammar is beneath a Profess'd Critic. (33–4)

*   *   *

[On *The Merchant of Venice*, 3.4.43f.]

'I thank you for your wish; and am well *pleas'd* To wish it back on you] I should rather think, Shakespeare wrote,

—and am well *'pris'd*;
from the French *appris*, taught, instructed,' &c. WARB. [II, 155

Why Mr Warburton should rather think so I cannot imagine, except for the sake of introducing a word of his dear French origine; but he takes a large fine for his *donum civitatis*, as he elsewhere calls it. Shakespeare neither uses French words so needlessly, nor does he hack and mangle his words at this rate to fit them for a place they were not designed for. . . (38)

*   *   *

[On *King Lear*, 1.1.37]

'*and 'tis our* fast *intent*, &c.] This is an interpolation of Mr Lewis Theobald, for want of knowing the meaning of the old reading in the Quarto of 1608, and the first Folio of 1623; where we find it,

and 'tis our *first intent,*

which *is as* Shakespeare *wrote it*, who makes Lear declare his purpose with a dignity becoming his character: that the *first reason* of his abdication was *the love of his people*, that they might be protected by such as were better able to discharge the trust; and his *natural affection for his daughters* only the second.' WARB. [VI, 4]

Had Mr Warburton, as he pretends, COLLATED ALL the former editions he must have known that FAST *intent* is not an interpolation of Mr Lewis

Theobald; and if he kept the reading of the second folio, for *want of* knowing the meaning of the other, Mr. Warburton would have done well to have followed him. For *our* FIRST *intent* can never signify the FIRST REASON of our intent, though he sophistically shuffles them upon us as expressions of the same import, and upon this change of the terms founds all his cobweb refinements about the dignity of Lear's character, his patriotism, and natural affection, his *first* and *second* reasons, not a word of which appears in the text, which seems to allude only to King Lear's age and infirmities.

> and 'tis our fast intent
> To shake all cares and business from our AGE;
> Conferring them on younger strengths, while we
> UNBURTHEN'D crawl tow'rd earth.   [1.1.37ff.]

Fast intent means *determin'd resolution*, which I think is the best reading. *First* must here signify *chief*, but neither of the readings affects the general sense of the passage. (40–1)

★   ★   ★

[On *Macbeth*, 2.3.114f.]

> their daggers
> Unmanly *breech'd* with gore,—

Breech'd with gore has, I believe, been generally understood to mean cover'd, as a man is by his breeches; and though the expression be none of the best yet methinks it might pass in a speech which, as Mr Warburton observes in his note on a line just before, is an unnatural mixture of far-fetched and common-place thoughts; especially since he urges this very circumstance as a proof of Macbeth's guilt.

But this is not sufficient, and therefore he says, 'This nonsensical account of the state, in which the daggers were found, must surely be read thus,

> Unmanly *reech'd* with gore—

Reech'd, soil'd with a dark yellow, which is the color of any *reechy* substance, and must be so of steel stain'd with blood. He uses the word very often, as *reechy* hangings, *reechy* neck, &c. so that the sense is, they were unmanly stained with blood; and that circumstance added, because often such stains are most honourable.' WARB. [VI, 368]

Mr Warburton should have shewed by some better authority than his own that there is such a word as *reech'd*, which I believe he will not find it easy to do. *Reechy* comes from recan, A. S. *fumare* (from whence our *reak* and *reaking*) and signifies with Shakespeare, *sweaty*, as *reechy* neck, *reechy* kisses or, by a metaphor perhaps, *greasy*; but does not mark any color. However the verb, being neuter, has no passive voice, and therefore there is no such participle as *reech'd*.

Nor is it true that a dark yellow is the color of all reechy substances. As to the *cook-maid's neck, that I suppose may be so, or not, according as her complexion happens to be. As to the hangings, if they hung a great while in London they had, it is probable, a great deal more of the sooty than the yellow in their tinct. If I were to ask Mr Warburton whether *reechy* kisses were of a dark yellow, he would tell me that they are not substances, and therefore are not within his rule. But if the kisses were *reechy*, the lips that gave them must be so too; and I hope Mr Warburton will not pay the king of Denmark so ill a compliment, though he was an usurper, as to say that his lips were soil'd with a dark yellow when he kissed his queen.

I cannot but add that it is far from being generally agreed that these same dark yellow stains are often most honorable. I know but one authority for it, which it would have been but fair in Mr Warburton to have produced, as it is evident that his whole criticism is founded on it. The passage is in the *Tragedy of Tragedies*, where Tom Thumb is represented as

Stain'd with the yellow blood of slaughter'd giants. (42–4)

*   *   *

[On *Richard III*, 1.2.251]

'My dukedom to a beggarly *denier*.

This may be right; but perhaps Shakespeare wrote *taniere*, French, a hut or cave.' WARB. [V, 226]

It is more than *perhaps*, that Shakespeare never thought of *taniere*, which is a den, *caverne, où les bêtes sauvages se retirent*: and when it is used figuratively for the habitation of a man it is considering him as living not like a poor man in a cottage but like a beast; *retraite*, says

---

*—The kitchen malkin pins
Her richest lockram 'bout her reechy neck,
Clamb'ring the walls to eye him.   [*Coriolanus*, 2.1.198ff.]

Furetière, *d'un homme sauvage et solitaire*. What put Mr Warburton upon this emendation, I suppose, was that he thought a dukedom to a penny was no fair bett; and that the wager would be more equal if the beggar were to *impone*, as Osric says, his cottage. Upon the same principle we should correct that line of Biron's speech in *Love's Labour's Lost:*

> I'll lay my head to any good man's *hat*. [1.1.287]

Read *heart*; for a head to a hat is too unequal a wager. (44–5)

*   *   *

[On *Timon of Athens*, 4.3.182]

'With all th' abhorred births below *crisp* heaven.

We should read *cript*, *i.e.* vaulted; from the latin *crypsa*, a vault.' WARB. [VI, 214]

Mr Warburton should have shewed by some authority that there is such a word as *cript* for vaulted, which he seems to have coined for the purpose. But if there is it should be spelt *crypt* not *cript*; and comes from *crypta* not *crypsa*, which indeed would give *cryps*, and that might easily be mistaken for *crisp*; as Mrs Mincing says, 'so pure and so *crips*.'[1] (45)

*   *   *

[On *I Henry IV*, 1.1.5f.]

'No more the thirsty entrance of this soil
Shall *damp* her lips with her own childrens blood.

Shall damp her lips] This nonsense should be read, shall *trempe*, *i.e.* moisten; and refers to thirsty in the preceding line.' WARB. [IV, 97] Why must this be nonsense? And why must Shakespeare thus continually be made to use improper French words, against the authority of the copies, instead of proper English? To *damp* signifies to wet, to moisten; which is the precise sense Mr Warburton and the context require. *Tremper* signifies something more, to dip, to soak, or steep: *je suis tout trempé*, I am soaked through.

But, says Mr Warburton, *trempe*, from the French *trempé*, properly

---

[1] Congreve, *The Way of the World*, 2.4.62.

signifies the moistness made by rain. If he speaks of *trempé* as an English word, since he coined it, he may perhaps have a right to give it what signification he pleases; but the French *tremper* signifies to dip, or soak, in any liquor whatsoever. *Tremper ses mains dans le sang: tremper les yeux de larmes: tremper du fer dans l'eau;* and figuratively, *tremper dans un crime.* (45-6)

* * *

[On *Coriolanus*, 5.2.17ff.]

> For I have ever *verified* my friends,
> (Of whom he's chief) with all the size, that verity
> Would without lapsing suffer.'

Verified here is certainly wrong, as Mr Warburton in a long note has shewn. To mend it he gives us a word which, if it is not his own, I doubt he can find no better authority for, than the Dictionary of N. Bailey, Philolog., who has taken care to preserve all the cant words he could pick up. However he gives the honor of it to Shakespeare, and says, 'without doubt he wrote

> For I have ever *narrified* my friends,

i.e. made their encomium. This too agrees with the foregoing metaphors of *book, read,* and constitutes an uniformity among them.' WARB. [VI, 541]

I suppose Menenius read his encomiums out of a book, or at least learned them there; and then *narrified* by rote. But though Mr Warburton makes no doubt of Shakespeare's writing *narrified* I must own I do; and if it were lawful for one who is not a critic by profession to make a conjecture after him, which yet I would not venture to thrust into the text without authority, I should imagine that possibly Shakespeare might have written

> For I have ever *varnished* my friends
> —with all the size, that verity
> Would without lapsing suffer.

that is, I have laid on as much praise as would stick. It is an allusion either to painting or white-washing: and the word *varnish* (or *vernish,* as it is sometimes spelt) agrees with the following metaphor of *size,* at

least as well as *narrify* does with *book* before. The only misfortune is
that the uniformity is broke: but that is of the less consequence, because
otherwise it would be knocked to pieces by the bowls which come in
in the very next line:

> nay sometimes,
> Like to a bowl upon a subtle ground
> Have tumbled past the throw—   [5.2.19ff.]

Whether this be right or no, I doubt *narrifying* with *size* will pass on
nobody but a Professed Critic. (47–8)

★   ★   ★

[On *Macbeth*, 4.1.4f.]

> 'Round about the cauldron go,
> In the poison'd *entrails* throw

Every thing thrown into the cauldron, is particularly enumerated, and
yet we find NO *poisoned entrails* among them—I believe Shakespeare
wrote,

poison'd ENTREMES—

an old word used for *ingredients*,' &c. WARB. [VI, 392]

If Mr Warburton means there is no mention afterwards of the entrails
being *poisoned*, what he says is true, but then it will affect his *entremes*
too. But he is mistaken if he affirms there are no *entrails* mentioned, for
the word *entrails* signifies the inward parts (*intestina, partes internæ*,
Skinner) in a larger sense than the viscera or guts, and so the maw of
the shark, liver of the Jew, gall of the goat, and tyger's chawdron, are
entrails; so that there is no need of Mr Warburton's *entremes*, which he
indeed says is an old word used for ingredients. But he should have
produced some authority for it, since his own will not go far with
those who know how easily he affirms things of this sort. (58)

★   ★   ★

[On *Hamlet* 3.2.125: see Warburton's note above, pp. 250ff.]

This is, as Mr Warburton says of Sir Thomas Hanmer, Vol. II p. 346,
amending with a vengeance. If every passage which our professed Critic
does not understand must thus be altered we shall have, indeed, a complete edition of Shakespeare. In this note, which I have quoted at length

that the reader may see the whole strength of Mr Warburton's reasoning, I know not which to admire most, the consistency of his argument, the decency of his language, or the wit of his lenten jest about shellfish, which makes so proper a conclusion. (79–80)

*   *   *

[On *The Winter's Tale*, 4.4.321f.]

—three swineheards, that have made themselves all *men of hair*, they call themselves *saltiers*.

that is, who have made themselves all over hairy (probably with goats skin) they call themselves *satyrs*.

But the servant's blunder in the name occasioned Mr Warburton's making one in the sense. I suppose *Saltiers* put him in mind of *saltare*; that, of *skipping* and *bounding*; and *bounding*, of *tennis-balls*, which produce this learned note:

'*all men of hair*] i.e. nimble, that leap as if they rebounded. The phrase is taken from tennis-balls, which were stuff'd with hair.' WARB. [III, 347] (83)

*   *   *

[On *Hamlet*, 3.4.48ff.]

In another passage of this play he has altered the text so as to make it point out a distant place, where is neither occasion nor authority for it.

> *Ham.*   Heaven's face doth glow
> O'er this solidity and compound mass
> With tristful visage; and, as 'gainst the doom,
> Is thought-sick at the act.
> *Queen.*   Ay me! what act,
> That roars so loud, and thunders in the *index?*

Where, I think, it is plain, that Shakespeare has used *index*, for *title*, or *prologue**. So he uses it in *K. Richard III*. 'The flattering *index* of a direful page' [4.4.85], or pageant, as others read. . . . But Mr Warburton says, 'This is a strange answer:' (I thought it had been a question) 'But the old Quarto brings us nearer to the poet's sense, by dividing the lines thus,

---

* The Index used formerly to be placed at the beginning of a book; not at the end, as now.

> *Queen.* Ay me! what act?
> *Ham.* That roars so loud, and thunders in the index.

Here we find the Queen's answer very natural. He had said, the Sun was thought-sick at the act. She says,

> Ay me! what act?

He replies (as we should read it)

> That roars so loud, *it* thunders *to* the *Indies.*

He had before said, heaven was shocked at it; he now tells her, it resounded all the world over. This gives us a very good sense; where *all* sense was wanting.' WARB.

Here Mr Warburton takes occasion, from what seems a mistaken division of the passage in the old Quarto, to represent an act as *thundering to the Indies,* that is, *making a noise all over the world,* as he explains it; which was probably known only to the murderer himself and to Hamlet, to whom his father's ghost had revealed it. And when he has made the mistake he contrives, as he frequently does, to commend himself by commending Shakespeare for what he never wrote or thought of: 'This', says he, 'gives us a very good sense; where all sense was wanting.' Modest enough for a Professed Critic! (90–2)

*   *   *

[On *The Tempest,* 5.1.286: quotes Warburton's note, above, p. 229]

The plain meaning of Shakespeare's words are, O, touch me not, for I am sore as if I were cramped all over. He must have a good nose at a conundrum who can hit it off upon so cold a scent as is here. But 'Sowter will cry upon it, though it be not as rank as a fox.' [*Twelfth Night,* 2.5.113] He suspects a jest here, which he cannot make out in English; and so, having suspected before that Shakespeare had taken or translated this play from an Italian writer, away he goes to his Italian Dictionary to hunt for some word whose like sound might be a pretense, though a poor one, for his suspicion. The best he could find was this same staffilato, which signifies simply *lashed,* not *well lashed,* much less flayed. But this it must signify, and this too must be *the real case of these varlets*; the one in defiance of the Italian language, and the other in defiance of Shakespeare, who fully explains their punishment, and this consequence of it, in Prospero's commission to Ariel:

> Go charge my goblins, that they grind their joints
> With dry convulsions; shorten up their sinews
> With aged *cramps*; and more pinch-spotted make them
> Than pard or cat o'mountain. [4.1.257ff.]

Had not the Dictionary helped Mr Warburton to this foolish conundrum I suppose this passage would have been degraded, as a nonsensical interpolation of the player; and I do not know which proceeding would have been more worthy of a Professed Critic, or have done more justice to Shakespeare.

I cannot help taking notice here of the unfair arts Mr Warburton uses to make his suspicion pass on his readers for truth. He first, to the word *lashed*, which *staffilato* does signify, tacks *flayed*, which it does not signify, as if they were the same thing . . . and then, to prove that this (flaying) *was the real case* of these varlets, he misquotes Shakespeare—

> pricking goss and thorns,
> Which enter'd their frail *skins*— [4.1.180f.]

insinuating as if they were torn and raw all over: whereas Shakespeare says,

> Which enter'd their frail *shins*—

Nor let Mr Warburton cavil that their shins could not be scratched without the thorns entering their skins, since scratched shins can never put a man in the condition which Stephano here represents himself in, or which he would have to be meant by his staffilato.

The instances above of corrections in pointing are brought, not to blame Mr Warburton for rectifying mistakes of that nature but to shew the unreasonableness of his ridiculing that care in others, when the want of it may make nonsense of the best of writings, and, as he acknowledges, has frequently done so in Shakespeare. (106–8)

* * *

[On *King Lear*, 1.2.20f.]

> 'Edmund the base
> Shall *be* the legitimate.

Here the Oxford editor would shew us that he is as good at coining phrases as his author, and so alters the text thus,

Shall toe the legitimate, i.e. says he, stand on even ground with him, *as he would with his author.*' WARB. [VI, 16]

Poor Sir Thomas! Woe be to you if you invade Mr Warburton's prerogative of *coining* words for Shakespeare! One may fairly say here that 'the toe of the *peasant* comes so near the heel of our *courtier* that it galls his kibe.' But Mr Warburton ought to have taken notice that the old reading is *shall* TO th' *legitimate*; which though it misled Sir Thomas, may perhaps direct to the right word,

> Edmund the base
> Shall *top* the legitimate.

which he would do if he got the inheritance from him, though that could not make him *be* the legitimate. (138–9)

*   *   *

CANON XXIV.

The professed critic may dispense with truth, in order to give the world a higher idea of his parts, or of the value of his work.

For instance,

1. He may assert that what he gives the public, was the work of his younger years, when there are strong evidences of the contrary. This Mr Warburton has done, in so many words, in his Preface, 19.

'These (observations on Shakespeare) such as they are, were among my younger amusements, when many years ago, I used to turn over these sort of writers, to unbend myself from more serious applications,' &c.

From a very great number of these notes one would think this to be true, though it is but a bad compliment to the public *at this time of day to trouble* them with such trash. But when one reflects on the passages in almost every page where Sir Thomas Hanmer's edition is corrected, and on the vast numbers of cancelled sheets, which give pretty strong evidence that the book was in a manner written while it was printing off, beside several other evident marks of haste, these circumstances render this assertion impossible to be true without construing away the obvious meaning of his words.

2. He may assert that he has collated the text of his author with *all* the former editions; when at the same time it appears undeniably in his work that he has not done it.

In the title page of his edition Mr Warburton says, that the text is collated with *all* the former editions; how truly this is said will appear by the following instances.

EXAMPLE I. *Much Ado About Nothing*. [4.1.63]

'Let them be in the hands of Coxcomb]—But the editor (Mr Theobald) adds, *the old Quarto gave me the first umbrage for placing it (this speech) to Conrade*. What these words mean, I do not know, but I *suspect* the old Quarto divides the passage as I have done.' WARB. [II, 72]

I SUSPECT! Is this the language of a man, who had actually collated the books? I am afraid from these words the world will more than *suspect* that he knew nothing of the matter, and that where he quotes the old editions it is only at second hand. (141-2)

EXAMP. II. *Tempest*. [4.1.151]

'And like the baseless fabric of *their* vision.

Not to mention the aukward expression of *their* vision, which Mr Theobald, *upon what authority I know not*, changed into *this* vision.' WARB. [I, 67]

It is strange that Mr Warburton should not know that it was upon the authority of the first Folio, which has this reading. (142-3)

*   *   *

[From the] ESSAY TOWARDS A GLOSSARY

*   *   *

CAP, 'property, bubble.' [VI, 221]

> Thou art the *cap* of all the fools alive.

Rather the *top*, *chief*.

CARBONADO'D *rectius* CARBINADO'D, 'mark'd with wounds made by a *carabine*.'

POPE confirmed by WARB. [III, 95]

So when Kent in *King Lear* says, *I'll carbonado your shanks for you*, he means, *I'll shoot you in the legs with a carabine*; which will carry the antiquity of that weapon much higher than Henry IV. of France.

But carbonaded means *scotched*, or cut as they do steaks before they make carbonadoes of them.

CEMENT, 'cincture or enclosure, because both have the idea of holding together.'

'Your temples burn'd in their *cement*.' [VI, 532]   (146–7)

*   *   *

CONSEAL'D a word of Mr Warburton's own invention, and which is as he says, '—a very proper disignment of one just *affianced* to her Lover.' [VIII, 69] (147)

*   *   *

EQUIPAGE, 'stolen goods.' [I, 280]

I will retort the sum in equipage.   (148)

*   *   *

FRAINE (another word of Mr Warburton's making) for 'refraine, keeping back farther favors.' [II, 62]

So one may upon occasion use 'fractory for refractory, 'bellion for rebellion, &c. (149)

*   *   *

To FROWN, 'to project or execute laws.' [VI, 493]

Than ever frown'd in Greece.

By the same rule of construction it may signifie to write angry notes, and call names. (149)

*   *   *

GENTLEMAN-HEIR, 'a Lady's eldest son.' [III, 132]

This is a phrase fresh from the mint. But Mr Warburton may take it back and lay it by for his own use: Shakespeare has no need of it, as any body will own who considers that Sir Toby was drunk, and interrupted in his speech by his pickled herrings.

'Tis a Gentleman here— a plague of these pickle herrings!

[*Twelfth Night*, 1.5.113] (150)

* * *

GROTH, 'Shape.' [*Romeo and Juliet*, 3.3.110ff.]

> Thy tears are womanish, thy wild acts denote
> The unreasonably fury of a beast,
> Unseemly woman in a seeming man,
> And ill beseeming beast in seeming* *both*,

This passage Mr Pope threw out as *strange nonsense*, and Mr Warburton restores it into absolute nonsense by a word of his own making, and wrong interpreting the word joined with it. For there is no such word as *groth*; and if he means *Growth*, that signifies *increase*, not *shape*; then what is *seeming shape*? —for I deny that *seeming* is used for *seemly*, as he says. Nor is there any reason for all this pother and amendment but that Mr Warburton cannot understand Shakespeare till he has brought him down to his level, by making nonsense of his words.

The meaning of the sentence, which is full of gingle and antithesis, is, 'You discover a strange mixture of womanish qualities under the appearance of a man, and the unseemly outrageous fury of a beast under that compound of Man and Woman.' (150–1)

* * *

OATS, 'a distemper in horses.' [II, 442]

> —the *oats* have eat the horses.

I hope Mr Warburton takes care to keep *his* horses from this dangerous distemper. (155)

* * *

PLOY'D, 'for imploy'd.' [VII, 328]

> —have both their eyes
> And ears so '*ploy'd* importantly as now.

This is Mr Warburton's word ('*ploy'd* for *imploy'd*, he should have

* *Groth.* WARB. [VIII, 70]

416

said *employ'd*) instead of *cloyed*. But Shakespeare never thought of circumcising his words at this rate, as our Critic does to fit them for any place which he wants them to fill. By the same rule we may say 'PTY and 'PIRE are English words, signifying *empty* and *empire*. (156)

*   *   *

PREGNANT, 'ready.' [III, 164]

       —most *pregnant* and vouchsafed ear.

Ready for what? (156)

*   *   *

RASH, 'dry.' [IV, 284]

       As strong as—*rash* gunpowder.

The true sense here is *sudden, easily inflammable.* (157)

*   *   *

To RETORT, 'to pay again.' [I, 280]

Hence, no doubt, comes a RETORT, a vessel used by the Chemists, because it *repays* the Operator whatever he puts into it with interest, Chemistry being well known to be a very gainful employment. (157)

*   *   *

To REVYE a man, 'to look him in the face.'

   Item, 'to call upon him to hasten.' WARB. [III, 90]
   '—And time *revyes* us.' A word of Mr Warburton's bringing into the text. (158)

*   *   *

SNIPE, 'a diminutive woodcock.' [VIII, 303]

   Just as a partridge is a diminutive pheasant. (159)

*   *   *

417

SPURS, 'an old word, for the fibres of a tree.' POPE, [VII, 311]

> —mingle their *spurs* together.

It is a common word and signifies the larger roots, in contra-distinction to the fibres or smaller roots: so the spur of a post is used in allusion to the large root of a tree. (160)

* * *

UNIMPROVED, 'unrefined.' [VIII, 120]

> Of *unimproved* mettle hot and full.

Shakespeare seems to use it for *unproved*. However that be, Mr Warburton has fully convinced the world that *refinement* and *improvement* are two very different things. (162)

* * *

UNTRIMMED bride, 'unsteady.' A term in Navigation: we say likewise *not well manned*. WARB. [III, 426] (162)

* * *

To conclude. I thought it a piece of Justice due to the memory of Shakespeare, to the reputation of Letters in general, and of our English language in particular, to take some public notice of a performance which I am sorry to say has violated all these respects. Had this been done by a common hand I had held my peace, and left the work to that oblivion which it deserves; but when it came out under the sanction of two great names, that of our most celebrated modern Poet and that of a Gentleman who had by other writings, how justly I shall not now examine, obtained a great reputation for learning, it became an affair of some consequence. Chimerical conjectures and gross mistakes were by these means propagated for truth among the ignorant and unwary; and that was *established for the *genuine* text, nay the *genuine* text *amended* too, which is neither Shakespeare's nor English.

As such a proceding is of the utmost ill consequence to Letters, I cannot but hope that this reprehension of it will meet with excuse from all unprejudiced judges, and then I shall have my end, which was to

---

* See Mr Warburton's Title-page.

defend Shakespeare, and not to hurt his Editor more than was necessary for that defense.

And now I hope I have taken my leave of Mr Warburton and his works, at least unless, to complete the massacre of our best English Poets, he should take it into his head to murder Spenser as he has Shakespeare, and in part Milton too; for by the specimen we have left I cannot with Dr Newton bewail the loss of the rest of his annotations on that Poet, though perhaps I and every body else may* 'apprehend what is become of them.' Upon the whole I leave it to the Public to judge which has been engaged AGAINST Shakespeare, Mr Warburton— or I, who have, in part at least, vindicated that best of Poets from the worst of Critics, from one who has been guilty of a greater violation of him than that on the authors of which he imprecated vengeance in his Epitaph,

> And curs'd be he, that moves my bones.

A violation which, were he not arm'd against the superstition of believing in Portents and Prodigies, might make him dread the apparition of that much injured bard. (172–3).

*   *   *

* See the Preface to Dr Newton's Milton.

128. Richard Hurd on Shakespeare

1751

From the 'Notes' and 'A Discourse concerning Poetical Imitation' added to Q. *Horatii Flacci Epistola ad Augustum. With an English Commentary and Notes* (1751).

For biographical details see the headnote to No. 120.

[On Christopher Sly as a satire on Epicureanism]

It unfortunately happens, to the infinite hurt and prejudice of this *mode of imitation* [painting] above all others, that the artist *designs* not so much what his own conscious idea of the dignity of his profession requires of him, or the general taste of those, he would most wish for his judges, approves; as what the rich or noble *Conoisseur*, who *bespeaks* his work, and prescribes the subject, demands. What this hath usually been, let the history of ancient and modern painting declare. Yet, considering its vast power in MORALS, as explained above, one cannot enough lament the ill destiny of this divine ART; which, from the chast hand-maid of *virtue*, hath been debauched, in violence to her nature, to a shameless prostitute of *vice*, and procuress of *pleasure*.

Our inimitable Shakespeare, who employed his great talents of poetry to other purposes, could not observe this corruption of a sister *art*, without a becoming indignation: and hath, accordingly, taken occasion, in one of his pieces, to satyrize this abuse with great force and spirit. I speak of the INDUCTION, as he calls it, to *The Taming of the Shrew*; which deserves, for the excellence of its moral design and beauty of execution throughout, to be set in a just light.

This *Prologue* sets before us the picture of a *poor drunken beggar*, advanced, for a short season, into the proud rank of *nobility*. And the humour of the scene is taken to consist in the surprize and aukward deportment of SLY; in this his strange and unwonted situation. But the poet had a further design and more worthy his genius, than this farcical pleasantry. He would expose, under the cover of this mimic fiction, the

420

truly ridiculous figure of men of rank and quality, when they employ
their great advantages of *place and fortune*, to no better purposes, than
the soft and selfish gratification of their own intemperate passions: Of
those, who take the mighty privilege of *descent* and *wealth* to lie in the
freer indulgence of those pleasures, which the beggar as fully enjoys,
and with infinitely more propriety and consistency of character, than
their *Lordships*.

To give a poignancy to his satire, the poet makes a *man of quality*
himself, just returned from the chace, with all his mind intent upon his
pleasures, contrive this metamorphosis of the beggar, in the way of
sport and derision only; not considering, how severely the jest was
going to turn upon himself. His first reflexions, on seeing this brutal
drunkard, are excellent.

> *O! monstrous beast! how like a swine he lies!*
> *Grim Death! how foul and loathsome is thy image!* [*Ind.* i. 34f.]

The *offence* is taken at *human nature*, degraded into *bestiality*; and at a
state of stupid *insensibility*, *the image of death*. Nothing can be juster, than
this representation. For these Lordly sensualists have a very nice and
fastidious abhorrence of such *ignoble* brutality. And what alarms their
fears with the prospect of *death*, cannot chuse but present *a foul and
loathsome image*. . . .

However, this transient gloom is soon succeeded by gayer prospects.
My *Lord* bethinks himself to raise a little diversion out of this adventure.

> *Sirs, I will practice on this drunken man.* [*Ind.* i. 36]

And, so, proposes to have him *conveyed to bed*, and blessed with all
those regalements of costly luxury, in which a selfish opulence is wont
to find its supreme happiness.

The project is carried into execution. And now the jest begins. Sly,
awaking from his drunken nap, calls out as usual for a *cup of ale*. On
which the *Lord*, very characteristically, and (taking the poet's design, as
here explained) with infinite satyr, replies,

> *O! that a mighty man of such descent,*
> *Of such possessions, and so high esteem,*
> *Should be infused with so foul a spirit!*
>
> [*Ind.* ii. 13ff.]

And, again, afterwards,

Oh! noble Lord, bethink thee of thy birth,
Call home thy antient thoughts from banishment,
And banish hence these lowly, abject themes.   [*Ind.* ii. 32ff.]

For, what is the recollection of this *high descent* and large *possessions* to do for him? And, for the introduction of what better thoughts and nobler purposes, are these *lowly abject themes* to be discarded? Why, the whole inventory of Patrician pleasures is called over; and he hath his choice of whichsoever of them suits best with his Lordship's improved palate. A long train of *servants, ready at his beck*: music, such as *twenty caged nightingales do sing*: couches, *softer and sweeter than the lustful bed of Semiramis*: *burning odours, and distilled waters*: *floors bestrewed with carpets*: the diversions of *hawks, hounds, and horses*: in short, all the objects of exquisite indulgence are presented to him.

But among these, one species of refined enjoyment, which requires a *taste*, above the coarse breeding of abject commonalty, is chiefly insisted on. We had a hint, of what we were to expect, before,

Carry him gently to my fairest chamber,
And hang it round with all my wanton pictures.
[*Ind.* i. 46f.]

And what Lord, in the luxury of his wishes, could feign to himself a more delicious collection, than is here delineated?

2. Man. *Dost thou love* PICTURES? *We will fetch thee straight*
ADONIS, *painted by a running brook;*
And CITHEREA *all in sedges hid;*
Which seem to move and wanton with her breath,
Ev'n as the waving sedges play with wind.
Lord.   *We'll shew thee* IO, *as she was a maid.*
And how she was beguiled and surprized,
As lively painted, as the deed was done.
3. Man. *Or* DAPHNE, *roaming thro' a thorny wood,*
Scratching her legs, that one shall swear, she bleeds,
So workmanly the blood and tears are drawn.   [*Ind.* ii. 51ff.]

These pictures, it will be owned, are, all of them, well chosen. But the servants were not so deep in the secret, as their master. They dwell entirely on circumstantials. While his lordship, who had, probably, been trained in the *chast* school of Titian, is for coming to the point more directly. There is a fine ridicule implied in this.

After these incentives of *picture*, the charms of *beauty itself* are presented, as the crowning privilege of his high station.

> *Thou hast a Lady far more beautiful*
> *Than any woman in this waining age.*
>
> [*Ind.* ii. 64f.]

Here indeed the poet plainly forgets himself. The *state*, if not the *enjoyment*, of nobility, surely demanded a *mistress*, instead of a *wife*. All that can be said in excuse of this indecorum, is, that he perhaps conceived, a simple beggar, all unused to the refinements of high life, would be too much shocked, at setting out, with a proposal, so remote from all his former practices. Be it, as it will, *beauty*, even in a *wife*, had such an effect on this *mock Lord*, that, quite melted and overcome by it, he yields himself at last to the inchanting deception.

> *I see, I hear, I speak,*
> *I smell sweet savours, and I feel soft things;*
> UPON MY LIFE I AM A LORD INDEED.   [*Ind.* ii. 72ff.]

The satyr is so strongly marked in this last line, that one can no longer doubt of the writer's intention. If any *should*, let me further remind him, that the poet, in this fiction, but makes his Lord play the same game, *in jest*; as the Sicilian tyrant acted, long ago, very *seriously*. The two cases are so similar, that some readers may, perhaps, suspect the poet of having taken the whole conceit from Tully. His description of this instructive scenery is given in the following words [quotes *Tusc. Disp.* Bk 5, 21]. . . .

The event, in these two dramas, was, indeed, different. For the philosopher took care to make the *flatterer* sensible of his mistake; while the poet did not think fit to disabuse the *beggar*. But this was according to the design of each. For, the *former* would shew the *misery* of *regal luxury*; the *latter*, its *vanity*. The *tyrant*, therefore, is painted *wretched*. And his *Lordship* only a *beggar in disguise*.

To conclude with our poet. The strong ridicule and decorum of this *Induction* make it appear, how impossible it was for Shakespeare, in his idlest hours, perhaps, when he was only revising the trash of others, not to leave some strokes of the *master* behind him. But the morality of its purpose should chiefly recommend it to us. For the whole was written with the best design of exposing that monstrous Epicurean position, *that the true enjoyment of life consists in a delirium of sensual pleasure.* And this, in a way the most likely to work upon the *great*, by shewing their pride, that it was fit only to constitute the *summum bonum* of one

> *No better than a poor and loathsome Beggar.*
>
> [*Ind*. i. 123]

Nor let the poet be thought to have dealt too freely with his *betters*, in giving this representation of *nobility*. He had the highest authority for what he did. For the great *master of life* himself gave no other of *Divinity*.

> *Ipse pater veri Doctus Epicurus in arte*
> *Jussit &* HANC VITAM DIXIT HABERE DEOS.
>
> PETRON. c. 132.[1] (66-71)

*   *   *

[On our involvement with characters in tragedy]

If the proper end of TRAGEDY be to *affect*, it follows, 'that *actions*, not characters, are the chief object of its representations.' For that which *affects* us most in the view of human life is the observation of those signal circumstances of *felicity or distress*, which occur in the fortunes of men. But *felicity* and *distress*, as the great critic takes notice, depend on *action*; [quotes *Poetics*, 6. 12: 'while character makes men what they are, it is the scenes they act in that make them happy or the opposite.'] They are then the calamitous *events*, or fortunate *Issues* in human action, which stir up the stronger *affections*, and agitate the heart with *Passion*. The *manners* are not, indeed, to be neglected. But they become an inferior consideration in the views of the tragic poet, and are exhibited only for the sake of making the *action* more proper to interest us. Thus our *joy*, on the *happy catastrophe* of the fable, depends, in a good degree, on the *virtuous character* of the agent; as, on the other hand, we sympathize more strongly with him, on a *distressful issue*. The *manners* of the several persons in the drama must, also, be signified, that the *action*, which in many cases will be determined by them, may appear to be

---

[1] *Satyricon*, 132: modern editions, however, read 'Ipse pater veri doctos Epicurus amare/ ussit, et hoc vitam dixit habere τέλος': 'Epicurus, the true father of truth, bade wise men be lovers, and said that therein lay the crown of life.' (Loeb translation by M. Heseltine)

carried on with *truth and probability*. Hence every thing passing before us, as we are accustomed to see it in real life, we enter more warmly into their interests, as forgetting, that we are attentive to a *fictitious scene*. And, besides, from knowing the personal *good, or ill, qualities* of the agents, we learn to anticipate their future *felicity* or *misery*, which gives increase to the *passion* in either case. Our acquaintance with IAGO's *close villainy* makes us tremble for Othello and Desdemona beforehand: and HAMLET's *filial piety and intrepid daring* occasion the audience secretly to exult in the *expectation* of some successful vengeance to be inflicted on the incestuous murderers. (76–7)

＊　　＊　　＊

[On originality in descriptions of nature in poetry]

This agreeable scenery is, for an obvious reason, the most frequent object of description. Though sometimes it chuses to itself a dark and sombrous imagery; which nature, again, holds out to imitation, or fancy, which hath a wondrous quickness and facility in opposing its ideas, readily suggests. We have an instance in the picture of that *horrid and detested vale* which Tamora describes in *Titus Andronicus*. It is a perfect contrast to Aelian's and may be called an *Anti-tempe*. Or, to see this opposition of images in the strongest light, the reader may turn to *L'Allegro* and *Il Penseroso* of Milton; where he hath artfully made, throughout the two poems, the same kind of subjects excite the two passions of *mirth* and *melancholy*.

When the reader is got into this train, he will easily extend the same observation to other instances of *natural description*; and can hardly avoid, after a few trials, coming to this short conclusion, 'that of all the various delineations in the poets, of the HEAVENS, in their vicissitude of times and seasons; of the EARTH, in its diversity of *mountains, valleys, promontories*, &c. of the SEA, under its several aspects of *turbulence*, or *serenity*; of the *make* and *structure* of ANIMALS, &c. it can rarely be affirmed, that they are *copies* of one another, but rather the genuine products of the same creating fancy, operating uniformly in them all.' . . .

For, though the *subject* of description be ever unvariably the same, and different poets may, or rather must, agree in the same *general* conceptions of it, yet is there enough left to the operation of true genius to distinguish the touch of a master from the faint and lifeless drawing of a bad poet. And this lies in what I call the *manner of expression*;

by which is not meant the *language* of the poet, but simply his *design*, or the *form* under which he chuses to present his imagery to the imagination. I shall be understood from the following instance.

Descriptions of the *morning* are very frequent in the poets. But this appearance is known by so many attending circumstances, that there will be room for a considerable variety in the pictures of it. It may be described by those *stains of light*, which streak and diversify the clouds; by the peculiar *colour of the dawn*; by its *irradiations* on the *sea*, or *earth*; on some peculiar objects, as *trees*, *hills*, *rivers*, &c. A difference also will arise from the *situation*, in which we suppose ourselves; if on the *sea shore*, this *harbinger of day* will seem to break forth from the *ocean*; if on the *land*, from the extremity of a large plain, terminated, it may be, by some remarkable object, as a *grove*, *mountain*, &c. There are perhaps many other *differences*, of which the same precise *number* will scarcely offer itself to two poets; or not the *same individual* circumstances; or not *disposed* in the same manner. But let the same identical circumstance, suppose the *breaking or first appearance of the dawn*, be taken by different writers, and we may still expect a considerable diversity in their *representation* of it. What we may allow to all poets, is, that they will *impersonate* the morning. And though this idea of it is *metaphorical*, and so belongs to another place, as respecting the *manner* of imitation only; yet, when once considered under this *figure*, the *drawing* of it comes as directly within the province of *description*, as the real, *literal* circumstances themselves. Now in descriptions of the morning under this idea of a *person*, the very same *attitude*, which is made analogous to the *circumstance*, before specified, and is to suggest it, will, as I said, be represented by different writers very differently. *Homer*, to express *the rise or appearance of this person*, speaks of her as *shooting forth from the ocean*:

ΑΠ ΩΚΕΑΝΟΙΟ ΡΟΑΩΝ ΩΡΝΥΘ [1]

Virgil, as *rising from the rocks of Ida*.
> *Jamque jugis summae surgebat Lucifer Idae,*
> *Ducebatque diem.* [2]

Shakespeare hath closed a fine description of the morning with the same *image*, but expressed in a very different manner.

---

[1] *Iliad*, 19.1f.: 'Now Dawn arose from the streams of Oceanus.'
[2] *Aeneid*, 2.801f.: 'And now above Ida's topmost ridges the day-star was rising, ushering in the morn.'

Look what streaks
Do lace the severing clouds in yonder east:
Night's candles are put out: and JOCUND DAY
STANDS TIPTOE ON THE MISTY MOUNTAINS TOP.
[*Romeo and Juliet*, 3.5.7ff.]

The reader of true taste pronounces, I dare say, on first sight, this description to be *original*. But why? There is no part of it, which may not be traced in other poets. The *staining of the clouds*, and *putting out the stars*, are circumstances, that are almost constantly taken notice of in representations of the morning. And the last *image*, which strikes most, is not essentially different from that of Virgil and Homer. It would express the *attitude* of a person impatient, and in act to make his appearance. And this is, plainly, the *image* suggested by the other two. But the difference lies here. Homer's *expression* of this *impatience* is *general*, ΩΡΝΥΘ. So is Virgil's, and, as the occasion required, with less energy, SURGEBAT. Shakespeare's is *particular*: that impatience is set before us, and pictured to the eye in the circumstance of *standing tiptoe*; the attitude of a winged messenger, in act to shoot away on his errand with eagerness and precipitation. Which is a beauty of the same kind with that Aristotle so much admired in the ΡΟΔΟΔΑΚΤΥΛΟΣ of Homer. 'This image,' says he, 'is peculiar and singularly proper to set the object before our eyes. Had the poet said ΦΟΙΝΙΚΟΔΑΚΤΥΛΟΣ, the colour had been signified too *generally*, and still worse by ΕΡΥΘΡΟΔΑΚΤΥΛΟΣ. ΡΟΔΟΔΑΚΤΥΛΟΣ gives the precise idea, which was wanting.'[1]

This, it must be owned, is one of the surest characteristics of real genius. And if we find it generally in a writer, we may almost venture to esteem him *original* without further scruple. For the shapes and appearances of things are apprehended, only in the gross, by dull minds. They think they *see*, but it is as through a mist, where if they catch but a faint glimpse of the form before them, it is well. More one is not to look for from their clouded imaginations. And what they thus imperfectly discern, it is not possible for them to delineate very distinctly. Whereas every object stands forth in bright sunshine to the view of the true poet. Every minute mark and lineament of the contemplated form leaves a corresponding trace on his fancy. And having these bright and determinate conceptions of things in his own mind, he finds it no

[1] *Rhetoric* III, ii, 13; 1405b: 'It makes a difference whether we say, for instance, "rosy-fingered morn" [*Iliad* 1.477 etc.], or "crimson-fingered", or worse still, "red-fingered".' (tr. R. C. Jebb).

difficulty to convey the liveliest ideas of them to others. This is what we call *painting* in poetry; by which not only the general natures of things are described, and their appearances shadowed forth; but every single *property* marked, and the poet's own image set in distinct *relief* before the view of his reader.

If this glow of imagery, resulting from clear and bright perceptions in the poet, be not a certain character of *genius*, it will be difficult, I believe, to say what is: I mean so far as descriptive poetry, which we are now considering, is concerned. (117-22)

*　　*　　*

[On inevitable similarities between Shakespeare and other writers on similar topics]

Those who are fond of hunting parallels, might, I doubt not, with great ease, confront almost every sentiment which, in the Greek tragedians, is made expressive of particular *characters*, with similar passages in other poets; more especially (for I must often refer to his authority) in the various living pourtraitures of *Shakespeare*. Yet he, who after taking this learned pains, should chuse to urge such parallels, when found, for proofs of his *imitation of the ancients*, would only run the hazard of being reputed, by men of sense, as poor a critic of human nature, as of his author. (127)

*　　*　　*

When the mind is at leisure to cast about and amuse itself with reflexions, which no *characteristic quality* dictates, or *affection* extorts, and which spring from no preconceived system of *moral or religious* opinions, a greater latitude of thinking is allowed; and consequently any remarkable correspondency of *sentiment* affords more room for suspicion of *imitation*. Yet, in any supposed combination of circumstances, one train of thought is, generally, most obvious, and occurs soonest to the understanding; and, it being the office of poetry to present the most *natural* appearances, one cannot be much surprised to find a frequent coincidence of reflexion even here. The first page one opens in any writer will furnish examples. The duke in *Measure for Measure*, upon hearing some petty slanders thrown out against himself, falls into this trite reflexion:

> *No might nor greatness in mortality*
> *Can censure 'scape: back-wounding calumny*
> *The whitest virtue strikes.*   [3.2.196ff.]

Friar Lawrence, in *Romeo and Juliet*, observing the excessive raptures of Romeo on his marriage, gives way to a sentiment, naturally suggested by this circumstance:

> *These violent delights have violent ends,*
> *And in their triumph die.*   [2.6.9f.]

Now what is it, in prejudice to the originality of these places, to alledge a hundred or a thousand passages (for so many it were, perhaps, not impossible to accumulate) analogous to them in the ancient or modern poets? Could any reasonable critic mistake these genuine workings of the mind for instances of *imitation*?

In *Cymbeline*, the obsequies of Imogen are celebrated with a song of triumph over the evils of human life, from which death delivers us:

> *Fear no more the heat o' th' sun,*
> *Nor the furious winter's rages, &c.*   [4.2.258ff.]

What a temptation this for the parallelist to shew his reading! yet his incomparable editor[1] observes slightly upon it: 'This is the topic of consolation, that nature dictates to all men on these occasions. The same farewell we have over the dead body in Lucian; ΤΕΚΝΟΝ ΑΘΛΙΟΝ, ΟΥΚΕΤΙ ΔΙΨΗΣΕΙΣ ΟΥΚΕΤΙ ΠΕΙΝΗΣΕΙΣ, &c.'

When Valentine in the *Twelfth Night* reports the inconquerable grief of Olivia for the loss of a brother, the duke observes upon it,

> *O! she that hath a heart of that fine frame*
> *To pay this debt of love but to a brother,*
> *How will she love, when the rich golden shaft*
> *Hath killed the flock of all affections else*
> *That live in her?*   [1.1.33ff.]

'Tis strange, the critics have never accused the poet of stealing this sentiment from Terence, who makes Simo in the *Andrian* reason on his son's concern for Chrysis in the same manner:

> *Nonnunquam conlacrumabat: placuit tum id mihi.*
> *Sic cogitabam: hic parvae consuetudinis*

---

[1] Warburton, edition of Shakespeare (1747), Vol. 7, p. 320.

Causâ hujus mortem tam fert familiariter:
Quid si ipse amâsset? Quid mihi hic faciet patri? [1]

It were easy to multiply examples, but I spare the reader. (133–5)

*   *   *

[Love is a variable emotion, yet] this Proteus of a passion may be fixed by the magic hand of the poet. Though it can *occasionally* take *all*, yet it delights to be seen in *some* shapes, more than others. Some of its *effects* are known and obvious, and are perpetually recurring to observation. And these are ever fittest to the ends of poetry; every man pronouncing of such representations, from his proper experience, that they are from *nature*. Nay its very irregularities may be reduced to rule. There is not, in antiquity, a truer picture of this fond and froward passion, than is given us in the person of Terence's *Phaedria* from Menander. *Horace* and *Persius*, when they set themselves, on purpose, to expose and exaggerate its follies, could imagine nothing beyond it. Yet we have much the same inconsistent character in JULIA in *The Two Gentlemen of Verona*.

Shall it be now said, that *Shakespeare* copied from Terence, as Terence from Menander? Or is it not as plain to common sense, that the English poet is *original*, as that the *Latin* poet was an *imitator*? (139)

*   *   *

[On originality and genius]

It is not therefore pretended, that the same images *must* occur to all. Sluggish, unactive understandings, which seldom look abroad into living nature, or, when they do, have not curiosity or vigour enough to direct their attention to the nicer particularities of her beauties, will unavoidably overlook the commonest appearances: Or, wanting that just perception of what is *beautiful*, which we call *taste*, will as often mistake in the *choice* of those circumstances, which they may have happened to contemplate. But quick, perceptive, intelligent minds (and of such only I can be thought to speak) will hardly fail of seeing nature in the same light, and of noting the same distinct features and proportions. The superiority of Homer and Shakespeare to other poets doth not lie in their discovery of *new sentiments or images*, but in the

---

[1] 109ff: 'All the time [my son] was in low spirits, and occasionally in tears. His behaviour pleased me at the time. If a scanty acquaintance, I reflected, makes the boy take the girl's death so much to heart, what if he had been in love with her himself? How deeply he will feel the loss of his father!'

forceable manner, in which their sublime genius taught them to convey and impress *old ones*. (145–6)

$$\star \qquad \star \qquad \star$$

[On genius and education]

. . . the culture of *education*, and the use and study of the best models of *art* may be thought expedient [for the poet]. Yet this may, after all, be wanting only to inferior wits. The truly inspired, it may be, have need only of their *touch* from heaven. And does not the example of the first of *our* poets, and the most honoured for his invention, of *any*, give a countenance to this enthusiastic conclusion? It is possible, there are, who think *a want of reading*, as well as a vast superiority of genius, hath contributed to lift this astonishing man, to the glory of being esteemed the most original THINKER and SPEAKER, since the times of Homer. (193)

129. Samuel Johnson on Shakespeare

1750–1

From *The Rambler*, Vol. 1 of the original Folio issue.

From *The Rambler*, No. 72 (24 November 1750)

$$\star \qquad \star \qquad \star$$

There are many whose Vanity always inclines them to associate with those from whom they have no Reason to fear Mortification; and there are Times in which the Wise and the Knowing are willing to receive Praise without the Labour of deserving it, in which the most elevated Mind is willing to descend and the most active to be at rest. All therefore are at some Hour or another fond of Companions whom they can entertain upon easy Terms, and who will relieve them from Solitude without condemning them to Vigilance and Caution. We are most inclined to love when we have nothing to fear, and he that always indulges us in our present Disposition, and encourages us to please ourselves, will not be long without Preference in our Affection to those whose Learning holds us at the Distance of Pupils, or whose Wit calls all Attention from us and leaves us without Importance and without Regard.

It is remarked by Prince *Henry*, when he sees *Falstaff* lying on the Ground, that *He could have better spared a better Man*. He was well acquainted with the Vices and Follies of him whom he lamented, but while his Conviction compelled him to do Justice to superior Qualities his Tenderness still broke out at the Remembrance of *Falstaff*, of the chearful Companion, the loud Buffoon with whom he had passed his Time in all the Luxury of Idleness, who had gladded him with unenvied Merriment, and whom he could at once enjoy and despise.

You may perhaps think this Account of those who are distinguished for their Good Humour not very consistent with the Praises which I have bestowed upon it. But surely nothing can more evidently shew the Value of this Quality than that it recommends those who are destitute of all other Excellencies, that it procures Regard to the Trifling, Friendship to the Worthless, and Affection to the Dull. (430–1)

*　　*　　*

No. 156 (24 September 1751)

Every government, say the Politicians, is perpetually degenerating towards Corruption, from which it must be rescued at certain Periods by the Resuscitation of its first Principles and the Reestablishment of its original Constitution. Every animal Body, according to the methodick Physicians, is by the Predominance of some exuberant Quality continually declining towards Disease and Death, which must be obviated by a seasonable Reduction of the peccant Humour to the just Equipoise which Health requires.

In the same Manner the Studies of Mankind (all, at least, which not being subject to rigorous Demonstration admit the Influence of Fancy and Caprice) are perpetually tending to Error and Confusion. The great Principles of Truth which the first Speculatists discovered have their Simplicity embarrassed by ambitious Additions or their Evidence obscured by inaccurate Augmentation, and as they descend from one Succession of Writers to another, like Light transmitted from Room to Room, lose by Degrees their Strength and Splendor and fade at last into total Evanescence.

It is necessary, therefore, to review the Systems of Learning, to analyse Complications into Principles and disentangle Knowledge from Opinion. It is not always possible, without a close and diligent Inspection, to separate the genuine Shoots of consequential Reasoning which grow out of some radical Postulate from the Branches which Art has engrafted on it. The accidental Prescriptions of Authority, when Time has procured them Veneration, are often confounded with the Laws of Nature, and those Rules are supposed coeval with Reason, of which the first Rise cannot be discovered.

Criticism, amidst her Endeavours to restrain the Licentiousness of Imagination and detect the Stratagems of Fallacy, has suffered her Provinces to be invaded by those restless Powers. Like the antient *Scythians*, by extending her Conquests over distant Regions she has left her Throne vacant to her Slaves, and suffered Prejudice and Error to reign unmolested in her own Dominions.

Among the innumerable Rules which the natural Desire of extending Authority or the honest Ardour of promoting Knowledge has from Age to Age prompted Men of very different Abilities to prescribe to Writers, all which have been received and established have not the same original Right to our Regard. Some are indeed to be considered as fundamental and indispensable, others only as useful and convenient; some as dictated by Reason and Necessity, others as enacted by Despotick Antiquity; some as invincibly supported by their Conformity to the Order of Nature and the Operations of the Intellect, others as formed by Accident or instituted by Example, and therefore always liable to Dispute and Alteration.

That many Rules of Composition have been advanced by Criticks without consulting Nature or Reason we cannot but suspect when we find it peremptorily decreed by the antient Masters *that only three speaking Personages should appear at once upon the Stage,*[1] a Law which the Variety and Intricacy of modern Plays has made impossible to be observed, and which, therefore, we now violate without Scruple and, as Experience proves, without Inconvenience.

The Original of this Precept was merely accidental. Tragedy was a Monody or solitary Song in Honour of *Bacchus*, which was afterwards

[1] Horace, *A.P.* 192.

433

improved into a Dialogue by the Addition of another Speaker; but remembering that the Tragedy was at first pronounced only by one they durst not for some Time venture beyond two; at last when Custom and Impunity had made them daring they extended their Liberty to the Admission of three, but restrained themselves by a critical Edict from further Exorbitance.

By what Accident the Number of Acts was limited to five I know not that any Author has informed us, but certainly it is not determined by any Necessity arising either from the Nature of Action or the Propriety of Exhibition. An Act is only the Representation of such a Part of the Business of the Play as proceeds in an unbroken Tenor without any intermediate Pause, Nothing is more evident than that of every real and, by Consequence, of every dramatick Action, the Intervals may be more or fewer than five; and indeed the Rule is upon the *English* Stage every Day broken in Effect without any other Mischief than that which arises from an absurd Endeavour to observe it in Appearance. For whenever the Scene is shifted the Act ceases, since some Time is necessarily supposed to elapse while the Personages of the Drama change their Place.

With no greater Right to our Obedience have the Criticks confined the dramatic Action to a certain Number of Hours. Probability indeed requires that the Time of Action should approach somewhat nearly to that of Exhibition, and those Plays will always be thought most happily conducted which croud the greatest Variety into the least Space. But since it will frequently happen that some Delusion must be admitted I know not where the Limits of Imagination can be fixed; nor have I ever observed that Minds not already prepossessed by Criticism feel any Offence from the Extension of the Intervals between the Acts, nor can I conceive it absurd or impossible that he who can multiply three Hours into twelve or twenty-four might image with equal Ease a greater Number.

I know not whether he that professes to regard no other Laws than those of Nature will not be inclined to receive Tragi-comedy to his Protection, whom, however generally condemned, her own Laurels have hitherto shaded from the Fulminations of Criticism. For what is there in the mingled Drama which impartial Reason can condemn? The Connexion of important with trivial Incidents, since it is not only common but perpetual in the World, may surely be allowed upon the Stage, which pretends only to be the Mirrour of Life. The impropriety of suppressing the Passions before we have raised them to the intended

Agitation, and of diverting the Expectation from an Event which we keep suspended only to raise it, may indeed be speciously urged. But will not Experience confute this Objection? Is it not certain that the tragic and comic Affections have been moved alternately with equal Force, and that no Plays have oftner filled the Eye with Tears and the Breast with Palpitation than those which are variegated with Interludes of Mirth?

I do not however think it always safe to judge of Works of Genius merely by the Event. These resistless Vicissitudes of the Heart, this alternate Prevalence of Merriment and Solemnity, may sometimes be more properly ascribed to the Vigour of the Writer than the Justness of the Design, and instead of vindicating Tragi-Comedy by the Success of *Shakespeare* we ought perhaps to pay new Honours to that transcendant and unbounded Genius that could preside over the Passions in Sport, who to produce or actuate the Affections needed not the slow Gradation of common Means but could fill the Heart with instantaneous Jollity or Sorrow, and vary our Disposition as he changed his Scenes. Perhaps the Effects even of *Shakespeare*'s Poetry might have been yet greater had he not counter-acted himself, and we might have been more interested in the Distresses of his Heroes had we not been so frequently diverted by the Jokes of his Buffoons.

There are other Rules more fixed and obligatory; it is necessary that of every Play the chief Action should be single, because a Play represents some Transaction through its regular Maturation to its final Event, and therefore two Transactions equally important must evidently constitute two Plays.

As the Design of Tragedy is to instruct by moving the Passions it must always have a Hero or Personage apparently and incontestably superior to the rest, upon whom the Attention may be fixed and the Expectation suspended. Of two Persons opposing each other with equal Abilities and equal Virtue the Auditor will indeed inevitably in Time choose his Favourite, but as that Choice must be without any Cogency of Conviction the Hopes or Fears which it raises will be faint and languid. Of two Heroes acting in Confederacy against a common Enemy the Virtues or Dangers will give little Emotion, because each claims our Concern with the same Right, and the Heart lies at rest between equal Motives.

It ought to be the first Endeavour of a Writer to distinguish Nature from Custom, or that which is established because it is right from that which is right only because it is established; that he may neither violate essential Principles by a Desire of Novelty, nor debar himself from the Attainment of any Beauties within his View by a needless Fear of breaking Rules which no literary Dictator had Authority to prescribe. (929-35)

No. 168 (26 October 1751)

It has been observed by *Boileau* that 'a mean or common Thought expressed in pompous Diction generally pleases more than a new or noble Sentiment delivered in low and vulgar Language; because the Number is much greater of those whom Custom has enabled to judge of Words than of those whom Study has qualified to examine Things.'

This Solution would be sufficient if only those were offended with Meanness of Expression who are unable to distinguish Propriety of Thought and to separate Propositions or Images from the Vehicles by which they are conveyed to the Understanding. But it is found that this Kind of Disgust is by no means confined to the ignorant or superficial; it operates uniformly and universally upon Readers of all Classes. Every Man, however profound or abstracted, perceives himself irresistibly alienated by low Terms, and they who profess the most zealous Adherence to Truth are forced to admit that she owes Part of her Charms to her Ornaments, and loses much of her Power over the Soul when she appears disgraced by a Dress uncouth or ill-adjusted.

We are all offended by low Terms, but we are not pleased or disgusted alike by the same Compositions because we do not all agree to censure the same Terms as low. No Word is naturally or intrinsically meaner than another, and therefore our Notions of Words, as of other Things arbitrarily and capriciously established, depend wholly upon Accident and Custom. The Cottager thinks those Apartments splendid and spacious which an Inhabitant of Palaces will despise for their Inelegance; and to him who has passed most of his Hours with the delicate and polite many Expressions will seem despicable and sordid which another, equally acute and judicious, may hear without Offence; but a mean Term never fails to displease him who considers it as mean, as Poverty is certainly and invariably despised, though he who is poor in the Opinion of some may by others be envied for his Wealth.

Words become low by the Occasions to which they are applied or by the general Character of them who use them, and the Disgust which they produce arises from the Revival of those Ideas with which they are commonly united. Thus if, in the most serious Discourse, a Phrase happens to occur which has before been successfully employed in some ludicrous Narrative, the most grave and serious Auditor finds it difficult to refrain from Laughter, when those whose Imagination is not prepossessed by the same accidental Association of Ideas are utterly unable to guess the Reason of his Merriment. Words which convey Ideas of Dignity in one Age are banished from elegant Writing or Conversation in another, because they are in time debased by vulgar Mouths and can be no longer heard without the involuntary Recollection of unpleasing Images.

When *Macbeth* is confirming himself in his horrid Purpose he breaks into the Violence of his Emotions into a Wish natural to a Murderer:

> Come, thick Night!
> And pall thee in the dunnest Smoke of Hell,
> That my keen Knife see not the Wound it makes;
> Nor Heav'n peep through the Blanket of the dark,
> To cry, hold, hold! [1.5.47ff.[1]]

In this Passage is exerted all the Force of Poetry, that Force which calls new Powers into Being, which embodies Sentiment and animates lifeless Matter; yet perhaps scarce any Man ever perused it without some Disturbance of his Attention from the Counteraction of the Words to the Ideas. What can be more dreadful than to implore the Presence of Night, invested not in common Obscurity but in the Smoke of Hell? Yet the Force of this Invocation is destroyed by the Insertion of an Epithet now seldom heard but in the Stable, and *dun* Night may come or go without any other Notice than Contempt.

If we start into Raptures when some Hero of the Iliad tells us that δόρυ μαίνεται,[2] his Lance rages with Eagerness to destroy; if we are alarmed at the Terror of the Soldiers commanded by *Cæsar* to hew down the sacred Grove, who dreaded, says *Lucan*, that the Axe aimed at the Oak would fly back upon them,[3]

> *Si robora sacra ferirent,*
> *In sua credebant redituras membra secures,*

we cannot surely but sympathise with the Horrors of a Wretch about to murder his Master, his Friend, his Benefactor, who suspects that the

---

[1] These lines are, in fact, spoken by Lady Macbeth.
[2] *Iliad*, 8.111: 'my spear also rages in my hands' grip.'
[3] *Pharsalia* 3.430f: 'believed that, if they aimed a blow at the sacred trunks, their axes would rebound against their own limbs.'

Weapon will refuse its Office and start back from the Breast which he is preparing to violate. Yet this Sentiment is weakened by the Name of an Instrument used by Butchers and by Cooks in the meanest Employments; we do not immediately believe that any Crime of Importance is to be committed with a *Knife*, and at last from the long Habit of connecting a Knife with sordid Offices feel Aversion rather than Terror.

Macbeth proceeds to wish, in the Madness of Guilt, that the Inspection of Heaven may be intercepted and that he may in the Involutions of infernal Darkness escape the Eye of Providence. This is the utmost Extravagance of determined Wickedness; yet this is so much debased by two unfortunate Words that in this Instant while I am endeavouring to impress on my Reader the Energy of the Sentiment I can scarce check my Risibility when the Expression forces itself upon my Mind; for who can, without some Relaxation of his Gravity, hear of *Divinities peeping thro' a Blanket*?

These Imperfections of Diction are less obvious to the Reader as he is less acquainted with the common Usages of the Age; they are therefore wholly imperceptible to a Foreigner who learns our Language only from Books, and will not so forcibly strike a solitary Academick as a modish Lady.

Among the numerous Requisites that must always concur to complete an Author, few are of more Importance than an early Entrance into the living World. The Seeds of Knowledge may be planted in Solitude, but must be cultivated in publick. Argumentation may be taught in Colleges, and Theories may be formed in Retirement, but the Artifice of Embellishment and the Power of securing Attention must be gained by general Converse.

An Acquaintance with the prevailing Customs and fashionable Elegance is necessary likewise for other Purposes. The same Injury that noble Sentiments suffer from disagreeable Language, personal Merit may justly fear from Rudeness and Indelicacy. When the Success of *Æneas* depended on the Favour of the Queen on whose Coasts he was driven, the Divinity that protected him thought him not sufficiently secured against Rejection by his Reputation for Bravery, but decorated him for the Interview with preternatural Beauty. Whoever desires (what none can reasonably contemn) the Favour of Mankind must endeavour to add Grace to Strength, to make his Conversation agreeable as well as useful, and to accomplish himself with those petty Qualifications which are necessary to make the first Impressions in his Favour. Many complain of Neglect who never used any Efforts to attract Regard. It is not to be expected that the Patrons of Science or of Virtue should be solicitous to discover Excellencies which they who possess them never display. Few Men have Abilities so much needed by the rest of the World as to be caressed on their own Terms, and he that will not condescend to recommend himself by external Embellishments must submit to the Fate of just Sentiments meanly expressed, and be ridiculed and forgotten before he is understood. (1001–6)

130. Unsigned essay on jealousy in *Othello*

November 1751

From *The New Universal Magazine*, November 1751, pp. 92–4. The piece is signed B*. It seems to be an imitation of No. 108 above.

REMARKS *on the* Tragedy *of* OTHELLO.

The chief subject of this piece is the passion of *Jealousy*, which the poet has represented at large, in its birth, in various workings and agonies, and in its horrible consequences. From this passion and the innocence and simplicity of the person suspected arises a very moving distress. *The most extravagant love*, says a certain author, *is nearest to the strongest hatred.*

The Moor is furious in both these extremes. His love is tempestuous, and mingled with a wildness peculiar to his character, which seems very artfully to prepare for the change which is to follow. How savage, yet how ardent is that expression of the raptures of his heart, when looking after *Desdemona* as she withdraws he breaks out,

> Excellent wretch! perdition catch my soul:
> But I do love thee; and when I love thee not,
> *Chaos* is come again. [3.3. 91ff.]

The deep and subtle villainy of *Iago* in working this change from love to jealousy in so tumultuous a mind as that of *Othello*, prepossessed with a confidence in the disinterested affection of the man who is leading him on insensibly to his ruin, is likewise drawn with a masterly hand. *Iago*'s broken hints, questions and seeming care to hide the reason for 'em; his obscure suggestions to raise the curiosity of the Moor; his personated confusion, and refusing to explain himself, while *Othello* is drawn on and held in suspence till he grows impatient and angry; then his throwing in the poison, and naming to him, in a caution, the passion he intends to raise,

O beware of Jealousy!   [3.3.169]

are inimitable strokes of art in that scene which has always been justly esteem'd one of the best which was ever exhibited on the theatre.

To return to the character of *Othello*. His strife of passions, his starts, his returns of love, and his threatenings to *Iago*, who had put his mind on the rack; his relapses afterwards to jealousy; his rage against his wife, and his asking pardon of *Iago*, whom he thinks he had abused for his fidelity to him, are touches which no one can over-look that has the sentiments of human nature, or has consider'd the heart of man in its frailties, its penances, and in all the variety of its agitations. The torments which the Moor suffers are so exquisitely drawn as to render him as much an object of compassion, even in the barbarous action of murdering *Desdemona*, as the innocent person herself who falls under his hands.

But there is nothing in which the poet has more shewn his abilities in this play than in the circumstance of the handkerchief, which is employ'd as a confirmation to the jealousy of *Othello* already raised. The very slightness of this circumstance is the beauty of it. How finely has *Shakespeare* expressed the nature of jealousy in those lines which on this occasion he puts into the mouth of *Iago*:

Trifles light as air
Are to the jealous confirmations strong
As proofs of holy writ.   [3.3.326ff.]

As the moral of this Tragedy (which ought to be the chief object of our attention) is an admirable caution against hasty suspicions, and the giving way to the first transports of rage and jealousy, which may plunge a man in a few minutes into all the horrors of guilt, distraction and ruin; I shall further inforce it by relating a scene of misfortunes of the like kind which really happen'd some years ago in *Spain* (where jealousy seems to have taken the deepest root) and is an instance of the most tragical hurricane of passion I have ever met with in history. It may be easily conceived that an heart ever big with resentments of its own dignity, and never allay'd by reflections which make us honour ourselves for acting with reason and equality, will take fire precipitantly. It will on a sudden flame too high to be extinguished. And the short story which follows is a lively instance of the truth of this observation, and a just warning to those of jealous honour to look about 'em, and begin to possess their souls as they ought; for no man of spirit knows how terrible a creature he is till he comes to be provoked.

Don ALONZO, a *Spanish* nobleman, had a beautiful and virtuous wife with whom he had lived for some years in great tranquility. The gentleman, however, was not free from the faults usually imputed to his nation; he was proud, conceited, suspicious and impetuous. He kept a Moor in his house whom, on complaint from his lady, he had punished for a small offence with great severity. The slave vow'd vengeance, and communicated his resolution to one of the lady's women, with whom he lived in a criminal way. This creature also hated her mistress, fearing that her wicked way of life was observed by her: she therefore undertook to make *Don* ALONZO jealous by insinuating that the gard'ner was often admitted to his lady in private, and promising to make him an eye-witness of it. At a proper time agreed on between her and the *Morisco* she sent a message to the gardener that his lady, having some hasty orders to give him, would have him come that moment to her in her chamber. In the mean time she had placed *Alonzo* privately in an outer room, that he might observe who passed that way: and it was not long before he saw the gard'ner appear. *Alonzo*, out of all patience, follow'd the fellow into the lady's apartment, struck him at one blow with a dagger to the heart; then dragging his lady by the hair, without further enquiry he killed her instantly on the spot. Here he paused, looking on the dead bodies with all the agitations of a demon of revenge; which so struck the wench who had occasion'd all these terrors that, distracted with remorse, she threw herself at his feet and in a voice of lamentation, without sense of the consequence, confessed all her guilt. *Alonzo* was overwhelmed with all the violent passions at one instant, and utter'd the broken voices and motions of each of 'em for a moment; till at last he recollected himself enough to end his agony of love, anger, jealousy, disdain, revenge and remorse by murdering the maid, the Moor and himself, with the very dagger that had slain the innocent objects of his jealousy.

131. William Mason, a proposal to revive the Chorus

1751

From Mason's *Letters* prefixed to *Elfrida, A Dramatic Poem. Written on the Model of the Ancient Greek Tragedy* (1752).

William Mason (1725–97), fellow of Pembroke Hall, Cambridge, and a prolific poet, was a friend of Gray, Hurd, Walpole and Warburton. He subsequently edited Gray's *Letters* in the form of a biography (1774).

LETTER I.

*   *   *

I meant only to pursue the ancient method so far as it is probable a Greek Poet, were he alive, would now do, in order to adapt himself to the genius of our times and the character of our Tragedy. According to this notion every thing was to be allowed to the present taste which nature and Aristotle could possibly dispense with; and nothing of intrigue or refinement was to be admitted at which antient judgment could reasonably take offence. Good sense, as well as antiquity, prescribed an adherence to the three great Unities; these therefore were strictly observed. But on the other hand, to follow the modern masters in those respects wherein they had not so faultily deviated from their predecessors, a story was chosen in which the tender rather than the noble passions were predominant, and in which even love had the principal share. Characters too were drawn as nearly approaching to private ones as Tragic dignity would permit; and affections raised rather from the impulse of common humanity than the distresses of royalty and the fate of kingdoms. Besides this, for the sake of natural embellishment, and to reconcile mere modern readers to that simplicity of fable in which I thought it necessary to copy the antients, I contrived to lay the scene in an old romantic forest. For by this means I was enabled to enliven the Poem by various touches of pastoral description; not affectedly brought in from the store-house of a picturesque imagination but necessarily resulting from the scenery of the place itself: A beauty so extremely striking in the COMUS of Milton, and the AS YOU LIKE IT of Shakespeare; and of which the Greek Muse (though fond of rural Imagery) has afforded few examples besides that admirable one in the PHILOCTETES of Sophocles. (i–ii)

LETTER II.

I am glad you approve the method I have taken of softening the rigor of the old Drama. If I have, indeed, softened it sufficiently for the modern taste, without parting with any of the essentials of the Greek method, I have obtain'd my purpose: which was to obviate some of the popular objections made to the antient form of Tragedy. For the current opinion, you know, is that by the strict adherence to the Unities it restrains the genius of the poet; by the simplicity of its conduct it diminishes the pathos of the fable; and by the admission of a continued Chorus prevents that agreeable embarrass which awakens our attention and interests our passions.

The universal veneration which we pay to the name of Shakespeare, at the same time that it has improved our relish for the higher beauties of Poetry, has undoubtedly been the ground-work of all this false criticism. That disregard which, in compliance merely with the taste of the times, he shewed of all the necessary rules of the Drama hath since been considered as a characteristic of his vast and original genius; and consequently set up as a model for succeeding writers. Hence M. Voltaire remarks very justly, 'Que le merite de cet auteur a perdu le Theatre Anglois. Le temps, qui seul fait la reputation des hommes, rend à la fin leurs defauts respectables.'

Yet notwithstanding the absurdity of this low superstition, the notion is so popular amongst Englishmen that I fear it will never be entirely discredited, till a poet rises up amongst us with a genius as elevated and daring as Shakespeare's, and a judgment as sober and chastis'd as Racine's. But as it seems too long to wait for this prodigy it will not surely be improper for any one of common talents who would entertain the public without indulging its caprice to take the best models of antiquity for his guides; and to adapt those models, as near as may be, to the manners and taste of his own times. Unless he do both he will, in effect, do nothing. For it cannot be doubted that the many gross faults of our stage are owing to the complaisance and servility with which the ordinary run of writers have ever humoured that illiterate, whimsical or corrupted age in which it was their misfortune to be born. . . .(iii–iv)

A Writer of Tragedy must certainly adapt himself more to the general taste, because the Dramatic, of all kinds of Poetry, ought to be most universally relish'd and understood. The Lyric Muse addresses herself to the imagination of a reader, the Didactic to his judgment, but the Tragic strikes directly on his passions. Few men have a strength of imagination capable of pursuing the flights of Pindar. Many have not a clearness of apprehension suited to the reasonings of Lucretius and Pope. But ev'ry man has passions to be excited, and ev'ry man feels them excited by Shakespeare.

But tho' Tragedy be thus chiefly directed to the heart it must be observed that it will seldom attain its end without the concurrent approbation of the judgment. And to procure this the artificial construction of the fable goes a great way. In France the excellence of their several poets is chiefly measur'd by this standard. And amongst our own writers, if you except Shakespeare (who indeed ought, for his other virtues, to be exempt from common rules) you will find that the most regular of their compositions is generally reckoned their *Chef d'oeuvre;* witness the *All for Love* of Dryden, the *Venice Preserved* of Otway, and the *Jane Shore* of Rowe. (v–vi)

LETTER III.

The scheme you propos'd in your last is, I own, practicable enough. Undoubtedly most part of the Dialogue of the Chorus might be put into the mouth of an Emma or Matilda, who with some little shew of sisterly concernment might be easily made to claim kindred with Earl Athelwold. Nay, by the addition of an unnecessary incident or two, which would cost me no more than they are worth in contriving, and an unmeaning personage or two, who would be as little expence in creating, I believe I could quickly make the whole tolerably fit for an English Audience.

But for all this I cannot persuade myself to enter upon the task. I have, I know not how (like many of my betters) contracted a kind of veneration for the old Chorus; and am willing to think it essential to the

Tragic Drama. You shall hear the reasons that incline me to this judgment. They respect the *Poet* and the *Audience*.

It is agreed, I think, on all hands that in the conduct of a fable the admission of a Chorus lays a necessary restraint on the *Poet*. The two Unities of Time and Place are esteemed by some of less consequence in our modern Tragedy than the third Unity of Action; but admit a Chorus and you must, of necessity, restore them to those equal rights which they antiently enjoyed and yet claim by the *Magna Charta* of Aristotle. For the difference which the use of the Chorus makes is this: the modern Drama contents itself with a fact *represented*; the antient requires it to be *represented before Spectators*. Now as it cannot be suppos'd that those Spectators should accompany the chief personages into private apartments, one single Scene or *unity of Place* becomes strictly necessary. And as these Spectators are assembled on purpose to observe and bear a part in the action the *time* of that action becomes, of course, that of the spectacle or representation itself; it being unreasonable to make the Spectators attend so long as the Poet, in bringing about his Catastrophe, may require. And this is usually the practice of the antient stage. The modern, on the contrary, regards very little these two capital restraints; and its disuse of the Chorus helps greatly to conceal the absurdity. For the Poet, without offending so much against the laws of probability, may lead his personages from one part to another of the same palace or city when they have only a paltry Servant or insignificant Confidant to attend them. He may think himself at liberty to spend two or three days, months, or even years in completing his story; to clear the stage at the end or, if he pleases, in the middle of every act: and, being under no controul of the Chorus, he can break the continuity of the Drama just where he thinks it convenient; and by the assistance of a brisk fugue and a good violin can persuade his audience that as much time has elaps'd as his *Hero*'s, or rather his own, distress may demand.

Hence it is that secret intrigues become (as Mr Dryden gravely calls them) the *beauties of our modern Stage*. Hence it is that Incidents, and Bustle, and *Business*, supply the place of Simplicity, Nature, and Pathos. A happy change, perhaps, for the generality of writers, who might otherwise find it impossible to fill *cette longue carrière de cinq actes*, which a Writer sufficiently experienced in these matters says *est si prodigieusement difficile a remplir sans Episodes*.

But whatever these Play-makers may have gained by rejecting the Chorus the true Poet has lost considerably by it. For he has lost a graceful and natural resource to the embellishments of Picturesque Description, sublime allegory, and whatever else comes under the denomination of *pure Poetry*. Shakespeare, indeed, had the power of introducing this naturally and, what is most strange, of joining it with *pure Passion*. But I make no doubt if we had a Tragedy of his formed on the Greek model we should find in it more frequent, if not nobler, instances of his high Poetical capacity than in any single composition he has left us. I think you have a proof of this in those parts of his historical plays which are called Choruses, and written in the common Dialogue metre. And your imagination will easily conceive how fine an ode the description of the night preceding the battle of Agincourt would have made in his hands; and what additional grace it would receive from that form of composition. (vi–ix)

*   *   *

LETTER IV.

*   *   *

In those parts of the Drama where the judgment of a mixt audience is most liable to be misled by what passes before its view the chief actors are generally too much agitated by the furious passions or too much attach'd by the tender ones to think coolly, and impress on the spectators a moral sentiment properly. A Confidant or Servant has seldom sense enough to do it, never dignity enough to make it regarded. Instead therefore of these the Antients were provided with a band of distinguish'd persons, not merely capable of seeing and hearing but of arguing, advising, and reflecting; from the leader of which a moral sentiment never came unnaturally but suitably and gracefully: and from the troop itself a poetical flow of tender commiseration, of religious supplication, or of virtuous triumph was ever ready to heighten the pathos, to inspire a reverential awe of the Deity, and to advance the cause of *honesty* and of truth. (x)

*   *   *

The character of PIERRE in *Venice Preserv'd*, when left entirely to the judgment of the audience, is perhaps one of the most improper for public view that ever was produced on any stage. It is almost impossible but some part of the spectators should go from the representation with very false and immoral impressions. But had that Tragedy been written on the antient plan, had Pierre's character been drawn just as it is, and some few alterations made in Jaffier's, I know no two characters more capable of doing service in a moral view when justly animadverted upon by the Chorus. I don't say I would have trusted Otway with the writing of it.

To have done, and to release you. Bad characters become on this plan as harmless in the hands of the Poet as the Historian; and good ones become infinitely more useful by how much the Poetic is more forcible than the Historical mode of instruction. (xii–xiii)

132. Thomas Gray, the Chorus rejected

c. December 1751

From Gray's Letter to Mason, *c.* December 1751; in *The Works of Thomas Gray* ed. J. Mitford, 5 vols (1835–43).

See head-note to No. 93.

* * *

I.

DEAR SIR,—very bad!—*I am* YOURS,—equally bad! it is impossible to conciliate these passages to Nature and Aristotle.

'*Allowed to modern caprice.*'—It is *not* caprice but good sense that has made these alterations in the modern Drama. A greater liberty in the choice of the fable and the conduct of it was the necessary consequence of retrenching the Chorus. Love and tenderness delight in privacy. The soft effusions of the soul, Mr Mason, will not bear the presence of a gaping, singing, dancing, moralizing, uninteresting crowd. And not love alone but every passion is checked and cooled by this fiddling crew. How could Macbeth and his wife have laid the design for Duncan's murder? What could they have said to each other in the Hall at mid-night, not only if a Chorus but if a single mouse had been stirring there? Could Hamlet have met the Ghost, or taken his mother to task in *their* company? If Othello had said a harsh word to his wife before *them*, would they not have danced to the window and called the watch?

The ancients were perpetually confined and hampered by the necessity of using the Chorus: and if they have done wonders notwithstanding this clog sure I am they would have performed still greater wonders without it. For the same reason we may be allowed to admit of more intrigue in our drama, to bring about a great action; it is often an essential requisite: and it is not fair to argue against this liberty from that misuse of it which is common to us, and was formerly so with the French, namely the giving in to a silly intricacy of plot in imitation of the Spanish Dramas. We have also since Charles the Second's time imitated the French (though but awkwardly) in framing scenes of mere insipid gallantry. But these were the faults of the writers and not of the art, which enables us with the help of a little contrivance to have as much love as we please without playing the petits maîtres or building labyrinths.

I forgot to mention that Comedy contrived to be an odd sort of Farce, very like those of the Italian theatre, till the Chorus was dismissed; when Nature and Menander brought it into that beautiful form which we find in Terence. Tragedy was not so happy till modern times.

II.

I do not admit that the excellencies of the French writers are measured by the verisimilitude, or the regularities of their Dramas *only*. Nothing in them or in our own, even Shakespeare himself, ever touches us unless rendered *verisimile*, which by good management may be accomplished even in such absurd stories as *The Tempest*, the Witches in *Macbeth*, or the Fairies in the *Midsummer Night's Dream*: and I know not of any writer that has pleased chiefly in proportion to his *regularity*. Other beauties may indeed be heightened and set off by its means, but of itself it hardly pleases at all. *Venice Preserved*, or *Jane Shore*, are not so regular as the *Orphan*, or *Tamerlane*, or *Lady Jane Grey*.

III.

Modern Melpomene.—Here are we got into our tantarums! It is certain that pure poetry may be introduced without any Chorus. I refer you to a thousand passages of *mere* description in the Iambic parts of Greek tragedies, and to ten thousand in Shakespeare, who is moreover particularly admirable in his introduction of pure poetry, so as to join it with pure passion and yet keep close to nature. This *He* could accomplish with passions the most violent and transporting, and this any good writer may do with passions less impetuous, for it is nonsense to imagine that Tragedy must *throughout* be agitated with the furious passions or attached by the tender ones. The greater part of it must often be spent in a preparation of these passions, in a gradual working them up to their height, and must thus pass through a great many cooler scenes and a variety of *nuances*, each of which will admit of a proper degree of poetry, and some the purest poetry. Nay, the boldest metaphors and even description in its strongest colouring are the natural expression of some passions, even in their greatest agitation. As to moral reflections, there is sufficient room for them in those cooler scenes that I have mentioned, and they make the greatest ornaments of such parts; that is to say, if they are well joined with the character. If not, they had better be left to the audience than put into the mouths of a set of professed moralists who keep a shop of sentences and reflections (I mean the Chorus), whether they be sages, as you call them, or young girls that learnt them by heart out of their samples and primers. (IV, 1–4)

133. Arthur Murphy, the Chorus rejected

September 1752

From *The Covent-Garden Journal* No. 62, 16 September 1752. For the ascription of this essay to Murphy see A. Sherbo, *New Essays by Arthur Murphy*, pp. 174-5.

No. 62 (16 September 1752)

To Sir ALEXANDER DRAWCANSIR, Knt.
Censor of Great Britain.

Bedlam, Apr. 9, 1752.

SIR,

I have been confined in this Place four Years; my friends, that is my Relations—but, as I call them, my *Enemies*—think me Mad; but to shew you I am not I'll send you a Specimen of my Present State of Mind.

About a Week ago a grave Gentleman came to the Grate of my Cell and threw me in a Pamphlet, written it seems by a Gent. of Cambridge. I read it over, and approve the Drama much, but I must send you some Thoughts that occur'd to me from Reading the Prefix'd Five Letters. The Author it seems lives at Pembroke Hall, in Cambridge, where Sophocles, Euripides, and Æschylus, have, I don't doubt, been his darling Studies, not forgetting the abominable Rules of Aristotle, who indisputably wrote very properly concerning Dramatic Poetry at his Time of Day, but what a Figure wou'd a Modern Tragedy make with his three Unities! If Shakespeare had observed them he wou'd have flown like a *Paper Kite*, not *soar'd like an Eagle*.

Again, Sir, as to his *Chorus* he is so fond of, why that did very well amongst the Greek Writers; but methinks this *Mr. Chorus* would be a very impertinent Fellow if he was to put in his Observations on any of Shakespeare's interesting Scenes. As, for Example, what do you think of this same *Chorus* if he was to be upon the Stage when, in the Play of *Othello*, Iago is imprinting those exquisite Tints of Jealousy upon Othello's Mind in the third Act; or suppose when Desdemona drops the fatal Handkerchief the *Chorus* was to call after her to bid her take it up again, or tell the Audience what was to happen in Case she did not?

450

Or suppose, Sir, this same *Chorus* was to stand by and tell us Brutus and Cassius were going to differ, but that they would make it up again—would not this prevent the noble Anxiety this famous Scene in *Julius Cæsar* raises in the Minds of a sensible Audience? Another Use this ingenious Gentleman finds out for the *Chorus*, and that is to explain the Characters and Sentiments of the several Personages in the Drama to the Audience. Now, Sir, there is a Nation in the World which has found out a way of doing this very effectually without *interrupting the Action*—and that is the *Chinese*; these People always make the Characters of the Drama come upon the Stage before the Play begins, and tell who they are, as thus, Sir:

Enter Dramatis Personæ.

1. I am Taw Maw-shaw, King of Tonchin, Brother to Hunfish, am to be dethroned by my Brother, and killed with the Sabre of the renowned Schimshaw.
2. I am Hunfish, Brother to Taw-Maw-shaw, I am to dethrone him, and usurp his Crown.
3. I am Schimshaw Master of the great Sabre which is to kill the King Taw-Maw-shaw.

Thus, Sir, do these wise People let you into the Characters of the Drama; which is to be sure a much wiser way than by a *Chorus*, who interrupt the Actors to cram in their stupid Remarks. Indeed, when Dramatic Poetry first appeared the whole was represented *by one Person*, and there it was necessary the *Chorus* should come in to give the poor Solo Speaker a little Breath. But as I have half a dozen Plays by me which I intend to bring upon the Stage I beg you will insist upon it that this learned Cantab says no more about his *Chorus*, for it would be very hard upon me if I had not the same Indulgence which has been shewn *to all my Cotemporaries*; which is to let the Audience find out the Meaning of my Characters if they can, of themselves; if not, let them depart as wise as they came.

I am, Sir, Yours in clean Straw,

TRAGICOMICUS.

N.B. I have no Objection to the Choruses of the immortal Handel.

If you observe, Sir, this learned Gentleman finds fault with Shakespeare's *Chorus* in *Henry the Vth*, and says it would do better in other Metre. If I had him here, I believe I should do him a Mischief.

451

134. Unsigned essay on *Hamlet*

1752

From *Miscellaneous Observations On the Tragedy of Hamlet* (1752). The authorship of this pamphlet remains obscure, although it has certain similarities of language and method with the essay by John Holt (above, No. 118).

PREFACE

Shakespeare, who first revived, or more properly form'd the Stage, was the greatest Dramatic Author this Country ever produced. By the Force of a sound Judgment, most lively Imagination, and a perfect Knowledge of human Nature, without the least Assistance from Art, he dispell'd those condense Clouds of Gothic Ignorance which at that Time obscured us, and first caused *Britain* to appear a formidable Rival to her learned Neighbours. Nothing but a liberal Education was wanting to raise this great Man to the Summit of Perfection, where he would for ever have flourish'd unrivall'd. But the Sun itself has its Spots; nor was any thing as yet ever form'd entirely compleat.

Had he been conversant with the ancient Critics and Tragedians his Genius, instead of being check'd or depress'd by an Observance of their Rules, would have soar'd a nobler and sublimer Height. A Critic of Eminence informs us that 'Grand Flights are never in more Danger than when they are left to themselves, without Ballast to poise, or Helm to guide their Course, but encumber'd with their own Weight, and daring without Discretion.'

The Unities of Time and Place he for the most part seems very little to regard; in his observance of the other he is more regular.

He indeed apologizes for this Absurdity in his Chorus in *Henry the Vth*:

> Vouchsafe to those, that have not read the Story,
> That I may prompt them; and of such as have
> I humbly pray them to admit th' Excuse
> Of *Time*, of Numbers, and true Course of Things,
> Which cannot in their huge and proper Life
> Be here presented.   [5 *Prol.* 1ff.]

452

This convinces us that he himself was conscious of the Error, but chose rather to proceed in the beaten Path than be at the Trouble of finding out a new one. But this is directly contrary to the Practice of the Ancients. *Aristotle* has laid it down as a Rule that the Time supposed to be employ'd in a Tragedy, should be confined to a single Day, or as little more as possible. . . . But I cannot see what Harm it can do us if we suffer ourselves to be deceived and pass over the length of Time necessary to produce the Incidents represented, and accompany the Poet in his Peregrinations from Place to Place, without being disgusted at the Absurdity or offended at the Imposition. Tho' *Shakespeare* did not bring Tragedy to the utmost Perfection yet he laid so noble a Base for its future Rise and Improvement as exceeded the most sanguine Expectations. Happy would it have been for us if his Successors could have maintained and supported it with equal Abilities! But alas! they were all unequal to the difficult Task, and sunk under the Weight their Master supported with Grandeur and Dignity. They are indeed more elaborate and correct, but the Sentiment and Diction can never be equall'd. Our Poet has particularly excell'd in clearly and fully marking and distinguishing the Manners of his principal Characters. Thus we know by his Discourse that *Macbeth* will break thro' all Laws human and divine to possess the Crown, tho' even at the Expence of his Peace of Mind. Nor are we at a Loss to determine whether the god-like *Brutus* will assist his enslaved Country, or tamely submit to the Usurpation of an ambitious Tyrant. (iii–vi)

*   *   *

Love, the usual Subject of modern Tragedies, our Poet has very wisely refused Admittance into his best Compositions. It is a Passion truly comic, and when introduced in Tragedy deserves our Contempt and Derision rather than Pity or Compassion. In *Romeo and Juliet* the Distress is real; yet there is none of the modern Gallantry so much admired. But the Play itself can be by no Means reckoned amongst his best Pieces. The following Speech of *Juliet* has been censured as ridiculous, but I believe without just Cause.

> Give me my *Romeo*, Night, and when he dies,
> Take him and cut him out in little Stars
> And he will make the Face of Heav'n so fine,
> That all the World shall be in Love with Night
> And pay no Worship to the garish Sun.   [3.2.21ff.]

This evidently alludes to the ancient fabulous Histories of Mortals being received into the Heavens and metamorphosed into Constellations. *Juliet*, by a beautiful Hyperbole, says that *Romeo*'s Body entire would not only make a Star but, divided in several Parts, would form so many different splendid Appearances. (vii)

*   *   *

Though *Shakespeare* has for the most Part caused his Kings and Heroes to maintain their Dignity without stooping into vulgar Phrase, yet he sometimes makes them descend from their Characters and use the Language of a Buffoon. Thus *Henry* the Vth, just before the Battle of *Agincourt*.

'Indeed the *French* may lay twenty *French* Crowns to one they will beat us, for they bear them on their Shoulders; but it is no *English* Treason to cut *French* Crowns, and To-morrow the King himself will be a Clipper,' and immediately after, falls into that beautiful Soliloquy,

> Upon the King! Let us our Lives, our Souls,
> Our Debts, our careful Wives, our Children, and
> Our Sins, lay on the King; he must bear all.
>
> [4.1.222ff.]

the Chorus in the same Play quibbles notoriously, speaking of the Conspirators who

> Have for the *Gilt of France* (O *Guilt* indeed!)
> Confirm'd Conspiracy with fearful *France*.
>
> [2 *Prol.* 26f.]

No Person hath been more commended for an honest Integrity of Heart than our Poet; but he is not free from that Court Vice, Flattery. In his *Macbeth* he openly digresses to pay a Compliment to the Prince then on the Throne; and whenever he has occasion to speak of Kings, makes use of the most religious Terms. (viii–x)

*   *   *

[On adaptations] Mr *Dryden* and Sir *William D'Avenant judiciously* made Choice of *The Tempest*, the most regular and correct of all our Poet's Works, and the Result was natural: they formed a very bad

Play out of a very good one. The Duke of *Buckingham*, observing that *Julius Cæsar* was spun out to the Death of *Brutus* and *Cassius*, resolved to divide it into two Plays; and after much Trouble and Pains at length presented us with the most wretched Performances that were ever exhibited on the *English* Stage. *D'Urfey* and *Cibber* hardly deserve our Notice; but we must not omit one *Tate*, a Writer devoid of all Spirit and good Taste, not deserving to be rank'd in the meanest Class of the meanest Poetasters, who thinking the Catastrophe of *Lear* too pathetic and moving cast aside the most beautiful Part and made us *ample Amends* by inserting his own vile Ribbaldry. Such has been the Fate of all those who have presumed to alter *Shakespeare*, without trying

> *Quid valeant humeri, quid ferre recusent.*[1]

And such will be the Fate of all future Pretenders unless their Fancy be as pregnant, their Judgment as strong, and their Knowledge as piercing and universal as the Poet's himself. (xi–xii)

OBSERVATIONS ON *HAMLET*

NOTE I.

> Last Night of all,
> When yon same Star that's Westward from the Pole,
> Had made his Course t'illume that Part of Heaven
> Where now it burns, *Marcellus* and myself,
> The Bell then beating One——
>
> *Enter the* Ghost.
>
> Peace, break thee off; look where it comes again——
>
> [1.1.35ff.]

The Poet has shown his Judgment in the Conduct of this Scene. The Time is Midnight, the Place a Platform before the Palace, upon which two Officers make their Appearance, and along with them a Gentleman (to whom they had communicated what they had seen two Nights successively) who wanted ocular Demonstration before he would credit the surprising Story. The Centinel is about to give a long circumstantial Narration when he is unexpectedly interrupted by the Entrance of the Ghost. The Truth of the Observation

---

[1] Horace, *A.P.* 39f.: 'ponder long what your shoulders refuse, and what they are able to bear.'

Segnius irritant animos demissa per aurem,
Quam quæ sunt occulis subjecta fidelibus.[1]

is here apparent.

The most artful and spirited Recital could never have raised the Terror that possesses the Spectators at the Appearance of the Phantom, who from first to last is grand and majestick, and maintains an equal Character. *Shakespeare* has strictly observed that Rule of *Horace*,

Nec Deus intersit nisi dignus vindice nodus.[2]

He has raised the dead, but it is to reveal a Secret which had never been discovered but by the Intervention and Assistance of a super-natural Power. None of his Plays are destitute of a Moral, this carries a noble one. 'Though a Villain may for a Time escape Justice and enjoy the Fruits of his Wickedness, yet divine Providence will at length overtake him in the Height of his Career, and bring him to condign Punishment.'

Raro antecedentem scelestum
Deseruit Pœna, pede claudo.[3]

It had been better for his Successors in the Drama had this Play never been written; for when they observed the universal Applause he received, and indeed very justly deserved, for introducing on the Stage this inimitable Piece of Machinery, they took Care to croud their Plays with Ghosts, tho' they had no other Effect than to frighten and delight the credulous and ignorant. Thus what in the Hands of an able Master is noble and sublime, attempted by a Bungler appears absurd and ridiculous.

The Rev. Mr *Upton* in his Observations on this Author has made a slight Mistake in calling *Horatio* a Soldier, who was in Fact a Student at *Wittenberg* (where an University at that Time flourished) along with young *Hamlet*, and came to *Elsinore* to be a Spectator of the Funeral of his Friend's Father. This is evident from the Prince's first Salutation:

Ham. What makes you from *Wittenberg, Horatio?*
Hor. A truant Disposition, good my Lord.

---

[1] *AP.* 180f.: 'Less vividly is the mind stirred by what finds entrance through the ears than by what is brought before the trusty eyes.'

[2] *AP.* 191: 'And let no god intervene, unless a knot come worthy of such a deliverer.'

[3] Horace, *Odes* 3.2.31f.: 'but rarely does Vengeance, albeit of halting gait, fail to o'ertake the guilty, though he gain the start.'

Ham. I know you are no Truant.
But what is your Affair in *Elsinore?*
Hor. My Lord, I came to see your Father's Funeral.

[1.2.168ff.] (9–11)

* * *

NOTE IV.

'Gainst that Season comes
Wherein our Saviour's Birth is celebrated;
The Bird of Dawning singeth all Night long:
And then, they say, no Spirit walks abroad;
The Nights are wholesome, then no Planets strike,
No Fairy takes, no Witch hath Power to charm,
So hallow'd and so gracious is the Time

[1.1.158ff.]

If *Ignorance is the Mother of Devotion* it is to be wished that this Age had not excelled the former in Knowledge. Our Ancestors believed *too much*, we *too little*. Pity it is but some Medium had been found between these Extremes that might have restrained Superstition and Atheism in closer Bounds. The Expression *no Fairy takes* is something obscure. The Meaning is that their Wiles and Deceits are frustrated on account of the Sacredness of the Time. He cannot be supposed to mean the innocent Part of that diminutive Species, who are reported to pass the Night very harmlessly in dancing round the Rings or Circles we often see in Pastures, but those unlucky and knavish Sprites who in the different Shapes of Horses, Hogs, Hounds, Bears, Meteors and various other Appearances, mislead benighted Travellers and play a thousand unlucky Pranks.

See the Midsummer Night's Dream.

NOTE V.

The chariest Maid is prodigal enough,
If she unmask her Beauties to the Moon:
Virtue itself 'scapes not calumnious Strokes;
The Canker galls the Infants of the Spring,
Too oft before the Buttons are disclos'd;

And in the Morn and liquid Dew of Youth,
Contagious Blastments are most imminent.

[1.3.36ff.]

This Play every where abounds with just, excellent and moral Precepts, which I cannot too warmly recommend to the serious Perusal and Consideration of every young Lady in *Great-Britain*; who, did they but seriously reflect that each unguarded Word or Action, however innocent the Intention may be, is liable to be basely misrepresented by the designing Arts of malicious Slanderers, would have a greater Regard to their Conduct and Behaviour than they seem to have at present. (14-15)

★   ★   ★

NOTE XXI.

That would be scann'd,
A Villain kills my Father, and for that,
I, his *sole* Son do this same Villain send
To Heaven.

[3.3.75ff.]

So all the Editions read except the last, the Editor of which hath the following Note on this Passage.

I his *sole* Son do this same Villain send

'The Folio reads *foule Son*, this will lead us to the true Reading, which is, *fal'n* Son, i.e. disinherited. This was an Aggravation of the Injury; that he had not only murther'd the Father, but ruined the Son.' I would not willingly differ from a Gentleman of Mr. *W*—'s Learning and Judgment but I cannot see any Want of an Emendation in this Place. The old Reading to me seems the more plausible. *Sole* in this Place is a very emphatical Expression. *Hamlet* means by it that he was his *only* Son, and consequently ought to be his chief Avenger instead of doing an Act of Kindness to the Assassin. Moreover *Hamlet* could not be said with any Propriety to be *fal'n*. The King had indeed, as he expresses it,

Popt in between th' Election and his Hopes.

[5.2.65]

458

But yet had done him the Justice to appoint him his Successor in the Kingdom.

> let the World take Note,
> You are the most immediate to our Throne.
> Our chiefest Courtier, Cousin, and our Son.
>
> [1.2.108f., 117]

NOTE XXII.

> A Bloody Deed; almost as bad, good Mother,
> *As kill a King*, and marry with his Brother.
>
> [3.4.28f.]

We are not expressly informed whether the Queen was conscious of, or concerned in, the Death of her Husband: but Probability must pass for Truth, as no Certainty can be obtain'd. The Ghost, in the Account he gives, says that his Brother was the Person who actually deprived him of his Life.

> Upon my secure Hour, thy Uncle stole,
> With Juice of cursed Hebenon in a Phial.
>
> [1.5.61f.]

It seems pretty plain that the Murtherer had obtained the Good-will of the Queen before he perpetrated the Fact.

> thy Uncle,
> That incestuous, that adulterate Beast,
> With Witchcraft of his Wits, with traiterous Gifts,
> Won to his shameful Lust,
> The Will of my most seeming virtuous Queen.
>
> [1.5.41ff.]

Had she not been Guilty of Murther as well as Incest what Occasion had the Ghost to desire his Son to offer her no Violence?

> But howsoever thou pursue this Act,
> Taint not thy Mind, nor let thy Soul contrive
> Against thy Mother ought; leave her to Heav'n,
> And to those Thorns that in her Bosom lodge
> To prick and sting her.
>
> [1.5.84ff.]

To corroborate other Circumstances, *Hamlet* in this Scene directly accuses her with the cruel Action.

> As bad, good Mother,
> As kill a King.

Nor does she in the least attempt to prove her Innocence but, confounded with Guilt, desires her Son to be silent on that Head.

> O *Hamlet* speak no more,
> Thou turn'st mine Eyes into my very Soul,
> And there I see such black and grained Spots
> As will not leave their Tinct. [3.4.88ff.]

This Play is said to resemble the *Electra* of *Sophocles*, and it is like it in many Respects. *Gertrude* and *Clytemnestra* are Characters nearly allied. Both were Queens, both Adulteresses, and both of them had their Hands imbrued in the Blood of their Lords and Masters. The latter had some Excuse for the bloody Deed, the former none at all. She was affectionately beloved by a King who had all the Bravery of *Mars* join'd with the Beauty of *Apollo*, and she rewarded him for his Tenderness by ent'ring into a Conspiracy with a cowardly Ruffian, and depriving him of his Life and Crown at the same Time. *Clytemnestra* was no less guilty but more open; she acknowledged the Fact and gloried in it. Nay, went so far as to declare, that it was Justice that struck him, not her alone. . . . But her Provocations were great. *Agamemnon* had enticed her Daughter *Iphigenia* to *Aulis*, and there sacrificed her on an Altar to favour the Cause of the *Argives*. This cruel Treatment incensed her so much that she vow'd Revenge and the very Night of his Return from *Troy*, assisted by *Egisthus*, assassinated him in his own Palace. (38–41)

* * *

NOTE XXIII.

Here *is* your Husband like a mildew'd *Ear* . . .

[3.4.64]

Allusions to Passages in Scripture are very frequent in all the Works of our Author, and his Ideas are often enriched by them. This Similitude has great Beauty, and the Contrast is finely heightened. He hints at *Pharaoh*'s Dream, mentioned in the 41st Chapter of *Genesis*. (43)

* * *

NOTE XXVI.

Enter two Grave-diggers.

Is she to be buried in Christian Burial, that wilfully seeks her own Salvation?   [5.1.1ff.]

Though this Scene is full of Humour, and had not been amiss in low Comedy, it has not the least Business here. To debase his sublime Compositions with wretched Farce, commonplace Jokes, and un-meaning Quibbles seems to have been the Delight of the laurelled, the immortal *Shakespeare*. Some of his foolish bigotted Admirers have endeavoured to excuse him by saying that it was more the Fault of the Age than his, that the Taste of the People was to the highest Degree vitious when he wrote, that they had been used to Buffoonery and would not be pleased without it, and that he was obliged to comply with the prevailing Taste for his own Emolument. This, instead of excusing, aggravates his Crime. He was conscious he acted wrong, but meanly chose to sacrifice his Sense and Judgment to delight an injudi-cious Audience, and gain the Applause of a Herd of Fools rather than approach too near to Purity and Perfection. To mix Comedy with Tragedy is breaking through the sacred Laws of Nature, nor can it be defended. The Ancients universally agreed in their Definition of Tragedy, that it was the Imitation of one *grave*, entire Action. Indeed the Adventures incident to human Life often, as they follow each other, form a motley Scene: but it is the Business of the Poet to select the grave from the ludicrous, and the grand from the mean. It certainly must be a great Honour to a Man who had an absolute Command over the Passions, to profane his noble, moral Scenes, with trifling, vain and impertinent Witticisms; who, when he had caused all Hearts to melt and all Eyes to swim at the well-painted Representation of human Woe could tear away the honest Impression for the Sake of a miserable Jest. A modern Author speaks very justly of him when he says.

[Quotes the lines on Shakespeare from Mallet's *Of Verbal Criticism* (above, p. 21f.) ending 'Sad *Hamlet* quibbles, and the Hearer sleeps,' and comments:] This incoherent Absurdity will for ever remain an indelible Blot in the Character of our Poet; and warn us no more to expect Perfection in the Work of a Mortal, than sincerity in the Breast of a Female. (46–8)

135. Bonnell Thornton on Shakespeare

February, March 1752

From *Have At You all, or The Drury Lane Journal* nos 6, 10 (20 February, 19 March 1752).

Bonnell Thornton (1724–68), was a poet and translator, a friend of Cowper, Robert Lloyd and George Colman the elder. He achieved most success as joint editor (with Colman) of *The Connoisseur* (1754–6) but was also involved in numerous other periodicals: *Student, St James's Chronicle, The Adventurer* and *The Drury Lane Journal*.

No. 6 (20 February 1752)

*   *   *

'Observations on the New Tragedy' [*Eugenia*, by Philip Francis]

Shakespeare, with all his imperfections, is the only tragic poet that seems to have written from the heart. Those who have succeeded him address themselves chiefly to the imagination: with them the tinsel pomp of declamation takes the place of passion and nature. I have been used to look upon this great poet in a very different light from the generality of people, who are prejudic'd with an opinion that he always wrote in an hurry because there are some strokes in every play of his that are incorrect blemishes. I am confident that all his capital scenes are work'd up with the most laborious exactness, as will plainly appear on a critical examination of them. 'Tis probable, indeed, that after he had prepar'd the greatest part of the drama he was oblig'd to get the play up in an hurry, and consequently to tack it together (if I may say so) with intervening speeches and whole scenes less polish'd and less interesting. (137–8)

*   *   *

No. 10 (19 March 1752)

'Some Reflections on the Theatres'

*   *   *

Theatrical exhibitions always afford a delicate entertainment to all whose hearts are capable of being touch'd with the more refin'd sensations; and it almost moves my contempt when I reflect that a mob of unmeaning two-legged creatures, the mere apes of humanity, will venture their precious limbs in jostling one another to have an opportunity of staring at the pretty feats of a dumb Harlequin, while the empty benches reproach their deficiency of understanding, when Shakespeare or Jonson in vain exert the affecting powers of reason and judgment. To the disgrace of common sense be it remembered that *Othello* has been play'd at *Covent-Garden* to the rejected refuse which has been disappointed of places at the other crowded house, because forsooth 'twas the twentieth night of *Queen Mab*. (227)

*   *   *

[On Mrs Cibber's Lady Macbeth] Nothing could be equal to that amazement which dwelt upon her brow just before and immediately after Macbeth had *done the deed*; and the contrition she shew'd when in her sleep she seem'd to smell to her fingers was painted on her countenance beyond the faint colouring of the most masterly artist.

There is a circumstance in this play of *Macbeth* which I always thought might be manag'd to more advantage. I would willingly confine all dumb ghosts beneath the trap-doors: the ghost in *Hamlet* is a particular exception as he is an interesting character, and not only speaks but is a principal engine in carrying on the fable:—otherwise their mealy faces, white shirts, and red rags stuck on in imitation of blood are rather the objects of ridicule than terror. I cannot help imagining that if the audience were not coldly let into the cause by the rising of the mangled Macduff our surprise would be much greater, and our terror more alarming while the imagination of Macbeth conjur'd up an airy form before him, though he were really looking only on a chair. There is no reason why a bloody dagger might not with as much propriety be let down by a wire over Macbeth's head, when in that fine scene he creates the air-drawn dagger of the mind.—At present I am sure by far the greatest part of the audience is chiefly taken up in contemplating the odd figure of Macduff and marking the opening or closing of the trap-doors;—as I once overheard an honest citizen in the first gallery observing to her neighbour, *he looks deadly like a ghost.* (228–9)

136. William Dodd on Shakespeare

1752

From *The Beauties of Shakespeare. Regularly Selected from each Play* . . . 2 vols (1752).

William Dodd (1729–77), a clergyman and literary figure (editor of *The Christian Magazine*, 1760–67) was executed for forgery. His anthology went through many editions, and was the format in which Goethe first read Shakespeare.

PREFACE

I shall not attempt any labour'd encomiums on *Shakespeare*, or endeavour to set forth his perfections at a time when such universal and just applause is paid him, and when every tongue is big with his boundless fame. . . . And wasteful and ridiculous indeed it would be to say any thing in his praise when presenting the world with such a collection of *Beauties* as perhaps is no where to be met with, and, I may very safely affirm, cannot be parallell'd from the productions of any other single author, ancient or modern. There is scarcely a topic common with other writers on which he has not excelled them all; there are many nobly peculiar to himself where he shines unrivall'd and, like the eagle, properest emblem of his daring genius, soars beyond the common reach and gazes undazled on the sun. His flights are sometimes so bold, frigid criticism almost dares to disapprove them; and those narrow minds which are incapable of elevating their ideas to the sublimity of their author's are willing to bring them down to a level with their own. Hence many fine passages have been condemned in *Shakespeare* as *Rant* and *Fustian, intolerable Bombast,* and *turgid Nonsense* which, if read with the least glow of the same imagination that warm'd the writer's bosom, wou'd blaze in the robes of sublimity and obtain the commendations of a *Longinus.* And unless some little of the same spirit that elevated the poet elevate the reader too he must not presume to talk of taste and elegance; he will prove but a languid reader, an indifferent judge, but a far more indifferent critic and commentator. I would not presume to say this is the case with *Shakespeare's* commentators, since many ingenious men, whose names are high in the learned world, are found in that list. Yet thus much in justice to the author must be avow'd, that many a critic, when he has met with a passage not clear to his conception and perhaps above the level of his own ideas, so far from attempting to explain his author has immediately condemned the expression as foolish and absurd, and foisted in some footy[1] emendation of his own. A proceeding by no means justifiable, for the text of an author is a sacred thing: 'tis dangerous to meddle with it, nor should it ever be done but in the most desperate cases. The best of critics will acknowledge how frequently they have found their most plausible conjectures erroneous; and readings which once appeared to them in the darkest and most unintelligible light afterwards clear, just, and genuine; which should be a sufficient warning to all dealers in such guesswork to abstain from presumption and self-sufficiency. False glory prevails no less in the critical than in the great world: for it is imagined by many a mighty deed to find fault with an author's word, that they may introduce an emendation (as they call it) of their own. Whereas there is nothing so easy as to find fault and alter one word for another; this the very dablers in learning can do. And after all, it may be said that a lucky hit is frequently superior to the most elaborate and brain-drawn conjecture. There is no true fame in work of this kind. But it is real honour to elucidate the difficulties in an author's text, to set forth his meaning, and discover the sense of those places which are obscure to vulgar readers, and stumbling-blocks to the tribe of *emending* critics. A commentator may by this shew his judgment and taste, and better display his knowledge of his author than by a motley fardel of miserable and blind conjectures. Nay, indeed, this is the principal business of every one who presumes to enter upon the work of commenting: it is but a modern device to explain by altering, and to exchange every word in

[1] 'Paltry; mean; insignificant' (*OED*).

the text improper in our *infallible* judgment for a sophisticated reading of our own.

But the editors, critics and commentators on *Shakespeare* have a deal to say in behalf of *alteration* and the absolute necessity of it; they tell you much of their author's inattention to, and disregard of his copies; how little care he took of their publication; how mangled, maimed, and incorrect his works are handed down to us. This they urge as a reason why they should strike out every word they cannot comprehend. And thus would they justify their barbarous inhumanity of cutting into pieces an author already sufficiently dilaniated, when one would have imagined they should have used all their endeavours to heal his slight wounds and to pour balm into his sores, to have amended the visible typographical mistakes and numberless plain errors of the press, for these very plentifully abound in the first editions: but they are in general so obvious, very little sagacity is required to discern and amend them. Nay, indeed, much of the rubbish hath been clear'd away by Mr *Theobald*, who approv'd himself the best editor of *Shakespeare* that has yet appeared, by a close attention to and diligent survey of the old editions, and by a careful amendment of those slight faults which evidently proceeded from the press and corrupted the text. As to the many other imaginary fountains of error and confusion, they may very justly be look'd upon (most of them) in the same light with Dr *Bentley*'s fantastic edition of *Milton*. The doughty critic, if he thinks proper, may support his combat and fight manfully with his dagger of lath against these shadowy existencies; but the judicious reader will easily discover he fights only with shadows, and will allow him a triumph over nothing but air, unless he should chance to baffle and conquer himself. The whole dispute then seems to rest here: *Shakespeare*'s inimitable compositions are delivered to posterity full of typographical errors and mangled by the blundering hands of printers (which none who considers the imperfection of printing amongst us at that time, and the great diligence that even at the present is required to print with tolerable accuracy will at all be surprised at). So that the business of an editor seems to be a close attention to the text and careful emendation of those errors. But he should not presume to alter (and to place these alterations in the text as his author's) any passages which are not really flat nonsense and contradiction but only such to his apprehension, and unintelligible solely to his unenliven'd imagination. Mr *Theobald*, as I before observed, has been successful enough in this, so far as he has gone, but he has left many passages untouch'd and unregarded which were truly difficult and called for the editor's assistance; and seems to have no notion of the further business of an editor than that of explaining obscure passages: 'tis true, he has sometimes, tho' rarely, done it.

It is plain, then, much work remained for subsequent commentators; and shall we add, still remains? For tho' succeeded by two eminent rivals we must with no small concern behold this imperfect editor still maintaining his ground; and with no little sorrow observe the best judges of *Shakespeare* preferring *Theobald*'s to any modern edition. The reason is obvious. Sir *Thomas Hanmer* proceeds in the most unjustifiable method, foisting into his text a thousand idle alterations without ever advertising his readers which are, and which are not, *Shakespeare*'s genuine words. So that a multitude of idle phrases and ridiculous expressions infinitely beneath the sublimity of this prince of poets are thrown to his account, and his imperfections, so far from being diminish'd, number'd ten-fold upon his head. Mr *Warburton* hath been somewhat more generous to us; for tho' he has for the most part preferred his own criticisms to the author's words yet he hath always too given us the author's words, and his own reasons for those criticisms. Yet his conduct can never be justified for inserting every fancy of his own in the text, when I dare venture to say his better and cooler judgment must condemn the greatest part of them. . . .

For endeavouring perhaps to avoid all reflections on Mr *Warburton* in this work the reader will sometimes condemn me: however, I had rather be blam'd on that head than for moroseness and snarling severity; and the good-natur'd will consider that impartiality is the first step to true judgment, and candor an essential in the dark work of criticism. For my own part I cannot but read with regret the constant jarring and triumphant insults, one over another, found amidst the commentators on *Shakespeare*. This is one of the reasons that has impeded our arrival at a thorough knowledge in his works: for some of the editors have not so much labour'd to elucidate their author as to expose the follies of their brethren. How much better would it have been for *Shakespeare*, for us, and for literature in general, how much more honour would it have reflected on themselves had these brangling critics sociably united; and instead of putting themselves in a posture of defence one against another jointly taken the field, and united all their efforts to rescue so inimitable an author from the *Gothic* outrage of dull players, duller printers, and still duller editors?

For my own part, in this little attempt to present the world with as correct a collection of the finest passages of the finest poet as I could, it has been my principal endeavour to keep myself clear as possible from the dangerous shelves of prejudice. And I have labour'd to the utmost to maintain an exact and becoming candor all thro' the work, not only because I am well convinc'd how much my own many imperfections and deficiences will claim the pardon of the reader but because it appears to me highly unbecoming a man and a scholar to blacken another merely for a mistake in judgment, and because it is in my opinion no small affront to the world to pester it with our private and insignificant animosities, and to stuff a book with *querrelous* jargon where information is paid for and justly expected. Indeed, it has sometimes been impossible for me not to take notice, and that with a little severity, of some particular *remarks*, in justice to truth and my author. However, for the most part I have omitted any thing that might give offence, and where it would have been easy for me, according to the custom of modern editors, to have triumph'd and insulted, have taken no notice of the faults of others but endeavoured to the best of my judgment to explain the passage. After all there perhaps remain some difficulties, and I think we may venture to pronounce no single man will ever be able to give the world a compleat and correct edition of *Shakespeare*. The way is now well pav'd, and we may reasonably, from the joint endeavours of some understanding lovers of the author, expect what we are greatly in need of. Thus much I must declare for my own part, that in several obscure passages in this work I have received great light by the conversation and conjectures of some very ingenious and learned men, whose names, were I permitted to mention them, would do high honour to the work and to whom I thus beg leave to return my most hearty and sincere thanks.

It was long since that I first proposed publishing this collection. For *Shakespeare* was ever, of all modern authors, my first and greatest favourite, and during my relaxations from my more severe and necessary studies at college I never omitted to read and indulge myself in the rapturous flights of this delightful and *sweetest child of fancy*. And when my imagination has been heated by the glowing ardor of his uncommon fire have never failed to lament that his BEAUTIES should be so obscur'd, and that he himself should be made a kind of stage for bungling critics to shew their *clumsy activity* upon.

It was my first intention to have consider'd each play critically and regularly thro' all its parts; but as this would have swell'd the work beyond proper bounds I was obliged to confine myself solely to a collection of his poetical *Beauties*. And I doubt not, every reader will find so large a fund for observation, so much excellent and refin'd morality, and, I may venture to say, so much good divinity that he will prize the work as it deserves, and pay with me All due adoration to the Manes of *Shakespeare*.

Longinus * tells us that the most infallible test of the true *Sublime* is the impression a performance makes upon our minds when read or recited. 'If,' says he, 'a person finds that a performance transports not his soul nor exalts his thoughts, that it calls not up into his mind ideas more enlarged than the mere sounds of the words convey, but on attentive examination its dignity lessens and declines; he may conclude that whatever pierces no deeper than the ears can never be the true Sublime. That, on the contrary, is grand and lofty which the more we consider, the greater ideas we conceive of it; whose force we cannot possibly withstand; which immediately sinks deep, and makes such impression on the mind as cannot easily be worn out or effaced: in a word, you may pronounce that sublime beautiful and genuine which always pleases and takes equally with all sorts of men. For when persons of different humours, ages, professions, and inclinations agree in the same joint approbation of any performance, then this union of assent, this combination of so many different judgments, stamps an high, and indisputable value on that performance, which meets with such general applause.' This fine observation of *Longinus* is most remarkably verified in *Shakespeare*; for all humours, ages, and inclinations jointly proclaim their approbation and esteem of him; and will, I hope, be found true in most of the passages which are here collected from him. I say most, because there are some which I am convinc'd will not stand this test: the old, the grave, and the severe will disapprove, perhaps, the most soft (and as they may call them) trifling love-tales, so elegantly breath'd forth and so emphatically extolled by the young, the gay, and the passionate; while these will esteem as dull and languid the sober *saws* of morality and the home-felt observations of experience. However, as it was my business to collect for readers of all tastes and all complexions, let me desire none to disapprove what hits not with their own humour but to turn over the page, and they will surely find something acceptable and engaging. But I have yet another apology to make for some passages introduced merely on account of their peculiarity, which to some, possibly, will appear neither sublime nor beautiful, and yet deserve attention as indicating the vast stretch and sometimes particular turn

---

* See *Longinus* on the *Sublime*, Sect. 7. The translation in the text is from the learned Mr *Smith*.

of the poet's imagination. Others are inserted on account of the quotation in the note from some other author, to shew how fine reflections have been built on a trifling hint of our poet's, and of how much weight is even one of his bullion lines. It would have been no hard task for me to have multiplied quotations from *Greek*, *Latin*, and *English* writers, and to have made no small display of what is commonly called *learning*; but that I have industriously avoided, and never perplex'd the reader (or at least as little as possible) with the learned languages, always preferring the most plain and literal translations, much to his ease tho' (according to the manner in which some judge) less to my own reputation. In the notes many extracts will be found from *Beaumont* and *Fletcher*, some, and indeed, the chief beauties of these celebrated authors. I have taken the liberty now and then to dissent from the ingenious gentlemen who have lately publish'd their works: and cannot but highly commend that good-nature and modesty with which they have conducted their remarks. One of them, Mr *Seward*, hath given us an agreeable preface, wherein he sets forth the merits of his authors and seems very desirous to place them in the same rank with *Shakespeare*. But alas! all his generous efforts in their cause are but fruitless, and all his friendly labours unavailing. For we have but to read a play of each and we shall not a moment hesitate in our judgment. However, so kind a partiality to his authors is by no means blameable, but on the contrary highly commendable.

As to the other passages in the notes they are in general such as are not commonly known and read, which sort it would have been easy to have multiplied. Indeed, there appears so little judgment in those who have made general collections from the poets that they merit very small notice, as they are already too low for censure.

There are many passages in *Shakespeare* so closely connected with the plot and characters, and on which their beauties so wholly depend, that it would have been absurd and idle to have produced them here. Hence the reader will find little of the *inimitable Falstaff* in this work, and not one line extracted from the *Merry Wives of Windsor*, one of *Shakespeare*'s best and most justly-admired comedies. Whoever reads that play will immediately see there was nothing either proper or possible for this work. Which, such as it is, I most sincerely and cordially recommend to the candor and benevolence of the world, and wish every one that peruses it may feel the satisfaction I have frequently felt in composing it, and receive such instructions and advantages from it as it is well calculated and well able to bestow. For my own part, better and more important things henceforth demand my attention, and I here, with no small pleasure, take leave of *Shakespeare* and the critics. . . . (I, v–xx)

[From the Notes]

[On *Love's Labour's Lost*, 4.3.340f.]

I read the lines in question,

> And when love speaks, the voice of all the gods
> Makes heaven drousy with the harmony.

Could the poet pay a finer compliment to love than to say that 'when he talk'd, all the rest of the gods seem'd to speak such nonsense, as was enough to make heaven drousy?' There is, I grant you, a critical inaccuracy in the lines, but it is such as is characteristical of your author, it is a *Shakespearism*. (I, 37)

* * *

[On *The Tempest*, 2.1.195f.: 'What might,
Worthy Sebastian? O, what might!']

There is not a more elegant figure than the *Aposiopesis*, when in threatening, or in the expression of any other passion, the sentence is broken and something is left to be supplied. *Shakespeare* excels greatly in it (as indeed he does in every poetical beauty) of which, the passage before us is a striking example. (I, 110).

* * *

[On *Antony and Cleopatra*, 2.2.195ff.]

The barge, &c.] As *Dryden* plainly enter'd the lists with *Shakespeare*, in describing this magnificent appearance of *Cleopatra*, it is but just the descriptions should appear together, that the reader may decide the victory. Partiality, perhaps, may incline me to think *Shakespeare*'s much the greatest; tho' I am greatly pleas'd in hearing it from *Antony*'s own mouth, in *Dryden*'s play.[1] (I, 156)

* * *

[1] See Vol. 1, pp. 175f.

[On *Antony and Cleopatra*, 5.2.311]

What should I stay, &c.] *Shakespeare* excels prodigiously in these breaks; so, *Percy* in *Henry IV, first part*, just departing,

> No, *Percy*, thou art dust,
> And food for—(*dies.*)
> *P. Henry*. Worms, brave *Percy*, fare thee well.
>
> [5.4.85ff.] (I, 169–70)

*   *   *

[On *Hamlet*, 1.4.69ff.: the Ghost might tempt Hamlet to 'the dreadful border of the cliff/That beetles o'er his base into the Sea'.]

See the famous description of *Dover-Cliff*, in *King Lear*, Act 4. Sc. 6. *Beetles*, i.e. hangs over, in the same manner as the head of a *beetle* hangs over, and is too big for the rest of its body: so we say a *beetle-headed* or *beetle-brow'd* fellow for a heavy, thick-headed one. The line,

> Which might deprive your sovereignty of reason,

has something in it truly *Shakespearian*. . . . (I, 224)

*   *   *

[On *Hamlet*, 1.5.77: 'Unhouseled, unanointed, unaneal'd']

. . . *Unaneal'd*, now alone remains unconsider'd: Mr *Theobald* says *it* must signify *without extreme unction*; Mr *Pope* explains it by *no knell rung*: . . . I apprehend the word should certainly have been *unaknell'd*, to bear the sense Mr *Pope* gives it: however, be that as it will, we must certainly allow Mr *Pope* to have been a *proper* commentator here. There are more arguments still to support the reading in the text. An attentive person must find great pleasure in looking, as it were, into the *mind* of his author; and as our thoughts on any subject always succeed in train and are nicely associated, be much delighted with finding out that train and tracing those *associations*. Let us see if we cannot do so in this passage. The poet is speaking of the misfortune of being cut off in the blossom of our sins, when we have had no means to attone for them or to receive the benefits of religion. These benefits then must naturally arise in the mind: the greatest of which it is natural to suppose would occur first, the *blessed sacrament*, the immediate consequence of which is, *extreme unction*, two so important and necessary branches of duty that the loss of these was the loss of all, and we may reasonably expect he should particularize no more, but add—'I was not only depriv'd of these but also of every other *preparation*, and without any kind of reckoning made, sent to my last and horrible account.' If we were to admit Mr *Pope*'s sense of the word we must imagine our author's thoughts carried still farther; 'without the host, without unction, without enjoying the benefits of the *passing* bell,' which used to *toll* while the person lay expiring, and thence was so called: nay, this shocking custom still prevails in some parts of *England*. The run of the line is no bad argument in support of the reading in the text. This manner of beginning each word with the same syllable is not unfrequent with the *Greek* tragedians, nor our best poets; and besides, it adds great strength and beauty.

> Unrespited, unpitied, unreprov'd.
> > *Milton, Par. Lost,* B.2.185.

> Unshaken, unseduc'd, unterrified.   B.5.899.

And numberless other instances, if necessary, might easily be brought. . . . (I, 229–30)

*   *   *

[On *Hamlet*, 3.1.59ff.]

The critics, greatly disgusted at the impropriety of *Shakespeare*'s metaphors, and not conceiving what he could mean by taking arms *against a sea*, have either inserted in their text or proposed *assail* or *assailing*, and the like: but there is *none so frigid a reader* of Shakespeare as to admit such alterations. Propriety in his metaphors was never one of the concerns of our author: so that if we were to correct every place where we find ill-join'd metaphors we may alter many of his finest passages. The expression of *taking arms* signifies no more than putting ourselves in a state of opposition and defence; by a *sea* of troubles, according to the common use of the word *sea* in the poets and other writers, he expresses no more than a *confluence*, a vast quantity, *&c.*— Besides, *a sea of troubles*, is generally used to express the approach of human ills and the misfortunes that flow in upon us, and it was amongst the *Greeks* a proverbial expression, κακων θαλασσα. Thus we may in a good measure justify the expression; at least it is plain enough to be understood, and I think we may with as much certainty pronounce it *genuine* as some critics pronounce it false. (I, 237–8)

*   *   *

[On *Hamlet*, 3.1.160: Ophelia describes Hamlet as 'Blasted with extasie']

Here is a striking instance of *Shakespeare*'s impropriety in his use of metaphors: the word *extasie* is used in the sense of the *Greek* word whence it comes, which signifies any emotion of the mind, whether it happens by madness, wonder, fear, or any other cause. (I, 241)

*   *   *

[On *Hamlet*, 3.3.73ff.]

It has been remark'd there is great want of resolution in *Hamlet*, for when he had so good an opportunity to kill his uncle and revenge his father, as here, he shuffles it off with a paltry excuse, and is afraid to do what he so ardently longs for. The observation may be confirm'd from many other passages: in the next page he himself observes *that all occasions do inform against him and spur his dull revenge*. But 'tis not my design in this work to enter into exact criticism on the characters. (I, 246)

*   *   *

[On *1 Henry IV*, 1.3.201ff.]

By heav'ns! &c.] I will not take upon me to defend this passage from the charge laid against it of bombast and fustian, but will only observe, if we read it in that light, it is perhaps one of the finest rants to be found in any author. (II, 4)

*   *   *

[On *2 Henry VI*, 4.1.3ff.]

And now loud howling wolves arouse the jades,
That drag the tragick melancholy night;
Who with their drowsie, slow, and flagging wings,
Clip dead men's graves . . .

No numbers can better express the *thing* than these. *Shakespeare* shews us that he can as well excel in that as in every other branch of poetry. None of the so celebrated lines of *Homer* and *Virgil* of this sort deserve more commendation: here the line, as it ought, justly *labours*, and the *verse moves slow*. However, I intend not to enter into any criticism on *Shakespeare*'s versification, wherein could we prove him superior to all other writers we must still acknowledge it the least and most trifling matter wherein he is superior. (II, 44)

*   *   *

[on *Julius Caesar*, 2.1.63ff.]

Between the acting of a dreadful thing,
And the first motion, all the interim is
Like a phantasma, or a hideous dream:
The genius, and the mortal instruments
Are then in council; and the state of man,
Like to a little kingdom, suffers then
The nature of an insurrection.

Either Mr *Theobald*, or Mr. *Warburton* (which who can pronounce, since the one prints the same words in his preface, which the other uses as his own in his notes? See *Theobald*'s preface Vol. 1. p. 25, and *Warburton* on the passage), either the one or the other of them have observed 'that nice critic, *Dionysius* of *Halicarnassus* confesses, that he could not find those great strokes, which he calls the *terrible graces*, any where so frequent as in *Homer*'. I believe the success would be the same, likewise, if we sought for them in any other of our authors besides our *British Homer, Shakespeare*. This description of the condition of conspirators has a pomp and terror in it that perfectly astonishes . . . . [Addison imitated it in his *Cato* (1.3) but] Mr *Addison* could not with that propriety bring in that magnificent circumstance which gives the terrible grace to *Shakespeare*'s description:

The genius and the mortal instruments
Are then in council.   (II, 87)

*   *   *

[On *Julius Caesar*]

It may perhaps be needless to inform the reader that the duke of *Buckingham*, displeas'd with what the critics esteem so great a fault in this play, the death of *Julius Caesar* in the third Act, hath made two plays of it; but I am afraid the lovers of *Shakespeare* will be apt to place that nobleman's performance on a level with the rest of those who have attempted to alter, or amend *Shakespeare*. (II, 115).

*　　*　　*

[On *Macbeth*, 2.1.55]

The reading in the old books is

　　　With Tarquin's ravishing *sides* towards, &c.

Which Mr *Pope* alter'd to that in the text. Mr *Johnson* is for reading

　　　With *Tarquin* ravishing, slides tow'rd, &c. [see above, p. 174]

Because a *ravishing stride* is an action of violence, impetuosity, and tumult; and because the progression of ghosts is so different from *strides* that it has been in all ages represented to be as *Milton* expresses it,

　　　Smooth *sliding* without step,

it seems to me the poet only speaks of the silence and secrecy wherewith the ghosts were supposed to move. And as when people walk with a stealthy pace, or as it is called on *tip-toe*, they generally take long *strides*, not stepping frequently, I should judge *strides* to be the proper reading. Beside, I think the two verbs coming in that manner together not entirely elegant; *slides towards his design*, and *moves like a ghost*, seem too near a tautology. I am the more explicit in this passage as any remark of so ingenious a person deserves all attention. (II, 141)

*　　*　　*

[On *Othello*, 1.3.140ff: 'of antres vast and . . . Cannibals']

I have omitted here five or six lines, which tho' indeed capable of defence, cannot well be produced as beauties. The simplest expressions, where nature and propriety dictate, may be truly sublime; such is all this fine speech of Othello. (II, 162)

*　　*　　*

[On *Romeo and Juliet*, 1.4.53ff.: the Queen Mab speech]

Tho' the following passages have something similar in general to this celebrated speech, yet they serve only to shew the superiority of *Shakespeare*'s fancy, and the vast range of his boundless imagination. (II, 200).

*   *   *

[On *Romeo and Juliet*, 5.2.74ff.]

I have given the reader this last speech of *Romeo* rather to let him into the plot and convince him of the merit of the alterations made in it, than for any singular beauty of its own; *Romeo*'s surviving till *Juliet* awakens, is certainly productive of great beauties, particularly in the acting. And indeed this play of our author's hath met with better success than any other which has been attempted to be altered. Whoever reads *Otway*'s *Caius Marius* will soon be convinc'd of this; and it is to be wish'd none would presume to build upon *Shakespeare*'s foundation but such as are equal masters with *Otway*. (II, 219)

A Select Bibliography of Shakespeare Criticism, 1733–1752

Note. Items which cover a wider range, including this period, which were listed in Volumes 1 and 2 are not repeated here.

(A) COLLECTIONS OF CRITICISM

See, in the previous volumes, collections edited by D. N. Smith, C. E. Hughes, W. H. Durham, H. H. Adams and B. Hathaway, E. S. Elledge, C. Williamson, and F. Kermode.

(B) INDIVIDUAL CRITICS: MODERN EDITIONS

SHERBO, A. (ed.), *Johnson on Shakespeare* (New Haven, 1968): vols 7 and 8 of the Yale Edition of the *Works* of Samuel Johnson.

SHERBO, A. (ed.), *New Essays by Arthur Murphy* (East Lausing, Michigan, 1963).

(C) HISTORIES OF LITERARY CRITICISM

See, in the previous volumes, the books by D. N. Smith, H. S. Robinson, L. Marder, P. S. Conklin.

(D) TEXTUAL STUDIES

See, in Vol. 2, works by R. B. McKerrow, H. L. Ford, and J. Isaacs.

(E) THEATRICAL HISTORY, ADAPTATIONS

See, in the previous volumes, the books by G. C. D. Odell, C. B. Hogan, G. C. Branam, A. C. Sprague, L. Hughes and C. H. Gray.

NOYES, R. G., *The Thespian Mirror. Shakespeare in the Eighteenth-Century Novel* (Providence, Rhode Island, 1953). Studies allusions to Shakespeare in 750 novels published between 1740 and 1780.

STONE, G. W. (ed.), *The London Stage, 1660–1800, Part 4: 1747–1776* (Carbondale, Ill., 1962), 3 vols.

PRICE, CECIL, *Theatre in the Age of Garrick* (Blackwell, Oxford, 1973).

Index

The Index is arranged in three parts: I. Shakespeare's works; II. Shakespearian characters; III. General index. Adaptations are indexed under the adapter's name, in III below. References to individual characters are not repeated under the relevant plays.

479

II SHAKESPEARIAN CHARACTERS

III GENERAL INDEX

IES

ld Smalley

McWilliams

Continued